LAW AND LEGAL PRACTICE IN EGYPT FROM ALEXANDER TO THE ARAB CONQUEST

The study of ancient law has blossomed in recent years. In English alone there have been dozens of studies devoted to classical Greek and Roman law, to the Roman legal codes, and to the legal traditions of the ancient Near East among many other topics. Legal documents written on papyrus began to be published in some abundance by the end of the nineteenth century; but even after a substantial publication history down to the present time, legal papyri have not received due attention from legal historians. This book blends the two usually distinct juristic scholarly traditions, classical and Egyptological, into a coherent presentation of the legal documents from Egypt from the Ptolemaic to the late Byzantine periods, all translated and accompanied by expert commentary. The volume will serve as an introduction to the rich legal sources from Egypt in the later phases of its ancient history as well as a tool to compare legal documents from other cultures.

JAMES G. KEENAN is Professor of Classical Studies at Loyola University Chicago.

J. G. MANNING is The Simpson Professor of Classics and History at Yale University.

URI YIFTACH-FIRANKO is Senior Lecturer in the Department of Classics in the Hebrew University of Jerusalem.

LAW AND LEGAL PRACTICE IN EGYPT FROM ALEXANDER TO THE ARAB CONQUEST

A Selection of Papyrological Sources in Translation, with Introductions and Commentary

EDITED BY
JAMES G. KEENAN
J. G. MANNING
URI YIFTACH-FIRANKO

CAMBRIDGE
UNIVERSITY PRESS

CAMBRIDGE
UNIVERSITY PRESS

University Printing House, Cambridge CB2 8BS, United Kingdom

Cambridge University Press is part of the University of Cambridge.

It furthers the University's mission by disseminating knowledge in the pursuit of education, learning and research at the highest international levels of excellence.

www.cambridge.org
Information on this title: www.cambridge.org/9780521874526

First published 2014
Reprinted 2015

Printed in the United Kingdom by Clays, St Ives plc

A catalogue record for this publication is available from the British Library

Library of Congress Cataloging in Publication data
Law and legal practice in Egypt from Alexander to the Arab conquest : a selection of papyrological sources in translation, with introductions and commentary / [edited by] James G. Keenan, J. G. Manning, Uri Yiftach-Firanko.
pages cm
ISBN 978-0-521-87452-6 (Hardback)
1. Egyptian law–Sources. 2. Law, Greek–Sources. 3. Roman law–Sources. 4. Egypt–History–Greco-Roman period, 332 B.C.–640 A.D.–Sources. I . Keenan, James G., editor. II. Manning, Joseph Gilbert, editor. III. Yiftach-Firanko, Uri, editor.
KL2814.5.L39 2014
340.5′32–dc23
2013045001

ISBN 978-0-521-87452-6 Hardback

Dedicated to the memory of
Traianos Gagos
(1960–2010)
and
Tomasz Markiewicz
(1974–2009)

Contents

List of figures

List of contributors

BARBARA ANAGNOSTOU-CAÑAS
CNRS, Paris

ANTTI ARJAVA
Secretary General, Finnish Cultural Foundation
Senior Lecturer
Institutum Classicum
University of Helsinki

ROGER S. BAGNALL
Professor of Ancient History and Leon Levy Director
Institute for the Study of the Ancient World
New York University

WILLY CLARYSSE
Emeritus
Department of Ancient History
KU Leuven

MARK DEPAUW
Head of Ancient History
KU Leuven

BRENDAN HAUG
Department of Classical Studies
The University of Michigan

ÉVA JAKAB
Chair, Department of Roman Law
University of Szeged

ANDREA JÖRDENS
Institut für Papyrologie
Universität Heidelberg

JAMES G. KEENAN
Professor of Classical Studies
Loyola University Chicago

CHRYSIE KOTSIFOU
Polonsky Postdoctoral Fellow
Van Leer Jerusalem Institute

CLAUDIA KREUZSALER
Austrian National Library
Department of Papyri

THOMAS KRUSE
Senior Research Scholar
Austrian Academy of Sciences
Institute for the Study of Ancient Culture
Division Documenta Antiqua

FRANÇOIS LEROUXEL
Maître de conférences
Université Paris IV
Paris Sorbonne

MYRTO MALOUTA
Lecturer in Greek Papyrology
Ionian University
Corfu, Greece

J. G. MANNING
The William K. and Marilyn M. Simpson Professor
of History and Classics
Yale University

†TOMASZ MARKIEWICZ
Department of Papyrology
Institute of Archaeology
University of Warsaw

CARY J. MARTIN
Honorary Research Associate

Institute of Archaeology
University College London

JOSEPH MÉLÈZE MODRZEJEWSKI
Professor Emeritus of Ancient History
Directeur d'études à l'École pratique des hautes études, Paris

BRIAN P. MUHS
Associate Professor of Egyptology
The Oriental Institute
The Department of Near Eastern Languages and Civilizations, and the College at the University of Chicago

BERNHARD PALME
Professor of Ancient History and Papyrology
University of Vienna

PROF. DR. T. SEBASTIAN RICHTER
Fakultät für Geschichte, Kunst- und Orientwissenschaften
Ägyptologisches Institut
Universität Leipzig

YOUVAL ROTMAN
Senior Lecturer
Department of Jewish History
Tel Aviv University

JANE ROWLANDSON
Department of Classics
King's College London

HANS-ALBERT RUPPRECHT
Emeritus
FB Rechtswissenschaften
Philipps-Universität Marburg

GEORG SCHMELZ
Institut für Papyrologie
Universität Heidelberg

REINHOLD SCHOLL
Professor of Ancient History
Universität Leipzig

JEAN A. STRAUS
Senior Lecturer
Université de Liège

RYOSUKE TAKAHASHI
Lecturer in History
Kawamura Gakuen Woman's University
Abiko, Japan

DOROTHY J. THOMPSON
Fellow of Girton College
University of Cambridge

JAKUB URBANIK
Chair of Roman and Antique Law
Faculty of Law and Administration
University of Warsaw

KATELIJN VANDORPE
Professor of Papyrology and Ancient History
KU Leuven

SITTA VON REDEN
Professor of Ancient History
University of Freiburg

URI YIFTACH-FIRANKO
Senior Lecturer
Department of Classics
Hebrew University

Preface

The idea for this book dates back a decade or so as one of the editors (JGM) came to believe that legal papyrology was being relegated to an ever-diminishing corner of ancient history. Papyrology itself, the decipherment and interpretation of documents written (mostly) on the ancient paper called papyrus, recovered (predominantly) from Egypt, is a highly technical, and therefore somewhat naturally isolated, discipline. The use, or neglect, of papyrological publications by ancient historians not trained as papyrologists remains a matter of constant concern. In addition, even if (from our perspective) the lesser languages of the wider discipline (e.g., Aramaic, Pahlevi) and the earlier forms of Egyptian are set aside, the field has traditionally suffered a linguistic split between Greek (and Latin) documents on the one side, and Egyptian documents (Demotic, Coptic) on the other. The former tend to be the concern of those classicists who have chosen to "major" in papyrology, the latter the concern of Egyptologists. Still more, the legal scholarship on the corpora of published documents in both language sets is predominately written in German. The present volume, accordingly, aims to introduce readers to this major source of ancient legal documents, to heal the linguistic divide by including documents in both major language traditions, and to distill the literature of juristic scholarship based on these texts for the benefit of the reader in English. We present in this volume some texts that are well known to papyrologists, others that have hardly been studied. The selection is limited to documents from Egypt.

The editors first met during the 24th International Congress of Papyrology in the Summer of 2004 in Helsinki to discuss the outline of the book with many of the present contributors. We had hoped to finish sooner, but the usual delays in projects with more than thirty contributors came in the way. Accidentally therefore, if not providentially, the present volume reached its final form a little over a century after Mitteis and Wilcken's four-volume *Grundzüge und Chrestomathie der Papyruskunde* was published in 1912. The present volume is in no way intended as a challenge or replacement to Mitteis' half of that endeavor (perish the thought!), but as an updated supplement. We nonetheless hope that this book will find a wider audience for its subject. It presupposes that there are legal historians of other times and places and students of ancient history who would wish to have an introduction to legal papyrology and access to samples of its rich variety of texts. We intend this volume to serve just such an audience. We present it as a work that provides an entrée into the field of legal papyrology, one that will give the reader a sense of the debates in the field along with an orientation to the types of texts preserved and to the subject's large bibliography. It is not a comprehensive guide nor is it a formal analysis of the system of law in any of the periods covered. That would demand a different and even larger volume. Rather we present here texts that reflect "law in action," evidence for how people used legal texts in "negotiating daily life," to borrow from the book title of our Yale colleague Valerie Hansen (*Negotiating Daily Life in Traditional China: How Ordinary People Used Contracts 600–1400*, Yale University Press, 1995).

A major difference between this volume and Mitteis' volumes is its range. The latter work concerned itself only with Greek and Latin texts. Its *Chrestomathie* presented the Greek and Latin originals without translations. The current one attempts to integrate Egyptian documents (Demotic, Coptic) and to blend the two usually distinct juristic scholarly traditions, classical and Egyptological. We also include more late material – though the Byzantine period is still not as well represented as it might have been. The fault may lie in the lesser attention devoted to the Byzantine period over the years (until lately), the original schema of topics set for consideration back in 2004 (as concretized in the present Table of Contents), or the special interests of scholars who were invited to contribute – or a combination of the above. While recognizing the problems of periodization, we have included under "Byzantine" several non-Greek documents that postdate the period and are not properly Byzantine. Whatever the reasons, the law of the Byzantine Egyptian papyri remains a field that begs special attention.

The reader will notice that a diversity of contributors results in a variety of forms, interests, and approaches. We have tried, as far as possible, to standardize citations, formatting, and translations of technical vocabulary while leaving personal freedoms intact. The reader may find a particular interest in distinguishing the (perhaps) more formal approach to the documents as evidenced in continental scholarship from the (perhaps) more sociological approach in Anglo-American scholarship. Some contributors give more material and textual information about their documents than do others. We were unable to supply parallel information for the rest, but simultaneously reluctant, just for uniformity's sake, to strip valuable information out when it was already present. The introduction to each chapter was mainly written by the editors, often with material supplied by the individual contributors.

A number of special problems need mention. We use the word Demotic to signify that particular stage of the ancient Egyptian language, and implicitly the script in which it was written. When information from the alternate side of a document is provided in translation we accept the contributor's identification of that side as a verso or a back, or reverse, side; this is a technical detail that need not concern our readers and something that can only be verified by inspection of each individual papyrus, impossible under the circumstances. In Ptolemaic dates, we have preferred keeping the three traditional Egyptian seasons based on the Nile's flood and ebb. In Roman dating formulas, we have a preference for "Emperor" (with capital E), representing the Greek *autokratôr*, but the reader will still find from time to time *autokrator*'s Latin equivalent *Imperator* in places where that seemed more elegant or appropriate. In translation from the Greek, we prefer writing out numbers when they are written out in the original (e.g., seven or seventh), using ciphers in English when there are ciphers in Greek (e.g., 7 or 7th). A Greek phrase found in clauses at the ends of many documents, *kathaper ek dikês* ("as if from a legal decision"), is variously rendered by contributors, but should be recognizable even in such variety. No doubt other inconsistencies remain; we can only hope that they do not detract from the readers' understanding when similar or the same meanings and the same linguistic phrases in the original are at issue.

Beyond the illustrations in the present volume, readers interested in considering in further detail the physical papyri upon which these and the volume's other legal texts have been written can find images of many of the Greek papyri by consulting www.papyri.info and using the codes for volume abbreviations to track individual papyri. We mark in their headings each text for which we have found this is possible. The same source will direct the reader to relevant printed plates. Online resources for Demotic and Coptic documents do not yet equal those for the Greek, but we try to indicate where photographic plates are conveniently available.

The editors wish to express a number of debts. Manning and Keenan met in Ann Arbor in June 2011 to do some final vetting of the manuscript.

One can find no better place than the University of Michigan and its famed Hatcher Library Room 807 in which to work. We are grateful to Arthur Verhoogt, Terry Wilfong, and Adam Hyatt for providing ideal surroundings in which to do this work, and for great company at day's end. We thank Jane Rowlandson for assistance with the editing of Chapter 9. We are grateful to the two anonymous Press readers who went through an early draft of the manuscript and produced numerous helpful ideas and criticisms. We thank all the contributors for their patience in sticking with the project through thick and thin. Additionally JGM would like to thank Peter Raulwing and Nicholas Venable of Yale College for their editorial assistance in the final editing of the volume, and to acknowledge the Earhart Foundation (Ann Arbor, Michigan) for a generous grant used in the initial phases of research. We are very grateful for the fine editorial skills of Malcolm Todd, copy-editor. Finally, but hardly least, we acknowledge Michael Sharp of Cambridge University Press, whose patience and encouragement over the years were essential both for the project's continuation and its completion.

Some contributions were received early in the process of composing this book, others somewhat later on. Editorial work at times proceeded feverishly, but there were intervals, some of them lengthy, of respite. The book received its final pre-press editing in April 2012, but by that time all contributions had been in hand for five years. All contributors provided rich bibliographies for their topics, but it has not been possible to bring these systematically up to date. Contributors should be exonerated for any fault in this regard.

Calendars

Egyptian season	Egyptian month name	Macedonian month name
First of *Akhet*	Thoth	Dios
Second of *Akhet*	Phaophi	Apellaios
Third of *Akhet*	Hathyr	Audnaios
Fourth of *Akhet*	Choiak	Peritios
First of *Peret*	Tybi	Dystros
Second of *Peret*	Mecheir	Xandikos
Third of *Peret*	Phamenoth	Artemesios
Fourth of *Peret*	Pharmouthi	Daisios
First of *Shemu*	Pachon	Panemos
Second of *Shemu*	Payni	Loios
Third of *Shemu*	Epeiph	Gorpiaios
Fourth of *Shemu*	Mesore	Hyperberetaios

Abbreviations

We follow the standard abbreviations for ancient texts cited in this volume. For papyri, see J. F. Oates *et al.*, *Checklist of Editions of Greek and Latin Papyri, Ostraca and Tablets*, 5th edn., available online at: http://scriptorium.lib.duke.edu/papyrus/texts/clist.html.

We follow the Periodical and Instrumenta abbreviations listed in the *Checklist* with the additions listed below.

For the texts of published Greek documents in this volume, see the Papyrological Navigator at: http://papyri.info/

The following cited abbreviations are listed for convenience:

CTh	*Codex Theodosianus.*
DDBDP	Duke Databank of Documentary Papyri. See now: http://papyri.info/
DDD III	S. Lippert and M. Schentuleit, *Demotische Dokumente aus Dime*, vol. 3: *Urkunden*. Wiesbaden, 2010.
FIRA I	*Fontes Iuris Romani Antejustiniani, pars prima: Leges*, ed. S. Riccobono, 2nd edn. Florence, 1941.
FIRA III	*Fontes Iuris Romani Antejustiniani*, pars tertia: *Negotia*, ed. V. Arangio-Ruiz, 2nd edn. Florence, 1943. Reprint Florence, 1969.
JEA	*The Journal of Egyptian Archaeology*. London.
JEgH	*Journal of Egyptian History*. Leiden.
JNES	*The Journal of Near Eastern Studies*. Chicago.
Jur.Pap.	*Juristische Papyri*, ed. P. M. Meyer. Berlin, 1920. Reprint: Chicago, 1976.
LexÄg	*Lexikon der Ägyptologie*. Wiesbaden.
LSJ	*A Greek–English Lexicon*, compiled by Henry George Liddell, Robert Scott, and Henry Stuart Jones. 9th edn. Oxford, 1968.

Mansi	Mansi, J.-D. *Sacrorum Conciliorum nova et amplissima collectio*. Florence, 1759–1927.
M.Chr.	L. Mitteis and U. Wilcken, *Grundzüge und Chrestomathie der Papyruskunde*. Vol. 2.2. *Juristischer Teil*. Leipzig, 1912.
P.Brit.Mus. Thompson	Herbert Thompson, *A family archive from Siut from papyri in the British Museum*. Oxford, 1934.
Sel.Pap.	*Select Papyri*. The Loeb Classical Library. 3 vols.
TAPA	*Transactions of the American Philological Association*. Baltimore.
UPZ	Ulrich Wilcken, *Urkunden der Ptolemäerzeit (Altere funde)*. 2 vols. Berlin, 1927–1937.
ZSS	*Zeitschrift der Savigny-Stiftung für Rechtsgeschichte: Romanistische Abteilung*. Weimar.

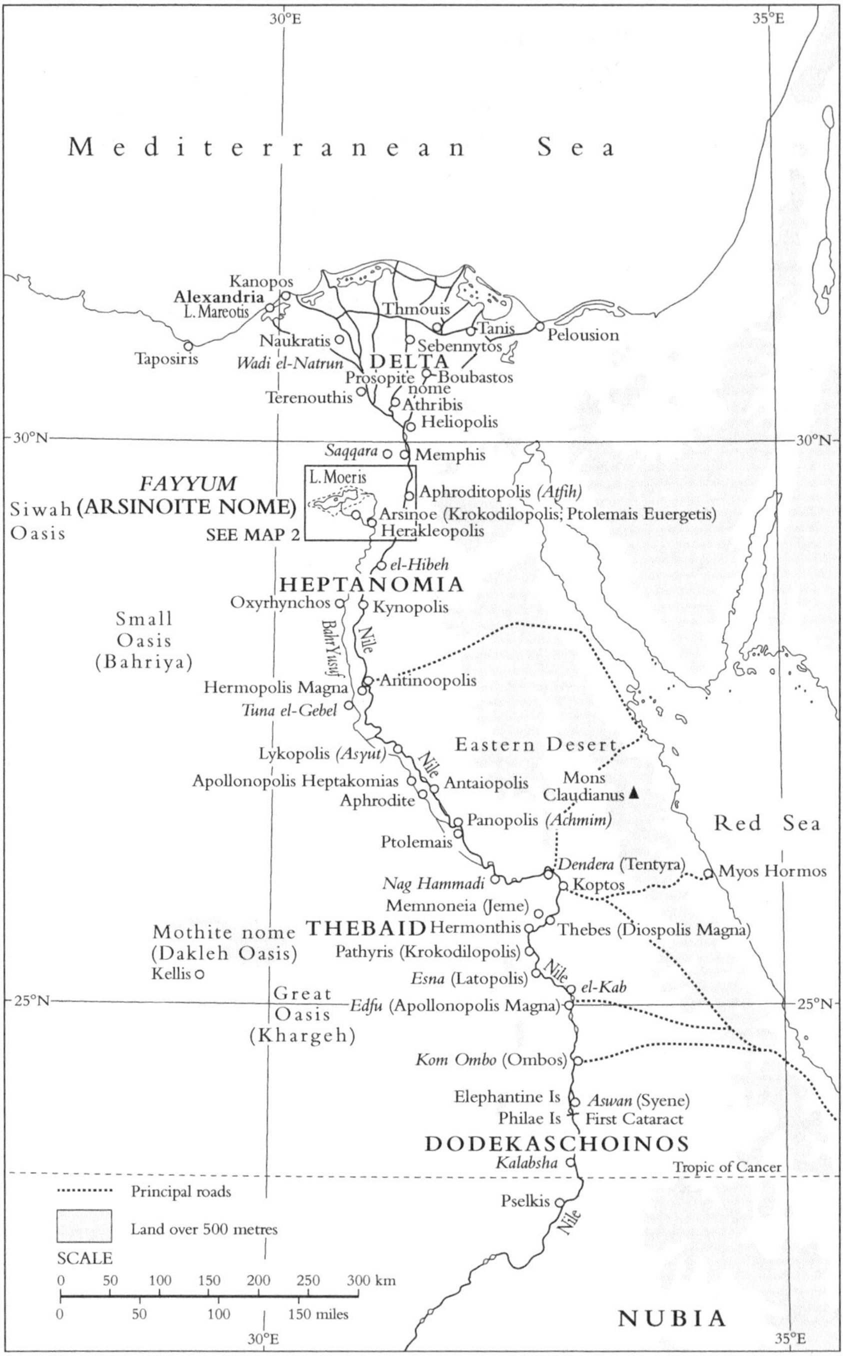

Map 1. Egypt, showing key sites of papyrus finds

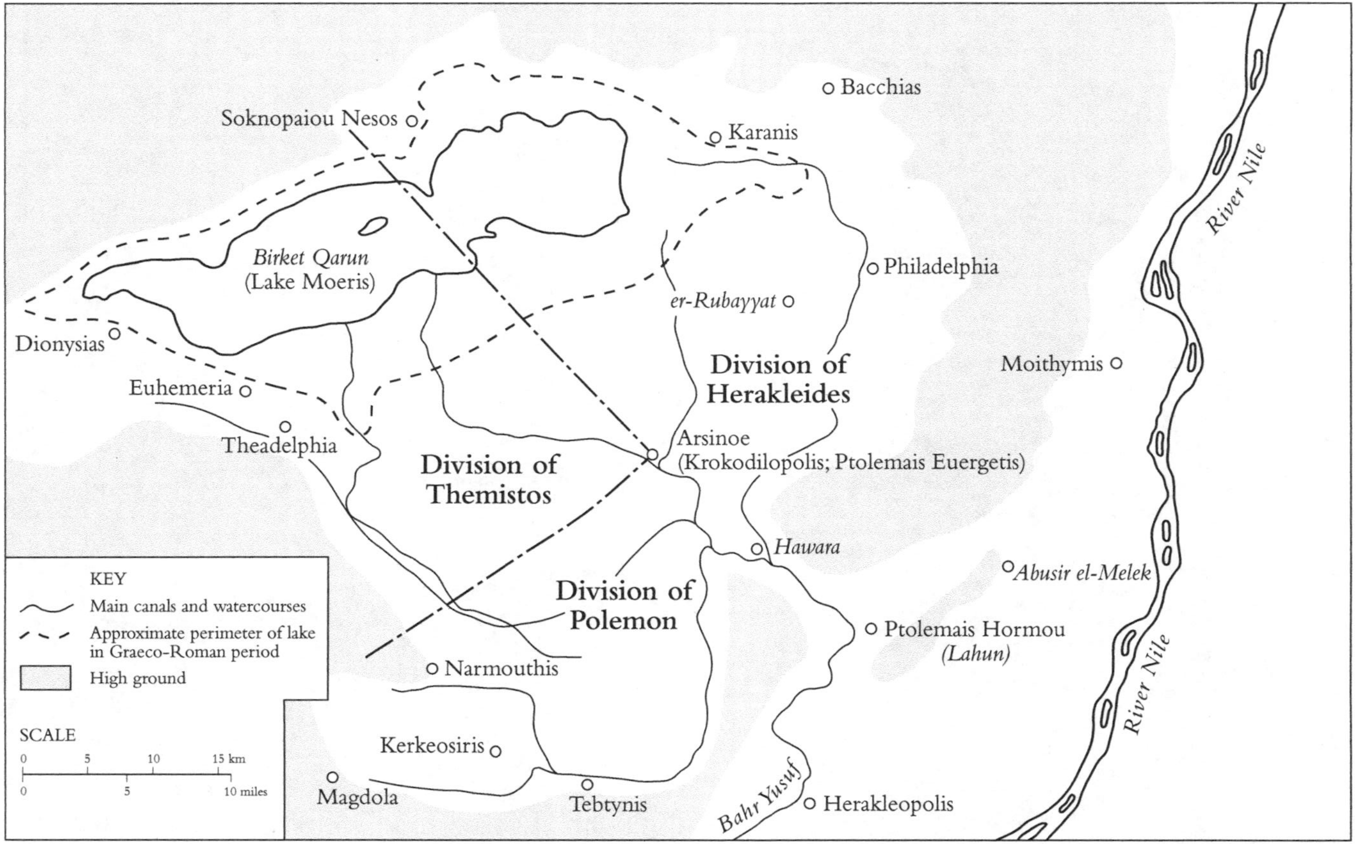

Map 2. The Fayyum (Arsinoite nome)

CHAPTER I

Introduction and historical framework

James G. Keenan, J. G. Manning, Uri Yiftach-Firanko, and T. Sebastian Richter

Introduction

J. G. Manning

The study of ancient law has blossomed in recent years. In the English language alone there have been dozens of monograph-length studies devoted to classical Greek and Roman law, to the Roman legal codes, and to the legal traditions of the ancient Near East including ancient Egyptian, biblical, and Coptic law, among many other topics. In 1995, an important conference was held at the University of California at Berkeley's law school (Boalt Hall) that brought together specialists in ancient legal documents and legal historians (*Chicago-Kent Law Review* 70–71 [1995]). Among the many important outcomes of that conference, two stand out. The first was the realization that ancient legal sources have value outside of the realm of those who specialize in the language and scripts of the ancient texts themselves. The second, and more immediately important, outcome for this volume was that pre-Roman legal systems could and indeed should be studied out from under the shadow of Roman law.[1]

Legal documents written on papyrus began to be published in some abundance by the end of the nineteenth century – not of course in time to be used by Henry Maine in his great *Ancient Law: Its Connection with the Early History of Society, and Its Relation to Modern Ideas* (1861). Even after a substantial history of publication down to the present time, however, legal papyri have not received due attention from legal historians, and have only gradually been incorporated into broader synthetic work. The legal papyri remain by and large in their own world although that world has now expanded beyond the Nile River valley.[2] The legal texts from Egypt, taken

[1] For one recent volume, although with little analysis of the papyri, examining ancient law from the point of view of economics, see Miller (2010). Several of the pieces in the volume derive from the Berkeley meeting.

[2] *Inter alia*, see Katzoff and Schaps (2005) on the Babatha archive from Roman Judea.

as a whole, are among the most valuable records from antiquity for the study of the ancient law, the ancient economy, and for social history more broadly. But that greater value of the papyri has often been lost in the technical occupation of publishing and correcting and commenting on an ever-growing corpus of documents.[3] The papyri are the raw material of history and the basis of institutional analysis, but the underlying questions, often unstated and problematic, usually center around questions like: what kind of history, and whose? This in turn relates to the bigger question of the presumptive status of Egypt in the Hellenistic and Roman periods as a place "set apart," and therefore easily dismissed as merely an unusual, if embarrassingly well-documented, part of the Mediterranean world.[4] This is referred to as the *Sonderstellung* problem.[5] Although legal papyrology has been a major aspect of the study of the papyri from the very beginning of the field in the late nineteenth century, the subject is generally known only to a small circle of specialists, and it is rarely taught as a regular feature of graduate programs in ancient or in legal history.

A recent treatment of ancient law, for example, did not mention the Greek or Egyptian papyri, or indeed any pre-Roman legal tradition outside of the Old Testament (Donahue 2006). We, however, believe strongly that the legal papyri are an important part of the story of law and of legal institutions. We hope, therefore, that this volume will serve as an introduction to the rich legal sources from Egypt in the later phases of its ancient history as well as a means by which to compare legal documents from other cultures. There are other languages that record legal agreements which we do not have the space to treat here. There was a long history of written legal instruments in ancient Egypt. There are also the Aramaic papyri from the island of Elephantine that are of special significance for the history of Aramaic legal forms and the interaction of Egyptian and ancient Near Eastern legal forms (Botta 2009). And indeed there is the burgeoning field of Arabic papyrology with more than its share of legal documents.

But, apart from two Arabic documents (**6.6.6** and **7.4.8**), the texts translated in this volume are written in three different languages, Greek, Demotic, and Coptic, the latter two being the final stages of the ancient Egyptian language. Some are bilingual: Demotic–Greek and Greek–Latin.

[3] On the estimate of total number of papyri, see Van Minnen (2007: 705–06).

[4] Bagnall (2011) is a brilliant exposition of the extensiveness of written documents throughout the ancient world.

[5] Keenan (2009b).

We can only hope to give an impression here of a very complicated linguistic environment.[6] Most of the documents were written on papyrus, the most common form of ancient "paper," some on ostraca (small sherds of stone or pottery), and some, in later periods, on parchment (**6.6.4**) and paper (**6.6.6**, Arabic). Some of the papyri from the Ptolemaic period were preserved in what is termed cartonnage, recycled documents, much like the Turfan documents from China, used in the wrapping of human mummy masks and sacred animal mummies.[7] The legal texts recorded in these languages are usually treated by different groups of scholars using a variety of approaches. The reader of this volume may come to perceive differences between the formal Continental approach and the socio-economic focus of Anglo-American tradition. These differences are intentionally preserved.

We have two primary aims in publishing these texts together. First, we intend this volume to serve as an orientation to the field of legal papyrology. Second, by translating and discussing Ptolemaic-, Roman-, and Byzantine-period texts together in thematic chapters, we hope to illustrate the continuities in language and conception of the law across more than a millennium of legal history in one place, Egypt, which was the core of the Ptolemaic empire before becoming in 30 BC a province of the Roman empire, and, later, a part of the Byzantine empire down to its conquest by Arabs in AD 642.

Papyrology has traditionally concerned itself solely with Greek texts written on papyri or ostraca.[8] Although Greek papyri have been found outside of Egypt, we shall focus on Egypt; but we shall include not only Greek texts but also texts written in Demotic and Coptic. These last two sets of documents tend to be treated as separate from Greek papyrology despite obvious overlaps (including bilingual archives). The documents included in the volume (with the notable exception of those in **2.6**) are in the main concerned with private law (not administrative or public law) because that represents the bulk of what the papyri have to offer. The volume's initial chapter organization ruled out including large or continuous extracts from some famous legal texts like the Alexandrian regulations in *P.Hal.* I (see extract at **6.5.3**) or the rules of the Gnomon of the *Idios Logos* in (mainly) *BGU* V 1210; for these and other "codes and

[6] See, for example, the eighth-century AD trilingual tax document discussed by Sijpesteijn and Clackson (2009), and **3.4** below.

[7] On the Chinese documents, see *inter alia* Hansen (1995).

[8] For a comprehensive survey of the field, see Bagnall (2009).

regulations" the reader is referred to the excerpts in *Sel.Pap.* II 201–206 (for the brief extracts in this volume, please refer to the Concordance). Important but lengthy Demotic papyri similarly have not been included here. The most important of these are *P.Mattha*, a kind of legal manual of document forms and of legal procedure, and *P.Brit.Mus.* 10591, a copy of a court transcript of a trial concerned with an inheritance dispute between relatives.[9] Our concern here, in the main, is less with the normative than with the actual functioning of law on the ground. How did the purchaser of land get his or her acquisition duly recorded? What procedures did a defaulting debtor face? How did a victim of violence seek justice? And so on.

This volume will focus chronologically on the Ptolemaic, Roman and Byzantine periods. We do this merely to put some limits on what could have become a large, multi-volume work. For example, if we were to go back before the Ptolemaic period, we could easily have covered both the earlier history of Egyptian law as well as the important corpus of legal material from Elephantine island written in Aramaic. If we were to extend ourselves beyond the Arab Conquest, we could have included many more Arabic documents.

Legal documents from Egypt indeed have a long history, extending almost back to the origins of the state *c.*3100 BC.[10] From the Old Kingdom there are preserved records of private conveyances of property recorded in tombs. By the Middle Kingdom, there are preserved wills, literary texts presenting an idealized version of private pleadings before officials, and by the New Kingdom, a fuller array of legal documentation, including a text recorded inside two officials' tombs known as "The Duties of the Vizier," an instruction manual of legal procedure and administration by the chief official in charge of the state legal system (van den Boorn 1988).

This long history of the use of written legal instruments in private contexts as well as the public administration of justice surely played a strong role in the continuity of legal practice under the Ptolemies and beyond. At the same time, there were enormous social, political, and economic changes brought about by successive regimes in the last millennium BC and the first millennium AD that had an impact on legal practice and on the form of legal documents.

[9] For *P.Mattha*, see briefly below, pp. 17–18. Both texts are discussed in Manning (2010: 165–206).
[10] For an excellent overview of Egyptian law, see Lippert (2008).

1.1 The Ptolemaic period (332–30 BC)

J. G. Manning

The Ptolemaic period began when Ptolemy, one of Alexander the Great's generals, established himself in Egypt, claiming the title "king" in 304 BC after having been proclaimed such by his army in the previous year.[11] The Ptolemaic empire, stretching into the Aegean, Cyprus, parts of Asia Minor, Judea, and Cyrenaica, became one of the largest and most powerful of the Hellenistic kingdoms. Greeks from around the eastern Mediterranean flocked to Egypt to seek their fortunes as soldiers, merchants, and in other occupations (**3.1**). Ptolemy II, one of Ptolemy's sons, enjoyed one of the most successful reigns of the ancient world, and effected reforms of the economic and legal systems as part of the larger process of state formation. The entire political system relied on local cooperation, and in particular that of the local priests who legitimated Ptolemaic rule throughout Egypt. Local legal traditions, including the property rights regime and local trials before priestly tribunals, were continued, but under Ptolemaic supervision.

The most important reforms included the introduction of a new taxation system, including payments required in coin in some cases, a household census (whose frequency is not known), the use of banks, and the issuance of tax receipts. The whole system suggests strong state supervision and monitoring, and an increase in the use of writing. There is good reason, however, to question both the existence of strong state supervision of the economic system as a whole and the normative use of written instruments.

The Ptolemaic state was challenged by outside powers, particularly that of the Seleukids to their east, and by internal unrest throughout the second and first centuries BC. While from the end of the third and throughout the second century BC the Ptolemies' external empire shrank, the legal papyri suggest gradual improvement in administrative capacity and control, as well as new types of contract forms, an increase in the bureaucratic supervision of private disputes, and an apparent decline in the use of older Egyptian contract forms such as the so-called witness copy contract (**2.2**). Civil and dynastic unrest, both in Alexandria and in the countryside, was a feature of the last two centuries of Ptolemaic rule. The Theban revolt (206–186 BC) removed Ptolemaic administrative control of much of the

[11] A good, short overview of the period is provided in Vandorpe (2009b). An excellent political history is provided by Hölbl (2001).

south of the country. Roman intervention to expel Antiochus IV from Egypt in 168 BC marks the beginning of direct Roman influence upon the dynasty. The last serious uprising occurred at Thebes from 88 to 86 BC and elicited a strong reaction from Ptolemy IX against the rebels. The last twenty years of the dynasty saw the rise of Kleopatra and the effort once again to establish Ptolemaic hegemony in the eastern Mediterranean. Octavian's defeat of the Ptolemaic fleet at Actium in 31 BC put an end to such dreams, as Egypt was added to the Roman empire.

1.2 The Roman period (30 BC–AD 284)

Uri Yiftach-Firanko

After 30 BC, Egypt became one of the most important provinces of the *imperium Romanum*. Not only did Egypt yield much of Rome's *alimenta* – according to Flavius Josephus the entire provision of a period of four months a year[12] – but also its strategic position on the Red Sea accorded Egypt paramount importance with regard to overseas trade with India and the Far East.[13] The unique position of Egypt finds expression in an especially tight control exercised over its administration by the emperors. Known and often cited is the prohibition of senators and other *illustres* from visiting Egypt without imperial authorization,[14] as well as the attempts to curtail any accumulation and manifestation of power by the heads of its administration, as manifested in the story of the rise and fall of Cornelius Gallus, the first prefect of Egypt.[15]

One way of securing the loyalty of Egypt was to keep it in the emperor's hands: Egypt became an imperial, not a senatorial province, and to decentralize power within the province it was managed by several *equites* (Roman "knights"), who were all appointed by the emperor in person and thereby owed allegiance to him rather than the local governor.[16] Besides the *Praefectus Alexandriae et Aegypti* himself, the following were strategically important: the *procurator* of Nea Polis, in charge of receiving, storing, and shipping grain destined for Rome and other places in need; the *procurator* in charge of the *dioikêsis*, the general office for administering state income; officials supervising domain lands (*ousiai*), the *bona caduca*, and *bona vacantia* (the *idios logos*) (see *BGU* V 1210, extracts from which are

[12] *BJ* 2.386; and Montevecchi (1988: 451–54, 456).

[13] See, in particular, the "Muziris Papyrus" (*SB* XVIII 13167, unknown provenance, mid-second century AD) and, e.g., Rathbone (2001b).

[14] Tacitus, *Ann.* 2.59. [15] Montevecchi (1988: 428). [16] Montevecchi (1988: 439).

at **2.6.4** and **4.6.6** in this volume); and the *iuridicus*, the only *procurator* with strictly jurisdictional competences. The province was divided into three, and eventually four *epistrategiai*, each headed by a Roman *eques*, appointed by the emperor in person as well.[17]

One of the first measures taken by the Romans was the abrogation of earlier status groups with their individual privileges. These included Egyptian priestly elites and the *politeumata* (for the latter see **10.2**). Egypt was now divided into three population groups: (1) Roman citizens, (2) citizens of the autonomous *poleis* (*politai*), and (3) the rest, conveniently labeled as "Egyptians," *Aigyptioi.*[18] The effort invested in keeping these groups apart is shown by many of the regulations of the Gnomon of the *Idios Logos.*[19]

Among these three groups, Roman citizens were an important though distinct minority, sometimes identifiable in the documentary papyri by their use of the traditional *tria nomina*, or variants thereof (e.g., Gaius Longinus Castor and the various participants in his mancipatory will, **3.3.1**), or, following the legal principle of personality, by their use of clearly Roman legal forms (see especially **3.3** and **4.3**). Roman citizenship was gradually extended in Egypt through various individual and group grants, whose beneficiaries adopted the gentile name (*gentilicium*) and sometimes the *praenomen* (first name) of the benefactor, often the emperor himself, to whom their citizenship was owed or could be traced (e.g., the Marci Aurelii in **4.6.5a-b**). By the *Constitutio Antoniniana* of AD 212, all free residents of Egypt became Roman citizens; those so blessed can be traced in the papyri by their use of Caracalla's *gentilicium* Aurelius without associated *praenomen* (see, e.g., **3.3.5**, **4.6.5a**). In some cases this is made explicit, as in those of "Aurelius Zosimus, before the divine gift called Zosimus son of Leonides" (*BGU* II 655, 16 August AD 215), and "Aurelius Aelurion, *kosmêtês* in office, councilor of the city of Athribis, before obtaining Roman citizenship, (called) Aelurion son of Zoilus, of the Neokosmian tribe and Althaian deme" (*P.Oxy.* XII 1458, AD 216/7).

Politai, more numerous than Roman citizens at the start of the Roman period, but still restricted in number, were associated with four specially designated *poleis*: in chronological order of foundation, Naukratis, Alexandria, Ptolemais, and Antinoopolis. Even though citizens of these *poleis* played a significant role in the country's administration, society,

[17] Montevecchi (1988: 436–39). [18] See Mélèze Modrzejewski (1989).
[19] *BGU* V 1210 (Theadelphia, after AD 149), especially articles 38–53.

and economy as individuals,[20] the civic bodies associated with their *poleis* as such did not play a role in the general administration of the province, at least not to the extent of the far more numerous cities in other provinces. Things changed, in this respect, only after the grant in AD 200 of civic status to the nomes' *metropoleis* throughout the *chôra* (the term given to the province of Egypt minus Alexandria).

The third group of Egypt's residents, the *Aigyptioi*, was by far the largest, comprising all those who were neither Roman nor *politai*. But within this mass the Romans did single out certain elite groups. Most significant in this respect is the fostering of Greek socio-cultural institutions, in particular the *gymnasion* of the *metropoleis*, whose members formed a privileged, closely monitored cadre through which Greek culture was preserved and disseminated throughout the Egyptian *chôra*.[21] The incentive was practical no less than cultural. In the course of the generations following the occupation, much of the land's administration was undertaken by local manpower. As the language of the administration had for some time been Greek, the propagation of local hellenized elites was essential for the functioning of this apparatus.

The Roman period was also marked by a growing sophistication in the engagement of manpower. In the early Roman period, the administration was not based on large numbers of permanent civil servants; like the rest of the Roman empire, the province of Egypt is usually considered, in Weberian terms, to have been "underbureaucratized." Rather, after initially adopting the Ptolemaic tax-farming system, the provincial administration of Egypt gradually introduced a system of liturgies, which involved the compulsory engagement of the inhabitants of the provinces in service to the state.[22] The place and nature of a liturgy were decided on by the person's individual status. If a liturgist, such as a tax collector, was unable to collect the due amount of taxes, he would initially have had to pay the deficit out of his own resources (*poros*). This was one (though by no means the sole) incentive for the rise of private property, in particular of landed property, in Egypt in the course of the early Roman period.

One of the most significant institutions introduced by the Romans was the *epikephalaion* or *laographia*, a new type of poll-tax, to be paid annually by all male *Aigyptioi* between the ages of 14 and 61.[23] The introduction of this tax not only had economic and social implications but also far-reaching bureaucratic consequences. As every male subject aged 14 or over

20 Montevecchi (1988: 442): Alexandrians as nome *stratêgoi*. 21 Montevecchi (1975).
22 Montevecchi (1988: 458–60). 23 Montevecchi (1988: 448).

was bound to pay the tax it was necessary to know who these subjects were. Every fourteen years, therefore, each individual head of a family had to submit a personal declaration (*kat' oikian apographê*), reporting the taxable residents in his household.[24] The said declaration could be updated by declarations of birth and death and by applications for recognition as members of privileged status groups. The system of individual declaration was also extended to other areas such as livestock and uninundated land.[25] These declarations naturally needed to be preserved for future reference and the information they encompassed to be forwarded to higher authorities. The new system promoted the development of archival and bureaucratic skills that were also put into use in other spheres of bureaucratic activity, including those of legal significance (see especially **2.6**).

In the course of the first and second centuries AD a set of archives, both local and Alexandrian, evolved, which allowed the processing of information on people and property in Egypt. The effectiveness of the bureaucratic system is shown, for example, in the case of tax reports. At the end of each month every tax collector had to send a report of his revenues to the nome's *stratêgos*. Within two weeks the material would have been processed in the *stratêgos*' office and would have reached the city of Alexandria.[26]

The source material of the early Roman period bears witness to constant changes in the province's administrative apparatus. Every decade is marked by some change. Thus, for example, the creation of new archives occurred in the Neronian, Flavian, and Hadrianic periods and a reform of the taxation system under Trajan. Yet the pace of the reforms may have accelerated in the third century with the introduction of the nome *metropolis* as a key player in the provincial administration. These changes culminate in the administrative, fiscal, and monetary reforms of Diocletian, the beginning of whose reign, AD 284, may be taken to mark the end of the Roman period.

1.3 The Byzantine period (AD 284–640)

James G. Keenan

The naming of the period that follows the Roman is an unsettled topic. In this volume we have adopted for convenience' sake the term "Byzantine,"

24 An excellent example of this type of declaration can be found in *P.Brux.* I 1–21, a *tomos synkollêsimos* with declarations from the Prosopite nome, dating to AD 174.
25 A thorough and relatively recent discussion by Kruse (2002: 63–251).
26 Cf, e.g., *BGU* III 981 (Diospolites Parvus, AD 77) and Wallace (1938: 37, 320).

as used by Mitteis and Wilcken in 1912 – though the papyrological Byzantine period, from AD 284 to 640 or thereabouts, is probably too early to suit professional Byzantinists, whose field stretches down to AD 1453. At times during the twentieth century, some papyrologists felt that a distinction should be drawn between an early and a late Byzantine period, though the cutoff between the two was never precisely determined, perhaps because of the difficulties caused by the dearth of fifth-century papyri. It is probably safe to say that the early Byzantine period roughly corresponded to what these days may be called, as Roger Bagnall did in his famous book (Bagnall 1993b), 'late antiquity', marking a beginning with Diocletian and an ending at *c.* AD 450.

This "Byzantine" label is of course keyed to political history, or perhaps administrative history, because from *c.* AD 330 the eastern half of the Roman empire was no longer ruled from Rome but from Byzantium, or, better, Constantinople. Other labels sometimes used for Egypt in this period, "Christian" and "Coptic," are based on religious, cultural, and, in the latter case, also linguistic criteria. The conversion to Christianity, progressive rather than radical, can be traced through the fourth century by, among other criteria, the changing repertoire of personal names (Bagnall 1982, 1987), including but far from restricted to names from the Old and New Testaments. From a fourth-century world in religious transition we arrive, by the fifth and surely the sixth century, at a world almost universally Christian.

In economic terms a distinctive feature of the Byzantine period derives from Constantine's stabilizing of the standard gold coin, the *solidus* (*nomisma* or *nomismation* in Greek), struck at seventy-two to the pound and itself notionally divided, depending on the applicable local standard, into from 18 (as in **5.5.3** = **8.2.4**, AD 569; *P.Lond.Herm.* introduction §5) to 24 carats (*keratia*); it can also be found in halves (as in **5.5.3** = **8.2.4**) and thirds (**6.6.2**, AD 758), which divisions corresponded to actual coins (*semisses*, *tremisses*). This is an innovation that outlasted the Arab conquest (see **6.6** *passim*). Meanwhile, Egypt remained an imperial "breadbasket," but now its grain, under the supervision of the Augustal prefect (despite the provincial divisions discussed in the next paragraph), was shipped through Alexandria to Constantinople instead of Rome. Overall control of Egyptian finances was in the hands of the *rationalis* (*katholikos* in Greek), also based in Alexandria.

In administrative terms the major innovation of the Byzantine period was the division of the Roman province of Egypt into a number of smaller provinces, each with its own governor and corresponding bureaucratic office (*taxis*, *officium*). Such experiments in administrative multiplication, which began early and whose details need not delay us here, were in some sense finalized by Justinian in his Edict XIII, dating to AD 539 (Keenan 2000: 612–17). Of the six provinces there established, or reestablished, two are of greatest concern to papyrologists. One is the province of Arcadia, with its capital at Oxyrhynchos, whose ash heaps have been the most important provenance of late papyri (and papyri in general). The other is the province of the Lower Thebaid, with its capital at Antinoopolis, but also encompassing major sources of papyri at Hermopolis, a major city across the Nile from Antinoopolis, and the village of Aphrodito (more properly in this period, the village of Aphrodite). An interesting set of large-sized, late sixth- to early seventh-century legal documents, the bilingual (Greek and Coptic) Patermouthis archive, comes from Syene (modern Aswan) on the First Cataract (Dijkstra 2008: 65–70 and *passim*; translations, Porten 1996). As an example from the archive see **6.6.1**, whose address illustrates one of the features typical of contracts of the period: the civilian party to this sale carries the status designation Aurelia (feminine), traceable to the *Constitutio Antoniniana* of AD 212 (see **1.2**); the cavalryman who purchases the house carries the higher designation Flavius, linked to the Byzantine imperial household. Both identify themselves as originating from or living in Syene, but if they had come from elsewhere, that would have been so stated (Keenan 2001).

A source like Syene only partly compensates for the disappearance of villages that lined the Fayyum's desert edge (Soknopaiou Nesos, Karanis, Tebtunis, Theadelphia, etc.), sources of so many papyri from the Ptolemaic and Roman periods (Keenan 2003). If, even for earlier periods, there was an urban bias to the evidence, so much the more for the Byzantine. Under the circumstances it may seem ironic that some scholars (e.g., Alston 2002) have seen in the Byzantine period a shift of wealth from city to country and a corresponding decline of cities as the predominant social, political, and economic units. This runs contrary to the pattern found in contracts of the period (no examples in this volume), where in loans, leases, and sales on delivery between city-dwellers and villagers, the creditors, lessors, and buyers are regularly city-dwellers, the opposite parties are villagers (Keenan 1981). Perhaps the impression of wealth moving into the country is to be linked to the large estates of the period, the subject of so much recent discussion, especially as represented by those of the Apion family of Oxyrhynchos, one of whose members reached the ordinary consulship in AD 539. How were these estates organized, how large were they, were they directly exploited or leased out (and in what proportions), what was the condition of their workforce? This last topic, the only one that surfaces in the present volume, may be conveniently approached through **8.2–3**.

The Byzantine period ended with the Arab conquest of the AD 640s. Papyri like those in the recently published volume *CPR* XXX evidence an early concerted public building program at the new capital at Babylon and the organization of vast "national" resources to that end. Greek remains a language of administration into the eighth century, then to be replaced by Arabic. Coptic in the eighth century experiences its heyday as a legal language, especially with its documents, e.g., **6.6.2**, from the town of Djême, built in the remains of the Pharaonic temple at Medinet Habu (Wilfong 2002). Coptic, like Greek, soon came to be replaced by Arabic. For both developments, see below **1.8** and further **2.7**, **6.6**, and **7.4**.

1.4 Monuments in juristic papyrology

James G. Keenan, J. G. Manning, and Uri Yiftach-Firanko

The study of legal documents in Greek (and Latin) and the study of legal documents in Demotic have tended to proceed as separate endeavors. In the former, although Mitteis' *Reichsrecht und Volksrecht in den östlichen Provinzen des römischen Kaiserreichs* of 1891 was a landmark in legal and intellectual history, it was still too early in the not-yet-named science of papyrology (Keenan 2009a: 61), too pre-papyrological, to be of much practical value to juristic papyrology today. The same does not apply to Mitteis' contribution to his and Wilcken's four-volume *Grundzüge und Chrestomathie der Papyruskunde* of 1912. This massive summation of documentary papyrology to date (Keenan 2009a: 64) was composed when Mitteis, educated in Vienna but since 1899 a member of the juristic faculty at Leipzig (Rupprecht 2007b, with photo), was at the height of his scholarly maturity. The set consisted of two halves, Wilcken's historical and Mitteis' juristic. Each half contained a basic introduction (*Grundzüge*) and a collection of illustrative texts (*Chrestomathie*). Although each volume in the four-volume set remains fundamental in its own way, the value of the two *Chrestomathie* volumes has perhaps been less dimmed by passage of time. In Mitteis' case the *Chrestomathie* (*M.Chr.*) encompassed 382 documents. To save space, texts were printed continuously (as in the other collections to be mentioned below) rather than printed line by line as in the originals; even so they run to 430 pages. The texts are keyed to the *Grundzüge* (and vice versa) and therefore appear in the *Chrestomathie* with only succinct but papyrologically valuable introductions and with juristically acute notes – but without translations. With the exception of a number of laws (*Gesetze*) in chapter 12, the texts are overwhelmingly Greek and feature, in terms of coverage, chapters on: Ptolemaic procedure (1), Roman civil procedure (2), types of documents (3), registration (4), loans and pledges (5), sale (6), marriage (8), and inheritance (9).

Not long after Mitteis, Paul M. Meyer (*Jur.Pap.*) presented his own selection of papyri, the ninety-two texts that he judged the most important from a juristic standpoint, plus an appendix with extracts from the just published (1919) *BGU* V 1210, the Berlin Gnomon of the *Idios Logos*. Here, though documents are fewer, introductions and commentaries are correspondingly longer than in *M.Chr.* – and still without translation. Meyer's principles of organization differ from those of Mitteis' *Grundzüge* and *M.Chr.* in that his book adheres more closely to what may be called the Roman institutional scheme (as found in Gaius' *Institutes*, and Justinian's) of subjects: the law of persons (Part A), the law of obligations (C), the law of things (D), and the law of civil procedure (F). Positioned between are a long section on *Urkundenwesen*, or "diplomatics" (B), and a short one on criminal procedure (E).

Papyri also figure prominently but far from exclusively among the texts collected by Victor Arangio-Ruiz (1884–1964; image at www.ulb.ac.be/assoc/aip/galerie_a-f.htm) in *Fontes Iuris Romani Anteiustiniani*, vol. III (*Negotia*), first edition 1940, second edition 1972, with translations and commentaries in Latin.

M.Chr., *Jur.Pap.*, and *FIRA* III are still convenient bases from which to acquire an orientation to many of the major documents of juristic papyrology (all three of course are now outdated), but require for any hopeful student a command of Greek and German, or Latin, and an understanding that these volumes skirt the broader reach of Egyptian law in Demotic and Coptic documents and tend to be thin on the Byzantine period, still the most neglected of the three traditional periods (Ptolemaic, Roman, Byzantine) of the papyrological millennium (see above **1.1–3**).

More general guidance through the arcana of juristic papyri of all periods was provided by Polish scholar Raphael Taubenschlag (1881–1958; image at www.ulb.ac.be/assoc/aip/galerie_s-z.htm) in his *The Law of Greco-Roman Egypt in the Light of the Papyri, 332 B.C.–A.D. 640*. Its first edition was published in 1944, when Taubenschlag, who had emigrated from Poland to France, then to the U.S., was at Columbia University in New York. It was approved by one reviewer (H. I. Bell, *CR* 59 (1945): 25–26) as an "up-to-date manual . . . meant not merely for legal experts . . . but also for editors and students of papyri." The book was revised and enlarged (484 pages to 789) after Taubenschlag's return to Warsaw in 1947.[27] The 1955 version, generally abbreviated as *Law*², has been probably the single most cited work on juristic questions that emerge from the papyri.[28] The book is largely but not exclusively organized according to Roman institutional principles (like *Jur.Pap.*), starting with the private law of persons (persons, domestic relations, inheritance), then property (real rights, obligations, sale, consensual contracts, etc.), then penal law (see **10.4** introduction), procedure and execution, political and administrative law. What may surprise first-time users will be the ratio of text (relatively sparse) to footnotes, extensive in their bibliographies, documentary citations, and excerpted quotations from the papyri.

H. J. Wolff (1902–1983; image at www.ulb.ac.be/assoc/aip/galerie_s-z.htm) was perhaps the most prolific legal scholar of the twentieth century's second half, despite his death in 1983.[29] His writings include seminal monographs, most conspicuously *Justizwesen der Ptolemäer* (1962, second edition 1970) on the court system of Ptolemaic Egypt as conceived in the third century BC and developed thereafter. In his articles he also studied the peculiar nature (from a Roman legal standpoint) of the Greek contract which was created by the surrender of an object to another person for a designated purpose; once the purpose of the delivery was accomplished, or for some reason could no longer be attained, the contract automatically came to an end.[30] Itinerant for much of his adult life, Wolff finally achieved a permanent position at Freiburg in 1955 (Simon 1987). It was in retirement that he dedicated his efforts to his masterwork, *Das Recht der griechischen Papyri Ägyptens in der Zeit der Ptolemäer und des Prinzipats*, whose first volume, on types of Greek legal documents in Egypt, was published in 1978. A second volume, edited by H.-A. Rupprecht and concerned with the various legal orders in Ptolemaic and Roman Egypt, would appear in 2002, long after Wolff's death.[31]

[27] See www.jewishvirtuallibrary.org/jsource/judaica/ejud_0002_0019_0_19632.html, by Reuven Yaron and Ruth Beloff, for biographical details.

[28] Taubenschlag was also founder of the *Journal of Juristic Papyrology* and author of numerous studies, many of which are collected in his two-volume *Opera Minora* (Warsaw, 1959). His *Das Strafrecht im Rechte der Papyri* (1916) is still the only comprehensive work on criminal law in Graeco-Roman Egypt. Other eventually repatriated exiles included H. J. Wolff (see below) and Fritz Pringsheim, author of *The Greek Law of Sale* (1950), both to Freiburg.

[29] He also acted as an advisor to several doctoral students, whose dissertations are still indispensable for students of the law of the papyri, especially in relation to the law of contract. We can only regret that most of them did not pursue scholarly activity after gaining their doctorates.

[30] See in particular Wolff (1957).

[31] See the review by Verhoogt (2004).

Although the field of legal or juristic papyrology has been blessed by the monuments of scholarship mentioned here, the field has mostly progressed over the years through specialist articles in specialist journals, in monographs on single topics, and in juristic dissertations at mainly German universities. The history of the field remains to be written. In the meantime Rupprecht (1994: ch. 3) provides a concise topic-by-topic survey with extensive bibliography for each. Many of the works there cited, together with more recent work, will be found in the Works cited of the present volume.

Before moving on, it is worth highlighting two points. First, most work during the formative period of the subject, in particular the decades 1890–1930, was conducted in Germany. Since, however, many of these scholars were also Jewish – for example, Adolf Berger, Fritz Pringsheim, Ernst Rabel, Andreas B. Schwarz, Raphael Taubenschlag, and H.-J. Wolff – Nazi racial policy, and ultimately the near-extermination of European Jewry, dealt a heavy blow to the field from which it never really recovered, even in spite of the eventual repatriation of Pringsheim, Taubenschlag, and Wolff.

Second, some of the scholars who started their work in legal papyrology at a later date achieved renown far beyond the narrow circles of the legal papyrological community: this was the case, for example, with Ernst Rabel, who made his first steps as a scholar of the law of the papyri and later became one of the founders of the discipline of comparative law.

The study of Demotic legal texts is nearly as old as the field of Demotic studies itself, even in some respects predating work on legal texts from Egypt in Greek and Latin as just discussed. Demotic is a distinct phase of the ancient Egyptian language in a cursive script that originated in the Delta around 650 BC and spread in use throughout Egypt as the Saite dynasty gained political hold of the Nile valley during the seventh and sixth centuries BC (Depauw 1997).[32] During most of the time when Demotic was in use, Egypt was ruled by foreigners. Under the Persians, Egypt was a province (satrapy) of the Persian empire. With new populations came new legal systems. Thus Aramaic legal papyri in the Persian period and the abundant Greek documentation and the legal traditions that these represent certainly interacted with the Egyptian legal tradition, although the process is not always easy to assess.[33] The use of Demotic as

[32] For a summary of the rise and spread of the Demotic script in Egypt, see Donker van Heel (1994). On the development of Demotic legal instruments during the first millennium BC, see Menu (1988).

[33] On the supposed "Jewish" law in Ptolemaic Egypt, see Mélèze Modrzejewski (2001). The acknowledgement of the receipt of a satisfactory price in Demotic sale contracts may have been

an independent language of legal instruments was in decline by the late Ptolemaic period. There are fewer published Demotic legal texts from the Roman period, by which time Greek had become dominant in legal instruments.[34] Demotic nevertheless continued to be used for tax receipts, temple accounts, and literary texts well into the second century AD.[35] The last Demotic contract is dated AD 175/6.[36]

It was in Paris that Eugene Revillout (1843–1913) established Demotic law as a field of investigation, although his rapidly produced studies, at a time when the language and script were not as well known as they are now, are on the whole unreliable by modern standards. Nevertheless, his *Cours de droit égyptienne* (1884) and *Les obligations en droit égyptien comparé aux autres droits de l'antiquité* (1886) formed the basis of all subsequent work on Demotic law. In the next generation, Wilhelm Spiegelberg (1870–1930; image at www.ulb.ac.be/assoc/aip/galerie_s-z.htm) in Germany, a superb editor of texts, was responsible for many of the first editions of Demotic legal texts in European collections. Two of his last students, Arthur Schiller (1902–77) and Erwin Seidl (1905–87; image at www.ulb.ac.be/assoc/aip/galerie_s-z.htm), contributed enormously not only to Egyptian law but to Ptolemaic Greek (Seidl) and Roman (Schiller) law as well.[37] Schiller's special interest in Coptic law is on display in his important edition and reference work, *Ten Coptic Legal Texts* (1932). (For Schiller's work in this area, see **1.8**.)

Before that, in 1920, Kurt Sethe (1869–1934; image at http://aaew.bbaw.de/wbhome/com/bg/imgSethe.html) and Josef Partsch (1882–1925; image at www.ulb.ac.be/assoc/aip/galerie_m-r.htm) had published a landmark work on one type of contract, *Bürgschaftsurkunden*, or contracts with third-party guarantees. It remains one of the most important contributions to Demotic papyrology. Other scholars have followed this model by collecting and studying particular types of legal instruments.[38] Another method of publishing legal texts is to group them by archives and dossiers

inserted into the contractual language under the influence of the Greek law of sale. See Pierce (1972: 99–100).

[34] Zauzich (1983), Lewis (1993), Bagnall (1993b: 235–40). Roman period Demotic legal texts come from Soknopaiou Nesos and Tebtunis in the Fayyum.

[35] Vleeming (1981), Pestman (1985b), Ray (1994).

[36] *P.Tebt.Botti* 3. On the decline of Demotic as a legal language see Lewis (1993), Manning (2003a: 173–77), Muhs (2005a).

[37] An excellent overview of Schiller's career is provided by Stein, P. (1986). For Seidl, see Rupprecht (1989).

[38] E.g., Lüddeckens (1960) on marriage contracts (**4.1** below), Kaplony-Heckel (1963) on temple oaths, Zauzich (1968) on instruments of sale (**2.2** below), Pierce (1972) on sale in advance of delivery, Felber (1997a) on leases (**7.1** below).

(Vandorpe 2009a), of which there are now some 370 known from *c.*650 BC to the Arab conquest (Clarysse 2010: 55).[39] In the second half of the twentieth century it has been the work of P. W. Pestman (1933–2010; image at www.ulb.ac.be/assoc/aip/galerie_m-r.htm) in Leiden that has contributed most to Demotic legal papyrology and in particular to the study of family archives of the Ptolemaic period.[40] At the same time studies like those inspired by Pestman have reduced the traditional gap between papyrology (in the limited sense of *Greek* papyrology) and Demotic studies and indicated that a full picture of the legal world of the Ptolemaic period (especially) requires mastery of both sets of evidence in combination.

1.5 Law under the Ptolemies

J. G. Manning

The complexity of law in the Ptolemaic period was the result of the political history of Egypt in the first millennium BC as well as ancient and more recent patterns of immigration. Well-established forms of written agreement (sales, leases, loans) were developed in the Demotic tradition from the middle of the seventh century BC. While the extent of successful state supervision of local society can be debated, it is clear that, beginning with the Ptolemaic period, scholars have available to them a far greater corpus of legal material than ever before. Indeed the legal papyri from Egypt constitute one of the single largest corpora of legal texts from the pre-modern world. Documents written in the interest of property rights constitute by far the largest corpus of Demotic texts. The same holds true with the Greek papyri.

The basic forms of Egyptian contract, as well as the legal traditions preserved by scribal practice, were carried over into the Ptolemaic period.[41] Greek and Egyptian traditions of contracting and adjudication came together, but were not systematized, in the period. At times within the same family Greek and Egyptian documents existed side by side (see **3.1**). It is Ptolemy II who is generally given credit for the major reforms of the state economic and legal administration during the 270s BC

[39] The Trismegistos site conveniently groups texts by archives: www.trismegistos.org/.

[40] For a review of Pestman's career see Sirks (2011).

[41] *P.Mattha* (Chapter 3 introduction), an important Demotic legal manual of forms and procedure dating to the third century BC, provides important but by no means the only evidence. See most recently Stadler (2004) and below, Chapter 3 introduction and **10.3**. On the question of legal "codes" from the period, see Lippert (2004); Lippert and Schentuleit (2010).

(Wolff 1960, below, **10.1**). Among the most important reforms in the sphere of law was the organization of the court system, subordinated, in theory although probably not very much in practice, to "royal law." There was, on the other hand, no overarching legislation that imposed a new legal order throughout Egypt. *P.Mattha* shows us that Demotic legal forms and procedures continued to be followed in the Ptolemaic and early Roman periods.

The *chrêmatistai* grew to be the main court by the second century BC for adjudicating Greek law in general, termed "laws of the cities," and probably referring to the various Greek traditions in the city states (**10.1**), while the *laokritai* ("the people's judges"), composed of a tribunal of Egyptian priests, heard local disputes involving Egyptians but with the presence of state officials (**10.1.4**).[42] For the Jewish population, Mélèze Modrzejewski argues (1995: 8–10), probably correctly, that the Septuagint translation of the Torah became the main source of Jewish law in Egypt.[43] Jews certainly used the Greek courts in Egypt (**10.1.3**). By the end of the second century BC it appears, however, that the language of the legal instruments involved in a dispute became the determining factor in a court's jurisdiction (**10.1.4**), although this is disputed by some scholars.[44] To be sure such a simple scheme was likely not always followed in any case. The role of the state can be seen not only in the monitoring of trials and in petitions, but also in the area of contract form (**2.1**), registration of contracts (**6.5**), in the control of land (**7.2**), in labor contracts (**8.1**), in the supervision of slavery (**9.1**), and in the use of public auctions to sell property (**6.3.4**).

Greeks (each with their own legal traditions from their city or region), Jews, and others who immigrated to Egypt in the third century BC brought with them to their new communities their legal traditions.[45]

[42] On the development of the Ptolemaic courts, see above all Wolff (1962, 2002: 84–85), Mélèze Modrzejewski (1995). A trial before the *laokritai* in the southern village of Asyut is preserved in a Demotic papyrus (P.Brit.Mus.EA 10591) dating to the mid-second century BC, on which see Manning (2010).

[43] The tradition, largely formed on the basis of the *Letter of Aristeas*, is that the Septuagint was written in the third century BC, and specifically at the request of Ptolemy II. This is a much-debated point. On the state of the debate, see Mélèze Modrzejewski (1995), Pearce (2007), van der Kooij (2007), and below, **10.1**.

[44] Below, **10.1.4**; Pestman (1985c).

[45] *P.Eleph.* 1, for example, a private marriage contract written in Greek, dated 310 BC (and therefore the earliest dated Greek document from Egypt), preserves old Greek legal forms (e.g., "upon all property . . . both land and sea") and might well also preserve a Dorian Greek legal tradition as well as reflect more recent, Hellenistic trends including the greater use of written records (Gagarin 2008: 236). See further Porten and Farber (1996: 408–10). Cf. **2.1.1** below.

The status of "Greek" law in the Hellenistic period has for many years been debated among legal historians. The Greek cities in Egypt (Alexandria, Ptolemais, Naukratis) were subject both to a separate body of civic law and to the royal edicts regulating norms.[46] Selected passages of such a "civil code" for Alexandria are preserved in a document that probably served as written "justifications" (*dikaiômata*) for legal arguments in several legal disputes.[47] Such written documentary support for a legal claim in a dispute, by the way, seems also to have been used in the famous trial held before the Egyptian *laokritai* that is documented in *P.Brit.Mus.* 10591 (Thompson, H. 1934). It was not only written documentary evidence that was presented as proof however. A "law of year 21" is cited as the controlling law in the dispute. It is not clear exactly what this "law" is, but it would appear to be a royal decree. If that is so, it would show that Ptolemaic law encapsulated re-stated Egyptian law, not a fusion of law, but an incorporation of legal tradition under new state sovereignty.

We know from other sources that Ptolemaic decrees had substantial and long-lasting effects on law throughout the period and well into Roman times. Royal law concerned with specific legal matters was certainly promulgated through written decrees and orders – *diagrammata* and *prostagmata*.[48] But there is unlikely to have been anything like a unified "Greek" law applied in Egypt. What centralized features there were were driven by state supervision of dispute resolution and to a certain extent of contract forms. It was perhaps the complexity of law, and the increased need for written evidence (Gagarin 2008: 235), that gave rise during the period to the need for professional lawyers, clearly in evidence, for example, in the famous Hermias trial recorded in *UPZ* II 162, one of the most remarkable legal documents from the pre-modern world.[49] Scribes and notaries played a major role in innovation of the legal forms as well as in procedure. "In many respects," Gagarin (2008: 241) concludes, "law in Ptolemaic Egypt resembled early common law in England."

[46] *P.Gurob* 2 (*c.*275 BC; = *CPJud.* I 19) is the main text.

[47] *P.Hal.* (= Bagnall and Derow 2004, no. 124), a mid-third-century papyrus deriving from the opposite end of the country, Elephantine. The papyrus also contains other forms of law, such as a letter from Ptolemy to an official clarifying the procedure for the billeting of soldiers. The text requires a new study. It has been summarized by Fraser (1972: 109–10).

[48] Fraser (1972: 107), Lenger (1964), Müller, B.J. (1968). Samples with English translation of such decrees can be read at *Sel.Pap.* II 207–32.

[49] See Chapter 10 below on trial reports and procedures.

1.6 Law in the Roman period

Uri Yiftach-Firanko

Information on legal institutions is gathered primarily from five documentary genres: contracts, petitions, minutes of court proceedings, laws, and letters, all genres that are commonly recorded on papyri, though much less frequently on ostraca. As early Roman papyri stem almost entirely from middle Egypt – in particular the Arsinoite, Herakleopolite, Hermopolite, and Oxyrhynchite nomes – this is also the region on which the study of law in this period focuses. Other regions are considerably less well documented – Upper Egypt (which yields quite a few documents in the Ptolemaic and Byzantine periods), for example, and naturally also the Delta and Alexandria. Within the area of middle Egypt, most finds stem from the Arsinoite nome's desert edges, while in the case of the Oxyrhynchite and the Hermopolite nomes most documentary finds stem from the nomes' *metropoleis* (capital cities).

Among the above-mentioned documentary genres, contracts are especially well studied: virtually every type of contract – e.g., loans, leases, sales, marriage contracts, and wills – has been studied in at least one monograph, occasionally more. Much less attention has been given to other sources: an exhaustive study of minutes of court proceedings and letters – all sources of major legal relevance – is still a desideratum (**10.3**). It goes without saying, then, that the following is a very tentative introduction, not a conclusive account of the legal history of Egypt in the Roman period.

The Ptolemaic legal system was based on the Greco-Egyptian dichotomy. Egyptians, that is the population that inhabited Egypt before the Macedonian conquest, were supposed to have their contracts documented by Egyptian scribes applying Egyptian language, terminology, and formulas. If the contents of these documents happened to be disputed, the judges to hear the case were the Egyptian board of the *laokritai*, where, apart from the laws of the king himself, an autochthonic set of regulations, "the laws of the land," was to be applied. The Greek settlers, on the contrary, were supposed to have their contracts drawn up by Greek scribes, in Greek, under the application of terminology and formulas that went back to the Greek world before Alexander. The regulations to be applied here, apart from the king's decrees, were the *politikoi nomoi*, perhaps the laws of the city of Alexandria (**10.1**).

This bipartite system, instituted through the legislation of Ptolemy II in the late 270s BC, was hardly applicable in later times, primarily because legally separating Greeks and Egyptians was no longer as practicable in later generations as it may have initially been (cf. **3.1**, **5.2**). The Ptolemaic state still endeavored to salvage some elements of this conceptual edifice,[50] but the Roman administration did not.

The Roman administration of Egypt promoted Greek language into the position of the sole language for recording legal activity – be they legal documents, petitions, minutes of court proceedings (cf. **3.2**). It achieved this goal both by limiting the scope of application of the Demotic script (see above, **1.5**) and subjecting it to requirements that would make its use generally unrewarding.[51] The same objective was also pursued by disseminating over the *chôra* a set of scribal offices that made the composition of Greek legal documents cheaper and more accessible than in the preceding period (**2.1**). The consequences of this policy are felt everywhere in the Roman period.

Within the Greek scribal system, the Roman period is marked by a richness and diversity of documents unattested in earlier times. Each region possesses its own particular scribal tradition, characterized by the use of unique formulas, unique terminology. Moreover, in each locality one could turn to more than one type of scribe for documenting his (or her) legal activities, and this scribe was capable of adapting existing schemes to the particular needs of the individual parties in question. The result is a continuing, perhaps growing conceptual and terminological diversification, as well as the evolution of new institutions and new concepts, many of which have not been sufficiently studied. In later times this evolution becomes a means by which the language of Greek contracts is gradually Romanized (**3.3**, **4.3**).[52] The role played by these scribes in furthering private economic activity should not be underestimated (see, e.g., the evolution in the Roman period of the new form of security without conveyance of title called *hypallagma*, compared with the older, and stricter form of the *hypothêkê* and security sales (discussed in **5.4**, cf. **5.5**).

Another element of the early Ptolemaic bipartite system that came to an end in the Roman period is the court system (**10.1**). The idea that two

50 Cf., in particular, *P.Tebt.* I 5 207–20 (= *M.Chr.* I, 118 BC), giving as criterion for the applicable court the language of the document, and not, as earlier, the nationality of the parties (**10.1.4**).

51 This, however, does not imply that Egyptian legal traditions per se were banned. See further Chapter 3, introduction.

52 Wolff (1956).

distinct courts should separately serve the two main ethnic groups, Greeks and Egyptians, was already compromised in the Ptolemaic period by the growing difficulty in drawing a clear distinction between them and by the introduction of new judiciary boards, most conspicuously the king's direct representatives, the *chrêmatistai*, as a popular alternative to the national courts. In this respect, too, the Roman conquest marks the end of a long development. The court of the *laokritai* and the Greek *dikastêrion* were abolished, and so were the *politikoi nomoi*.

In the new system, as it evolves in the early Roman period, justice is not administered by special boards, but normally by major officeholders in the province. Parties would report their grievances to local potentates and officeholders, to the nome's *stratêgos*, as well as to Roman equestrian officers in Alexandria, especially the *praefectus Aegypti* and the *iuridicus* (**10.3**). The hearing by these officials took the informal form of an interview by the judge of the litigants and their advocates. In these "interviews" the parties gave account of the issue at stake and brought forward pieces of evidence that seemed to support their cases (**10.4**).

In these hearings, the parties could introduce any piece of evidence, any source of law they deemed fit, and the judge, who as in the preceding period was not in possession of an exhaustive law code, was at liberty to decide which of these sources he would take into consideration. Still, in the course of the Roman period there evolved several sources that judges would consider on a regular basis. One such source was rulings by other high-ranking officials in similar cases. For this reason, minutes of legal hearings became widespread as a documentary genre in the early Roman period (**10.3.6**). Roman judges also took into consideration the practices of their non-Roman subjects. To get acquainted with these practices, the provincial administration had these practices documented in a source called "the laws of the Egyptians." This treatise, incorporating regulations of Greek and Egyptian origin alike, was interpreted in court by the *nomikoi*, provincial legal experts.[53]

One of the sources, surprisingly rarely applied in early Roman Egypt, in courts as elsewhere, is precepts of Roman origin, those stemming from *ius civile*, *ius honorarium*, *senatus consulta*, or imperial constitutions. Such precepts seem to be applied primarily where the parties are Roman citizens *and* the issue at stake relates to the law of succession, family, or personal status (cf. **3.3**, **4.3**). In other spheres they are manifestly absent, as is

[53] Yiftach-Firanko (2009: 550–55).

Roman legal documentation in general, primarily because claims were not formulated and introduced to court in the highly professional language and terminology of the edicts of the Roman city magistrates that emerged in the republican period.[54] Rather, petitions to officials, written by ordinary persons, reflect "legal" understanding and categories of these people and not those of Roman law (**10.3.4**, **10.4.1**).

The growing sophistication of the Roman archival system (**2.6**) was used also for legal purposes. State interest in monitoring land conveyances is evident in all times. In the Ptolemaic period it meant that every land sale had to be registered with special officials, the *tamiai* in the case of the city of Alexandria, the *agoranomoi* in the case of the *chôra*. As these officials were not available everywhere – the *agoranomoi* were primarily located in the nomes' capitals – the time and money involved in performing the act formed a disincentive for land conveyances, and for all transactions for which registration was necessary (e.g., security sales in the case of loans) (**6.5**). In the mid-first century, the responsibility of registering property transfers was taken over by a new archive, the *bibliothêkê enktêseôn*.

The new archive was located, just as the old *agoranomeion*, in the nomes' capitals, but now the parties did not need to attend this office in person. They would address the local scribe of the village *grapheion* (record office), and the scribe would draw up the sale contract after he procured from the *bibliophylakes* a confirmation that no conflicting property rights were registered in their files (**2.6**, **5.3**). By registering the new conveyance, the *bibliothêkê*'s files were then kept up to date. This new archival system, as other systems (e.g, the *dêmosiôsis*, **2.6**), spurred private economic activity in early Roman Egypt.[55]

1.7 Law in the Byzantine period

James G. Keenan

Just as 1891, the *annus mirabilis* marked by a number of significant publications, is often said (in retrospect) to have introduced papyrology as a significant and modern scholarly discipline (Keenan 2009a: 59–61; there are competing dates), the same may be said of what has been its chief ancillary field, juristic papyrology. But here the date's significance is marked by a single classic work, Ludwig Mitteis' *Reichsrecht und Volksrecht* (Mitteis 1891; see **1.4**). Today probably more cited from respect than read with care, Mitteis' book may at least be credited with having set

[54] Yiftach-Firanko (2009: 553–55). [55] Cf. in particular F. Lerouxel (forthcoming).

the important questions that papyrus documents (and inscriptions) of the Roman period may be used to address: namely, questions about the knowledge and efficacy of imperial law in provincial context. A glance at Mitteis' *Quellenverzeichniss* (list of sources), however, will show how few papyri were then at his disposal, and a look at his text shows that he was less interested in the late period (likewise in Mitteis' *Grundzüge* and *M.Chr.* of 1912), but greatly keyed into the problem of the *Constitutio Antoniniana* of AD 212 and its impact on the provinces of the Eastern Empire, including Egypt, where, he held, the "Volksrecht" remained strong and effective down to the Arab conquest (Mitteis 1891: 58; see **1.8**). For the Byzantine period, and for Egypt, the analogous problem is posed by the papyri in conjunction with the imperial law codes, especially with those compilations emanating from Justinian's legislative program of the late 520s into the 530s, and with the "new laws," or "novels" (*novellae*), that followed; in other words, the problem-filled attempt "to weave together the bits and patches of the papyri with the tangled skein of the Codes and Novels" (Jones 1951: 271)[56] and the difficulty of tracing norms in relation to practice (Keenan 1975; cf. **4.2** introduction).

For years the traditional view, Raphael Taubenschlag's in articles dating back to the 1930s (grand summation in Taubenschlag 1955), was that, as with earlier Roman law (*contra* Mitteis), Justinian's laws were known and effective in Egypt and were in identifiable instances specifically cited in the papyri (cf. Taubenschlag 1959: esp. 113–14). A collection of the relevant papyrus texts was subsequently assembled by Amelotti and Luzzatto (1972; 2nd edition Amelotti and Migliardi Zingale 1985). But in the early 1970s, this view was provocatively challenged by A. Arthur Schiller in two revisionist articles (Schiller 1970, 1971).[57] The first rejected the idea that Justinian's laws were known, much less practiced, in Egypt; the second proposed that civil courts in Egypt had disappeared in the course of the sixth century (rebuttal to the latter, Simon 1971, and see below). Schiller dismissed the idea that references in the papyri were to specific enactments of Justinian or that Justinian's laws had any specific "impact upon the private law of Egypt ... What imperial law is reflected in the instruments drafted by Egyptian notaries of the sixth and later centuries ... flows from imperial decrees incorporated into notarial practice a century or more before Justinian" (Schiller 1975: 585–86). He found Taubenschlag's

[56] Though the papyri, as some selections in this volume make clear, are often more than "bits and patches."

[57] My offprint of the latter bears the publisher's date of 1969, hand corrected by Schiller to 1971.

identifications of imperial laws in the documentary papyri illusory and the general picture based on them "just too slick . . . [for] having first hand knowledge of Haile Selassie's new legislation in the province of Eritrea, I suspect the picture is the same. Within fifty miles of Addis Ababa the new western law is observed, or at least an attempt at observation. But in the provinces, Gojjam, Wollo, Eritrea, there is absolutely no attention paid to it. For Addis Ababa substitute Byzantium" (letter of September 1, 1975).[58]

The whole matter of "Schiller's radical thesis" was recently reexamined in detail by Joëlle Beaucamp (Beaucamp 2007), who basically returns, though with more nuance, to Taubenschlag's earlier position. She accomplishes this on the basis of recent scholarship (2007: 276 n. 17 – not after all very much) and a significant increase in the papyrological evidence since 1970 (2007: 272, 276). Interestingly, many of the leading documents in her presentation are those that have been known for a century, more or less, which allude specifically to imperial enactments or show familiarity with their contents. These include *P.Cair.Masp.* I 67028, with its reference to a law of the Emperor Leo "forbidding the second wife to receive more property than one child of the first marriage" (Beaucamp 2007: 274); *P.Cair.Masp.* II 67151 and III 67312, wills that reproduce in Greek the Latin words of a Justinianian constitution (*CJ* 6.23.21) on seven-witness wills (Beaucamp 2007: 274–75, cf. 277),[59] and *PSI* I 76, a document clearly familiar with the language of Justinian's Novels and Edicts on the *constitutum debiti alieni* (informal agreement to pay another's debt, often involving bankers) (Beaucamp 2007: 280–81, cf. Keenan 1978). Of special interest is Justinian's Novel 47 (31 August 537) mandating the inclusion of regnal years in dating formulas in addition to consular and indictional dates (cf. **6.6.1** with introduction), a rule whose implementation can be seen by 4 April 539 in Egypt (*P.Harr.* II 238),[60] though not consistently till mid-century. Legal literary fragments add to the sum, especially now *P.Oxy.* LXIII 4400 and Addendum, a fragment of Justinian's Edict XIII on the administrative reorganization of Egypt in AD 539. The result is that, in the face of evidence that is not statistically overwhelming, we can at least say with Beaucamp that the elite of Alexandria and the Egyptian

[58] The letter, to Keenan, was in response to Keenan (1975).

[59] The latter also refers to a *ius Falcidium* ("Falcidian right") deriving from a Republican law on legacies of 40 BC and subject of a chapter in Justinian's *Institutes* (2.22) and titles in the *Code* (6.50) and *Digest* (35.2) – Beaucamp (2007: 274, cf. 273), on *P.Bodl.* I 47. For *P.Cair.Masp.* III 67312, see also Keenan (2000: 618–25).

[60] Even earlier, by 10 May AD 538, in Petra; see *P.Petra* I, p. 17.

metropoleis (e.g., Antinoopolis, Oxyrhynchos) and studious gentlemen like Dioskoros of Aphrodito (van Minnen 2003) display knowledge of the imperial laws, even if at times only to mention them so as to set them aside (*P. Oxy.* I 125 intro., 136.37–39 and note; Beaucamp 2007: 282–83). At other times, known laws are tacitly violated (*Nov.* 134, see **5.5.3**). We are less certain when it comes to the villages, whose evidence disappears in the late period, and their peasants. Here Schiller (and Mitteis, in principle) may well be right.

At the same time, no matter the conclusions to which the above leads, it is clear that the documentary evidence of the Byzantine period had experienced a significant shift from the Roman period. From a recent discussion (Palme 2009),[61] a number of conclusions can be drawn. Above all, the spectrum of document types had contracted – and changed. The late documentation is increasingly vested in large archives. Contrary to expectation, Christianity did not eradicate divorce or slavery in Egypt or their attendant documentations (divorce: see **4.2** introduction and **4.2.3** especially; slavery: see **9.3** introduction and **9.3.3** especially). Acts of adoption are new to the typology of the Byzantine period (366), along with single acts of emancipation and disownment. We see in this period the disappearance of the legal guardianship of women (**4.3.2**). Census returns (e.g., **4.4.2**, **4.4.6**) also disappear, but there are extensive sixth-century tax records preserved no longer on rolls but on codices (383, see Gascou 1989). Contracts develop new formularies with increasingly florid language (see **5.5.3**, **6.6.1** with introduction, cf. Tiersma 1999), script, and preference for the *transversa charta* format according to which the papyrus roll was rotated ninety degrees, the left side of the roll now becoming the top of the contract (or will), with its writing proceeding across the fibers and the roll's former height converted into the document's width. In place of registration (see **2.6**), contracts find enforceable backing by being witnessed and "notarized" (386; see Diehart and Worp 1986, and see below). There is an increase of the document type commonly referred to as "sales on delivery," most of which date to the sixth and seventh centuries and are often concerned with wine (368; see Kruit 1992b). Loans without fixed terms of repayment become common (369). Leases of land are still found in the Arsinoite nome, but are rare in the Oxyrhynchite. The hereditary (and long-term) leasehold known as *emphyteusis* makes its first appearance in the late period (369). Common document types largely specific to the great estates of the Apion family

61 Unadorned page numbers in parentheses in this paragraph all refer to Palme (2009).

are personal guarantees against flight on behalf of agricultural workers (*enapographoi geôrgoi*) (**8.3.4**) and receipts for broken or worn-out parts of waterwheels (**8.3.2**; see Tacoma 1998).

As far as legal procedure is concerned, reports of judicial proceedings diminish after about 300; the fifty or so bilingual (Greek and Latin) reports of proceedings cluster in the earlier part of the Byzantine period (377; see **10.4.5**). Fifth- and sixth-century reports, bilingual or not, are rare.[62] The reports disappear almost completely about AD 530 (387) – a telling silence for Schiller's argument on the disappearance of the courts themselves. In any case, as the argument now goes, civil disputants, mainly concerned with inheritance claims, tended to try to reach settlement privately without going to court. To put the procedure in the simplest form, they might agree to go to arbitration, such agreements being recorded in documents known as *compromissa* (Gagos 2008). Or they might submit to mediation and have the ensuing settlement recorded in a document known as a *dialysis* (387; see Gagos and van Minnen 1994). Often involved in resolving such disputes were bishops and monks and clerics (**10.5** and **10.6**). The numerous petitions of the period, like other documents, come with increasingly florid addresses and detailed, rhetoricized narrations (378; see Fournet and Gascou 2004; cf. Keenan 2008).

It should be noted with regard to all the above that Greek remained the prevailing legal language in Byzantine Egypt. And Schiller (see above) was surely correct in insisting on the importance of Greek notaries in Byzantine Egyptian legal practice. Numerous notaries have been identified by names and idiosyncratic signatures (Diethart and Worp 1986, with plates), somewhat reminiscent of the sample of the London scriveners; but they and their practices are not well enough known to be able to allow composition of a work like (say) Kathryn Burns's on the colonial archives of Peru (Burns 2010).[63] Nevertheless, it seems Dioskoros of Aphrodito, sometimes rather loosely but conveniently referred to as a "lawyer," was after all a notary. Only his drafts, none of the notarized work from his years in Antinoopolis, *c.* AD 566–73, have survived, but this, I would wager, is the stuff of a book waiting to be written.

When Coptic legal documents made their appearance in the later sixth century they were obviously influenced by Greek notarial forms (cf. **6.6.2**, also *transversa charta*, with introduction). They are at first to be found in a

[62] A recently published example in Gascou (2009); see also *P.Mich.* XIII 660–61, the famous Aphrodito "murder mystery," on which see Keenan (1995).

[63] Reference thanks to Ari Z. Bryen.

few bilingual archives, mainly in the forms of arbitrations (*compromissa*) and settlements (*dialyseis*). The first Coptic contract dates to AD 608; they do not become prevalent till the eighth century (for a sketch of surviving types, MacCoull 1991; translations, MacCoull 2009). When this did happen, the Coptic formularies prove to have been modeled on existing Greek formularies, and the documents' technical vocabulary of course was also lifted from the Greek (**3.4**; see Förster 2002, Fournet 2009). This Coptic prevalence was, relatively speaking, short-lived, Coptic being displaced by Arabic, beyond the chronological limits set for the present volume (but see, especially, **6.6** and **7.4**).

1.8 The law of Coptic legal documents

T. Sebastian Richter

As early as the late nineteenth century, soon after the first Coptic papyri had been discovered and edited, legal historians started trying to categorize the kind of law underlying the legal practice as attested by these new pieces of evidence. At that time the issue was shaped and focused by the binary perspective of Ludwig Mitteis' (1891) seminal work on *Reichsrecht* versus *Volksrecht* in the eastern provinces of the Roman empire. Mitteis had argued that in contrast to the linguistically as well as culturally largely Romanized western provinces, in the eastern part of the Roman empire substantial remains of native legal thought and practice had resisted the reception of Roman law and even survived the most efficacious impacts of it, including the *Constitutio Antoniniana* of AD 212, and the introduction of Justinian's code and novels in the sixth century (cf. Steinwenter 1952; Wolff 1956; Taubenschlag 1930 and 1940/41). Mitteis' methodological innovation was to treat the broad historical evidence for deviations from Roman legal norms no longer as secondary sorts of vulgarized, sunken bits of originally Roman law, but as traces of a substratum, actually pointing to pre-Roman legal traditions. During the whole twentieth century, the question whether or not the Coptic legal documents were conveying pre-Roman, "Demotic" or "Egyptian," law remained a debated matter. Two leading contemporary historians of the law, the Austrian Arthur Steinwenter of the University of Linz and the American A. Arthur Schiller of Columbia University, even acquired some knowledge of Coptic in order to treat the issue *a fontibus*.

The evidence for an inner, legal continuity of Egyptian law was often seen in close connection with the possibility of proving an external, linguistic continuity of schemes, clauses, and phrases between Demotic and Coptic legal documents. While earlier assumptions as to the transmission of parts of the Demotic legal language in Coptic documents could not be proved (Richter 2002b: 37–57), there could be some instances of pre-Roman Egyptian law that might have been transmitted in changed clothes, as it were, first by Greek and later by Coptic documents. But in many cases it is almost impossible to distinguish vertical, diachronic connections (continuity) from horizontal, synchronic relationships (coherence). For example, the donation of boys to the Upper Egyptian monastery of Phoibammôn near the town of Djême evidenced by more than twenty mid- to late eighth-century Coptic documents has often been related to earlier priestly practices in Egypt, particularly evidenced by the Demotic dossier of self-dedication documents in favor of certain gods and temples.[64] Nevertheless, as has been shown recently, the practice of child donation attested in that Coptic dossier had a broad Byzantine background, including also the western medieval European institution of the *oblatio puerorum* "conveyance of boys" (cf. Papaconstantinou 2002a and 2002b; Richter 2005). Or, to quote another example, the tendency to avoid lawsuits at courts by forming settlements with the aid of arbitrators as attested by late Roman and Byzantine Greek and eighth-century Coptic *dialysis* documents has been thought by some scholars an Egyptian peculiarity (Schiller 1932: 252; Allam 1985, 1991, 1994a), while Gagos and van Minnen (1994) treated the Greek *dialysis* dossier in terms of merely synchronic conditions, namely kinship and social relationships, asking under a quasi-ethnographic perspective, "how [did people] manipulate laws, rules, customs, and principles to get the best deal they could – without unduly damaging the relationships that existed between them?" (p. 37), and giving reasonable explanations without any particularly Egyptian implications (on arbitration outside of the courts, cf. also **10.4** and **10.5** below). Fields of law that have always been considered conservative strongholds of native legal customs and manners are the laws of family, marriage, and marital property; but the latter in particular are scarcely attested by Coptic documents.

Arthur Schiller, who tended to a maximalist estimation for the continuity of Egyptian law in the Coptic papyri, used to speak about "Coptic law." This term, implying a virtually independent, or at least, distinguished legal tradition evidenced by Coptic texts, was challenged by Arthur Steinwenter, who replaced it by the term and concept of "the law of Coptic documents" (cf. Schiller 1938: 360–64, Wenger 1939: 281–82, and Steinwenter 1955: 1–3). Although himself far from denying the possibility of legal continuity,

[64] See Schiller (1931: 212 and 1932: 252), Thissen (1986), Richter (2002b: 136–42).

in doubtful cases Steinwenter preferred to look for Byzantine sources of law, and often did so successfully. His term "the law of Coptic legal documents" is therefore chosen in the heading of the present section.

Still, the overwhelming impression of a largely Romanized law underlying the legal relations of the people of Byzantine and early Islamic Egypt may be a good deal shaped by a merely philological perspective looking through the lens of written records. In the case of sales and leases, for example, we have to admit that the vast majority of legal events might have happened simply unrecorded (cf. introductions to **6.6** and **7.4**). Not only does the form of putting a legal matter have some influence on that matter, but already the parties' choice of a certain way of managing, or a certain scheme of recording, their legal and business affairs does imply their favor for the legal implications and consequences connected with this particular way. Thus reliance on these formally drafted documents may simply lead to a sort of self-fulfilling prophecy.

CHAPTER 2

The historical development of the form, content, and administration of legal documents

Mark Depauw, Thomas Kruse, J. G. Manning, †Tomasz Markiewicz, T. Sebastian Richter, Katelijn Vandorpe, and Uri Yiftach-Firanko

Introduction

This chapter provides an overview of the form, content, and method of state administration of legal instruments from the Ptolemaic to the Byzantine period and beyond. While the basic types of transactions remained fairly consistent (sales, loans, marriage arrangements, and leases), the documents show a wide variety of forms and considerable development, and, in some cases, mutual influence. From the modern perspective there was considerable overlap between types of contracts and their uses. The *misthôsis* contract, for example, the standard contract of lease, was also used in labor contracts (e.g., **8.2.10**) and could be combined with loans. Demotic sales could be used to secure loans and to guarantee the maintenance of a woman in marriage (**2.2**).

In both Demotic and Greek texts, sale (Chapter 6), the signature contract in many legal systems, was one of the most common types of contracts. In Greek, in sale and other contractual types, the so-called objective homology, i.e., a declaration in the third person: "NN (i.e., the seller) acknowledges that he has sold to NN (i.e., the buyer) . . .," was at first the prevalent form; but gradually the subjective homology, written in the first person, prevailed: "X to Y, greetings. I acknowledge that I have sold to you . . .".[1] Demotic contracts also prefer the latter: "I acknowledge that I have received from you the satisfactory price for my house . . .". Despite the seeming informality of the subjective form, the contracting parties were always carefully identified at all periods according to the style of their times (as discussed in Chapter 1 and elsewhere and as evidenced in many of the selected documents), while the documents themselves tend to

[1] Palme (2009), who provides an excellent summary of the types of Greek documentary texts preserved in the papyri.

be full of back-referring words like "above-written," "aforementioned," and variants so familiar from modern contractual boilerplate.

Both the Greek and the Demotic traditions preserve a basic documentary distinction between a formal legal text (Demotic *sẖ*, Greek *syngraphê*) and an informal or private agreement (Demotic *šᶜ.t*, Greek *cheirographon*). Greek had other words for agreements, while the Egyptian scribes divided document types into two basic categories, either the *sẖ*, a notarial instrument (literally a "written thing") or the *šᶜ.t*, a "letter." Both the Egyptian and Greek traditions of written contracts had histories before the Hellenistic period, although writing, and the degree of literacy, may have meant that "written law" played a different role in Egyptian and Greek societies (Gagarin 2008). In both, however, the use of written instruments to document private agreements appears, over time, to have played an increasingly important role. Parties had a choice whether to record their agreements in writing to begin with, and whether to choose a professional scribe or to record the agreement more informally. The rise of the *agoranomos* scribe in the third century BC presented a new method for recording private agreements. This scribe acted truly as a notary, no witnesses were required, and the document was registered in the local registry. State supervision of private contracts, and the development of local registries, appear to have been increasingly centralized from the Ptolemaic period onward (**2.1**).

There are other types of contracts not treated in this volume. These include state licenses to perform certain kinds of work such as beer brewing or tax collection in a specified area (de Cenival 1973). There was regional and temporal variation in the types of Greek documents used (Wolff 1978: 129–35 and **2.1**). The Demotic instruments (**2.2–4**) also show regional differences in their contractual clauses (Zauzich 1968). Indeed there is considerable regional variation in the forms of Greek legal texts as well. In some cases we have a document type from only one place (**8.3**, especially **8.3.2** and **8.3.4**).

The registration of private agreements was not new with Ptolemaic rule. In pharaonic times it was the vizier who supervised the deposit of important written documents in official archives. The registration of private agreements seems to have been done in the Third Intermediate period, perhaps tied to the collection of the sale tax (Muhs 2005b: 19). By the reign of Ptolemy II, Greek subscriptions to Demotic sale contracts from Upper Egypt (Thebes[2] and Edfu[3]), Memphis, and the Fayyum

[2] *P.Fam.Theb.* 14 (264 BC). [3] *P.Hausw.*

(Hawara[4]) note that the document had been "deposited in the box," perhaps a reference to the official registration of the contract. The state function of registration appears to have been tied, as earlier, to the collection of the sale tax (Muhs 2005b: 20).

In addition to being notarized, private Demotic contracts were also recorded in registers. A third-century Demotic register shows a mature system of noting the type of private agreement and the parties involved.[5]

Notarial offices also seem to be involved in the enforcement of loans, where loans are registered but also paid back. The evidence suggests there was no rigid bureaucratic uniformity in how private agreements were registered.[6] Occasionally, for example, red stamps were used as a means of authentication on some Greek and Demotic contracts, bank receipts, and petitions.[7] While Greek contracts were drawn up and recorded in a different tradition than the Demotic, there were also some innovations in Greek practice in Ptolemaic Egypt. Notary scribes, called *agoranomoi*, are attested in the third century BC, although such scribes are better known in the middle of the second century BC in the Pathyrite nome.[8] These notary scribes replaced older methods of documenting contracts that required the presence of witnesses.[9] Such public notary scribes may have also been intended to replace the ancient Egyptian system of recording private agreements with sixteen witnesses, although private Demotic agreements continued to be written throughout the third and second centuries BC. Although such contracts are written in Greek, on high-quality papyrus, and the scribes have Greek names, the scribes that Pestman (1985c) has studied were Egyptians, showing us how some local scribal families adjusted to Ptolemaic administrative practice.

In 146 BC, an administrative order was published requiring Demotic instruments to be registered in order to be valid, and summaries in Greek of the contents of such agreements to be made on the Demotic text; another summary, in Greek and Demotic, was to be deposited in the records office.[10] Nevertheless, a recently published register of contracts

4 E.g., *P.Chic.Haw.* 9 (= Hughes and Jasnow 1997: 52–58, Hawara [Fayyum], 239 BC).

5 *P.Sorb.* inv. 264 + 265 (= de Cenival 1987, Ghoran [Fayyum]).

6 Some amount of regional variation in scribal traditions is clear. At Pathyris and Krokodilopolis, the notary office is called the *archeion*, on which see Vandorpe (2004).

7 Vandorpe (1997: 254–55). Generally known from the Fayyum, but one Demotic example is known from the Memphis area, discussed by Martin (2009b: 112).

8 E.g. *P.Hib.* I 29. On these scribes see Seidl (1962: 62–63), Pestman (1985a), Vandorpe (2000b, with previous literature, and 2004).

9 The Greek "six-witness agreements." See Wolff (1978: 571).

10 *P.Par.* 65; analyzed by Pestman (1985d).

from the agoranomic office in Pathyris dated to 110 BC records complete copies of agreements, minus the dating protocol, not just abstracts.[11] We cannot be certain, given the current state of the evidence, whether such public notary documents were designed to replace an earlier system of registering Demotic contracts, or were merely an attempt to bring uniformity to the system.[12]

Pierce's study (1972) of a small group of late second-century BC Demotic papyri (see **6.2.2**) has demonstrated that, by the later Ptolemaic period, transactions could be recorded using a hybrid form of Greek sale/loan. Demotic scribes could add to the Demotic tradition a Greek institution such as the payment of a fine to the state for breach of contract (Pierce 1972: 159–78). In **5.4.5**, a loan in Greek is secured by a Demotic sale of property. Chapter 7 (introduction) presents us with the hybrid form known as *misthoprasia*, lease-sale, for ships (Rathbone 2007b). Other types of "mixed transactions" include the labor contracts discussed in **8.2**, which combined concepts of loan or lease with labor arrangements.

The first section of this chapter provides a survey of Greek texts that illustrate the pivotal role played by the state in the creation and development of different schemes of Greek legal documents. One such scheme, the double document, was subject to three regulations – around 275 BC, 125 BC, and AD 14 – that left clear marks on its shape and eventually caused its transformation into the *grapheion* document. The reform of the double document (**2.1.1**, **2.1.2**) around 125 BC coincides, so it seems, with the introduction of the *cheirographon*, a handwritten agreement (see Chapter 7), in the form of a letter, of the terms of the contract written by, or on behalf of, the debtor (**2.1.3**). The two measures are complementary: in the late Ptolemaic period contracting parties could document the transaction in a double document, and thus have the act attended by witnesses and registered in a state *grapheion*; or they could do away with both the witnesses and the registration if they decided to draft a *cheirographon* (**2.1.4**, **2.1.5**, **2.1.6**) The former option was more cumbersome and expensive, but provided enhanced security for the transaction and the document itself. Composing a *cheirographon* was simpler and cheaper, but lacked these securing measures.

Many options in documenting a transaction are also evident in the Roman period: legal documents could still be drawn up by the parties in person (in most cases autographically) in the form of a *cheirographon*. Alternatively, the transaction could be documented at a *grapheion* and

[11] Vandorpe (2004). [12] Cf. the comments of Muhs (2005b: 21).

thus benefit from the security accorded by the deposition of the document in the *grapheion*'s files. Yet now, unlike in the Ptolemaic period, we note a connection between the type of transaction recorded and the format chosen for its documentation. One of the clearest expressions of this connection is to be found in the lease contracts recorded in Oxyrhynchos from the very beginning of the Roman period in the format of the "private protocol" (**2.1.9**) and in the Arsinoite in that of the *hypomnêma* (**2.1.10**, **2.1.11**).

The Byzantine period is the era of the *cheirographon*. Already in the early Roman period the *cheirographon* was taken to be the default format by professional scribes in Oxyrhynchos. This practice, which is evident outside Egypt as well, finally led in the Byzantine period to the assumption of the *cheirographon* as the routine scheme for composing legal documents everywhere in Egypt, and probably everywhere in the Greek East (**2.1.7**, **2.1.8**). But in this regard, too, the change came from above, brought about by state act, or probably several acts, in the course of the late Roman and Byzantine periods.

2.1 Evolution of forms of Greek documents of the Ptolemaic, Roman, and Byzantine periods

Uri Yiftach-Firanko

In this section I illustrate the common schemes that were used in Greek legal documents in Ptolemaic, Roman, and Byzantine Egypt. Some schemes (in particular the bank *diagraphê* and the Alexandrian court *synchôrêsis*) are left out of the present discussion. For those schemes that are discussed, I focus on changes in the structure of the documents themselves rather than on the documents' methods of archivization or economic uses.[13] I will present some of the main types of documents and show how they changed during the long period under discussion, starting with the so-called double document. (See further **5.2**.)

From the double document to the *grapheion* document

2.1.1 Early Ptolemaic double document (loan of money)

P.Cair.Zen. I 59001 (= *Sel.Pap.* I 66) (Pitos, Memphite nome, 273 BC). Image: Figure 1.

[13] The most recent comprehensive work on the subject is Wolff (1978).

Fig. 1. Loan of money. *P.Cair.Zen.* I 59001. Pitos (Memphites), Spring 273 BC

The double document is the earliest Greek legal document attested in Egypt. Its earliest example, *P.Eleph.* 1 (= *M.Chr.* 283, *Sel.Pap.* I 1, *Jur.Pap.* 18), dates to 310 BC. It is also found outside Egypt. The earliest non-Egyptian sample dates to 88/7 BC and comes from Avroman in

Kurdistan; but there is no reason to believe that the form was not in use throughout the Hellenistic world much earlier, as early as the fourth century BC. In its earliest form, the Greek double document in Egypt consisted of two *identical* texts of the contract, written one above the other across the fibers on the same papyrus sheet. The upper text was then sealed by the six witnesses who attended the act as well as by the parties to the contract themselves. The completed document was kept by one of the witnesses, the *syngraphophylax,* for future use. If the contents of the lower, open text were later subject to dispute, its authenticity could be established by breaking open the upper text and comparing the two versions. The present document, *P.Cair.Zen.* I 59001, represents the double document of the early Ptolemaic period.

Translation in the main follows *Sel.Pap.* I 66.

Inner text: the body of the document: In the 12th year of the reign of Ptolemy son of Ptolemy, in the priesthood of Leontiskos son of Kallimedes, in the month Peritios, at Pitos in the Memphite nome. Dionysios son of Apollonios, Gazaean, in the service of Dinon, has lent to Isidoros, Thracian, of the troops of Lykophron, holder of 40 arouras, 34 drachmas of silver, this being the price of the royal grain, on interest at the rate of 2 drachmas each month on each mina. Isidoros shall repay the loan to Dionysios in the month of Artemisios of the 13th year with the interest. If he fails to repay in the stated time, he shall forfeit one and a half times the amount of the loan, and Dionysios shall have the right of execution upon the property of Isidoros and that of his surety, making exaction in whatever way he chooses in respect of debts to the Crown. Surety of Isidoros for payment to Dionysios of the loan and all the liabilities of the contract: Demetrios son of Damon, Thracian, a part-holder. This contract shall be valid wherever produced by Dionysios or by the person to whom Dionysios transmits it.

Inner text: list of the witnesses: Witnesses: Terepes, Thracian, holder of 40 arouras, Hebryzelmis, Thracian, holder of 40 arouras, Posidonios, Thracian, holder of 70 arouras, Bithys, Thracian, holder of 110 arouras, Dionysios, Thracian, holder of 60 arouras, Zipyros, Thracian, part-holder with Bithys, all belonging to the troop of Lykophron.

Outer text: the body of the document: In the 12th year of the reign of Ptolemy son of Ptolemy, in the priesthood of Leontiskos son of Kallimedes, in the month Peritios, at Pitos in the Memphite nome.

Dionysios son of Apollonios, Gazaean, in the service of Dinon, has lent to Isidoros, Thracian, of the troops of Lykophron, holder of 40 arouras, 34 drachmas of silver, this being the price of the royal grain, on interest at the rate of 2 drachmas each month on each mina. Isidoros shall repay the loan to Dionysios in the month of Artemisios of the 13th year with the interest. If he fails to repay in the stated time, he shall forfeit one and a half times the amount of the loan, and Dionysios shall have the right of execution upon the property of Isidoros and that of his surety, making exaction in whatever way he chooses as in respect of debts to the Crown. Surety of Isidoros for payment to Dionysios of the loan and all the liabilities of the contract: Demetrios son of Damon, Thracian, of the troops of Lykophron, a part-holder. This contract shall be valid wherever produced by Dionysios or by the person to whom Dionysios transmits it.

Outer text: list of the witnesses: Witnesses: Bithys, Thracian, holder of 110 arouras, Tereites, Thracian, holder of 40 arouras, Hebrydzelmis, Thracian, holder of 40 arouras, Posidonios, Thracian, holder of 70 arouras, Zipyros, Thracian, part-holder with Bithys of 60 arouras, Dionysios, Thracian, holder of 60 arouras, all belonging to the troop of Lykophron. Keeper of the contract: Bithys.

Outer text: acknowledgement by Bithys, the syngraphophylax: I have received the contract, being valid.

Verso:

Docket: Contract with Isidoros concerning 34 drachmas.

A comparison of the inner and outer texts exhibits some differences: the designation of the surety as a co-holder of 40 arouras, which appears in the outer text, is missing in the inner text. Some elements that are interlinear in the inner text are on the line in the outer one. The order in which the witnesses are listed is different in the two versions. The autograph confirmation of the *syngraphophylax*, which appears in the outer text, is missing in the inner one. Otherwise the two texts are identical, written equally spaciously and in an equally careful hand.

The aforesaid features are upheld in virtually all double documents from Egypt down to *c.*125 BC. This is not accidental: *BGU* XIV 2367, a law promulgated by Ptolemy II around 275 BC, prescribed these features as *sine qua non* for the validity of the document – *inter alia*, probably the drafting of a complete version of the document in the inner text. Still, in the late third century BC, double documents began to be registered and deposited in archives, a deposition that guaranteed the authenticity of the document, in addition to, and eventually instead of, the inner script. Consequently, while the inner script is still written, following the precepts of the law, *in extenso*, in the later third and second century it becomes very dense, occasionally illegible (cf., e.g., *P.Bad.* II 2, Hermonthis, 130 BC).

2.1.2 Later Ptolemaic double document (loan of wheat)

P.Dion. 14 (= *P.Rein.* I 14, *M.Chr* 132) (Akoris, 15 October 110 BC). Image at Papyri.info.

The consequences of the change were drawn in the course of a reform of the scheme of the document around 125 BC. In this reform the double document became subject to *anagraphê*, that is, the registration of its contents in a state bureau, *grapheion*. On that occasion, the inner script ceased to encompass the entire text of the contract; it reported just the particulars of the transaction that were recorded in the *grapheion*'s files. The reform affected other sections of the document as well: late Ptolemaic double documents contain, besides the succinct inner script, the debtor's autograph confirmation (*hypographê*) of the terms of the transaction as well as the *syngraphophylax*' autograph acknowledgement of the receipt of the deed.[14] Late Ptolemaic double documents also contained an account of the *anagraphê* itself. *P.Dion.* 14, recording a loan of twenty artabas of wheat by Dionysios son of Asklepiades to Dionysios son of Kephalas, exhibits the traits of the double document after 125 BC.

> *Inner text:* (*4th hand*) On the 26th of Thoth, in the eighth year. Loan of Dionysios son of Asklepiades to Dionysios of 30 artabas of wheat. Let him return in the month of Payni of the eighth year. The penalty for each (undelivered) artaba will be 3,000 drachmas and to the royal treasury 60 drachmas.
>
> *Body of the document, outer text:* (*1st hand*) In the eighth year of the reign of Kleopatra and Ptolemy, the gods Philometores Soteres, during the priesthood in Alexandria of him who is a priest of Alexander and the gods

[14] This last element appears already in *P.Cair.Zen.* I 59001 (**2.1.1**), and seems to become common in the early second century BC.

Soteres, and the gods Adelphoi, and the gods Euergetai and the gods Philometores and the gods Epiphaneis and the god Eupator, and the god Philometor, and the god Neos Philopator, and the god Euergetes, and the gods Philometores Soteres, during the priesthood of the *hieros pôlos* of Isis, the great mother of the gods, during the priesthood of the *stephanêphoros* of queen Kleopatra, goddess Soteira Dikaiosyne Nikephoros, and during the priesthood of the *kanêphoros* of Arsinoe Philadelphos, and the priestess of queen Kleopatra, goddess Soteira Dikaiosyne Nikephoros, and the priestess of Arsinoe Philopator, all those priests and priestesses who are in Alexandria, on the twenty-sixth of the month Dios, twenty-sixth of Thoth, in Tenis also known as the village of Akoris of the Hermopolite nome. Dionysios son of Asklepiades, Persian of the katoikic cavalry of Apollophanes and Exakon, has lent to Dionysios son of Kephalas, Persian of the *epigonê*, twenty artabas of wheat, which Dionysios has received for his own use, at an interest rate of 50 percent, amounting to ten artabas. Let the borrower return all thirty artabas of wheat to Dionysios in the month Loios, which is Payni, of the eighth year,[15] new, clean and pure wheat according to the measure relating to bronze. Let the artabas be delivered to the harbor that is in the vicinity of the village of Akoris without suit or judgment or any excuse. And if the debtor does not pay in accordance with the terms of this document, let him pay to Dionysios as a compensation for each (undelivered) artaba three thousand bronze drachmas and to the royal treasury in money of the ancient currency sixty sacred drachmas and nothing less. Let the execution be available to Dionysios for the wheat and all the things reported in the *syngraphê* from Dionysios the debtor himself and all his assets as if resulting from a court sentence. Let the document be applicable. Witnesses are Dionysios son of Ptolemaios, Macedonian, *hypêretês tagmatos*, [Apollonios – –], Dionysios son of Apollonios, Herakleides son of Her[– –], Hermophilos son of Ammônios, all four being Persians from those made klerouchoi by Kleopatra, Ptolemaios son of Anaxagoras, Milesian. *Syngraphophylax*: Dionysios.

The debtor's autograph confirmation: (*2nd hand*) I, Dionysios son of Kephalas, Persian of the *epigonê*, received the said thirty artabas of wheat in accordance with the above contract and gave the document valid to Dionysios.

The syngraphophylax' *confirmation of the receipt of the document:* (*3rd hand*) I, Dionysios, received the document valid.

[15] *c.*July 109 BC, nine months after the start of the loans.

Registration of the document by the grapheion *official:* (*4th hand*) On 26th Thoth of the eighth year, in the village of Tenis of the Mochite toparchy. Registered by Ptolemaios.

2.1.3 Records office document (loan of money)

P.Tebt. II 312 (Tebtunis, AD 123/4). Image at Papyri.info.

After the reform of 125 BC, the *grapheion* official became involved in the composition of the document itself. This involvement is especially evident in cases like **2.1.2**, where the same person certifies the registration of the document in the records office, or *grapheion*, and drafts the body of the document. It can also be assumed in all cases where the registration of the document by the *grapheion* scribe follows the drafting of the body of the document within a short interval; in **2.1.4** both occur on the same day.

The close involvement of the *grapheion* scribe in the drafting of the document finally paved the way to a second reform, around AD 14. In the second reform, which can be studied primarily thanks to the rich finds of early first-century Tebtunis and Soknopaiou Nesos, the inner script was done away with, as was any mention of witnesses, or a *syngraphophylax*. The resulting new document consisted of the body of the document (formerly: the outer script), the parties' autograph confirmations, and the scribe's confirmation that the document was deposited in his files.

The reform of AD 14 also introduced new elements into the document. In the Ptolemaic period, it was common to record in some types of documents the ages of the parties as well as detailed accounts of their physical appearance – stature, skin and hair color, shape of face and nose, and visible physical defects such as scars and moles. But in the Ptolemaic period this means was applied rather selectively, primarily in documents of economic importance, such as wills and deeds of land sales, as well as in abstracts of double documents and Demotic documents registered in regional, probably state archives. After the reform of AD 14, the same means was massively employed for the identification of all parties to contracts drawn up in Arsinoite *grapheia*, regardless of their roles in the transaction. Yet in order to make such a massive application possible, the *grapheion* scribes had to do away with many of the old means of identification: in the *grapheia* the physical description focuses on the scars and moles alone.

The reform introduced another new element. The autograph confirmation, which in the course of most of the Ptolemaic period exhibited a lapidary formulation, became in the late Ptolemaic and early Roman period increasingly detailed and elaborate, frequently recounting most terms of the contract. Drawing up this account was particularly complicated for the illiterate and semi-literate. In Tebtunis and Soknopaiou Nesos, with their predominately Egyptian population, this was an especially acute problem. With this in mind the reformer of AD 14 introduced the position of the *hypographeus*, a private person who wrote the document on the party's behalf. The results of the reform were documents with the following three parts: the body of the document written by a scribe with an account of the ages of the parties and their visible physical defects; a long autograph confirmation issued by the parties in person or by their respective *hypographeis*; and, finally, a confirmation by the scribe of the registration of the contract in his files. The early Roman source material contains no less than 900 documents of this type. *P. Tebt.* II 312 is a *grapheion* document of the early Roman period.

Translation follows the *editio princeps*.

Body of the document (the former outer script): The eighth year of the Emperor Caesar Traianus Hadrianus Augustus . . . at Tebtunis in the division of Polemon of the Arsinoite nome. Paopis son of Paopis the younger son of Paopis, exempted priest of the [.]fourth[16] generation, Persian of the *epigonê*, aged about thirty-five years, having a scar on the right . . ., acknowledges to Maron son of Marepsemis, also a priest, aged about thirty years, having a scar on the right arm, that he, the acknowledging party, has received from him, Maron, forthwith from hand to hand out of his house a loan (*chrêsis*) of the capital sum of one-hundred twenty silver drachmas bearing interest, and the acknowledging party Paopis is bound to repay to Maron the capital sum of the loan, 120 silver drachmas, and the interest, in the month Mecheir of the coming ninth year of Hadrianus the lord without any delay or excuse, Maron having the right of execution upon Paopis and all his property as if in accordance with a legal decision.

Autograph confirmation by the debtor: (*2nd hand*) I, Paopis son of Paopis, declare that I have received from the said Maron as a loan (*chrêsis*) bearing interest one-hundred twenty silver drachmas, which I shall repay in the month of Mecheir of the ninth year without delay as written above.

Autograph confirmation by the creditor: (*3rd hand*) I, Maron, (declare that) the declaration was made (towards me).

[16] I.e., fourth, fourteenth, or twenty-fourth generation.

Confirmation of registration by the grapheion *official:* (*4th hand*) The document was registered through the *grapheion* of Tebtunis.

Verso:

Docket: Deed of acknowledgement of Paopis on the receipt of a loan of 120 drachmas from Maron.

The letter format (*cheirographon*)

2.1.4 Third-century bc *cheirographon* (payment for reed propping)

P.Col. IV 76 (Philadelphia, 15 December 247 BC). Image at Papyri.info.

The use of the letter for documenting transactions and contractual obligations is probably current in any literate society, and is attested in Egypt from the very beginning of the Ptolemaic period. This is the case, for example, in the following text. The document is introduced through the address clause ("Athenodoros to Eukles and Agathokles, greetings"). At the end of the document we find the farewell formula: "good-bye." The dating formula is abbreviated: year and day number without the names of the rulers.

Translation follows the *editio princeps.*

Athenodoros to Eukles and Agathokles, greeting. I have received from Herakleides, farmer, pay for reed propping to the number of 65,500 reeds at 4 obols per ten thousand, total 4 drachmas 2 obols, on the understanding that I will furnish them at the farms being listed from your office for the vineyard operations of the 40th year or pay back 4 drachmas per ten thousand and the indemnity. This is the remainder of the money paid me for cutting vine props in the 38th year.

Verso: And (in case of non-fulfillment) I will pay back in addition at the same time also 4 drachmas 2 obols paid me on the 23rd of Phaophi for the 65,000 reeds. Good-bye. Year 39, Phaophi 23.

2.1.5 Second-century bc *cheirographon* (settlement of a debt)

P.Adl. 4 (Pathyris, 28 May 109 BC).

In the second century BC, one applies the above format (see **2.1.4**) for the creation of a new type of instrument: the *cheirographon*, or simply *cheir* ("hand"). The document was originally autograph, written by the prospective debtor in person. As in the third century, the document opened with the formula "A to B, greetings." This was followed by an acknowledgement of the performance of the act that created the contract. Yet the scribe dispensed with some of the routine elements in regular letters, such as the farewell (*errôso*), and introduced new ones typical in other types of legal documents: the execution (*praxis*) and validity (*kyria*) clauses. In Ptolemaic and Roman Egypt the date was given in an abbreviated form at the end of the document. Unlike the double document, the *cheirographon* was written along the fibers, in a relatively narrow, columnar format (30–50 letters a line). It contained just one text of the contract, and was not drawn up before witnesses. Usually the *cheirographon* was not deposited in an archive.[17] The document was expected to be written by the prospective debtor in person, and did not contain, for that reason, his autograph confirmation. The case of *P.Adl.* 4, recording a settlement regarding preexisting debt, is interesting inasmuch as the debtor is illiterate, and the contract is written by a third party on his behalf.

Translation follows the *editio princeps.*

> Psemminis son of [. . .]os to Horos son of Nechoutes, greeting. I acknowledge that I received from you three (?) talents of bronze coinage (?), free of interest (?). These are what is still owing to you according to the contract of Taïsis, your daughter, which I shall repay to you up to Pachon 30 of the year 9 without trial and judgment. And if I do not return them by the fixed time, I shall give you the same twice over compulsorily. And you shall have the right of execution (*praxis*) both upon me and upon all my property as if in accordance with a legal decision. Dionysios son of Archidemos, of the demos Berenike, wrote on behalf of Psemminis by his request as he is illiterate. Year 8 Tybi 24.

Cheirographa in Roman Oxyrhynchos

2.1.6 Oxyrhynchos *cheirographon* (repayment of money loan)

P.Oxy. XLIX 3487 (Oxyrhynchos, 1 October AD 65). Image at Papyri.info.

Most *cheirographa* of the Roman period maintain the features of their late Ptolemaic predecessors: the document is written by the declaring party in person; it is structured as a letter, features columnar format, is written along the fibers, and records no witnesses or act of

[17] Exceptions in the case of the *cheirographa* of the archive of Dionysios son of Kephalas of late second-century BC Akoris. Cf., e.g., *P.Dion.* 32.

registration (cf., e.g., *BGU* I 100, AD 159, Arsinoite nome). But there were also exceptions. *Cheirographa* of early Roman Oxyrhynchos commonly exhibit autograph confirmations, which means that the body of the text was not written by the declaring party in person. Oxyrhynchite *cheirographa* show other peculiarities as well: a wide format (60–90 letters a line), proficient, probably professional scribal hand in the body of the document, and a frequent reference to a bank, located in the quarter of the Sarapeion (Temple of Sarapis), in which the financial aspects of the transaction were managed. The document also contains a confirmation by the banker himself of the money transfer. It can be assumed that in Oxyrhynchos, the *cheirographon* was the routine format used by private scribes working next to and in cooperation with banks in the vicinity of the local Sarapeion. In the early Roman period, Oxyrhynchite *cheirographa* record primarily loans and other credit-related transactions. From AD 160 onwards they also record conveyances of title to landed property. One of the Oxyrhynchite *cheirographa* is *P.Oxy.* XLIX 3487.

Translation follows the *editio princeps.*

Body of the document: Tausoreus daughter of Panemgeus, one of those from the city of the Oxyrhynchi, with her kinsman Kephalas son of Kephalas as guardian, to Sarapion son of Ptolemaios, who lives with me as husband according to the laws, one of those from the same city, greeting. I acknowledge that I have back from you, at the Sarapeion, by the city of the Oxyrhynchi, through the bank of Dionysios, sometimes called "of Faustos," and partners, a capital sum of thirty-two drachmas of silver in imperial coinage, which are part of the capital sum of seventy-two drachmas of silver which I lent to you by a *cheirographon* and a bank transfer through the bank of Apion son of Andromachos the representative of the aforementioned Dionysios, which is established at the same Sarapeion, in the month Neroneios Augustus of the tenth year of Nero Claudius Caesar Augustus Germanicus Imperator, without detriment to my interests in the exaction of the remaining capital sum of forty drachmas and the interest on these from this point and also in my rights under the contract of marriage which you owe me, which is normative in all the points set out in it. This *cheirographon* is normative. Twelfth year of Nero Claudius Caesar Augustus Germanicus Imperator, Phaophi 4.

Autograph confirmation by the declaring party: (*2nd hand*) I, Tausoreus daughter of Panemgeus, have back the capital sum of thirty-two drachmas of silver out of the seventy-two drachmas of silver, without detriment to my interests in the exaction of the remaining forty drachmas and in my rights under the contract which you owe me as aforesaid. I, Zoilos son of Horos, wrote for her since she is illiterate. Twelfth year of Nero Claudius Caesar Augustus Germanicus Imperator, Phaophi 4.

Autograph confirmation by the guardian of the declaring party: (*3rd hand*) I, Kephalas, have been appointed her guardian.

Account of the money transfer through the bank: (*4th hand*) Twelfth year of Nero Claudius Caesar Augustus Germanicus Imperator, Phaophi 4. The bank-transfer has been made through the bank of Faustos and partners.

The Byzantine period

Early Roman documents with the letter format composed outside Egypt are structured differently from their Egyptian counterparts: in *P.Yadin* 20 of AD 130 Maoza (Arabia), for example, the dating formula appears at the beginning of the document, before the address clause, and ends with the parties' *hypographê*, that of the witnesses who attended the act, and finally, with an autograph confirmation of the scribe who composed the document. In the Byzantine period, this became the routine format in *cheirographa* from Egypt. The change was gradual: first, in the early fourth century, the dating clause was inserted at the beginning of the contract, first in addition to the date clause at the end of the contract, later in its stead, and the scribe, commonly termed *symbolaiographos* in Byzantine Egypt, added his autograph confirmation at the end of the document. Witnesses first emerge in the early fifth century and become routine in the sixth. In the same period the document opens with the number 643, the isopsephism for *Theos Boethos* ("God (the) Helper"), and with an oath by the Holy Trinity. The following two papyri, *P.Sakaon* 64 (= *P.Thead.* 10, Theadelphia, AD 307) and *P.Ant.* I 42 (= *C. Pap.Jud.* III 508, Lenaiou, Antinoite nome, AD 542), exhibit the two stages of the development of the *cheirographon* in the Byzantine period.

2.1.7 The "new *cheirographon*": earlier format (money loan)

P.Sakaon 64 (= *P.Thead.* 10) (Theadelphia, 3 April AD 307). Image: Figure 2. Translation follows relatively closely the editor in *P.Sakaon*, p. 159.

Dating formula 1: In the consulship of our lords Severus Augustus and Maximinus Caesar, consuls for the 1st time

Body of the document: Aurelius Sakaon son of Satabous and Thermouthion, from the village of Theadelphia in the Themistos division, about 50 years old, with a scar on his . . . left shin, to Aurelius Koyles son of . . . from the village of . . . greeting. I acknowledge that I have received from you hand-to-hand three talents and three thousand drachmas of silver, equal 3 tal., 3,000 dr., as a loan for one month, counting from the present day, and that I shall perforce repay you the aforementioned sum on the seventh day of the coming month of Pachon without delay; and that should I fail to repay by the appointed day, I shall forfeit to you for the overtime the interest agreed between ourselves; and that on formal demand you are to have the right of execution both upon me and upon all my property, as one does when bringing a case; and on formal interrogation I so acknowledged.

Dating formula 2: In the 15th, 3rd, and 1st year of our lords Maximinus and Severus, Augusti, and Maximinus and Constantinus, the most noble Caesars, Pharmouthi 8th.

Autograph confirmation by the declaring party: I, Aurelius Sakaon son of Satabous, acknowledge that I have received from hand to hand the three talents and three thousand drachmas of silver, and shall repay them as stated above. I, Aurelius Serenus son of Sotas, wrote for him since he is illiterate.

Autograph confirmation by the scribe: Composed by me, . . ., notary.

Verso:

Docket: Note of hand (*cheirographon*) of Sakaon, from the village of Theadelphia. Receipt for 3 talents, 3,000 drachmas

2.1.8 The "new *cheirographon*": later format (sale in advance of delivery)

P.Ant. I 42 (= *C.Pap.Jud.* III 508; Lenaiou, Antinoite nome, 26 September AD 557)

Translation in the main follows the *editio princeps*.

† 643

Dating formula: In the reign of our most sacred master, Flavius Justinianus the eternal Augustus and Emperor, the twentieth year, the thirtieth day in the year after the consulate of the most distinguished Flavius Basilius, Thoth 29, the sixth indiction.

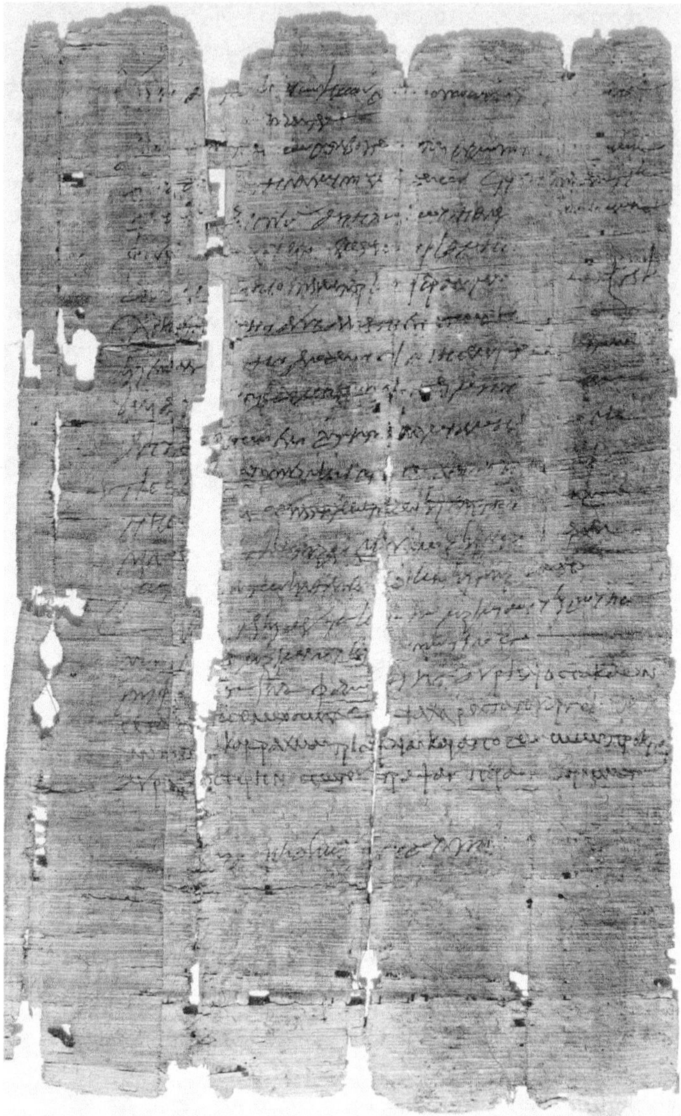

Fig. 2. New *cheirographon P.Sakaon* 64. Theadelphia (Arsinoites), April AD 307.

Body of the document: (*1st hand*) Aurelius Peieuous son of Apollos and Thekla, together with his surety Aurelius Petrus son of Psas and Thermouthia, who goes bail for him in respect of any pledge and payment mortgaged to you for this my debt, both being farmers and natives of the village of Lenaiou in the Antinoite nome and now residing there in the said village of Lenaiou, to Aurelius Josephius son of Sourous, a Jew by religion, of the same village of Lenaiou in the same Antinoite nome: greeting. I, the aforesaid Peieous, with Petrus my surety, acknowledge through this my written bond that I have had and received in full from you in complete and due amount one hundred and twenty-one and a half small jars of new wine, fragrant, of the best quality, each jar containing five Jewish *sextarii*, total 221½ small jars of wine each containing 5 *sextarii*. And this I am prepared to supply to you at the time of the vintage in the month Mesore of this forthcoming seventh indiction at the harvest. Should any of the said wine be found to be sour or unfit for keeping or musty up to and including the month of Tybi in the same indiction, I am to exchange it for better wine of good quality. And this said amount of wine we will deliver to the door of your house in the village at my expense and freightage without any delay or dispute. And should this time have elapsed without my paying the said amount of wine, I am prepared to give you without fail in respect of its value five gold *solidi* forthwith, our property being mortgaged to you in respect of this debt as though by legal decision. This deed is valid and confirmed and, on being asked the formal question, I gave my consent.

Autograph confirmation by the debtor: I, the above-mentioned Aurelius Peeus, accompanied by Petrus as surety, agree with all the above terms. Aurelius Kyriakos, notary (*nomikos*), having been requested, wrote the document on his behalf, since he does not know writing.

Autograph confirmations by the witnesses: (*2nd hand*) I, Flavius Stephanus son of Kyros, bear witness to this agreement, having heard declarations from the person executing it.
(*3rd hand*) † I, Phoibamon Pollon, deacon, bear witness to this agreement, having heard declarations from the person executing it.†

Autograph confirmation by the scribe: (*1st hand*) †Composed by me, Kyriakos.

The "private protocol" and the *hypomnêma*

In the Ptolemaic period, every type of contract – a *cheirographon*, a double document, and others – could be used for the documentation of almost any type of transaction. The format of the document and its production costs were also independent of the nature and value of the transaction recorded.

Things changed in this respect at the beginning of the Roman period. In the *grapheia* (see above on the format of the *grapheion* document) the scribe would apply a narrow, columnar format for instruments documenting low-cost, short-term transactions, and a wide format for high-cost instruments documenting long-term and high-value transactions.[18]

Another expression of the same policy is the removal of the documentation of certain types of contracts from the state notaries (including the *grapheia*) into the hands of private scribes, who applied new formats for documenting transactions. Such a change is manifested particularly in relation to leases. In the Oxyrhynchite nome, lease contracts still take in the late Ptolemaic period the shape of a double document, or are composed by state scribes. This is still the case in *P.Oxy.* XIV 1629 drawn up in 44 BC, that is, just before the Roman conquest. *P.Oxy.* II 277, however, drawn up in 19 BC, fairly soon after the Roman conquest, adopts a new scheme.

2.1.9. "Private protocol" (land lease)

P.Oxy. II 277 (= *P.Lond.* III 1188 descr., Oxyrhynchos, 6 September 19 BC). Image at *P.Lond.* III, Plate 13.

The new document type, called by scholars a "private protocol," is marked by its extremely narrow format: 20–40 letters a line. The text begins with an account of the act undertaken by the lessor that set the contract in motion: "X has leased to Y," and ends with the date and place clause. Occasionally the body of the document is followed by an autograph confirmation by the tenant of the terms of the lease, as is the case in the foregoing document. Private protocols rarely report the identity of the scribe who issued them. The private protocol remains the sole means of the documentation of leases in Roman Oxyrhynchos.

> *Body of the document:* Dionysios son of Alexandros, hipparch over men, has leased to Artemidoros son of Artemidoros, Macedonian, hipparch over men, 36$\frac{3}{4}$ arouras which Dionysios possesses near Pamis of the allotment land of Philon, on the condition that Artemidoros sow the land in the course of the 12th year with wheat, in return for half share of all the future fruits and crops, on the condition that the transport costs and the instruments for mowing will be upon Artemidoros, while the costs of reaping will be paid (by the lessor and the lessee) in common. If any demand be made upon Artemidoros for the government or for any other

[18] I discuss this phenomenon in Yiftach-Firanko (forthcoming).

purpose on account of Dionysios, let a deduction be made of half a . . . and let Dionysios guarantee the lease by every warranty. The warranty having been made, let them convey the crops jointly to the threshing floors that are located near Pamis, and of what has been collected each will get his own half a share.

Autograph confirmation by the lessee: (*2nd hand*) I, Artemidoros, have leased the land for half a share as written above.

Dating formula: Year 12 of Caesar, Thoth 9.

2.1.10 *Hypomnêma* (vineyard lease)

P.Ryl. IV 600 (Karanis, 29 October 8 BC)

In the Arsinoite nome the process was more gradual. Down to AD 40, one still recorded leases in the public *grapheion* document. The one outstanding exception is when the contract relates to the lease of vineyards, olive or palm groves, and the fruits have already ripened, and in some cases fallen from the trees, and need to be gathered with haste. In these cases, to avoid the costly and especially time-consuming composition of the document by a public scribe, one applies a different scheme, that of a contractual offer (*hypomnêma*). The present document, *P.Ryl.* IV 600, was composed on Phaophi 20 (October 29) and the crop had to be gathered within the next five weeks, by Hathyr 30 (November 11) of the same year.

The format is very narrow, measuring *c.*25–35 letters a line. The lease opens with the address clause: the prospective lessee addresses the manager of an estate of an absentee landlady. In the following clause, the actual appeal is opened by the formula, "I/We wish to lease. . .," with an account of the object and the terms of the lease. The date clause appears next, followed by autograph confirmation of additional prospective lessees and by an endorsement by the prospective lessor. The verso exhibits a docket.

Translation follows the *editio princeps.*

Appeal by the prospective lessee: To Poseidonios, factor to Theanous daughter of Alexandros, from Ammonios son of Archedemos and Dorion son of Dorion, partners. From the newly planted olive grove near Karanis belonging to Theanous we wish to lease the fruits formed in the 22nd year of Caesar and falling in the 23rd year at a total rent of 40 silver drachmas, which we will pay by the 30th of the month Hathyr, we being mutual sureties for payment in full without any delay or equivocation; it will be lawful for you to relet to anyone making higher bid. We will gather the crop in the month of Hathyr of the 23rd year of Caesar. 23rd year of Caesar, Phaophi 20.

Autograph confirmation by the co-lessee: I, Dorion son of Dorion, agree that I am a partner to the lease made agreeably to the above-mentioned conditions, and I will, as partner, pay in full the rent on which I have agreed. 23rd year of Caesar, Phaophi 20.

Autograph confirmation by the landlady's agent: I, Posidonios, factor to Theanous daughter of Alexander, have granted the lease on the above-mentioned conditions, and it shall be lawful for me to relet to anyone making a higher bid. 23rd year of Caesar, Hathyr 2.

Verso:

Docket: 23rd year of Caesar, Phaophi 20.

2.1.11 *Hypomnêma* (lease of land with date palms)

P.Corn. 10 (Philadelphia, 23 August AD 119). Image at Papyri.info.

By AD 50 the *hypomnêma* became the most popular means of documentation of leases in the Arsinoite nome. The change did not take place overnight, and hence was probably not brought about by a formal decree. At the same time, the change is across the board, sweeping enough to assume some guiding hand. It can be assumed, that is, that sometime in the course of the Julio-Claudian period measures were taken that made the composition of lease contracts at the state *grapheia* increasingly unrewarding, prompting the employment of private scribes instead. The outcome of this policy is shown in the structure of **2.1.11**.

Unlike **2.1.10**, **2.1.11** records a regular long-term lease for a period of four years. The document is structured as an appeal, in this case too to an absentee landlord through his agent; at the end of the appeal appears the formula "if it is agreed to make the lease," to which the lessor adds his endorsement, indicating that he has accepted the proposal upon the terms detailed in the appeal. After the landlord added his endorsement, the document was presumably handed back to the lessee.

Appeal by the prospective lessee: To Lucius Longinus Fronto, through Frontinus Longinus Apella, from Lucius Vettius . . . I wish to lease from you one and a half arouras of land near Philadelphia belonging to Fronto, in which are scattered date palms, whatsoever he may now be growing, the land being also an undivided portion of a three-aroura plot, for four years, namely four fruit crops, four sown crops, (reckoning) the date palms on the basis that all the hanging fruits of the present 3rd year of Hadrian Caesar our lord are included in the 4 years' crops, and the farm plot as (leased) from the coming 4th year, the rent of the farm land and the date palms to be one hundred and twenty drachmas annually without deduction and without risk, the farm labors resting upon me, the lessee. And I will pay the rent as follows, in . . . forty drachmas, and the remaining eighty drachmas in the month of . . . And at the end of the time I will hand back the farm plot after the harvest, if it is agreed to make the lease.

Endorsement by the lessor: (*2nd hand*) I, Lucius Longinus, through Apella, have made the lease on all the foregoing conditions as laid down above.

Dating formula: Year 3 of Hadrian our lord, Mesore 30th.

2.2 Demotic sales

J. G. Manning

The normal shape of a formal Demotic sale was broad and rectangular (i.e., a small number of very long lines of text) in the Ptolemaic and Roman periods.[19] At times these texts could reach great lengths, stressing the ceremonial nature of these texts but also perhaps functioning as a protection against forgery.[20] The broad horizontal format of traditional Egyptian instruments of sale and cessions documented, from the beginning of Demotic sale contracts in the seventh century BC, with blank papyrus that, once the document was rolled up, would be wrapped around the written text, may also have been purposefully designed to protect the writing since these texts were crucial in securing long-term property interests.[21] Other types of sale could take the narrow format, as **6.2.2** illustrates. The basic formula of the Demotic sale, as with the cession discussed below, was developed during the Saite period (664–525 BC). The legal formulas became more elaborate, and the sale and cession

[19] Demotic sale texts from the Saite and Persian periods could be either of an older "narrow format" and have four witnesses or of a newer, broad format with sixteen witnesses.

[20] One of the third-century BC *P.Hausw.* originating from Edfu, for example, is over four meters in length. Cf. the comments by Thompson (1994: 80–81).

[21] See Jasnow (2003a and b) for a summary of pre-Ptolemaic Demotic legal texts.

became distinct acts, i.e., the real sale consisted of a sale and a cession text, in the later fourth century BC.[22]

The written sale document is one of the most common Demotic documents and is attested from the seventh century BC to the late first century AD, although the majority of preserved Demotic "sale" texts date to the Ptolemaic period.[23] There was considerable variation among regional scribal schools in the use of specific clauses.[24] A sale of property was completed by "satisfying the heart" of the vendor with a "purchase price" that is routinely left unmentioned. The phrase "to sell" in Demotic is rendered literally as "to give [something] in exchange for money." Despite this phraseology, Demotic "sales" were not always cash sales: The instruments could be used as security for other types of transactions including temporary conveyance of property. Indeed a Demotic sale text could be written to serve as a guarantee by a husband to his wife that she will be maintained with the husband's property. Should he default on the obligation, the husband was required to draw up a cession document to complete the conveyance of property to the wife (Martin 2009b: 70).

The sale and the cession instrument could in fact be deployed for a variety of transactions from real sales to pledges. Most commonly they are a complement to what is generally called a "sale" or a "document concerning silver" (*sẖ n ḏbꜣ ḥḏ*). In this case they often concern a piece of real estate, such as a house, and were frequently written on the same papyrus sheet as the sale. It has been suggested that sales would only transfer the legal right to *use* the property, while cessions would actually transfer the *ownership*. In fact, however, it seems far more likely that cessions do not transfer anything but served merely as confirmation on the part of the seller that he/she no longer had any rights whatsoever vis-à-vis the object of the sale.[25]

The "quitclaim" or cession document (**2.3**) apparently confirmed a permanent transfer of title.[26] In some cases the quitclaim was written several years after the sale.[27] In straightforward sales, the two texts were

22 The first known occurrence seems to be the fragmentary P.Inv.Sorbonne 1276 + 1277 (= de Cenival 1972), 343 BC.

23 The latest known Demotic contract of the "broad" type is P.Vienna D 10086 (AD 85/6). I thank Sandra Lippert for the information. For Roman Demotic legal texts see Lippert and Schentuleit (2010).

24 Studied in detail by Zauzich (1968: 115–24). Cf. Botta (2009: 151–68).

25 Depauw (2000: 4–7).

26 Cf. Depauw (2000: 5). In P.Louvre 9416 (Thebes, 214 BC), for example, a woman "sold" to a Greek man three arouras of land that she had acquired from another Greek seven years earlier by sale instrument alone.

27 For such a "split" transaction, see, e.g., *P.Ryl.* 19 (118 BC) + 24 (113 BC) and the remarks of Pierce (1972: 118–19).

often written on the same sheet of papyrus side by side, but they could also be split up into two separate documents. Normally a list of witnesses was placed on the verso of the text.

The entire text written by a professional scribe was occasionally copied in full by some of the witnesses (the so-called "witness-copy" form, **6.1.1**).[28] This was an ancient feature of witnessing agreements that became moribund by the end of the third century BC. It may have been a traditional method of training future scribes. The exact day of the agreement was not written until 186 BC, no doubt as part of a larger Ptolemaic administrative reform (Manning 2003a: 211).[29]

The essential elements of the sale contract were as follows:[30]

Dating protocol – Regnal year, month, of king Ptolemy; the names of eponymous priests in the Ptolemaic dynastic cult who served that year.

Statement of satisfactory price – Vendor has declared to buyer: "I am paid in full (not a universal clause). You have satisfied my heart with the purchase price of my land."

Specification and location of property – "Located within the temple estate of god so-and-so . . . (or within the royal fields)."

Specification of the neighbors, or a landmark (the desert edge, a canal etc.) – Neighboring property, normally in the order South, North, East, West.

Conveyance of the property in exchange for money – "I have given the plots to you in exchange for money. You have given me the value of the plots in money."

Acknowledgement of receipt of price – "I have received the money, it is complete, there is no balance. I am satisfied."

[28] On the history of this type of contract, see Depauw (1999). For an example with ten-witness copies, see *P.OI* 17481 (= *P.Chic.Haw.* 1, Hawara [Fayyum], 365/4 BC) published by Nims (1958), re-edited by Hughes and Jasnow (1997, text 1 and Plate 7 for the list), which has a list of thirty-six witnesses. Other texts might simply list the names of witnesses to the agreement. For the distinction, see Pestman (1994c: 26–27); Vleeming (1998: 169 n. qq). By the Ptolemaic period, this number was fixed at sixteen for the "broad" contracts as is confirmed in a text from the famous probate dispute from Asyut dating to the mid-second century BC (P. Brit.Mus. EA 10591, rto. iii, 5) which states that the document in dispute was valid, "it being complete with sixteen witnesses." On the location of the witness list on the document, see Donker van Heel (1995: 57). The number of witnesses does not appear to have been standard everywhere at all times in the Ptolemaic period. The use of twelve witnesses, for example, in sale instruments does occasionally occur, and some Demotic leases (e.g., **7.1.2**) had sixteen witnesses.

[29] Specific-day dates were in fact written in the so-called Abnormal Hieratic tradition in the Theban area earlier.

[30] Zauzich (1968: 113–24, esp. 114); Menu (1988). I summarize here *P.Hausw.* 1a (Edfu, 265 BC).

Statement of clear title – "This is your property, no one else has any claim to it."

Declaration of guarantee by seller – "Anyone who comes against you about the property I will remove him from you."; "You have a right to all documents pertaining to the property."; "I will swear an oath in court to guarantee to prove your rights to the title of this property."

Signature of scribe

The names of sixteen witnesses on the verso

The terms of the clauses in quitclaim documents overlap considerably with sale documents (see further **2.3**). The essential difference in the wording comes at the beginning, where the seller states that he/she is "far" from the buyer concerning the property being sold.

It is not known with certainty why it was felt necessary to have two separate but heavily overlapping documents to effect a real and permanent transfer of property. It is likely that the early development of written legal instruments that distinguished between the conveyance of property and its permanent transfer simply continued into Ptolemaic Demotic legal instruments. The retention of two separate documents for permanent conveyance of property may have been the result of the conservative tendency of scribes to preserve old forms. By the Roman period the cession was nearly otiose.

2.3 Demotic cessions

Mark Depauw

Evidence for the secondary role of cessions (Dem. *sẖ n wy*, lit. "document of being far") in comparison with sales is abundant. Cessions themselves often refer to the sales they accompany, while the opposite is never the case.[31] In the contract type in which witnesses write out the contract in full, the so-called "witness copy" document (see **6.1**), the cession is copied by fewer witnesses than the sale (see below, **6.1.1**) or even completely lacks copies.[32] There are examples of Greek translations of Demotic documents with sale and cession which meticulously render every element of the original, including the autograph subscriptions, but make do with a simple reference to the cession at the end (see below). Finally, cessions are often absent in the sense that a *sale* of a house is the only document preserved of

[31] Zauzich (1968: 151–52). [32] Depauw (1999: 96–97).

a specific transaction. Such an argument *e silentio* can be very dangerous because so much evidence is lost, but in some private archives found in sealed jars (a so-called "closed" archive) it seems highly unlikely that the cessions would have been discarded while the sales were carefully preserved.[33] If therefore the vendor in the sale states "I have given you my house; it is yours," while he states in the related cession "I am far from your house," this makes clear that the house was already owned by the second party when the cession was drawn up. An existing situation is confirmed rather than a new one created, which is nicely illustrated by the use of a form (the "Qualitative") of the Egyptian verb "to be far" rather than the infinitive "to remove."

From this observation follow the other practical applications of cession documents, such as after a verdict in a trial, when the losing party can be forced to make a document in which he refrains from further action on the object of litigation (see **6.2.5**), the so-called "withdrawal after judgment" (*Streitverzichterklärung*).[34] A cession could also be drawn up to confirm that an obligation had been fulfilled (see **6.2.4**), for example, when the document stipulating the obligation could not be given back for some reason. Another typical use is when ownership changed at the occasion of an inheritance and the heirs and new owners wrote cessions to confirm that they had no claims on the portions of other parties.[35] In all these cases, like in the cessions accompanying sales, the seller acknowledged an existing, albeit often recently changed situation, to remove all doubts concerning the validity of the buyer's claims.

The basic structure of a Ptolemaic and Roman Demotic land cession was as follows:[36]

Dating protocol – Regnal year, month, of king Ptolemy; the names of eponymous priests in the Ptolemaic dynastic cult who served that year.

Statement of removal – "I am far from you with respect to the rights over the property."

Specification and location of property – "Located within the temple estate of god so-and-so . . . (or within the royal fields)."

Specification of the neighbors, or a landmark (the desert edge, a canal etc.) – Neighboring property, normally in the order South, North, East, West.

[33] Depauw (2000: 4–7). [34] Allam (1994a). [35] Pestman *et al.* (1977, vol. 2: 6–7).
[36] I summarize here *P.Hausw.* 1b (Edfu, 265 BC). For full examples, see below, Chapter 6.

Declaration of no rights retained by seller – "I have no right, no complaint, nothing at all with regard to the property."

Declaration of rights being conveyed by seller – "No one has authority over the property except you."

Declaration of guarantee by seller – "Anyone who comes against you about the property I shall remove him, and will guarantee you clear title to the property."

Signature of scribe

The names of sixteen witnesses on the verso

2.4 Demotic loans

†Tomasz Markiewicz

The formula of loan contracts with its many clauses developed gradually during the Late Period (*c.*664–332 BC) and seems to have been fully established by the time of Alexander's conquest in 332 BC. No clear influence of Greek law can be traced in them, even though Egyptians had to accept some Hellenic customs. Among these was the introduction of offerings to the royal cult as penalty ("mulct," see below). Local variants in the clauses can be observed, notably between documents from Thebes/Gebelen and those from Middle Egypt (Tehne; Hawara), attesting to the existence of independent legal traditions in those regions. Above all, the wording of an individual document depended on its legal form (full notary contracts being more wordy than the less formal documents in epistolary style). The object of debt – money or kind – also had a bearing on the choice of clauses used in contracts. Money debts are consistently expressed in traditional Egyptian units of weight, *debens* (*c.*91 grams) and *kite* (*c.*9 grams), even though in the Ptolemaic period it was surely coins that actually changed hands. Debts in kind concern grain (wheat or barley), or, less commonly, wine and occasionally other commodities, such as bricks and clay (*P.Gebelen* 32).

A fully developed Ptolemaic debt acknowledgement agreement contained the following clauses (explored more fully below, **5.1**):

Dating protocol – Documents were dated according to the regnal year of the ruling pharaoh and, in Ptolemaic notary contracts, the pontifical years of the priests attending to the royal dynastic cult of the Ptolemies and Alexander the Great.

Introduction of the parties – Egyptian deeds were unilateral in form and contained declaration of the debtor as received by the creditor in front of the notary and witnesses. The actual body of the contract was thus introduced by a formula "A said to B." The only exception to this rule were the so-called *hn.w* – agreements which contained declarations of *both* parties as received by the trustee.

Acknowledgement of indebtedness clause – The crucial statement in which the debtor confirmed his debt and stipulated to repay it by a certain date. In Ptolemaic documents from Upper Egypt this clause had the following form: "You have 'x' with me in the name of money/grain that you gave me and I shall give it back to you before a particular date." Deeds containing this clause can be safely labeled as "loans" as they mention both transfer of property and an ensuing obligation to repay it. If the transfer is not mentioned (as, e.g., in *P.Hausw.* 18), we cannot speak of a loan, since the debt could have resulted from any other transaction, for instance a division of inheritance. Middle Egyptian documents from Hawara, Tehne, and Akoris employ a slightly different formula: "You gave me 'x'."

Delivery clause – This clause appears only in debts concerning commodities. It governed the conditions under which the repayment should be effectuated: the quality of the commodity in which the debt was to be settled, its measure, and also frequently the place of delivery. Since it was no doubt troublesome and expensive to transport larger amounts of commodities, the contracts settled the matter in advance. It was usually required of the debtor to deliver to the house of the creditor, but, for example, in Tehne it was customary to deliver the goods to the harbor – the creditor apparently had to fetch them from there. Some deeds explicitly say that the costs of delivery are to be covered by the debtor (e.g., *P.Dion.* 2).

Penalty clause – This clause contains contractual indemnities for the case when the debtor fails to repay the debt on time. Demotic documents show a great variety of such penalties: *hêmiolion* or 50 percent increase of the sum due; a fixed amount of money to be paid instead of a commodity as a multiple of the market price;[37] *mulct* – money to be paid by the defaulting debtor to the burnt offerings and libations of the kings;[38] and some other hybrid forms. Forfeiture of pledged real estate in conditional sales (see **6.2.1**) was also part of the

[37] Boswinkel and Pestman (1982: 19–20) suggested that the multiplier was 2.5 in the loans from the archive of Dionysios son of Kephalas.
[38] Pierce (1972: 159).

penalty clause, even though from the legal point of view the pledge of property was a method of securing the repayment of the loan.

Guarantee clauses – Under this heading we can label together various clauses in which the debtor ensured the creditor's claims would be satisfied and obligations resulting from the contract would be fulfilled properly. Here we may find anything from specific securities of real value (pledges) to employment of sureties to verbose declarations of goodwill and diligence on the part of the debtor. The commonest form of guarantee was one establishing security for debt on the entire property of the debtor. Pledges could be established on real estate (e.g., P.Brit.Mus. EA 10425), a title deed (e.g., *P.Adl. Dem.* 10), or movables (*e.g. P.Tor.Botti* 13). Other types of security were conditional sales of property and "mortgages" (see below, **5.1.1**, **6.2.1**). Sometimes additional guarantees denied the debtor the right to postpone the payment beyond the date set in the penalty clause (e.g., *P.Tor.Botti* 26). Some documents named formal conditions that had to be fulfilled so that the obligation could be considered extinguished: the original deed had to be handed over to the debtor and/or a written receipt had to be produced for the latter (e.g., *P.Tor.Botti* 26). *O.Tempeleide* 150 translated below (**5.1.4**) highlights a situation when such conditions were not fulfilled and the case was brought to court as a result.

Proxy clause – In this clause the debtor acknowledges the creditor's right to appoint a proxy and promises to perform on the proxy's demand as if he were the creditor himself. The need to appoint a proxy was obviously not always felt and this clause is only occasionally present. However, it can also be found in other types of Demotic deeds such as marriage agreements and leases.

Clause of joint and several responsibility – We find this clause in a few documents stipulating joint liability of several persons for one debt. This would happen when several debtors took up a loan together (see, e.g., *P.Chic.Haw.* 10 discussed below, **5.1.3**) or when a surety was jointly responsible for the debt (e.g., *P.Survey* 20). The creditor could choose to proceed against one of them or all of them. Each had full responsibility for the entire amount of debt. This clause was greatly advantageous to the creditor; we also find it in Demotic leases. A close parallel can be traced in the *praxis* (i.e., execution) clause of Greek loans.

Waiver of claims clause – Several documents contain a declaration of a third person (a woman) who expresses her assent to the contract.

In some documents she is the debtor's mother (e.g., *P.Recueil* 5), in one his wife (*P.Schreibertrad.* 8). It is unclear why this was necessary. The woman's assent can be interpreted as her assuming the role of a guarantor (a co-debtor in effect) who would be held liable for the debt alongside with, or instead of, the male debtor. Alternatively such assent may have been regarded as necessary when the transaction involved family property, such as a house or a field pledged for debt. The debtor's mother (or wife) was thus effectively regarded as co-owner of the family property.

Signature of the scribe

Signatures of witnesses

2.5 Greek loans

Katelijn Vandorpe

Greek loan contracts, explored more fully below (**5.2**), whether these were constructed as six-witness-contracts, notary contracts, or *cheirographa*, usually had the following clauses:[39]

Dating formula – Loan contracts may have short dating formulas mentioning only the date, the place of redaction (**5.2.3**); or more elaborate protocols, including the names of the reigning kings and the names and/or titles of the eponymous priests in Alexandria and Ptolemais (**5.2.2**).

Introduction of the parties – Both parties, creditor and debtor, were introduced in the third person, except for the *cheirographa*, which were unilateral declarations by the debtor. Greek loan contracts could record the physical description either of both contracting parties (**5.2.1**) or of the debtor alone.[40]

Acknowledgement of debt – Mentioning the loan object and the interest, discussed above.

Delivery clause – This clause contains details on the date the loan object has to be returned. In case of loans of consumer goods, the amount lent has to be returned after the harvest in a good condition, and the measure to be used is specified.

Penalty clause – When a loan of money was not paid back in time, a fine of 50 percent of the total amount lent was imposed. In addition, a customary interest of 2 percent was to be paid for each month that

[39] Compare Rupprecht (1967); Boswinkel and Pestman (1982: 23–30, 176–93, 246–52, 280–82); Vandorpe (2002a: 105–12, 118–19).

[40] E.g., Vandorpe (2004, document 6).

the loan was not paid off. In case of loans of consumable goods or seed a fine of 50 percent was customary, including interest: some loans required the defaulting debtors to pay a fixed price per artaba due (e.g., *BGU* X 1969), whereas other contracts demand one and a half times the prevailing market price of the total debt (Sosin 2004).

Sureties clause – In case of multiple debtors, the borrowers were sureties for each other.

***Praxis* clause** – The creditor could hold responsible the debtor (of his choice, in case of multiple debtors) and he could have a claim on the entire property of the debtor(s), "as if there were a legal decision."

***Kyria* clause** – This clause stipulated that the deed was valid wherever it was presented.

2.6 Archives and registration in Roman Egypt

Thomas Kruse

The keeping of archives and the deposition and registration of written records and legal instruments, building on Ptolemaic and earlier recording practice, continued to be important throughout the Roman period. They guaranteed legal certainty for contracting parties on the one hand, and the control of the actions of the civil authorities on the other. Archives – the Greek technical term for them being *bibliothêkê* ("library") – existed as central archives in Alexandria and on the level of local administration in the individual nomes of the Egyptian *chôra* as well. There were two different types of archives: on the one hand, there were central and local archives which received private contracts and served to control private legal transactions and provided documentary evidence for contracting parties in case of legal dispute; on the other hand, there were archives in which the official records (the *dêmosioi logoi* or *dêmosia biblia*) of the several authorities of the civil administration were deposited.

In the following, the latter type of archive is represented in our documentation by **2.6.6** (Arsinoite nome, AD 98), which impressively illustrates the problems of the specific internal organization of such a local record office, in particular when it had to receive and handle masses of documents from a very large administrative district. As **2.6.7** will show, this archive also received the legal instruments that were drafted in the several local notary bureaux (*grapheia*) and other records connected to them. On the level of central administration **2.6.8a** and **2.6.8b** provide evidence for the deposition of official records of local civil authorities in the "Archive in the Patrika" in Alexandria.

But the focus here will be mainly on the organization and functioning of those record offices that were in particular concerned with legal instruments and private legal transactions. Not only was this whole branch of the administration reorganized in the Roman period, it was to a very large extent a completely new creation. It differed considerably from the system of local registration of private contracts in the Ptolemaic period by means of a procedure called *katagraphê*.[41] The Roman administrative actions concerning archival matters can be illustrated by a number of important texts, including prefectural edicts and decisions. On the level of central administration, the Romans established from the very beginning a central record office in Alexandria called the *Nanaion* to receive legal instruments from the whole province. About AD 127 another central record office for the same purpose was created with the so-called "Library of Hadrian" (*Hadrianê bibliothêkê*), which was superior to the preexisting *Nanaion*. For both record offices the so-called "Catalogue" (*katalogeion*), which was placed under the direction of the "Chief Justice" (*archidikastês*), served as a sort of "clearing house" for receiving documents at first hand and (after having them checked) transferring them to both the aforementioned record offices. In the following, the functioning and interaction of these three Alexandrian archives will be illustrated by two edicts of the *praefectus Aegypti*, T. Flavius Titianus (**2.6.1**), and by an example of an application for "publication" (*dêmosiôsis*) of a private contract (**2.6.5**), a legal procedure that entailed registration and deposition of legal instruments through the Alexandrian archives. Also connected to this aspect is a regulation in the so-called "Gnomon of the *Idios Logos*" (**2.6.4**) concerning the obligation of private notaries to register the documents drawn up by them in Alexandria.

On the level of local administration, the famous edict of the prefect M. Mettius Rufus (**2.6.2**) provides evidence about the purpose and organization of the recently established "property record office" (*bibliothêkê enktêseôn*) in each nome. This was a special archive that mainly recorded legal transactions concerning landed property. The composition and the functioning of this archive can be seen in an excerpt of such records concerning the village of Soknopaiou Nesos in the Arsinoite nome (**2.6.3**).

The various documents on archival matters to be treated here demonstrate that the organization of the central and local public record offices in

[41] For the Ptolemaic *katagraphê*, above all illustrated by the famous *P.Par.* 65 (= *UPZ* I 126, 145 BC), see **6.5** below.

Roman Egypt was structured according to the different levels of the country's civil administration. By this structure, on the level of central administration in Alexandria as well as on the level of local administration in the nome *metropoleis*, were established archives that served the registration and deposition of private legal instruments and official documents respectively. These institutions allowed a considerably high degree of control of private legal transactions and of the business of the various officials when measured against the normal conditions of political communities in classical antiquity. The public records offices on the local level (e.g., the *bibliothêkê enktêseôn*, see below) and the central archives in Alexandria (*Nanaion* and "Library of Hadrian") guaranteed, through the obligation to deposit legal instruments in these institutions and through the procedure of *dêmosiôsis*, legal certainty for the country's population and their legal transactions on a large scale. The great interest of the administration in the upkeep and smooth functioning of the country's public archives, which were essential elements of an administrative and legal system widely dependent on written records, is impressively illustrated by the edicts and decisions of several prefects of Egypt that express permanent concern for archival matters.

The hierarchic organization of the archives and the various administrative and legal procedures connected with the deposition and registration of documents were for the most part an achievement of the Roman administration. For most of its elements Ptolemaic precedents are unknown. An important aim of the rebuilding of the administration's archival branch by the Romans was, first of all, to centralize (not to say "monopolize") the registration of private legal transactions in Alexandria. To this the tightly knit network of *grapheia* all over the Egyptian countryside functioned as a necessary complement by being connected with the Alexandrian archives through the obligation for deposition in the *Nanaion*, and (later) in the "Library of Hadrian," of all contracts drafted in the local *grapheia*. It is also important to emphasize that through the establishment of this system the notaries' offices, which appeared in Ptolemaic times in the form of the *agoranomeia* in the nome *metropoleis*, were from now on also present on the village level.

As a safeguard for the connection between the local *grapheia* and the Alexandrian archives the *katalogeion* was crucial. This was under the direction of the *archidikastês* and functioned as a "clearing house" by which every document destined for deposit in the *Nanaion* and the "Library of Hadrian" was carefully examined. It also controlled the process of *dêmosiôsis* of private legal instruments.

Another important innovation by the Romans was the *bibliothêkê enktêseôn*, established in each nome *metropolis* and aimed in particular at increasing the efficiency of the control of legal transactions concerning landed and other immovable property.

What (due to the insufficient sources for the early Roman period) remains until now unclear is the exact date by which the various Egyptian archives were established. Owing only to its name, for the "Library of Hadrian" a range of dates at least can be suggested: AD 117–38. For the two other known Alexandrian archives (the *Nanaion* and the "Library in the Patrika") and for the archives in the countryside (the public records offices and the *bibliothêkê enktêseôn*)[42] information about dates of establishment can only come from new sources. It appears nonetheless that the establishment of the *bibliothêkê enktêseôn* is in some way connected with the extension and dissemination of the liturgical system that gradually involved nearly all social strata of the Egyptian population. This may have prompted the government to seek to establish a sounder record of property ownership and transfers because liturgists were liable for their nominations to the extent of the property they owned. Furthermore, the establishment of the *bibliothêkê enktêseôn* doubtlessly aimed at providing a greater security for the contracting parties because the edict of Mettius Rufus prescribed that any disposition on real estate had to be authorized by the *bibliothêkê enktêseôn*, which had to check whether the property in question was free of any legal liabilities (e.g., mortgages).

Even more uncertain than the establishment dates of the various archives are the date, circumstances, and motivation of another important reform, which radically changed the procedure of registration and deposition of private legal instruments as described above. With this reform is connected the disappearance of the village *grapheia* and the publicly registered deeds drafted by them, the *dêmosioi chrêmatismoi* (which from now on were only sporadically drafted in the *agoranomeion* in the *metropolis* of the nome), and the emergence of a new type of private legal instrument styled as a letter to the contracting party and without witnesses, the so-called *cheirographon*. No more was there any obligation to deposit such documents in duplicate in the Alexandrian archives, but the contracting parties themselves had them registered at the very moment when they became the subject of legal proceedings.

[42] With respect to the probable date of establishment of the *bibliothêkê enktêseôn* see **2.6.2** – the edict of Mettius Rufus. The *bibliothêkê enktêseôn* is for the first time attested in AD 53 (cf. *P.Oxy.* XLVII 3332; *P.Mich.* IX 539; 540); see also Burkhalter (1990: 209–11).

2.6.1 Two edicts of the prefect T. Flavius Titianus

P.Oxy. I 34 verso (= *M.Chr.* 188) (Alexandria [found at Oxyrhynchos], 2 October AD 127)

The verso of this papyrus from Oxyrhynchos contains three documents. The first two are copies of two edicts of the prefect of Egypt T. Flavius Titianus dating from the eleventh year of Hadrian (AD 126/27). The first one (cols. I–II) deals with the relationship between the so-called "Catalogue" (*katalogeion*) – a record office in Alexandria under the direction of the "Chief Justice" (*archidikastês*), which received all private contracts – and two other central state archives, the *Nanaion* and the "Library of Hadrian" (*Hadrianê bibliothêkê*); the latter must have been established shortly before the promulgation of the edict. The *Nanaion*, or "Library of the *Nanaion*" (*bibliothêkê tou Nanaiou*) as it is called in other texts,[43] was the central record office that the Romans established in Alexandria during the reign of Augustus. It appears that it was connected in some way with a sanctuary of Isis, because *Nanaia* was an epithet of this goddess (after the name of the Babylonian goddess *Nana* who was identified in Egypt with Isis). The central concern of the first edict is to place the new archive alongside the existing *Nanaion* and to subordinate the latter to the newly established "Library of Hadrian." The second edict (col. III) was published a couple of months after the first one and confirms the regulations of the latter by threatening violators with punishment. The third document (col. IV, not translated here) is an official letter of a certain Apollonios to another official named Horos. Both men were most probably keepers of an archive in Oxyrhynchos. In this letter Apollonios informs Horos that for better understanding of its regulations he added a copy of the prefect's edict; there follows another copy of the second edict of Titianus already written down in col. III.

The first edict is incomplete because at least one preceding column is lost and therefore the sense of the opening lines of col. I remains obscure. In these lines certain regulations about the filing of administrative documents are continued and it appears that documents from the financial administration, which had till then been given to the *Nanaion*, should from now on for the sake of greater security also be deposited in the "Library of Hadrian" (col. I, lines 1–7). Since the meaning and context of these regulations remain unclear, we will omit them in the following

[43] See, e.g., *P.Oxy.* IX 1200.49 (AD 266); XII 1475.44–45 (= **2.6.5**) (AD 267).

translation and begin with the regulations concerning the deposition of private contracts.

First of all the prefect ordered the clerks of the *katalogeion* to make abstracts of the contracts stored in the local record offices throughout the country and to deposit them in the *Nanaion* and in the "Library of Hadrian." To them they should add the names of the notaries and of the contracting parties and also the index number (*arithmos*) of the documents, signifying probably the ordinal number of the actual roll and that of the sheet on which the legal instrument in question was written. Also the "copyists" (*eikonistai*), who obviously were attached to the "Catalogue," should very accurately examine the rolls consisting of single documents that were pasted together and intended for deposition in the archives;[44] they should make written records of any erasures or insertions in the documents that were not properly indicated as such and deposit copies of these notes in both archives. It is obvious from these regulations that the *katalogeion* functioned as a sort of "clearing-house" for documents destined for deposition in the *Nanaion* and in the "Library of Hadrian." A number of documents indicate that in the course of this procedure the "Library of Hadrian" received the originals of the legal instruments while the *Nanaion* accepted the copies.[45] This was intended to provide greater protection against falsifications.

The following regulation concerns the position of the superintendent of the *Nanaion*, who is prohibited from lending out documents or even letting them be inspected without the formal approval of the superintendent of the "Library of Hadrian." The reason for this is an affair (which apparently happened not long before the edict's publication) involving the superintendent of the *Nanaion*, who had acted contrary to the regulations and was accused of having "tampered" with the documents entrusted to him.[46] So, this quite recent affair may have given the prefect the occasion and the motivation to reorganize the central record offices in Alexandria and to put the *Nanaion* under the control of the superintendent of the "Library of Hadrian."

Having published his edict the governor obviously got the impression that its various regulations were not implemented fast enough by the responsible

44 On these "pasted rolls," see Clarysse (2003).

45 See Burkhalter (1990: 207) and below with respect to *P.Oxy.* XII 1475 (= **2.6.5**).

46 It seems doubtful to me whether the superintendent of the *Nanaion* really wanted to "falsify" documents as Abbott and Johnson (1926: no. 443) translate the Greek passage in lines 9–10 (*paralogisasthai ti boulêtheis tôn deontôn*) because the formulation at this point appears to me too vague for such an explicit accusation. It seems to mean only that the superintendent had acted contrary to the regulations and thus probably "tampered" in some way or another with the documents entrusted to him.

officials and therefore five months later followed it up with a second (this time short) edict by which he once again enjoined his earlier regulations and threatened potential violators with due punishment (col. III).

Col. i, lines 7–17: ... The accountants up to now in the *katalogeion*, called secretaries (*grammateis*) according to the old usage, shall make short abstracts of the contracts including the names of the notaries and those of the contracting parties and the index-number of the documents as well as the type of the contracts and they shall deposit these in both archives (i.e., the *Nanaion* and the Library of Hadrian). Those named copyists (*eikonistai*), when they examine the so-called composite roll destined for deposition, shall make notes on the margin of each document if there has been anything erased or if any illicit additions have been made; and they shall deposit a copy (i.e., of those notes) on a separate sheet in both archives – for I command that the regulations applied in the Arsinoite and [. . .]polite nomes shall be observed in the rest of Egypt.

Col. ii: And they shall add the page numbers and the names of the contracting parties. The so-called clerks (*epi tês dialogês*) of the Bureau of Examination of the officiating *archidikastai* shall do the same and deposit reports every five days. The superintendent of the *Nanaion* is forbidden to lend out documents committed to his charge or to allow any inspection of them or to make any disposition of such a document before having received an order of the superintendent of the Library of Hadrian, because he is liable to the charge of being willing to act contrary to the regulations. Let the officials in the city (i.e., Alexandria) deposit the contracts in both archives from the first of Pharmouthi (i.e., 27 March), those in Egypt likewise from the first of Pachon (i.e., 26 April). Year 11 of the Emperor Caesar Traianus Hadrianus Augustus, Phamenoth 26 (i.e., 22 March AD 127). Let this be made public.

Col. iii: Edict of Titus Flavius Titianus, prefect of Egypt. It has not escaped my notice that the private notaries in Egypt, believing that they could escape punishment for their illegal acts, rather deposit their documents anywhere than in the Library of Hadrian, which was established mainly for this very purpose of preventing the concealment of irregularities. I therefore command them and all city officials (i.e., of Alexandria)[47] to comply with the

[47] In my opinion the translation of *tous politikous pantas* in col. III, line 10 as "all officials whom it may concern" in *P.Oxy.* I, p. 74 (see also Abbott and Johnson 1926: no. 443) doesn't hit the meaning of

orders of my edict, for they should know that I will punish any violator of it whether it is from mere disobedience or by seeking a reason for his illegal deeds.[48] Let this be made public. Year 11 of the Emperor Caesar Traianus Hadrianus Augustus, Mesore 27 (i.e., 20 August AD 127).

2.6.2 Edict of the prefect M. Mettius Rufus

P.Oxy. II 237 col. VIII, lines 27–43 (= *M.Chr.* 192, *Sel.Pap.* II 219, *Jur.Pap.* 59) (Alexandria [found at Oxyrhynchos], 31 October AD 89). Image at Papyri.info.

The edict of the prefect M. Mettius Rufus is part of the large dossier of official documents that Dionysia, daughter of the former gymnasiarch Chairemon from Oxyrhynchos, included in AD 187 in her famous long petition to the prefect Pomponius Faustinianus to strengthen her position in a legal dispute with her father. The edict is the most important source for the nature and structure of the "property record office" (*bibliothêkê enktêseôn*) and was occasioned by defects that had occurred there in the Oxyrhynchite nome. In AD 89 the prefect took these grievances as an occasion for an incisive reorganization of the archive and for outlining the basic principles of its work. The property record office was by then about thirty years old and had originated most probably from a splitting up of the local public record office (the *bibliothêkê dêmosiôn logôn*) of the nome.[49] There was a state institution for the control of legal transactions and private property in each nome that collected documentation of the private assets of the population, especially those connected with landed property. For that purpose every owner had to report any change of the legal condition of his property like sale or mortgage by submitting a return (*apographê*) to the property record office. In the *bibliothêkê enktêseôn*, then, the documents concerning the landed property of each owner were collected under an *onoma* ("name") – a sort of a "personal file" – and for each such file was compiled an "abstract sheet" (*diastrôma*). The most

the Greek text, because I believe that *hoi politikoi* in this context means "city (i.e., Alexandrian) officials" as opposed to the *apo tês Aigyptou nomikoi* ("the notaries from Egypt") who are addressed by the prefect in the first place (line 3).

48 Again I am not quite convinced of the translation of the editors in *P.Oxy.* I, p. 74 (see also Abbott and Johnson 1926: no. 443), who translate *aphormên zêtountas hamartêmatôn* in col. III, l. 12 as "to serve their own nefarious purposes." I think the prefect here wants to distinguish two groups of persons who are violating the orders of his former edict: the first one being merely disobedient while the other is seeking reasons or pretexts for their wrongdoing, which are (of course) in the prefect's opinion insufficient and unjustified reasons.

49 The earliest dated return (*apographê*) to the property record office is probably *SB* XII 10788 A from Oxyrhynchos dating from AD 61; see Wolff (1978: 230–32) (but cf. Cockle [1984: 113], who by following the older opinion pleads for an establishment of the *bibliothêkê enktêseôn* in AD 72).

essential parts of these files were the *apographai* concerning the property rights that the individual proprietors had to submit personally.

The legal character of the *bibliothêkê enktêseôn* was determined initially by Hans-Julius Wolff (2002: 222–55). Wolff proved that contrary to earlier scholarly opinions the *bibliothêkê enktêseôn* could not be identified with a land register where the registrations provided substantive legal protection; rather the *bibliothêkê enktêseôn* was simply an instrument for controlling legal transactions and private assets. With respect to the latter, the main interest for the government lay in the seizure of the property in case of its owner's eventual liturgical service as well as in providing greater security for contracting parties legally disposing of landed property. In his edict Mettius Rufus ordered that property rights be reported to the *bibliothêkê enktêseôn* within six months. Eventual proprietary claims which, according to Egyptian law, a wife could lay against her husband and children against their parents should also be reported. Furthermore, the recorders of legal instruments and the notaries were ordered not to execute any contract drafted by them without the formal consent of the *bibliothêkê enktêseôn*. Older *apographai* should be stored carefully in the archive together with the abstract sheets (*diastrômata*) so that in case of an eventual investigation because of false statements they could provide documentary evidence and serve as legal proof. Finally the prefect ordered that the keepers of the archive (*bibliophylakes*) should renew the *diastrômata* every five years so that they could further be used in the future. To this purpose the *bibliophylakes* should transfer the most recent information about every individual *onoma* to new abstract sheets.

> Edict of Marcus Mettius Rufus, prefect of Egypt. Claudius Areios, *stratêgos* of the Oxyrhynchite nome, has informed me that neither private nor the public affairs receive the appropriate administration, because for a long time the abstract sheets in the property record office have not been kept in the proper way, despite the fact that my predecessors have on many occasions ordered that these abstract sheets should receive the necessary corrections. This cannot be done in the right way unless copies are made from the beginning. Therefore I order that all owners should register their property at the property record office within six months, that all lenders should register their mortgages and that all others having claims on property should register them likewise. They should file their return by individually declaring the sources from which the property came into their possession. Also wives shall make additional statements in the property-statements of their husbands if in accordance with any native Egyptian law they have a claim over their husband's

property, and children shall in the same way proceed with the property-statements of their parents where the usufruct of the property has been guaranteed to the parents by public contracts but the right of ownership has been settled upon the children, in order that contracting parties may not be deceived through ignorance. I also instruct all scribes and recorders of contracts not to execute any contract without an order from the record office, for they should know that failure to observe these orders not only will invalidate their proceedings, but they themselves will suffer the due punishment for their disobedience. If the record office contains any registrations of property of earlier date, they should be preserved with utmost care. This applies likewise to the official abstracts of them, in order that, if any investigation is conducted hereafter concerning the improperly made registrations, the evidence can be collected from these documents. Therefore, in order that the use of the official abstracts may stay permanent and reliable and prevent the necessity of another registration, I command the keepers of the property record office to revise the official abstracts every five years and to transfer to the new abstract sheets the last statement of property of each person arranged according to villages and kinds. The 9th year of the Emperor Domitian, Domitianos, 4.[50]

2.6.3 Abstract sheet of the property records office

BGU III 959 (= *M.Chr.* 194, *Jur. Pap.* 61) (Arsinoite nome [Fayyum], after 27 August AD 148)

Though not an original but only an official extract from the *diastrôma*[51] of the village of Soknopaiou Nesos in the Arsinoite nome (Fayyum), the following text is of special interest because it illustrates how these abstract sheets were organized. The names of the owners of immovables in such a *diastrôma* were arranged in sections according to their initial letters and within a section according to the individual sheets (*kollêmata*). The text therefore offers valuable insight into the details of record keeping in the *bibliothêkê enktêseôn*. It contains an extract from the file of the minor Herieus concerning the registration of an acquisition of three arouras of katoikic land through Herieus that was held in common together with other proprietors.

[50] I.e., 31 October AD 89. The Egyptian month Hathyr was renamed (briefly) for the Emperor Domitian.

[51] For an original *diastrôma* cf., e.g., *P. Oxy.* II 274 (= *M.Chr.* 193, *Jur.Pap.* 60, AD 97).

Extract from the abstract sheet of Soknopaiou Nesos, roll for the letter Epsilon, sheet 17. The girl Herieus daughter of Stotoetis son of Stotoetis, and of the mother Taphiomis, a minor acting through her guardian Ar. . . son of Panephremmis son of Stotoetis, 11 years old [registered(?)] in the 11th year of Antoninus Caesar the lord on the 4th day of the epagomenai (i.e., 27 August AD 148) the [.]th part of a plot of three arouras of katoikic land held in common and undivided belonging to the village of Apias, (purchased) at a price of 160 drachmas from Chrysarion daughter of Heron son of Hermanoubion, citizen of a *polis*, who registered her purchase of the whole plot on the same day.

2.6.4 Extract from the Gnomon of the *Idios Logos*

BGU V 1210 §100 (= *Sel.Pap.* II 206, *Jur. Pap.* 93) (Theadelphia [Fayyum], after AD 149)

The so-called Gnomon of the *Idios Logos* is a collection of rules based on precedent cases of special interest for the administration of the *Idios Logos* ("private account"; see further **4.6.6** below). This office was attached to the central administration in Alexandria and goes back to the Ptolemaic period. After Egypt became a Roman province the office was administered by an equestrian procurator (*epitropos pros tôi idiôi logôi*). The name of the office is due to the original competence of its holder for the private income of the Ptolemaic kings. In the course of time the office also gained responsibility for the diverse sources of all irregular income, e.g., certain fines. In addition the income out of the *bona vacantia* (abandoned property) and of confiscated property fell within its competence as did the finances of the Egyptian temples.[52]

The Gnomon of the *Idios Logos* was compiled, as stated explicitly in its preamble, during the reign of Augustus, whereas the text preserved in *BGU* V 1210 dates from the time of the Emperor Antoninus Pius. In the preamble we are told that the following text is not the complete Gnomon (to it in the course of time were added numerous decisions of the emperors, the Roman senate, and several prefects), but an extract in form of a compilation of several regulations that had been modified only a short time ago.[53] Obviously the compilation should serve the purposes of a local civil authority (the village administration of Theadelphia maybe), since the local officials were of course often concerned with administrative matters that fell within the competence of the *Idios Logos*.

[52] For the nature of the office see Swarney (1970). [53] See Uxkull-Gyllenband (1934: 8–10).

The section (or paragraph) bearing the number 100 concerns the obligation of the private notaries (*synallagmatographoi*), recorders of legal instruments possessing a license from the government, to register with the Alexandrian archives the documents drafted by them within a prescribed limit of time. Different time limits were prescribed for notaries in Alexandria and for those in Upper and Lower Egypt. Those who failed to register in time were to be fined 100 drachmas.

> It was ordered, that the private notaries should register (viz. the contracts) here [in the town(?)][54]: (the ones) from the Thebaid within 60 days, from the other nomes within 30 days, from the town itself (i.e., Alexandria) within 15 days. People who failed to register were fined 100 drachmas [and were ordered(?)] to register until the 5th of the following month.

2.6.5 Application for registration of a deed

P.Oxy. XII 1475 (Alexandria [found in Oxyrhynchos], 20 March AD 267). Image at Papyri.info.

The cooperation of central and local archives can be observed particularly well in connection with the procedure of "publication" (*dêmosiôsis*) by means of which a privately drafted document (e.g., the *cheirographon* drafted in the style of a letter to the contracting party; see **2.1.4–8**) was made a public and thereby legally valid deed.[55] The central element of the *dêmosiôsis* was the incorporation of the legal instrument in the two Alexandrian archives, the *Nanaion* and the "Library of Hadrian." This procedure fell to the exclusive competence of the *katalogeion* under the direction of the "chief justice" (*archidikastês*) and was launched by a memorandum (*hypomnêma*) of the interested contracting party to this official. The applicant had to submit the *hypomnêma* personally in Alexandria or through an authorized representative. It was stated in the *hypomnêma* that the applicant had paid to the *polis* of Alexandria the fixed charge for *dêmosiôsis* of twelve drachmas and another fee whose meaning and purpose are not clear. In addition, the *hypomnêma* contained the complete copy of the contract. It culminated in the request to deposit

[54] There is a lacuna in the text in line 222, which the editor supplemented as "*apo tês* | [*poleôs*]," pointing out that the mention of the relevant office or archive would make more sense here; but "*epi tês* | [*dialogês*]," as was suggested by Seckel (cf. the commentary to the passage by the editor), meaning "the office of examination" in the *katalogeion* (see above with respect to **2.6.1**), seems too long for the space.

[55] For details see Wolff (2002: 129–35).

the original of the contract – which apparently had to be added to the application – together with the *hypomnêma* in the "Library of Hadrian" and a copy of it in the *Nanaion*. Finally, at the end of the application is a request to deliver a copy of the record on *dêmosiôsis* (which is now styled *prosphônêsis*) to the property record office (*bibliothêkê enkteseôn*) in the applicant's nome. This delivery had to be made by the applicant himself, who for that purpose received a duplicate of his application together with an accompanying letter of the *archidikastês*.

In **2.6.5** the order of the central elements of the *dêmosiôsis* procedure presents itself as follows:

(1) Application to the *archidikastês* for *dêmosiôsis* of a contract of sale (lines 6–9 and 41–47).
(2) Copy of a contract of sale of arable land in the holding of the village Paimis (lines 10–40; we omit most of this section in the following translation of the text).
(3) Another application to the *archidikastês* to pass on the record on *dêmosiôsis* to the keepers of the *bibliothêkê enktêseôn* of the Oxyrhynchite nome (lines 4–5 and 48–49).
(4) Endorsement on behalf of the *archidikastês* that the required steps should be taken (line 50).
(5) The required letter of the *archidikastês* to the keepers of the *bibliothêkê enktêseôn* of the Oxyrhynchite nome concerning the passing on of the record on *dêmosiôsis* (lines 1–3).

Lines 1–2: Aurelius Gaius also called Harpokration, priest and *archidikastês*, to the keepers of the property record office of the Oxyrhynchite nome, greetings. A copy of the official report which has been executed is appended. Good-bye.

Line 3: The 14th year of Gallienus Augustus, Pharmouthi 18 (i.e., 13 April AD 267). The official of the Bureau of Examination of the city: It was signed through me, Aurelius Alexandros.[56]

Lines 4–5: (*2nd hand*) To Aurelius Gaius alias Harpokration, priest and *archidikastês*, and superintendent of the *chrêmatistai* and the other

[56] The reading of the signature in line 3 is problematic (see the editor's remarks on *P.Mich.* XI 614, line 8, cf. *BL* VI 102); but it is certain that the Bureau of Examination of Documents, which was part of the *katalogeion*, must be involved here. The signature probably indicated that the proper fees for *dêmosiôsis* have been paid by the applicant.

courts, from Aurelia Thaisous also called Lolliane. A copy of the *dêmosiôsis* that has been executed is appended.

Lines 5–9: To Aurelius Gaius alias Harpokration, priest and *archidikastês* and superintendent of the *chrêmatistai* and the other courts, from Aurelia Thaisous alias Lolliane daughter of Sarapion alias Agathos Daimon, former *agoranomos* of the city of the Oxyrhynchites. A copy of the deed issued to me in duplicate together with the signature succeeding the date is appended.

In lines 10–37 follows the copy of a contract of sale by means of which Aurelius Agathinus alias Origenes, son of Varianus alias Klaros and Origenia, sells to Aurelia Thaisous alias Lolliane eleven arouras of grain-bearing and other land belonging to him in the area of the village Paimis in the western toparchy of the Oxyrhynychite nome. This contract is dated Hathyr 23 in the 14th year of the Emperor Gallienus (i.e., 19 November AD 266). Then follows in lines 37–40 the signature (*hypographê*) of Aurelius Agathinus:

I, Aurelius Agathinus alias Origenes, have sold and ceded to Lolliane alias Thaisous the aforementioned property and all the constructions pertaining to it and have received for the price 1 talent 3,700 drachmas of silver, and I will guarantee the property from claims in my name only, and I consent to the publication to be made by you, and in answer to the formal question have given my consent.

Now it is again Aurelia Thaisous who is speaking, applying for the *dêmosiôsis* of the aforesaid contract (lines 41–49):

Wishing that one copy of the duplicate deed should be made public, I pay to the city the prescribed 12 drachmas and the sum that is prescribed for the publication, and I request that you – by receiving the deed from Aurelius Neilos, whom I have dispatched with the confirmation written by himself, that the signature after the date is the autograph of Aurelius Agathinus alias Origenes – will deposit the original together with this application in the Library of Hadrian and a copy of it together with this application in the *Nanaion*, in order that I may be lawfully entitled to the rights deriving from it, as from a public deed, because Aurelius Agathinus alias Origenes has given his consent to the publication of the deed. The 14th year of Gallienus Augustus, Phamenoth 24 (i.e., 20 March AD 267). And whereas I wish that this should be communicated to the keepers of the property record office of the Oxyrhynychite nome, I request that, on receipt of the aforementioned and properly signed application for *dêmosiôsis*, you will give instructions for a letter written to them so that they will know.

There follows the endorsement on behalf of the *archidikastês*:

(*1st hand*) Let the necessary steps be taken. The 14th year of Gallienus Augustus, Phamenoth 27 (i.e., 23 March AD 267).

2.6.6 Petition to the prefect M. Iunius Rufus

P.Fam.Tebt. 15, lines 75–98 (Arsinoite nome [Fayyum], 15 May AD 98)

On the level of local administration the most important archive was the public record office (*bibliothêkê dêmosiôn logôn*), found in every single nome of the country, in which, as indicated by its name, all official documents (*dêmosioi logoi*) were deposited for the corresponding administrative district. In the beginning, this archive received the documents concerning the ownership of landed or other immovable property and those concerning slaves as well. Subsequently, the official documents of the civil administration, such as the official journals and the official correspondence of the individual authorities (in particular that of the two leading officials of the nome, the *stratêgos* and the royal secretary, *basilikos grammateus*), were also deposited there, as were files concerning taxation, census declarations, and census lists. Probably about AD 60 the *bibliothêkê dêmosiôn logôn* was divided into two separate archives. One continued to be the public record office, being styled as before the *bibliothêkê dêmosiôn logôn*; the second became a special archive for the registration of immovable property, therefore called the *bibliothêkê enktêseôn*.[57] The *bibliothêkê dêmosiôn logôn* continued to receive the official documents of the administration mentioned above and later, in addition, the documents concerning the business of the city council after the Emperor Septimius Severus had granted the right to establish such a *boulê* in each nome *metropolis*.

2.6.6 is a petition from AD 98 incorporated in a report dating from AD 115 and containing a large collection of copied official documents dating from earlier periods. They reveal great disorder and mismanagement in the public records office in the Herakleides district of the Arsinoite nome (which had been receiving the official records of all three *merides* of this, the largest nome of the whole country). Also related to this affair is *P.Fam.Tebt.* 24 from AD 124, containing the minutes of a trial before the nome *stratêgos*. Both documents are concerned with a legal dispute about the liability for defects in the administration of the public records office of the Arsinoite nome.

[57] See above, **2.6.2**, concerning the organization of this archive in the edict of Mettius Rufus.

This dispute was incited by the fact that in AD 90 a document from the *bibliothêkê demosiôn logôn* was presented to the prefect of Egypt, M. Mettius Rufus, as he was conducting his annual *conventus* (judicial "assizes") of the nome. The document lacked its beginning. Upon closer investigation it turned out that during the past decades the public records office of the Arsinoite nome had been in such disarray that a large number of documents were not only heavily damaged but many of them also irrecoverably destroyed. Out of this the said dispute arose between the officials responsible for the archive, which is closely connected with the specific organization of this office.

At the head of the *bibliothêkê demosiôn logôn* stood two keepers of records (*bibliophylakes*), whose office was a municipal liturgy. With the exception of certain formal procedures in which they had to be involved, the main responsibility for the routine service of the archive lay with their secretary (*grammateus*). He was hired and paid by the *bibliophylakes*. His office was not a liturgy but a professional occupation pursued for many years or even for a lifetime. Contrariwise, as a rule, the term of office of the liturgical *bibliophylakes* lasted for a shorter (not always exactly defined) period of years until (beginning with the reign of Trajan) the regular term of office for liturgists was set at three years. Upon retirement they transferred the archival records to their successors. This official transfer of records, called *paradosis* ("a handing over") or *paralêmpsis* ("a taking over"), was executed by the *grammateus* but had to be confirmed by the *bibliophylakes* through their signatures for every single record they received. Because of this the *bibliophylakes* were of course anxious to take over only such documents as were in an orderly condition because otherwise they would run the risk that their own successors in office would refuse to take over damaged documents and they themselves accordingly would be held responsible for the damage of the records. For this reason the transfer of records offered ample opportunity for conflict.[58]

It emerges from *P.Fam.Tebt.* 15 and 24 that between AD 87 and AD 114 the *grammateus* Leonides worked for at least five different pairs of *bibliophylakes*. But in the course of time the public records office got into deplorable condition and numerous documents were damaged or lost. The legal dispute between the officiating and the former *bibliophylakes* and between the *bibliophylakes* and the *grammateus* Leonides, respectively, and later between the heirs of the meanwhile deceased litigants as well,

[58] See also Burkhalter (1990: 193).

was initiated because Leonides refused to take over a part of the records in question; that is, he insisted on the clarification of the issue on whose risk he eventually would take over such documents. He also claimed compensation from the *bibliophylakes* and their predecessors in office for repairs made by him to the documents or for their replacement. In AD 124/5, after three successive prefects of Egypt and several *stratêgoi* of the nome had been involved, the dispute was finally settled between the heirs of the meanwhile deceased opposing parties, who were under the legal obligation to assume the liability for their ancestors' administration of office. The sentence was passed that the heirs of the *grammateus* Leonides should bear the costs for the repair or replacement of those documents that he had taken over without the participation and consent of the *bibliophylakes*.

Of the documents copied in *P.Fam.Tebt.* 15 the petition to the prefect M. Iunius Rufus dating from 15 May AD 98 (lines 75–98 = **2.6.6**) demonstrates particularly well the extent of the disorder into which the public records office of the Arsinoite nome had fallen during the past decades.

> Copy of a letter: To Iunius Rufus, the most excellent prefect of Egypt. Isidoros and Protogenes, <former> keepers of the public records office of the Arsinoite nome, greetings. When the former prefect Mettius Rufus held the *conventus* of the nome,[59] a document was presented to him out of the archive which missed the beginning. When he asked why it was missing its beginning, we(?) pointed out that not only this one in the archive missed its beginning but also many others, and that they had been transferred to us in this condition by our predecessors, Apion and Isidoros. And Mettius ordered that Apion, who was still alive, should appear before him and should render account of the transfer of documents being in such a state. Heliodoros and Zopyros, the keepers of the archive who were appointed after us, also submitted a petition, one of them, Heliodoros, to Mettius, the other, Zopyros, to you, the lord, concerning the documents in the archive that missed their beginnings and were utterly damaged. And Mettius wrote to Archelaos, the former *stratêgos*, to keep an eye on us that we(?)[60] should copy the missing parts from the documents deposited in Alexandria and supply in

[59] This *conventus* of the Arsinoite nome was held in spring AD 90.

[60] The text here wrongly speaks of the *bibliophylakes* in the third person (*hin' eklabôsi*) because in the original letter to the *stratêgos* Mettius Rufus of course did so and the scribe who copied this passage forgot to change into the appropriate person (*hin' eklabômen*); see *P.Fam.Tebt.* 15, 84n.

the archive the documents that miss their beginnings.[61] You also, lord, wrote to Claudius Hermias, former *stratêgos*, that the order of Mettius should be executed. Since, most high prefect, Heliodoros and his partner made this new request in an unprecedented way against the custom, and we ourselves were appointed a very long time ago, and taking over from the former keepers of the archive documents that in most cases missed their beginnings, whereas some of them are also utterly damaged, and others are pasted together; and since the successive *stratêgoi* and royal scribes in the same way having delivered to us the documents in whatever state they were, and because of the mass of documents lying in disorder one upon the other, it happened through frequent and continuous consultation day by day – the nome being very large[62] – that some of the other documents could not be saved from being destroyed by the long lapse of time, that others were partly damaged and others again eaten away at the top. Now again a period of eight years has passed since we resigned the office, and the documents in the course of time were even more seriously damaged and destroyed. Therefore we request, if it may please your most gracious provision and benevolence to all people, that you order a letter to be written to Arrius Herakleides, the *stratêgos* of the Herakleides division, to oblige Heliodoros and his partner to have the transfer done immediately and to take over the documents that are preserved in their contents, but the other utterly damaged ones and those without the beginning exactly as they are. We have also subjoined a copy of a letter concerning a similar case. Before all we pray for your health. First year of the Emperor Caesar Nerva Traianus Augustus, Pachon twentieth (i.e., 15 May AD 98).

2.6.7 Deposition of documents

P.Flor. III 357 (= *M.Chr.* 184) (Oxrhynchite nome, 1 September AD 208)

In each toparchy of a nome and in many of the larger villages there existed a notary's bureau (*grapheion*) under the direction of a

[61] The archive where the documents were deposited, most probably, was the *en Patrikois bibliothêkê* ("Library in the Patrika"), which in particular received the documents of the civil administration (see also below with respect to *BGU* III 981 [**2.6.8a**] and *P.Vind.Bosw.* 1).

[62] As was already pointed out in the introduction to this document, the public record office of the Arsinoite nome (the modern Fayyum) received the documents from all three administrative divisions (namely the Herakleides, Themistos, and Polemon divisions), these districts (*merides*) being administered independently and reaching the size of some average-sized nomes in the Nile valley; the Arsinoite being thus by far the largest nome in the whole country.

superintendent, the *pros tôi grapheiôi* or *nomographos* or *nomikos* ("notary")[63] as he is called in other documents.[64] He conducted the *grapheion* by virtue of a license from the government for which he had to pay a proper license fee and was answerable to the competent authorities for his business. While the contracting parties received copies of the documents drafted in the *grapheion*, the originals were numbered and pasted together in chronological order and thus formed long rolls of documents that were glued together (*tomoi synkollêsimoi*, "pasted rolls"). In addition to that there was made a summary of its content for every single legal instrument and this was entered on a chronological list of all contracts made in the *grapheion*, which list was called the *eiromenon*. Another list, which was called the *anagraphê*, contained only the titles of the contracts and functioned as an index for the summaries of the *eiromenon*. Furthermore, the *anagraphê* also served as formal registration for every single legal instrument and attested the payment to the clerk who had drafted the document. The superintendent of the notary's office had to deposit all these records, that is to say *tomoi synkollêsimoi*, *eiromena*, and *anagraphai*, periodically in the public records office of the nome (*bibliothêkê demosiôn logôn*) and in the "Library in the Patrika" (*en Patrikois bibliothêkê*) in Alexandria. This procedure is to be distinguished from the official registration of single contracts from the *chôra* of Egypt in Alexandria that we have dealt with in connection with the edict of T. Flavius Titianus (**2.6.1**) and §100 of the Gnomon of the *Idios Logos* (**2.6.4**) respectively.

2.6.7 is a *hypographê* ("signature," "endorsement") of the superintendent of an Oxyrhynchite notary's office affixed to a *tomos synkollêsimos*. By this he confirms that he deposited the roll properly and, with it, also the corresponding *eiromenon* and *anagraphê*.

> Apollonios alias Didymos, son of Apollonios, superintendent of the notary's office of the western toparchy of the Oxyrhynchite nome.
> I have deposited the above pasted roll (*synkollêsimon*) of the legal instruments drafted by me in the month of Mesore of the current year in 21(?) days,[65] and also the corresponding list of abstracts (*eiromenon*) and the corresponding list of titles (*anagraphê*); because in nine days (i.e., of

[63] As, e.g., in the edict of T. Flavius Titianus concerning the Alexandrian archives (see above, **2.6.1**, with respect to *P.Oxy.* I 34 verso).

[64] See Boak, *P.Mich.* V, pp. 1–2.

[65] In line 8 is written *chrêmatismou a* (=1), but this is presumably (as Mitteis suggested in *M.Chr.* p. 198) a haplography for *chrêm() hêm()*, meaning *chrêm(atismou) hêm(erôn)*, which (combined with the following sentence that there haven't been drafted any contracts for nine days of the month) leads to the assumption that the scribe, by indicating the number of days on which legal instruments were actually drafted, omitted a kappa as well and therefore wrote a single alpha instead of kappa-alpha.

the said month) there have not been drafted any legal instruments.[66] 17th year of the Emperors Caesars Lucius Septimius Severus Pius Pertinax Arabicus Adiabenicus Parthicus Maximus and Marcus Aurelius Antoninus Pius Augusti [[and Publius Septimius Geta Caesar Augustus]],[67] Thoth 4 (i.e., 15 September AD 208).

2.6.8 Deposition of the records of administrative officials

Local administrative officials had to deposit the official records of their administration (*dêmosioi logoi*) as well as their official journals (*hypomnêmatismoi*) not only in the public records office of their respective nomes but also in Alexandria. This is illustrated in our papyrological sources in particular for the two leading nome officials, the *stratêgos* and the royal scribe (*basilikos grammateus*). For the purpose of deposition in Alexandria the records were entrusted to special couriers "for receipt and delivery of records to be sent to Alexandria" (*hoi pros paralêmpsin kai katakomidên bibliôn pempomenôn eis Alexandreian*).[68] On the one hand, the records that were delivered by these couriers served as a means for the audit of local authorities that fell within the competence of the "auditors" (*eklogistai*) for each nome who were attached to the prefect's office in Alexandria. On the other hand, these records were deposited in one of the Alexandrian archives, as already pointed out in connection with *P.Fam.Tebt.* 15, lines 75–98 (**2.6.6**). There the keepers of records of the *bibliothêkê demosiôn logôn* of the Arsinoite nome are ordered by the prefect to restore by means of the duplicates deposited in Alexandria the missing parts of certain damaged documents kept in their local archive. Although we are not told the name of this central Alexandrian archive, here it is very probably the "Library in the Patrika" (*hê en Patrikois bibliothêkê*) to which the Arsinoite *bibliophylakes* should refer because it can be demonstrated with the help of other texts that this archive received the official records of the administrative authorities. The institution presumably derived its name from its location in a quarter of the city named "Patrika"[69] and was most probably established not long after the Roman conquest. As far as we know there was no Ptolemaic predecessor.[70]

66 Presumably because of religious holidays.

67 The name of the co-Emperor Geta is (as usual) crossed out in *damnatio memoriae.*

68 With respect to these couriers see, e.g., *P.Amh.* 69, 2–4 (AD 154); *SB* XII 10883 (AD 158); *P.Ryl.* II 83 (AD 138–161); *P.Flor.* III 358 (AD 146); *P.Princ.* II 127 (AD 159/60); *BGU* II 362 col. II 14 (AD 215/16).

69 Though this district isn't mentioned in Fraser (1972).

70 The earliest dated document that mentions the "Library in the Patrika" is *P.Vind.Bosw.* 1 (at line 19), 25 July AD 49; see also Burkhalter (1990: 208 with n. 72).

Although the two texts that follow are both concerned with the deposition of official documents in the "Library in the Patrika," each deals with it from a different point of view.

2.6.8a Beginning of a labor contract

BGU III 981 Col. 1, lines 1–11 (Diospolis Parva, 15 April AD 77). Image at *ZPE* 107 (1995), Plate 1.

This is the beginning of a labor contract (see Chapter 8) between Chairemon, royal scribe (*basilikos grammateus*) of the nome of Diospolis Parva in Upper Egypt, and a certain Ptolemaios, who is employed by him as one of his clerks or "secretaries" (*grammateis*).

Unfortunately this document, which is of great interest for the administrative history of Roman Egypt,[71] is severely mutilated. Among the various tasks of Ptolemaios' occupation is also mentioned the obligation to deposit regularly the records compiled by him in the public records office of the nome as well as in the "Library in the Patrika."

> Copy of an agreement: Ptolemaios son of Ptolemaios to Chairemon son of Andromachos, from the tribe Agathodoteios and the deme Althaieus,[72] royal scribe of the Small Diospolite (nome) [. . .] greetings. I herewith agree to serve as a scribe for you [. . .] for [. . .] years [. . .] and to provide the office [. . . and of the?] *stratêgos* with all the necessary lists drafted man by man[73] and the accounts for the main sums, and also to submit copies of them to the offices [of the *eklogistês* and . . . (?)] and to the archive in the Patrika and to the archive on the spot[74] as it was ordered . . .

2.6.8b List of journals followed by endorsements

P.Lips. I 123, cf. *BL* I 216 (Mendesian nome, 15 April AD 136). Image at Papyri.info.

The document consists of two parts. The first is a list (*anagraphê*) of various official journals (*hypomnêmatismoi*) filed for deposition in the "Library in the Patrika" by the *stratêgos* of the Mendesian nome that was

71 For further details see Kruse (2002: 782–811).

72 Chairemon possesses the Alexandrian citizenship, and therefore his *phylê* ("tribe") and *dêmos* ("deme") are mentioned

73 The so called *kat'andra*-lists in which persons are listed by name for different purposes, e.g., lists of inhabitants of villages and town quarters, lists of payments for the diverse taxes.

74 The formulation *eis tôn epi topôn bibliothêkên* is surely to be understood as "in the local public record office" and thereby meaning the *bibliothêkê demosiôn logôn* of the nome.

located in the eastern part of the Nile Delta. The second part presents the endorsements of the competent officials of the archive by which they confirm that they had received the records.

> From Philiskos, *stratêgos* of the Mendesian nome. List of the official journals for the 20th year of Hadrianus Caesar the lord (i.e., AD 135/6), which have been deposited in the archive in the Patrika. They are the following: from Hadrianus[75] 21 to Tybi 21 (i.e., 18 December AD 135–17 January AD 136), one roll; and from Tybi 22 to Mecheir 5 (i.e., 18–31 January AD 136), one roll; and from Mecheir 6 to the 21st of the same month (i.e., 1–16 February AD 136), one roll; and from Mecheir 22 to Pharmouthi 4 (i.e., 17–29 February AD 136), one roll. That is, [altogether], four rolls. 20th year of the Emperor Caesar Traianus Hadrianus Augustus, Pharmouthi 20 (i.e., 15 April AD 136)
>
> (*2nd hand*) D[. . .], I have(?) the aforementioned official journals in four rolls.
>
> (*3rd hand*) Marcus Ulpius Phanippos Tryphonianos, there have been received through the responsible officials the above-mentioned four rolls, that is, 4 rolls. 20th year of the Emperor Caesar Traianus Hadrianus Augustus, Pharmouthi 20 (i.e., 15 April AD 136), 4 rolls.
>
> *Verso:* Receipt of the keeper of the archive in the Patrika, from Hadrianus 21 to Phamenoth 4 (i.e., 18 December AD 135–28 February AD 136), in 4 rolls.

2.7 Byzantine sales: some aspects of the development of legal instruments in the later Roman and Byzantine period

T. Sebastian Richter

In the late nineteenth and parts of the twentieth centuries, papyrologists considered treating Byzantine documents an unpleasant duty, hard to avoid because of the sheer quantity of material, but worth doing for some bits of historical information – at any rate a depressing encounter with the sad decline of classical standards in the society and language of late antiquity. Both the Eurocentric, pejorative view on the history of the later Roman empire in the succession of Gibbon and the positivist disgust for the rhetoricality underlying the early papyrologists' way of treating the Byzantine evidence have now become *passé*. The old views have been replaced by

[75] This is the Egyptian month Choiak that was renamed after the Emperor Hadrian.

a new esteem for Byzantine society including its rhetorical tendencies. The result is a favorable view and a new approach to the sources.

It has become usual in papyrology, and is entirely reasonable in a pragmatic sense, to make the break between Roman and Byzantine Egypt fall in the reign of the Emperor Diocletian (AD 284–305) (see above, **1.3**). Some of the long-lasting changes initiated by his efforts to rebuild the administrative, military, and economic organization of the Roman empire are directly mirrored in the papyri, thus formally distinguishing the documentary evidence of the fourth to seventh from that of the first to third centuries. These changes included the administrative status and subdivision of the land of Egypt into smaller provinces, the names and functions of officials at all levels of administration, a fiscal reform leading to a new way of formally dating legal documents, and a currency reform creating a new monetary system based on the gold standard with its new coin called the *solidus* in Latin, *nomisma* in Greek, and *holokottinos* in Coptic.

Apart from such changes in substance, the visual and linguistic appearance of legal documents also experienced changes beginning under Diocletian, resulting in new standards in the diplomatic and calligraphic practice of the chancelleries along with the development known as the "rhetorization of the style" (see below). Two centuries after the administrative interventions of the zealous reformers Diocletian and Constantine (AD 306–37), the jurisprudential zeal of the Emperor Justinian (AD 527–65) left its own heavy impact on the layout and the language of legal documents. By Justinian's code and his own legislation, the professional organization of private notaries was thoroughly regulated and closely linked to certain diplomatic and phraseological features of the legal instruments to be drafted by them (cf. Steinacker 1927/1975: 79–81; Sachers 1932). Justinian's codification of law also supported the standardization of Latin legal terms and their Greek equivalents and itself introduced many new legal words and phrases.

In what follows, the characteristics of Byzantine schemes will be dealt with from two points of view: first, the development of Greek documentary schemes, and, second, the emergence and development of Coptic schemes.

Greek schemes

As an overall tendency, we find a diplomatic standardization and unification of Greek legal instruments in the Byzantine period. All but one of the formerly used schemes successively disappeared, while one type, the *cheirographon*, became increasingly ubiquitous for recording private legal affairs.

The *cheirographon* is a scheme that uses a subjective style, which means that all relevant matters of a given legal or business event are put in a "speech" made by the issuer, referred to in the first person, to the addressee, in the second person. This adlocutive attitude had its pattern in the epistolary style from which certain phrases were actually borrowed, such as the address formula *ho deina tôi deini chairein* "A to B, greetings!" Like almost all Demotic and Greek legal instruments (see above, **2.1** and **2.2**), the *cheirographon* too was a *unilateral* kind of statement, just the opposite of what modern contracts used to be: The content of the issuer's fictional speech is what he or she promises to do, or to refrain from, in favor of the addressee. This asymmetric sort of statement implies an asymmetry of the parties' interests, even (as has been argued) revealing differences in the parties' social status and economic power. The first was certainly the case with business or legal affairs implying obligation of one party only. The latter may be particularly true of those sorts of business with an intrinsic social and economic inequality between two parties, such as land-leasing, with one party possessing and the other one seeking access to land.

Emphyteusis contracts, long-term leases of estates or buildings, were one of the very few sorts of *bilateral* records that emerged in the Byzantine period. These typically included the different points of view of the two parties, and mentioned their respective rights and duties. These types of contracts were typically used by ecclesiastical institutions to liquidate estates that had come into their possession as pious endowments. Other examples of bilateral, mutual schemes are Byzantine deeds of divorce and the kind of Byzantine Greek (and Coptic) labor contract typically enough called a *symphônon* "concordant agreement."

A general feature of the Byzantine *cheirographon* is its *homología* ("agreement, declaration") style. Subsequent to a set of introductory formulas, the body of the contract begins with the phrase *homologô* (plural *homologoumen*), "I/we (i.e., the issuing party/-ies) agree/declare." All the following conditions and details of the business, as numerous as they may be, are put then in a string of subordinate clauses in indirect discourse depending on this opening phrase, so that the whole content of the contract's body grammatically forms one single complicated sentence.

This brings us to the most striking feature of Byzantine records: their pretentious style.[76] In contrast to earlier Greek documents, Byzantine records grow increasingly long, simply due to the abundant application of linguistic figures of adjection (*figurae per adiectionem* in terms of classical

[76] Cf. Zilliacus (1956, 1967); Gagos and van Minnen (1994: 27–30).

rhetoric). The results are characteristic pairs of homonymous or complementary words and expressions, such as: "voluntarily and being convinced"; "to have sold and signed over to you"; "at my own expense and expenditure"; "to infringe or to violate"; "(wherever the document will) be produced and exhibited"; "(the purchase price) which we agreed upon with each other and which pleased both of us," to quote only a few examples from the deed of sale *P.Münch.* I 11 (see **6.6.1**). Also to be found in this document are strings of expressions patterned by this rhetorical figure, such as the clause declaring the issuer's free will and soundness of mind: "without any fraud or fear or violence or deception or compulsion or robbery or flattery or contrivance, without any malice or malignity or knavery or any reduction, but with voluntary awareness and guileless decision and clear conscience and right-mindedness." Note also the clause declaring the transfer of ownership rights: "and you (i.e., the purchaser) shall be lord and proprietor, and be governing and administering, and constructing and selling, and donating and reselling, and exchanging, and leaving to children and grandchildren, and doing and acting with it (i.e., the object of sale) in every way, undisturbed and unprevented."

This new-fashioned Greek chancellery style, transforming hitherto unpretentious pieces of simple everyday prose concentrated on pure facts into highly elaborate specimens of rhetoric, forms part of an overall contemporary tendency directed toward the saturation of written text genres by rhetorical means of expression, which has therefore been labeled "the rhetorization of the style." Applied to legal records, the style neatly worked as a proper *function style*, fit to make any relevant point of a legal event certain and unequivocal by means of a linguistic "dissection," as it were, of its terms into their conceptual components by means of these synonymous and complementary words and phrases. At the same time the style may have been meant to impress and to please. But by no means should we, like early papyrologists, disdainfully regard the results as empty bombast without connections to contemporary social realities.[77]

Who were the draftsmen who could put concrete legal events with all their peculiarities into appropriate schemes and clauses with the added grace of rhetorical ornaments? The ability and formal responsibility for this resided with a professional group of private notaries who called themselves *tabelliones* in Latin, *nomikoi* or *symboulaiographoi* or the like in Greek and Coptic. Formally trained and educated scribes, possessing some bits of knowledge of the law though not qualified as learned

[77] Cf. Gagos and van Minnen (1994: 27–30).

lawyers, they were certified by the government and held offices in cities, towns, and even in larger villages where they offered their services to paying customers. Every Byzantine *cheirographon* originating from these certified professionals was finished off by a handwritten signature, the so-called *plerôsis* or *compleusis*, in Latin *completio* ("completion note") of the authorized notary even if the document itself was written by an assistant. These signatures, sometimes carried out in a hybrid combination of Greek language written in oddly shaped Latin characters, looked something like this: *di emou NN nomikou egraphê* "written by me, NN, the notary." Besides such professionally drafted documents, there is also a good number of legal records that were designed and drawn up by occasional scribes who were more or less successfully copying or imitating the schemes of their professional colleagues without being formally authorized as notaries (e.g., **6.6.1**) – a difference, however, that did not affect the formal validity of a document as a means of legal evidence. Many Coptic documents after the conquest, when an authorizing government no longer existed, came into being through the efforts of non-professional notaries, often clergymen by their original profession. But even then, and onwards to the later eighth century, the titles *nomikos* and *symboulaiographos* remained in use in Coptic documents.

The general scheme of a Byzantine *cheirographon* or *homología* ran something like this:

Invocation formula – † *En onomati tou theou* etc. "In the name of God, etc.!"

Dating formula – From the fourth to seventh centuries, documents are usually dated according to the yearly consulate and postconsulate, and additionally according to a year within the 15-year fiscal cycle called *indiction*; later in the sixth to seventh centuries, the emperor's regnal year was used again, as had been usual in earlier Roman documents.

Address formula – "A to B, greetings!"

Deed corpus – *homologô* . . . "I declare . . ."

***Kyria* clause** – "This (so-and-so) deed is valid" (literally: *kyria* "having authority").

Stipulation of the deed and subscription by the issuing party –*kai eperôtêtheis hômologêsa* "And in answer to the formal question I have given my consent."

Signature of witnesses

Completion note of the notary – *di emoû NN egraphê* "Written by me, *NN*."

As mentioned, all common types of legal and business affairs, from the law of domestic relations and the law of inheritance up to any kind of transfer of property and rights, were recorded in the *cheirographon*/*homología* scheme in Byzantine times. Well-attested sub-types and their names are the following:

- sale of real estate, animals, or any objects, called *prasis* "sale' or *ônê* "purchase" (cf. below, **6.6**);
- sale on delivery (cf. **2.7.1a and 2.7.1b**) and the acknowledgement of indebtedness called *asphaleia* "security";
- lease of land, buildings, devices, animals, or any usufructuary rights, e.g., fishing rights, as well as the hire of labor, all of them called (in the singular) *misthôsis* (cf. below, **7.4** and **8.3**);
- long-term lease, called *emphyteutikê homologia*;
- deed of gift *inter vivos*, called *dôrea*, *dôreastikê homologia*, or the like;
- will, called *diathêkê* "testament";
- deed of surety, called *eggyê* "bail, guaranty";
- final settlement after arbitration, called *dialysis* "separation" (cf. below, **10.4**);
- deed of divorce, called *dialyseôs* or *rhepoudíou* (< Latin *repudium*) *homologia* "agreement of separation/divorce" (cf. below, **4.3**);
- receipt, one of the most common types of documents, called *entagion* "receipt" or *apodeixis* "proof," usually drawn up in a rather short and plain *cheirographon* scheme.

It goes without saying that our evidence for all of these types is regrettably discontinuous, so that some places in Egypt and certain periods of time are well documented while others are poorly or not at all attested. (Most glaringly, the entire fifth century displays an odd lack of evidence.) Typical provenances of Greek legal documents from Byzantine and early Islamic times are, from north to south, the *poleis* and nomes of Arsinoë, Herakleopolis, Oxyrhynchos, Hermopolis (cf. **7.4.3**), and Antinoopolis, the Komê ("village") Aphroditês, the town of Apollônos Anô, and the town of Syênê (cf. **6.6.1**). Sometimes when the evidence permits us to compare one certain type of business as found in different regions of Egypt, we find amazing variations. For example, there is a striking difference between the economic conditions agreed to by the tenants in Byzantine land leases from the Fayyûm and those from Middle and Upper Egyptian nomes (cf. below, **7.4** and Jördens 1990 and 1999). This striking phenomenon might find explanation in the decentralized administration of Egypt in the aftermath of Justinian's administrative reform by his Edict XIII of AD 539, which turned Egypt into a number of separate provinces or eparchies, each under a governor enjoying both civil and military power.[78]

Coptic schemes

Because of the sociolinguistically conditioned circumstances of the emergence of Coptic legal instruments (below, **3.4**), it comes as no surprise to find the Coptic legal terminology and the whole repertoire of Coptic schemes heavily influenced by Greek prototypes: The sixth/seventh-century lease formulary of Hermopolis as instanced by the Greek *P.Lond.* III 1012 (= **7.4.3**) and the Coptic *CPR* IV 114 (= **7.4.1**), *CPR* IV 117 (= **7.4.4**), or the elaborate sixth-century sale formulary of Syene (*P.Münch.* I 11 = **6.6.1**) and an eighth-century Coptic counterpart from Djême (*P.KRU* 6 = **6.6.2**) are striking examples. Developed by virtually bilingual notaries as a "branch line" of the fully evolved post-Justinianian Greek instrument, the Coptic legal instrument and its schemes generally bear *additional* evidence for sixth- and seventh-century Greek schemes. Of course, "additional evidence" means more than a pure accumulation of evidence: it implies variations on all levels, enlarging our stock of knowledge based on Greek evidence proper.

By contrast, attempts to prove traces of continuity between Demotic and Coptic instruments have failed to succeed (see **1.8**): Unsupported by written transmission for more than three centuries, only small bits of the native Egyptian legal terminology, hardly more than a few single lexical items, survived.[79] One of those was the Theban Coptic expression *sahne* "lease," "to lease out to somebody" (in Demotic *sḥn* "(to) lease," literally: "to commit something to someone's charge," cf. **7.1**), which also might have been calqued in the Greek designation of Coptic lease documents from that area (cf. below, **3.4.2**).

The universal scheme of Coptic instruments is the *cheirographon* stylized as a subjective, unilateral declaration in accordance with its Greek prototype, with the exceptions mentioned above: the long-term lease, designated in Coptic as in Greek by the term *emphyteutikê homologia*, and the type of labor contract called *symphônon*, using its Greek designation, were bilateral and sometimes objectively stylized. The most elaborate phenotype of the Coptic *cheirographon* scheme, mainly used for more important transactions such as leases, sales of real property, and donations, looks like its Greek pattern, with some slight variations:

[78] Bell (1929: 279–80); Rouillard (1928: 15–24); Jones (1964: 281).
[79] Cf. Richter (2002a) and Richter (2002b: 37–57).

Invocation formula – "In the name of God, etc.!," "God willing!," or the like, written in Greek or Coptic.

Dating protocol – Dating to consulates is not attested in Coptic, and due to their chronological position, only a negligible minority of all Coptic documents give dates according to regnal years of the last Byzantine emperors to rule over Egypt. Instead some documents are dated to local eponymous officials (cf. *P.KRU* 6 = **6.6.2**). In the vast majority of Coptic documents, however, only one of the three dating methods of Byzantine documents is still used, the reference to a year within the 15-year *indiction* cycle. The counting of *indiction* years operates in a small, relative chronological frame, which presumably was perfectly comprehensible to contemporaries, but cannot possibly be fixed by us without additional dating criteria. This is why so many Coptic documents are only tentatively datable even if the text is completely preserved. Only the ninth- to eleventh-century late Coptic documents (cf. *P.Lond.Copt.* I 673 = **6.6.4**; *P.Teshlôt* 2 = **6.6.5**; *P.Lond.Copt.* I 487 = **7.4.7**) are regularly dated in an absolute way, either by the era of Diocletian (counting from AD 284) or by the *hijra* year (counting in lunar years from AD 622).

Address formula – "I, A, am writing to B": The Coptic way of referring to the addressee, unlike its Greek counterpart always operating with the verb "to write to," corresponds with the Coptic epistolary formula. A more striking difference between Greek and Coptic addresses is the almost entire lack of the ubiquitous status designations *Aurelius* and *Flavius* in the Coptic documents.

Deed corpus – The Greek term *homologein* "to declare" does sometimes occur, but more frequently the key term of the particular sort of business opens the deed corpus: "I lease from you," "I sell to you," etc.

***Kyria* clause** – "This (so-and-so) deed is valid at any place where it will be produced."

Stipulation of the deed and subscription by the issuing party – Renderings of the classical stipulation formula of Roman civil law "in answer to the formal question I have given my consent" into Coptic do occur, but the more frequent stipulation formula used in Coptic legal documents is the simple statement "I assent," operating with the Greek term *stoichein* "to assent, to agree."

Signatures of witnesses

Completion note of the notary or scribe – "Written by me, *NN*," in Greek or Coptic.

The most prominent sites that have yielded Coptic legal documents are:

- the Fayyum (cf. *P.Lond.Copt.* I 673 = **6.6.4**), mainly eighth-century documents, but a few documents date even to the ninth and tenth centuries;
- the region of Hermopolis/Ashmunein, including the towns (*poleis*) of Ashmunein (cf. *CPR* IV 34 = **2.7.1**, *CPR* IV 114 = **7.4.1**, *CPR* IV 117 = **7.4.4**, and *P.Lond.Copt.* I 487 = **7.4.7**) and Antinou, the Hermopolite monastery of Apollo called Bawît (cf. *P.Mon.Apollo* 24 = **6.6.3**), and sites in the south of Ashmunein (cf. *P.Teshlôt* 2 = **6.6.5**), evidence from late sixth to ninth centuries, a number of late Coptic documents even tenth and eleventh centuries;
- the Komê ("village") Aphrodito, in Coptic called Jkôw, including an assemblage of late sixth-century texts, and an early eighth-century dossier forming part of the correspondence of the Arab governor Qurrah ibn Sharîk (his governorship in Egypt AD 709–14);
- the Theban area, including the town of Djême (cf. *P.KRU* 6 = **6.6.2**), the local monastery of Phoibammon, the monastery of Epiphanius nearby, and the more distant surroundings (cf. *BKU* I 48 = **7.4.6**; *O.Crum Ad.* 15 = **7.4.2**; and *O.Crum VC* 33 = **7.4.5**), evidence from around 600 to the late eighth century, including a large number of ostraca used for short kinds of documents such as receipts, acknowledgements of indebtedness, *epitropê*-leases, and labor contracts;
- the town of Syene, evidence from late sixth to early seventh century, a few Coptic papyri belonging to the archive of Patermouthis (for this archive cf. *P.Münch.* I 11 = **6.6.1**), mainly acknowledgements of indebtedness written on ostraca.

The Coptic evidence of particular business types differs a lot among these provenances. Marriage and divorce are almost unattested; the most important items are an early seventh-century betrothal declaration from Thinis, a single agreement of divorce, and two very late marriage agreements, addressed by the fiancée to her prospective father-in-law, both of them clearly patterned on Arabic documents. Sales, donations, and wills are almost exclusively attested in the Theban dossier, with a few examples in the Ashmunein dossier; sales on delivery are mainly instanced by Fayyumic texts. All *emphyteusis*-leases and the great majority of *misthôsis*-leases belong to the Ashmunein dossier, while the Fayyumic and the Theban dossiers provide us with other types and names of lease-like documents, such as the above-mentioned *epitropê* type. Also: Coptic labor contracts vary a lot from region to region. Ubiquitous types of documents attested in all of the local dossiers are acknowledgements of indebtedness and receipts acknowledging the fulfillment of any obligations.

Despite the aforementioned difficulty of precisely dating large numbers of Coptic legal documents, one gets an overall impression of their age. Depending on and overlapping the late Byzantine Greek instruments, the production of Coptic legal documents considerably increased after the Arab conquest when Greek, though still playing an important role in the administration during early Islamic times, gradually withdrew from the realm of private legal and business affairs. Between the late seventh and the mid-eighth century, the production of Coptic legal documents may have been at its peak. After the eighth century, the number of Coptic documents shrank sharply, and, even more conspicuously, their schemas underwent a striking transformation. The former dominance of Greek patterns faded away, while Arabic patterns started influencing the terminology and formulas of late Coptic legal documents, pointing to private legal and business contacts between Christians and Muslims. Striking examples of that transformation of late Coptic schemes are the deeds of sale *P.Lond.Copt.* I 673 (= **6.6.4**) and *P.Teshlôt* 2 (= **6.6.5**) (cf. the Arabic deed of sale *P.Cair.Arab.* I 57 = **6.6.6**), and the lease document *P.Lond. Copt.* I 487 (= **7.4.7**; cf. the Arabic lease *Chrest.Khoury* II 29 = **7.4.8**). All in all, the age of the Coptic legal instrument was a roughly 500-year period from the later sixth to the later eleventh century.

2.7.1 Greek–Coptic specimen forms of sales on delivery

CPR IV 34, lines 1–41 (=*P.Rain.Unterricht* 112, Hermopolis/Ashmunein, seventh century)

Vienna, papyrus collection of the National Library, inv. K 4912B, two fragments of 10 cm and 50 cm in height by 32 cm in width; forty-four lines preserved, many gaps, beginning and ending of the papyrus scroll wanting. On the recto (K 4912A, vertical fibres), one of the two extant Coptic wills within the Ashmunein dossier, *CPR* IV 177, is preserved. Since the later part of the text, which should have borne signatures of the issuer, witnesses, and notary, is lost, we do not know whether the text was the legal instrument itself or only a draft or copy. The back side of the large papyrus was used, or re-used, for a kind of exercise unique in the papyrological evidence, but perhaps fairly common at that time, if one takes the relationship between Greek and Coptic schemes into account.

Three sales on delivery are subsequently written on the very same papyrus, although their addressees are different. The texts are subdivided into paragraphs, each of them written twice, once in Greek and once in Coptic, but none bearing signatures of the issuers, witnesses, or scribe. The purpose of this kind of text was obviously to provide specimen forms of sales on delivery in the two languages. The first, partly damaged text (lines 1–14) concerns a sale of 50,000 pieces plus 30 bundles of reeds. The issuer, whose name is lost in a gap, acknowledges he has received their full price in advance from the addressee, promises to deliver them in time and in good quality, and accepts liability by pledging his fortune. The second text (lines 15–41) is a sale on delivery of 600 *kouphon*-vessels and 200 *kollathon*-vessels. The potter Aurelius Johannes acknowledges the receipt of their price from Flavius Gennadios and promises their timely delivery in good condition, accepting liability by pledging his fortune. It is striking to find the addressee's status designation "Flavius" properly translated into Coptic as "the great one." The third text (lines 41–44) breaks off at the beginning of the deed corpus, *homologô ekousiôs* "I declare voluntarily . . .," and is not given here in translation.

Literature: Till (1953: 201–08); Till (1958: 39–42, no. 34); for specimen formularies see von Druffel (1915/1970); for sales on delivery, Ernst (1997).

2.7.1a Sale on delivery of reeds

CPR IV 34, lines 1–14 (Hermopolis/Ashmunein, seventh century)

Introductory formulas: (*Both Greek and Coptic section lost*)
(*Receipt of the price in advance*)
(*Greek section lost*)
(*Coptic section*) [. . . I received and am paid in full by you with the] fair and just [price] for the fifty thousand (pieces) of reeds and the thirty bundles,

Promise of timely delivery in good quality: (*Greek section*) which reeds I declare I will deliver to you in the month of Mecheir of the – God willing! – coming fifth (year of) indiction [. . .] as good, new reeds, acceptab[le and well-]pleasing, the one half [. . .] the other half, however, [. . .] of the reeds
(*Coptic section entirely lost in the gap*)

Guarantee clause: (*Greek section*) [However, if I will not pay you in full with these reeds at the aforementioned delivery date, then (I declare) I will give you twelve *nomismata* for their price at my risk, my] entire fortune [being in pledge], whereas I swear by God the Almighty, and the salvation of those ruling over us, not to violate the legal force of the present document; the present document is valid and sure, and in answer to the formal question I have personally given my consent.

(*Coptic section*) However, if I should not have paid you in full with these reeds at the aforementioned delivery date, then I will give you twelve gold *holokottinoi* for their price at my risk and the entire stock of my fortune in pledge, swearing by God, the Almighty, and the salvation of those who rule over us, that I shall not violate the legal force of this document, as this document is valid and sure, and (when) they asked me, I agreed.

2.7.1b Sale on delivery of *kouphon*-vessels

CPR IV 34, lines 15–41 (Hermopolis/Ashmunein, seventh century)

Introductory formulas: (*Greek section*) Aurelius Iohannes, the vessel-potter, the son of the late Dios, of the village [. . .,] to Flavius Gennadios [. . .] from the same town of Hermopolis[, greetings! I declare I have received] and been paid out by you for the full and fair [price of the] *kouphon*-vessels, their inside coated with pitch, of the great(?) *aggeion*-measure, [. . .] (each) bearing a lid(?), with four handles, hundred [. . . . .]

(*Coptic section*) [I, Iohannes], the vessel-potter, the son of the late Sia (*sic*), inhabitant of the village [. . .] of this town Shmoun – (to) you, the great Gennad[ios, son] of the late, memorable Theodore, inhabitant of the same town [of Shmoun,] I have [received and I am paid out by you for the full, fair, and just p]rice of the six hundred *kouphon*-vessels [. . .] and the two hundred *kollathon*-vessels [v] of clay [. . . each of them with four] handles,

Promise of timely delivery in good quality: (*Greek section*) which *kouphon*-vessels I declare I will deliver to you in the month [. . .] of the – God willing! – coming fifth (year of) indiction as new, good [. . .] and well-pleasing *kouphon*-vessels; and I declare I am liable for these very [. . .] at the drying place and beyond, two hundred, without any delay or contradiction or judgment or lawsuit.

(*Coptic section*) + These *kouphon*-vessels now, I declare to give them to you [in the month . . .] of this coming – God willing! – fifth year of indiction as new, good, and w[ell-pleasing] *kouphon*-vessels; (and)

I declare that I am liable to you for them [. . .] at the drying place, without [. . .]; without any delay or contradiction or judgment or lawsuit.

Guarantee clause: (*Greek section*) However, if I will not pay you in full with these *kouphon*-vessels at the aforementioned delivery date, then (I declare) I will give you [fifteen] nomismata [for their price] at my risk, my entire fortune being in pledge, whereas I swear by God the Almighty, and the salvation of those ruling over us, not to violate the legal force of the present document; the present document is valid and sure, and in answer to the formal question I have given my consent.

(*Coptic section*) However, if I should not have paid you in full with these *kouphon*-vessels at the aforementioned delivery date, then I will give you fifteen *holokottinoi* for its price at my risk and the entire stock of my fortune in pledge, swearing by God, the Almighty, and the salvation of those who rule over us, that I shall not violate the legal force of this document, whereas this document is valid and sure, and (when) they asked me, I agreed.

CHAPTER 3

The languages of law

James G. Keenan, J. G. Manning, Brian P. Muhs, T. Sebastian Richter, and Katelijn Vandorpe

Introduction

In the Egyptian millennium covered by this volume two major languages were spoken and written. Egyptian was the larger in terms of number of speakers, while Greek, certainly spoken in Egypt during much of the first millennium BC, became in the Ptolemaic period the dominant language of administration and the language of law. The Egyptian language is represented in its two last phases by two different scripts. The first, which developed in the Delta during the seventh century BC and spread through Egypt by the fifth century BC, is known as Demotic, characterized by a highly cursive script that developed out of the cursive Hieroglyphic writing known as Hieratic.[1] The second phase, Coptic, began to be written around AD 300 and came to be used in legal documents by the sixth century AD, though it did not become a dominant contractual language until after the Arab conquest (**3.4**).[2] This last stage of the Egyptian language deployed a Greek alphabet to which were added several signs left over from Demotic that preserved phonemes in Egyptian not found in Greek.

Thus during the three traditional phases of Egyptian political history documented in this volume (Ptolemaic, Roman, Byzantine) Egypt was a serially bilingual society.[3] Of course, the Romans through their conquest introduced Latin as a language prominent in certain military and legal contexts (**3.3**, **4.3**). This notwithstanding, Greek remained for Egypt, whether ruled from Rome or Constantinople, the chief administrative and legal language. It continued as such past the Arab conquest into the early eighth century AD (**3.4**).

There are several different circumstances in which bilingualism features in legal papyri. The first occurs at the intersection between the interests of

[1] For a good overview, see Thompson, D. J. (2009).
[2] Bagnall (2011: 75–94)
[3] For a recent overview, see Papaconstantinou (2010).

the state (taxation and registration) and the making of private contracts. That intersection can be seen in the "archival dockets" recording the sale tax on Ptolemaic Demotic documents beginning with the reign of Ptolemy II (Pierce 1972: 179–88). Bilingualism can be seen, for example, in Demotic contracts with Greek registration dockets (**3.2.1**), or in those contracts where the contractual language was Greek or Demotic and the subscriptions in the opposite language (**3.2.2–3.2.3**). Official Greek wills might bear signatures of priestly witnesses "in the native script" (**3.1.2** and introduction) if there were not enough "Greeks" on hand. We also see bilingualism in trials in which Greeks and Egyptians were involved. The state official present at the Asyut family dispute (called an *eisagôgeus*, an "executive officer" [Taubenschlag 1955: 483], or "clerk of the court," a state official in charge of supervision of the trial and perhaps responsible for the enforcement of the judgment), for example, presumably knew enough spoken Egyptian to follow the proceedings.[4] In certain cases, it may have been the case that Demotic contracts had to be translated into Greek to be adjudicated by Greek courts (Mairs and Martin 2008–09).

The two different courts of the Ptolemaic period, one hearing cases in Greek, the other in Egyptian, must have created the need both for bilingual speakers and for interpreters (Rochette 1994). This also held true for the Roman period, when reports of legal proceedings record the testimony of Egyptophone witnesses as rendered into Greek through interpreters (*hermêneis*, e.g., *P.Sakaon* 32 [AD 254/68], *SB* XVI 12692 [17 May AD 339]). The Roman period saw the introduction of written records of court proceedings with framework and speakers' cues in (highly abbreviated) Latin and the substance of questions and answers in Greek (**10.3.6**, **10.4.5**). The Byzantine period brings to papyrological prominence the bilingual Greek–Coptic notary Flavius Dioskoros, whose knowledge of the law suggests he must have had at least a smattering of training in Latin as well (van Minnen 2003; see Rowlandson 1998: 151–55, **4.2.3** and **8.2.12** for samples of his work).

Another good example of the use of an interpreter is to be found in one of the most famous texts from Roman Egypt.[5] Therein, as part of a lengthy petition to the prefect over a property dispute, minutes before a regional Roman official (an *epistratêgos*) were cited verbatim as evidence in support

[4] On this trial, see Manning (2010: 193–96). On the official, see the discussion by Allam (2008), who argues that the official was a continuation from pharaonic law courts.

[5] *P.Oxy.* II 237, Col. VII, lines 37–38. Trans. Rowlandson (1998, no. 138). Part of this large text is treated above in **2.6.2**.

of the complaining party's claims. Part of the minutes from 14 October AD 133 states that an interpreter was deployed to translate, and thus to make plain before the official, the wishes of an Egyptian woman. Bilingual archives, whether Demotic–Greek or Coptic–Greek (Clarysse 2010, Clackson 2010, **3.4**), are perhaps the richest source for relations between ethnic groups, and it is the Dryton archive (see **3.1** and **4.5.3**) that offers the best glimpse at the use of Greek and Egyptian legal forms and traditions within a single family.

In the Ptolemaic period, the maximum Greek population represented between 5 and 15 percent of the total population of Egypt.[6] There were, of course, many other ethnic groups living in Egypt, Idumaeans, Arabs, Jews, for example. Occasionally they were organized into distinct communities (*politeumata*, see **10.2** below). Greek became the dominant administrative language. Many Egyptians of the scribal class learned enough Greek to function in the new bureaucratic system, while certain among the Greeks who immigrated to Egypt adapted to their new local surroundings by learning Demotic.

The military families of Upper Egypt that are documented in archives such as Dryton's used both Greek and Demotic texts to record their transactions. Dryton, whose father was probably from Crete, served as a cavalry officer in Upper Egypt during the second century BC. His bilingual archive is especially important because it contains three versions of his Greek will, linked to three milestones in his life: his first and second marriages and his impending death. Taken together these Greek wills, along with the Egyptian "deeds of division" found in other archives, demonstrate quite clearly how Egyptian and Greek traditions of intergenerational property transfer interacted and influenced each other to form "Greco-Egyptian" documents (Vandorpe 2002a: 26).

The social status of the parties may have influenced the choice of language and the type of document selected for a particular transaction. Military communities like Pathyris (in the south, modern Gebelein) were certainly places in which ethnic interactions were more likely. The Greek of the papyri does show some influence from Egyptian; on the contrary, Demotic, with the exception of some technical loanwords, shows notable isolation both from Greek and from Egyptian, even though many Greek loanwords must have been borrowed into spoken Egyptian already during the Ptolemaic period. Such a formal distinction between documentary and spoken language was, theoretically, a standard feature of Egyptian

[6] Thompson, D. J. (2009: 401). For the low estimate see now Fischer-Bovet (2011).

(Ray 1994). The Greek of the Byzantine period borrowed numerous Latin technical terms (Daris 1991 *passim*), while Coptic of all periods gets a goodly portion of its vocabulary from Greek, with technical terms, once again, significant in such borrowing (**3.4**, cf. Crum 1939a: 879–939).

Bilingual Demotic and Greek contracts continued to be written in the Fayyum following the disappearance of purely Demotic contracts at the beginning of the Roman period, but even these bilingual contracts gradually begin to disappear in favor of purely Greek ones in the late first and early second century AD. The gradual nature of this disappearance argues against an outright administrative proscription of either the Demotic language and script or the Egyptian legal tradition.[7] Indeed, documents from Oxyrhynchos outside the Fayyum suggest that the Egyptian legal tradition continued to be recognized well into the Roman period. The proclamation of the prefect of Egypt Marcus Mettius Rufus, dated to AD 89–90, is preserved as a citation in the petition of a certain Dionysia to another prefect of Egypt in AD 186 (see above, p. 97).[8] This proclamation makes it clear that claims arising out of the Egyptian legal tradition were recognized at least as late as AD 89–90, as long as those claims were properly registered in Greek, while the petition suggests that such claims could be recognized well into the second century AD.[9] This latter possibility is supported by a Greek translation of the Demotic legal manual of Hermopolis dating to the second century AD found in Oxyrhynchos.[10]

P.Mattha, referred to on several occasions in the present volume but too big to include, is dated by palaeography to the third century BC. It contains in some cases what appear to be legal rules that are earlier, so the text may be an updated version of something created before the Ptolemaic period. It consists of a series of legal rules and particular forms of legal texts (how to make out a lease of land, the proper form of an annuity, the rules of inheritance, and so on). This legal manual, or book of forms, and its Roman period copy (*P.Oxy.* XLVI 3285), demonstrate that Egyptian legal traditions and forms of text were still in use throughout the Ptolemaic and early Roman (at least) periods.[11]

Thus, the disappearance of bilingual contracts in favor of purely Greek ones is likely to have been the long-term consequence of the administrative

[7] Lewis (1993); Muhs (2005a: 100–04).

[8] *P.Oxy.* II 237, Col. VIII, lines 27–43 (= **2.6.2**).

[9] The very use of the *katochê* by Dionysia shows that this Egyptian institution was still applied towards the end of the second century.

[10] *P.Oxy.* XLVI 3285. For Demotic legal "codes," see Lippert (2004).

[11] *Ed. pr.* Mattha and Hughes (1975). See further Donker van Heel (1990). For the connections to actual praxis, see Muhs (2002).

changes made at the beginning of the early Roman period. It has been shown that the texts of Greek subscriptions of first contracting parties could closely parallel the texts of Greek contracts proper. In fact, the subscriber for the first contracting party could largely restate the Greek contract proper in the first person, when the contract proper was written before the subscription. Similarly, the *grapheion* officials could largely restate the Greek subscription of the first contracting party in the third person, when the subscription was written before the contract proper. In contrast, bilingual Demotic and Greek contracts always required a translation, either on the part of the subscriber when the Demotic contract proper was written first, or on the part of the *grapheion* official when the Greek subscriptions were written first. The elimination of the separate administrative systems of Demotic notaries and Greek contract scribes made it easier to choose the language and script of a contract, and the requirement that contracting parties subscribe their contracts in Greek may thus have made Greek contracts more attractive than bilingual Demotic and Greek ones, especially for a population that was probably largely illiterate in both Demotic and Greek. In addition, the Ptolemaic state requirement that Demotic contracts be registered in order to be valid appears to have led to a decline in their use.[12] The Roman state centralized even further the registration of private agreements.[13]

Coptic documentary papyri reveal a large number of phenomena related to societal bilingualism and individual bilingual skills of different degrees, sometimes as components in Greek–Coptic bilingual archives.[14] The social milieus and affairs reflected by Coptic literary and documentary texts give the impression that the Egyptian vernacular was functioning as a low-variety language, regularly learned as the first, hardly as a second language, spoken and occasionally written by native speakers within, socially and functionally, rather narrow surroundings.

A strong obstacle to drawing a reliable and nuanced picture of Greek–Egyptian bilingualism and legal biculturalism in Byzantine Egyptian society is the narrow limits placed on conclusions based on the evidence of written texts: What we see is only the tip of an iceberg. This is true both of the linguistic contours of the documents and of their legal content. We have no appropriate criterion to decide whether or not, or to what extent, the linguistic appearance and the legal practice evidenced by our texts represent the usual linguistic behavior of Egyptians and the overall

[12] *P.Par.* 65 (146 BC) on which see above, Chapter 2, introduction.
[13] *P.Oxy.* I 34 verso (= **2.6.1**). [14] Clackson (2010).

legal customs of Byzantine Egypt. Still, the surviving evidence is a wide area full of complexity, one that will not stop prodding us to imagine how the language of legal and business communication functioned in Byzantine Egypt.

3.1 Ethnic diversity in a wealthy household

Katelijn Vandorpe

The papers of Dryton, his wife, and their offspring constitute only one of the family archives originating from Ptolemaic Pathyris. Archives from this town are especially important for studying the degree of hellenization of the local people and the initiatives taken by the government to encourage this.[15] The town of Pathyris was established in the aftermath of a fierce inland revolt that ravaged Upper Egypt *c.*207–186 BC (Veïsse 2004). Ptolemy V tried to suppress the uprising and several measures were taken in the decades following to bring peace to the region. Strategic sites like Pathyris, located south of Thebes, received military bases. Soldiers bought land and settled in this town. One of them was the Greek cavalryman Dryton son of Pamphilos, of Cretan descent and citizen of Ptolemais, the Greek *polis* in Upper Egypt. He was attached to the military camp of Ptolemais, but served in other Upper Egyptian places where control was necessary. In a later stage of his career he was promoted to cavalry officer (Vandorpe and Waebens 2010, §36).

When he was about forty years old, Dryton married for the second time. His wife, a teenager, was the daughter of a soldier who served in the same unit as Dryton. After the marriage Dryton moved to Pathyris, where his wife and her family lived. His new spouse, who was as well off as he, belonged to a local family of Egyptian origin. But her grandfather or father had managed to be enrolled in the fiscally privileged class of the Greeks and had assumed the ethnic designation "Cyrenaean." Enrollment in this class implied a degree of hellenization. Henceforth several family members adopted Greek names alongside their Egyptian ones and thus bore double names. Dryton's wife, for instance, was called Apollonia alias Senmonthis. (See Figure 3.)

It is not always easy to distinguish between people whose ancestry was purely Greek (like Dryton) and those who were hellenized Egyptians

[15] See, for instance, the archives of Harsiesis son of Schotes, Horos son of Nechouthes, Pelaias son of Eunous, and Peteharsemtheus son of Panebchounis. All these archives originate from Pathyris: see Vandorpe and Waebens (2010).

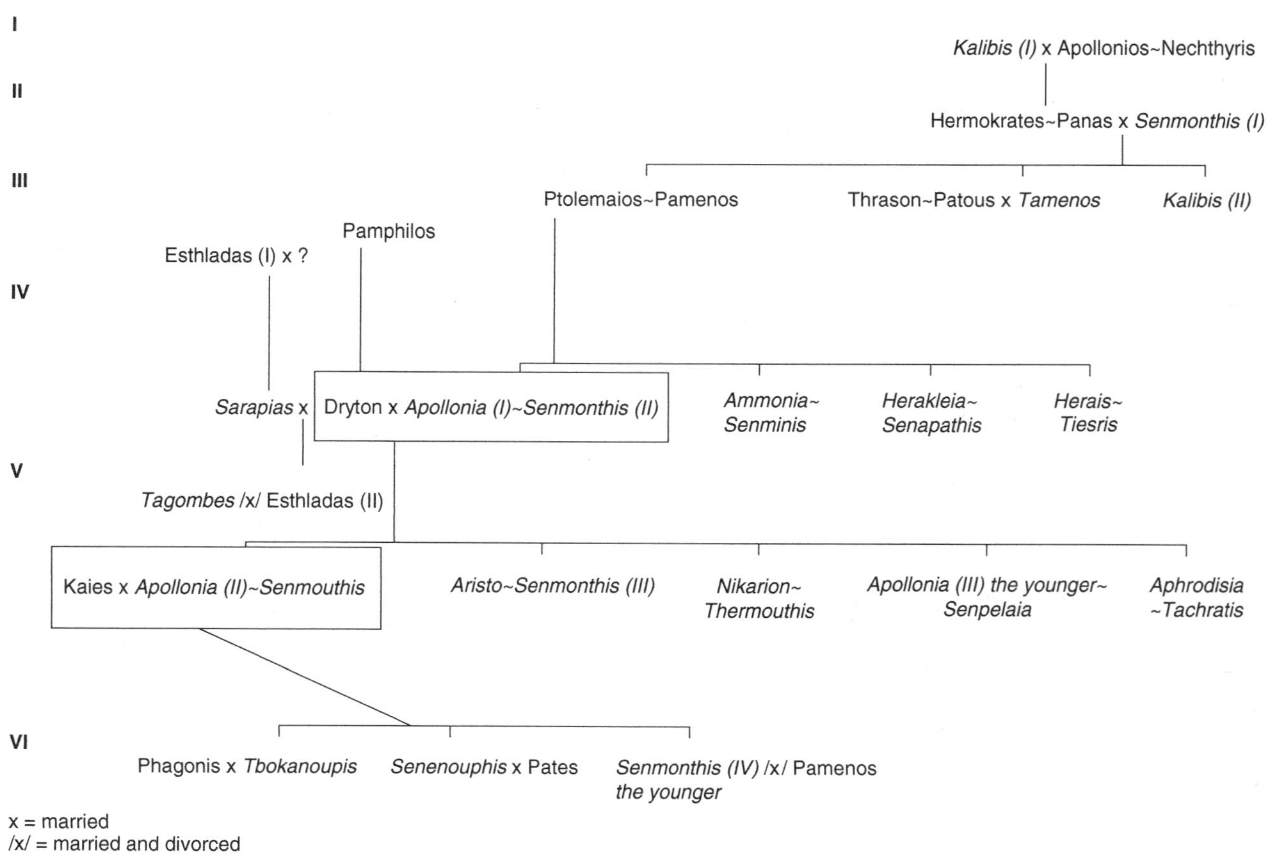

Fig. 3. Family tree of Apollonia alias Senmonthis, wife of Dryton

(like those in Apollonia's family). Both used Greek contracts (**3.1.1**), both submitted Greek petitions to higher officials (**3.1.3**), both had or had adopted Greek names, and both have preserved Egyptian documents in their private archives (Vandorpe and Waebens 2010, §31).

One important difference concerns the mother tongue, which can be retrieved by turning to private documents such as accounts and lists. Dryton's accounts are indeed all written in Greek, whereas his wife's Egyptian background is betrayed, for instance, by her Egyptian name, Senmonthis. Another difference concerns traditions about inheritance, marriage, and divorce, which differ according to the Greek or Egyptian origins of the individuals concerned (**3.1.2** and Chapter 4).

In their "mixed" marriage, Dryton lived in accordance with Greek tradition (**3.1.2**) and Apollonia clearly adjusted herself to Greek customs: she became a businesswoman who presented herself to society as a Greek woman in every respect (**3.1.1**). But the Greek range of influence was not maintained after Dryton's death. His son Esthladas, who enjoyed a Greek education, married and divorced an Egyptian girl according to local tradition. Although Dryton's five daughters bore Greco-Egyptian double names, none of them followed in their mother's footsteps: they all married Egyptians and, consequently, did not continue the Greek tradition of their parents, nor did they become businesswomen as had their mother. They lived according to Egyptian custom (**3.1.4**) and no longer gave their children Greek names. Thus, the Greek "flare-up" within Apollonia's family, brought about by her marriage to a Greek officer, was entirely unmade in the third generation.

The return of Dryton's children and grandchildren to Egyptian tradition symbolizes what was going on in Upper Egypt at that time. Around 100 BC, the Greek initiatives in Upper Egypt on the part of the government disappeared. Greek notaries, Greek banks, Greek tax farmers, Greek jurisdiction had dropped out of the picture. In the 80s BC Upper Egypt revolted once more against Ptolemaic rule.

3.1.1 Greek loan by Apollonia

P.Dryton 19 (= *P.Lond.* III 616 desc., *P.Grenf.* I 20) (Pathyris, 7 November 127 BC)

Apollonia was a young girl who used her marriage with the Cretan cavalryman Dryton as an opportunity to present herself as a Greek lady – and with every reason, since she had married a Greek husband and was herself descended from a hellenized (Cyrenaean) family. In her view, she was better off presenting herself in this way since Greeks were more respected than Egyptians in Ptolemaic society. Consequently she became a part of the upper class. She was quite well off, having inherited real estate from her father, and she derived a substantial income from giving loans in money and in kind. Dryton helped her, where necessary, with her business activities.

As long as there was no Greek notary's office in Pathyris she negotiated loans in the presence of an Egyptian notary and conducted business without a guardian in accordance with Egyptian legal forms. But, contrary to the other women of her village, she presented herself as a "Greek woman," bearing a Greco-Egyptian double name with the Greek name mentioned first. In 136 BC a Greek notary's office was installed in Pathyris and from then on Apollonia contracted Greek loans as a "Cyrenaean" woman, accompanied by a male guardian (or *kyrios*) as Greek law required. In the loan mentioned below she was assisted by her husband and lends 10,000 bronze drachmas for a period of five months. In the amount of 10,000 drachmas the interest was already included, a practice attested in all loan contracts from Pathyris.

Year 44, month of Phaophi, day 15, in Pathyris in the presence of the Greek notary Asklepiades.

Has lent Apollonia daughter of Ptolemaios, Cyrenaean, having as guardian her own husband Dryton son of Pamphilos, Cretan, cavalry officer in charge of men at the head of those of the *epitagma*-unit and one of the *Diadochoi*, to Solon alias Sleis, son of Horos, and to Harmais son of Horos, Persians of the *epigonê*, and to Tebos daughter of Phageris, Persian, having as guardian her own son Sleis mentioned above, one talent and 4,000 drachmas of bronze, without (further) interest (i.e., with interest included), for a period of five months, from Phaophi onwards until 10 Mecheir of the 44th year.

This loan the borrowers shall return to Apollonia in the month of Mecheir, (before) the 30th day. If they fail to return it within the time stated, they shall immediately return (it) increased by 50 percent and for the overtime (they shall pay) interest at the rate of 2 drachmas per mina each month.

Sureties for each other for the payment of all liabilities described in this loan contract are the borrowers themselves. Apollonia shall have the right of execution upon the borrowers, upon each and every one of them and upon whomsoever she chooses and upon all their property, as if in accordance with a legal decision.

I, Areios, subordinate of Asklepiades, have dealt with (this contract).

On the verso: Loan of Apollonia to Sleis and others, of 1 talent, 4,000 drachmas in bronze.

3.1.2 Greek will by Dryton

P.Dryton 3 (= *P.Lond.* III 640 descr., *P.Bour.* 9, *P.Grenf.* I 44, *Pap.Lugd.Bat.* XIX 4, *P.Lond.* III 687 a and e descr.) (Pathyris, 29 June 126 BC) (English translations in: *Sel.Pap.* I 83 and Rowlandson 1998, no. 86). Image at *P.Dryton*, Plate 3.

Dryton wrote at least three wills, a record for Greco-Roman Egypt. The earliest was drawn up north of Thebes, in Little Diospolis in 164 BC, on the occasion of his first marriage with Sarapias, who subsequently gave birth to a son called Esthladas. He altered his will when he married Apollonia in 150 BC (see **4.5.3**). Shortly before his death, in 126 BC, he produced a third and last will, given below. By that time Dryton had been promoted cavalry officer and bears the court title of *Diadochos*. His second wife had borne him five daughters. As children of a mixed marriage, the five girls gained from both traditions: they inherited real estate in accordance with Egyptian tradition and received dowries in accordance with Greek custom. The oldest son, Esthladas, born out of his first marriage, inherited half of Dryton's property as well as his military equipment. This privileged position of the oldest and single son fits into both the Greek and Egyptian traditions.

Dryton made his wills in the standard Greek form (cf. **4.5.3**). A Greek will required six witnesses, who signed the document in Greek. In Dryton's will four of them, however, were Egyptian priests, who signed in Demotic. The official copy with the Demotic signatures is no longer extant, but in the surviving copy the original signatures were translated into Greek. In the town of Pathyris the majority of the inhabitants were Egyptians, the elite partly or completely unable to write Greek. Even some of the Greek notaries, descended from a local, Egyptian family, did not sufficiently master the Greek language.

Year 44, month of Payni, day 9, in Pathyris, in the presence of the Greek notary Asklepiades.

These are the testamentary arrangements by Dryton son of Pamphilos, Cretan, one of the *Diadochoi* and cavalry officer over men, at the head of those of the *epitagma*-unit, while he was healthy, of sound mind and in possession of his wits.

"May I be master of my property in good health. But if I should suffer mortal fate, I bequeath and give all my immovable and movable property, cattle, and whatever I may acquire besides:

"The horse on which I campaign and all my armor (I leave) to Esthladas, my son by Sarapias daughter of Esthladas son of Theon, a citizen (of Ptolemais), with whom I used to live as my wife in accordance with the laws and with the will that was drawn up in the record office in Little Diospolis, before the Greek notary Dionysios, in the 6th year of the reign of Philometor (164 BC), and that records among its dispositions the appointment of Herm(a/o)philos as guardian, being a relative; of the 4 household slaves (I give to Esthladas) those named Myrsine and her (child) – –; the remaining 2 female slaves called Eirene and Ampelion, (I leave) to (my daughters) Apollonia and her sisters, being 5 girls in all; and (to Esthladas I leave) the vineyard site belonging to me on the Kochlax on the east bank of the Pathyrite nome, the wells in it made of baked brick and the other appurtenances; (I) also (leave to him) the wagon with its equipment, the dovecote, the other, half-finished dovecote, a courtyard whose neighbors are, on the south: vacant lots of the said Esthladas, on the north: a vaulted room of Apollonia the younger, on the east: a lot [. . .] of Petras [. . .] son of Esthladas, on the west: a vacant lot of Esthladas, as far as the door that opens to the west.

"The remaining rooms with appurtenances, on old [. . .], a vacant plot intended for a dovecote down from the door of Esthladas and to the west of the vaulted room, I give to Apollonia, Aristo, Aphrodisia, Nikarion, and Apollonia the younger, my 5 daughters by Apollonia alias Senmonthis, the wife with whom I am living in accordance with law. They are to possess the 2 female slaves and the cow in equal shares for their households according to the division I have made.

"Esthladas shall give, from the vacant plot granted to him facing his door to the west, four square cubits as space for an oven.

"Of the remaining building(-site)s and vacant plots in the Ammonieion (-quarter) in Great Diospolis (Thebes) and in the Potters' Quarter, Esthladas is to have half, Apollonia and her sisters half. All my remaining belongings, my warrants for grain and cash as well as all my furniture, will be divided in half shares.

"Esthladas, Apollonia, and her sisters shall pay in common the expenses of building the dovecote, (that is) the intended dovecote until they have finished it.

"(Esthladas, Apollonia and her sisters shall jointly give) to Apollonia alias Senmonthis, my wife, for (a period of) four years, if she remains in my house irreproachably, for the maintenance of herself and her two daughters, each month $9\frac{1}{2}$ (artabas) of wheat, 1/12 (artaba) of castor oil (and) 200 bronze (drachmas). After 4 years they shall make the same provisions from the common fund for the two younger daughters for 11 years. They (Esthladas and his sisters) shall give to Tachratis for a dowry 12 bronze talents out of the common fund. Of whatever properties Senmonthis appears to have acquired as belonging to herself, while living with Dryton, she shall be the owner. Those who will proceed against her for these acquisitions, [. . .]."

Year 44, 9 Payni.

Testator was Dryton son of Pamphilos, Cretan, of the *Diadochoi* and cavalry officer over men, at the head of those of the *epitagma*-unit.

Witnesses: [Has signed – – – – – – – – – – – – – – – -]

Has signed NN son of NN, priest of Aphrodite and Souchos, of the first *stolistai* and the *pterophoroi*, about 35 years old, tall, with a honey-colored complexion, straight hair, a flat face, straight nose, (and) a scar on his right temple.

Has signed Nechoutes son of Thotortaios, Persian, priest, first *stolistês* of the temple in Pathyris, about 50 years old, of medium stature, with a honey-colored complexion, straight hair, a long face, straight nose, (and) a scar on his forehead on the right.

Has signed Patous son of Herieus, Persian, priest, first *stolistês* of the same temple, about 50 years old, of medium stature, with a honey-colored complexion, straight hair, a flat face, straight nose, (and) a scar on his forehead to the left.

Has signed Patous son of Horos, *hypepistatês* (vice mayor) of Pathyris, Persian, of the infantry, about 40 years old, with a honey-colored complexion, straight hair, a long face, straight nose, (and) a scar.

These four (witnesses have signed) in the native script because there was not the same number of Greeks on the spot.

Has signed Ammonios son of Areios, Persian, one of the soldiers-serving-for-pay, about 30 years old, of medium stature, with a honey-colored complexion, slightly curly hair, a long face, straight nose, (and) a scar in the middle of his forehead.

3.1.3 Greek petition from Dryton's daughters

P.Dryton 34 (= *P. Lond.* II 401, pp. 12–14, *M.Chr.* 18, *C.Ptol.Sklav.* I 58) (Pathyris, 115–110 BC) (English translation in: Rowlandson 1998, no. 87)

Dryton's two oldest daughters, Apollonia alias Senmouthis and Aphrodisia alias Tachratis, petitioned in Greek to one of the highest officials of the country, Phommous, *epistratêgos* and *stratêgos* of the Thebaid, acting also in the name of their three younger sisters. They described how their father left them half of his property. Among the immovables was a vineyard with appurtenances on the Kochlax, on the east bank of the Pathyrite nome, of which they had inherited a half share. See **3.1.2**.

When in a period of unrest (probably due to dynastic troubles) they were not able to inspect their property, Ariston, a man from Thebes, occupied the vineyard plot and planted part of it. The sisters ask the *epistratêgos* Phommous to summon Ariston and to investigate the matter.

In general, both Greeks and hellenized Egyptians addressed Greek petitions to high officials. But the girls were able to impress the Greek authorities by adding their ethnic designation "Cyrenaean," thus stressing their belonging to the class of the Greeks. In addition, they tried to raise compassion, as they were wronged by a man who had used violence and despised them because they were women.

To Phommous, Kinsman (of the King), *epistratêgos* and *stratêgos* of the Thebaid.

From Apollonia alias Senmouthis and Aphrodisia alias Tachratis, both daughters of Dryton, living in Pathyris.

There belongs to us and to our sisters Aristo alias Senmonthis, Nikarion alias Thermouthis and Apollonia the younger alias Senpelaia, a half share of our father's plots of land, being 4 in number, in the Peritheban and Pathyrite nomes, and similarly (a half share) of the domestic slaves. Among the plots of land, there is on the Kochlax on the east bank (of the Nile) in the said Pathyrite nome, a half share of a vineyard plot of about $2\frac{1}{2}$ arouras and to the east of this a garden, wells, farm buildings, a wine press, a plot of dry land, another plot of non-revenue-yielding land and all the appurtenances that our father owned as long as he lived.

After his death, we were owners of the rest (of the inheritance), (but) Ariston son of Athenodotos, from Great Diospolis (Thebes), forcefully occupied the said vineyard and its appurtenances in times of unrest and he unjustly lays claim to the half share that belongs to us. He has planted a certain part with vines, looking down (upon us) because we are women and are not able easily to go to the property referred to, since we live in another place.

Therefore, having fled to you, we ask, if it seems (good to you), that you summon him and investigate, and, if things are as we write, that you compel him to vacate the half share of the vineyard described by us and the plants growing in it and the adjoining places, and also to compensate

for the crops he has removed therefrom. As regards the violence he has committed, (we ask that you), as one who hates wickedness, condemn him so that we may obtain redress.
May you prosper.

3.1.4 Demotic divorce agreement for Dryton's granddaughter

P.Dryton 8 (= *P. Baden* 1, pp. 9–11, no. A.6) (Pathyris, 21 September 100 BC)

After Dryton's death his wife Apollonia alias Senmonthis probably lived with her oldest daughter Apollonia alias Senmouthis and her husband Kaies. Henceforth, from *c.*118 BC onwards, that is eight years after Dryton's death, the family archive was enriched with several papers of Kaies, who apparently took over the business activities of the family. The latter had a stable marriage with Senmouthis, but two of her sisters and one of their children were not so fortunate and divorced in accordance with Egyptian legal forms, resulting in three Demotic divorce agreements drawn up by the Egyptian temple notary. Contrary to marriage contracts, divorce agreements did not mention the financial consequences of divorce. They only treated the status of the woman, allowing her to take another husband.

The following document recorded the divorce of Senmonthis the younger, daughter of Kaies and Senmouthis, granddaughter of Dryton. The agreement is signed by four witnesses, but only two signatures are preserved. Her former husband Pamenos, son of Nechouthes and Senthotis, was married again four years later.

Year 15, month of Thot, day 5, of King Ptolemy (X) also called Alexander, and Queen Berenike his sister (and) wife, (and the year of the priests) who are appointed in Rakotis (Alexandria).

Has spoken the Greek, born in Egypt, Pamenos son of Nechouthes, his mother being Senthotis, to the woman Senmonthis the younger, daughter of Kaies, her mother being Senmouthis:

"I have repudiated you as a wife. I am far from you in respect of (the) right (to you) as (my) wife. I have nothing in the world to claim of you in the name of the right (to you) as (my) wife.

"I am the one who says to you: 'take yourself a husband.' I will not be able to stand in your way in any place to which you wish to go to take yourself a husband. If I find you together with any man in the world, I will not be able to say to you: 'you are my wife' from this day on and afterwards, forever."

Has written Nechthminis son of Nechthminis, who writes in the name of the priests of Hathor, mistress of *Inty* (Pathyris), (priests) of the five *phylai* (= priestly classes).

Has signed Pasouchos son of Onnophris.

Has signed Nechthminis son of [. . .]

3.2 Greek and Demotic in the Roman Fayyum

Brain P. Muhs

The Fayyum, and particularly the towns of Soknopaiou Nesos and Tebtunis, preserve a large number of legal documents from the end of the Ptolemaic period through the early Roman period (30 BC – *c.* AD 100), especially when compared to the rest of Egypt.[16] These documents make it clear that the Egyptian and Greek legal traditions coexisted at this time, but for primarily administrative reasons: purely Demotic contracts soon gave way to bilingual ones, which in turn gave way to purely Greek contracts.[17]

The Egyptian and Greek legal traditions had also coexisted in the preceding Ptolemaic period (332–30 BC), each with its own independent administration system. Thus verbal agreements in the Egyptian language were recorded by Egyptian notaries in the Demotic script according to Demotic schemes, and agreements in the Greek language were written by Greek contract scribes in Greek using Greek schemes. The vast majority of the population was illiterate, so witnesses literate in Demotic and Greek respectively signed the contracts to confirm that the written texts agreed with the verbal agreements. Nonetheless, from the middle of the second century BC onwards, literate contractors, especially the first contracting party, usually also subscribed to contracts in Demotic or Greek to confirm them.[18] Lawsuits arising from these agreements were even sent to separate courts, depending on the language of the contracts from which the lawsuits arose.[19] The state kept track of the activities of these two separate but parallel systems by requiring that both types of contracts be registered in *grapheia*. Both Demotic and Greek contracts occasionally received short Greek registration texts to show that the contracts had been registered, or sometimes just red stamps with the same significance.[20]

16 See now Lippert and Schentuleit (2006a), (2006b), (2010).

17 Lewis (1993). 18 Depauw (2003: 66–88).

19 *P.Tebt.* I 5, re-edited as *C.Ord.Ptol.* 53, lines 207–20 (**10.1.4**), discussed by Mélèze Modrzejewski (1975) and Pestman (1985c).

20 Muhs (2005a: 93–96).

In the early Roman Period, these two legal traditions continued to coexist, as suggested by the Greek translation of the Demotic legal manual of Hermopolis mentioned in the introduction to this chapter. Contracts could still be written either in Demotic according to Demotic schemes or in Greek according to Greek schemes. In any case, the separate but parallel administrative systems of Demotic notaries and witnesses and Greek contract scribes and witnesses disappeared very early in the Roman period, probably as the result of deliberate centralization by the state. Instead, the *grapheia* previously responsible for registration were made responsible for writing both Demotic and Greek contracts. As before, a short Greek registration text or stamp could be added to contracts to confirm that they had been registered. The role previously played by witnesses in confirming contracts was now fulfilled by the personal subscriptions of the contracting parties. In particular, the subscription of the first contracting party in Greek seems to have become mandatory on both Demotic and Greek contracts. Subscriptions in Demotic and Greek had in fact become common and perhaps even mandatory in the second century BC, but now Demotic subscriptions were replaced by Greek ones, even on Demotic contracts. Those who could not write and women relied on guardians to subscribe for them.[21]

3.2.1 Demotic house sale and cession with Greek registration

P.Brit.Mus. 262 + *M.Chr.* 181 (= *DDD* III 5) (Soknopaiou Nesos, 21 November AD 11). Image: Figure 4.

The early Roman innovations in the administration of contracts affected the appearance of Demotic contracts much more seriously than that of Greek contracts. The presence of Greek subscriptions as well as Greek registration texts below ostensibly Demotic contracts rendered the contracts in effect bilingual. In this way, purely Demotic legal documents rapidly disappeared from public contexts in the early Roman Fayyum. **3.2.1** is one of the earliest of these bilingual contracts. It is a house sale from the town of Soknopaiou Nesos ("The Island of Soknopaios") on the northern edge of the Fayyum, and dates relatively early in the Roman period to 21 November AD 11. The upper part of the papyrus contains a Demotic sale contract and a Demotic cession contract written next to each other. In the Ptolemaic period, the Demotic sale contract had come to be viewed as a conditional sale that was completed only when the seller drew

[21] Depauw (2003: 89–105); Muhs (2005a: 96–99).

Fig. 4. Demotic house sale. *P.Brit.Mus.* 262 / *P.Lond.* 262. Soknopaiou Nesos, November AD 11

up a parallel cession contract or died.[22] Consequently, in the course of the Ptolemaic period one finds increasing numbers of paired sale and cession contracts for sales intended to be complete from the start. Early in the Ptolemaic period these paired sale and cession contracts were most often written on separate papyri, each with its own set of witness signatures, usually on the verso. Later in the Ptolemaic period they were frequently written next to one another on the same papyrus, as here, but with a single shared set of witness signatures, which this papyrus lacks. Instead, the lower part of the papyrus contains the subscriptions of the two contractors, that of the seller in Greek and that of the buyer in Demotic, as well as a Greek registration text.

> *Demotic sale:* Year 41 of the victory of Caesar, the god, the son of the god, third month of the *akhet*-season, day 24. Has said the servant of Neith, the prince, the noble, the prophet, the son of a prophet, Chairemon son of Herodes, whose mother is Tasis, to the lord of purity, the chief of the lake "The Great Green" of Nephersatis,[23] Satabous son of Herieus the younger, whose mother is Satabous:[24] "You have satisfied my heart with the money, the price of my house, which is built, which is furnished with beams and doors, below to above, and of its seat(?) which is to the north, and of its light well and of its vacant lot which are to the south, and of everything belonging to them, which is in the Sobek-town 'The Island of Soknopaios the great god,' in the Herakleides district in the Arsinoite nome, with every measurement which belongs to them. Their neighbors: south, the wall of the town; north, the house of Horos the son of Horos; west and east, the streets of Pharaoh, life health prosperity. They belong to you from today onwards. No one on the earth, myself likewise, shall be able to exercise authority in them apart from you from today onwards. The one who shall come against you on account of them, I shall cause that he be far away from you, compulsorily, without delay. And I will cause them to be clear for you from every document, every judgment, every claim on the earth, of brother, sister, son, daughter, every man on the earth. To you belongs every document that has been made concerning them, and every document that has been made for me concerning them, and every document that has been made for my

[22] In contrast, Ptolemaic Greek sale contracts were rendered conditional by leaving them incomplete; see Pestman (1985a: 56–57).

[23] "The Great Green one of Nephersatis" is Lake Moeris in the Fayyum. See www.trismegistos.org/geo/detail.php?tm=1384.

[24] Notably the son and mother have the same name. See the discussion by Schentuleit (2001: 138–39).

father and my mother concerning them, and every document, every judgment, everything in which I have been justified in their name. The oath and the proof that will be placed after you in order to cause that I do it in their name, I will do it," while the woman and servant of Sobek, Temsais daughter of the prophet of Neith, Chairemon, whose mother is Tamestasythmis, his wife, says: "Write and do everything that is written above. My heart is satisfied with it."

Demotic cession: See below, **6.2.5**

Greek registration: Year forty-one of Caesar, day twenty-four of the month of Hathyr. Registered in Psinachis in the Themistos district, a sale and a cession of a house and a seat(?) and light well[25] and vacant lot and everything belonging to them in Soknopaiou Nesos in the Arsinoite nome in the Herakleides district which Chairemon, the son of Herodes whose mother is Thasis, prophet, has executed for Satabous, the son of Heriopsemis whose mother is Satabous. Tomsais the wife of Chairemon, the daughter of Chairemon, whose mother is Tamesthasythmis, has consented.

Subscription of the seller, in Greek: (*2nd hand*) We, Chairemon son of Herodes, whose mother is Thasis, prophet, and his wife, Themsais daughter of Chairemon, whose mother is Tamesthasythmis, agree that Chairemon has sold to Satabous son of Heriopsemis, whose mother is Satabous, the house belonging to me with the veranda(?) on the north side and the light well and the adjoining vacant lot on the south side and everything belonging to them in Soknopaiou Nesos in the Herakleides district, of whatever size it is, with the measurements, the neighbors: south, the town wall; north, the house of Horos son of Horos; west and east, the royal street. And I have received the complete agreed-upon price in full immediately from hand to hand out of the house and I undertake to guarantee with every guarantee for all time. And I, Themsais, agree to the sale and will not make any claim, as is written above. I, the above-named Chairemon, prophet and first *stolistês* of Sobek, the twice-great god, have written for her because she does not know letters, and I am forty-three years old, with a scar on the middle of the forehead, but Themsais is forty years old without distinguishing marks.

[25] For a discussion of these architectural features, see Lippert and Schentuleit (2010: 117–18).

Subscription of the buyer, in Demotic: In the writing of Satabous son of Herieus the younger, whose mother is Satabous:[26] I have received this house in exchange for silver, from Chairemon son of Herodes, whose mother is Tasis, the prophet of Soknopaios, which is in the Sobek-town "The Island of Soknopaios the great god." He shall cause that it is clear for me according to every word that is written above.

3.2.2 Greek sale of a priest's dwelling with Demotic subscription

P.Ryl. II 161 (with *BL* I 389, V 87, VII 172) (Soknopaiou Nesos, AD 81). Image at *P. Ryl.* II, Plate 10.

The early Roman administrative innovations applied equally to Greek contracts and to Demotic contracts, but the appearance of Greek contracts was less seriously affected. Already in the Ptolemaic period, the first contracting party frequently subscribed to Greek contracts in Greek,[27] so the main change in the early Roman Period was the disappearance of witness signatures. **3.2.2** is an example of such a Greek contract. It is a sale of a *pastophorion*, a kind of chapel or priest's dwelling, from the town of Soknopaiou Nesos, and dates to AD 81. The upper part of the papyrus contains a Greek sale contract, while the lower part contains the Greek subscriptions of the two contractors as well as a Greek registration text. The seller was a woman, and therefore her guardian, her brother, signed for her in Demotic, presumably because he could not write Greek. This Demotic subscription was then followed by a Greek subscription written on behalf of the seller and her guardian. Note that this Greek subscription largely restates the Greek contract proper, except that it is written in the first rather than the third person. This format was typical of publicly registered Greek contracts throughout the Roman period.[28]

Greek sale: Third year of the Emperor Titus Caesar Vespasian Augustus, on the tenth day of the month Artemisios, Phamenoth 10, in the village of Soknopaiou Nesos in the Herakleides district of the Arsinoite nome. Thases daughter of Panephrimmis son of Panephrimmis, about forty-five years old with a mole on the right cheek, with her guardian and sibling Stotoetis son of Panephrimmis son of Marres, about thirty years old with

[26] "His mother is Satabous" is erroneously omitted from the translation in *DDD* III 5, p. 153.
[27] Depauw (2003: 85–86); and see for example *P.Tebt.* I 104 and 105, dated to 92 and 103 BC respectively.
[28] Wolff (1978: 40–41). See **2.6**.

a scar on the right shin, agrees with the husband of her daughter Stotoetis, Stotoetis son of Satabous son of Herieus, about thirty-two years old with a scar on the left shin, that she the agreeing party has sold to him according to this agreement, from the present day for all time, the one-fourth part of a two-storied *pastophorion* and courtyard, common and undivided, and everything belonging to it, belonging to her, Thases, within the enclosure of the temple of the god Soknopaios in the eastern part of the same temple; the neighbors of the whole *pastophorion* and courtyard are: south, the shared entrance and exit; north, the *pastophorion* and courtyard of Stotoetis son of Satabous and the vacant lot of the children of Tesios son of Haruotes; west, plots belonging to the same temple; east, the aforementioned enclosure; and she, Thases, the agreeing party, has received from Stotoetis the complete price agreed upon for the one-fourth part sold of the *pastophorion* and courtyard, in full immediately from hand to hand out of the house, [. . .]8 silver drachmas; and Thases, the agreeing party, and those belonging to her guarantee Stotoetis and those belonging to him with every guarantee from all public and private fees, and from poll-taxes from previous times until the coming census, from public and private fees and every claim for all time, and building, completing, and repairing both entrances and exits; and that the agreeing party and those belonging to her make no claim and will make no claim, and will not dispute or proceed against it in any manner, breaking none of the aforementioned provisions. But if she does not guarantee or does not provide, she will pay double the damages and costs and a fine of [. . .] silver drachmas and the same to the public treasury. The subscriber of the agreeing party and her guardian is Satabous son of Herieus, about 21 years old without mark; and that of the purchaser is Onnophris son of Onnophris, about thirty-two years old with a scar on the right side of his forehead.

2nd hand, subscription of the guardian on behalf of the seller, in Demotic: Stotoetis son of Panephrimmis son of Marres, I act as guardian (?) of Thases daughter of Panephrimmis, she having been paid (?) its price. . .

3rd hand, subscription on behalf of the seller and her guardian, in Greek: Thases daughter of Panephrimmis with guardian and sibling Stotoetis son of Panephrimmis son of Marres, I agree to have sold to the husband of my daughter Stotoetis, Stotoetis son of Satabous son of Herieus, according to this agreement from the present day for all time, the one-fourth part of a two-storied *pastophorion* and courtyard, common and undivided, and everything belonging to it, belonging to me, within the enclosure of the temple of the god Soknopaios in the eastern portion of the same temple. The boundaries are: south, the shared entrance and exit; north, the *pastophorion* of Stotoetis son of Satabous and the plot of the children of Tesios son of Haruotes; west, plots belonging to the temple; east, the enclosure of the same temple. And I have received the price in full, [. . .]8 silver drachmas, immediately from hand to hand out of the house; and I guarantee with every guarantee as stated above. Satabous son of Herieus wrote for them because they do not know letters.

4th hand, subscription of the buyer, in Greek Stotoetis son of Satabous has purchased as stated above. Onnophris son of Onnophris wrote for him because he does not know letters.

5th hand, registration of the sale, in Greek: It has been registered in the *grapheion* in Soknopaiou Nesos.

3.2.3 Greek subscription to a Demotic contract of sale

P.Mich. v 301 (extract) (Tebtunis, between AD 7 and 56)

The early Roman administrative innovations may not have severely affected the appearance of Greek contracts, aside from the disappearance of witness signatures, but the remains of the archive of the *grapheion* in early Roman Tebtunis, dating between AD 7 and 56, reveal that the procedures for writing contracts, both Greek and bilingual Demotic and Greek ones, were profoundly altered. The archive contains many incomplete versions or copies of Greek, and to a lesser extent bilingual contracts, some of which contain only the Greek subscriptions of the contracting parties at the foot of the papyrus. Clearly, in some cases at least, the Greek subscriptions were written first, and the contract proper afterwards.[29] **3.2.3**, an extract from *P.Mich.* v 301, is an example of such a Greek subscription, for the sale of a vacant lot "according to Egyptian contracts." The subscription is undated, but was surely written in the first half of the first century AD along with the rest of the *grapheion* archive. The scribe regularly substitutes omicron-iota for upsilon or beta in names. There is a large blank area at the top of the papyrus where the contract proper would eventually have been written, perhaps a single Demotic sale contract,[30] or perhaps paired Demotic sale and cession contracts.[31] Below the Greek subscription are descriptions of the contracting

[29] Husselman, in *P.Mich.* v, pp. 3–11. [30] As in *P.Mich.* v 253. [31] As in *P.Mich.* v 249 and 250.

parties, which would perhaps have been worked into the Greek registration text when it was written, since Demotic contracts used titles rather than descriptions for identification.

This translation reproduces the original rather than the normalized Greek spellings of the Egyptian names.

> We, Mieous and Herakles, both sons of Harmioisis and our mother Taarpaesis, and the wife of Mieous, Tabneoitoinis daughter of Psonsneus and her mother Taarmioisis, agree that we, Mieous and Herakles, have sold according to Egyptian contracts to Psonsneus son of Orseus and his mother Tapesoures the part belonging to us from our father of the vacant lot that is partly walled, and everything belonging to it, common and undivided, in Tebtoinis in the division of Polemon. The measurements of the whole vacant lot are: south to north, eight cubits, west to east, five cubits, as many cubits as there may be. The neighbors are: south, the open space of the temple of the god Herakles Kallinikos; north, the house of Mieous son of Kouthis; west, the house of the purchaser Psonsneus; east, the house of Panther and in part the shared entrance and exit. And we have received from the purchaser, immediately from hand to hand out of the house, the entire price agreed upon in full; and we guarantee with every guarantee for all time. I, Tapneoitoinis, the aforementioned wife of Mieous, consent to the preceding sale and that neither I will proceed against it, nor anyone else on my behalf for all time, and that I will make no claim; and we will do the other things and agree to them as stated above. Marepsemis son of Marepsemis wrote for them because they do not know letters.
>
> *2nd hand, descriptions of the contracting parties, in Greek, at the bottom of the papyrus:* Mieus about 48 years old with a scar on the right side of the face. Herakles about 30 years old with a scar on the left cheek. Tapnebtunis about 45 years old with a scar on the left side of the face under hair. Psosneus about 50 years old a scar on the little finger of the left hand.

3.3 Roman law in Egyptian documents

James G. Keenan

In a footnote to his *Egypt in Late Antiquity* (Bagnall 1993b: 233–34 n. 16) Roger Bagnall provided a list of thirteen documents that either were or contained Greek translations of legal documents from Latin originals.[32]

[32] See also Adams, J. N. (2003: 527–641) for examples and full discussion.

The footnote appears in the course of a discussion not on law, but on "Languages, Names, and Ethnicity." Nevertheless, its references also provide a suitable point of departure for discussion of Roman law in documents from Egypt: Greek, Latin, and bilingual. Of interest is that the documents listed all date from the second and third centuries; more precisely, from *c.* AD 150 to AD 300. They therefore fall on either side of AD 212, the year in which the Emperor Caracalla issued the *Constitutio Antoniniana*, the edict by which (virtually) all inhabitants of the empire became Roman citizens. Of the thirteen documents, two are securely dated and one is editorially assigned to the second century; the rest for all practical purposes belong to the third. Though the numbers are small, the distribution may suggest an extension in use of Roman legal forms in third-century Egypt as part of a more general legal Romanization following Caracalla's edict. The persons involved were in the main city dwellers, with residents of Oxyrhynchos especially well represented.

The documents in which these people figure are of legal interest both for what they concern and what they do not. They include mancipatory wills (*BGU* I 326 [= **3.3.1**], *Pap.Lugd.Bat.* XIII 14); assorted claims to inheritance rights (*P.Oxy.* IX 1201, XIX 2231; *SB* VI 9298); registrations of inheritances (*P.Oxf.* 7; *PSI* XIII 1325 = *SB* V 7630, with a translated copy of the will itself); requests for guardianship (*P.Oxy.* XII 1466 [= **3.3.5**], XXXIV 2710 [= **4.3.2**], cf. *P.Harr.* I 67); a release from paternal power, *patria potestas* (*CPR* VI 78 [= **4.3.4**], with will appended in Greek translation); and an informal manumission "among friends" (*P.Oxy.* IX 1205).[33] In sum, the documents concern inheritance and family (including household slaves); or, to put this in institutional terminology, the law of succession and persons, not obligations or actions (in general, Wolff 2002: 99–200). It is even tempting to consider that the documents concerned with the law of persons were themselves aimed at legal adjustments anticipated or required by complications arising from inheritance. This is clearly true in **4.3.4** (Arjava 1999b), where a daughter's inheritance from her mother is conditioned on a release from paternal power (*patria potestas*).

The list of translations of Latin legal documents can be extended for present purposes by adding Greek documents that are obviously

[33] *P.Oxy.* XX 2276, last in Bagnall's list and not mentioned here, is a private letter concerned with a legal case whose substance is beyond recovery. Lines 6–7 refer to a papyrus roll (*chartê*) on which a Latin text and its Greek translation were inscribed. *P.Oxf.* 7 seemingly refers to "a copy of a translation" (line 12, with the core of the word for "translation" entirely restored), but the translation referred to is not to be found in *P.Oxf.* 7 itself (see *P.Thomas* 20 intro., p. 178).

translations, but whose headings identifying them as such have been lost, for example:

(1) *P.Hamb.* I 73 (= Migliardi Zingale 1997: 65–67, no. 13) (second century AD), fragment of the protocol of the opening of a Roman mancipatory will (cf. **3.3.1** and **3.3.3** below);
(2) *P.Lips.* II 151 (AD 246/7), another manumission *inter amicos* ("among friends");
(3) *P.Oxy.* XII 1467 (= **4.3.3**) (AD 263), a woman's petition for the *ius trium liberorum* ("right of three children").

Clearly bilingual documents also bear mention, for example:

(1) *P.Oxy.* XXXVIII 2857 (= **4.5.5**) (AD 134), a draft of a Roman mancipatory will (cf. **3.3.1**) where the Greek version is nearly complete but the Latin very fragmentary;
(2) *M.Chr.* 362 (= *Jur.Pap.* 8 = *CPL* 172) (AD 211), still another manumission *inter amicos*, on a wooden diptych. Here is found a full Latin text followed by a Greek summary, extensive enough but not reproducing the Latin in all its detail;[34]
(3) *P.Oxy.* VIII 1114 (AD 237), a Latin declaration (*professio*) of an inheritance followed by an affidavit in Greek;
(4) *P.Thomas* 20 (AD 269/70), a bilingual petition to the prefect to confirm possession of an estate (*agnitio bonorum possessionis*), the decedent in this instance being a woman who had died childless and intestate. The headings of both the Latin original and the Greek translation are lost.[35]

Additions like these[36] in no way alter the conclusion already reached on the basis of the original thirteen documents cited in Bagnall's footnote: namely, that Roman legal documents in Greek are by and large translations from the Latin. As such, they are presumably accurate representations of Roman law both before and after the *Constitutio Antoniniana*. The

[34] It is the formulaic Latin of this document that suggests the Latin underlying *P.Lips.* II 151 cited above. On the document type: Scholl (2001).

[35] Cf. **4.6.5a** (bilingual) and *P.Oxy.* IX 1201 (bilingual), both in "the list of thirteen" translations, and the other references in *P.Thomas* 20 introduction. *Agnitiones bonorum possessionis* were requests addressed to the praetor for grants of possession of an inheritance according to praetorian (as opposed to civil) law (Berger 1953: 358 s.v. *Agnitio bonorum possessionis*); in Egypt the prefect substitutes for the praetor and the request is made by petition.

[36] Others may be culled from Migliardi Zingale (1997), who also reproduces many of the documents cited thus far.

additions also reinforce the predominance of documents of third-century date and the frequency of Oxyrhynchite provenance.

It is further possible in some cases that the documentary transformation was not merely linguistic, from Latin into Greek, but that it also entailed an exchange of writing surfaces, with waxed wooden tablets being replaced by sheets of papyrus (Meyer 2004).[37] This is what likely happened in **3.3.1**, the longest and most famous example in the list of thirteen, one of a handful of wills from the classical period of Roman law that survives in something like its complete though not original form (Champlin 1991: 29). Its Roman character[38] and complexity make it an ideal text for presenting some of the practical workings of Roman law in Egypt. This will be followed by a series of texts (**3.3.2–5**) that explore some of the implications of the will itself, in effect constituting a commentary on the will. Together, linguistically, they will reveal the mixed use of Greek and Latin in Egyptian documents of Roman legal content.[39]

3.3.1 Roman will (*testamentum per aes et libram*)

BGU I 326 (= *M.Chr.* 316, *Jur.Pap.* 25, *Sel.Pap.* I 85 [with tr.], *FIRA* III 50, Pestman 1994b, no. 50, Migliardi Zingale 1997: 58–64, no. 12; tr. Rowlandson 1998, no. 139) (Karanis, 18 October or 17 November AD 189 [the will]; 21 February AD 194 [the opening])[40]

Strictly speaking, the document presented here is not a will but a subsidiary record (Amelotti 1966: 173–74), commissioned by an interested party, of the will's opening. It includes the will's text in Greek translation as well as subsequent codicils along with rather complicated notices about the signatory-sealers. The will was opened on 21 February AD 194; it had been drawn up on 18 October (or 17 November) AD 189. It was presumably first committed to several waxed tablets tied together, perhaps to form a polyptych like the will of Antonius Silvanus (*FIRA* III 47 = *CPL* 221 = Migliardi Zingale 1997: 30–36, no. 5) with its five tablets (plates in Pestman

[37] Perhaps the earlier Near Eastern substitution of papyrus (in double document, or *Doppelurkunde*, form) for clay tablets is comparable.

[38] "One of the very few examples of pure Roman law found in Egypt" (Pestman 1994b: 202).

[39] I am grateful to Uri Yiftach-Firanko for his close observations and to Antti Arjava for advice, especially in the selection of texts. I have also benefited from seeing the latter's contribution to this volume (**4.3**) in an early draft.

For a sensible discussion of "Greek as a legal language" under the Roman empire, broader in scope than what is presented here, see Kaimio (1979: esp. 143–53).

[40] For wills from Egypt in their historical development, see **4.5**. For a list of wills from Ptolemaic, Roman, and Byzantine Egypt, see Salomons (2006: 232–36).

1994b: 205 and Migliardi Zingale 1997: 35–36). Accordingly, translation of the will from Latin to Greek also in this instance entailed the substitution of papyrus (in a sheet cut from a roll) for wooden tablets. Tablets since early times had held for the Romans a certain religious mystique that attached both to the tablets themselves and to the style of Latin with which they were inscribed: concise, abbreviated, archaic (or archaizing), full of word play – above all meant for "recitation" in a ceremonial environment (Meyer 2004; **3.3.3** below). At the end of **3.3.1** the text indicates that Gaius Longinus Castor's codicils to the will had also first been written on wooden tablets; but since the text was brief, a diptych, or double tablet, was apparently sufficient for them.

The text has been available in English translation since 1932 (*Sel.Pap.* I 85), more recently as Rowlandson (1998), no. 139. The latter in its presentation (following Keenan 1994, in turn building upon Watson 1966) assumes that the primary and secondary heirs of the testator, Gaius Longinus Castor, a veteran of the Roman navy, were all members of his "natural family" whose biological connections to the testator remain unacknowledged (for such problems, see **4.4** introduction). The primary heirs, by this view, were two "common-law wives," the slave women Marcella and Cleopatra, who were freed by the terms of the will. The secondary heirs were their respective sons by Gaius Longinus Castor, namely, Marcella's sons, Sarapion, Socrates, and Longus, and Cleopatra's son, Nilus. The interests of Cleopatra's daughter, Sarapias, were to be satisfied through a legacy, possibly to serve as a dowry.

As a will that has been labeled "one of the very few examples of pure Roman law found in Egypt" (Pestman 1994b: 202, already cited), we expect Gaius Longinus Castor's to satisfy the legal requirements for a Roman civil law will; and since the will, a *testamentum per aes et libram*, presents itself as replicating the archaic civil-law ritual of *mancipatio*, we expect it to adhere to the ritual model. Archaic in form and in its underlying ceremony, the mancipatory will was nonetheless the most common form of Roman will under the empire (see Wolff 2002: 133).

Gaius Longinus Castor's will does in fact fulfill the expected requirements and follow the expected form of the mancipatory will. Among other considerations, the testator, as a Roman citizen after his honorable discharge from the navy (cf. **3.3.2**), had the capacity to make a will (*testamenti factio*). He names his heirs in solemn form in the imperative mood: "Let them in equal shares be my heirs" (cf. Gaius, *Institutes* 2.116–17). He disinherits everyone else: "Let all others be disinherited" (cf. Gaius,

Institutes 2.128 for the Latin form: *ceteri omnes exheredes sunto*). He allows his heirs time to decide whether or not to assume their inheritance: "Let them enter upon the inheritance, each for her own share, whenever it seems proper to each to bear witness that she is my heir . . .". See **3.3.4** introduction for the technicalities.

Gaius (*Inst.* 2.104) describes in capsule the procedure of making a mancipatory will (full discussion: Amelotti 1966: 111–90). The testator writes out his will and mancipates the property to someone in name only. The property-purchaser then says, "I declare that your family and your property are in my administration and custody. Let them be bought by me with this bronze and (as some add) with bronze scales, so that you can legally make a will according to public statute." Then he strikes the scale with the bronze and gives it (i.e., the bronze) to the testator in place of a price. Then the testator, holding the tablets of the will in his hand, says: "These things, as they have been written in these wax tablets (*tabulae cerae*), I thus give (*do*), I thus bequeath (*lego*), I thus attest (*testor*); and so, you, Roman citizens, bear witness for me."

This last statement was called the declaration (*nuncupatio*), giving general confirmation to the specifics written out in the will proper.

According to Gaius (*Inst.* 2.102–07), the ceremony required for its personnel, besides the testator himself, the following actors, all Roman citizens with full legal capacity:[41] a "property-purchaser" (*familiae emptor*), a "scale-holder" (*libripens*), and five witnesses (*testes*). In **3.3.1** Julius Petronianus performs the first function, Gaius Lucretius Saturnilus, the second. All five witnesses are present (Marcus Sempronius Heraklianus, Gaius Longinus Acylas [Aquila], Julius Volusius, Marcus Antistius Petronianus, and Julius Gemellus), but only the first of the five is recorded in the context of the will proper. The other four are only listed after the will's opening and reading. So the list of the requisite five is cobbled together from two separate places and times. It can only be assumed that "the remaining sealers" listed in the context of the will's opening were present and filled out the five required by the will's creation, but this cannot be certain. Their seals, by the way, would have been affixed to the outer text of the will's original wooden tablets. Note that Gaius Longinus Castor's codicils are also witnessed by five men, one of whom is named Gaius Longinus Castor![42] All involved

[41] **4.5.5** interestingly leaves blank spaces for the later addition of the requisite participants (lines 28–30).
[42] See *FIRA* III, p. 152 n. 2 for the whole problem; cf. Champlin (1991: 79 and nn. 49–50).

seem to have been military comrades of the testator and in one case at least a relative.[43]

Col. I: Translation of a will.[44] Gaius Longinus Castor, honorably discharged veteran of the praetorian fleet of Misenum, has made a will. I order that Marcella my slave, over thirty years of age,[45] and Cleopatra my slave, over thirty years of age, become free. Let each in equal shares be my heir. Let all others be disinherited. Let them enter upon the inheritance, each for her own share, whenever it seems proper to each to bear witness that she is my heir; it shall not be possible to sell or mortgage it. But if the above-written Marcella suffers the lot of humanity, then I wish her share of the inheritance to devolve upon Sarapion and Socrates and Longus. Likewise for Cleopatra, I wish her share to devolve upon Nilus. Let whoever becomes my heir be liable to give, to do, to provide all these things that have been written in this my will, and I commit them to her trust.

Let my slave Sarapias, daughter of Cleopatra my freedwoman, be free; to her I also give and bequeath:[46] five arouras of arable land that I possess in the vicinity of the village of Karanis in the place called Ostrich; likewise, one and a quarter arouras of wadi-land; likewise, a third share of my house and a third share of the same house that I earlier bought

[43] See Alston (1995: 125–27) for detailed prosopographical connections with other documents; cf. Champlin (1991: 78–79).

[44] Roman wills had to be in Latin until, according to the common view (e.g., Taubenschlag 1955: 193–94; Amelotti 1966, no. 54, pp. 57–58; Migliardi Zingale 1997: 96–97, n. 1; Wolff 2002: 134 with n. 107), Greek was universally permitted by a constitution of Severus Alexander (AD 222–35). The only direct evidence for this is the fragmentary *Stud.Pal.* XX 35 (= *SB* I 5294.12–14 = Amelotti 1966, no. 13, pp. 271–72), a will in Greek referring in a seriously damaged context (lines 12–14) apparently to its own "Greek [letters] (*[grammasin] Hellenikois*) according to the divine [constitution] (*theia* [*diataxei*], *SB* I 5294; *theia n*[*omothesia*], *Stud.Pal.* XX 35; *theia k*[*eleusei*], Amelotti)" of the emperor. But whether, apart from its problematic reading, the approval was universal rather than local (e.g., restricted to Egypt), or otherwise restricted (i.e., to certain groups such as new Greek-speaking citizens), cannot be known for certain. Even before the constitution of Severus Alexander, the rules for the Roman wills of soldiers and veterans had been relaxed, allowing for the use of Greek (Taubenschlag 1955: 199). It is therefore curious that Gaius Longinus Castor did not avail himself of this leniency, but rather had his will drafted in Latin.

[45] An implicit allusion to a provision in the Augustan Lex Aelia Sentia, AD 4, restricting owners' freedom to manumit their slaves by last will and testament. According to Gaius (*Inst.* 1.18), "The requirement about the age of a slave was introduced by the Lex Aelia Sentia. For this law's intention was that slaves manumitted under 30 become Roman citizens only if they were freed 'by the rod' with the council's approval of the valid reason (*iusta causa*) for the manumission." See also the Gnomon of the *Idios Logos* (*BGU* V 1210) §§19–21.

[46] Of the four types of legacies named by Gaius (*Inst.* 2.192), this one is a "proprietary legacy" (*legatum per vindicationem*) both in form (Latin *do lego*) and in substance (transmitting ownership of specific things). See Gaius, *Inst.* 2.193–200; Taubenschlag (1955: 196–97).

from Prapetheus son of his mother Thaseus; likewise, a third share of a palm-grove that I possess closest to the canal that is called

Col. II: Old Canal. I wish my body to be carried out and wrapped by the care and piety of my heirs.[47] If I leave behind anything in writing after this, written in my own hand, in any form whatsoever, I wish this to be valid. Let evil malice be absent from this will.

Julius Petronianus bought the household and property of the will just made for one sestertius, the scaleholder being Gaius Lucretius Saturnilus. (He acknowledged.) He (i.e., the testator) called as witness Marcus Sempronius Heraklianus. (He acknowledged.) The will was made in the village of Karanis in the Arsinoite nome on the 15th day before the Kalends of November in the consulship of the two Silani, in the 30th year of Emperor Caesar Marcus Aurelius Commodus Antoninus Pius Felix Augustus Armeniacus Medicus Parthicus Sarmaticus Germanicus, Hathyr 21. If I leave behind any additional document written in my own hand, I wish this to be valid.

Opened and read in the Arsinoite *metropolis* in the Augustan Forum in the office of the five percent tax on inheritances and manumissions on the 9th day before the Kalends of March in the consulship of the present consuls, in the 2nd year of Emperor Caesar Lucius Septimius Severus Pertinax Augustus, Mecheir 27. The remaining sealers: Gaius Longinus Acylas (= Latin Aquila) – he acknowledged; Julius Volusius, Marcus Antistius Petronianus, Julius Gemellus, veteran.

Translation of codicils in diptych form (*kôdikilloi diptychoi*):[48] I, Gaius Longinus Castor, honorably discharged veteran of the praetorian fleet of

47 This wish is formulated as a trust (*fideicommissum*) that was morally but not legally binding on heirs until Augustus gave it legal force (Berger 1953: 470–71 s.v. *Fideicommissum*). Compare, more generally from above, the command, "Let whoever becomes my heir be liable to give, to do, to provide all these things that have been written in my will, and I commit them to her trust." According to Meyer (*Jur.Pap.* 25 commentary; also Taubenschlag 1955: 196), the form is that of a legacy *per damnationem*. This of course embraces the requirement to execute both the legacy in Sarapias' favor and these burial instructions. Taubenschlag (1955: 216) interestingly suggests that the act of seeing to the burial of a testator could be construed as the heir's intention to enter upon the inheritance. Of cultural rather than legal interest is that the word for "wrapped" implies the Egyptian practice of mummification.

48 These codicils are in the category of *codicilli testamento confirmati* ("codicils confirmed by testament": Berger 1953: 392–93 s.v. *Codicilli*; cf. Taubenschlag 1955: 200). When Gaius Longinus Castor did add codicils (just below), they were written, presumably in Latin, on doubled tablets (*kôdikilloi diptychoi*), physically separate from the tablets of the will itself. **4.5.5** also allows for the addition of codicils, but spells out, in Greek, the possible physical formats so as to include "tablets (*pinakes*), codicils (*codicilli*), papyrus (*charta*), or any other medium." Here *pinakes* refers to tablets joined end to end in concertina form, *codicilli* to tablets bound in book form (Haran 1996). Cf., in

Misenum, have made codicils.[49] I have made Marcus Sempronius Heraklianus, a friend of worthy repute, guardian (*epitropos*) on his own good faith. To my kinsman, Julius Serenus, I give and bequeath 4,000 *sestertii*. I have written this in my own hand on the 7th day before the Ides of February. Longinus Acylas and Valerius Priscus have sealed them. Sealers: Gaius Longinus Acylas – he acknowledged; Julius Philoxenus, Gaius Lucretius Saturnilus – he acknowledged; Gaius Longinus Castor; Julius Gemellus, veteran.

Opened and read on the same day on which the will was untied.

2nd hand: I, Gaius Lucius Geminianus, expert in Roman law (*nomikos Romaïkos*), translated the above copy and it is in conformity with the original will.

Verso: [The will of?] Gaius Longinus Castor.

3.3.2 Military diploma

CIL XVI 122 (on p. 109), appendix to *CPL* 119 (= *P.Mich.* VII 441) (exact provenance unknown, 30 April AD 166). Image at *P.Mich.* VII, Plate XII d and e.

The text, a diploma bestowing rights upon veterans, is in Latin, heavily abbreviated in its imperial titulatures and elsewhere.[50] It is also heavily but reliably – because of the conservatively formulaic nature of such documents – restored throughout. It survives on a bronze tablet broken into unequal halves. The text upon which the translation is based is a composite of inner and outer texts. Although other diplomas of Egyptian provenance are better preserved, this one has two special merits for present purposes: (1) It is for veterans of the praetorian fleet of Misenum (although the word for Misenum is almost entirely restored, the restoration is secure) and (2) its

Latin, *P.Hamb.* I 72 (= *CPL* 174; Amelotti 1966, no. 10, pp. 266–67; Migliardi Zingale 1997, no. 1, pp. 15–18, lines 9–16, second/third century): *codicillis charta membrana aliove quo genere*. Note in this short list the inclusion of parchment (*membrana*), rare in Egypt.

49 The codicils, besides imposing another legacy on the estate, a money legacy *per vindicationem*, appoint a guardian. The Greek term for this guardian, *epitropos*, suggests the testator was seeing to the legal protection of children under age (see **4.4.1**, **3.3.4b**), but this is not absolutely certain here (Amelotti 1966: 50 n. 1). Marcella and Kleopatra themselves would both have needed guardians, *kyrioi* (Roman law *tutores*), since neither had borne the four children required by law for the exercise of the "ius liberorum" by freedwomen. See **3.3.5** below. On another interpretation (Taubenschlag 1955: 198), the *epitropos* named in the codicils had nothing to do with guardianship but was to be the executor (*procurator*) of the will, while in a very brief note (to *New Papyrological Primer* no. 50, line 39), Pestman (1994b: 204) limits the executor's competence to the codicils.

50 For abbreviation as a feature of tablet style: Meyer (2004: esp. 63–66).

Fig. 5. Military diploma. *T.Duk.* inv. 2. Unknown provenance, April AD 166

date is very near the date when Gaius Longinus Castor could himself have been discharged (Keenan 1994: 103), toward the close of Lucius Verus' Parthian campaign. Significant with relation to Gaius Longinus Castor's will (**3.3.1**) are the grant of citizenship accorded to veterans of the Misenum fleet after twenty-six years' service, and to their sons (or children – the gender of *filisque* is ambiguous), together with a grant of *conubium*, that is, the right to marry according to Roman law with their common-law wives provided the union was monogamous. For a later (AD 209), better-preserved diploma for a sailor of the Misenum fleet, see Figure 5. As here, the veteran's name is lost. He had served for twenty-eight years. (See Oates 1972.)

Emperor Caesar Marcus Aurelius Antoninus Augustus Armeniacus, *pontifex maximus*, with tribunician power for the 20th time, *imperator* for the 3rd time, consul for the 3rd time, Father of the Country (*pater patriae*), and Emperor Caesar Lucius Aurelius Verus Augustus Armeniacus Parthicus Maximus, with tribunician power for the 6th time, *imperator* for the 3rd time, consul for the 2nd time, proconsul, sons of the divine

Antoninus, grandsons of the divine Hadrian, great-grandsons of the divine Trajan, great-great-grandsons of the divine Nerva, to those who have served in the praetorian fleet [of Misenum], which is under Julius Crescens as prefect, and completed twenty-six years of service with an honorable discharge, whose names have been written below: to them and their sons (or: children) whom they have acknowledged from women whom they prove they have lived with according to the allowed custom, they (*sc.* the co-emperors) have granted Roman citizenship and the right of marriage with the women whom they then had with them when citizenship was given to them, or, if they did not then have them, with those whom afterwards they took as wives, provided (the marriage is with) one wife apiece.
On the 2nd day before the Kalends of May . . .

3.3.3 Formal opening of Roman wills

3.3.1 indicated toward its end that it was "opened and read in the Arsinoite *metropolis* in the Augustan Forum in the office of the five percent tax on inheritances and manumissions."

The formal opening and reading of Roman wills was an ancient practice. When the 5 percent inheritance tax was introduced by Augustus in a Julian law of AD 5 or 6, it was attended by the requirement that this be done in the presence of a competent magistrate (cf. the *stratêgos* in **3.3.3a** and **3.3.3d**, the *curator civitatis* in **3.3.3b**) in some sort of official venue. Forum and basilica are specified in Paul's *Sententiae* (4.6.2). Compare **3.3.1** as just quoted; **3.3.3b** (Temple of Hadrian); **3.3.3c** (Augustan [Forum]); **3.3.3d** (office of the Oxyrhynchite *stratêgos*); see also, e.g., *P. Oxy.* LIV 3758.181–213 (the gymnasium). Those who had witnessed and sealed the will would, if still alive and available – a majority of the original witnesses seems to have been required (**3.3.1**, **3.3.3b** [four out of seven], **3.3.3c** [majority], **3.3.3d** [majority]; Paul, *Sententiae* 4.6.1 [*testes vel maxima pars eorum*]) – identify their seals on the outside of the tablets. It was important that the seals be recognized as sound, i.e., unbroken (Paul, *Sententiae* 4.6.1, Vandorpe 1995b: 15–16). This guaranteed the will's authenticity (Champlin 1991: 77). The will would then be opened and, ceremoniously (Meyer 2004: *passim* but especially chapter 4), read aloud. Official copies of the will and the record of its opening would then be archived (Berger 1953: 364 s.v. *Apertura testamenti*). They were therefore available to be consulted by interested parties – and copied in whole or in part, whether directly from the Latin or in Greek translation. It has been argued (Yiftach-Firanko 2002: esp. 160–64) that in Egypt, for Greek wills (*diathêkai*) before the *Constitutio*

Antoniniana, citizens of the *metropoleis* also took advantage of the enhanced security afforded by the Roman procedures of will-opening as just sketched.

Presented here are a petition initiating the process of *apertura testamenti* (**a**), a report of proceedings concerning the opening of a will (**b**), and two extracts (**c–d**) preserving notations of wills' having been opened.

3.3.3a Request to open a will

M.Chr. 309 (= *P.Lond.* II 171b, p. 176; Amelotti 1966, no. 16, p. 276) (Herakleopolis, third century AD)

In Greek: To Aurelius Rhesus, *stratêgos* of the Herakleopolite (nome), from Antonia Nemesilla daughter of Kronion, honorably discharged veteran and landowner in the village Phebichis of the Koite (toparchy), acting without guardian (*kyrios*) by right of children. Since my husband Serenus, a soldier, going away on assignment to his auxiliary unit (*vexillatio*) in the Thebaid, entrusted me with his will (*diathêkê*) under seal, but I have learned now that he has died, of necessity I bring this and ask that it be opened in your presence according to custom so it may be possible to ascertain the will (*boulêma*) written therein. Year 2 of the Emperors Caesars . . . (the text breaks off)

3.3.3b Report of proceedings

P.Oxy. LIV 3758, lines 134–55 (Oxyrhynchos, 18 March AD 325). Image at Papyri.info.

The papyrus contains, in Greek, a report of proceedings before the *logistês* (*curator civitatis*) of Oxyrhynchos. Two segments, lines 134–55 and 181–213, record the openings of wills. They are equally valuable in substance, but the former, somewhat briefer and less damaged, has been chosen for presentation here. The purely Egyptian name of the testatrix is noteworthy; so is the opening of the will a mere day after its composition.

Year 19 and 9, Phamenoth 21. In the Temple of Hadrian, in the presence of Berenicianus, assistant (*boêthos*), and Theodorus alias Horion and Ammonas and Ischyrion son of Anoubion, the four of them sealers, and Diogenes, notary (*tabellio*), and Horion, assistant (*hyperetês*). Diogenes, notary, said, "Tanechontis, falling ill, summoned me and asked that a will (*boulêmation*) be written for her [. . .] Heraklas, record-keeper (*bibliophylax*) [. . .] in the event of her death [. . .] for opening (*lysis*). Well, then, since she has died, her will is today presented to Your Grace." The *logistês* said, "Were you, Heraklas, entrusted with presenting the document (*grammation*) for opening?" He replied, "Yes." The *logistês* said to Diogenes, "Did you compose the document in accordance with the intention (*gnômê*) of Tanechontis?" He replied, "Yes." The *logistês* said, "In whose presence?" He replied, "The sealers'." The *logistês* said, "How many sealers are there?" Diogenes said, "Seven; four are present." The *logistês* said, "Let the four subscribe that they have recognized their seals." And after the four sealers, being present, subscribed that they recognized their own seals, the *logistês* said, "Let the document be opened and read." And the document of Tanechontis, a local person, having been opened (*inserted above the line*: and read), dating to the (*cancelled*: same) present consulship, Phamenoth 20 – after the reading the *logistês* said, "The body of the deceased will be handed over for burial. The inscribed heirs shall take care, upon giving copies of the document, to take the original (*authentikon*) . . .".

3.3.3c Opening of a will

P.Coll.Youtie I 64, lines 18–20 (= *P.Diog.* 10, *ChLA* XLVII 1403) (Ptolemais Euergetis [Fayyum], 3 June AD 211). Image at *P.Coll. Youtie* I, Plate XX.

In Latin, heavily abbreviated: Opened and read in the Augustan [Forum] in the Arsinoite *metropolis*, the 3rd day before the Nones of June, in the consulship of Quintianus and Bassus, in the same year, in the month Payni, 8th day, in the presence of the majority of the sealers who affixed their seals.

3.3.3d Opening of a will

P.Oxy. XXII 2348, lines 50–56 (= Migliardi Zingale 1997, no. 21, pp. 90–94, Col. II, 20–25) (Oxyrhynchos, 21 July AD 224). Image at Papyri.info.

In Greek: Opened and read in the same city [*sc.* Oxyrhynchos] in the presence of Aurelius Harpocration, *stratêgos*, in his office (*logistêrion*), and in the presence of the majority of the sealers who had acknowledged and sealed, on the day before the Ides of October under the same consuls (*sc.* Claudius Julianus for the 2nd time and Bruttius Crespinus), in the fourth year of the Emperor Caesar Marcus Aurelius Severus Alexander Pius Felix Augustus, Thoth 15.

3.3.4 *Cretiones* (formal acceptances of inheritances)

In **3.3.1** Gaius Longinus Castor expected his heirs, Marcella and Cleopatra, to make solemn declarations of their respective acceptances. A normal period was 100 days (see the formula in Gaius, *Institutes* 2.165 and below, **4.5.5** = *P.Oxy.* XXXVIII 2857, lines 7–8, cf. *CPL* 221 = *FIRA* III 47 = Migliardi Zingale 1997, no. 4, pp. 26–29, lines 9–11: 100 days for primary heirs, 60 for secondary), but Gaius Longinus Castor leaves the matter in more general terms: " . . . whenever it seems proper to each to bear witness that she is my heir . . ."; see *P.Oxy.* VI 907 = *M.Chr.* 317 = *FIRA* III 51 = Migliardi Zingale no. 24, pp. 101–05, line 3; more generally, Taubenschlag (1955: 214–16). This declaration of heirship was technically called *cretio.* It was oral in nature, but came to be documented in writing. *FIRA* III reproduces two of these, both incidentally by women, both on waxed tablets: *FIRA* III 59 and 60. Both have Latin texts with Greek subscriptions. The former is longer and more elaborate; both replicate the essential formulaic language for *cretiones* (*adeo cernoque*) as presented in Gaius, *Institutes* 2.166 (Berger 1953: 418 s.v. Cretio); but in their nature as affidavits rather than exact records of oral proceedings, they change the heirs' statements from the first person of the oral declarations ("I enter upon and formally declare . . .") to infinitives in indirect discourse (Meyer 2004: 207–08).

3.3.4a *Cretio*

FIRA III 59 (= *PSI* IX 1027, *CPL* 213) (Ptolemais Euergetis [Fayyum], 5 December AD 151). Image at Papyri.info.

Wooden tablet (diptych or triptych).
The text is corrected to make proper sense. (Problems remain.)

In Latin, on wax: In the matter of the testament that Lucius Herennius Valens made or is said to have made, which testament having been made he died and by this testament had instituted Herennia Helene his daughter as his *ex asse* heir (i.e., heir to the whole estate; *OLD* 179 s.v. *as* 4), for this reason Herennia Helene through Marcia Athenais her mother, under the authorizing guardianship (*tutore auctore*) of Lucius Valerius Onnus, testified in the presence of those who were about to sign that she said that she was [entering upon (*adire*)] the inheritance of Lucius Valerius Herennius her father, and [on wood] was formally declaring (*cernere*) this according to the tablets of his testament (*secundum tabulas testamenti huius*).

Done in Egypt, in the Arsinoite nome at the *metropolis*, on the Nones of December, in the consulship of Sextus Aquilius Condianus and Sextus Quintilius Maximus, year XV of the Emperor Caesar Titus Aelius Hadrianus Antoninus Augustus Pius, in the month of Choiak, 8th day.

In Greek: I, Marcia Athenais, bore witness that my daughter Herennia Helene entered upon the inheritance of Lucius Herennius Valens my husband as stated above. I, Gaius (*sic*) Valerius Onnus, have written in her behalf as she is illiterate, I being registered (also) as her guardian (*kyrios*).

3.3.4b *Cretio*

FIRA III 60 (= *M.Chr.* 327, *CPL* 214, *Jur.Pap.* 26) (Ptolemais Euergetis [Fayyum], 29 September AD 170)

This is a wooden diptych, with its interior writing (sides 2–3) on wax and the exterior writing (sides 1 and 4) in ink (now very faded). The text presented here is a composite of the two texts. The interior text of the original is, as frequently, somewhat more abbreviated than the exterior and it does not include the exterior's Greek subscription. Noteworthy is that Valeria Serapias made *cretio* on the very same day for the estate of her paternal grandmother (*avia de patre*), Lucretia Diodora, in the exact same format and wording as here, barring essential changes (*Jur.Pap.* 26 = *CPL* 215). I have therefore, though at the risk of introducing confusion, taken the liberty of borrowing the seals (*signa*) and adjacent names (in the genitive, see Meyer 2004: 179–80) of the seven witnesses, one line devoted to each, from *CPL* 215, as exemplifying what probably stood on the exterior text, page 1, of the present declaration, where the seals and names only survive in traces. This assumes the seven witnesses were the same in both, without guaranteeing they sealed the two documents in the exact same order.

The role of Serapias' brother as both guardian (in some sense) and seventh witness has been subject to scholarly remark.

In Latin: (seal) of Gaius Lucceius Sempronianus
(seal) of Titus Flavius Iulianus
(seal) of Lucius Ignatius Numerianus
(seal) of Gaius Julius Antonius
(seal) of Gaius Rufus Ptolemaeus
(seal) of Gaius Julius Herminus
(seal) of Lucius Valerius Lucretianus

Valeria Serapias, Antinoite, a minor (*virgo*), through her guardian (*procurator*) L. Valerius Lucretianus alias Plutinius, an Antinoite, her brother, has testified that she has entered upon (*adiisse*) the inheritance of Flavia Valeria, her mother, and has formally declared (*crevisse*) herself to be heir according to the tablets of her testament.

Done in Egypt, in the Arsinoite nome at the *metropolis*, 3rd day before the Kalends of October, in the consulship of M. Cornelius Cethegus and Sex. Erucius Clarus.

In Greek: I, Valeria Serapias, have entered upon the estate of my mother in accordance with her testament (*diathêkê*). I, Lucius Valerius Lucretianus, being her guardian (*epitropos*), have written in her behalf since she is under age (*aphêlix*).

3.3.5 Bilingual request for a guardian

P.Oxy. XII 1466 (= *ChLA* XLVI 1361, *CPL* 204) (tr. Rowlandson 1998, no. 140b; Evans Grubbs 2002: 36–37) (Oxyrhynchos, 21 May AD 245). Image at *P.Oxy.* XII, Plate I.

Of interest in **3.3.1** is that Gaius Longinus Castor, because he was not related to them, could presumably not name guardians (*tutores mulierum*) for his two (presumed) common-law wives, both of whom became Roman citizens upon their testamentary emancipations. (Cf. **4.4** introduction.) Marcella, with her (presumed) three sons, Sarapion, Socrates, and Longus, would not have been entitled to the Augustan *ius liberorum*: the right was available to free women (women born free) with three children but freedwomen had to have four. Like Cleopatra, with her (presumed) two children, a son and a daughter, she would have needed to apply for a guardian, as illustrated in the present document – unless, that is, by some irregularity, the naming of an *epitropos* in Gaius Longinus Castor's codicils was intended not for underage children (see, however, **3.3.4b**, where the *epitropos* is *procurator* for an underage female) but for Marcella and Cleopatra, and was somehow legally effective. This is a puzzle that the brevity of the statement in the codicils both creates and fails to resolve. This is why Taubenschlag's notion that the *epitropos* named in the codicils was intended as the executor of the will (not a guardian for either the women or their children) merits attention even if it is not fully argued.

What follows is a bilingual request for a guardian.[51] The Latin parts are italicized in the present translation. Restorations are derived both internally (the Greek text supplementing the Latin and vice versa) and from *P.Oxy.* IV 720 (= *M.Chr.* 324) and IX 1201. Note the archiving of the documentation in the prefect's files as "Sheet 94, roll 1."

[51] For parallels, see **4.3.2** introduction.

The Julian and Titian Law regarding the appointment of guardians was of Augustan date. It granted competence in this matter to provincial governors (Berger 1953: 555 s.v. *Lex Iulia e Titia*), in Egypt, the prefect.[52]

> *To Valerius Firmus, prefect of Egypt, from Aurelia Arsinoe. I ask, my lord, [that you grant me as guardian in accordance with the Julian and Titian Law and decree of the Senate Aurelius] Herminus.* (Year) 2, Pachon 26. Sheet 94, Roll One.
>
> Translation of the Latin: (*2nd hand*) To Valerius Firmus, prefect of Egypt, from [Aurelia Arsinoe. I ask, my lord, that you grant me] as guardian (*kyrios*), registered according to the Julian [and Titian Law and decree of the Senate, Aurelius Herminus. Presented on] the 12th day before the Kalends of June in the consulship of Emperor [Philippus Augustus and Titianus]. I, Aurelia Arsinoe daughter of Sarapion, [have submitted this petition, requesting that Aurelius Hermi]nus be registered as my guardian. I, Aurelius Tima[genes(?) have written in her behalf] since she is illiterate. I, Aurelius Herminus son of Diony[sius, consent to the request. Year 2, Pachon 26?].
>
> (*3rd hand*) Unless you have the right to another guardian, [I grant the guardian] whom [you request].

3.4 Greek and Coptic in the Byzantine era

T. Sebastian Richter

3.4.1 The sociolinguistics of Greek and Coptic in Byzantine Egypt

Greek and Coptic papyrologists frequently have different experiences in confronting different kinds of documents. The Greek scholar, for instance, is usually familiar with administrative records from the middle and high levels of the administration of Byzantine Egypt, while the Coptologist does not learn anything of this except, say, the modest response given by troubled subjects down from the village. There are reasons for this. As different languages are usually valid in different segments of multilingual societies, so Greek and Coptic had different patterns of social distribution, or functional domains, in Byzantine Egyptian society.

[52] For a succinct discussion of the guardianship of women, based on legal and papyrological sources and therefore largely concerned with Egypt, see Arjava (1996: 112–23).

Coptic was a socially delineated and functionally limited written code from its beginnings. When it came into being around or shortly before AD 300, it was a linguistic medium first and foremost centered upon *religion*, certainly not invented, but refined and properly put into circulation by Egyptian worshippers of late antique *Offenbarungsreligionen* – by Gnostics, Manichaeans, and, above all, by Christians, when their missionaries passed the boundaries of urban settlements, that is, the boundaries of linguistic hellenization, towards the countryside and its inhabitants, Egyptian native speakers. Thus the earliest evidence of Coptic comes from religious texts, mostly translations of Greek compositions, such as parts of the New Testament and the Septuagint version of the Old Testament, as well as Gnostic, Manichaean, and apocryphal writings.

Moreover, the earliest Coptic documentary texts, fourth-century AD private and business letters (e.g., *P.Kell.Copt.*, *P.Lond.* VI 1920–22; *P.NagHamm.*, *P.Neph.* 15–16, *P.Ryl.Copt.* 268–76), can be attributed to Christian and Manichaean contexts. The use of Coptic for letter-writing enabled monolingual Egyptians confined to their native language to communicate over distances without the aid of translators for the first time for centuries. This was because the earlier written form of Egyptian, the Demotic language and script, had ceased to be used in everyday written communication after the first century AD, from that time more and more becoming a linguistic register of merely religious and magical use. As Willy Clarysse (1993: 201) put it:

> From about 100 AD until the introduction of Coptic, a period of more than two hundred years, an Egyptian wanting to write a letter to a fellow Egyptian had to do so in Greek, even though in many cases both writer and addressee needed a translator to understand what was written.

In the three centuries after the introduction of Coptic, the new written medium entered a few functional domains in the realms of religious and everyday language use, but a great many literary genres as well as administrative, economic, and legal matters were still treated in Greek only. For estimating the functional confines of Coptic, it is instructive to realize that Coptic was not, and never became, a language, let alone the *original* language, of higher education, contemporary sciences, and scholarship. It never served as a language of administration and justice beyond the bottom level, and only *after* the Arab conquest did Coptic become a common linguistic means of modest private representation in epigraphy and of recording legal and business matters inside Christian communities.

During the fourth, fifth, and almost the whole of the sixth century, private legal documents were recorded exclusively in Greek. For a number of reasons – governmental requirements, for example, or the desire for greatest possible security combined with a preference for traditional manners, or the advantage of using the subtle means of expression provided by Greek as a long-established and highly developed language for law's special purposes – it was probably not before the mid-sixth century that Coptic was first taken into consideration as a linguistic means of recording legally relevant and effective writings. The earliest known legal records in Coptic are documents written by the bilingual poet and notary Dioskoros of Aphrodito in the 60s and 70s of the sixth century. And it was only after the Arab conquest of Egypt in AD 641 that private legal documents drawn up in Coptic became more common and widespread for a century and a half.

Thus in terms of sociolinguistics, Coptic in Egypt was always a sort of linguistic "low variety" versus Greek, and later Arabic, as the respective "high varieties" (in conspicuous contrast to the contemporary language situation in the Christian kingdoms of Nubia, where Greek *and* Coptic functioned as "high varieties" versus the "low variety" of the Nubian vernacular). Already in Ptolemaic and Roman times, the prestige of Egypt's native language had been dropping, and this was still the case under Byzantine and, the more so, under Islamic rule, when it eventually became a minority language bound to die.

3.4.2 Greek–Coptic interferences from a linguistic point of view

The emergence of Coptic around AD 300 was in some respects the result of long-lasting Greek–Egyptian language contact and a gradual cultural hellenization of Egypt. One sign of hellenization is written, as it were, in the face of Coptic: Its writing system does not depend on hieroglyphs but is based on the Greek alphabet. Even more significant is the huge number of loanwords of almost all semantic and grammatical categories borrowed into Coptic from Greek. In terms of quantity, we can only guess, since no complete dictionary is available at present. Nevertheless, some figures are provided by compilations based on large textual corpora, such as Hans Förster's dictionary of Greek words in the Coptic documentary texts (Förster 2002), comprising about 2,500 Greek lemmata, or Louis-Théophile Lefort's concordance of Greek words in the Sahidic New Testament (Lefort 1950), amounting to nearly 1,000 words. Obviously, lexical borrowings from Greek formed an important source of written

Coptic vocabulary; even small corpora and single Coptic texts yield significant numbers of them. The crucial question remains: What conclusions can be drawn from the incorporation of so many lexical items from almost all semantic fields and all but a few grammatical categories into Coptic *written* texts in terms of societal as well as individual bilingualism? Principally there are two scenarios. There was a proper "hellenization" of the *entire* language, that is, there was a deep impact on the written *as well as the spoken* language, supported by a broad base of bilingual individuals. Or the impact was superficial, limited to the uppermost linguistic registers of the *written language only*, supported by a rather small group of really bilingual individuals. Elsa Oréal (1999) has argued for the latter.

But what about the other way around? Was there also a significant Egyptian impact on the Egyptian variety of Byzantine Greek? Certainly not. Even granted a number of subtle linguistic interferences between peculiar Egyptian means of expression and certain recurrent syntactic deviations of Egyptian Greek from the Greek *koinê* norm not recognized as yet (see Gonis 2005), traces of the impact of Egyptian on Greek texts remain very limited. We find a few lexical borrowings mainly of the new-things-and-concepts type, which have at last been dealt with by Fournet (1989) and Torallas Tovar (2004b), and a number of examples for calquing that have never been systematically compiled.

A typical example of an Egyptian loanword in Byzantine Greek texts is the term *(t)khrêre* occurring in sixth-century sale documents from Syene, among them **6.6.1**, where it served to designate a certain house-part somewhere beneath the staircase. Obviously, the Greek terminology for buildings and their parts did not provide a precisely appropriate designation for this particular location, so that Greek-writing notaries had recourse to *transcribing* its Egyptian name.

Some calques – words etymologically Greek although semantically coined by underlying Egyptian terms – even occur in the legal terminology of Greek documents from Egypt, mirroring interferences between the Demotic and Greek legal languages that may go back to the chancellery practice of Egyptian scribes writing Greek (Clarysse 1993). Three examples follow:

(1) The legal meaning "to take proceedings against somebody, to take somebody to court" carried by the Demotic and Coptic verbal phrase *ei (ebol) e-*, lit. "to come (out) to somebody," may have been transferred to the corresponding Greek term *eperchesthai*.

(2) The conspicuous use of *epitrepein* "to authorize" and *epitropê* "authorization" occurring in Theban texts as designations,

respectively, of "to lease" and "lease document" (cf. **7.4.6**) can presumably be traced to the Demotic term *s-ḥ-n* "to lease," literally "to entrust something to somebody," which also survived in the local Theban variety of Sahidic Coptic (*sahne* "lease").

(3) Some technical meanings of the Egyptian verb *m-ḥ* (Coptic *moukh*), literally "to fill," as in "to pay off somebody," or "being complete" in connection with amounts of money and crops, recur in respective uses of the verb *plêroun* "to fill" in Greek documents from Egypt.

All this notwithstanding, these and like instances cannot change the overall impression that lexical borrowing in Byzantine Egypt was far from a reciprocal, mutual relationship: it was a highly asymmetrical process with (mainly) one donor language, Greek, and (mainly) one recipient language, Egyptian.

3.4.3 Greek–Coptic interferences in Byzantine and early Islamic documentary evidence

As is well known, documentary evidence from Byzantine and early Islamic Egypt is bi- or even trilingual. In many cases we cannot treat an issue and draw conclusions on the base of a monolingual set of sources, since our body of evidence also includes documents recorded in the other languages. This is true of the evidence for many historical issues, and likewise true of the evidence for single individuals and their business affairs as attested in archives. Of course merely monolingual archives do exist. Many archives from the second to the fourth century AD, the time when Demotic had already ceased to be used as a written language for everyday purposes while Coptic was not yet in use, provide monolingual Greek (if not bilingual Greek–Latin, cf. Rochette 1996) evidence. But the great bulk of Coptic documents comes from the seventh and eighth centuries, when Greek still and Arabic already played prominent roles in everyday written communication.

Ex. 1: The Nepheros archive (*P.Neph.*) and the Meletian correspondence (from *P.Lond.* VI) form part of a dossier centered around a Meletian monastery flourishing in the 30s of the fourth century AD. The Meletian community was a schismatic Christian denomination, alienated from the Alexandrian patriarch by different attitudes toward the issue of martyrdom during the persecution in the days of Diocletian. Two documents out of a total of forty-two items from the Nepheros archive and three out of nine Meletian documents from

P.Lond. VI are written in Coptic, the earliest datable Coptic documentary texts of all. These altogether five Coptic texts are personal letters, as are almost all fourth-century Coptic documentary texts.

Ex. 2: The Apa Abraham dossier (around AD 600). This fascinating personality, as bishop of Hermonthis and abbot of the Theban monastery of St. Phoibammon at the time of the Alexandrian patriarch Damianos (AD 578–607), had a wide range of responsibilities, which are mirrored in great detail by the extant remains of his correspondence. The dossier consists of around 200 Coptic ostraca (kept in London, Berlin, Leipzig, and elsewhere), his correspondence, and one papyrus, *P.Lond.* I 77, the bishop's will in Greek. The complete correspondence is written in Coptic. Actually almost all late sixth- to late eighth-century documents with a Theban provenance are Coptic texts. This landscape, structured at that time by a number of small and medium-size settlements, like Djême with its 1,000 to 2,000 inhabitants, and a number of monasteries and dwelling places of single hermits, seems to have been a particularly Coptophone region; even in written communication Coptic seems to have been the preferred language. It is only here that Coptic papyrological evidence far exceeds the Greek. The bishop himself, as is clear from a passage in his Greek will, was unable to speak or even to read Greek. But why did he draw up his last will in that language? This is again an issue of functional domains: Coptic might still have been an idiom simply forbidden for recording testaments; at the very least it might have been felt inappropriate for such an important purpose or somehow unfit for the technical requirements of recording a Byzantine will. It may be worth mentioning, for appreciating the ongoing processes in the realms of literacy and written culture at that time, that the wills of Abraham's successors, the abbots of the monastery of Phoibammon in the later seventh and eighth centuries, are recorded in Coptic.

Ex. 3: Two documents from the archive of Philemon, *P.Budge*, the Coptic record of a hearing that happened in AD 646, and the Greek *dialysis*-settlement *P.BLOr.* 2017 issued in AD 647, witness two stages of a lawsuit brought by the deacon John against the farmer Philemon for the ownership of a house (see Schiller 1964 and 1968; Allam 1991). Obviously both parties were Coptic native speakers. This might have been the reason to record their hearing before the arbitration committee in Coptic, the language actually spoken and heard in the proceedings. After the decision favored Philemon, John had to withdraw formally from his earlier claim by drawing up a *dialysis* document, and this was done now in Greek: At the time immediately after the Arab conquest, Coptic was just about to become a more common language of legal instruments (cf. **3.4.1**), and we actually know a considerable number of early- to mid-eighth-century *dialysis* documents in Coptic. But in the seventh century, Greek seems still to have been preferred in such cases (see Gagos and van Minnen 1994).

Ex. 4: The large correspondence of Qurrah ibn Sharîq, early eighth century AD, consists of documents written in three languages, Arabic, Coptic, and Greek (cf. Abbott 1938; Bell in *P.Lond.* IV; Bell 1929; Cadell 1967). At the highest administrative level, the chancellery of the governor Qurrah ibn Sharîq himself in the new capital Fustât, documents written in Arabic and also in Greek were produced. At the middle administrative level, as in the office of the pagarch of Aphrodito, Greek was used. Only at the bottom level, some local administrative bodies of the surrounding villages made use of Coptic. In communication between Arabic-speaking authorities and Coptic-speaking subjects concerning matters such as tax revenue, mustering workmen, and justice, Greek still served as a lingua franca into the first decades of the eighth century.

3.4.4 Greek–Coptic interferences in the legal documents

In everyday spoken communication, it is a speaker's linguistic competence and social awareness of language behavior that serve him or her in spontaneously making appropriate language choices. By contrast, language choice for written communication is less a spontaneous decision than a result of prior consideration. Moreover, using a language as a written medium does not even depend on the author's own ability in speaking, or writing, this language, provided only that he or she is able to pay a scribe. It rather depends, apart from the existence of an alphabetic code as a basic condition, on the possibility of recurring to *genres*, on the availability of linguistic means qualified to express opinions and to address issues in a way that virtually meets the recipients' expectations: appropriate terminologies, common rhetorical strategies, and literary conventions as to the relation of form and content. Such means of expressions can be generated within the development of a literary tradition of one language, or can be borrowed from a still existing literary tradition of another language. As is pointed out above (**2.7**), the *genre* of legal documents was applied by later sixth-century bilingual notaries to Coptic, with the result that Greek terminology and schemes influenced and shaped the language and form of Coptic legal documents. Thus to consider Greek–Coptic interferences in legal documents means to speak about the usual appearance of those sorts of Coptic texts, that is, about normal cases.

Case 1: One papyrus, two languages

Often a single piece of papyrus bears evidence of more than one language. Commonly, this is a matter of lexical borrowing, abundantly occurring in documentary as in any Coptic texts. But what is meant here are linguistically *coherent* paragraphs, sentences, or strings of words of different languages occurring side by side in the same text or on the same papyrus.

Ex. 1: Often in Coptic legal documents, parts of the scheme to the extent of full sentences are written in Greek, especially at the beginning and ending of deeds, such as the invocation formula, the dating, and the completion note of the scribe (cf. above, **2.7**).

Ex. 2: Stereotyped Greek *syntagmata* beneath the sentence level could be inserted somewhere in the Coptic text, embedded amidst Coptic syntactic structures, such as *pote kairo ê chronô* "at any moment or time," *ek cheiros eis cheira* "(payment) from hand to hand (i.e., in cash)," *alla en pasê kalê prohairesei* "but in every nice decision," *katharos kai apokrotôs* "pure and unchangeable," or the routine repetition of amounts (cf. below, case 4).

Ex. 3: Two languages can occur, one on the recto and one on the verso side of one papyrus. Usually papyrus documents received a registration note (docket) on the verso, a kind of summary of the text, which remained visible even when the papyrus was folded and sealed. This permitted persons to perceive the content of the text inside without breaking the seal. These *dockets* often are written in Greek even when the deed itself was drafted in Coptic. Being a second text in a sense, a paratext as we could call it, this docket belongs immediately to the text summarized by it. Nevertheless, aside from these and similar cases of obvious textual connections, recto and verso side may also contain texts not *immediately*, or not *obviously* belonging to each other, such as a Greek or Arabic verso in some way related or not related to a Coptic recto (cf., e.g., the Coptic will on the recto of the Greek–Coptic specimen forms discussed at **2.7.1**). But even in such cases there must be some kind of relationship, if only from the fact of their having been written on the same piece of writing material. Being paratexts, as it were, of the second or third degree to each other, they do bear evidence for a specific circulation of documents in a bilingual setting.

Case 2: Greek deeds in Coptic dresses

This crucial issue has already been dealt with in a more detailed way (above, **2.7**) and only need be recalled here briefly. Over centuries, Greek had undivided sovereignty over written discourses in legal, business, and all everyday affairs, so that when Coptic entered the field, many Coptic schemes were simply molded on a Greek matrix. Revealing instances of this technique are the Greek and Coptic versions of the Hermopolite scheme of *misthôsis*-leases (**7.4.1**, **7.4.3**, and **7.4.4**), and the deed of sale form used by eighth-century Coptic documents from Djême (cf. **6.6.2**), its Greek pattern being attested by sixth-century documents from Syene (cf. **6.6.1**).

Case 3: Byzantine rhetorical style applied to Coptic speech

A kind of cross-linguistic interference often neglected, despite its being a revealing phenomenon of language contact, is the impact of one language on another at the level of rhetorical style. From the early Byzantine age, the Greek chancellery style underwent a dramatic change from a simple prose concentrating on facts to an elaborately rhetorical prose (cf. above, **2.7**). A most striking feature of this new style was the excessive use of rhetorical figures of adjection (*figurae per adiectionem*). As Coptic legal documents are so closely related to Greek patterns, rendered from Greek schemes and in many cases written by scribes whose proficiency was presumably applicable also to the production of Greek documents, these rhetorical figures were introduced into the style of Coptic documentary texts in a most natural way.

Ex. 1: Monolingual tautological word pairs, consisting of Greek words, such as *kakonoia nim hikakoêtheia* (*P.KRU* 98, lines 35–36), "(without . . .) any wicked mind and malice."

Ex. 2: Monolingual tautological word pairs, consisting of Coptic words, such as *emnsôrm ebol hisromrm shoop mmoi* (*P.KRU* 74, lines 38–39), "while no hallucination and confusion happened to me."

Ex. 3: Bilingual tautological word pairs, such as *eiêtei eisops* (*P.KRU* 16, line 8), "while I am asking and begging"; *pros taaitêsis toei mmin mmoi mnpaouôsh nhêt* (*P.CLT* 7, lines 9–10), "according to my decision and my heartfelt desire."

Ex. 4: Tautological strings composed of more than two homonymous words, such as *tnshtôre tnkindyneue awô tno neggyyê awô tno nenaichesthai* (*P.Lond.* IV 1494, line 9), "we are warranting and we go bail and we are warrantors and we are liable."

Ex. 5: Bipartite paraphrastic phrases (expressions somehow complementing each other) with antithetic parallelism, such as *euplêrou emnteuaposia e[may]* (*P.Lond.* IV 1588, line 15), "in full and without deficit"; *hnoushepshôp awô para ta[pro]sdoqia* (*P.KRU* 74, lines 20–21), "suddenly and against my expectation."

Ex. 6: Bipartite paraphrastic phrases with opposite parallelism, such as *oude hanhêt oude hanarês* (*OMH* 88, lines 4–5), "neither in the north nor in the south" (i.e., nowhere); *kan sahêt kan sarês* (*P.Bal.* 188, lines 13–14), "be it in the north, be it in the south" (i.e., anywhere); *mpehow mnteoushê* (*P.KRU* 87, line 16), "day and night" (i.e., always); *hmpamou ê hmpaônh* (*P.KRU* 68, lines 77–78), "during my death or during my life" (i.e., always).

Ex. 7: Paraphrastic word pairs with *homoioteleuton* (rhyme), such as *aih**itou** aij**itou*** (*P.KRU* 7, line 32), "I measured them, I received them"; *aihô**rize** ayw aidô**rize*** (*P.KRU* 81, line 29), "I determined and donated"; *tariq**opf** ajn h**opf*** (*P.Lond.* IV 1528, lines 12–13), "that I catch him without hiding him"; *oude hipt**oou** oude hmpm**oou*** (*BKU* III 350, line 11), "neither on the mountain nor in the water" (i.e., nowhere).

Ex. 8: Complex paraphrastic strings, consisting of three and more complementary expressions, such as *eite hiptoou eite hnkême eite hntsôshe* (*P.KRU* 65, line 44), "be it on the mountains, be it in the Nile valley, (or) be it on the field"; *eite hntpolis Ermont eite hnpkastron eite kômê eite chôrion* (*P.KRU* 65, lines 57–58), "be it in the town Hermonthis, be it in the kastron (Djême), be it a village, be it an estate"; *eite kamoul eite eiô eite esoou eite baampe* (*P.KRU* 65, line 57), "be it a camel, be it a donkey, be it a sheep, be it a goat" (note the arrangement of the different animals obviously following the natural order *de majore ad minorem*).

Case 4: Awareness and instrumentalization of bilingual speech

Sometimes we catch a glimpse of something like awareness of bilingualism as a bilingual professional scribe might have possessed it. A revealing example occurs in a Djême document written by the very skilled scribe Aristophanes son of John. In an otherwise routine punishment clause of a sale (*P.CLT* 7, line 53), a Coptic legal term is formally glossed by its Greek equivalent: "If anybody dares, . . . to take proceedings (Coptic: *ei ebol*, literally 'to come out') or (*êgoun*) to bring lawsuit (Greek: *enagein*) for anything concerning this room." The Greek particle *êgoun* "or even, or at least, or also, namely" is used here the same way as it occurs in philological treatises to gloss strange words, "or" as "that means," thus forming an explicit statement for the equivalence of two technical legal terms from two different languages. Similar strategies are known from medieval European documents, where vernacular glosses are usually introduced by phrases such as: *quod vulgo dicitur* "what is called in common speech," *vulgariter nuncupatum* "commonly designated," *seu* "or," and *vel* "or."

A sort of instrumentalization of bilingual writing can be found in the Coptic phraseology around the amounts in money and in kind: in Coptic documents, the chancellery tricks of fixing the amount twice in different ways also include the shift from Coptic to Greek, such as: *maab nrir gi (netai) choir(oi) 30*, "(*Coptic*) thirty pigs, (*Greek*) makes pigs 30."

CHAPTER 4

The family

Barbara Anagnostou-Cañas, Antti Arjava, Willy Clarysse, J. G. Manning, Myrto Malouta, and Jakub Urbanik

Introduction

The fact that papyrus documents are often associated with family archives shows us that the family was an important factor behind the production of private contracts. That is immediately clear in marriage contracts (**4.1**), for example, and in disputes over inherited property, as well as conflicts over broken marriage promises and outright resistance to an arranged marriage (**10.5.4**). Underlying the conveyance of property, wills, and often sales of property lay family relationships and their expectations. Among the strongest of these was the expectation that children would inherit the property of their parents.

In the previous chapter we have seen the extent to which the language of law was bound up with the various and diverse ethnic groups living in Egypt. One of the key issues in studying the papyri is the presence of Roman law found in the Egyptian documentation (**3.3**). Indeed Roman law had an important impact on family life, not only in the structure of particular texts such as wills but also in the realm of behavior. The reader may wish to start with **4.3** to gain a sense of the impact of Roman law on the family as it is reflected in the papyri.

The ancient family has been a popular research topic in ancient history for some three decades. While in the beginning the emphasis was mainly on the family in classical Greece and Italy, gradually the perspective widened to embrace family history in the provinces of the Roman empire, including the Byzantine period.[1] True, our sources for provincial life are meager and ambiguous. We lack abundant information on families even in Palestine, an exceptionally well-known province with sources like Josephus, the Gospels, and Acts, with Rabbinic literature, inscriptions, and papyri.[2]

[1] See, e.g., Arjava (1996), Bremen (1996), Evans Grubbs (2002), George (2005).
[2] Williams (2005); cf. Bremen (1996: 198–201).

Most other cultures in the Mediterranean have left no written record of their family structures. This lack is especially evident in the west, where written culture and the epigraphic habit were late imports by the Romans. For pre-Roman Gaul there are a few stray remarks by Caesar, for Spain some passages of Strabo, for most other areas not even that. In the east, the sources are not much better. A partial exception is Asia Minor, which abounds in inscriptions especially from the second and third centuries. This leaves the papyri from Roman Egypt, by far the best source material for gauging the everyday life of the provincial middle classes. Nevertheless, legal and social historians, perhaps deterred by their sheer bulk, have shrunk from employing them to their full extent.

In Hellenistic and Roman Egypt the legal order of succession on intestacy was for the most part founded on indigenous Egyptian custom and on Greek custom. The latter reveals common points with the law of succession of Dura-Europos, a Greek military colony founded by Seleukos I. This fact shows that the changes that occurred in Egypt in the regulation of the devolution of a property to an heir reflect the common evolution of Greek institutions in the Hellenistic period towards greater individualism. The data of our documents show the weakening of male preponderance within the Greek family, a relative emancipation of Greek women in the Hellenistic period, and the fact that the father and mother of the deceased were not excluded by the collaterals in succession. These innovations correspond to the political and social transformations that occurred because of the transition from the world of the classical cities to the world of the Hellenistic monarchies and then to the Roman empire.

As in Egyptian and in Greek law, marriage in Hellenistic and Roman Egypt did not give the surviving spouse a right of inheritance in intestacy. Nevertheless, this deficiency was compensated for by testamentary provisions in favor of the surviving spouse, in particular from husbands in favor of wives.[3]

Statutes on intestacy occur either to protect the economic interests of a group on which the king leaned, soldiers for example, or to legalize a de facto situation, while displaying the humanity of the ruler (**4.6.1a**, **4.6.2b**, **4.6.3**).

The role of the state in inheritance was that of a regulator. But it also had a title to the estate of anyone who died intestate and without legal heirs, and could bring an action to assert its rights (**4.6.6**).

[3] Rupprecht (1985: 292–93).

In recent years, the principal contributions to the law of succession have been W. Clarysse's critical edition of the register listing Arsinoite Greek wills drawn up between 238 and 226 BC (*P.Petr.*[2] 1) and L. Migliardi Zingale's collection (1997) of Roman wills preserved in Egyptian documents dating from the first to the fourth century AD. A renewed global study of the law of testate and intestate succession, following the now ancient example of H. Kreller (1919) and establishing comparisons among Egyptian, Greek, Hellenistic, and Roman laws, is something truly to be desired.

In the case of fatherlessness (**4.4**), we shall encounter a boy who recently lost his mother (**4.4.1**), a young woman owning property inherited from her grandmother (**4.4.2**), a couple registering their young daughter (**4.4.3**), a man asking to benefit from the privilege of the corn dole (**4.4.4**), a woman whose family proved that there was an important inaccuracy in her stated pedigree (**4.4.5**), and another woman who had married and divorced a man from an eminent family (**4.4.6**). The characteristic that all these people shared was that they all had to designate themselves as fatherless.

These particular documents were chosen because they were deemed to be the most interesting texts relating to fatherlessness. It must be pointed out, however, that the types of texts included here (mostly census-related) are not numerically representative of the types of texts in which most references to fatherless individuals occur. Indeed most fatherless people appear in receipts for work in the dikes, lists of workers, and tax lists, none of which would be of interest if seen in isolation or appropriate for a collection of sources such as the one at hand. A word of caution is therefore due regarding the biases that the present selection by necessity presents. This concerns the social standing and gender of fatherless individuals: a survey of all known cases of fatherlessness places the individuals in question in a middling social position, with identified cases spanning from dike workers to village officials (Malouta 2009: 126–29), while the kinds of documents in the present selection are clearly more representative of the higher end of that scale. Also, judging from the above texts, one would conclude that the phenomenon of fatherlessness is equally attested among men and women; this is not so. Of the total attestations of fatherlessness only 11 percent refer to women (ibid., 123–25).

The significance of the texts presented in **4.4** below is that, while they may not be the most representative numerically, they are the ones that challenge anachronistic assumptions about fatherless individuals. With their help, and based on the entire body of evidence, one can conclude that fatherless individuals were not stigmatized by their status. The legal absence of a father could on occasion cause difficulties, but these difficulties were practical, especially in the eyes of Roman law, not social or moral. No document explains the reasons for any given individual's fatherlessness. The assumption, based mostly on the duration of the phenomenon in the Roman period, as well as the contexts in which it is attested, is that it was based on a Roman legal institution, probably regarding marriage. Its occurrence is another manifestation of dissonance between the legal systems of Rome and Egypt that required compensation.

The last two sections of this chapter are concerned with wills and with intestacy. At this moment about 200 Greek and Latin wills from Egypt have been published, as listed by Salomons (2006: 232–38) and Yiftach-Firanko (2002). Three types can be distinguished: Greek *diathêkai*, Greek *mesiteiai* or *synchôrêmata*, and Roman *testamenta*. The middle group, which comes up in the Roman period, is influenced by Egyptian law, but also by the law of contracts. The graph in Figure 6 shows the distribution over time. After the *Constitutio Antoniana* (AD 212) the differences are less clear as Roman formulas enter Greek wills. The corpus of Petrie wills accounts for a large portion of the third-century BC documents.

The documents on intestacy presented here have been chosen either because they contain a rule of law or of custom, or because they attest its

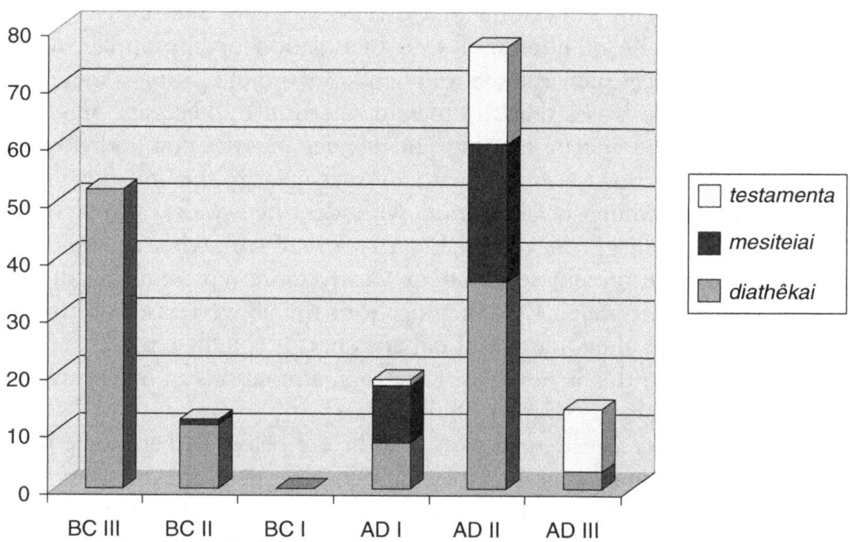

Fig. 6. *Testamenta*, *mesiteiai*, and *diathêkai* – distribution over time

application, or because they reveal the facts that lay behind the legislator's intervention. They confirm for the Ptolemaic period as well as for the Roman, for the indigenous as well as for the Greek population, the two fundamental principles of intestate succession: (1) children, sons or daughters, prevailed over all natural heirs and inherited from their fathers as well as from their mothers;[4] (2) in the absence of descendants, it was the intestate decedent's father and mother who came into succession.[5]

4.1 Marriage

J. G. Manning

The most famous marriage contract is *P.Eleph.* 1 (17 July–15 August 310 BC). As one of the earliest Greek documents from Egypt, it has been extensively discussed and will not be reproduced here.[6] It is remarkable in preserving a purely Greek marriage tradition, in this case recording the marriage between a man from Temnos and a woman from Kos. The husband is in the stronger position, and since no institutions are documented here, the enforcement of the contract is purely by the community, in this case one related to the important military garrison in the far south of Egypt. In neither the Egyptian nor the Greek traditions was a written contract required for a legally valid marriage.[7] Many of these texts were probably composed at some point after the marriage. In 16 percent of Demotic marriage contracts, children had already been produced (Smith 1995: 49). The property interest of the woman – her dowry, the

[4] As for the Egyptian law, the provisions in *P.Mattha* concerning inheritance have confirmed the position of the eldest son as a privileged heir; this position is attested by practical documents in Demotic and in Greek; cf. Manning (2003a: 221–24). In Greek law, according to a principle common to the various known legislations (Athens, law of succession attributed to Solon: Dem. 43 *Contra Macart.* 51; Naupactus, *IG* ix.1^2, 3, 718, lines 16–20, fifth century BC) the descendants were the first to inherit, the sons, whether natural or adopted, excluding the daughters, except in the law of the Cretan city of Gortyn, which granted a more favorable situation to the daughters (*Code* V 9–27; IV 23–48; V 1–9). In Egypt, following the disintegration of the *oikos*, that is the entity of persons, of estate, and of rites which was the fundamental element of the Greek city, the daughter of a man who died without sons did not become *epiklêros*, which means that the nearest male kin of her father coud not claim to marry her so as to beget a son who would perpetuate the *oikos* of his maternal grandfather: Harrison (1968: 132–38), and *Code of Gortyn* VII 15 – IX 24.

[5] As in Egyptian law (Pestman 1969: 70), and contrary to the Athenian law and to the law of Gortyn. The Athenian law provided that after the descendants, the intestate takers were first the paternal and then the maternal collaterals (Harrison 1968: 138–42). The *Code of Gortyn*, V 9–27 also remains silent about the rights of the ascendant line.

[6] *P.Eleph.* 1 = *M.Chr.* 283; *Sel.Pap.* I 1; *Jur.Pap.* 18; Bagnall and Derow (2004, no. 145). See further Rowlandson (1998, no. 123), Porten and Farber (1996: 408–10).

[7] In general for the structure of Greek marriage contracts, see Yiftach-Firanko (2003).

expectation of maintenance during the marriage, and a payment in case of divorce – tell us the primary purposes of such documents.

4.1.1. Ptolemaic Demotic marriage contract

P.Louvre 2433 (= Lüddeckens 1960, no. 14, Smith 1995: 64–65) (Thebes, January/February 252 BC)

The Egyptian tradition of written marriage contracts goes back to the Third Intermediate period.[8] Pestman (1961) divided Demotic marriage contracts into two basic types, which in part reflects regional variation. These arrangements protecting the rights of the wife and future children stand in sharp contrast to *P.Eleph.* 1. In both types the Demotic marriage contract was drawn up to provide a maintenance for the wife during the marriage, to provide for the disposal of property upon divorce and, finally, to endow any children produced during the marriage with the property of the husband (Smith 1995: 48). In Pestman's "Type A," the husband provides for a nominal "gift" to the wife, "the wife's gift," with the promise of an annual maintenance. The second type, "Type B," also documented in the Memphis and Fayyum region, records a gift from the wife to the husband, and the promise of the husband to maintain the wife with this endowment. These two basic types of arrangement produced differently structured texts. In Type A, a "woman's document" (Dem. *sẖ n s.ḥm.t*) was written, whereas in Type B, a sale document (**2.2** above) functioned as a recognition by the husband of the woman's dowry, and a maintenance document (*sẖ n sʿnḫ*) specified the yearly obligation of the husband's maintenance of his wife. The following text is an example of Pestman's Type A. Unlike the norm it does not have a list of the woman's personal possessions that are brought into the marriage. There are special clauses at the end that give over to the wife the documents that the husband's mother had made for him that conveyed to him half of his father's property. The children of the present marriage are also forbidden from coming against the wife, their mother, with respect to the property.

> Regnal year 33, fourth month of *akhet* of pharaoh Ptolemy son of Ptolemy, the god, Aetos daughter of Dionysios is *kanêphoros* before Arsinoe Philadelphos. The *pastophoros* of Amenope in the west of Thebes, Pa-Item son of Pa-khel-Khonsu whose mother is Tay-heter, to the

[8] The standard corpus of Demotic marriage texts and their analysis is Lüddeckens (1960). Egyptian marriage: Pestman (1961), Smith (1995). See also Lippert (2008: 166–70).

woman Ta-qetem daughter of Relu, whose mother is Ta-netem: I have made you wife. I have given you one *deben*, equaling five *statêrs*, that is one *deben*, as your woman's gift. And I will give you six (loaves) of bread, their half is three, that is six (loaves) daily, and three *hin*-measures of oil per month, that is 36 *hin*-measures yearly, and one *deben* and two *kite* for clothing allowance yearly, and one *kite*, that is one-half *statêr*, that is one *kite* for spending money monthly, making one *deben* and two *kite*, making six *statêrs*, making one *deben* and two *kite* for spending money yearly. This is the total of your food and clothing and your spending money yearly. And I will give it to you yearly. You are entitled to the arrears of your food and clothing and your spending money that are my obligation, and I will give it to you. Your eldest son, <who is> my eldest son, is the owner of everything that belongs to me, and <all that> I will acquire. If I divorce you, whether because I hate you or I want another woman, I will pay you twenty *deben*, that is 100 *statêrs*, that is twenty *deben*. Everything that belongs to me, and <everything> that I will acquire, is the guarantee for every word and everything written above until I do for you accordingly, without bringing any dispute or anything at all against you. The documents that my mother, Ta-heter daughter of Djed-hor, has made for me of half of everything that belongs to Pa-khel-Khonsu son of Pa-na my father that he conveyed by writing to me, and the rest of his documents in my possession – they are yours, along with the rights <established in them>. You are the one who possesses the rights in them. The son or the daughter of mine who comes against you with respect to them, he (*sc.* they) will pay you twenty *deben*, equaling 100 *statêrs*, that is twenty *deben*. He (*sc.* they) will be far from you regarding them, without any subterfuge.

The Theban scribe and priest of Amun Horemheb son of Nes-min has written.

Greek registration docket: Year 33, Choiak 17 in Diospolis Magna. Deposited into the register. Polyaratos, ordered by the *oikonomos* Leon, has officiated.

On the verso is the list of sixteen witnesses (see Chapter 2 introduction).

4.1.2 Greek marriage contract

BGU IV 1052 (= *Sel.Pap.* I 3) (Alexandria, 15 April 13 BC)

Many more examples of Greek marriage contracts survive from the first two centuries AD, more than two-thirds of the total (Yiftach-Firanko

2003: 21). The following text specifies, as does **4.1.3**, the reciprocal duties of the couple. Both reflect an "urban Greek milieu" (Lewis 1983: 55).

The following translation is that of *Sel.Pap.* I 3.

> To Protarchos from Thermion daughter of Apion, with her guardian Apollonios son of Chaereas, and from Apollonios son of Ptolemaios. Thermion and Apollonios son of Ptolemaios agree that they have come together to share a common life, and the said Apollonios son of Ptolemaios acknowledges that he has received from Thermion hand-to-hand from the house a dowry of a pair of gold earrings weighing 3 quarters and [. . .] silver drachmas; and from now Apollonios son of Ptolemaios shall furnish to Thermion as his wedded wife all necessities and clothing in proportion to his means and shall not ill-treat her nor cast her out nor insult her nor bring in another wife, or he shall straightaway forfeit the dowry increased by half, with right of execution upon both the person of Apollonios son of Ptolemaios and all his property as if by legal decision, and Thermion shall fulfill her duties towards her husband and their common life and shall not absent herself from the house for a night or a day without the consent of Apollonios son of Ptolemaios nor dishonor nor injure their common home nor consort with another man, or she again if guilty of any of these actions shall, after trial, be deprived of the dowry, and in addition the transgressing party shall be liable to the prescribed fine. The 17th year of Caesar, Pharmouthi 20.

4.1.3 Byzantine marriage contract

P.Cair.Masp. III 67310 + *P.Lond.* V 1711 (tr. Rowlandson 1998, no. 155) (Antinoopolis, AD 566–73). Image at Papyri.info.

This document survives in two halves, one in Cairo, the other in London. The Cairo piece appears to have been a draft or model document. There are corrections in the text, and there is no scribal signature. The London half, the actual document, is heavily damaged at the beginning. Both texts come from the famous lawyer and poet Dioskoros' archive. See also **4.2.3**. The detailed expectations of behavior are notable, while the basic agreement is comparable to what is found in earlier Demotic documents.

The translation follows that given in Rowlandson. The contract is in the form of a *cheirographon* (see **2.1.4–8**), with the husband in the first person addressing his wife in the second.

> Lately, and in accordance with friendly and peaceful disposition, I joined myself to your propriety by a giving[9] in legal marriage, based on sound expectations, if God should think best, also for the procreation of legitimate children; and, having found your sacred and secure virginity, I have proclaimed it. Wherefore I have come to this guarantee in writing by which I agree that I owe and am indebted for your wedding gifts or gifts before marriage, agreed upon and pleasing between me and you, for 6 good-quality imperial *solidi*, less 36 carats, by the scale and standard of Antinoopolis. And I am ready to furnish these to your nobility whenever you want, without any neglect or delay, at the risk and wealth and expense of my property, general and particular. And I agree no less in addition to support you legitimately and to clothe you in likeness to all my family members of like status and in proportion to the wealth available to me, as far as my modest means will allow; and not to show contempt for you in any way or to cast you out from marriage with me except by reason of unchastity or shameful behavior or physical misbehavior established through three or more trustworthy free men, be they country residents or city residents; and never to leave your marriage bed or to run to other disorder or wickedness, provided however that your propriety is obedient to me and preserves all benevolence towards me and sincere affection in all fine and useful deeds and words, and is subject to me in all ways that it befits all women of nobility to display toward their own well-endowed and most beloved husbands, withour insult or fickleness or any other type of disdain whatever; rather you are to be full-time housekeeper and husband-loving on my account, in keeping with the good and proper disposition that will be displayed to you by me.

The second part of the text is taken from the London text, the actual contract itself:

> But if it should happen that I at some point in time disdain you in the above-proclaimed manner, or cast you out without reasonable cause as above written, I, your aforementioned husband Horouonchis, am ready to furnish to your propriety, by reason of penalty for the said disdain, 18 *solidi*, deposited by me on demand withour any prevarication or delay of trial or judgment or any pretext or blame or any kind of indisputably

[9] The term here is *ekdosis*, the key concept in marriage whereby the woman gives herself, or in normative Greek practice the father gives the bride, in marriage. See further Mélèze Modrzejewski (1981), Yiftach-Firanko (2005).

legal exception; you, too, however, my aforementioned bride and wife Scholastikia, being liable to the very same penalty if you should disdain me with respect to the above set forth agreements . . . [and] I your husband additionally agree not to invite any inconsequential man home to your presence or to hold a drinking-party in your presence with friends or relatives or anyone else if you are opposed to their presence. And for the security of either party and for our mutual-loving marriage, I have drawn up this agreement of union, or marriage contract, it being authoritative and secure wherever it is produced. And, having been asked the formal question, I have willingly and voluntarily agreed, not overcome by duress or fraud or violence or deceit or compulsion; and I have issued to you for security that which is written below (*sic*), and for each and every one of the clauses contained in it and for the payment of the penalty (if this should happen), putting under mortgage to you all my property, present and future, by way of pledge and by right of mortgage. And I the aforementioned Horouonchis agree in addition that I cannot at any occasion or time introduce other wives above my lawful wife, and if I do so I shall pay the same penalty.

4.2 Divorce

Jakub Urbanik

Our imagination of the matrimonial reality of the Roman world has been haunted by women counting their age by their husbands instead of consuls (Seneca, *de ben.* 3.16.2) and the notorious Cato–Marcia–Hortensius triangle (Plutarch, *Cato* 25–27). This stereotype of the poor durability of ancient marriages has been challenged by Susan Treggiari (Treggiari 1991a, 1991b). Having counted the divorces recorded in the classical literary sources (sixty-odd until the reign of Domitian, some of them involving the same persons), she concluded that this picture was simply a byproduct of the *topoi* of the kind of moralistic, satirical literature that relished blaming women for every kind of matrimonial trouble – recall the renowned fragment of Apuleius, *Apol.* 92: "In either case it is the woman who is to be blamed, who either has been so unbearable that she had to be sent away, or so audacious to initiate a divorce."[10] And yet we must observe that the literature hardly ever concerns the lives of simple people whose realities can only be retrieved from the documents of legal practice.

[10] *Utramvis habens culpam mulier, quae aut tam intolerabilis fuit, ut repudiaretur, aut tam insolens, ut repudiaret.*

Prima facie the scarcity of the documentation seems to corroborate Treggiari's thesis. At present there are known fewer than fifty deeds dealing directly with divorce. These predominantly date to the Roman and Byzantine periods; some of them are only preserved as fragments. These documents have been traditionally termed by their editors "contracts of divorce," "contrats de divorce," "contratti di divorzio." This label, however, is rather misleading: the parties never agree to divorce from one another in the documents proper, simply stating that their separation has already occurred.[11] The actual object of these agreements is to settle the financial duties resulting from the dissolved union, above all confirmation of dowry-return and renouncing of claims between the ex-spouses. Occasionally, the fate of the common children could be decided upon, and the rights of the ex-couple to remarry secured as well. If we recall that according to Roman law a marriage was created by the mere (even if not openly expressed, much less documented) will of the parties and dissolved by the simple lack of it, we may better understand the supposed paucity of the documentation.[12] Divorce therefore is totally formless; a simple desertion of one spouse by the other will amount to a dissolution of the marriage bond (see also the comments on **4.2.4**, **4.2.5**, **4.2.6**).

We may therefore put forward the notion that, in the majority of cases, the ends of marriages, just like their beginnings, were simply not recorded. No one would doubt that people generally married in Greco-Roman Egypt and yet the number of preserved marriage contracts is not so spectacular either.

The "normality" of divorces is further confirmed by papyri that are not directly concerned with divorce. First, in all the "contracts" of marriage there is a clause stipulating the duties of the parties in case of separation, whether by default of one of the parties or in case of a joint decision to end the union. This can be seen even in the later Christian period, as in the case of a Coptic marriage contract of a priest or a priest's son: *P.Bal.* 152 (see below, toward the end of this discussion). This simply means that a dissolution of marriage was always contemplated at its formation and that the parties saw nothing bizarre in mentioning it. We also deal with a few petitions lodged by one spouse against the other (or even the other's parents, see **4.2.4** and **4.2.5**) in cases of maltreatment or desertion; they add to the panorama illustrating tendencies toward unilateral divorce.

[11] The only exception is *P.Tebt.* III 809 (156 BC), which speaks in fact about the *future* separation of the spouses; unfortunately its poor condition is not very elucidating at to the reasons for such an unusual formula.

[12] See above all Volterra (1940), (1975), and (1980).

One particular document may serve for a better approximation of the actual ratio of marital separations. It is a copy of a census return republished by Thorolf Christensen and now accessible as *SB* XXIV 15987 (Arsinoite nome [Tebtunis?], *c.* AD 208; the original return dates from AD 188/9). This text offers a fascinating example of a "multi-nuclear" family (see Figure 7). Didymos son of Kallinikos registers his house and slaves as well as the slaves belonging to his present wife, Sarapias daughter of Sabeinos. We learn that a forty-three-year-old Sarapias is the third spouse of the declarant and that she registered herself in the previous census as a single person. A ten-year-old son of Didymos and his former wife Hermione, named Didymos as well, lives with the couple. Another son of the declarant, Xenophon, is mentioned as the co-owner of three slaves belonging to Didymos. The youth himself is declared, however, with his mother, whose name has sadly not been preserved, another former

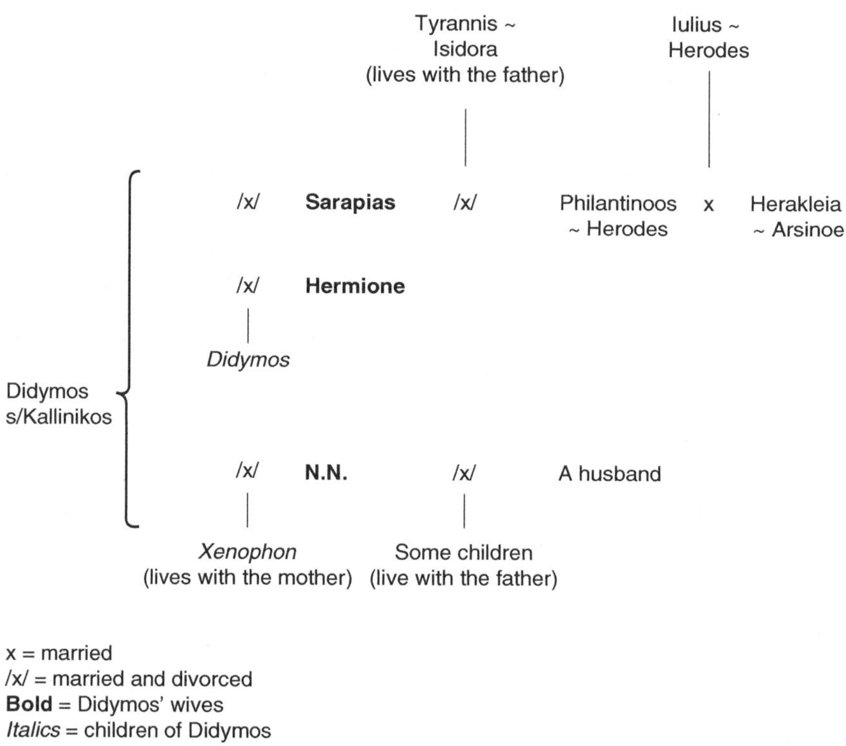

Fig. 7. The "multi-nuclear" family tree of Didymos son of Kallinikos and his three former wives (Tebtunis, AD 150–205/6)

wife of Didymos. The return informs us as well that Xenophon's mother has remarried and then divorced another man and that she has had children by him who presently live with and are declared by their father. The picture is completed by various items from the Tebtunis Family Archive. In *P.Fam.Tebt.* 48 (AD 202/3), another census-return, Sarapias, now aged fifty-seven, is declared as a single woman; meanwhile her daughter Tyrannis, also known as Isidora, born in AD 188, is in turn registered in Antinoopolis with her father Philantinoos-Herodes. The latter must have married again around the time of the AD 202/3 census a woman called Herakleia-Arsinoe and fathered a child by her. This time, for a change, the marriage was ended by Philantinoos' death around AD 206 as the post-dated texts *P.Tebt. Fam.* 49–53 deal with the guardianship of his orphan Iulius-Herodes.

To make the picture even clearer: Didymos married and divorced thrice, two of his wives had been at least twice married and divorced, and their respective spouses contracted new unions, too. The children of the separated couples stayed normally with the fathers but at least in one case joined the mother's new family. In this extended and rather wealthy family divorce was but a normality, which, in this case, may have depended on the financial as well as personal factors of those involved. But on the assumption that separation of the spouses was normal among ordinary people, it may not be so far from the truth that divorce was just the anticipated complement of marriage.

Divorce settlements: format

For the reasons expressed above I prefer calling the documents in question "divorce settlements." This preference is further justified because *dialysis* and *perilysis*, words used both in the papyri and in the legal sources (the *Basilika* and the Greek *novellae*) for divorce documents, generically denote any kind of settlement. Quite often the papyri use verbal forms meaning "to end," "to cut off," "to release," depending on *homologô* (*P.Lips.* I 27, Arsinoite, AD 123;[13] *P.Oxy.* XLIII 3139, third–fourth century AD; *P.Oxy.* XXXVI 2770, AD 304); or, in case of the Alexandrine format, *synchôrô* (*BGU* IV 1102 and 1103, Alexandria, 13 BC). In the Byzantine period we frequently find the Latinism *repoudion* (= *repudium*), often strengthened with synonyms like *dialysis*, *apozygê*, or *diaisis* (e.g., **4.4.3**).

[13] Similarly, *CPR* I 23 (second century), *P.Kron.* 52 (AD 138), *P.Mil.Vogl.* III 185 (AD 139), *P.Brook.* 8 (AD 178).

The most important elements of a divorce settlement are always the same (cf. Préaux 1962, Rupprecht 1971: 43–50):

- first, the dowry-receipt clause, the wife's declaration that the dowry had been returned (note that some documents lack the dowry receipt; this may be because the wife did not bring a dowry or because she decided to forfeit it);
- second, the quitclaim clause, declared by each of the ex-spouses, occasionally supplemented by securing the right to the ex-spouse to enter a new union.

These clauses are set in a pattern that in the most general lines hardly changed throughout the period. After the date and the specification of the parties, with the wife possibly assisted by her *kyrios* or in some cases her mother, the parties declare – *homologousi(n)*, or in two Alexandrine documents *synchôrousin* – that they have ended their married life. The use of the past tense infinitive indicates once more that the document was executed only after the divorce proper took place.

Normally there follow the dowry-receipt and the quitclaim clauses. The first one usually employs the present infinitive of the verb *apechô*. Subsequently, the ex-spouses declare that they do not have any claims in regard to their joint life or any other thing until the present day of separation/execution of the document. The settlement of claims may be further supplemented by a mutual consent for the new marriage of the ex-partner. A typical formulation can be found in one of the earliest examples, *BGU* IV 1103 (13 BC): "(they agree) that Zois or anyone on her behalf shall not sue Antipatros as to the return of the dowry, and both of them (shall not sue) each other, neither as to their married life nor as to any other dispute up to the current day." In the later documents the formula becomes more elaborate, addressing any possible matters between the ex-spouses; a good example would be *P.Fam.Tebt.* 13, lines 21–26 (AD 113/4): "and none of the aforementioned persons shall proceed against one another in any way, neither on account of the possessions regarding the marriage nor on account of any other matter written or unwritten, a debt or any kind of contract whatsoever, from the former times up to the present day." Lastly, the convention is declared valid, and the penalty clause preventing breach is included.

From the later Byzantine period we have nine Antinoopolitan papyri (there are only seven deeds: two papyri are duplicates) and two possibly coming from Hermopolis. A mere glimpse at the otiose phrases with their repetitions and redundancies allows their immediate identification. Theoretically, a written form of divorce became compulsory with *Nov.Theod.* 12.1

of Theodosius II from AD 439, but the documentary material does not really prove the efficacy of the rule. It is true that the clauses describing the actual separation of the spouses are present in all the documents and that they have become much longer and more elaborate: the parties, seemingly trying to justify their divorce, recall their decision to be joined in wedlock under best auspices and in hope for procreation of children in the best and highest spirits. Each document differs from the others by its unique wording of the separation clause. Two patterns are most often used as bases: the first one describes the activity of preparing a letter of repudiation (**4.2.3**, lines 6–7: "I am preparing and sending you this *repudium* of divorce in the following words," cf. *BGU* XII 2203, *P.Flor.* I 93 and its copy *P.Lond.* V 1713); the second applies the verb *erchomai* (as in *P.Lond.* V 1712, lines 10–11: *kata touto eis tautên elêuthamen pros heautous tên engraphon dialusin*). For the separation itself an "evil daimon" is blamed, *ek kakou daimonos*.

The quitclaim clause is also, as expected, long and detailed. A typical one lists all possible grounds for future claims: dowry, written and unwritten things, earnings during marriage, *hedna* (bridal gifts), anything that comes and does not come to mind at the moment of executing the document; for example, *P.Lond.* V 1712, lines 11–17: "we declare that each of us has fully received his/her own, and that we have no claim, nor shall have any claim against each other, neither in regard to the equipment, nor any goods, nor in regard to the bridal gifts, nor the married life, nor in regard to any matter whatsoever, be it small or big, written or unwritten, which is now considered, and which is not considered, which comes to mind, and which does not, which is registered and which is unregistered, that we do not sue one another and neither shall ever sue be it in court or out of it, and that through it (the settlement of divorce) we have set each other free and fulfilled (all duties to one another) and we have got settled among ourselves. . . "

Divorce in documentary practice vs. imperial law

The material chosen for the present section may well serve to illustrate one of the perennial questions of juristic papyrology, i.e., the possible compliance of regional practices with the *Reichsrecht*. See above, **1.4**, **1.7**, and **1.8**.

The first problem would concern the effectiveness of the imperial limitations imposed upon unilateral divorces dating back to the (in)famous Constantinian law of AD 331, *CTh* 3.16.1. The traditional liberty of marriage, built into the Roman *ordre publique* (cf. *CJ* 8.38.2–2.02, AD 223, Alexander Severus; *Pauli Sententiae* 2.19.2, cited below, n. 15), got pricked by the proverbial hairpin, evoked in the picturesque Constantinian sanction against a woman who would dare illegal divorce (*CTh* 3.16.1: she is to lose all her property, "up to the last hairpin"). Any possible traces of the legislation would obviously have to be searched for among the petitions on papyrus, as neither Constantine nor his successors until Justinian tried to ban consensual divorces. Sadly, the papyri neither confirm the success of the law nor its supposed subsequent revocation by Julian. The six extant texts containing petitions of deserted spouses are either too imprecisely dated or too ambiguous in their interpretation (see **4.4.4** and its introduction). Nor can we trace the imprints of various barriers imposed on divorce throughout the fifth century (for which there is little papyrological material), unless, as argued above, we consider the development of the formulary of the sixth-century divorce settlements the result of Theodosius II's introduction of compulsory letters of divorce. Justinian's prohibition against any kind of divorce, promulgated with *Novella* 22, likewise cannot be traced back in the papyri. Divorce settlements coming from his reign are too poorly dated to provide any evidence for or against the real application of such a harsh norm.

Another question worth considering through the papyri is the role of fathers in the creation and dissolution of their children's unions.[14] This seemingly unimportant fragment of Roman family law allows us to follow the dissemination of Roman concepts in Egypt. One of the possible explanations of the formation by the end of the Republic of the very unpractical juristic concept of Roman marriage could have been the increasing emancipation of women and adult children from the traditional power of the head of the household (*patria potestas*). The idea that marriage is created and dissolved, as long as other prerequisites like age, citizenship, right to marry (*conubium*) are fulfilled, by the mere will of the marriage partners implies that no external interference is wished for or approved.[15] Obviously such a practice could hardly be observed in a society with strong family ties reinforced by a father's near absolute authority. Therefore we find traces of the dissolution of children's marriages against

[14] See Volterra (1948), Urbanik (2002).

[15] Cf. the celebrated – even if possibly post-classical – passages from *Works of Ulpian*, 5.2: "A valid (legitimate) marriage is made, when there is *conubium* between the contracting parties, and if the man is adult and the woman is able to procreate, and if both of them agree, if they are autonomous, or also their fathers, if they are still in their power"; supplemented by *Pauli Sententiae*, 2.19.2: "The marriages of these who are under their fathers' power are not legally contracted without their will, but once contracted, they cannot be dissolved (by the father's will)." Consideration of the public interest prevails over commodity of the private.

their will not only in the papyri, but also in the purely juridical texts, including one that states: "Divine Pius has forbidden the father to separate a well-harmonized marriage, likewise the patron in case of a freedman, likewise the parents in case of a son or a daughter, unless an investigation is made as to where their (i.e., spouses in their fathers' power) permanence would be more appropriate" (*Pauli Sent.* 5.6.15).[16]

Let us notice that not only are fathers barred from too strict an employment of their *patria potestas*; the imperial rescript speaks generally of "parents," which implies that in some cases it was the mothers who meddled with their children's marriages.[17] Practical examples of such practices in the papyri led Taubenschlag (1929) to develop the concept of a *materna potestas* that would be almost as strong as the *paterna potestas* in the law of the papyri. The thorough examination of the sources, however, makes us believe that these phenomena are rather of social than legal nature. Even if (which is neither certain nor unquestionable) the laws of the Greek *poleis* (see **1.5**), imported with their ancient citizens to Egypt, originally allowed fathers to perform *apospasis*, i.e., to snap away daughters from their nuptial houses, this custom was barred by the Roman judges. The *Petition of Dionysia*, *P.Oxy.* II 237 (AD 186; the four precedents cited by the woman date back to AD 86–137; extract in **2.6.2**), shows how Roman justice, confronted by fathers wishing to recover their daughters from their husbands and *ipso facto* to dissolve their marriages, left the decision to the daughters themselves. The *epistratêgos* Paconius Felix, dismissing the absoluteness of the father's claims over his daughter's autonomy in the third case cited by Dionysia (*P.Oxy.* II 237 Col. VII, lines 29–38), characterized the law from which they arose as inhuman (line 35).[18]

The last point to be addressed is the popular belief that Christianity had a dramatic impact on family customs. Modern studies have shown convincingly that changes in ancient society happened gradually. In the case of marriage and divorce practices we can clearly observe the continuity of ancient traditions. Above all, notwithstanding the pastoral teaching and the early collections of ecclesiastical laws, divorce apparently remained common. The frequently repeated condemnation of divorce proves that the Christian flock was not really ready to follow the evangelical principle

[16] *Bene concordans matrimonium separari a patre divus Pius prohibuit, itemque a patrono libertum, a parentibus filium filiamque: nisi forte quaeratur, ubi utilius morari debeat.*

[17] In reaction to one more case of such mother's intervention Diocletian remarked that *a daughter's divorce is not in the power of the mother* (30 December AD 294, *CJ* 5.17.4).

[18] On this problem see most recently Kreuzsaler and Urbanik (2008), *passim*.

of the indissolubility of marriage apart from adultery. A Coptic ostracon, *O.Crum* 72, a pastoral letter very likely authored by the famous Abraham, bishop of Hermonthis (seventh century AD; see above, **3.4.3**), bears witness to such a practice. The writer, being informed about some people among his congregation who practiced divorces unjustified by previous fornication of the divorced spouse, decreed their excommunication. The Church seems to have been more influential in the case of a maltreated Christian wife (*P.Oxy.* VI 903 [fourth century AD], Rowlandson 1998, no. 153).[19] In the petition by which she finally ends her marriage, the woman tells a story of marital abuse and of failed trials of reconciliation recommended by the bishop. One may only guess why the woman did not divorce her abusive husband earlier: apart from the financial reasons (the couple seems to have been wealthy and high-ranked), there may have been the conviction that she should silently bear her cross as the typical Christian wife should do (cf. the slightly later example of Saint Thomais of Lesbos, who sanctified herself by bearing silently her husband's cruelty).[20]

Meanwhile, the normality of divorce for the common people is shown by the constant inclusion of the divorce clause in marriage deeds even in the case of a Coptic marriage contract of a priest or priest's son, *P.Bal.* 152, dated to the eighth century AD, where this clause is further secured by an oath on the Holy Trinity. The same may be deduced from a totally "sinless" attitude of the parties to divorce settlements. In *P.Cair.Masp.* I 67121 (AD 573), Aurelios Isakos and Aurelia Tetrompia not only secure each other's rights to remarry, but also agree not to protest the other's entering monastic life; the only one to blame is an evil daimon (see above) that had brought malice to the couple's life and caused the dissolution. Interestingly this evil daimon is actually a pagan element first appearing in AD 305 in *P. Gren.* II 76 (see introduction to **4.2.2**).

The most interesting piece of evidence in question is a very late papyrus coming not from Egypt but from Arab Palestine (see further Urbanik 2005). *P.Ness.* III 57 (AD 689) documents a consensual divorce of a priest, Ioannes, and his wife Nonna. Three high-ranking clerics assist and witness this act among seven other witnesses; obviously they do not represent the Church, they simply appear in the deed as respectable and important members of their community. Not only was a divorcing priest something unimaginable in Church discipline, but the mere intercession of clerics at a divorce resulted in their excommunication, at least according to the oriental canons attributed to St. Basil and St. Athanasius

19 See further Montserrat (1996: 99–100). 20 Talbot (1996).

of Alexandria,[21] which should reflect the Church order of seventh-century Palestine.[22] We may also recall that in the second part of the epistle cited above, *O.Crum* 76, the bishop excommunicated anyone, be it a lay person, be it a cleric, who would dare prepare an *apost(asia)*, that is, a deed of divorce. Explanation of the Nessana story may dwell in pastoral practice. Perhaps the clergymen of the town approving of Nonna and Ioannes' separation chose the lesser evil – just like Justin II, who, lifting his predecessor's ban on consensual divorces (*Novella* 140, AD 566), praised the ban as aimed at securing stability in marriage, but at the same time found it unacceptable to uphold when he considered the misery of unhappily married couples.

4.2.1 Repayment of part of a dowry

P.Lond. II 178 (provenance unknown [Alexandria?], 5 April AD 145). Image at *P.Lond.* II, Plate 52.

In this short deed Petronia Sarapias confirms having received back a smaller part of her dowry, 400 drachmas, from her ex-husband Iulius Apolinarios, a soldier in the First Apameian Cohort of the century of Iulianus. She also retains the right to proceed for the remaining 600 drachmas. The dowry was presented to her husband a mere year earlier under the pretense of a deposit (yet another proof of the fleetingness of marriages and normality of divorces). Claudia Kreuzsaler (**5.5.4** below) comments on the luckily preserved *parathêkê* agreement, *BGU* III 729 (Alexandria, AD 144), which cloaked a marriage contract between the couple. In the present instance, Petronia and Iulius Apolinarios obviously circumvented the law forbidding soldiers to marry (see above, **3.3.1–2**). Petronia was lucky to be able to retrieve her dowry; her illegal husband proved to be a sincere man. We can be almost certain that she would not

[21] According to W. E. Crum, canons attributed to St. Basil took their final shape in the sixth century; the Athanasian canons (which actually might be authored by the bishop himself: personal communication of Ewa Wipszycka, of 18 February 2006) are dated to the late fourth century.

[22] *Can. Bas.* 63: *Wer von seiner Frau geschieden werden wünscht.* b. "Daß ein Presbyter oder Diakon seine Frau nicht ohne Grund fortschicken oder entlassen darf"; *Can. Bas.* 71: *Wenn jemand eine Frau entläßt und ein Kleriker den Scheidenbrief für sie schreibt.* "Wenn jemand eine Frau entlassen will und ein Kleriker den Scheidenbrief für sie schreibt, so soll er ausgeschlossen werden, bis die Ehe zwischen beiden wieder zusammengekommen ist" (ed. Riedel 1900); *Can. Ath.* 45: "No priest shall put away his wife without reason of adultery. And if any shall put away his wife and dwell with another, above all if he hath gotten children by her, he shall be excluded"; 46: "No priest shall be go-between in the putting assunder of a marriage. If any be found that he hath done this, he shall be excluded until the marriage be brought together" (ed. Riedel and Crum 1904).

have won the case had it found its end in court. A ruling of the prefect M. Rutilius Lupus leaves no doubt as to the possible fate of the proceeding (*P.Catt.* recto Col. 1, lines 5–13 [Alexandria, 5 January AD 117]):

> In the year 20th of the divine Trajan, the twentieth day of the month Tybi. As Lucia Macrina through attorney Phaneios said that she sued for a deposit from the belongings of Antonius Germanus, the late soldier, Lupus said, "We know that such deposits are dowries. From such causes I do not grant a judgment, as a soldier is not allowed to marry. And if you sue for dowry I, granting a judgment, shall have to be persuaded that the marriage is valid.

A simulated legal transaction was valid as long as it did not breach the law. In this case, the prefect is inclined to refuse an action on a deposit because, he is convinced, it conceals a dowry. Nor would the woman be able to proceed with an action for return of the amount since a *condictio* (personal action) was not given if the initial payment was executed, as here, to obtain an illegal goal.

The document itself lacks the separation clause perhaps because the couple did not want to put their transgression even more clearly into evidence. The dowry-receipt clause uses the verb *apechô* in the perfect infinitive form *apeschêkenai.* Such a verbal construction is known from two earlier Alexandrine *synchôrêseis, BGU* IV 1102 and 1103 (already cited), and one much later Oxyrhynchite text, *P.Oxy.* XLIII 3139 (all other dowry-receipt clauses are formulated with the present infinitive). Seeing that the couple's "marriage contract" was executed in Alexandria, we may suggest the provenance of the present text is Alexandria or a place influenced by its notarial practice.

The parties are Roman citizens. The woman is assisted by a tutor (*kyrios*), her brother C. Petronius Marcellus. Roman women became quite independent juridically toward the end of the Republic; still a guardian's authorization was needed – at least purely formally – for them to conduct more important transactions (cf. **3.3.5**, **4.3.2**), as in this case where a considerable sum is at issue. The document is made in two copies; the other was kept by the woman as a proof of her right to proceed for the remaining 600 drachmas. The parties assure publicity of the act as well.

> Petronia Sarapias, with as *kyrios* her brother Gaius Petronius Marcellus, to Iulius Apolinarios, soldier of the First Apamean Cohort of the century of Iulianus, greetings.
>
> I acknowledge (*homologô*) that I have received from you four hundred drachmas of silver according to the public standard, which I brought you as a dowry, from your own hands, retaining the right to the

remaining six hundred drachmas. The document was written in a double copy without additions and cancellations and be it lawful as if it were deposited in a public registry. In the eighth year of Emperor Caesar Titus Aelius Hadrianus Antoninus Augustus Pius, Pharmouthi 10.

(*2nd hand*) I, Petronia Sarapias, with as *kyrios* my brother Gaius Petronius Marcellus, am getting back four hundred silver drachmas into the account of my dowry, retaining the right to six hundred drachmas, as stated above.

I, Gaius Petronius Marcellus, have been inscribed as *kyrios* of my sister, and have signed for her as she is illiterate.

4.2.2 Divorce settlement

P.Stras. III 142 (= *SB* V 8024, tr. Evans Grubbs 2002: 215) (Arsinoite nome, 16 October AD 391)

4.2.2 may be characterized as a classic example of a divorce settlement. It bears some interesting features. The series of laconic elliptical sentences present in the earlier acts is substituted for here by much more elaborate proclamations (especially in the cases of the quitclaim clause and the separation clause), much closer in style to the sixth-century Byzantine documents from Aphrodito than to its second- and third-century counterparts from the Fayyum.

Two points are of particular interest here. First, in a true spirit of amicable divorce, neither of the parties is blamed for the separation; instead an "evil daimon" bears the guilt. *Prima facie* the flavor of this reference seems very Christian. It is found repeatedly in all the later divorce settlements. But the first occurrence of the daimon as the cause of divorce dates to AD 305, in *P. Grenf.* II 76, a divorce settlement between Soulis and Senpsais, two probably pagan gravediggers.

The other curious feature of **4.2.2** is that Allous, the wife, was assisted by her mother. It is not the only act in which an ex-wife is aided by her mother. Recall as one instance *P.Ness.* III 57, mentioned in this section's introduction. In addition, **4.2.4**, along with Diocletian's admonition quoted above in note 17, shows that a mother may have played an important role in her daughter's divorce. Obviously, as argued above, deciding upon her daughter's divorce or marriage was not a mother's *legal* prerogative; it should rather be understood in terms of social influence, as prevails till this very day in some communities. Our instance is different, however. Nothing in **4.2.2** hints at the active undertaking of Apina: it is Allous herself who has divorced her husband. Apina's presence may be explained by the settlement nature of the deed. In the fourth century AD mothers had already obtained the right of guardianship (curatorship to be more precise) over their children, specifically when there was no other close relative to undertake such duties. Any act of disposition (and such is, par excellence, a renouncement of claims) of a person younger than twenty-five had to be approved by a *curator*; otherwise, in virtue of the mid-republican *Lex Laetoria*, it might have been declared void as potentially harmful to the minor's estate. It is true that Apina is not termed as a curatress. But her presence is described by the word *metasynestôs* ("standing together with"), normally denoting legal assistance to an act. It may have been that Apina had to approve of the final renunciation of claims, and hence she was present when the transaction was executed.

During the consulship of Tatianus, the most illustrious prefect of the Holy Praetorium, and of Flavius Symmachus, the most illustrious, on the 18th of Phaophi of the 5th indiction.

Aurelia Allous daughter of Onnophrios, assisted by her mother Aurelia Apina, from the village Nestos of the Arsinoite nome, to Aurelius Elias son of Ariston, from the village Onniton of the same nome. After I, Allous, lived with you, Elias, for some time, it seemed best, by reason of an evil daimon [that] came suddenly upon us, that (we), being freed from our married life, go away; and because of this I, Allous, acknowledge that I do not have any claim against you, Elias, in regard to our married life, and any other written or unwritten debt or demand, charge, search, once and for all, completely; and that you, Elias, have power to contract another marriage without being reproached for that; and let the divorce (*per[i]lusis*) be [valid?] and being asked formally (of the above) I have given my consent. Aurelia Allous, the above, assisted by her mother Apina has given. . .

The remainder is much damaged; it does include evidence of the familiar illiteracy clause in its last line.

Verso: divorce (*[per]ilusis*) of Allous daughter of Onnophrios

4.2.3 Divorce settlement

P.Cair.Masp. II 67153 (= *P.Cair.Masp.* III 67253) (Antinoopolis, 7 May AD 568)

4.2.3 is a divorce settlement of Aurelius Menas, son of Horouonchis and Tsia, probably a cabbage-seller, and Aurelia Maria, daughter of Victor and Herais. We luckily possess its duplicate copy (*P.Cair.Masp.* II 67253) executed by the woman for the ex-husband. The text bears far-reaching lexical and formulary similarities to the other seven divorce documents coming from the archives of Dioskoros, the lawyer and poet from Aphrodito.[23] Its style is highly elaborate, full of synonyms and tautologies, but its object is exactly the same as its earlier counterparts'. The deed therefore contains a separation clause and a quitclaim clause. The formulation of the latter corresponds perfectly to the renunciation clauses in the settlements of claims (see for example a particularly rich formulation in *P.Münch.* I 1, lines 32–42, Syene, 11 March AD 574). One element of this clause calls for particular attention. Menas gives assurance that "It will not be allowed to me to seek justice with you either in a court or out of it." The meaning of this phrase seems simple enough: the parties not only exclude the possibility of any judicial proceeding in regard to the dissolved union, but also renounce any recourse to private arbitration. A. A. Schiller, however, persuaded by the high number of private arbitrations (see **10.5–6**) and the absence of records of judicial proceedings in civil law cases in Byzantine Egypt (see **10.3**, cf. **10.4.5** and **1.8**), deemed this formulation to be purely ornamental.[24]

By a penalty clause the parties subject themselves to a fine of no less than six *solidi* of gold, should they transgress the terms of the agreement. The question of the reality of such a harsh penalty remains open, but research on the settlements of claims allows some indications that these could have been actually exacted (cf. *P.Münch.* I 14 with Urbanik 2007). Finally, let us observe that neither *P.Cair.Masp.* II 67153 nor 67253 constitutes a legally binding act as they both lack witnesses' subscriptions, unlike, for example, 67155, a settlement of divorce between Aurelius Sarapion and Aurelia Maria. Both texts must have been copied by Dioskoros for the use of his law office if not for purposes of scholarly reference.

> + During the reign and consulship of our most pious lord Flavius Iustinus, the eternal Augustus and Emperor, in the third year, Pachon the twelfth, at the beginning of the second indiction, in Antinoopolis the most splendid.

[23] *P.Cair.Masp.* II 67154 recto, *P.Cair.Masp.* II 67155, *P.Lond.* V 1712, *P.Lond.* V 1713 (the other copy of *P.Flor.* I 93 = *M.Chr.* 297), *P.Cair.Masp.* III 67311 (all from Antinoopolis), *P.Cair.Masp.* I 67121 (Aphrodito). For a marriage contract from this archive see **4.1.3**.

[24] See Schiller (1971); *contra* Simon (1971) and Urbanik (2007).

+ Aurelius Menas son of Horouonchis, of mother Tsia, *krampis* (a cabbage-seller?) from Antinoopolis, to Aurelia Maria daughter of Victor,[25] once joined to me as wife, would that this had never happened!, of the same city.

I am preparing and sending you this deed (*repoudion* = Latin *repudium*) of divorce (*apozugê*)[26] in the following words: I was earlier joined together with you for marriage and community of life in hopes for the best and for procreation of children wishing to complete with you a peaceful and holy married life. On the contrary, I do not know for what reason, because of some malicious and evil daimon, some odious hate has arisen between us two and has caused us to separate one from another as to our common married life and no longer to live in the same household with one another any further in the future. And in accordance with this I, the above-written Menas, acknowledge,[27] by this my written act of divorce (*dialysis*), that is, separation (*diaisis*), that neither have I nor will I have any claim against you henceforth from this time at any time in regard to any matter written or unwritten, either in regard to marriage, or *hedna* (bridal gifts), or expenses in marriage, or dowry, or any house furniture whatsoever brought in by one side for the other's benefit; because of the fact that I have been released and divorced with respect to you on all counts, and you with respect to me on all counts; and that it shall not be allowed to me to seek justice against you either in court or out of it, regarding any matter small or large, concerning anything at all; and that it shall be allowed to either one of us to join in another marriage, because both of us have sent this act of divorce (*repoudion*) to one another. And if it should happen that one of us breach these above-written things and proceed against the other one regarding any matter whatsoever, the party in breach shall render to the non-breaching one six(?) gold *solidi* according to the public standard of Antinoo(polis), that will be really and unconditionally executed[28] and that

[25] The version of *P.Cair.Masp.* II 67253 reads in lines 5–8: "+ Aurelia Maria, daughter of Victor, of mother Herais, from the city of Antinoe to Aurelius Menas son of Horouonchios, once joined to me as husband, would that this had never happened!, who happens to be *krampitês* [cabbage-seller *or* grower] originating from the same Antinoopolis."

[26] Lit. "this repudiation of divorce/separation/release": the papyrus actually uses two synonyms, a Latinism *repoudion* and its exact Greek counterpart.

[27] *P.Cair.Masp.* II 67253 reads in line 16: "I, the above-written Maria, acknowledge . . .".

[28] Cf. *P.Münch.* I 4, line 34 with L. Wenger's commentary and the English translation in *The Elephantine Papyri in English*, D34, p. 489 and n. 23, where *ergo kai dynamei* is rendered by "by (court) judgment and authority." According to Berger (1911: 97–99) the formulation had no practical meaning and was a typical repetition. Wenger, with caution, referred to St. Braßloff's idea, 'Zu den Quellen der byzantinischen Rechtsgeschichte: II. Zur Gesichte der Konventionalstrafe',

will be paid with no protest, without (a need of) trial or court decision and without quibble of any kind. And the letter of this repudiation (*repoudion*) we have executed for each other twice in writing and we have issued it with the signature of the one[29] who is signing in our behalf, and having been asked the formal question we have consented. + I, Aurelius Menas son of Horouonchios, the cabbage-seller(?), the above-written, have made this deed of divorce (*to repoudion tês dialuseôs*) under all the inscribed conditions on the penalty, as stated above. + I, Aurelius Magistor son of Horouonchios from Anti(noopolis), having been asked, have signed for him since he does not know letters, him being in my presence and having spoken to me face to face, as stated above.

Fourth century *AD* documents relating to unilateral divorces

The three following texts, two petitions (**4.2.4–5**) and a report of legal proceedings (**4.2.6**), introduce data on the unilateral dissolution of marital unions. Even more interesting, they all date to the fourth century AD, the time of great change in Roman marriage law owing to the limits Constantine imposed on divorces. **4.2.4** (AD 362) is a petition of Aurelius Serenos directed against his mother-in-law. Apparently, the woman had deceitfully caused her daughter's return and given her into a new marriage. In **4.2.5** (AD 363) a husband demands the arrest of his wife, who has deserted him and stolen his things. A similar situation can be found in two more petitions: the above-discussed petition of the maltreated Christian wife, *P.Oxy.* VI 903 (last quarter of the fourth century AD, Oxyrhynchos), and the complaint of Aurelia Herais, expelled from her marriage home by her husband (*PSI* I 41, roughly fourth century AD, Antinoopolis). In all four petitions the petitioner, notwithstanding the actual desertion of the spouse, still terms him or her as husband or wife. Scholars have used these texts to advocate for the successful application of Constantine's reform,[30]

ZSS 25, pp. 302 ff., who had thought the possibility of using the extra-court help of a judge "tatsächlich (*ergo*) und mit Hilfe der staatlichen Gewalt (*dynamis*) d.i. vom Richter eingetrieben werden," finally opting for a possible facilitation of the execution, but without a firm conviction. As there are no examples of such state aid aimed at execution of a conventional penalty, I have chosen to translate this clause as suggested by Preisigke, *WB* ("unbedingt und tatsächlich").

29 [At this point the document shows its first sign of confusion, losing the sense that it is being drafted with both parties in cooperation (indicated by grammatical plurals) and continuing (or so it seems) as if its only client is Menas (with singulars; some late plurals in the translation are based on editorially resolved abbreviations). Note that we have only the subscription for Menas by his subscriber, none for Maria. – eds.]

30 Cf. Levy (1925: 122); Merklein (1967: 60). Differently: Erdmann (1941: 53–54).

seeing in them proof that desertion of a spouse did not result in divorce, as unilateral divorces had been made illegal. Such an approach, however, seems problematic.

In fact, both **4.2.4** and **4.2.5** may post-date the possible repeal of Constantine's legislation by Julian. But such a consideration, especially in view of the merely hypothetical suggestion of Julian's return to the customs of the forefathers, may still seem inconclusive. More importantly, neither Constantine nor any of his successors until Justinian dared to declare illegal divorces to be void. They were punishable, but nonetheless still effective. Thus, there must be some other explanation of the petitioners' perception of their troublesome partners as still married to them. I would suggest that even if their marriages had legally ended (in the case of Herais ten years before the petition!), they were not ready to accept it. The Christian wife of *P.Oxy.* VI 903 and Herais of *PSI* I 41 probably decided only with the present petitions to give up hope of reconciliation; hence Herais' lament uses the expressions typically found in the divorce documents: "had I not looked at him, had I not been united with him at the beginning." In **4.2.4** Serenos sees Tamounis as his lawfully wedded wife because her mother had no right to take her away. The deserted and robbed husband in **4.2.5** might have still not decided for divorce; he is more concerned with the things snatched by his wife than with the future of his marriage. Curiously, however, he accuses his wife of having performed an "illegal exit." This might be – with due reservations as the document is dated to Julian's last regnal year – the only indication of Constantine's norm in practice.

There is one more direct reference to "the laws." In **4.2.6** Olympiane's attorney suggests that she obtained the right to divorce her husband once he deserted her. The date of the document is problematic again. Nevertheless, even if the original text (most probably we have at our disposal a copy made for scholarly use) had been executed under the rule of *CTh* 3.16.1, this mention does not find any plausible explanation. Constantine allowed women to repudiate their husbands in case of three very specific grave crimes: homicide, poisoning (or magic), and destruction of tombs. Any minor offenses, like a husband's womanizing, drunkenness, or gaming-addiction, were not enough: leaving a husband under these pretexts was labelled as "deprived debauchery." It is obvious therefore that Olympiane's attorney cannot have meant the Constantinian regulation.

I suggest therefore that we cannot draw from the papyrological material any conclusion as to the efficacy of Constantine's reform. We also have to bear in mind that with consensual divorce still permitted, the party willing to divorce might still be able to induce the other to separate, be it by financial or social means. An adequate parallel may be provided by the so-called "ransom divorce" practiced under Koranic or Talmudic law, a situation in which the woman, forfeiting her dowry, persuades her husband to divorce her.

4.2.4 Petition for unilateral divorce

P.Cair.Preis. 2–3 (Hermopolis, AD 362). Image at Papyri.info.

4.2.4, surviving in two almost identical copies, was addressed to the police officials, *riparii*, of the Hermopolite nome. The translation is based on the version of *P.Cair.Preis.* 3, as it bears a very interesting variant of the text at the end of line 13 of the original Greek text.

Serenos complains that during his absence for a business trip his mother-in-law gave his wife Tamounis to another man. Serenos had married Tamounis six years before; on that occasion she received *hedna* (bridal gifts). The unlucky husband claims to have tried to fulfill his marital duties as well as he could. After three years of married life, the evil mother-in-law intervened, taking Tamounis back to her home under pretenses of her daughter's possession by a daimon.

The translation of the concluding, much disputed, lines of the papyrus depends on their reconstruction. In the translation I have preferred the restoration suggested by Beaucamp ("[the mother-in-law] has given this (my) wife to another man without [her consent]")[31] to the one postulated by Yiftach-Firanko ("without [a document/dutiful proceeding of divorce]")[32] and to the one suggested in *Berichtigungsliste* I ("without [my consent]"). As for the latter proposal: it would be bizarre to expect that Serenos would put forward that invalidity of his divorce depended on lack of his approval of the new marriage. I repeat: unilateral divorces even in the times of Constantine's reform were still effective even if sanctionable. An ex-consort never had the prerogative to give consent to the subsequent marriage of his/her former partner. The former restoration does not convince either in view of the lack of any compulsory divorce proceeding whether in papyrological practice or under imperial law; as stated above, a document of divorce, at least until the reform of Theodosius II, was by no means obligatory. It is therefore more plausible that the petitioner

[31] Beaucamp (1992: 122 with n. 117). [32] Yiftach-Firanko (2003: 217 with n. 77).

regards the divorce as invalid because it was imposed by the mother, who (*contra* Taubenschlag 1929: 330 and n. 37) never had the prerogative to dissolve her daughter's union – unless, of course, the daughter approved. In such a case, in the line of the precedents cited by Dionysia, separation would be considered to have been executed and wished for by the daughter herself.

Unfortunately the document breaks off before exposition of the object of the petition, so we do not know whether Serenos has given up the idea of marriage with Tamounis altogether and demanded back only the *hedna* and the expenses, or whether he has claimed the return back home of his wife as well.

> During the consulship of Mamertinus and Nevitta, the most illustrious. To Aurelii Nilos son of Gennadios and Theodoros son of Komasios,[33] the *riparii* of the Hermopolite nome, from Aurelius Serenos son of Pinoution from the village Enseu in the same Hermopolite nome. Six years ago I married a wife, Tamounis by name, [born] from her father Demetrios and I gave to the same wife the customarily given bridal gifts (*hedna*), and I fulfilled the laws of marriages and the custom of marriages, and I lived three years of married life with her. But the mother of the above-written fooled me that my wife was possessed by a daimon. Therefore, when I was away from home on personal business, as I was looking for an opportunity to make my life longer, she (the mother) gave the same spouse to another man of name Paeuti from the village Achilleus of the same Hermopolite (nome) without [her consent?] . . .

The object of the petition is lost, as also in the copy, *P.Cair.Preis.* 2.

4.2.5 Petition to the *stratêgos*

P.Lond. V 1651 (Hermopolis, 20 April AD 363)

4.2.5, submitted by Aurelius Dios against his wife Hermione, brings out a little family scandal. When Dios was away, Hermione left the marital household taking away some valuable objects belonging to him. Dios seems especially worried ("not being able to sit in peace") that the woman

33 The papyrus actually gives the patronymic in the dative, but Wilcken in *Archiv* 3 (1905: 115) already pointed out the mistake.

has also robbed some important documents: loans and the deed of sale of (his?) house, which as we know from the Byzantine sales of real estate (e.g., **6.6.1**) constituted proof of ownership and was transmitted to the new owner. In line 10 Dios accuses his wife of having performed an illegal exit. This might be the only indication in the documents of the Constantinian norm in actual legal practice (see above). Dios was certainly interested in encumbering his (former) wife with the gravest accusations: he requests her arrest until the "fortunate" arrival of the *praeses* (civil governor) of the Thebaid, who will be able to decide the lawsuit. Dios was probably contemplating the possibility of summoning Hermione by means of an *actio rerum amotarum*, used in cases of theft between spouses. The regular action for theft, the *actio furti* as infamatory, was not admissible.

During the consulship of our lord Julianus the eternal Augustus for the 4th time and Flavius Sallustius, the most illustrious prefect of the Holy Praetorium.

To Aurelius Hermeias son of Heliodoros, leading councilor and sitting *stratêgos* of Hermopolis the most illustrious, from Aurelius Dios son of Apollon of the same city. Since the month of Mesore my wife Hermione, having waited for me to be absent, as I was spending time at a village, took away all things that were in our house, including essential records (*anangkaia biblia*), and, sneaking off, she has committed an illegal exit. And many times I kept sending [. . .] Then when it all turned out that [. . .] and above all she did not give back the deeds of sale of my house property (*oikopeda*). Therefore, I, not being able to sit in peace, submit to your Sagacity this petition (*biblia*), asking that she be brought from whatever place and kept in custody until the fortunate arrival of my lord most eminent *praeses* Cerealis Telephios Hierokles, as I am intending on making a petition (*entuchia*) about this. Farewell!

In the above-mentioned consulship, Pharmouthi 25. I, Aurelius Dios son of Apollon, have submitted. I, Aurelius Olkoueis son of Pathermouthis, have written for him as he does not know letters.

4.2.6 Courtroom speech on behalf of an abandoned orphan

P.Lips. I 41 (= *M.Chr.* 300) (Hermopolis, last quarter of the fourth century AD)

4.2.6, dated by its palaeography and context, is a copy of a courtroom speech with occasional insertions by a second hand. In the speech, the attorney Nilammon represents Olympiane, an orphan deserted by her husband Besarion. A few years before, the girl married Besarion with her *curator*'s consent. The groom, who was not ready to provide the customary marriage gifts that he had promised, executed an IOU to secure the fulfillment of the matrimonial promises. When the wife, assisted by her *curator*, requested the promise's fulfillment, Besarion left the "family hearth," taking some of his wife's property that he probably later sold (if we understand correctly lines 11–12 of the Greek text). The attorney warns that the woman thereby has obtained the right to divorce the man. As argued above, **4.2.4**, this renunciation is not very clear: if the document dates back to the times of Constantine's ban on divorce, a mere desertion did not constitute a rightful ground (*iusta causa*) for divorce. Since the attorney cannot have addressed the marriage document (our document preserves the last mention of a marriage started without a document, *agraphos gamos*), can he possibly have had in mind the terms of the IOU mentioned at the beginning of his speech? At the end of his discourse Nilammon petitions that the *hedna* finally be delivered, the stolen things returned, and marital harmony restored.

It is interesting to observe the *curator*'s role in the whole story. He seems to have taken the place of the woman's late father. Kastor was asked for Olympiane's hand. According to Wilcken (1913), he also may have received some gifts on the occasion of the engagement, just as a father would. Mitteis' interpretation of the *hedna* in lines 4 and 5, *M.Chr.* 300, that the former would be the bridal gifts promised by the groom, the latter the counter-gifts actually presented by the girl, is unconvincing: *hedna*, a technical term, always means the gifts provided by the groom.

According to Mitteis (*P.Lips.*, p. 140), the *curator* also had to give consent to the girl's divorce. This, however, seems quite strange, especially in view of *Dig.* 24.2.4, which expressly excludes such a prerogative even in case of the ward's insanity (see Urbanik 2002). Either we are dealing here with an application of local rules contradictory to imperial law (cf. *Liber Syro-Romanus* § 81 [ed. Selb and Kaufhold]), or perhaps a *curator* was needed because a ward's divorce implied financial settlements and these had to be approved by the guardian (see introduction to **4.2.2** as well). I reject the alternative restoration hesitantly offered by Wilcken (1908: 475–76) in favor of the original editor's reconstruction.

Ni(lammon?) for Olympiane daughter of Dionysios the ex-*primipilaris*,
with as *curator* Kastor, the councilor of the illustrious city of
Hermopolites. The ward is an orphan by both parents. And since her

curator, the above-named[34] Kastor, was asked with some gifts[35] by a certain Besarion, ex-*beneficiarius* of this holy office,[36] to take the girl for himself (as wife) – if she wanted so – the *curator* with the consent of the ward welcomed the unwritten-marriage of the ward upon the condition of agreeable marriage-gifts (to be given to the bride). But because the groom[37] was not ready to provide the gifts, he issued a document for the ward[38] with her guardian, so they thought that he would provide the gifts in accordance with the security[39] of the document, on which account they contracted the marriage. These things having been done and the marriage on these terms [. . .] having been arranged – but not for long. After he (the groom) formed the intention to demand return of the gifts from the *curator* and the bride herself, with what intention we do not know, he did not give them, but he even left the family hearth in which the marriage had been completed, taking away with him not only his own things, but also some of his wife's. And now he has not only not given the gift, but he also owes, and moreover he has sold (things belonging) to the wife but still has got (their value) in money, and having let her live just by herself, he has gone away. So that according to the laws it is allowed to her, putting forward these demands, and assisted by her *curator*, to send him away: first of all that the gift owed by writing be given to her, and then that the things he has carried away, he will restore to the home-place. If these things are thus accomplished, the harmony of the marriage will also likely be restored.

4.3 The Romanization of family law

Antti Arjava

The Egyptian papyri can be used to investigate many aspects of the family that would be difficult or impossible to investigate elsewhere – for example, the demographic structure of families in a Roman province.[40] Another fundamental question, and one to be addressed in this section, is

[34] "above-named" according to Wilcken clearly refers to the fact that we deal here with a court speech. Instead of the usual "above-written," the author uses a rare *pro-onomazo*: Olympiane's guardian has already been named during the proceedings, in the earlier part of the document which is now lost.

[35] For discussion between Wilcken and Mitteis on the understanding of the *hedna* in these places, see the preceding paragraphs. The text begins with *hedna* in the plural before shifting to *hednon* in the singular.

[36] Presumably the provincial *officium* of the Thebaid, of which Dionysios, as ex-*primipilaris*, had also been a member.

[37] Lit. "the one willing to marry."

[38] Lit. "to the one who is presently under the guardianship."

[39] *pistis* in Greek, Latin *fides*.

[40] Bagnall and Frier (1994).

when and how far family life in the outlying regions of the empire was Romanized. Evidence from late antiquity suggests that in the course of time a substantial part of the empire's inhabitants had adopted the Roman family model, with many of its legal peculiarities, including the strong position of women. To understand the beginnings of this development, we should focus our attention on the third century, around the time of the universal grant of the Roman citizenship in AD 212 by the *Constitutio Antoniniana*. Fortunately, this is also the period when the papyri from Egypt are the most abundant. On the basis of this material, legal historians have concluded that in Egypt Roman private law was adopted only to a small extent, and hardly at all before Diocletian's reforms at the end of the third century;[41] but owing to the accumulation of new evidence, this idea, as the examples presented below will show, needs revision. (See also above, **3.3**.) Lastly, family law in the provinces is part of an even wider picture. If we get some idea of the way the legal rules were put into practice in one province, this contributes to a better understanding of how the empire as a whole was governed and to a clearer sense of the extent to which it was legally and socially integrated.

To observe cases of Romanization in any provincial society, it is important to determine how far the Roman family differed from other family models in the Mediterranean area. Many differences in customs between cultures are only minor details when seen from a wider perspective. Thus, in the work of the anthropologist Jack Goody, the Roman, Greek, Germanic, Near Eastern, and Chinese families are closely related subgroups within the Eurasian family system; the real continental divide was between it and the African system.[42] That is why a study of Romanization must concentrate on those aspects of family life where a difference between Roman and indigenous practice is sufficiently clear.

The best example of this is sibling marriages, certainly the most peculiar feature of Romano-Egyptian families. Such marriages, between siblings and half-siblings, were so frequent in the second century that perhaps one-fourth of the married population lived in brother–sister unions. As far as we know, this was not a Pharaonic custom but a novelty of the Greco-Roman period. In Roman law, close-kin marriages were criminally incestual, not tolerated among citizens, though the authorities evidently did not try to prevent them among non-citizens in Egypt. Brother–sister marriages disappear from Egyptian documents around AD 212, certainly

[41] E.g., Wolff (2002: 6–7, 148–9; cf. 113–48), Maehler (2005: 137–40).
[42] Goody (1990), cf. Bremen (1996: 202).

as a consequence of the *Constitutio Antoniniana*. Marriages contracted before it may have been allowed to continue; the custom may have survived longer though concealed in the documents.[43] It is as yet an open question how far the Egyptian population faced the vastly increasing infant mortality and grave genetic disorders that would be the expected biological consequences of close inbreeding.[44]

Another major area where the influence of imperial law can be traced is guardianship. In Roman law of the early third century, a guardian (*tutor*) was responsible for every orphan below puberty (twelve years for girls, fourteen for boys). After that, a *curator* was appointed for young people until they were twenty-five years old. Women received additionally another kind of guardian, *tutor mulieris*, though he had only a passive role.[45] In Greek legal culture, there were originally two types of guardians. An *epitropos* took care of orphan children up to puberty; a *kyrios* supervised the affairs of adult women. Accordingly, the only guardians we meet in Roman Egypt before the third century were *epitropoi* and *kyrioi*. The first *curator* appears just before AD 212 (*BGU* III 705), but he is a lonely exception because he was linked with a Roman citizen who was probably not a native of Egypt. The next *curator* is recorded in the published papyri only in AD 231/2 (*SB* XXII 15868). Obviously the Roman system of guardianship had not been adopted very quickly, or at least not so widely that it would be reflected in the surviving material. Beginning in AD 249, we find several *curatores* in the documents (as in **4.3.1** below). They continued into the fourth century, when the terms for guardianship, for unknown reasons, disappeared from the papyri. Hence, it appears that around the mid-third century the Roman rules for guardianship and the Latin loan-word *curator*, together with the Roman concept of legal majority, had become an acknowledged part of life in Egypt.[46]

The Greek word *kyrios* was used for a guardian of adult women both in the Greek tradition and in Roman law. Thus, if a document after AD 212 used the word *kyrios* without further explanation, it may be difficult to know if the people thought they were following Roman law or their old

43 Hopkins (1980); Bagnall and Frier (1994: 127–34), Scheidel (1995), Wolff (2002: 128). For Roman attitudes towards close-kin marriage, see Gaius, *Inst.* 1.58–64; *Dig.* 23.2.57a, 48.5.39.4; *Coll.* 6.4 (295) and 6.5 (291); Evans Grubbs (2002: 136–43). The Gnomon of the *Idios Logos*, *BGU* V 1210 §23 (second century AD, an extract of which is at **2.6.4**), contains a direct ban on sibling marriage for Roman citizens in Egypt.

44 Scheidel (1996: 9–51). See now also Huebner (2007), Remijsen and Clarysse (2008), Rowlandson and Takahashi (2009).

45 Gaius, *Inst.* 1.190; Arjava (1996: 112–18).

46 Arjava (1999a); cf. also Wolff (2002: 155–56).

local customs or if the result was some kind of mixture of these. Often the guardian in the papyri is styled "guardian according to Roman custom," to avoid confusion with the local guardianship. Moreover, in the middle of the third century several papyri show women approaching the prefect of Egypt and requesting that a guardian be appointed "according to the Julian and Titian Laws and the decree of the Senate," as the proper Roman formula went (see above, **3.3.5**, below, **4.3.2**). Before the *Constitutio Antoniniana*, when women approached regional magistrates to ask for a guardian in their traditional law, they used a different formula, stressing that the guardian was meant for just one specific transaction.[47]

There was one important feature of Roman guardianship that distinguished it from all comparable systems: ever since the Augustan marriage laws it was possible for women to receive an exemption by giving birth to three living children. The *ius liberorum* was widely known in the eastern Mediterranean, especially after AD 212 (as in the petition **4.3.3** below). In dozens of papyri women are said to "act without a guardian by the right of children."[48] Besides Roman legal texts and the Egyptian papyri, the *ius liberorum* appears generally in the third century in Greek inscriptions of the eastern Mediterranean.[49]

Roman influence can be seen indirectly also in the decreasing number of those women who actually had a guardian in third-century AD Egypt. Documents where women record that they act "with a guardian" are frequent in the period before the *Constitutio Antoniniana* and continue so for some two decades after it. There are over one hundred cases from between AD 181 and 235. But then the evidence dwindles. From between AD 236 and 310 there are only twelve documents where a *kyrios* is present. The decline after the decade AD 231–40 is significant compared with the overall distribution of datable papyri (see Figure 8).[50] From the same period, AD 236–310, we know over fifty women who announce that the

[47] E.g., *P.Oxy.* I 56 (= *M.Chr.* 320, *Jur.Pap.* 15, Evans Grubbs 2002: 35–36); see further Rupprecht (1986). For the competent magistrates, see Gaius, *Inst.* 1.185; *Dig.* 1.20.2, 38.17.2.23.

[48] Sijpesteijn (1965), Arjava (1996: 112–23, 1997), Sheridan (1996), Beaucamp (1992: 193–267), Evans Grubbs (2002: 37–43), Wolff (2002: 134–36). See Figure 8.

[49] Syria: *P.Euphr.* 15 (parchment), in Feissel and Gascou (2000: 189–92). Asia Minor: *TAM* III 383, 482, 669, 705, 714, V 1126; *SEG* IV 544, XLI 1270; Marek (2006, no. 171). Greece: *IG* V 586, 589, 596, 603, 608. Macedonia: *IG* X.2.2 18A; Gounaropoulou and Hatzopoulos (1998, nos. 51–53); Petsas *et al.* (2000, nos. 6, 27, 52, 73, 76, 89, 91, 92; cf. p. 41). For Moesia, see Feissel and Gascou (2000: 189 n. 134).

[50] The numbers of papyri with a guardian derive from a search in the DDBDP, supplemented with papyri published after 1995. The numbers of papyri with the *ius liberorum* are based on Sheridan (1996: 118–24), with the addition of *P.Graux* II 17–19; *P.Hamb.* IV 279; *P.Kell.* I 19a App.; *P.Lips.* II 151; *P.Matr.* 5; *P.Neph.* 28; *P.Oxy.* LXV 4489; *SB* XVIII 13305, XXII 15604 = *SP* XX 74. I have omitted

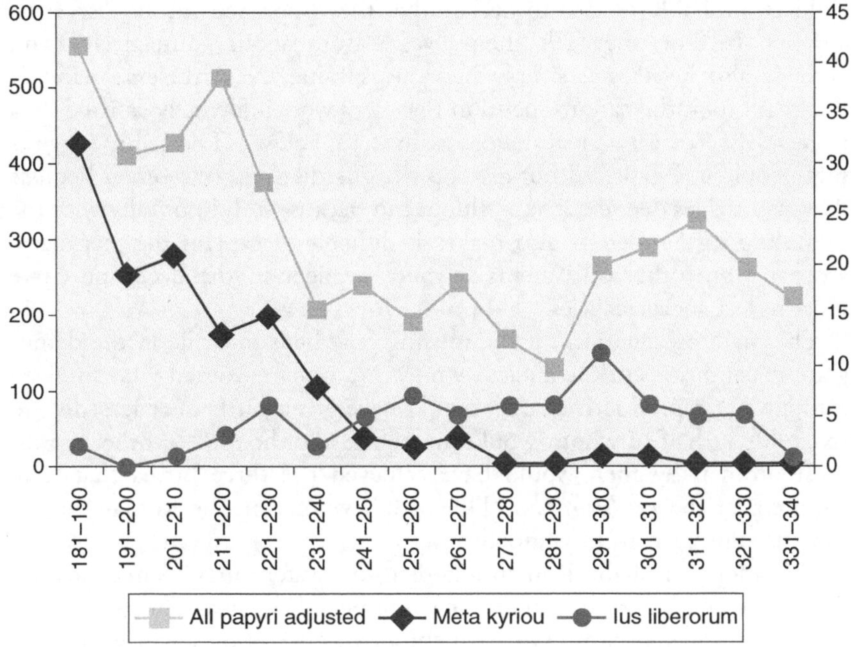

Fig. 8. Number of papyri per decade, AD 181–340, in which women appear acting with and without guardians

ius liberorum exempted them from guardianship, and there is no comparable decrease in their number.

Admittedly, in practice there were not many occasions on which Roman law required a guardian's presence. For example, alienation of provincial land did not need his authorization. The making of a last will was the most important legal act that could not be performed without a guardian. There are two papyri in the third century that display women's wills, *P.Princ.* II 38 and *P.Lips.* 29 (= *M.Chr.* 318). The first woman has a guardian, and the second appeals to the *ius liberorum*. In general, however, mothers of three

P.Bad. 24 (Sheridan 1996, no. 16) as too uncertain. In Sheridan no. 35, *P.Oxy.* XIV 1637 is a misprint for XLVII 3354. There are also a few inaccurate datings in Sheridan's list, as compared with the actual stand of the Heidelberger Gesamtverzeichnis (August 2006). The curve of all papyri from Egypt is adjusted from the Gesamtverzeichnis by omitting, besides *P.Dura*, many large homogeneous archives that have no relevance for this question but distort the statistics (like *P.Bub.* and *P.Panop.Beatty*), recording names or prices, etc. The most important omission is the Heroninos correspondence in the decades between 241 and 270; the other adjustments tend mainly to flatten the curve, without affecting its general shape. It should be clear that the resulting curve is only a very rough guide.

children probably tended to declare that they possessed the *ius liberorum* anyway, because they felt themselves unsure about Roman law, and perhaps also because it simply had status value. Nevertheless, many of them still took the care to mention that they were informally assisted by a male relative or an acquaintance (as in **4.3.1** below). The habit suggests that people in Egypt did not give up the guardianship of women because they themselves deemed it superfluous but because it did not tally with the prevailing legal order. It also makes it difficult to explain the guardians' absence from other documents by pure negligence: the declining curve must reflect social realities.

The main explanation for the missing guardians must lie in the demographic conditions of the ancient world. An average woman who survived through her reproductive career would have given birth to at least five to six children, half of whom would die before adulthood.[51] In other words, most ordinary women would have achieved the three births that were required for the *ius liberorum*. Thus, adult women in the Roman empire were usually freed from guardianship.[52]

The adoption of the Roman guardianship system may seem a positive development because it reduced the number of women who were compelled to have guardians. The frequent appearance of other male supporters indicates that the change was not so radical. Males continued to advise and control their female relatives, but in an unofficial manner. Although a woman could now refuse to have anyone assisting her, our sources are not likely to have explicitly recorded such cases.

The father's dominant position is a further area where a clear difference existed between Roman law and practically all the other family systems in the ancient Mediterranean.[53] The Roman father exercised an almost absolute authority, *patria potestas*, over his descendants until his own death. They had no independent ownership rights: everything they acquired through purchase, gift, or inheritance, became legally his property. True, as Roman men married relatively late and died early by modern standards, most adult Romans had already lost their fathers when they reached their full majority at the age of twenty-five. Moreover, the father could release his descendants from *potestas* by a procedure called *emancipatio*, making them as independent as if he had died. Emancipation was rarely mentioned in the Latin literary sources of the early empire; it seems to have been an exceptional measure, motivated by political or familial reasons.

51 See, e.g., Bagnall and Frier (1994: 138–39).

52 Arjava (1996: 114–16).

53 See Gaius, *Inst.* 1.55; Arjava (1998).

In the Byzantine period there was a tendency to emancipate children when they reached adulthood, though it always remained a father's personal decision. This habit may have had its origins in the third century, when an increasing number of new citizens were trying to cope with Roman family law in their everyday lives.

The most famous quarrel between a father and child in Roman Egypt is the trial of Dionysia in AD 187 (*P. Oxy.* II 237, excerpted in **2.6.2**). Both father and daughter were non-citizens. The case was judged by the prefect, and for her support Dionysia, or her lawyer, duly pleaded several earlier judgments and legal opinions connected with similar cases in the provincial court. Nevertheless, the legal principles to which she refers are not Roman. Above all, she claims that daughters who had been born from an unwritten marriage were more dependent on their father than those who had been born from a written marriage. The precise logic and contents of this rule are not known, but another Oxyrhynchite woman refers to the same principle in her petition from the year AD 223. It is one of those documents that seem to attest good knowledge of imperial law: she cites appropriate rescripts as precedents and appeals to "the law of the Romans." Against this claim, it is confusing that she still adduces the fact of being from a written marriage, an argument that had no meaning in Roman law.[54]

In the papyri of the third century, we have evidence of very good knowledge of *patria potestas* (notably **4.3.4** below), but also many cases where paternal power appears to be treated in a perfunctory or distorted manner (as in **4.3.5** below). According to an older theory, people in Egypt had never really understood *patria potestas*, equating it with the guardianship for minor children.[55] As the connection is never explicitly made in the papyri, it seems more likely that *patria potestas* was often identified with a lifelong guardianship, that is, children owned separate property under the father's supervision. In practice, this did not conflict too harshly with Roman legal requirements, because the same document could be interpreted in different senses. It also remains possible, although few papyri explicitly mention such a practice (see **4.3.4** below),[56] that fathers emancipated their children by some more or less formal method that satisfied the authorities.

[54] *P. Oxy* LXXIII 4961 (AD 223). David Thomas very kindly provided me with the transcript before publication. He also commented on the draft of this section in a most helpful way. For written and unwritten marriages, see most recently Yiftach-Firanko (2003: 81–104). A further quarrel between father and daughter, this time citizens, is discussed in *BGU* VII 1578 (late second or early third century).

[55] Taubenschlag (1916b), followed by many others ever since.

[56] Arjava (1998: 156–59), cf. also Wolff (2002: 139–42).

Every new papyrus must be interpreted in the light of such possibilities. The papyri should also be read against the third-century imperial rescripts of Justinian's Code (*CJ*), addressed mainly to petitioners in the eastern Mediterranean. The rescripts regard *patria potestas* as a commonplace institution that the addressees were assumed to understand without difficulty. This assumption was certainly based on the petitions themselves. Although the petitions are no longer extant, their contents can often be inferred from the rescripts: they had clearly provided detailed legal information on the petitioners' families, including emancipated and unemancipated family members.[57]

In sum, there is substantial evidence that such Roman legal concepts as paternal power, curatorship, and the guardianship of women, or rather the lack of guardianship, had been adopted in the provinces between the third and sixth centuries. We are best informed of affairs in Egypt, but the evidence is sometimes echoed elsewhere, in Palestine, Syria, Asia Minor, North Africa, Spain, and Gaul. In Egypt the *ius liberorum* appears in the sources already in the second century but spreads quickly after AD 212. Brother–sister marriages disappear at the same time. Guardians of women become rare after the AD 230s, *curatores* emerge around the mid-century and paternal power around AD 260. Keeping in mind the low absolute number of cases it is not certain that this reflects accurately the pace of development. But it does indicate that, one or two generations after the *Constitutio Antoniniana*, a significant number of Egyptian families had become conscious of the basic rules of Roman family law. The major shift had therefore clearly taken place before the reign of Diocletian, the alleged hinge of legal Romanization in the papyri. In any case, the relative frequency of documents displaying concepts of Roman family law in the later third and early fourth century is noteworthy, and it is not paralleled by comparable material afterwards. Whether this is only due to the general decrease of documentation or has other reasons is a question that urgently begs an answer.

4.3.1 Sale of land by siblings

P.Vind.Bosw. 6 (cf. *BL* VIII 197) (Hermopolis, AD 250). Image at Papyri.info.

Two brothers and two sisters sell a plot of land, owned in common, through a banker's deed (*diagraphê*). The younger brother has a *curator*.

[57] Arjava (1998: 155–56).

They have thus lost their father and this son is below the age of twenty-five. Both sisters, each having borne three children, are exempt from the guardianship of women. For the ability to write, see **4.3.3** below. Note that the older brother owns a bigger share of the land than the three other children: it may indicate that he was favored in their parents' will. The old Egyptian practice had been to give the eldest son a double share.[58] Primogeniture is not attested in the Roman world, but a few papyri suggest that in Roman Egypt the eldest son may sometimes have received more than his brothers and sisters, though this was by no means a universal habit: often all children received equal shares, as in *P.Oxy.* IX 1208 (**4.3.5** below).

Although the two sisters are formally free from tutelage, they are both assisted by a male: the elder by her husband and the younger by a man who was not her husband. This may indicate that she is currently not married, though it is also possible that her husband is temporarily absent. The presence of male support in cases where women expressly state that they have the *ius liberorum* and need no guardian is common in the papyri of the later third century. Often the assisting male (*synestôs* or *symparôn*) is the woman's husband, as here. The terms probably had no precise legal significance: they meant just any person who was present and supported the woman in her transaction.

The two brothers are mentioned before the two sisters. This may not establish their order of birth, since the women are not said to have a *curator* while the younger brother, named second out of four, did. According to imperial law (see *CJ* 5.37.12, AD 241), the *ius liberorum* did not free women from the need to have a *curator* if they were below legal age. Nevertheless, deviation from the letter of the law remains possible. In *P.Princ.* II 38 (*c.* AD 264, tr. Rowlandson 1998, no. 146) a woman has her husband as her *kyrios* and another male as her *kouratôr* (from the Latin *curator*). This document causes us to puzzle over what precise role the two men played in the transaction.

The present translation reproduces only the subscriptions to the original document (beginning at line 7). These essentially recapitulate the information found in the main text.

(*3rd hand*) We the undersigned are Aurelii Achillianos alias Maximus and Herminos alias Saprion and Demetria alias Tinoutis and Charina alias Artemidora, the two women acting without guardian by the right of

58 Maehler (2005: 133–34).

children according to the Roman custom and able to write, all four being children of Hermes alias Maximus, former *gymnasiarch*, chief priest, and councilor of the great, old, illustrious, and most respectable city of Hermopolis, registered in the Western Fort District. Herminos alias Saprion is accompanied by his *curator* Aurelius Dioskoros alias Menches; for the women, Demetria alias Tinoutis is assisted by her husband Aurelius Apollon alias Areios, former *exêgêtês* and chief priest, and councilor of the same city, while Charina alias Artemidora is assisted by Aurelius Theon son of Hermeinos.

We have been present when this banker's deed (*diagraphê*) was drawn up, and we have sold from now on and forever to Aurelius Maximus alias Korellianos, councilor of the same city, three arouras of obligatory katoikic land belonging to us in the area of Armotnis from the allotment (*klêros*) of Timonides, from three and one-sixth arouras that are part of nine and one-half arouras of undivided katoikic land. Of these arouras Achillianos owns two-fifths, previously separated, and the others in equal parts the remaining three-fifths. These arouras we shall give over to him fit for sowing and fully measured with the standard katoikic measuring cord, free from public compulsory cultivation and any such encumbrance. The neighboring plots are [. . .] in three directions, private land.

The mutually agreed price of one thousand silver drachmas (1,000 dr.) we have received at once in full from the buyer through this banker's deed. The buyer and his beneficiaries will control and govern the land, using and managing it in any way they choose from now on and forever. We the sellers shall be responsible for all the taxes and additional contributions accumulating from previous times up to the past sixth year and the sixth year itself (*sc*. of the Emperor Philippus), while the buyer will be responsible for them since the present 1st year (*sc*. of the Emperor Decius), because to him belong the rents and revenues of the same first year.

We the sellers shall forever confirm with full guarantee the buyer's title to this property, nor shall we or any other in our name bring a legal action against the buyer or against his beneficiaries on account of anything connected with this sale in any way. If we bring a legal action or do not defend his title, the action will be invalid and we, or whoever acts in our name, shall pay to the buyer or to his beneficiaries the damages and expenses, and as a penalty, like a personal debt, double the purchase price and an equal amount to the state, and nevertheless the sale will be valid. We have been formally asked whether all this has taken place correctly and well, and we have agreed to it. In the first year of the Emperor Caesar Gaius Messius Quintus Traianus Decius Pius Felix Augustus, Tybi 21.

(*4th hand*) I, Aurelius Achillianos alias Maximus, son of Hermes alias Maximus, have sold (the land) and received the price and shall guarantee (the sale) as stated. (*5th hand*) I, Aurelius Hermeinos alias Saprion . . .

(the papyrus breaks off)

4.3.2 Request for a guardian

P.Oxy. XXXIV 2710 (Mélèze Modrzejewski 1974: 271; Pestman 1994b: 63) (Oxyrhynchos, AD 261). Image at Papyri.info.

A woman applies for a guardian (*kyrios*) to be appointed for her according to Roman laws. This is the last of a number of similar documents from the third century.[59] Those are bilingual (Latin and Greek), while the present text is a Greek translation from Latin and, as it is broken at the top, may well originally have been preceded by a Latin sentence, as in *P.Oxy.* XII 1466 (**3.3.5** above). To these can be added two Latin wax tablets from second-century Egypt: in each of these the prefect of Egypt nominated a guardian for a woman according to her petition, which had been presented by a male proxy.[60] Finally, there are two tablets from Herculaneum that show Italian municipal magistrates performing the same task in the first century.[61] Most of these have been usefully reprinted and discussed.[62] As far as can be seen, the wording of the requests and grants, with their formal references to the *Lex Julia Titia* and a *senatusconsultum*, followed rather faithfully a common Latin model. Some of the texts additionally specified that the guardian newly appointed upon the woman's request was not intended to replace a legitimate guardian, in case such existed. This phrase is missing in the present document.

Although the original editor of the text modestly commented that "It is of interest chiefly for the form of the date," there is another aspect worth noting: it is the chronologically last clear proof anywhere in the ancient Mediterranean for the requirement that women in the Roman empire have guardians. The requirement was most likely abolished in the AD 320s, on which see Arjava (1996: 116–20).

59 *ChLA* XI 503 (219); *P.Mich.* III 165 (= *C.Pap.Lat.* 203 = *ChLA* V 290 (236)); *P.Oxy.* XII 1466 (= *C.Pap.Lat.* 204 = *ChLA* XLVI 1361 [245]); and *P.Oxy.* IV 720 (= *FIRA* III 24, *M.Chr* 324, *C.Pap. Lat.* 205, *ChLA* IV 269 [247]).

60 *C.Pap.Lat.* 200 (2nd c.); *SB* III 6223 (= *FIRA* III 25 = *C.Pap.Lat.* 202 [198]).

61 *FIRA* III^2 25bis.

62 Mélèze Modrzejewski (1974); see also Rowlandson (1998: 190–91), and Evans Grubbs (2002: 36–37).

Translation from Latin: To Lucius Mussius Aemilianus, the most sublime prefect of Egypt, from Aurelia Heras daughter of Kastor and Syra, from the city of Oxyrhynchos. I ask you, lord, to give me as a guardian, to be registered according to the Julian and Titian law and the decree of the Senate, Aurelius Chairemon son of Diogenes, former chief priest (*archiereus*) of the same city. Given in the 2nd consulship of our lords Emperors Macrianus and Quietus, year 1, Pachon 22.

4.3.3 Request for the *ius trium liberorum*

P.Oxy. XII 1467 (= *Jur.Pap.* 14; *FIRA* III 27; *Sel.Pap.* II 305; *New Docs.* II 29–30; Pestman 1994b, no. 65; tr. Rowlandson 1998, no. 142; Evans Grubbs 2002: 39; cf. *BL* VIII 246) (Oxyrhynchos, AD 263)

A woman asks the prefect to record her exemption from guardianship because she has borne three children. It is not likely, however, that such an official registration was legally required from women if they wished to appear without guardians. At least this is the only specimen of its kind. Three years later, the same woman appears in another papyrus buying landed property (*P.Oxy.* XII 1475), where she is duly recorded as having the *ius liberorum*.

The woman also claims that her case is strengthened by the fact that she can read and write. In several documents of this period (like the sale contract **4.3.1** above) women who possesed the *ius liberorum* also stated that they were literate. Nevertheless, this hardly reflects a generally accepted link between literacy and this legal right. In Roman law literacy was no prerequisite for the *ius liberorum*, and at least one-quarter of those women who appear having it in the papyri are actually illiterate. Moreover, women could mention their ability to write even without the *ius liberorum*.[63]

[. . . there have for a long time been laws], most sublime governor, that give women, if they have been honored with the right of three children, the authority to take care of themselves and to act without a guardian in any affairs they conduct, the more so if they know letters. Thus, as I am myself blessed with the grace of many children, being also literate and perfectly able to write with ease, I approach confidently your greatness through this petition of mine, so that I may without

[63] See Sheridan (1998: 194–99) for the evidence.

hindrance carry out the affairs that I henceforth conduct. I ask you to keep this petition in the office of your sublimity, without prejudice to my rights, so that I shall be aided and shall forever acknowledge my gratitude toward you. Farewell.

I, Aurelia Thaisous alias Lolliane, have sent this for submission. In the year 10, Epeiph 2x.

Your petition shall be kept in the [office].

4.3.4 Inheritance on condition of emancipation from paternal power

CPR VI 78 (Arjava 1999b) (Hermopolis, *c.* AD 265)

Aurelia Apollonia alias Tinoutis approaches the *stratêgos* to secure her share of her mother's inheritance. The mother, Dioskorous, had instituted Apollonia heir on the condition that her father emancipate her from paternal power. Otherwise the inheritance would have become the father's property. The inclusion of such a condition in the last will was a practice that was often mentioned in contemporary Latin legal and literary sources, e.g., *Dig.* 5.3.58, 26.5.21.1; *CJ* 6.25.3; Sueton, *Vitell.* 6; Pliny, *Ep.* 4.2, 8.18. In her request, Apollonia attaches a translated copy of the document by which her father had emancipated her. She had also a maternal half-brother, Aurelius Neilos, apparently a freed slave, who received part of the inheritance by Dioskorous' will and might have received Apollonia's share, too, if the father had not fulfilled the testamentary condition. The end of the request suggests that Neilos may at the moment have been in possession of the entire estate.

Dioskorous must have begun her life as a slave: Neilos had been born before she was freed and Apollonia after it. It is remarkable how a freed slave mother could use the same legal methods as the Roman upper classes to ensure that her estate really devolved on both her children. Apollonia apparently had also another half-brother, but he must have been from the father's side, so he did not play any role in the maternal inheritance.

Only the beginning of the attached document of emancipation is preserved, so we can say little of its contents. Just one very fragmentary Latin emancipation has been preserved in the papyri, *FIRA* III 14 (= *C.Pap. Lat.* 206, *Jur.Pap.* 9, *ChLA* XII 521; Oxyrhynchos, third century AD);[64] but to judge from its slight traces, the present document does not follow any known Latin model. Why it had originally been written in Latin is not clear.

[64] Cf. Wolff (2002: 138–39).

Roman wills could be written in Greek since the reign of Alexander Severus (see *SB* I 5294 = *SP* XX 35), and it is difficult to understand why stricter rules would have applied to emancipation more than thirty years later. On the whole, emancipation is rarely mentioned in the papyri. Besides this text, it appears only in a series of documents from around 300, *CPR* VI 12–30, where two men are characterized as "freed from paternal power."

The translation follows the text of Arjava (1999b).

> To Flavius Paniskos Longos, *stratêgos* of the Hermopolite nome, from Aurelia Apollonia alias Tinoutis, inhabitant of Hermopolis, registered in the Western Fort District, emancipated [from paternal power, and accompanied by my guardian/assistant NN son of –]mon. My mother [Aurelia Dioskorous, freedwoman of Demetrios . . .] instituted me and my other, maternal half-brother [Aurelius Neilos her heirs in equal shares on the condition that I shall be freed] from paternal power or, if this does not happen, she decreed that my share [of the inheritance should devolve on my above-mentioned brother]. As I have been freed [from paternal power by my father] in accordance with the will within the prescribed time [through a document whose] copy I attach below, I request you to let [. . .] the above-mentioned freedman Aurelius Neilos be informed of it, so that he knows [. . .]
>
> The following is a translation of the emancipation from paternal power: "I, Marcus [Aurelius NN son of NN], from the great, old, illustrious, and most respectable city of Hermopolis, registered [in the Western Fort District, set free from my power Aurelia Apollonia] alias Tinoutis, from the mother Dioskorous, freedwoman of Demetrios . . ." (*traces of nine lines*).

4.3.5 Joint sale of land by father and son

P.Oxy. IX 1208 (Volterra 1966: 577–81; cf. *BL* I 333; VI 101; VIII 242; XI 148) (Oxyrhynchos, AD 291)

Aurelius Thonios sells 0.8 arouras of arable land to Aurelia Thermuthion alias Tanechotis. He, together with his four siblings, inherited it from his mother. Note that in this case, unlike in **4.3.1** above, all five children inherited equally a fifth part of the mother's total four arouras, although admittedly we cannot be sure that this plot constituted her entire estate.

Aurelius Thonios, whose age is not given, is explicitly said to be still in the paternal power (*hypo têi kheiri*) of his father Thonios. In contrast to **4.3.4** above, the text does not display any clear awareness that in Roman law the son's inheritance should have devolved upon his father: the son is consistently treated as the real successor of his deceased mother. The scribe describes the younger Thonios as the owner and seller of the inherited land and is careful to state repeatedly that the father was present and sanctioned the sale. The latter circumstance suggests that he perceived the ownership to be somehow restricted or divided. Such a text would hardly have been appreciated by an imperial jurist, but in practice the disagreement with Roman law may not have been fatal, and the wording may have been sufficiently safe to ensure that no one could contest the sale's validity. It is impossible to tell how accurately the parties themselves understood the juridical situation.

The buyer Aurelia Thermuthion is underage, probably below twelve years, and she is acting through her father (*dia tou patros*). Evidently she was not even present at the transaction. Again, if she had not been emancipated, she would not have been able to own any property: the document does not specify her status in this respect. The practice of buying or registering certain property in the name of one's children sometimes appears in the papyri, and it is echoed in a contemporary imperial rescript, *Epit. Cod. Greg. Vis.* 3.8.2 (= *FIRA* II 661).[65]

The copy of the sale contract was included in a further document (*ekmartyrêsis*), where it was publicly confirmed the following year. Only the contract, beginning at line 6, is here translated.

> Aurelius Thonios, son of Thonios and Artemidora, from the illustrious and most illustrious city of Oxyrhynchos, with the joint guarantee of his father Aurelius Thonios, son of Serenos and Isarous, from the same city, who also has him under his paternal power according to Roman law, greets Aurelia Thermuthion also named Tanechotis daughter of Nepheros and Tanechotis, from the village of Pakerke of the eastern toparchy, not yet of legal age, acting through her father, Aurelius Nepheros son of Dionysios, from the same village.
>
> I acknowledge I have sold and ceded to you from now on and forever the property that is mine by right of inheritance and formerly belonged to my said mother Aurelia Artemidora, daughter of Pausiris and Isis, from the same city, who died leaving as her heirs her five children, me and my siblings, my full brother Aurelius Demetrios and my maternal half-siblings Aurelii Diogenes and Isidoros and Isis, the latter three from

[65] See further Arjava (1998: 158).

the father Herminos. My mother also held the property by right of inheritance, as it had formerly belonged to her father Aurelius Pausiris, son of Dionysios and Artemidora, from the same city, and she had received it according to his will, which he had left in the 2nd year of Claudius, which was the 1st year of Aurelian, in the month Tybi x, and which was opened after his death. Pausiris had bought it from Aurelius Herammon, son of Pausanias alias Eutyches and Hermione, from the same city, by an autograph deed of sale and cession made in the 12th year of Gallienus, Pachon 23, in the village Pakerke of the eastern toparchy [. . .] The property in question consists of the fifth part of four arouras of private arable land, that is four-fifths of an aroura, which are part of eight arouras held in common with Horion son of Akrono[. . .], these again being part of altogether approximately twenty-eight arouras equipped with a watering system and irrigator with all wooden and iron equipment, the sold property being entitled to its proportionate share of the watering system and irrigator. The neighbors of the whole are to the south a road and from the other three directions a canal.

The price and transfer payment of the fifth part of the above-mentioned four arouras of private land with its proportionate share of the watering system and irrigator we have mutually agreed to be nine thousand imperial silver drachmas, which is one talent and three thousand drachmas of silver, and I have received them at once from you through the same father of yours in full from hand to hand. It has been given to you, as you state, through an irrevocable and irreversible deed of gift. And asked by you whether I have been paid off in full, I affirm I have done so with my father, who accompanies me and receives the money together with me.

You are thus entitled to govern and control with your descendants and successors the fifth part of the four arouras of private arable land and its share of the watering system and irrigator, which I have sold and ceded to you as related above, and you have the power to use and manage it as you choose. No right is left to me or to anyone acting in my name to bring a legal case on account of this property or a part of it in any way. And I shall in all circumstances convey it to you, so that your title to it is always defended against everything with all possible guarantee. It is free from public or imperial compulsory cultivation or any such encumbrance or debt or public or private burden and civic or municipal or any other possible imposition, and from the maintenance and surveillance of dikes, and free from all kinds of public dues payable on them and additional charges and contributions up to and including the current 6th and 5th year, because from the coming seventh and sixth year the revenues of this property will belong to you the buyer and recipient, and you will also be liable for all the public dues and additional charges from the end of the same current sixth and fifth year. If any person in any way will raise a legal action or claim this property or part of it, I shall in all circumstances at once avert him at my own expense, as if from a court decision.

This deed of sale and cession is valid, made in three copies, and you can have it publicly confirmed whenever you wish, not needing my further approval, because I hereby assent to an eventual public confirmation. We have been asked by you through your father whether this has taken place correctly and well, and we have agreed to it. In the sixth and fifth year of our lords Emperors Diocletian and Maximian Augusti, Epeiph 11.

I, Aurelius Thonios son of Thonios, have sold and ceded the fifth part of four arouras with their share of the watering system, and I have received as the price and transfer payment one talent and three thousand drachmas of silver, and I shall guarantee the buyer's ownership and I assent to the public confirmation, as I have agreed to when asked. I, Aurelius Thonios, also guarantee the fifth part of the *arouras* and assent to the sale, as I have agreed to when asked. I, Aurelius Apion alias Theon, have written on his behalf, as he does not know letters. The copy ends here [. . .]

4.4 Fatherless persons

Myrto Malouta

The annexation of Egypt into the Roman empire brought about numerous changes to its legal and administrative system and had a profound impact on its social configuration. Some changes took effect early on, while others occurred gradually, to suit the changing conditions and to cater to the particular demands of the valuable province (Bowman and Rathbone 1992). Strangely and suddenly, just before the beginning of the second century, some individuals began to identify themselves officially as fatherless. This phenomenon continued through the remainder of the second century and for most of the third.[66] It is found predominantly in documents of administrative character, mostly related to the census. The practice involved replacing an individual's patronymic, which

[66] The earliest known attestation of this phenomenon is *P.Oxy* I 104 (AD 96). The latest known reference is *P.NYU* I 12 i.19, re-dated to AD 336–7.

would accompany his name in official documents, with the designation "fatherless," transliterated from Greek here as *apatôr*, plural *apatores*. This was commonly followed by the name of the mother. Whether or not this means of identification implied an actual or a physical absence of a father is immaterial. The point is that although the word *apatôr* seems merely to describe an irregular family setup, it in fact designates a legal status whereby the individual identified as *apatôr* was for some reason prevented from being legitimately recognized as his or her father's offspring. This must have had legal consequences both for the "fatherless" person (it was after all a determining factor of his or her identity) and for the unnamed father.

This form of identification had no recognized precedent in the legal and administrative practices of Ptolemaic Egypt, so it must have emerged as the modification of a Roman institution. The traditional view, prevalent for the last three decades at least, holds that this sort of fatherlessness had its roots in the prohibition of the marriage of soldiers (Calderini 1953: 361; Youtie 1975a: 737). Youtie especially suggests that many of the fatherless were soldiers' children; others owed their status to other restrictions on marriage, such as between some ethnic groups (Youtie 1975a: 738). Indeed, although the ban on the marriage of soldiers is likely to have been part of the explanation, it fails of full corroboration because there are numerous occurrences of *apatores* long after *c.* AD 197 when Septimius Severus lifted the ban on soldiers' marriages (Phang 2001: 115–36). Undeniably, attestations to *apatores* in the third century are fewer, in fact less than half those of the second century; but this reflects the decline in the number of published papyri from the third century rather than a diminishing trend (Malouta 2009: 132–35).

The overwhelming majority of documents mentioning fatherless individuals come from the Oxyrhynchite and Arsinoite nomes; other areas of Egypt are underrepresented (Malouta 2009: 135–38). An idiosyncrasy of the Oxyrhynchite documents is that rather than using *apatôr*, the term elsewhere in universal use, they invariably describe a fatherless person as "designated as the son of (his) mother," *chrematizôn mêtros* (Malouta 2007). There is no apparent difference in the intended meanings of the two expressions; they just go about it from opposite directions.

The following texts illustrate different situations in which people would have been expected to designate themselves, or be designated by others, as fatherless; they therefore allow us to observe how this was done both by the fatherless persons themselves and by others. More interestingly, the texts focus on situations where being fatherless could have been critical in determining the lot of the individual in question, or that of their offspring.

Two of them are census returns (**4.4.2** and **4.4.6**; cf. **4.4.5**), and one includes the text of a census document, while it involves a case of disputed inheritance (**4.4.5**). One is the registration of a child (**4.4.3**), and another a request to the *iuridicus*[67] regarding the welfare of a fatherless minor (**4.4.1**). There is also one that contains an application of a fatherless man for a share of the corn dole (**4.4.4**).

4.4.1 Request for a guardian

P.Diog. 18 (duplicate of *P.Harr.* I 68 = *FIRA* III 28) (probably Philadelphia, 12 January AD 225). Image at *P.Diog.*, Plate 13.

The application, preserved in two copies, was first published as *P.Harr.* I 68. When a third copy came to light, it was edited and published as *P.Diog.* 18. In this text Marcus Aurelius Diogenes took steps to manage matters arising from the death of his intestate sister for the benefit of her three underage sons. As the three sons were the product of three different fathers, their circumstances at their mother's death varied: one was (and had been) in his father's custody, but a second son was "fatherless" in the legal sense and the third was literally fatherless: i.e., his father was dead. Their maternal uncle, Marcus Lucretius Diogenes, as the next of kin, requested legal guardianship over the last two boys. One son, Marcus Aurelius Iulas, was able to enter into the inheritance (according to Roman law) because he was in "paternal power" (*patria potestas*). His half-brothers, Lucretius and Rufus, were not in paternal power. Thus, as minors, they could not enter into the inheritance until a guardian had been appointed for them. Hence the petition.[68]

This text is the clearest confirmation that the kind of fatherlessness meant by the terms *apatôr* (used here) and *chrematizôn mêtros* have nothing to do with being orphaned of one's father. Furthermore, it gives insight into social attitudes toward the legally fatherless: although such documents do not usually go into too much detail, it is interesting to observe that the setting is that of a well-off Antinoite family; that the fact that the three sons are the product of three unions is stated matter-of-factly without any hint of moral censure; and, finally, that the fatherless child is treated equally with his brothers in his uncle's effort to secure his upbringing and preserve his patrimonial rights.

[67] A high official appointed by the emperor to assist the prefect of Egypt in jurisdiction, but who also had judicial powers of his own (Kupiszewski 1953–54).

[68] Observation owed to one of our anonymous readers, slightly modified.

To Aurelius Didymos *stratêgos* of the Arsinoite nome, district of Herakleides, from Marcus Lucretius Diogenes, Antinoite. A copy of the petition that I submitted to Claudius Herennianus, most excellent *iuridicus* and vice-prefect, along with the subscription that I obtained, is appended below, and I request that the following come to pass, namely, that you appoint a guardian for the below-named minors, in order that they might lose nothing that is theirs, in accordance with the laws. Here is the text:

"To Tiberius Claudius Herennianus, most excellent *iuridicus* and vice-prefect by imperial order, from Marcus Lucretius Diogenes, Antinoite. Submitting to you a petition befitting your kindness, I am hopeful that I shall obtain justice from you. I shall lay down the matter in a few words. In the month of Phaophi last my sister Octavia Lucretia died intestate, having left behind as heirs three sons from different marriages, Marcus Aurelius Iulas, Marcus Aurelius Lucretius, and Marcus Aurelius Rufus, all minors. One of them, Iulas, being under the authority of his own father, Marcus Aurelius Heron, has received his due part of the inheritance. Of the others, however, Lucretius happens to be fatherless, while Rufus' father has died, and no kinsman of theirs is closer than I, Lucretius Diogenes. It is in their name that I make this request, and I ask you, if it should seem worthy to your Fortune, to order by way of a revered subscription from yourself to the *stratêgos* of the division of Herakleides of the Arsinoite nome, where their property is found, to appoint me a guardian of the orphan boys, in order that I may manage their inheritance, so that it may be safeguarded until they become of age."

Farewell. I, Marcus Lucretius Diogenes, have submitted this through Aurelius Sarapion.

The *stratêgos*, under pain of consequences for himself, shall settle the appointment of a guardian for the minors. Sheet number 68.

(*2nd hand*) Lucretius [. . .]

(*3rd hand*) Year 4 of Imperator Caesar Marcus Aurelius Severus Alexander Pius Felix Augustus, Tybi 17.

4.4.2 Census return with property of a fatherless woman

BGU I 90 *et al.* (see discussion following) (Soknopaiou Nesos, 28 July AD 161)

This census return has been preserved in six different copies: *BGU* I 90 and II 537 addressed to the village scribe, I 224 and II 410 to the *stratêgos*, I 225 to the *laographoi*, and *P.Grenf.* II 55 to the royal scribe.

The following translation is based on a compound text (Calderini 1922), and therefore omits the address.

In this document we see three people sharing a house. The declaration is submitted by a man called Hatres; he lives with his wife, Isarion. In the same house lives Tapetsiris, a woman one year younger than his wife. Her relationship to the couple is not specified, though there are reasons to think she was Hatres' cousin (Bagnall and Frier 1994: 240–41). Isarion, who is declared as fatherless, is identified by the names of her mother and maternal grandfather.

The interest of this text lies in its references to inherited property. Hatres owned a house, inherited from his mother; Isarion owned two houses and a quarter of one, inherited from her grandmother; and Tapetsiris owned property separately inherited from her grandfather and grandmother. Thus we can conclude that Isarion found no obstruction in her condition as *apatôr* in inheriting from her grandmother and owning property on equal terms with her husband, and with Tapetsiris, who is not *apatôr*.

From Hatres son of Satabous, grandson of Panephremmis, his mother being Segathis, from the village of Soknopaiou Nesos.

I declare myself and my family in the house-by-house declaration for the previous, twenty-third year of Divus Aelius Antoninus, in which I live in the house inherited from my mother, in the village. I am the aforementioned Hatres, 25 years old, with no distinguishing marks; (I also declare) my wife Isarion, fatherless, her mother being Tanephremmis daughter of Panomieus, 13 years old,[69] with no distinguishing marks. She owns in the village two houses and a quarter of the house inherited from her grandmother. (I also declare) Tapetsiris daughter of Stotoetis, granddaughter of Panephremmis, her mother being Tapetsiris, 12 years old, with no distinguishing marks. Tapetsiris owns two houses and a courtyard and a quarter of the house inherited from her grandfather and a quarter of the house inherited from her grandmother.[70] I therefore submit the declaration.

Year 1 of Imperator Caesar Marcus Aurelius Antoninus Augustus and Imperator Caesar Lucius Aurelius Verus Augustus, Mesore 4.

[69] The age of thirteen years may surprise the modern reader but is within the realm of ancient expectations.

[70] Or: "a quarter of two houses and a courtyard, etc." The ambiguity exists in all six exemplars.

4.4.3 Registration of a child with fatherless parents

P.Petaus 2 (Ptolemais Hormou, 14 February AD 185). Image at Papyri.info.

There are two copies of this document sent to two different officials, both written on the same day and at the same place and published as *P.Petaus* 1 and 2. The text presented below is that of *P.Petaus* 2, chosen because it contains some evidence for the administrative process of such a declaration after submission.

The document is addressed to the royal scribe of the Arsinoite nome, district of Herakleides, and the copy published as *P.Petaus* 1 to the village scribe of Ptolemais Hormou. The declarants are the father of the child in question and his sister, who is also his wife, for whom he is acting as guardian (*kyrios*). This copy contains a docket addressed to the village scribe.

This papyrus is one of the few published registrations of girls. The reason for registering a girl's birth is a matter for speculation. The consensus is that such documents could be useful in providing proof of status for the benefit of future children rather than having any immediate and personal administrative impact.[71] From the point of view of fatherlessness, the interest of the present text lies in the fact that at least one, and probably both parents are *apatores*: the father explicitly describes himself as such and the mother is said to have been his sister of the same mother.[72] No father is mentioned. This document therefore seems to contradict arguments about the purpose of registering girls, since the fatherless ancestry of the child whose birth is registered here will not lend distinction to her future children.

> To Hermophilos, royal scribe of the Arsinoite nome, district of Herakleides, from Apynchis, *apatôr*, his mother being Tapholemis, and his sister of the same mother Tapasis, who is also his wife, from the town of Ptolemais Hormou, his wife having as a *kyrios* himself, Apynchis.
>
> We declare the daughter born to the two of us, Taesis, who is, during the current twenty-fifth year, eight years old. We therefore submit this notification of birth.
>
> (*2nd hand*) To the village scribe of Ptolemais Hormou. See to this in accordance with similar cases, for the responsibility and consequences lie with you if anything should be carried out in an improper way.
>
> Year 25 of Marcus Aurelius Commodus Antoninus Augustus Pius, Mecheir 20.

[71] For the ongoing debate, see the introductions to *P.Oxy.* XLIII 3136, *P.Petaus* 1 and 2, *P.Ups.Frid.* 6; also: Montevecchi (1947), Mertens (1958: 48–65), Cohen (1996), Jördens (2000).

[72] On sibling marriage see **4.3** above.

4.4.4 Application for the corn dole in Oxyrhynchos

P.Oxy. XL 2913 Col. II (Oxyrhynchos, 19 February AD 269). Image at Papyri.info.

The following text comprises the second column of *P.Oxy.* XL 2913, published in the volume dedicated exclusively to the corn dole in Oxyrhynchos. It is an application to the officials in charge of the dole from an inhabitant of Oxyrhynchos who asks to be added to the list of entitled recipients. This selection contains the only certain example of a fatherless individual who thought himself eligible to receive the dole (there is only one other possibly fatherless applicant: *P.Oxy.* XL 2912, 4). This is curious, since eligibility to receive the corn dole depended on belonging to one of three groups of citizens (*epikrithentes*, *rhemboi*, and *homologoi*), all of which, to different degrees, required proof of status.[73] The applicant in the text below belongs to the last and lowest of the three, which would have been the only one available to him: the two higher groups required their members to have passed the *epikrisis*, or proof of status, by giving evidence of both their parents' status (Rea 1972: 2–5; further, Carrié 1998). But even if the group of *homologoi* to which he belonged had a concessionary claim, the fact remains that receipt of the dole was a privilege. That a fatherless individual could be a beneficiary may be taken as proof that fatherlessness did not excite bias against such a person's status.

The process the present applicant Aurelius Herakleon underwent had two stages. The first required an application to the phylarch. If this was favorably received, a second application was submitted, this time to the officials in charge of the dole. In the present case, because of the phylarch's past mistake, there was a long delay between the two applications: the first was submitted in AD 250–251, and the second in AD 269. The text here in fact is a request to have his name added to the list of the phylarch from which it had been dropped.

To the examiners in charge of the corn dole, from Aurelius Herakleon, designated as the son of his mother Iseis daughter of Achilleus, from the illustrious city of the Oxyrhynchites, registered at the South Street quarter.

Having been registered and become a member of the list of minors in the first year of the Decii (= AD 250–1) in accordance with the official

[73] These three status groups had differential rights to the receipt of grain; the higher the status the more stringent the requirements for proof of status. See Rea (1972: 5).

records, but having been omitted from the submitted records by the phylarch of the quarter, having proven that my personal circumstances are as declared, I request to be included among the names to be announced for the distribution of the corn dole, so I may also benefit from the donation.

Year 1 of Imperator Caesar Marcus Aurelius Claudius Pius Felix Augustus, Mecheir 25.

(*2nd hand*) I, Aurelius Herakleon, submit this request.

I, Aurelius [. . .]ammon, wrote it on his behalf, because he is illiterate.

4.4.5 A case of concealed fatherlessness

P.Lond. II 324 (= *W.Chr.* 208) (Prosopite nome, AD 161). Image at *P.Lond.* II, Plate 62.

The provenance of the papyrus alone is a significant feature, since documents referring to fatherless individuals from nomes other than the Oxyrhynchite and the Arsinoite are rare. On the geographical distribution of such documents see Malouta (2009).

Here Anikos writes to his sister Thamistis.[74] To his letter he appends copies of the two previous census records of their family. In these it is stated that Anikos and Thamistis had both times been declared as siblings of the same mother and father. It therefore comes as a surprise that in the letter, which follows the census copies, Anikos addresses Thamistis as "my sister of the same mother, *apatôr*."[75] The date of the document is significant, since the census following those quoted in the usual fourteen-year cycle would have been just composed, or, more probably, about to be. So, when Anikos refers to the need for proof of his sister's status, he must be alluding to an imminent situation, whereby her status will appear as different from one census to the next.

[74] Thamistis appears in the letter as Tamystha. The variation in spelling of transliterated Egyptian names is very common, and occurs in most names in this document, most impressively Thenthnoupis or Khentmouphis or Khenthnouphis or Kenthnoupis. Since the document contains a great number of people, I have decided to normalize the spellings in multiple references to the same person to avoid confusion. I have not normalized the spelling when a name is used by different people (Herpaesis and Herpsaesis are assumed to be different people, though conceivably they could be the same, which would make Thaneutis and her husband Pathermouthis cousins).

[75] The letter itself must be seen as an official cover letter, rather than just a note to Thamistis from her brother. In the latter case it would not have explicitly included her official status or Anikos' patronymic, which is not the practice in private correspondence among family members.

The reasons for this change of status are not clear from the document. It has, however, been plausibly suggested that Thamistis' status as *apatôr* had so far been concealed, only to become relevant after the death of the mother and possibly also of the alleged father. At this point issues regarding inheritance may have gotten the better of some family members (Youtie 1975a: 724–25). This example indicates that on occasion attempts were made to conceal the status of *apatores* from the authorities, and indeed many may have been more successful than the present one in this attempt (Youtie 1975a: 725).

Since the census returns are just copies from the record office they do not include the opening lines that are found in originals, which would contain the address to the responsible officials.

> Copy of a copy [of] sheet 9–70[76] from the public record office of the census in the sixteenth year of the lord Hadrianus Caesar carried out in the Prosopite nome, volume 2: Pathermouthis son of Anikos [?] in which (are registered): I, Pathermouthis son of Anikos and Thaseis, grandson of Pathermouthis, quarry worker,[77] 47 years old; Thaneutis daughter of Tithoenathymis, granddaughter of Herpsaesis, my wife; Thaesis, my daughter; Anikos, her brother of the same parents; Thenthnoupis son of Anikos, grandson of Pathermouthis, his mother being Thaseis (daughter of?) Herpaesis, 45 years old; Demetrous daughter of Soterichos and Thamistis, his wife; Thamistis their daughter, [. . .] years old; Anikos her brother of the same parents, a minor, 6 years old; Herpaesis son of Anikos, grandson of Pathermouthis [. . .], his mother being Thaseis daughter of Herpaesis, 42 years old; [. . .]esies daughter of Horos, his wife, her mother being Tertia daughter of Kapito(n), 29 years old; Anikos, son of both parents, 20 years old; Thaesis, his sister of the same parents, 8 years old; Tertia, his other sister, 4 years old; Pantbeus son of Anikos, grandson of Pathermouthis, his mother being Thaseis daughter of Herpaesis, 38 years old; Thaesis, his wife, her mother being Thaubastis daughter of Piesieeus, 21 years old; Anikos, son of both parents, a minor, 4 years old.
>
> Similarly in the ninth year of the lord Antoninus Caesar, from the same public record office, sheet 5[.] of the volume, Thenthnoupis son of

[76] This is the figure that appears in the editions; the sequence of these letters cannot of course make up one number, and must be an archival sorting code, an attested practice, perhaps roll number followed by sheet number. There may have been space for more digits before the 9; see the transcript of Wessely as indicated by *BL* I 245.

[77] Bagnall and Frier (1994: 218).

Anikos, grandson of Pathermouthis, his mother being Thaseis daughter of Herpaesis, quarry worker, 52 years old; Anikos his son, his mother being Demetrous daughter of Soterichos, 20 years old; Thamistis, his sister of the same parents, 24 years old.

(*2nd hand*) Anikos son of Thenthnoupis to my sister of the same mother Thamistis, *apatôr*, greetings. I delivered to you the present copies of the census returns, of which I shall present the same in the registry, whenever there may be need to prove that I am your brother of the same mother.

Year 24 of the lord Antoninus, Phamenoth 28.

Verso: Anikos son of Thenthnoupis

4.4.6 Census return of the ex-husband of a fatherless woman

SB XXIV 15987 (= P.Hafn. inv. 24, *SB* XIV 11355, Bülow-Jacobsen and Ebbesen 1971: 3–15) (Tebtunis,[78] *c.* AD 208)

The fatherless woman who features in this document admittedly does not play a big part, but it is interesting to observe the circumstances in which she did a stint as one of Didymos' three wives. Didymos is currently married to a 43-year-old woman, Sarapias, who is declared with her entire lineage of father, paternal grandfather, and mother, as well as location during the last census. In the present census it transpires that Didymos has been married twice before, once with Hermione, the fatherless woman in question, by whom he has a son, and once with an Antinoite woman (name lost), by whom he also has a son. It is difficult to say which wife succeeded the other, since the age of the son he had with the Antinoite, which would function as a *terminus post quem* for the divorce, has not survived. Bagnall and Frier (1994: 125; 187-Ar-22 is a misprint for 187-Ar-32) name this as the most complicated case of divorce and remarriage recorded in a census return.[79]

What is important here is that an *apatôr* married into a landed and privileged Greek family with a pedigree stretching back a century or more (Van Groningen 1950: 11–13). The present document attests to the financial aspect of this by the large number of slaves declared, and – if the opinion of the scholars who claim that divorce was uncommon in the

[78] Its provenance, initially seen as uncertain, is probably Tebtunis, since the document is connected to the well-known "Family Archive of Tebtunis." See Bagnall and Frier (1994: 279), Christensen (1998: 29–30).

[79] A genealogical table of the known members of this family can be found in Bülow-Jacobsen and Ebbesen (1971: 6).

lower strata of society is correct – also to the family's high social standing.[80] The copy of the census that we have is part of a volume of the record office, as indicated by the preservation of the sheet number.[81] The original was addressed to the *stratêgos* of the relevant division of the nome.

Copy of a house-by-house declaration of the twenty-eighth year, of sheet 165.

(*2nd hand*) To Ammonius, *stratêgos* of the Arsinoite nome, division of Herakleides, from Didymos son of Kallinikos and Tephorsaeis, grandson of Didymos, metropolite, registered in the Gymnasium quarter.

I own in the quarter of Moeris one-sixth of a house in which I register myself and my family for the house-by-house declaration of the past year 28 of Aurelius Commodus Antoninus Caesar the lord in the same quarter in which I registered myself for the house-by-house declaration of the fourteenth year.

I am Didymos, mentioned above, private payer of poll-tax, [. . .] years old, with a blank left eye. (I also declare) my current wife, Sarapias daughter of Sabinus, granddaughter of Kronion, her mother being Eudaimonis, 43 years old, with no distinguishing marks, who registered herself in the previous census in the quarter of Syriake. (I also declare) the son born to me from my former and divorced wife Hermione, fatherless, her mother being Herois, Didymos, registered in the list of minors, 10 years old. (I also declare) my own seven slaves: Euprepos, slave son of [female name lost] [. . .] years old, and Sarapammon, slave son of the same, 29 years old, and [name lost] slave son of Tapaeis, [.]9 years old, and a slave bought from [. . .], called Alexandra, 49 years old; and the slave of my current wife in the current twenty-ninth year who came from further down the river, Elpis, 12 years old, with a scar on her left shin; also half of the bought slaves mentioned below: Isis, also known as Memphis, slave daughter of [*name lost*] [. . .] years old, and her slave son Sarapammon not registered in the list of minors, 6 years old, the other half of whom was registered in the quarter of Syriake by Kronia and Taorsis.

(I also declare) my son Xenophon, [. . .] years old, born to me from my ex-wife [name lost], who is an Antinoite, and he is registered with his mother in Antinoopolis. The rest of the children, who do not belong to

80 Bagnall and Frier (1994: 123), Treggiari (1991a: 482), Treggiari (1991b: 41–46).
81 On such archival methods see Clarysse (2003).

me but [name lost], who had become her husband but is now divorced, were registered with their father. I therefore submit the declaration.

4.5 Deeds of last will: Demotic, Greek, and Latin

Willy Clarysse

At the death of a person something has to happen to his possessions. Usually the inheritance goes more or less automatically to the next of kin, in the first place of course the children, according to fixed legal rules. In Egyptian law the oldest son often received a double share, daughters being on an equal footing with the younger sons; in Greek law daughters who had received a dowry no longer entered into account. If, however, a person wanted to deviate from the *ab intestato* rules or wanted to be more specific than those rules, he could draw up a last will, by which he made a number of dispositions that would take effect only after his death. A will is always unilateral and therefore not a normal contract (in which there are two parties). Typical of wills is that the stipulations become effective when the testator is no longer alive and has no personal control over what will happen and that they may be unilaterally revoked by the testator at any time as long as he is alive.

Egyptian law did not have a special type of document for this purpose. If a person wanted to deviate from the normal rules, he could draw up a deed of sale, by which he divided his property among his next of kin or donated (part of) his property to somebody. The deed does not mention when it will become effective, but by not drawing up a corresponding deed of cession and/or by keeping the deed of sale to himself until the end of his life the donator postponed its effects (**4.5.1**). In one example a Demotic gift (in the form of a deed of sale) is dated the day before the death of the testator; this *donatio inter vivos* is in fact used as a will.[82] Greek wills form the majority of our documentation. They can be general (for the whole estate) or consist of specific legacies, leaving the rest of the property to the *ab intestato* rules (**4.5.2**, **4.5.3**). Roman wills often follow the traditional pattern of a *testamentum per aes et libram*, though soldiers had a greater freedom in using different forms of wills (Gnomon of the *Idios Logos* §34). The wills of other Roman citizens are much more uniform and adhere to a strict pattern of formulas (**4.5.5**).

[82] See Pestman (1995b: 79–80).

4.5.1 Donation of the woman Eschonsis to her son

P.Brit.Mus. Andrews 1 (Thebes, Dec. 265–Jan. 264 BC). Image at *P.Brit.Mus. Andrews*, Plate 1.

This Demotic text belongs to the family archive of Pachytes son of Pchorchonsis, which contains some twenty documents ranging from 334 to 199 BC.[83] Pachytes' descendants belong to the famous Theban *choachytai* in the second century BC.[84]

The contract is written by the notary Zminis son of Phibis, as can be seen from his signature at the end of the notarial copy. There is a list of sixteen witnesses on the back and four of these have copied the entire text in their own hands. This is one of the latest of the so-called witness copy contracts (see Chapter 2, and Depauw 1999).

Eschonsis leaves half of her property to her son Panas by means of a sale ("you have satisfied my heart with the silver"). A full Demotic sale consists in fact of two documents, a deed of "sale" and a deed of "cession" (see **2.2** above). Because the latter is missing here, the transaction was not finalized. By this fictive sale the family property is passed on from one generation to the next; moreover, the transaction will only become final after the death and burial of Eschonsis. Although in this case the sons apparently receive full rights to the property in exchange for a monthly ration of food, clothing, and oil to their mother, the final clause about the burial will only apply after her death. Moreover, as long as Eschonsis is alive, she will receive half the income of the tombs. This turns the *donatio inter vivos* into a kind of sale *propter mortem*.

The property consisted of two houses in the "House of the Cow," a city quarter near the temple of Karnak, and one house in Djême (the Greek Memnoneia) on the Theban west bank, and of two groups of tombs, in Djême and in Hermonthis. The history of the second Theban house can be followed over three generations (330–252 BC).[85] The tombs and their mummies were an important source of income for the *choachytai*, who were paid by the families of the dead for making regular offerings on the tombs. Notice that in the Egyptian tradition women can also own priestly funerary rights.

[83] See Seidl (1962: 20–21, no. 3).

[84] For recent discussion of the *choachytai* and their archives, see Martin (2009b) for the Memphis region; and Pestman (1993) for Thebes. They were a kind of funerary priest, literally "libation pourer," responsible for the care of the dead. See in general the superb summary of Thompson (1988: chapter 5), with 2nd edn. 2012.

[85] See Pestman (1987: 279–80).

From the clauses it is clear that Eschonsis gave the other half of her property to a second son Patemis. This deed is also preserved; it is written two years earlier and deals with the other half of house A and the rest of the tombs, but not with the house in Djême (*P.Louvre dem.* 2424 = Zauzich 1968, no. 11). In accordance with the Egyptian tradition the older son received a larger part. The translation here follows the conflated transliteration of the first edition.

Year 21, Thoth, under pharaoh Ptolemy (II) son of Ptolemy (I) and Ptolemy his son, when Timarchides son of Asklepiodotos was priest of Alexander and of the brother gods, when Xeinorode daughter of Agesipolis was *kanêphoros* of Arsinoe Philadelphos.

Has declared the woman Eschonsis daughter of Teos, her mother being Thabis, to the *pastophoros* of Amenophis in the west of Thebes, Panas son of Pchorchonsis, his mother being Eschonsis, my eldest son:

You have satisfied my heart with the silver for half of my house, which is built and roofed, and the half of its courtyard to its west, whose other half to its east belongs to Patemis son of Pchorchonsis, my son, your brother, completing the entire house, and its courtyard, which is in the northern quarter of Thebes, in the House of the Cow. (... *There follow here the neighbors South, North, East, and West* ...) You may go out by the middle door of the above-mentioned house. You may inhabit the forehall of the house corresponding to your half. You may work with the equipment of the above-mentioned house in accordance with the (half) share. This is the total of the neighbors. And (you have satisfied my heart with the silver for) my (second) house, which is built and roofed, and its courtyard which is in the above-mentioned quarter (*There follow the neighbors South, North, East, and West*). These are the neighbors of the entire house and its courtyard. (*There follow the neighbors South, North, East, and West*). ...

And (you have satisfied my heart with the silver for) the half of my (third) house, which is built and roofed and the half of its courtyard which is near the market of Djême (... *There follow the neighbors South, North, East, and West* ...) These are the neighbors of my entire house and its courtyard of which I have given you their half. Its other half belongs to Patemis son of Pchorchonsis my son, your brother. This is the total of the neighbors. And (you have satisfied my heart with the silver for) half of my duty as *choachytês* in Hermonthis, (whose revenues come) from the countryside and from the town, whose other half belongs to Patemis son of Pchorchonsis my son, your younger brother. And (you have satisfied my heart with the silver for) my duty as *choachytês* in the tombs that are in the necropolis of Djême. (*There follows a list of the tombs in Djême, one by one . . .*)

I have given them to you. They belong to you as follows: your half of the house and its courtyard and its vacant lots to its west, your house and its courtyard and your half of the house which is in Djême and its courtyard, your duty as *choachytês* in Hermonthis and your duty as *choachytês* in the tombs of the saints and the tombs of the people which are specified above. No person at all, myself included, will be able to exercise authority over them except you, from this day onward. As for anyone who shall proceed against you on account of them in my name or in the name of anyone on earth, I shall cause him to be far from you. And I shall clear them for you from my title, from anything at all at any time. To you belong their title deeds wherever they will be. Every document that has been drawn up concerning them and every document by virtue of which I am entitled concerning them, they belong to you, and (also) the right conferred by them. To you belongs that by virtue of which I am entitled concerning them. The oath or the proof which will be imposed upon you in the courthouse concerning the right(s conferred) by the above-mentioned document, which I have drawn up for you, to cause me to swear it, I will swear it, <without alleging any title or anything at all against you>. And you will give me two cooked cakes daily, a shawl of woven stuff, one garment yearly and one *hin*-measure of oil monthly. This is the total of my subsistence daily, monthly, and yearly for my lifetime. And you shall give me half of all the rations which will be given to you for the duty of *choachytês* for my lifetime. And you shall carry out my embalming and my burial completely in conformity with the manner of men – without alleging any title or anything at all against you. I have written this.

4.5.2 Will of the officer Dion, including manumission of slaves

P.Petrie 1^2 3, lines 9–38 (Fayyum, 238 BC). Images at *P.Petrie* 1^2, Plates 5–6.

Fragments of one or more chronological registers of wills were found among the papyri that Flinders Petrie extracted from mummy cartonnage. They range from 238 to 225 BC and some fifty wills are preserved, often in a very fragmentary state. They all come from the Arsinoite nome (Fayyum) and are written in Greek according to a uniform pattern of formulas:

a full date, with eponymous priests and Macedonian month, an introductory formula in the objective style ("NN has made the following will"), followed by the stipulations themselves in the first person singular ("I bequeath . . ."). The king and queen are named as testamentary executors; they were supposed to give legal protection to the will. At the end come the usual six witnesses, with full physical description. No notary is mentioned, perhaps because they all come from the same notarial office.

Most of the Petrie wills leave the entire property to one or more persons, often the wife and children of the testator. Apparently some people found that the legal rights of their spouse were not sufficiently guaranteed. These "general legacies" are usually followed by a clause of disinheritance for all other persons. Specific legacies deal with part of the inheritance only, leaving the rest to the *ab intestato* rules. Many deal with military possessions of the testator, his military allotment, billet, and horse. At his death these returned in principle to the Crown and by his will he tried to secure them to his family. In the present case the testator leaves to his wife and children "the possessions which they already hold," whereas what remains is to be used for his funeral. But the main clause is the manumission of the slave Melainis and her son Ammonios, who is the testator's son. They will be free at his death on condition that they serve him faithfully during his lifetime. One has the impression that Dion is estranged from his legal family. There is perhaps a holdover from earlier Greek practice of manumission in the temple, but the relevant passage is unfortunately damaged.

Dion was an officer and the witnesses belong to the category of the *epigonê*, a group which is linked to the army. As is the case for most testators in the Petrie wills Dion had reached an advanced age (65 years) when he drew up his will.

In the reign of Ptolemy (III) son of Ptolemy (II) and Arsinoe, brother gods, [year 10]; while Apollonides son of Moschion was for the second time priest of Alexander and the brother gods and the benefactor gods, while Menekrateia daughter of Philammon was for the second time *kanêphoros* of Arsinoe Philadelphos, on the 30th of the month Audnaios, in Krokodilopolis of the Arsinoite nome, Dion of Herakleia, of the company of Damon, commander of five hundred infantrymen, kleruch, about 65 years old, short, [with a honey-colored complexion], bald forehead and round face, with a scar on his cheek beside his [left] eyebrow and another one in the middle of his forehead above his right eyebrow, being of sound mind and in possession of his wits, has made the following will:

May I enjoy good health and manage my own affairs. But if I should suffer the fate of man, my wife and sons may keep the possessions they hold; the rest I leave for my funeral.

Melainis [and] her [son] Ammonios, whose father I am, and whom (both of them) I reared, I set free, if they stay with me as faithful servants as long as I live. [I remit] them the payment of maintenance. They shall be free as from a sale to the god (?). Nobody shall have the right on any pretense to lay hands on them.

I choose for executors king Ptolemy son of [king Ptolemy] and of Arsinoe, brother gods, and queen [Berenike], the sister and wife of [king Ptolemy] and [their children.]

Witnesses: (The first two witnesses are missing because part of the papyrus is lost here)

[NN son of – –]s, Persian of the *epigonê*, [about x years old, – –], with a [long] face and a scar in the middle of his forehead and another one below his chin,

[– –]s son of Theokles, Macedonian of the *epigonê*, about 31 years old, of honey-colored complexion and medium stature, with straight hair and a scar on his nose,

Euphris son of Euphris, Cyrenean of the *epigonê*, [about x years old, of medium] stature and honey-colored complexion, with hair brushed up and a scar [on his forehead] on the left,

Archestratos son of Nikandros, Carian of the *epigonê*, about 24 years old, [of medium stature] and honey-colored complexion, with straight hair, a long face, and a scanty beard.

4.5.3 Will of the cavalry officer Dryton on the occasion of his marriage

P.Dryton 2 (= Vandorpe 2002a: 59–68) (Latopolis [Esnah], 4 March 150 BC). Image: Figure 9.

Dryton was a cavalry officer of Cretan origin and a citizen of Ptolemais in Upper Egypt.[86] He wrote at least three wills (*P.Dryton* 1–3), in 164 BC (in favor of his first wife Sarapias), in 150 BC (in favor of his son Esthladas and the children of his new marriage), and in 126 BC (division of his property between Esthladas and his five daughters of the second marriage, with maintenance for his wife (Vandorpe 2002a).

[86] Dryton's family presents a fascinating picture of a mixed legal tradition. See Vandorpe, above, **3.1.2.**

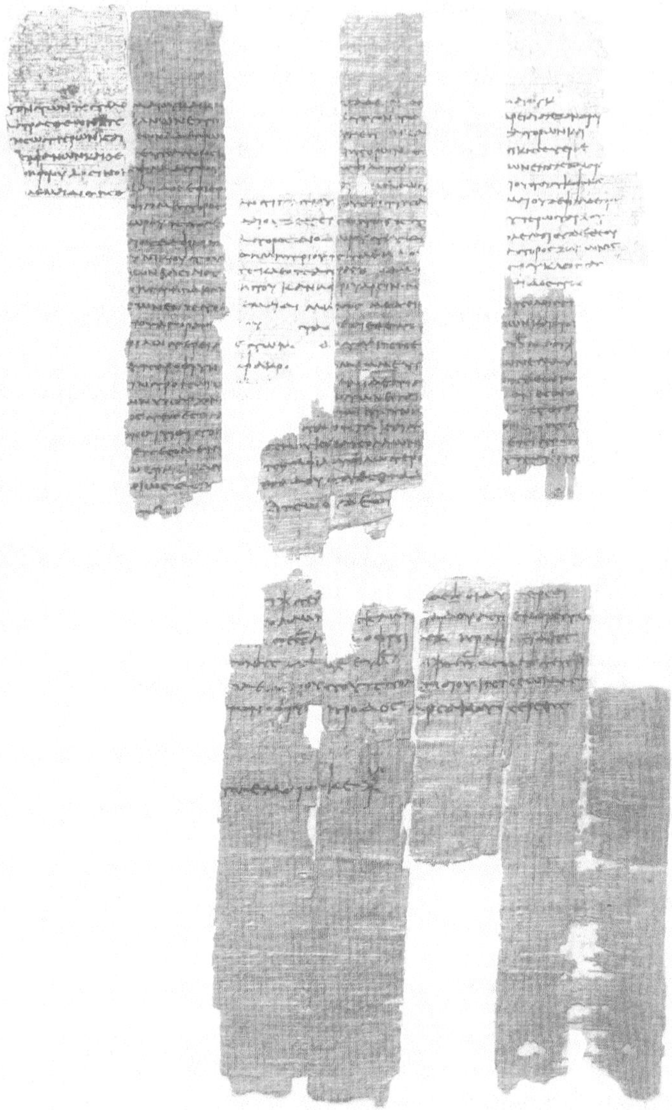

Fig. 9. Will of cavalry officer. *P.Dryton* 2. Latopolis (Esnah), March 150 BC

The present will was drawn up on the very day that Dryton married his second wife Apollonia, as is clear from the docket on the back. The couple lives in Pathyris, but as there is no notary there, they have their will drawn up in Latopolis (Esnah). The will apparently functions also as a marriage contract. Marriage contracts similarly contain provisions for the wife and her children in case the husband died.[87]

By a general legacy Dryton divides his present and future property in two halves, one half for Esthladas, the son of his first marriage, the other for the future children of his young new wife Apollonia. Esthladas, who was also in the army, inherits the military possessions of his father, his armor and his horse. A family member functions as testamentary executor.

The will is very similar to **4.5.2** and stands firmly in the Greek tradition. Apollonia, however, came from a hellenized Egyptian family.

In the reign of Ptolemy (VI) and Kleopatra (II) his sister, children of Ptolemy (V) and Kleopatra (I), the gods who appear (to humans), year 31, when NN was priest of Alexander etc. (. . . *here follows a long list of eponymous priests in Alexandria and Ptolemais* . . .) on the sixth of Mecheir in Latopolis [of the Thebais, before] the notary Ptolemaios.

[Dryton son of Pamphilos . . .] of the demos Philotereios, belonging to the cavalrymen of Diodotos, [about 42 years old,] of medium stature and honey-colored complexion, [with straight hair, a long face, hair brushed up, a hooked nose, and] a scar near the top of his left eyebrow.

May I enjoy good health and be master over my own affairs and manage them as I wish. But if I should suffer the fate of man I be[queath and give of] my possessions in land and movables:

to Esthladas my son by Sarapias daughter of Esthladas, the wife with whom I have lived, to Esthladas my above-mentioned son, the half share as well as the weapons and the [horse] on which I serve in the army;

the remaining (I give) to the children which will be born from me and from Apollonia.

I [leave] as executor Hermophilos son of Pamphilos, belonging to the deme Philotereios, a relative of Dryton son of Pamphilos, and equally of Esthladas son of Esthladas. I do not bequeath nor give anything else to anybody else. Witnesses [. . .]

The list of witnesses is severely damaged: one is from Aspendos, another is a Persian (with a Persian patronymic) and a third is a cavalryman.

On the verso there is a docket reading:

The marriage of Apollonia with Dryton took place in Latopolis before the notary Ptolemaios in year 31, 6 Mecheir.

[87] E.g., *P.Eleph.* 2 (= *Jur.Pap.* 23).

4.5.4 Division of property among the children (*donatio mortis causa*)

P.Mil.Vogl. II 84 (= *P. Kron.* 50) (Tebtunis, 13 June AD 138). Image at *P.Mil.Vogl.* II, Plate 8.

Kronion's archive was found by A. Vogliano in Tebtunis in 1934. About seventy texts, all in Greek, ranging from AD 106 to 153, were grouped by D. Foraboschi in 1971 (*P.Kron*); some ten more have been added since.

Aged 75, Kronion equally divided his property after his death between his sons Harmiysis and Harphaesis and his granddaughter Tephorsais (born from the endogamous marriage between his children Kronion II and Taorsenouphis). His first-born son Kronion II was disinherited because of misconduct. A few months later Kronion II divorced his sister-wife and he was in serious financial trouble (*P.Kron.* 51, 52, and 16). Perhaps Kronion the father was here protecting his family against this prodigal son. Two other daughters, Tephorsais and Taorsenouphis, had already received a dowry and now got only a sum of money. Harmiysis, Harphaesis, and the younger Tephorsais have to pay for his funeral and possible debts.

This was a family of rather poor villagers, belonging to the lower ranks of the priesthood (*pastophoroi*), and owning only a few acres of land (seventeen arouras). They leased some more land (twenty arouras) from other landowners, but had difficulties in making ends meet, as is clear from the more than twenty loans in the archive. Perhaps the younger Kronion functioned as *phrontistês* for one or more Greek landowners in Tebtunis.

The will was written in the objective style by the notary and introduced by the verb *homologei*, which is borrowed from contracts (**2.1**). The testator distributed his property among his children and grandchildren, excluding one son. There was a provision for the author's burial rites. Six witnesses signed in their own hand and sealed the document with their signets. Because the testator was illiterate his subscription was written by a third person.

This type of will, clearly differentiated from the traditional Greek *diathêkai*, was typical of the villages, as opposed to the *metropoleis*, in the early Roman period and was especially well attested in the Arsinoite nome. Here it was called a *synchôrêma* ("agreement") in line 17; in the first century this type of will was called a *meriteia* ("division") (Yiftach-Firanko 2002).

In the twenty[-second] year of the Emperor [Caesar Trai]anus Hadrianus Augustus, 19 Payni, in Tebtunis of the *meris* of Polemon of the Arsinoite nome.

Kronion son of Cheos and Taorsenouphis, grandson of Harmiysis, from the village of Tebtunis, about seventy-five years old, [with a scar on] his right [hand] acknowledges that he has ceded after his death to Harmiysis and Harphaesis, the sons born to him from his deceased wife Thenapynchis daughter of Patynis, and also to Tephorsais, the [minor] daughter of Kronion and Taorsenouphis, the other children of Kronion, the three of them as heirs, all things that their father Kronion will leave behind, all kinds of possessions and movables and household goods and furniture and other things and all things that are due to him and other things as well by whatever means, for each equally according to one third. For the [three] other children of Kronion, Kronion and Taorsenouphis and Tephorsais, he has bequeathed to Kronion only forty drachmas because, as his father Kronion says, he was wronged by him in many instances in the course of his life, and to his two daughters Taorsenouphis and Tephorsais he gives, besides the gifts he says he has arranged for them in gold, silver, jewels, and cloths, as a present to each [twenty?] drachmas. The funeral and the mummification and the distribution of the above-mentioned legacies and whatever he will eventually appear to owe in private and public debts are the duty of the three heirs, Harmiysis, Harphaesis, and his minor granddaughter Tephorsais. As long as the declarant Kronion is alive he will himself have the power over all his property to administer it as he likes.

Undersigner: Onnophris son of NN, about sixty-two years old, with a scar on his forehead.

Witnesses: Hippalos son of Chrates, about sixty-eight years old, with a scar on his right arm; Soterichos son of Eutychos, about forty years old, with scars on both his eyebrows; K[ronio]n son of Tyrannos, about thirty-two years old, with a scar on his left shin; Zoilos alias Tyrannos son of Kronion, about thirty years old, with a scar on his right knee; Arretion son of Ision, about forty years old, with a scar on his right foot; Diogenes son of Horion, about twenty-six years old, with a scar on his forehead, all six of them witnesses to the present cession (*synchôrêma*).

(*2nd hand*) I, Kronion son of Cheos, recognize that I have ceded after my death to my children Harmiysis and Harphaesis and to my grandchild Tephorsais, the three of them as common heirs with equal rights, all that I will leave behind, of all kinds of possessions and all household goods and the rest. To my son Kronion I have bequeathed, because he wronged me, only forty drachmas, to my daughters Taorsenouphis and Tephorsais each [twenty?] drachmas in addition to the payments as stipulated above. And I will seal with a signet of Isis and Harpochrates. I, Onnophris son of NN, have written for him because he does not know how to write.

(*3rd hand*) I, Hippalos son of Chrates, witness and I will seal with a signet of Harpochrates.

(*The other five witnesses similarly sign and seal.*)

In the twenty-second year of the Emperor Caesar Traianus Hadrianus Augustus, on 19 Psyni. It was registered in the notarial office at Tebtunis.

4.5.5 Draft of a Roman will (*testamentum per aes et libram*)

P.Oxy. XXXVIII 2857 (= Migliardi Zingale 1997, no. 4, pp. 26–29) (Oxyrhynchos, 17 May AD 134). Image at Papyri.info.

In Roman law the heir succeeded to all rights and obligations of the testator. The present will strictly follows the formulaic requirements of Roman wills. The introductory formula *testamentum fecit* is preceded by the name of the testator, the freedman Tiberius Claudius Alexander, followed by the formula *heres esto* and the name of his heir, and presumed wife, Claudia Theanous. All other persons are explicitly excluded from the inheritance (*exhereditatio*). In the *cretio* clause the testator imposes upon his heir the requirement that she accept the inheritance within one hundred days. The heir's (and presumably also the testator's) son Tiberius Claudius Ptolemaios is named substitute heir in case Claudia Theanous does not accept the inheritance. Then come two legacies of 100 drachmas to fellow freedmen and a wish that another 100 drachmas be set aside for the funeral that was to be carried out by the heir. (Changes remained possible as long as the testator survived.) Next come the clause *dolus malus abesto*, and the mancipatory clause by which "the purchaser of the household and chattels" (*familiae emptor*) bought the estate for a nominal sestertius. In ancient times the money was put on a scale, hence the name of this type of transaction: *per aes et libram*, "by money and scale." The names of the estate purchaser, scaleholder, and chief witness have not been filled in. The document ends with both Roman consular and Egyptian regnal dates. It is signed, in Greek, by the testator in his own hand.

Wills of Roman citizens had to be written in Latin up to the time of Hadrian (but cf. **3.3.1** n. 44 on this; **3.3.1** in general for other pertinent matters). Of the Latin version of this will – not the original, which was on wax tablets, but a copy on papyrus – only a few fragments remain below. The Greek translation, which is well preserved, had no legal effect, but recorded the contents in the language of the testator, who no doubt dictated his testamentary wishes in Greek. This was then translated into Latin by the notary, and later translated back into Greek. In the present will this was expressed by the words written by the testator: "I have read my will (*sc.* in Greek), in consonance with which I wished my Roman will to be written."

Tiberius Claudius Alexander, freedman of Tiberius, has made a will.

Let Claudia Theanous, my fellow freedwoman, be my heir to all that belongs to me, and let all others be disinherited in respect to me. And let her be under the obligation to give (and) to do all things that will have been written in this will without evil guile (*dolus malus*). Let her publicly claim my inheritance within the first 100 days when she will be aware and able to testify that she is my heir. But if she does not publicly claim or testify let her be disinherited [. . .] Let Tiberius Claudius Ptolemaios, her son, be my heir in the second grade, and let [all others] be disinherited. And let him be under the obligation to give (and) to do all things that his mother the [first] heir [was to give (and) to do]. Let him publicly claim my inheritance within the first [100] days without evil guile. Whoever [will be] my heir, I entrust to his faith to give.

To Tiberius Claudius Theonas, my fellow freedman, I give (and) bequeath one hundred drachmas. To Tiberius Claudius Demetrios, my fellow freedman, I give and bequeath one hundred drachmas. The care for my body I leave to my heir and I wish that there be spent for this no less than one hundred drachmas. If I leave anything, subsequently to this my will, on tablets, codicils, papyrus, or any other [writing material], written or signed and sealed by me, on the basis of which I will instruct or forbid anything to be given or happen or be supplied, I wish it to be as valid as this my will. May evil guile be absent from this will. Purchaser of the household and chattels in the making of this will: (BLANK), for 1 sestertius, the scale-holder being: (BLANK). Chief witness: (BLANK).

The will was made up in the city of Oxyhynchos in the Thebaid on the 16th before the Kalends of June, in the consulship of Lucius Iulius Ursus Servianus for the third time and Titus Vibius Varus, year 18 of the Emperor Caesar Traianus Hadrianus Augustus, Pachon 22.

(*2nd hand*) I, Tiberius Claudius Alexander, have read my will, in consonance with which I wished my Roman will to be written.

For I agree with everything as written above.

4.6 Intestate succession

Barbara Anagnostou-Cañas

The evidence for statutes that establish the rules of intestate succession in Greek and Roman Egypt is limited. In this branch as in the other branches of civil law the legislator intervened only incidentally. The main source for determining the legal order of succession was not law but custom. Composed of two sources of civil law, the Egyptian and the Greek, this custom enjoyed the state's sanction through first the Ptolemaic and then the Roman courts. Therefore, it is mostly from legal documents, contract clauses, and administrative documents that it is possible to determine facts that enable us to set the next of kin into a hierarchy.[88]

The Ptolemaic period documents presented (**4.6.1.a** and **4.6.1b**) show the pragmatism of the royal power that confirmed and completed the development of a system of testate succession concerning the land allotments of the Ptolemaic soldiers (see **6.4**). As to the Roman period, the documents here (**4.6.2a**, **4.6.2b**, **4.6.3**, **4.6.4**, **4.6.5**, and **4.6.6**) contain direct or indirect testimony to Roman statutes and local customs concerning successions.

4.6.1 Inheritance of soldiers' land allotments

4.6.1a Rules of an ordinance (*prostagma*)

BGU IV 1185 (= Wilcken 1920: 403–6, lines 1–15; *Jur.Pap.* 56d, lines 16–19; *C.Ord. Ptol.* 71) (Herakleopolite nome, *c.*60 BC)

In order to form a permanent army in Egypt the Ptolemies granted military settlers (*kleruchs*) the usufruct for life of a parcel (*klêros*) taken from the royal domain on the understanding that the beneficiary was subject to mobilization in time of war (see further **6.4**). Although they knew that after their deaths the usufruct of their parcels would be granted to their descendants, from the third century BC on the kleruchs disposed of it in their wills (*P.Petr.*^{2} 22, *P.Lond.* VII 2105). In an ordinance from the years 122/1–118/7 BC, Ptolemy VIII Euergetes II, Kleopatra II, and Kleopatra III granted to kleruchs the hereditary holding of their parcels (*P.Tebt.* I 124 = *C.Ord.Ptol.* 54). In his ordinance of the year 60 BC, Ptolemy XII on the one hand extended this measure to the billets occupied by the cavalry kleruchs and on the other hand established that if the cavalry kleruchs died

[88] Kreller (1919: 137–200), Taubenschlag (1955: 181–89).

intestate, their land allotments would be inherited by their nearest kin. In this way the king assimilated the land allotments to private property and acknowledged implicitly to cavalry kleruchs the right to dispose of them in their wills. By this decision the king extended to cavalry kleruchs of the Herakleopolite nome rights to a rule that he had enacted earlier concerning the cavalry kleruchs of the Arsinoite nome.

The first part of this ordinance (lines 1–12) also contains a penal and fiscal amnesty granted by the king to the cavalry kleruchs.

The translation follows Lenger's (1964) edition.

Col. I (lines 1–15): By order of the King.

[. . .] the cavalry kleruchs who observed their ancestors' attitude of devotion towards the power and who in crucial circumstances brought without difficulty their "crowns" in corn and in specie[89] will be amnestied together with their wives, their children, and their [. . .] the involuntary and intentional offenses that they committed, the convictions, the [. . .], all the legal proceedings started against them; they will be exempted from additional contributions [. . .] from fines, from illicit collections that they conduct, from pecuniary penalties called *epitima* and *prostima* [. . . until] (the year) 19, relieved of all the arrears owed to the royal treasury.

They and their descendants will continue to have the possession of the land allotment that they occupied and the billet [. . .] without having to fear either denunciation or accusation or confiscation for any motive.

Col. II (lines 16–19): And if some of them die intestate, their land allotments will be inherited by their nearest kin, as is the case with the cavalry kleruchs of the Arsinoite nome . . .

4.6.1b Petition regarding succession

SB VIII 9790 (tr. Rowlandson 1998, no. 167) (Herakleopolite nome, mid-first century BC)

Rhodokleia, daughter of an Herakleopolitan cavalry kleruch who had died without male descendants, indicates to the *stratêgos* that the cavalry kleruchs' accounts office acknowledged her as successor to a land allotment in accordance with royal legislation. The ordinance to which Rhodokleia

[89] From the end of the third century BC on, the word "crown" indicates an annual land tax paid in corn or *in specie* collected over the land allotments of the kleruchs: Préaux (1939: 394–95).

refers seems to be that promulgated by Ptolemy XII in the year 60 BC (see **4.6.1a**).[90]

The translation follows Kiessling's edition.

To Alexander, *stratêgos* of the Koites (toparchy), from Rhodokleia daughter of Menippos, an orphan from (the village of) Phebichis. After the death of my above-named father, according to the ordinances of the greatest kings, I was acknowledged by the cavalry kleruchs accounts office (to have inherited) the 20 arouras left by my father from the land allotment near (the village of) Molothis, because there were no male descendants and because the ownership of the rest of the property [. . ..] has fallen to my [. . .]

4.6.2 Legitimacy and inheritance

4.6.2a A prefect's decision about soldiers' marriages

P.Catt. recto Col. IV, lines 1–15 (= *M.Chr.* 372; *Jur. Pap.* 22b; *FIRA* III 19b) (Alexandria [provenance unknown], 4 June AD 115)

Considering military life to be incompatible with marital life, Romans for a long time did not allow soldiers to marry. This prohibition did not impede de facto unions, particularly in Egypt, a province whose importance to Rome required the presence of a significant garrison. Nevertheless, the papyrological evidence shows that Roman soldiers lived there as husband and wife with Roman, but more often with peregrine women. The recto of *P.Catt.* is a collection of seven precedents dating from AD 114 to 142 concerning litigation resulting from the prohibition of soldiers' marriages. The Chrotis case (col. IV, lines 1–15) was judged by the prefect M. Rutilius Lupus. Chrotis and Isidoros, both Alexandrian citizens, had lived together as man and wife. Isidoros joined the Roman army, became a Roman citizen, and took the name Iulius Martialis. During his military service they had a son, Theodoros. Martialis subsequently died leaving a will in which he appointed his son as his sole legatee. Chrotis asked that her son be exempted from the Roman 5 percent tax on inherited property, an exemption that could be claimed only by the next of kin of a Roman citizen.[91] Through this reasoning, she asked implicitly that her son be recognized as his father's legitimate son. The prefect refused to proclaim

[90] *C.Ord.Ptol., All.* 96.

[91] Dio Cassius 77.9.5; cf. Kreller (1919: 103 n. 3 and 105).

Theodoros the legitimate son of Iulius Martialis but he recognized that his father had appointed him his heir legally.[92]

The translation follows Mitteis' edition (*M.Chr.* 372).

> (Year) 18 of the reign of Trajan, Payni 10. Chrotis having said through the intermediation of the advocate Philoxenos that, being an Alexandrian citizen, she had lived with Isidoros, an Alexandrian citizen himself, as husband and wife, and that afterwards, the latter having enlisted in the cohort, she had from him a son, Theodoros, on whose account she petitions, requesting, if it has been neglected, his exemption from the one- twentieth-portion tax; that the testament which the former wrote makes it clear that the latter is his son, since he appointed him his sole legatee; the testament of Iulius Martialis, soldier of the First Cohort of the Thebans, having been read, Lupus said, after having consulted his friends:
>
> Martiali(o)s being a soldier, could not have a legitimate son; but he legally appointed him his legatee.

4.6.2b Imperial constitution about rights of soldiers' children

BGU I 140 (= Wilcken 1902 [with improved readings]; *M.Chr.* 373; *FIRA* I 196; *Sel.Pap.* II 213) (Alexandria?, AD 119). Image at *BGU* I, Plate II.

Gaius states that the citizen soldiers had the faculty to appoint peregrines as their heirs.[93] This privilege enabled many of them to make wills in favor of their children born from their concubines, but an inequality remained between the children of a provident father and those of a negligent one. Therefore the Emperor Hadrian decided to grant to the children of Roman soldiers conceived during their fathers' military service the right to inherit on intestacy in the following way: in the absence of a testament of a decedent, the praetor in Rome could call to the possession of his estate (*bonorum possessio*) different classes of persons (*bonorum possessores*); Hadrian placed illegitimate soldiers' children in the third class, which was that of the consanguines (*cognati*). **4.6.2b** contains the copy of a constitution in the form of a letter that Hadrian addressed on this subject to the prefect of Egypt Q. Rammius Martialis. In this letter the Emperor granted the illegitimate children of soldiers *bonorum possessio unde cognati*. They could therefore obtain the possession of the paternal estate in the

[92] Gaius, *Inst.* 2.109–10. [93] *Inst.* 2.109–10.

absence of legitimate children of their father, born before or after his military service, and of agnatic relatives.

The translation follows Mélèze Modrzejewski's edition.

Copy of a letter of the Lord, translated [. . .], which was displayed in the 3rd year of Trajan [Hadrian Augustus], in the consulship (of Hadrian) [consul for the third time] and of Publius Dasumius Rusticus, [at Alexandria(?)] in the winter camp of the [legion III] Cyrenaica and the legion XXII Deioteriana, the day before the Nones of August, which is II Mesore, at headquarters.

I know, my Rammius, that individuals whose parents begot them during the period of the father's military service have been hindered from inheriting their fathers' property and it did not appear hard since (their fathers) were acting contrary to military discipline. But I seize with great pleasure the opportunity to interpret more humanely the measures which were decided with more severity by the emperors before me. That is the reason why, although those who were begotten during the period of (their fathers') military service are not legitimate heirs of their fathers, I order that they be allowed to claim possession of the property in accordance with that portion of the edict that grants this possession to the kinsmen by blood. It will belong to your duties to make this favor of mine well known to my soldiers and to my veterans, not in order that I may appear to take great importance in their eyes, but in order that they may use this measure in case they don't know about it.

4.6.3 Minutes of court trial: representation in succession

BGU I 19, lines 1–19 (= *M.Chr.* 85; *FIRA* I 190) (Arsinoite nome [Fayyum], AD 135). Image at *BGU* I, Plate I.

Chenalexas, an Egyptian woman, starts legal proceedings against her uncle and her cousin, who were in possession of all the inheritance of her paternal grandmother; she requests the successoral part of her deceased father. The affair came before the prefectural court (*conventus*) and was judged by Herakleides, an officer judging by delegation of the prefect. Chenalexas claimed before him that her father had acquired his part of the maternal succession, while her opponents asserted that he couldn't have done this because he had died before his mother. The affair was deferred for administration of proof. But the plaintiff could not produce documents to prove her allegations, since before Menander, the new judge, she demanded to be accorded the advantages of a constitution of Hadrian.

The Emperor had granted the grandchildren of Egyptians the right to represent deceased heirs and Chenalexas produced a precedent, that is, the decision of an *epistratêgos* who had already applied that imperial measure. Despite this, Menander, before he gave a verdict, consulted the prefect M. Petronius Mamertinus for two reasons: first, because the affair was important, second, because the imperial grant was made after the death of Chenalexas' grandmother. The prefect responded the same day ordering the retroactive enforcement of the constitution. The term "Egyptians" employed in Hadrian's constitution is used in the papyri of the Roman period to indicate all the residents of the province who were not Roman citizens or citizens of Alexandria or the three other Greek cities. That is, "Egyptians" were the inhabitants of the chief towns of the nomes and of the villages of the country (*chôra*) without ethnical distinction.[94] Because the principle of representation in succession was known to the Romans and to the Greeks and also to native Egyptians, it is probable that Hadrian wanted to confirm this principle for all the inhabitants of the country and to dispel the doubts that its application as custom could arouse among the provincial judges.[95]

The translation follows Mitteis' edition (*M.Chr.* 85).

Copy. By delegation of Petronius Mamertinus, prefect of Egypt. Year 19 of Hadrian Caesar the lord, Mecheir 17, in the case of Chenalexas versus Petesouchos and Dionysios. Menander the judge told the litigants: "I postponed the present affair, because it was in the general interest, until I should write to His Excellency the prefect to ask him if the inheritance of the grandmother's estate was given to the grandsons and to the granddaughters of the Egyptians by virtue of a grant of the lord Hadrian Caesar. So, the letter I wrote to His Excellency the prefect and the one he sent me in response will be read." He ordered that both of them be read and inserted in the minutes, their content being verbatim as follows:

"To His Excellency the prefect Petronius Mamertinus, Menander, former royal scribe of the Arsinoite nome, greetings. At the last *conventus*, Chenalexas daughter of Alexander, Egyptian, was involved in a lawsuit with her paternal uncle Petesouchos and her cousin Dionysios before the judge Herakleides, about the part of the inheritance of her grandmother which she said had fallen to her father from his mother. As those around Petesouchos confirmed that the latter had died before his mother in the first year of the reign of Hadrian Caesar the lord (AD 117/8),

[94] Bickerman (1930: 42–43). [95] Katzoff (1970).

whereas (Chenalexas said he died) in the fifteenth year (AD 131/2), she promised to prove it with documents. The judgment was deferred for administration of proof. Now, all of them having been sent to me for trial, she claimed to benefit by the grant of the god, the most illustrious Emperor, who allowed the Egyptians to inherit their grandmothers' estate, and she brought a precedent of His Excellency the *epistratêgos* Gellius Bassus, who had judged that the children's children also inherit the estate of the grandmother. After other things, his decision was written as follows: 'All the paternal estate that falls to the person in question from the testament of Eudaimonis or in any other way, will come to his children.' The matter being also about the question whether with the grandmother being dead intestate the ninth year before the Emperor's grant, the granddaughter will take the part of the succession of her father, I write to you, my Prefect, so that you may command what in your opinion is to be done. I pray for your health, Lord Prefect. Year 19 of the Emperor Caesar Trajan Hadrian Augustus, Mecheir 14."

To which letter it was answered:

"Petronius Mamertinus to Menander, former royal scribe of the toparchy of Polemon, greeting. If no judgment has been pronounced on the affair between Chenalexas and Petesouchos [. . .] paternal uncle and Dionysios, cousin, concerning the estate of her grandmother, it is advisable that, according to the letter of the lord, you allow Chenalexas, through your judgment, to succeed to the part of the paternal estate her father would have inherited if he had survived. Goodbye. Year 19, Mecheir 14."

He pronounced the following decision:

"It seems advisable, according to the letter of His Excellency the prefect, that Chenalexas should succeed to the part of the paternal estate her father would have inherited (from his mother) if he had survived."

4.6.4 Minutes of court trial: limits to freedom of testation

CPR I 18 (= *M.Chr.* 84; *Jur.Pap.* 89; *FIRA* I 189) (Arsinoite nome [Fayyum], AD 124)

This document is a record of a trial that was held subsequent to a nullity suit started by a father concerning the will made by his deceased son. The Roman judge had to choose between two solutions: either to recognize the incapacity of a son born of an unwritten marriage to make his will in favor of a third person, even if the latter was a cousin or a brother, whereas his father, who was his legal successor, was still alive; or to recognize the principle of freedom of testation. The two solutions are presented as belonging to the local custom known as the "law of the Egyptians."[96] The judge pronounced in favor of the right claimed by the privileged ascendant. Thus, he chose a solution in accordance with the Roman theory of the *querela inofficiosi testamenti*, which protected nearest kin against a testator's caprices.[97] As regards the unwritten marriage, attested from Greek documents of Egypt under Roman rule, it was a type of union based on the mutual consent of the spouses and on their living together without any written documentation of marriage.[98]

The translation follows Mitteis' edition (*M.Chr.* 84).

In the district of Herakleides of the *stratêgia* [i.e., nome] of the Arsinoite. Extract from the roll of the minutes of Blaesius Marianus, prefect of the First Flavian Cohort of Cilician cavalrymen. By delegation of his Excellency the prefect Haterius Nepos, the eighth year of the Emperor Caesar Trajan Hadrian Augustus, Pharmouthi eighteenth. In the presence of Claudius Artemidoros, jurist, Aphrodeisios son of Apollonios, versus Ammonios son of Apion. Aphrodeisios stated through the advocate Soterichos that, after having lived with a certain Sarapous in an unwritten manner, he had from her Origenes, who died, and other sons; and that, whereas the law calls fathers to the estates of children born of an unwritten marriage, the opposing party wants to be testamentary heir of Origenes, although in accordance with the laws, the latter did not have the right to write a will to the advantage of a third party while his father was alive. The testament being unjust and illicit with respect to the opposing party, he (Aphrodeisios) claims what was bequeathed by his son.

Ammonios responded through the advocate Marcianus that the law of the Egyptians gives to all those who make their wills the right to bequeath their property to whomever they want and that he himself is a cousin of the deceased and that he was designated heir with another son of the opposing party and that the will has the required number of witnesses.

Blaesius Marianus (said) : "Let the will of Origenes be read." After the will was read, the eighth year of Hadrian the Lord, Choiak thirtieth, Blaesius Marianus, prefect of the First Flavian Cohort of Cilician

[96] On the problem of the origins of the rules of the "law of the Egyptians," see Mélèze Modrzejewski (1988 and below, **10.1**).

[97] Watson (1971: 61–70). [98] Yiftach-Firanko (2003: 81–104).

cavalrymen, having deliberated upon the case with the jurist Artemidoros, dictated a decision which was read and which was verbatim as follows:

"The late Origenes having been born of an unwritten marriage seems to leave his property to the father, without having the right to make a will while his father was alive."

And Ammonios having said that Origenes had been born of a written marriage whereas Aphrodeisios having confirmed that he was born of an unwritten marriage, Blaesius Marianus, prefect of the First Flavian Cohort of Cilician cavalrymen (*said*):

"Aphrodeisios will prove this very thing within 60 days."

Aphrodeisios having claimed that, under these circumstances, an inventory of the inheritance left from him (*Origenes*) be made, Blaesius Marianus ordered Isidoros, a prefectural assistant, to make the inventory in duplicate and to give a copy to the parties involved, the key of the house with seals on its door staying in Ammonios' control. A little later, Isidoros having announced that the order had been executed, Blaesius Marianus (said):

"I have ordered that this debate should be entered on the minutes."

Claudius [. . .] keeper of the record office (*bibliophylax*), (said): "The text is in the rolls." The eighth year of the Emperor Caesar Trajan Hadrian Augustus, Epeiph twenty-first.

4.6.5 Application for succession to an inheritance

SB I 1010 + *SB* VI 9298a+b (**A:** *Jur.Pap.* 27; *FIRA* III 61; *CPL* 216; **A+B:** *ChLA* 486; Pestman 1990, no. 61) (Oxyrhynchos, AD 249). Image at Papyri.info.

This petition of a minor successor acting with the assistance of his father, who is mentioned as his tutor, concerns the succession to his deceased mother's estate. There is no mention of a will. The document has come down to us in two copies. The first one (**4.6.5a**) contains the copy of the original petition in Latin signed in Greek; then, in Latin, the decision of the prefect, who grants the possession of the maternal estate; then, in Greek, reference to the prefectural register, which was a roll made with papyri containing requests on the same subject pasted together; and finally the beginning of a Greek translation of the petition. The second copy (**4.6.5b**) contains the registered copy of the literal translation of the petition in Greek authenticated by the Roman lawyer who drew up and translated the document.

As indicated by their *tria nomina* (Marcus Aurelius NN), the petitioner and his father were upper-class Roman citizens of Egypt who traced their citizenship to Caracalla's *Constitutio Antoniniana* of AD 212 or possibly even before that (D. Hagedorn 1979). The young orphan asks the prefect to grant him the possession of his mother's estate in accordance with the portion of the edict of the praetor that granted lawful successors (*unde legitimi*) the possession of the estate. This petition is the proof of the application in Egypt of the *senatus consultum Orfitianum*, adopted under the reign of Marcus Aurelius and Commodus in AD 178, which called children to the succession of their intestate mothers before the agnates.[99]

The translations follows Pestman's edition.

4.6.5a Bilingual request for *bonorum possessio*

SB I 1010 (Oxyrhynchos, AD 249)

In Latin: To Aurelius Appius Sabinus, the most illustrious, prefect of Egypt, from M. Aurelius Chaeremon, also called Didymos, minor, acting with the assistance, as guardian, of his father M. Aurelius Chaeremon, also called Zoïlos, conqueror in the games, citizen of Antinoopolis. I beg you, my lord, to grant me the possession of the estate of my mother Aurelia Hammonilla daughter of Heraclas [. . .] from the town of Oxyrhynchites, in accordance with that portion of the edict in which you undertake to give the possession of the estate to the lawful heirs.

This application was presented the 18th day before the Kalends of October in the consulship of Aemilianus, consul for the 2nd time, and of Aquilinus.

In Greek: (*2nd hand*) Aurelius Didymos, also called Chairemon, minor, acting with a guardian, my father Aurelius Chairemon, also called Zoïlos. I ask for the possession of the estate of my mother.

(*3rd hand*) The seventh year, Thoth 18.

In Latin: (*4th hand*) "In accordance with the edict. I have seen it."

In Greek: Sheet 51, of the second papyrus-roll.

(*5th hand*) Translation.

To Aurelius Appius Sabinus, prefect of Egypt, from Marcus Aurelius Didymos, [. . .] also called Chairemon, minor, acting with a guardian, his father, Marcus Aurelius Chairemon also called Zoïlos, conqueror in the games, citizen of Antinoopolis.

[99] Volterra (1966: 582).

4.6.5b Request in Greek for *bonorum possessio*

SB VI 9298a+b (Oxyrhynchos, AD 249)

Copy. To Aurelius Appius Sabinus, prefect of Egypt, from Marcus Aurelius Didymos, also called Chairemon, minor, acting with a guardian, the father, Marcus Aurelius Chairemon also called Zoïlos, conqueror in the games, citizen of Antinoopolis. I beg you, my Lord, to grant me the possession of the estate of my mother Aurelia Ammonilla daughter of Heraklas, from the town of Oxyrhynchos, deceased, in accordance with that portion of the edict in which you undertake to give the possession of the estate to the lawful heirs. This application was presented the eighteenth day before the Kalends of October in the consulship of Aemilianus, consul for the second time, and of Aquilinus, the 7th year of the Emperors Marci Iulii, Thoth 18, sheet 51 of the second papyrus-roll. I, Aurelius Aegyptus, and however I am styled, Roman jurist, translated the present copy and it is in agreement with the original document which is in the register and which I composed.

4.6.6 Devolution of inheritances without heirs

BGU V 1210 §4 (= *Jur.Pap.* 93, *FIRA* I 99) (Theadelphia [Fayyum], after AD 149)

BGU V 1210 contains the Gnomon of the *Idios Logos* (**2.6.4** above), a collection of 121 rules, perhaps precedent cases, addressed from the imperial departments in Rome to the *Idios Logos*, an equestrian procurator who was an administrator of state property in Egypt as head of the department of the *Idios Logos*, originally a Ptolemaic creation (see Swarney 1970). Paragraphs 4 to 22 and 27 to 54 of the Gnomon regulate succession.

§4 provided that, in the absence of legal heirs, intestate estates were appropriable to the fiscus. This rule reflects Roman law because it orders to be reserved for the fiscus the *bona vacantia* that the *lex Iulia de maritandis ordinibus*, voted under Augustus, granted the Roman people.[100] But it seems that §4 also preserves a Hellenistic principle, that of the devolution of inheritances without heirs to the state. We do not know of any Ptolemaic statute giving this privilege to the state, but documents of the Ptolemaic period attest indirectly that the royal treasury could acquire the intestate estates of the inhabitants of the *chôra*. They mention sales,

[100] Gaius, *Inst.* 2.150; *Regulae Ulpiani* 28.7. Cf. Rathbone (1993).

made by the department of the *Idios Logos* acting for the royal treasury, of confiscated or ownerless property, the latter being composed not only of property abandoned by its owners but also of intestate estates deprived of legal heirs.[101]

This privilege of the Ptolemaic Crown is also indirectly attested for Alexandria by the Gnomon through §9, which reflects Alexandrian law. It provides that, if the *libertus* (freedman) of an Alexandrian citizen died intestate and without children, it was his *patronus* or his *patronus*' son who inherited his property if they claimed it as inheritance before the court; if they renounced the inheritance, the fiscus could claim it. This rule offered to the royal treasury of the Ptolemies the possibility of inheriting a share of the inheritances of Alexandrians.[102] In a different geographical area, in the kingdom of the Seleukids, a copy of the law of succession of Dura-Europos was preserved on a parchment written in the third century AD but with rules going back to the Hellenistic period. They lay down a hierarchy of heirs, in which women and ascendants are possible heirs, and provide that "if there be none of these, let the property be the king's."[103]

The Ptolemaic documents just referred to, along with the provision regarding Alexandrians of Gnomon §9 and the law of Dura-Europos, allow the hypothesis that the devolution to the royal treasury of inheritances without heirs was a principle in force in Ptolemaic law as well as in the law of the Seleukids. §4 of the Gnomon thus appears as a general rule referring to Roman law and to the Ptolemaic fiscal system, applicable to Roman citizens as well as to peregrine inhabitants of Egypt.

The translation follows Modrzejewski's edition.

> *§4* The estate of those who die intestate, and who besides don't leave any legal heir, is awarded to the fiscus.

101 *UPZ* II 220–221 (130 BC), *P.Baraize* (= *SB V* 8033, *Et. de Pap. II*) (165–158 BC), and *P.Haun. II* (158 BC).

102 Hypothesis of Reinach (1920: 46–47).

103 *P.Dura* 12, lines 14–16.

CHAPTER 5

Capital

Claudia Kreuzsaler, François Lerouxel, †Tomasz Markiewicz, Hans-Albert Rupprecht, and Katelijn Vandorpe

Introduction

The loan is among the most common types of Egyptian contracts recorded in Greek (Palme 2009: 368). It is also well represented in the Demotic legal tradition. The present chapter explores the types of loans represented in Demotic, and the variety of Greek loans from the Ptolemaic and Roman periods, as well as one (**5.5.3**) from the Byzantine. We begin with three examples of Demotic loans of the Ptolemaic period and a text dealing with the litigation concerning a loan (**5.1**). These are followed by: selected Greek loans of the Ptolemaic (**5.2**) and Roman (**5.3**) periods; examples of the use of real security in the Greek papyri (**5.4**); and Greek loans that were components of other transactions (**5.5**).

In classical Athens, the credit market was populated by professional bankers and private lenders who provided large maritime loans as well as smaller amounts of credit. Recent research has pointed to the segmented image of the private credit market in Athens: the rich preferred to lend to the rich, citizens to citizens, foreigners to foreigners, whereas bank credit circulated more between social groups.[1] In Ptolemaic Egypt, however, the credit market was dominated by private lenders, who tended to lend out to relatives, fellow villagers, or colleagues. Because of the nature of the documentation, mainly small-scale loans are attested.

The Ptolemaic state became increasingly involved in the process of private lending. In the Greek documentation, despite regional variations, private creditors were protected by clauses that are remarkably alike from contract to contract. The private double document, whose contents were usually negotiated in the presence of six witnesses, was at first popular, but by the later Ptolemaic period it was outstripped in some regions by the notarial contracts, administered through a

[1] Chankowski (2008).

registration system controlled and thus protected by the state, as well as by the *cheirographon*, a self-written acknowledgement of debt drawn up without the presence of witnesses, in which the scribe applied several clauses from more formal contracts. In addition, six-witness contracts and self-written acknowledgements could be registered in the later Ptolemaic period (Boswinkel and Pestman 1982, §3d) and thus were protected by the state.

Lending money or consumable goods in Ptolemaic Egypt was a non-professional activity between private persons. There may be one exception: concessionary banks, a kind of exchange office, apparently lent out money, under strict conditions, to those who frequented the market and to merchants. Nevertheless, this type of bank, appearing in the reign of Ptolemy II Philadelphus, did not survive the third century BC.[2] We may suppose that a good deal of private lending occurred without written contract and on a more informal basis.

The same kind of lending as in the Ptolemaic period prevailed in the Roman (**5.3**) – that is, small-scale private lending. Noteworthy is a return to the predominance of money loans following the monetary instability of the latter half of the Ptolemaic period and consequent prevalence of loans in kind. Also noteworthy are the reduction in the maximum legal interest on money loans from 24 percent to 12 percent, the proliferation of types of credit instruments, and the development of institutions that encouraged larger-scale transactions by firmly securitizing them (**5.4**). Banks, for example, helped to link credit lines between city and village, while the office of property registers (*bibliothêkê enktêseôn*) facilitated the recording of liens against property as backing for loans (cf. **2.6.3**). Of course, conversely, ownership of property eased access to credit, a process itself facilitated by the extension of private ownership of land under the Romans. Loans continued to be important in the Byzantine period (not well represented here, but see **5.5.3**). An interesting feature is the number of late loans in which the creditors were city-dwellers and villagers the debtors (Keenan 1981). This is a pattern, together with that of the so-called sales in advance of delivery (cf. **2.1.8** for the document type), that implies an earnest attempt to remonetize village economies so as to keep up with the generally highly monetized Egyptian economy of (especially) the sixth century AD (e.g., Banaji 2007).

[2] *P. Rev.*, Cols. 77 and 78; Bogaert (1984), Geens (2008).

5.1 Ptolemaic Demotic loans

†Tomasz Markiewicz

Except for the dubious Greek tradition about the legislation of Bocchoris (Markiewicz 2008) and a very fragmentary Demotic legal manual (*P.Zauzich* 41), normative sources for Egyptian law governing loans are lacking. Loan contracts, on the contrary, are common, and the incentive for their composition is clear: recording the act of loan in writing and placing the document with the creditor provided an important means of security. Debt acknowledgements are known already in the Third Intermediate period (1069–664 BC), the oldest being the abnormal hieratic *P.Berlin* 3048 verso B from about 837 BC; but the bulk of evidence is Ptolemaic.[3]

Legally these texts are varied in their form as well as in their contents. Besides lengthy loan contracts we find more abstract debt acknowledgements, renewals of existing debts, confirmations of repayment (in full or in part), various contracts establishing securities, cessions of property in satisfaction of debts, temple oaths resulting from lawsuits over unpaid debts, etc. Demotic sales on delivery also belong to this category since they used almost exactly the form of a debt acknowledgement rather than that of a sale.

In keeping with the prevailing Egyptian legal custom, the agreements are unilateral in form and "spirit." In other words, they imposed duties, obligations, and restrictions on one party only – the debtor. The other party, the creditor, is silent and passive. His only action, the delivery of the thing being lent, is presented as a *fait accompli* (whether this is really the case, or is just a formulaic fiction, we do not always know). All paragraphs and clauses seem to have one common purpose: to diminish the creditor's risk and to strengthen his position in case of litigation. We do not know whether debtors enjoyed protection against (unjust or excessive) claims of the creditors. If they did, they may have relied on state legislation. Diodorus (1.79.3) reports a dubious tradition by which it was the pharaoh Bocchoris who abolished slavery for debt, claiming that the body of every subject belonged to the king alone. Accordingly, no private person could enslave the king's subjects.[4]

The question of personal liability and slavery for debt in Egypt is perhaps the most interesting legal problem connected with loans.[5] The tradition quoted by Diodorus suggests that enslavement of insolvent debtors was known in Egypt at least before Bocchoris. Greek evidence attests that it was known in Ptolemaic Egypt, but we cannot tell whether it

[3] Möller (1921). Good examples of fifth-century BC Demotic loans are fully discussed in Vleeming (1991: 156–88).

[4] Markiewicz (2008).

[5] I treat this issue more fully in Markiewicz (2005: 142–46).

was a native Egyptian custom or something introduced from Greece or Macedonia or both. Among various guarantees, Demotic deeds often contain a clause that may be called "the clause of personal liability," as in the phrase, "the right of this document which is above will be on my head and (on the head of) my children" (*P.Dryton* 12, lines 14–15). The legal function of such a clause may have been (a) to submit the very body of the debtor and his children as security for debt; (b) to prevent his children from objecting to the alienation of their patrimony in payment of their father's debt; (c) to assure the liability for the debt beyond the lifetime of the original debtor. Due to the rather vague and brief "clause of liability," I am inclined to favour the last of the three possibilities. Egyptian contracts of the Ptolemaic period are usually quite detailed and something as serious as enslavement of the debtor and his family would no doubt have been treated more explicitly.

Although published Demotic texts pertaining to debts are relatively few, they document a vivid Egyptian legal tradition providing potential lenders and borrowers with an array of legal instruments that could be used even for complicated transactions. This tradition seems to have been almost fully developed even before the Macedonian conquest of Egypt and was hardly influenced by Greek legal practices in the Ptolemaic period. The creditor was in the stronger position in the contract. If this is a reflection of socio-economic circumstances, we may assume that the credit market belonged essentially to the creditors, with potential debtors willing to go to great lengths in order to get access to ready capital. It is not clear whether slavery for debt was practiced in Pharaonic Egypt, but it was definitely known in the Ptolemaic period (**9.1** below), as attested by royal legislation that sought to protect parts of the population from excessive oppression by creditors. We must not forget, however, that the position of the creditor may often have been a precarious one, as it was probably not easy to extract payments from a defaulting debtor. Egyptian legal procedure provided the latter with a relatively easy means of denying his obligation, if he was prepared to take an oath to that effect. It is therefore not surprising that creditors sought to protect themselves with various securities and heavy penalties.

5.1.1 Loan with conditional sale

P.Schreibertrad. 14 (= *P.Louvre* 2443) (Thebes, March/April 249 BC)

This Demotic loan of money belongs to the category labeled by Spiegelberg as "conditional sale" ("Kaufpfandvertrag").[6] It is characterized by

[6] Spiegelberg (1909: 91–106).

certain assets, in this case priestly liturgies, used as security for the debt. The loan transaction was secured by a sale document (above, **2.2**) incorporated into the body of a loan contract. If the debt was not paid on time the conditional sale converted into a real one. In such cases an additional document of cession (Dem. *sẖ n wj*, above, **2.3**) had to be drafted to make the sale legally binding in accordance with the Egyptian law (we find such a case, e.g., in *P.Hausw.* 18).[7]

The interest is set at 30 percent per year or 2.5 percent per month. It was in the period of this document (middle of the third century BC) that Ptolemy II issued a *diagramma* reducing the maximum interest rate to 2 percent per month.[8] **5.1.1**, dated to March/April 249 BC, could provide a *terminus post quem* for the said *diagramma*.

The guarantee clause in **5.1.1** is chiefly concerned with securing Taketem's rights in the future. Should anyone contest her rights to the pledged property, this person is required not only to pay the whole sum of 5 *deben* 7 *kite* (capital plus interest) back to her, but also to pay interest for the whole period from the day on which the document was drafted. The mention of a marriage document and the unusually long duration of the loan (three years) both suggest that we are actually dealing with a marriage agreement of some sort disguised as a loan. Perhaps Patoumis was unable or unwilling to give his newly wed wife Taketem the bridal gift of three *deben* and postponed it by three years, securing her rights by means of this contract. Another possibility is that he wanted to transfer all his property to his new wife and disinherit his children by a previous wife. In such cases the loan was altogether fictitious and the three years may be seen as a sort of "trial period" for the marriage.

> Year 36, second month of *peret* of the pharaoh Ptolemy son of Ptolemy the god, when Epainetos son of Epainetos was the priest of Alexander and the gods Philadelphoi and Echeitime daughter of Menneas was *kanêphoros* before Arsinoe Philadelphos. The *pastophoros* of Amun in the West of Thebes, Patoumis son of Pchorchonsis and Neschonsu, has said to the woman Taketem daughter of Lelous and Tainetem:

[7] Treated below in **6.1**. Conditional sales have to be distinguished from first-century AD Greco-Egyptian arrangements resembling more closely the modern concept of mortgage, such as *P.Zauzich* 39. Here a Greek loan is accompanied by Demotic sale (*sẖ n ḏb3 ḥḏ*) and Demotic withdrawal (*sẖ n wj*) plus a Greek sale. The security consisted of an unconditional sale and when the debt was paid a re-conveyance of the pledged property was necessary. On this type of security see Markiewicz (2005: 156–58).

[8] The precise date of this regulation is not known, but Pestman (1971: 7–8) has suggested that it was enforced between 250 and 245 BC.

"You have with me 3 silver *deben*, being 15 *statêrs*, being 3 silver *deben* again, in the name of the money that you have given me. And I shall give you for them 5 *deben* 7 *kite*, being 28.5 *statêrs*, being 5 *deben* 7 *kite* again, before the last day of the first month of *peret* of the year 39, which makes 3 years, which makes 36.5 months.

"If I don't give you the above 5 *deben* 7 *kite* until the last day of the first month of *peret* of the year 39, the above date, then you have caused my heart to be satisfied with the money of my half share of a house. . ."

(There follows a lengthy description of the pledged real estate with all clauses typical for a *sẖ n ḏbꜣ ḥḏ* agreement plus a specification of no less than twenty-five tombs in the *necropoleis* of Djême and Hermonthis for which the debtor serves as a *choachytês*; these liturgies are also pledged.)

. . . "Whoever shall oppose you because of them (i.e., the pledges), I shall cause him to go away from you. A son or a daughter of mine who would oppose you because of the above things, you have a claim on him regarding the above money and its interest. [. . .text damaged. . .] who shall oppose you because of the above things that I have issued you (this) document about, he shall give you the above money and its interest (accruing) from the day on which I issued you this document until the date on which he opposes you, compulsorily, without delay. You are after me regarding the right (*hp*) of the marriage document that I had issued to you before. And I shall fulfill it for you at any date independent of the above document without going to court with you about anything at all."

Written by Harmaios son of Nesminis.

5.1.2 Loan of wheat

P.Dryton 27 (Vandorpe 2002a: 201–05) (Pathyris, 12 February 112 BC)

This is a typical Ptolemaic loan of grain in Demotic from the Thebaid. It belongs to the bilingual archive of the soldier Dryton and his family from Pathyris (**3.1**, **4.5.3**). Dryton and his wife Apollonia, as well as their daughter Senmouthis and son-in-law Kaies, had attained some prosperity, and they were frequently involved in economic activities involving credit, usually as lenders. The archive contains no less than twenty documents pertaining to loans of wheat, barley, spelt, salt, and bronze money.

5.1.2 does not mention any interest. Nevertheless, there are good reasons to believe that the loan was not interest-free. Whereas in money loans the interest depended on the duration of the loan, in commodity loans it was usually fixed at 50 percent.[9] This was not necessarily mentioned on the papyrus, but a suspiciously large number of deeds feature amounts easily interpretable as the principal plus 50 percent (e.g., 3, 9, 15, 30, or 45 units), thus suggesting that it was common practice to "hide" the increase in the amount stipulated by the agreement. The 50 percent increase, known as *hêmiolion* in Greek documents, was probably of a very ancient date and was connected with fluctuations of commodity prices throughout the year.[10] In **5.1.2** the total sum stipulated by the debtor (15 artabas) most probably represents capital (10 artabas) plus interest (5 artabas). It should be noted that *hêmiolion* could be also used as a penalty: the contract above explicitly mentions an addition of 50 percent (to 22.5 artabas) if the debtor failed to pay on time.

Year 5, first month of *peret* day 26, of Queen Kleopatra (III), (granddaughter of) the gods Epiphaneis, and Pharaoh Ptolemy (IX) Soter and (the priests) who are appointed in Alexandria (and in) Ptolemais in the district of Thebes.

The man receiving pay (i.e., soldier) while he is registered at Krokodilopolis, Siepmous the younger, son of Psenpathes, said to the man receiving pay while he is registered at Krokodilopolis, Kaies son of Pates:

"You have with me (i.e., I owe you) 15 artabas of wheat – their half is 7½, being 15 artabas of wheat again – in the name of the grain that you gave me, while their interest is in them.

"I shall give them to you before year 6, first month of *shemu*, last day, in grain that is pure, without adulteration (or) chaff, while they are measured, transported, and delivered within your house in Pathyris according to the measure that you had measured them for me.

"If I do not give them to you within the above date, I shall give them (to you) with their increase of 50 percent in the month following the above month, compulsorily, without delay.

"I shall not be able to give them on another date except for the above date. I shall not be able to say 'I have given to you money, grain (or) anything whatsoever' without a valid receipt. I shall not be able to say <BLANK SPACE> 'I have performed for you <BLANK SPACE> the right of the *symbolon* (i.e., contract)' while the above *symbolon* is in your hand.

"Everything, all things that belong to me together with those that I shall acquire (in the future), are security for the above words until I have acted in accordance with them, compulsorily, without delay."

9 An exception to this universal rate is found in the documents from Pathyris, where the interest rate was apparently fixed by the authorities every year (depending on the harvest?). See Vandorpe (1998).

10 Markiewicz (2006).

Written by Nechtminis son of Nechtminis, who writes in the name of the priests of Hathor, Lady of Pathyris, of the five *phylai* (= priestly classes).

There follow signatures of four witnesses.

5.1.3 Partial repayment of a money loan

P.Chic.Haw. 10 (Hughes and Jasnow 1997: 59–61) (Hawara, February/March 221 BC). Image at *P.Chic.Haw.*, Plate 56.

The original debt of two silver *deben* must have been jointly contracted by two men, Akhomnevis and Nakht. This is a Demotic receipt issued by the creditor to Akhomnevis, who repaid his part of the debt. The persistence of the obligation of the other debtor is stressed. The original loan agreement probably remained in the hands of the creditor Marres as proof of the outstanding liability. The translation here follows Hughes and Jasnow (1997: 60).

Year 1, first month of *peret* of pharaoh Ptolemy son of Ptolemy and Arsinoe Philadelphos (*sic*) the gods Adelphoi, Berenike, when the priest of Alexander and the gods Adelphoi Euergetai was Nikanor son of Bakchios, and Aristomache daughter of Ptolemaios was *kanêphoros* before Arsinoe Philadelphos.

The *choachytês* of the pharaoh Maare (Amenemhat III) Maare (*sic*), Marres, son of Nakht-pa-Ra, whose mother is Ta-remetet[. . .] to the god's sealer and embalmer Akhomnevis son of Pasis, whose mother is Haunchis:

"You gave me 1 *deben* – its half is 5 *kite*, being 1 *deben* again – as your half share from 2 *deben* about which you wrote a document for me together with Nakht son of Petesouchos. I have received the above 1 *deben* from you.

"My heart is satisfied therewith, they being paid in full, without remainder. I have nothing at all against you on account of the above document with regard to your half share. As for him who might oppose you concerning it, I will make him go away from you necessarily, without delay. I am (still) after (i.e., still have a claim on) Nacht son of Souchos with regard to 1 *deben* in accordance with the document mentioned above. I have nothing at all against you on account of it from today onward."

Written by Thotmosis son of Nakht-Her-heb (?).

Written by Maa[. . .]

There follow signatures of twelve witnesses.

5.1.4 Litigation over a loan

O. Tempeleide 150 (Thebes, Ptolemaic)

The following Demotic text documents litigation arising out of an unpaid debt. The case was brought before an Egyptian court, which ruled that the defendant must swear a so-called temple oath regarding his debt. The case shows the importance of formal procedures for extinguishing a debt, i.e., handing over of the original deed *and* drafting of a receipt. As long as these were not fulfilled the burden of proof lay with the debtor.

The plaintiff in **5.1.4**, Onnophris, holds a deed of loan (Demotic *tnn* = Greek *daneion*) that was issued for his (deceased?) brother by the defendant Psenchonsis. It is explicitly stated that the *tnn* is "in the hand" of the plaintiff. Yet the defendant contested the obligation resulting from the deed, claiming that the debt had been partly repaid and the amount due has been reduced to five *deben*. If he swears an oath to that effect he will have to pay only five *deben*. Should he fail to do so, he will have to return the whole (unknown) sum. We can imagine that the original *daneion* deed was not handed over to Psenchonsis, since the debt was not fully repaid. After the death(?) of the first creditor the document was found among his papers by his heirs and became a cause of action, as the debtor could not produce any receipt.

> Words of the oath which Psenchonsis son of Petemonthes shall take in the gate of Djême, in the Temple of Montu-Lord-of-Meten, in the year 23, fourth month of *shemu*, day 27, to Onnophris son of Erianoupis, to wit:
>
> "By the Bull of Meten (i.e., local god) that rests here with those who rest with him! As for the *daneion*-deed that is in your hand – I have paid your elder brother for it. He does not have anything with me except for 5 *deben*, which are his."
>
> If he (Psenschonsis) takes the oath, he shall give 5 *deben* to Onnophris, with whom he had made the *daneion*-deed (i.e., loan). And he (Onnophris) shall give a withdrawal. If he refuses to take it, everything that he (Onnophris) will reveal, he (Psenchonsis) shall give it.

5.2 Ptolemaic Greek loans

Katelijn Vandorpe

The creditor was protected by written arrangements, secured by specific clauses, by the presence of other persons who acted as witnesses or as notary, or by the use of seals to secure the contents of the document against alteration. Already in the third century BC the so-called double documents (**2.1.1**; cf. **2.1.2**)[11] were introduced by the Greeks for loans and other transactions (e.g., *P.Corn.* 2). These agreements are inscribed twice on one papyrus: the upper part (or *scriptura interior*) is sealed so that its contents cannot be altered; the lower part (or *scriptura exterior*) is left unsealed and can be consulted whenever necessary.[12] Six witnesses may be present when the double document is drawn up; one of them, the *syngraphophylax*, keeps the document under his surveillance as long as the contract runs (**5.2.2**). With the spread of Greek notarial offices in the second century BC, Greek loan contracts by these notary scribes became popular (**5.2.3**). In these the transaction was secured by the presence of the notary, a governmental official who as a rule entered the contract in a register[13] and afterwards recorded the repayment.

In small-scale loans between people who trusted each other, a simple acknowledgement of debt written by the debtor in his native language might suffice (in Greek this was called a *cheirographon*, see **2.1.4–8**). Only if the debtor was illiterate, a third person was involved who wrote down the acknowledgement for him. From the second century BC onward, a more formal type of Greek *cheirographon* was established, the clauses of which are similar to those of the notarial and six-witness contracts, but which did not require witnesses, notary, or seals. The second-century BC archive of Dionysios son of Kephalas (Boswinkel and Pestman 1982) includes all the above-mentioned Greek types of loan contracts as well as Demotic temple contracts, thus allowing a detailed comparison of different types of loans.[14]

Only exceptionally did creditors demand a mortgage (see **5.2.1**). Provisional purchases, where real estate is sold in a contract that becomes valid only when the loan has not been returned (Pestman 1985a), were a concealed form of loan secured by real estate.

Creditors negotiated loans in order to increase their capital through interest (*tokos*) (for loans with other purposes, the so-called antichretic loans, attested in the Ptolemaic period but more frequent in the Roman, see below, **5.5**). Nevertheless, some loans are said to be "without interest" (*atoka*). Goodwill could have played a role in some cases, but the term *atoka* is misleading, since loans "with interest included" are usually involved, continuing an Egyptian practice.[15]

[11] Yiftach-Firanko (2008b). [12] Vandorpe (1997).

[13] For an example of such a register, see Vandorpe (2004).

[14] Boswinkel and Pestman (1982: 23–30, 176–93, 246–52, 280–82).

[15] Pestman (1971) and Vandorpe (2002a: 108–10).

Interest in loans of money was fixed by the month. Up to about 249 BC (**5.1.1**) a rate higher than 2 percent a month could be charged, but Ptolemy II reduced the maximum interest rate to two drachmas per mina (2 percent) monthly or 24 percent a year (**5.2.1**; see also **3.1.1**). For loans in kind (wheat, barley, spelt, salt, wine), an interest of 50 percent (*hêmiolion*) was common regardless of the duration of the loan (Pestman 1971; Lewis 1945). In some cases, especially when loans of seed were involved, a varying interest seems to have been agreed on, depending on the harvest to be expected (Vandorpe 1998).

When the loan was repaid, the debtor either received back the expired contract (**5.2.2**), or a receipt (**5.2.4**), or even both (e.g., *P.Dryton* 29). Only exceptionally a new notarial contract, called *epilysis* or *katabolê*, was drawn up to confirm the repayment. Such a contract was needed, for instance, when the loan had been returned too late or only in part (e.g., *katabolê*: *P.Grenf.* II 19; *epilysis*: *P.Grenf.* I 26).

5.2.1 Loan secured against mortgage (*hypothêkê*) of a house

P.Tebt. III.1 817 (= *CPJ* I 23, *SB* I 4232) (Krokodilopolis [Fayyum], 4 November 182 BC). Image at Papyri.info.

This Greek loan drawn up by a notary scribe is written on a papyrus that also contains other, now damaged, documents or notes. Both contracting parties are Jews. 15,000 drachmas of bronze money are lent "without interest" for one year. It is not clear whether the interest is already included in the total amount. If the interest is included and the usual rate of 2 percent per month is calculated, the original amount lent was 12,500 drachmas. The Biblical prohibition against Jews lending money at interest may not apply here, since interest is imposed only in case the loan is not returned in time. Nevertheless, similar contracts show that Jews did lend money to Jews at regular interest.[16]

The loan is, uncommonly, secured by a mortgage of real estate: a house and appurtenances, measuring 20 by 20 cubits. The exact location in the town of Apias is described. If the debtor Sostratos does not repay the loan in time, the creditor Apollonios may lay claim to the mortgage in accordance with a royal ordinance (*diagramma*) regulating this juridical question.[17] If there appears to be a problem with the mortgage, the debtor has to repay the loan, otherwise the usual fine for money loans will be imposed.

[16] *CPJ* I 20 and 24, and pp. 35–36.

[17] See the comment in *CPJ* I, p. 164, l. 20.

For further discussion of **5.2.1**, see **5.4.2** below.

In the reign of King Ptolemy son of Ptolemy and Arsinoe, the gods Philopatores, in the twenty-fourth year, at the time of the office of the priest who is appointed in Alexandria, (priest) of Alexander and the gods Adelphoi and the gods Euergetai and the gods Philopatores and the gods Epiphaneis, at the time of the office of the *athlophoros* of Berenike Euergetis appointed in Alexandria, of the *kanêphoros* of Arsinoe Philadelphos appointed in Alexandria, of the priestess of Arsinoe Philopator appointed in Alexandria, twenty-eighth day of the month of Dystros, Thoth twenty-eighth, in Krokodilopolis in the Arsinoite nome.[18]

Apollonios son of Protogenes, Jew of the *epigonê*, has lent to Sostratos son of Neoptolemos, Jew of the *epigonê*, a loan of two talents and three thousand drachmas of bronze money, interest-free, for one year from the above-written date, upon condition of a mortgage (*hypothêkê*) of the house and courtyard belonging to him including its appurtenances, located in the village of Apias in the district of Themistos, whose measurements are from south to north twenty cubits and from west to east twenty cubits. The neighbors are: south, house of Sopatra; north and east, streets; west: house of Harpalos and Sostratos, (belonging) to them at the date above-written. Sostratos shall return the loan to Apollonios within the year. If he does not pay back as written, then Apollonios shall have a claim on the mortgage pursuant to the royal ordinance (*diagramma*).[19] Sostratos shall guarantee this mortgage to Apollonios and shall guarantee it free of any encumbrances, unpledged, and free from other loans and free of royal claims (*basilika*, i.e., taxes). If he does not guarantee it or protect it as written or if any risk regarding this mortgage arises either for the whole or for a part of it in any way whatsoever, then Sostratos shall pay back the loan to Apollonios immediately within the year. If he does not pay back as written, then Sostratos shall pay to Apollonios immediately as a penalty the loan plus 50 percent of the lent sum (*hêmiolion*), and overtime interest of two drachmas per mina per month (= 24 percent). The document shall be valid everywhere.

In a more cursive script: Through Boubakes alias Stheneus.

Names and descriptions of the parties, in large characters: Apollonios, about 35 years old, tall, with honey-colored complexion, rather blue-eyed and with protruding ears.

[18] The dating follows the synchronization of the Macedonian and Egyptian months after 202 BC.
[19] On this royal edict (*diagramma*) see Wolff (1960).

Sostratos, about 35 years old, of middle height, with honey-colored complexion, [. . .], with a scar above his right eyebrow.

5.2.2 Six-witness loan contract of wheat

P.Dion. 16 (= *Pap.Lugd.Bat.* XXII 16, *P.gr.Rein.* I 16) (Tenis-Akoris, 15 February 109 BC). Image at Papyri.info.

Dionysios son of Kephalas was waiting to be recruited as an infantryman of the Ptolemaic garrison at Tenis-Akoris in Middle Egypt, and went into business in order to make a living. His substantial archive informs us about these activities.[20] Most texts are loan contracts of several types: Greek six-witness contracts, Greek and Demotic notarial contracts, and Greek self-written acknowledgements (*cheirographa*). Below is a six-witness contract. All six witnesses are signatories, one of whom, the syngraphophylax, or "guardian of the contract," is also custodian of the physical document for as long as the contract runs. The contract is written twice: the *scriptura exterior* is a full version, while the *scriptura interior* is a shortened version, rolled up and sealed[21] so that the important data of the text cannot be falsified. The parties and all the witnesses are present at the sealing and write their names around the three seals, which in this case are lost. The repayment of the loan was recorded on the back of the contract and the contract was returned to the debtors.

In February 109 BC, the leader of the rear-guard Dionysios son of Apollonios lent $166\frac{2}{3}$ artabas of wheat to Dionysios son of Kephalas and his mother, at the usual interest of 50 percent (the interest is called 1/3, that is, 1/3 of the total amount to be returned = 250 artabas). The debtors have to return the wheat after the harvest, in June/July of the same year. The quality of the wheat (new, compact, unadulterated), the measure to be used (an equivalent of the bronze standard measure, present in each nome), and the place and conditions of repayment are specified. If the debtors do not return the loan in time, they have to pay a fixed price of 3,000 drachmas per artaba.

Scriptura exterior: full contract, not sealed: In the reign of Kleopatra and Ptolemy, the gods Philometores Soteres, year 8, at the time of the office of the priest who is appointed in Alexandria, (priest) of Alexander, the gods

[20] Boswinkel and Pestman (1982). See the description of the archive of Dionysios son of Kephalas by B. Van Beek at www.trismegistos.org/arch/index.php.

[21] See above, **5.2** introduction.

Soteres, the gods Adelphoi, the gods Euergetai, the gods Philopatores, the gods Epiphaneis, the god Eupator, the god Philometor, the god Neos Philopator, the god Euergetes, and the gods Philometores Soteres; at the time of the office of the *hieros polos* of Isis the mighty mother of the gods, of the *stephanêphoros* of queen Kleopatra the goddess Philometor Soteira Dikaiosyne Nikêphoros, of the *athlophoros* of Berenike Euergetis, of the *phôsphoros* of queen Kleopatra the goddess Philometor Soteira Dikaiosyne Nikêphoros, of the *kanêphoros* of Arsinoe Philadelphos; of the priestess of queen Kleopatra the goddess Philometor Soteira Dikaiosyne Nikêphoros, of the priestess of Arsinoe Philopator: the priests and priestesses who are appointed in Alexandria; in the month of Dystros the 29th day, Tybi the 29th day, in Tenis also called the village of Akoris, in the district of Mochites, in the Hermopolite nome. Dionysios son of Apollonios, Persian, leader of the rear-guard, has lent to Dionysios son of Kephalas, Persian of the *epigonê*, and to the latter's mother Sarapias alias Senabellis, daughter of Heliodoros alias Herieus, Persian, with as guardian her own son Dionysios, mentioned above, compact wheat 166⅔ artabas of which they received from him from his house, at an interest of one third for each artaba of wheat, that is 83⅓ artabas. The borrowers shall return all the artaba*s* of wheat, 250 artabas, to Dionysios or his representatives, in the month of Loios which is also Payni, of the 8th year, in wheat that is new, compact, unadulterated, by a measure that is in conformity with the measure of bronze, delivered at the quay along the town of Akoris, at their own expense, without trials nor judgment and without any malpractice. If they fail to return the loan or if they do not act as prescribed, the borrowers shall pay to Dionysios or to his representatives, as price for each artaba, 3,000 bronze drachmas and nothing less. Sureties for each other for the loan, for the payment in full and for all liabilities described in the contract, are the borrowers themselves. Dionysios shall have the right of execution for this loan upon Dionysios and Sarapias themselves, mentioned above, upon each one of them both and upon whomsoever he chooses and upon all their property, as if by legal process. This contract shall be valid wherever it is produced.

Names and ethnics of six witnesses: Ptolemaios son of Anaxagoras, Milesian; Agenor son of Barkaios, Spartan; Arimmas son of Dionysios, Charistêrios;[22] Herodes son of Herakleides, Alexandrian; Eumenes son

[22] On this designation, see Boswinkel and Pestman (1982: 199).

of Polykrates, Persian; [Apollonios son of . . . Persian], one of those registered to Kleopatra [. . .]

The first witness is also the keeper of the contract, who identifies himself as such: [Keeper of the contract: Ptolemaios][23]

Subscription by the debtors (2nd hand): We, Dionysios son of K]ephalas, Persian of the *epigonê*, and his mother Sarapias alias Senabellis daughter of Heliodoros alias Herieus, Persian, with as guardian her above-mentioned son, the above-mentioned Dionysios, we have received the 250 artabas of wheat as stated and we shall act according to the other written conditions and we have handed over the valid document to Ptolemaios. I, the above-mentioned Dionysios, have also written for my mother Sarapias because she is illiterate.

Subscription by the keeper of the contract (3rd hand): I, Ptolemaios, have the valid document.

Scriptura interior: shortened version of the contract, to be sealed: Year 8, 29 Tybi. Loan of Dionysios to Dionysios and Sarapias of 250 artabas of wheat. The borrower shall return it in Payni of year 8 at the village of Akoris by a measure that is in conformity with the measure of bronze. Fine: 300 drachmas of bronze per artaba. Keeper of the contract: Ptolemaios.

Verso: names of the parties and the six witnesses, displayed to the right and left of the three seals

Verso: summary Loan of Dionysios to Dionysios and Sarapias, of 250 artabas of wheat.

Verso: note after the loan was returned. Dionysios. Repayment on 12 Payni.

5.2.3 Notarial loan contract of wine

P.Amh. II 48 (27 August 106 BC)

Nahomsesis daughter of Sebtitis was a successful Egyptian businesswoman from Pathyris, an Upper Egyptian town that has produced about one hundred Greek and Demotic loan contracts and receipts from the Ptolemaic period. Nahomsesis acted as creditor in Greek loans of wheat and wine.

[23] Restored from the *scriptura interior.*

Her papers turned up in the archive of her grandson Pelaias son of Eunous.[24] The loan object is eight jars of wine, "without interest." This is an expression found in all loans of consumable goods from Pathyris; it appears to be the equivalent of the clause "while the interest is included" found in the Demotic loans from the same town. Grapes in Egypt are harvested in the period August–September. Hence, the loan is negotiated in August and is to be returned one year later, by 30 Epeiph, that is, by the middle of August. The wine is to be returned at the wine-press:[25] here the grapes are crushed, probably in the presence of the creditor, and the juice is collected in empty vessels provided by the debtor and measured by a private measure of someone called Pelaias. Laid up in a storehouse, the wine ferments for three months until 30 Hathyr or mid-December and, if of a good quality, is then delivered to the house of the creditor.

The loan presented here was drawn up by the subordinate of the local Greek notary. It is common practice that the notary or his clerk add a Greek summary on one of the two sides of the rolled-up loan contract. On the side that was left blank, the Egyptian holder of contracts (in Greek, the *syngraphophylax*) sometimes added a private, Demotic summary.[26]

Year 11 that is also year 8, 13 Mesore, in Pathyris before Hermias, subordinate of the *agoranomos* Paniskos. Nahomsesis daughter of Spemminis, Persian, has lent to Psenthotes son of Alukis, Persian of the *epigonê*, eight jars of wine without interest. This loan he shall return to Nahomsesis on the 30th day of the month of Epeiph of the 9th year, at the wine-press, by the measure of Pelaias, furnishing very good vessels, and he shall provide wine that will keep until 30 Hathyr of the tenth year, and he shall deliver it to her at her house at his own expense. If he fails to return it within the stated time, he shall repay one thousand drachmas of bronze for each jar. Nahomsesis shall have the right of execution upon Psenthotes and upon all his property, as if by legal process.
I, Hermias, subordinate of Paniskos, have dealt with this contract.

Verso: Greek summary (1) Loan: Psenthotes son of Alukis, (2) eight jars of wine.

[24] Pestman (1981b). For a short description of the archive see Vandorpe and Waebens (2010: §44).

[25] For the Greek term *lênos*, "wine press," the equivalent of the Demotic expression "constructions to tread," but sometimes also "fermentation vat," see Kruit (1992a: esp. 268–69), Vandorpe and Clarysse (1998).

[26] Vandorpe (2000b).

5.2.4 Repayment of a loan of money

P.Dryton 21 (Pathyris, second half of the second cent. BC)

In this *cheirographon* or self-written receipt, Zois alias Onchasis acknowledges having received twelve talents of bronze from the priest Patous who represented Esthladas son of Dryton. Since the lady did not master Greek, a representative wrote the receipt. According to the Demotic summary on the back, the receipt was issued in the Greek notary's office, or *archeion*, where the repayment of this loan had to be registered.

> Zois alias Onchasis daughter of Isidoros, to Patous, one of the priests of the temples in Krokodilopolis and Pathyris, greetings. I have received from you on behalf of Esthladas son of Dryton, twelve talents of bronze, three thousand drachmas and I cannot charge anything against you.
>
> Has written (*name of the writer is lost*).
>
> *Verso: Demotic summary* Greek document which Onchasis has made in the *archeion*.

5.3 Greek loans in the Roman period

F. Lerouxel

As indicated in the chapter introduction, loans are the most frequent type of contract in Greek papyri from Roman Egypt, money-lending being a daily activity even in small villages. Interestingly, this pervasive activity is non-professional: there were private banks but they were not money-lending institutions. What the papyri document are private individuals lending to other private individuals. This simplicity was not an obstacle to large transactions. For example, the office of property registers (*bibliothêkê enktêseôn*), created in the beginning of the Flavian period, enabled borrowers to give creditors more reliable real securities. Consequently, in the following decades, the credit market became increasingly dynamic, the sums lent clearly rose and women had better access to the credit market.[27]

With the Roman conquest, two major changes occurred in the credit market. First, Augustus put an end to the monetary instability that prevailed during the last two centuries of Ptolemaic rule. In the Ptolemaic period, the monetary instability had led to a clear preference for loans in kind, which represented 60 percent of financial transactions. After Augustus, perhaps as a

[27] Lerouxel (2006).

result of his new measures, they make up just 15 percent. The second major change is reduction of the interest rate from 24 percent to 12 percent.

The financial system of the Egyptian economy has been described as archaic and responsible for a so-called economic stagnation. More recent research has shown that the credit market had its own historical characteristics and its own, increasingly complex, ways of functioning. In Roman times, not all types of contracts were to be found in every place and at every period. Some contracts, some types of securities, some methods of interest payment became scarce as new ones evolved. Loan contracts have their own history, shaped by the interaction of the economy with the society of Roman Egypt. Innovations in contractual practices seem to be decisively linked to changes on the economic front.

The texts below have been chosen to show this diversity and growing complexity of loans in Roman Egypt.

5.3.1 is a loan in kind. In this contract, two men borrow wheat and barley for seed. The transaction takes place in Tebtunis, a village in the Arsinoite nome. It is a loan without security, one of the simplest loans we can imagine.

5.3.2 is a loan of money. A woman and her son, from Tebtunis, borrow 1,300 drachmas at the rate of 12 percent a year from a former gymnasiarch, presumably a resident of the nome capital, Ptolemais Euergetis. This transaction is more complicated than the first one because two institutions are involved: a private bank located in Ptolemais Euergetis and the office of property registers of the nome (*bibliothêkê enktêseôn*). The private bank does not lend the money, it just pays it out. It may also have acted as a go-between. This financial intermediation may help connect local credit markets and may create financial links between the villages and the capital of the nome. On the other side, the office of property registers of the nome (*bibliothêkê enktêseôn*) gives greater efficiency to real securities, land and dwellings for the most part, which attend the largest loans. After the creation of this institution, the sums lent increase.[28]

5.3.3 consists of the cancellation of a loan contract after its full repayment. From a geographical and a financial point of view, this transaction takes us another step forward. It takes place in Alexandria, the largest city in Egypt and the second city in the Roman empire after Rome. The sum lent is huge: 13 talents (78,000 drachmas). The loan has been repaid in several installments made through two different banks.

[28] Lerouxel (2006).

The last text, **5.3.4**, is a private letter from Oxyrhynchos. It is neither a contract nor the cancellation of a contract. It allows us to catch a glimpse of the world of pawnbroking, another feature of the credit market, which is absent from written loan contracts, as numerous and informative as these may be.

5.3.1 Loan of wheat and barley

P.Kron. 9 (*BL* IX 115; *BL* X 90) (Tebtunis, 22 November AD 111)

This text belongs to the "archive" of Kronion and his family (see **4.5.4**). These Egyptian farmers lived in Tebtunis in the second century AD.

In this contract, written and registered through the record-office (*grapheion*) of Tebtunis, two peasants, Orsenouphis and Kronion, borrow twenty artabas of wheat and twenty artabas of barley from a man named Didymus. Orsenouphis and Kronion are brothers-in-law and they probably farm land together. They borrow the grain in the month of November for seeding and they bind themselves to repay in June (the Egyptian month of Payni), at harvest time. Almost all loans in kind (mainly cereals) or mixed loans (loans in both kind and money) are repaid in Payni at harvest time, whereas loans of money may be repaid at any time during the year. The contract is a *chrêsis*, a kind of loan frequent in Tebtunis. No interest is stated, which is normal in *chrêseis* in kind. The interest may have been included in the sum lent. Orsenouphis and Kronion are jointly liable for the repayment. No precise security is mentioned. According to a hypothesis generally admitted, the status of "Persians of the *epigonê*," a legal fiction during the Roman period, subjects them to expeditious enforcement in case of default.[29]

> In the fifteenth year of Emperor Caesar Nerva Traianus Augustus Germanicus Dacicus, month of Neos Sebastos 25, at Tebtunis in the Polemon district of the Arsinoite nome. Orsenouphis son of Patunis, grandson of Mesoeris, about forty-five years old, a scar on his right forearm, and Kronion son of Cheos, grandson of Harmiusis, about fifty years old, a scar on the little finger of his left hand, both of them Persians of the *epigonê*, acting as mutual sureties for the repayment, acknowledge to Didymus son of Didymus, grandson of Maron, about thirty-four years old, a scar on his right shin, that they have received on loan (*chrêsis*) from him, Didymus, twenty artabas of new, pure and unadulterated wheat and twenty artabas of new, pure and unadulterated barley, all by the

[29] Oates (1963), Vandorpe (2008).

four-*choinix* measure owned by Didymus himself; and the debtors, Orsenouphis and Kronion, are bound to repay Didymus the loan, twenty artabas of wheat and twenty artabas of barley, in the month of Payni of the present fifteenth year of Traianus Caesar the lord without any delay or subterfuge, Didymus having the right of enforcement (*praxis*) against the debtors and against each of them whomsoever he chooses, and against all their property. Signatory: Marepsemis son of Pakebkis, about 36 years old, a scar on the left side of his nose.

(*2nd hand*) We, Orsenouphis son of Patunis and Kronion son of Cheos, both acting as mutual securities for repayment, acknowledge that we have received on loan from Didymus son of Didymus, twenty artabas of new, pure and unadulterated wheat and twenty artabas of barley, by the four-*choinix* measure owned by Didymus, and that we shall repay in the month of Payni of the present fifteenth year as stated above. Pakebkis son of Psoiphis wrote for them since they are illiterate.

(*3rd hand*) Didymus son of Didymus: the contract came into my possession as stated above. Registered through the record-office (*grapheion*) of the village of Tebtunis.

5.3.2 Loan of money

SB XII 10786 (Tebtunis and Ptolemaïs Euergetis, 22 June AD 133). Image at Papyri.info.

Two inhabitants from Tebtunis, a woman named Taonnophris and her son Sarapion, borrow 1,300 drachmas from Herodes, a former gymnasiarch of the Arsinoite nome, who may have lived in Ptolemais Euergetis, the capital of the nome. Once again, the contract is a *chrêsis*. In Roman Egypt, in most cases, women needed the assistance of a guardian in order to make a contract. In this document, Sarapion is the guardian of his mother. They borrow for one year at the rate of one drachma per mina per month, that is 12 percent a year, the usual interest rate in loans of money in Roman Egypt (and the maximum legal rate allowed by the Gnomon of the *Idios Logos* §105). The total amount of the interest, 156 drachmas, is mentioned, which is rather unusual. The loan is paid through the private bank of Apollonios and Sabinus in Ptolemais Euergetis. The bank does not lend the money,[30] it just transfers it from the lender to the borrowers. The amount of the loan is important: it is larger than the annual pay of a Roman legionary (1,200 drachmas).[31] The loan is secured with real property (a tract of land)

[30] Lerouxel (2008). [31] Alston (1995: 106).

because of the large amount of money that is being lent. The *hypallagma*, a kind of mortgage (see **5.4.3**), is made at the nome's office of property registers (*bibliothêkê enktêseôn*). The aim of the final clause is to preserve Herodes' rights on another debt recorded in a second loan made the same day (*SB* XII 10787, loan of 1,200 drachmas), in case of foreclosure. The end of the second contract is lost and we do not know why the debtors did not borrow 2,500 drachmas at once. What follows is the editor's translation[32] modified in small details.

> In the seventeenth year of Emperor Caesar Traianus Hadrianus Augustus, Payni 28, at Tebtunis in the Polemon district of the Arsinoite nome. Taonnophris daughter of Kronion the elder, granddaughter of Amaeis, from Tebtunis, about forty-eight years old, a scar on her left hand, and her son Sarapion son of Herakles, grandson of Herakles, about twenty-two years old, a scar on his right forearm, both of them Persians of the *epigonê*, the said Taonnophris with her son Sarapion as guardian and surety for repayment, acknowledge to Herodes also called Diogenes son of Didymus the younger, formerly gymnasiarch, about forty-eight years old, having no distinguishing mark, that they have received a loan from him, Diogenes, forthwith through the bank of Apollonios and Sabinus in the Treasuries' quarter at the *metropolis*,[33] the capital sum of one thousand three hundred silver drachmas for one year from the present day at interest of a drachma per mina monthly; and the debtors, Taonnophris and her son Sarapion, on mutual security, are bound to repay Diogenes the capital sum, one thousand three hundred drachmas, plus the accompanying one hundred fifty-six drachmas for the year's interest at the one-drachma rate, in all, one thousand four hundred fifty-six silver drachmas, on the twenty-seventh of the month Payni in the coming eighteenth year of Hadrianus Caesar the lord, without any delay or subterfuge; and as security for the above-mentioned capital plus interest Taonnophris has willingly and voluntarily mortgaged to Diogenes through the office of property registers, in all, nine and one-quarter arouras of an estate in two parcels belonging to her in the vicinity of Tebtunis, subject to purchase in part, and, in the village, lots measuring nine *bikoi*, one hundred sixty-four and one-half cubits, Herodes also called Diogenes suffering no diminution with respect to what the debtors owe him according to the other

[32] Keenan (1970: 79–80).

[33] Ptolemaïs Euergetis is the *metropolis* (capital) of the Arsinoite nome where Tebtunis is located.

contract of the present day, the capital sum of one thousand two hundred silver drachmas plus interest . . . (*the papyrus breaks off*)

5.3.3 Cancellation of a loan contract (*synchôrêsis*)

P.Oxy. XXVII 2471 (Oxyrhynchos, *c.* AD 50). Image at *P.Oxy.* XXVII, Plate X.

In AD 48, in Alexandria,[34] Chairemon borrowed thirteen talents (78,000 drachmas) at interest from two high-ranking Alexandrians who were also Roman citizens, Demetrius and Isidorus. It is by far the largest financial transaction known in Roman Egypt, maritime loans excluded. The original loan contract was not a *chrêsis* but a *daneion*. The legal differences between the two types of loans have sometimes been overestimated, and may probably be explained by the place and time of the document's composition.[35] The original contract, a *synchôrêsis* in form, which is cancelled in the document below, had its own peculiarities. It is a public contract of a type used in Alexandria. It is drawn up as a letter addressed by the parties to the *archidikastês*, one of the most important officials of the province, who was in charge of the *katalogeion* (record-office) in Alexandria. The two lenders are bankers but they did not make that loan as bankers. The money has instead been paid through another bank, the exchange-bank (*kollybistikê trapeza*) of Narcissus in Alexandria, which wrote a *diagraphê*, a document attesting to the payment of the money. The loan was repaid by Chairemon and by other people, acting as his representatives, which is rather unusual. It was repaid in several installments, through the bank of Demetrius and Isidorus, and through the exchange-bank of Narcissus. A *diagraphê* was written for each installment. Chairemon himself made the last installment. The document below aims at legally cancelling the loan contract, the *synchôrêsis*. Since it was found there, Chairemon or his heirs may have settled in Oxyrhynchos after the date of the document.

The editor's translation is used, with very slight modifications.

To [. . .] *archidikastês* and superintendent of the *chrêmastistai* and the other courts, from Tiberius Claudius Demetrius and Tiberius Claudius Isidorus, sons of Bion, of the tribe Quirina [. . .] Demetrius and Isidorus, both sons of Bion [. . .] Demetrius, priest and gymnasiarch and one of those exempt from taxes and maintained in the Museion, and from

[34] Bogaert (1983[4]). According to Bogaert, the exchange-bank of Narcissus, which figures in the present loan, was located in Alexandria. The operations of the exchange-banks are no different from the operations of the other private banks. See **5.3.2**.

[35] Tenger (1993: 27–47).

Chairemon son of Ale[. . .] We agree between ourselves as follows: whereas Demetrius and Isidorus have received from Chairemon – through Chairemon himself and through others, by the former *diagraphai* of the exchange-bank of Narcissus son of Archias, and by the *diagraphai* of the bank of Demetrius and Isidorus themselves, and by the present *diagraphê* made by Chairemon and executed through the aforesaid exchange-bank of Narcissus – the thirteen talents that they lent to Chairemon himself by a *synchôrêsis* through the *katalogeion* (record-office) in Pharmouthi of the eighth year of Tiberius Claudius Caesar Augustus Germanicus Imperator (March/April AD 48), together with the interests, that the loan *synchôrêsis* be null and void as well as the *diagraphê* made through the aforementioned exchange-bank of Narcissus and that neither Demetrius nor Isidorus nor any other person on their behalf proceed against Chairemon regarding the aforesaid loan and the interests or any other transaction whatsoever, written or unwritten, from times past until the present day [. . .] (*the papyrus breaks off*)

5.3.4 Private letter about redemption of pawned clothing

P.Oxy. III 530, lines 1, 10–32 (Oxyrhynchos, second century AD)

The following text is rather exceptional. It is not a contract but a private letter written by Dionysios to his mother Tetheus in Oxyrhynchos. In the first part of the letter (not quoted here), Dionysios replied to his mother who wrote to him about some taxes. He also sent money to her through the bearer of the letter, Chairemon. He wanted her to repay Sarapion in his name and to redeem the clothes he has put in pawn in order to secure the loan. Dionysios wrote that he borrowed to repay the loan, but it is difficult to verify this since he obviously did not send his mother as much money as she wanted to prepare a festival. It is not possible to calculate the interest rate because the duration of the loan is unknown.

Pawnbroking is almost always invisible in contracts. Usually the objects pawned are clothes or jewels (e.g., *P.Oxy.* I 114; *P.Coll.Youtie* II 96). For those petty loans, there was no written contract. Writing a contract costs money and that cost must have been prohibitively disproportionate in the case of small loans. Therefore, loan contracts do not cover the full range of financial life in Roman Egypt.

The editor's translation is used with minor variations.

Dionysios to Tetheus his mother, greetings. [. . .] Please receive from Chairemon the bearer of this letter one hundred twelve drachmas of silver, of which you will give to my friend Sarapion son of Apei one hundred drachmas and redeem my clothes, with eight drachmas on account of interest, and keep four drachmas for yourself for the expenses of the festival. If I had had more I would have forwarded a further sum; I have borrowed to send even this. So pay him the money and get my clothes back safe and put them in a secure place. Do not be anxious about us, for there is nothing the matter with us and we are at harmony with each other. Theonas salutes you. Salute the boys Apion and his brother Hermatois, Dionytas, those with Nike and the little Thaisous, all those with [. . .] , Heras and his household, Leontas the proud and his household, those with Taamois, and Thermoutharion. Goodbye. The 20th of the month Kaisareios.

In the left margin, at right angles: Send me word about this immediately after the festival, whether you received the money and whether you recovered my clothes. Salute Dionytas and Theon.

Verso: To my mother Tetheus.

5.4 Real security

Hans-Albert Rupprecht

To insure claims and to guarantee credit the creditor requires a security or securities. In addition to personal securities such as the guarantee, which will not be discussed here, real (*in rem*) securities are common. In such cases the creditor is secured by a specified object (*res*), which is preferably available for satisfaction only to him, to the exclusion of other creditors.

In the following, the different forms of real securities will be briefly sketched. But first it must be noted that Greek law, whether in Greece proper or in the Hellenistic states, including Egypt, did not employ a specific juristic terminology, that is, a well-defined, specialized vocabulary. Thus, we can only proceed on the basis of a more or less fixed use of technical terms. If therefore in what follows, terms like creditor, debtor, claim, ownership, possession, or lien are used, this only serves for a simplified exposition, whereby the individual legal situations described in the papyri are not tied to a particular juristic construction as in Roman law, whose legal foundations are different from those of Greek law.

Common forms of security are the pledge (*enechyron*) and the mortgage (*hypothêkê*), and, in papyri of the Roman period, the *hypallagma*. The transfer by means of a secured conveyance is also found. We also come across many forms that now and then must be assigned to the middle ground between the drawing up of legal documents and their execution. Below will be found: the pledge (5.4.1), the mortgage (*hypothêkê*) (5.4.2), and the *hypallagma* (5.4.3) as common examples. Exceptional cases are the *menein*-contract (5.4.4) and the combination of purchase with loan (5.4.5).

Liens in the proper sense of the word are restricted to pledges and mortgages. The difference between the two turns principally upon the issue of possession: in whose possession is the object of the pledge, the creditor's or the debtor's? Basically we can assume that the personal pledge (*enechyron*) is a "possession-pledge" by which the creditor obtains possession of the thing (*res*). In the mortgage (*hypothêkê*), however, the pledge is "possession-less" and therefore remains with the debtor.

Objects of security in pledges are movables, especially clothing (as in 5.3.4), jewelry (as in 5.4.1), and implements. The reason for borrowing in such cases is necessity, of the kind that sometimes openly threatens one's very existence. Objects of mortgage are normally houses (as in 5.4.2), or shares thereof, courtyards, gardens, vineyards, and also slaves. Mortgages (as opposed to pledges) were concerned with normal business loans.

Common to both these basic types of real security, pledge and mortgage, are the legal consequences in case the loan is not repaid. The pledge used as security is, according to Greek law, a "substitute pledge." This means that the pledged object substitutes for the loan amount. For the debtor, this means that if the object is worth less than the loan, the creditor cannot make additional claims, and, vice versa, that the creditor is not obliged to pay out any eventual overage to the debtor. Pledge and mortgage are, furthermore, a "forfeit pledge." This means that for the pledge in possession, i.e., of the creditor, the object *ipso iure* is transferred into the property of the creditor; special actions of realization are not necessary. In case of the possession-less pledge, the *hypothêkê*, the thing likewise becomes the creditor's property. The creditor obtains the object only after a legally regulated procedure through *embadeia* and *epikatabolê*; self-help is not permitted. A further consequence of this is that after forfeiture of the pledge there will not be any right of execution on other assets of the debtor.[36]

For the establishment of the personal pledge, documents as a rule were not created; at least no such documents survive. What have survived are lists of objects that were pledged with professional pawnbrokers or complaints against creditors who refused to accept payments and return the pledged objects. The mortgage (*hypothêkê*), on the contrary, was as a rule certified by a document. In the Roman period a record of the

[36] See further Rupprecht (1997).

establishment of the mortgage was generally made on the creditor's personal page in the office of property registers (*bibliothêkê enktêseôn*). The mortgage required payment of a 2 percent tax on the amount of the loan; likewise for an extension of the length of the contract.

An instrument that differs from this is the *hypallagma* (**5.4.3**, cf. **5.3.2**). Here there is no creation of a lien in the narrower sense of the word. Rather, the creditor is granted a special position insofar as the debtor keeps the object in his possession and has to protect it for future execution. He is consequently forbidden to dispose of it for the course of the loan.

In case of non-fulfillment the creditor can avail himself of a general execution against the property of the debtor and against the objects reserved for *hypallagma*; usually these were land, slaves, or livestock. In some instances (when land is at issue), the creation of the *hypallagma* is recorded on the debtor's page in the office of property registers (*bibliothêkê enktêseôn*): see **5.2.1**, **5.4.2**.

The *menein*-contract is a special type of contract limited in time to the first and second centuries AD, and in geography to the Oxyrhynchite nome. This type of agreement later apparently fell out of use for whatever reason. Here it is a matter of a loan contract coupled with a subsidiary agreement regarding forfeiture of the object/s used to secure the loan. The debtor confirms his receipt of the loan and promises repayment within a given time; if he does not repay, the pledged objects should "remain" (*menein*) with the creditor. Pledged objects in this type of contract are houses (as in *P.Oslo* II 40b – see **5.4.4** introduction) or parts of houses, land, and (as in **5.4.4**) slaves. Whether the creditor obtained possession of the thing is, owing to ambiguity in the contract's wording (see **5.4.4**), uncertain. A record of the transaction on the debtor's page in the office of property registers (*bibliothêkê enktêseon*) is sometimes provided. At maturity, the creditor has the choice between acquisition of the object under pledge and the right of execution against the person and property of the debtor, including the specified pledged object. The above-named choice between seizure and execution speaks against an *ipso iure* acquisition without further procedure (details remain as yet unknown).

The texts often mention the transfer of the pledged object used to secure the transaction. To date there is no surviving document concerned with such a transfer; the term *ônê en pistei* (conditional sale in case of failed redemption of the loan) as a successor to the *prasis epi lysei* (sale on annulment) in Greece is all that is mentioned.

In addition to the so-called sale with pledge contracts (see **6.1**), we have to mention the combination of loan and purchase on a single papyrus sheet (see 5.4.5). In such a document the creditor has combined the loan document with the sale. Upon repayment of the loan the creditor must return the papyrus sheet to the debtor, thereby simultaneously nullifying the contract of sale. The debtor was meanwhile probably protected by the fact that several copies of the document had been issued.

We can summarize real security as follows: The pledge (*enechyron*) and mortgage (*hypothêkê*) continued from the Greek tradition. The *ônê en pistei* – heretofore mentioned in other texts but not documented as such – is the continuation of the *prasis epi lysei*. The *hypallagma* is a new form created in the first century AD, but not based upon or occasioned by Roman law. The *menein*-contracts reflect a highly complicated and coherent type of construction. Whether evidence for *menein*-contracts is only documented for a short period of time because this type of contact was not recognized or because it did not prove itself useful, we do not know. The combination of Greek and Egyptian legal documents is likewise a new type of legal practice. This was possible because both legal traditions existed side by side. They were not, however, merged with one another but open for equal use by both Greeks and Egyptians.

The often-presumed personality principle (Egyptian law for Egyptians, Greek law for Greeks) was no obstacle for this side-by-side existence of legal forms. In addition, juristic competence, in view of the availability of claims for enforcement (= *coercitio*) by administrative officials or the *chrêmatistai* (judges of the Ptolemaic period), or the later jurisdiction of the Roman prefects, cannot have been a problem. Furthermore it is noteworthy that here, as elsewhere, new or further development of legal models or formulas was not the work of jurists, but the result of notarial practices that were introduced by documentary scribes who were able to deal directly with the changing requirements of economic life.

Future studies need to devote special attention to connections between Greek and Egyptian documents. In view of the increasing publication of new documents in both areas, surprising new results are possible in the history of credit instruments in Greco-Roman Egypt.

5.4.1 Personal pledge of jewelry as security for a loan

Stud.Pal. XX 2 (= *CPR* I 12) (Fayyum, 29 September AD 93). Image at Papyri.info.

This *enechyron* (personal pledge) is a pledge entailing possession of an object that is normally given over to the creditor. The transaction was a common one when credit could only be obtained against security. As a rule, objects are household movables. This makes the *enechyron* a security transaction for the emergencies of daily life, and probably also in most cases for short-term needs. Apparently, legal documents were not normally drawn up for this. In the text at hand we are dealing with gold jewelry that has been given as short-term security for a very large sum of money for less than a month. The weight is given as 184 grams according to the local standard. The interest was set at four obols per mina per month = four obols per one hundred drachmas a month, which equals 8 percent per year. The annual interest agreed upon is therefore lower than the 12 percent maximum allowed in the Roman period. The conveyancing of the jewelry is here formulated in terminology proper to the contract of deposit (*depositum*). In case of non-redemption through failure to repay the loan, loss occurs on the side of the debtor. He loses the object pledged, ownership of which is now transferred to the creditor. The acquisition is secured through an explicit renunciation on the part of the debtor/owner regarding the enforcement of claims and an attendant waiver of rights to legal proceedings.

> Lucius Snanoubas to Dionysios, the son of Didymos, greetings. I have deposited with you as pledges: a pair of clasps with dangling heart-shaped pendants weighing seven and a half minas of genuine gold measured according to the locally used standard against two thousand one hundred and sixty silver drachmas (= 2,160 silver drachmas) at an interest of four silver obols per mina, and I will necessarily redeem them before the thirtieth of the current month Phaophi of the current thirteenth year of Domitian Caesar the lord. If not, I will forfeit the aforementioned clasps and will not assert any claims.
>
> In the thirteenth year of the Emperor Caesar Domitian Augustus Germanicus, on the 2nd of Phaophi.

5.4.2 Loan secured against mortgage (*hypothêkê*) of a house

P.Tebt. III.1 817 (= *CPJ* I 23) (Krokodilopolis, 4 November 182 BC). Image at Papyri.info.

For another discussion, taking a contrary position, and for the translation of this text, see **5.2.1** above.

For a loan of 15,000 bronze drachmas a mortgage (*hypothêkê*) on a house with courtyard and appurtenances was created. Both parties were "Jews of the *epigonê*," which means that they probably had some connection to the military.[37] The reference to bronze coinage, not silver, was standard practice. The sum was considerable, and the term was specified as one year. The loan is designated as interest-free. Since both parties were Jews, it is highly probable that the loan really was interest-free, and the interest has probably not been calculated as capitalized into the loan.[38] The house is described in more detail according to its position in relation to its neighbors; this was common practice, but the mention of the dimensions of the property (here 20 × 20 cubits, 100.25 m^2) is rare.

If the repayment of the loan fell outside of the due date, the creditor could lay claim to the mortgage, i.e., the house, pursuant to a royal edict. This means that we are in the present case concerned with a forfeit-pledge and a substitute-pledge that excluded the right of execution for the loan amount. The usual warranty was a liability for deficiency in title. The house was free of debts *in rem* and third-party claims. Furthermore, there were no liabilities in arrears to the state that otherwise would be transferred to the creditor. In addition to the warranty clause, derogations were forbidden either through the debtor himself or through third parties. Therefore the usual provisions against alienation by the debtor in the Roman period were absent because they were effectively covered by the warranty clause. If the security failed or the mortgage, i.e., house, was at risk, the loan must be paid back immediately, even before the expiry of its term. If this agreement should be violated, the penalty clause, valid only for this, provided for a penalty of 150 percent of the loan amount and the payment of 24 percent per year on interest in arrears. In general, 24 percent interest rates were common in Ptolemaic times. Despite the Jewish prohibition of interest, this rate apparently also prevailed for Jews. In the *Diaspora* the enforcement of the prohibition was apparently less strict.

5.4.3 Loan against mortgage (*hypallagma*)

P.Ryl. II 177 (= *SP* I 63) (Hermopolis, 1 September AD 246)

In this *cheirographon*, a document in the form of a letter, two debtors assume an interest-bearing loan of 1,920 silver drachmas. The term of the loan cannot be exactly determined because of damage to the text, but it lasted less than a year. Security was guaranteed by half of a house jointly owned by the debtors. How the joint ownership was created cannot be determined; it may have been a question of shared acquisition through inheritance.

37 Vandorpe (2008). 38 Pestman (1971).

Here it is not a mortgage (*hypothêkê*) but a so-called *hypallagma* that is established. The usual means of execution against the person and his assets remained valid. The only purpose of the *hypallagma* was to preserve the secured asset for the general right to execution on the property. To this corresponded the restrictions of disposal and the general warranty against legal defects. The *hypallagma* is therefore neither a forfeit-pledge nor is it a substitute-pledge (**5.4** introduction). The secured asset does not thereby come into the property of the creditor, but the execution is still necessary. Since the warranty is all-encompassing, a provision for the possibility of execution on account of other, old debts of the debtor was necessary. Both debtors were jointly liable; the creditor thereby could by his choice proceed against both or just one alone.

The following translation has been slightly abridged. It is designed to highlight the mortgage elements of the loan. There is a conveniently accessible English translation, following that of the original edition, down to the concluding date and signature.

> Aurelius Melas [. . .] and Silvanus [. . .], both from the village of Magdola Mire in the district of the lower town, to Aurelius Sois, greetings.
>
> We acknowledge that we have received from you from hand to hand out of the house an interest-bearing [. . .] (at 12 percent?) loan of one thousand nine hundred twenty silver drachmas (= 1,920 drachmas), which we will pay back to you as joint debtors by [. . .] of the current 4th year [. . .] without delay. As security for repayment we reserve (*hypallassomen*) for you by this document the half share that we commonly own of the new house with courtyard and appurtenances and furniture as well as entries and exits, which formerly belonged to Pekysios of the same village. The neighbors of the whole property are: south, the house of Teres son of Menches; north, . . .; [east], a road for entry and exit; west, the courtyard of Phoibammon son of Tryphon. The half part of the house that is given as security (*hypêllagmenon*) we preserve inalienably and unencumbered until we will pay back or become subject to execution, as written above. You are entitled to the enforcement against us jointly or individually, as you choose, because we are co-debtors, and from our total property and against the mortgage (*hypallagma*) as if based upon a legal process. And we will guarantee you with all warranty from public and private claims and liabilities, all of them completely, there remaining in effect the debts that one of us, Aurelius Melas, owes you. That this has been done with complete correctness, we, having been formally asked by you, have given our consent.

Year 4 of Emperor Caesar Marcus Julius Philippus Pius [Felix and Marcus Julius Philippus, the most noble] and brilliant Caesar, Augusti, Thoth 4.

I, Aurelius Kopreas alias Eudaimon, [have written in their behalf since they do not know letters . . .]

5.4.4 Mortgage in the form of a *menein*-contract

P.Oslo II 40a (Oxyrhynchos, 14 April AD 150)

P.Oslo II 40 presents two contracts of loan between the same parties. One (a), for 600 drachmas, is dated 14 April AD 150. The other (b), for 1,400 drachmas, is dated 26 August AD 150. The collateral in (a) is a nine-year-old female slave, in (b), a house. The legal arrangement of the warranty was identical in both cases. The loan was given under the usual conditions. On the one hand, the creditor was granted a right to acquire the object offered as collateral, and on the other the possibility of general execution against the person and his property, including the security; both options were according to the choice of the creditor after maturity of the claim of the loan and non-performance by the debtor.

Regarding the establishment of security through the female slave in **5.4.4**, the warranty clauses were borrowed from the law of sale. That this follows a schematic, formalized pattern is documented by the mention of descendants of the nine-year-old female slave. The debtor assumed the warranty and subjects himself to restrictions on its disposition for the time down to repayment. If the loan matured and was not repaid, the creditor could acquire the female slave as "property." The amount of the loan and the interest were then applied to the purchase price. The price is probably reasonable. In this case, the debtor also assumed the payment of the sales tax. Whether the realization of the interest, and assumption of possession as agreed, was possible without legal proceedings, we do not know.

The factual circumstances behind the transaction are unclear and are further complicated by the second loan. Three days after maturity of this first loan, on 23 August AD 150, the debtor assumed a second, higher loan with the same creditor, namely on 26 August AD 150. This second text makes no reference to the first loan. We do not know if the seizure of the security was realized and the second loan was assumed in addition to the first; or if – contingently – the first loan was integrated into the second loan and the first was thereby legally renewed and the first security thereby released. Both contracts on a single sheet of papyrus, were evidently copies, not the original loan contracts. Offered here is a translation of *P.Oslo* II 40a only.

Ptolemaios son of Apion, grandson of Apion, his mother being Sarapous, from the city of Oxyrhynchos, Persian of the *epigonê*, to Apion alias Petosorapis son of Petosorapis, grandson of Petosorapis, former *kosmêtês* of the same city, greetings.

I confirm that I have received from you from hand to hand six hundred silver drachmas of the imperial mint as capital, to which nothing is added, at the interest of one drachma per mina per month (= 12 percent a year) from the current month Pharmouthi onward. I will repay you the capital including interest on the thirtieth of Mesore of the currrent thirteenth year of Antoninus Caesar the lord without any delay.[39]
If I do not repay you, then I confirm that instead of the capital and the interest, the ownership (*kratêsis*) and the right of disposal (*kyrieia*)[40] will remain with you and your legal successors regarding the female slave Isarous, about nine years old, free of defects with the exception of the sacred disease (i.e., epilepsy) and leprosy. I will pay the upcoming taxes for her if you take her. And you shall be master over her and over the descendants henceforth brought into the world by her, as if a sale had taken place; and you shall be entitled to take her offspring and sell her to others and use her as you like, without any claim remaining to me. I will guarantee warranty to you and your descendants for the female slave and her descendants from now on in every way, without my being allowed to sell, to pledge the slave Isarous or her descendants or to make any transaction regarding them if I do not first repay the six hundred drachmas and interest. You are free to choose, whether you according to your will, without legal proceedings, after the appointed time for the six hundred drachmas plus interest, will become master of the female slave and her possible descendants, or if you want to initiate the execution for the complete sum and the interest for late payment of twelve percent against my person and the female slave Isarous and her descendants and my other assets. Neither escape nor death nor bodily injury of the female slave Isarous or her descendants, if such a thing should happen, will cause damage to the capital or the interest or a part of it, because they are free of every risk. This personally written *cheirographon*, which I have written in two copies, is valid. Thirteenth year of the Emperor Caesar Titus Aelius Hadrianus Antoninus Augustus Pius, Pharmouthi 19.

[39] Period of time: 1 April to 23 August.

[40] The terms *kratêsis* and *kyrieia* designate actual control of the thing and its legal possibilities. They correspond, respectively, to the Roman terms for ownership and possession.

5.4.5 Greek loan with a Demotic sale of property

SB XII 10804 + *DDD* III 23 (Soknopaiou Nesos, 28 February AD 47). Image at *DDD* III, Plate 37.

Both contracts reflect the following situation. On one side Stotoetis appears as the buyer and creditor; on the other side are Soueris as the (female) seller and debtor, with her husband Onnophris as her guardian, and as debtor. Both contracts were written on the same sheet of papyrus. The Demotic sale and cession contract, dated to the second day of Phamenoth, is on the left; the Greek loan contract, dated to the same day, is on the right.

The connection between the transactions is not explicitly stated; but is known from other documents of this time and place (*P.Ryl.* II 160c and 160d). It can be assumed that the main reason for the contract was to guarantee a loan, and the purpose of the sale was to provide the creditor with security. This would mean that with the repayment of the loan the sale would also become invalid. This is evident through the common practice of returning loan documents to the paying debtor tied together with the pertinent documents of sale. If this assumption is correct, then we have here an example of the documentary practice that established a form for the conveyance of security. Whether one can go so far as to interpret this as an example of the *ônê en pistei* (i.e., conditional sale) must remain an open question. Furthermore, it is interesting that here two Egyptian parties use forms of Egyptian and Greek law for one and the same economic and legal transaction without there being any obvious problems.

Note the different standing of the female party, Soueris, in the Greek loan and the Demotic sale. In the Greek contract she appears with her husband as *kyrios*, in the Demotic she acts alone. In Greek law a woman needed the support of a male guardian, either her father or, in the case of a married woman, her husband; for widows, if applicable, the eldest son could act as legal guardian. According to Egyptian law a guardian was not required.

5.4.5a Greek loan contract

SB XII 10804

Seventh year of Tiberius Claudius Caesar Augustus Germanicus Imperator in the month of Phamenoth, second day, in Soknopaiou

Nesos of the Herakleides district of the Arsinoite nome. Stotoetis son of Horos, about forty-six years old with a scar on his right wrist, has given a loan (*edaneisen*) to Soueris daughter of Satabous, Persian, about twenty-eight years old, with a scar on her left shin, with her own husband Onnophris son of Harpagathes, about forty-two years old, with a scar in the middle of his forehead, as guardian, and to the same Onnophris, Persian of the *epigonê*, the two as mutual guarantors for repayment of the eighty-four drachmas of silver minted coin as capital which she (*sic*) received immediately from him from hand to hand out of the household chest at an interest of one drachma per mina per month (= 12 percent a year). The capital and interest will I (*sic*), the debtor, as above written, pay back to Stotoetis in the month Mecheir of the coming ninth year of Tiberius Claudius Caesar Augustus Germanicus Imperator (= January/February AD 9). If I do not repay as written, then . . . (*rest of the text is lost*).

5.4.5b Demotic sale and cession

DDD III 23[41]

7th year 2nd Phamenoth. The woman Soueris has declared to Stotoetis.

You have paid out to me in full. You have made me agree with all my heart to the amount of money[42] corresponding to the price for my share that equals one share of two, which equals again a share, of the house, which has been built and has been equipped with beams and doors . . . (*there follows a more detailed description of the house and the neighbors; then the text breaks off*).

5.4.6 Procedure for execution against a debtor's property

BGU XIV 2376 (Herakleopolis, 28 February–29 March 35 BC)

We are well informed about the procedure of execution primarily by evidence from the period of the Principate. New evidence has shown that the essentials of the procedure were already existent under the Ptolemies. It is the creditor who initiates the execution; the procedure is thus unilateral. Protection of the debtor and eventually concerned third parties is

[41] Both the Greek and the Demotic text have been republished by Lippert and Schentuleit (2010). This document is not translated in full.

[42] Because the exact purchase price is not mentioned, the loan amount cannot be determined.

guaranteed by the chance to raise objections (*antirrhêsis*) at various steps of the procedure.

The procedure of execution is complicated in its details. The presentation given here is based, in addition to the secondary literature, on the combination of a mass of observations that in the end, because of the fragmentary condition of the individual documents, offers a mosaic rather than a systematic portrayal. **5.4.6** demonstrates that modifications through new finds are possible.

All in all the picture seems to be consistent and self-evident. The procedure's continuity from the Ptolemaic to the Roman period is very interesting. Its adoption by the Romans is consistent with the principle of introducing changes only when it appears necessary. The procedure in its entirety is marked by the fact that in its individual steps the creditor had to take the initiative, but at the same time the execution was the responsibility of the state administration. The debtor is protected in the individual steps by the opportunity to raise objections; the same is true for the protection of third parties.

I. Execution based on judgment
   (1) The basic point of departure is the assumption that the sentence in a Greek trial was limited to a decision about the admissibility of a validly made claim by the creditor himself. It did not aim at a court order compelling specific performance by the debtor. In such a case, the procedure for execution ran against the property of the debtor, in which procedure we may assume the following steps (in the Ptolemaic and Roman period; see Rupprecht 1997).
   (2) The individual steps
      (a) Up to the seizure of property in pledge (*enechyrasia*): The sentence of the court forms the basis for execution, the *chrêmatismos*, which must at the same time also have contained the order for execution issued to the collector (*praktôr*). This *chrêmatismos enechyrasias* was sent to the *stratêgos*, or rather to the *praktôr xenikôn*. It did not designate the object to be seized. Attached was a petition of the creditor to the *praktôr* for distraint (*sc.* of the pledge). For this purpose the creditor designated the object (*paradeixis*) that then was to be seized by the *praktôr* (*enechyrasia*). In the case of real estate an entry was made (*katochê*) in the debtor's personal page in the register of properties (*bibliothêkê enktêseôn*). Before the sale by auction, a delay,

probably for at least ten days, was prescribed, to allow for the debtor as well as third parties to raise objections (*antirrhêsis*).

(b) Auction sale: The liquidation of the pledged object occurred by auction and was knocked down to the highest bidder (*prosbolê*). It is not yet entirely clear whether the purchaser had to conclude a sale contract (with the owner or the *praktôr*). From the proceeds of the auction sale the creditor's interests were satisfied.

(c) In the case of real estate there follows the *katagraphê*, i.e., the entry of the acquisition in the register of properties. Further examination is needed to determine whether *antirrhêsis* against this *katagraphê* was permitted.

(d) The procedure was concluded when the purchaser was put into possession (*embadeia*), presumably after the filing of a petition with reference to the preceding *katagraphê*. The petition had to be approved by the *chrêmatistai* (judges) with an order to the *stratêgos* to put the purchaser into possession. Then, instructed by the *stratêgos*, the *praktôr* puts the purchaser into possession and expels the former owner, unless he has already left the property or raised *antirrhêsis* within a period of ten days after receiving the court order.

II. Execution based on executory deeds: Execution is frequently attested as the result of executory documents. Whether these documents had to contain a "*praxis* clause" (clause of execution) remains a matter of dispute. In any case, with the inclusion of a *praxis* clause, the following procedure, sketched here in brief, was followed.

(1) Execution (see above, I(2)) was preceded by an admonitory proceeding. This was initiated by a petition from the creditor, fortified by an oath, to the *archidikastês* (chief judge) with a statement of the basis of the debt and a demand for payment. It was followed by the official notice of payment due (*diastolikon*), sent by the *archidikastês* to the *stratêgos*. Next came the petition from the creditor to the *stratêgos* and the notification to the debtor. The debtor had the right to raise objections (*antirrhêsis*) with the *archidikastês*. To the extent that this was a matter of documents privately drafted, the public declaration of the document (*dêmosiôsis*) had first to be effected.

(2) After this was a ruling of the *chrêmatistai* concerning the *enechyrasia* and further steps (see above, I); title and object of the petition and the ruling of the *chrêmatistai* nevertheless constitute the *diastolikon*. This is preceded by yet one more assurance under oath of the creditor that the facts are correct and that he has received no payment from the debtor. If the debtor introduces no objections (*antirrhêsis*) within a period of ten days after receiving the ruling on the *enechyrasia*, the *enechyrasia* takes place.

III. If the issue was a claim secured by mortgage (*hypothêkê*), the procedure followed was as under II; however, *paradeixis*, *enechyrasia*, *prosbolê*, and *katagraphê* were lacking. In place of these was an *epikatabolê*. This was not, however, the case in instances of *hypallagma*. For this was not the basis for lien but only caused the appropriation of assets for execution (see Rupprecht 1995: 429). The procedure then was as under II, including the *enechyrasia*.

IV. A brief note on personal execution. The stipulation for this belongs to an inherent part of the *praxis* clause of the documents. Apparently, arrest as a means to compel performance was allowed in an orderly administrative procedure, but not debt-bondage for working off debts or sale into slavery.

In **5.4.6** the procedure for liquidating a debtor's assets to satisfy a loan takes place through the *praktôr xenikôn* in an auction sale that was initiated and endorsed by a *chrêmatismos* of the *chrêmatistai* on the 10th day of the month of Thoth of the 16th = 1st year of Kleopatra VII (= 10 September 37 BC).

The *chrêmatistai* still functioned in the late Ptolemaic period (unlike in the Roman) as a regular trial court. The *chrêmatismos* was the sentence in a trial and allowed, in this case, for compulsory execution for a sum of 3,080 silver drachmas and five bronze talents. The basis for the two sums is not stated, but one may assume they derived from a loan (see Llewelyn 1994: 202), though other bases, such as, for example, a lease, a deposit, or a delict, are also possible. They did not derive from a guarantee. Therefore there was no admonitory proceeding, since a *diastolikon* is not mentioned.

The procedure ran as described above (I), but the specifics are as follows:

The parties involved were Ptolemaios son of Heroides as plaintiff and Herakleides alias Harthotes son of Hephaistion as defendant. A piece of real estate, which the plaintiff had designated (through *paradeixis*) to the *praktôr*, had been pledged. The piece of real estate, however, was designated as belonging to (Iss)akleides alias Lochos (according to the editor a reading of "Herakleides" is absolutely impossible). That means that the property of a third party had been pledged. The protection of the third party was assured through the possibility of raising an objection (*antirrhêsis*) before the auction; but the text indicates that no one had raised any objections against the execution. The value of the pledged piece of property was set at two bronze talents; it is not clear by whom, but it was probably by the *praktôr*.

In the *chrêmatismos* there would have further been reserved to the plaintiff the right of execution for amounts not covered through the designated piece of property and against other possessions of the debtor that he, the creditor, might still discover. This reservation was probably necessary because of the nature of the creditor's right of security as established through the *enechyrasia* as a compensatory pledge (see above), according to which the object when due took the place of the guaranteed claim without the possibility of a subsequent claim for the uncovered amount.

The auction procedure would then take place after the course of the prescribed delay of probably ten days – here in fact more than ten days – through a heraldic summons to the marketplace in the presence of the plaintiff and the deputy of the royal scribe (*basilikogrammateus*). As no one made a bid, the object was knocked down to the plaintiff. That concluded the auction procedure. It would have been conducted as prescribed by the *diagramma*, presumably the great judicial *diagramma* of Ptolemy II Philadelphus (285–246 BC).

Then the steps as described under I (2) (c) and (d) were left to be completed.

This text documents the arrangement of execution as it is evidenced for the Ptolemaic period as being essentially the same as that for the Roman period. *P.Tebt.* III.1 814 (after 227 BC) had already suggested that. One may conclude from this that the Ptolemaic procedure was adopted, or at least continued, by the Romans (Wolff 1983: 451–53).

The text, originally from mummy cartonnage, was transmitted in two documents, *BGU* XIV 2376 and 2377, in two columns that are verbatim copies of one another. That allows for mutual restorations, although it is still impossible to restore the text in its entirety. The grammatical construction – the text's core is all just one long sentence – is rather complicated. Presented here is Column 1 based on the English translation by Llewelyn (1994: 197–200) but with some modification.

In the reign of Kleopatra, goddess, the younger, Philopator and Philopatris, and Ptolemy also called Caesar, god, Philopator and Philometor, year 17 which is also the year 2,[43] at the time of the priest of Alexander officiating in Alexandria and of the others so recorded in Alexandria, in the month of Artemisios = Phamenoth, in Herakleopolis above Memphis. Mousaios, *praktôr xenikôn* and *nomophylax* of the aforementioned nome,[44] has knocked down (*sc.* at auction) to Ptolemaios son of Heroides on the basis of the verdict which he (Ptolemaios) transferred from the court which is dated the past year 16 which is also year 1, Thoth 10 (= 10 September 37 BC), with respect to the complaint he brought before the *chrêmatistai* (*sc.* board of judges) holding court locally and Dorotheos, their administrative officer (*eisagôgeus*), against Herakleides also called Harthotes son of Hephaistion, regarding a right of action (*praxis*) for 3,080 silver drachmas and damages and expenses amounting to 5 bronze talents,[45] the land designated by him (*sc.* Ptolemaios son of Heroides) for distraint in the present proceedings belonging to [Issa]kleides(?) son of Lochos.[46] There remains to him (*sc.* Ptolemaios son of Heroides) the right of action for the remaining capital sum both from him and whatever other property he finds belonging to him (*sc.* Herakleides, also called Harthotes); not only the days determined for the distraint and knocking down (*sc.* at auction) having passed but also (further days) having elapsed.[47] No one in the meantime has yet come forward for the sworn denial or retraction of that which has been distrained or, following what was written by us to the royal scribe (*basilikogrammateus*), has spoken out suitably in opposition; inasmuch as

[43] 17th year = 2nd year, in the month Artemisios = Phamenoth, in Herakleopolis. The double dating possibly refers to Kleopatra and Caesarion.

[44] Mousaios, *praktôr xenikôn* and *nomophylax* of the mentioned district (nome), had awarded to Ptolemaios, son of Heroides, the piece of real estate owned by (Iss)akleides alias Lochos which he (Ptolemaios) had designated in this procedure for distraint.

[45] 3,080 silver drachmas equal 17 talents, 5,800 drachmas bronze (Brashear 1980, see note on line 18); altogether this gives in bronze a claim of 22 talents and 5,800 drachmas.

[46] Mousaios has done this pursuant to the *chrêmatismos* of the court, which had been in session in the past (16th = 1st) year on the 10th of Thoth. Before this court, the locally competent *chrêmatistai*, and their *eisagôgeus* (manager) Dorotheos, he, Ptolemaios, introduced a complaint against Herakleides alias Hathotes, son of Hephaistion, for the execution of 3,080 silver drachmas and 5 bronze talents for damages and expenditures. Designation of the piece of real estate: *eis to paron* presumably refers to the "current" procedure (Wolff 1983: 448).

[47] The prescribed period of delay begins with the notification to the royal scribe. During this period no one has stepped forward for an independent oath nor for delivery of the contested object or raised objection against the impending auction, neither the third party, Issakleides, nor the debtor, Herakleides. The verb *antiphônein* can also be understood as "to stand surety" (see Preisigke, *WB*, vol. 1 s.v.), meaning that no surety stepped forth for Ptolemaios' claim and thereby the auction was rendered superfluous.

the land has been proclaimed by a herald when the marketplace (*agora*) was full, in the presence of Ptolemaios and the deputy of the royal scribe, Herakleides son of Herakleides; and inasmuch as no one has come forward whether to make a higher bid or even a lower one(?):[48] it has been knocked down to Ptolemaios, the one who has distrained, about 38 years old [. . .] honey-skinned, white-haired, manly, with a scar on his chin. Redeemable upon 2 bronze talents as the decree (*diagramma*) specifies.[49] All the property is in the village of Sobthis near the city (*sc.* Herakleopolis), consisting of a deserted orchard with trees and a well, 2¾ arouras or however many they are, with the attached appurtenances, the half at 2 bronze talents. The neighboring properties of the whole orchard are: south, a canal called "the Navel"; north, a royal road and Tekbe; east, dry land belonging to [Iss- or Her-]akleides(?), west, a village and (property?) formerly belonging to Eumelos.

5.5 Loan contracts serving other purposes

Claudia Kreuzsaler

Loan contracts may incorporate provisions other than the standard loan formulas that reflect other interests of the parties. In some cases, a loan becomes merely a means to an entirely different end from the original economic purpose of a loan, the transfer of money.

Most commonly, a loan is modified into a mixed contract through the inclusion of an antichretic agreement. Instead of receiving interest in cash, the creditor was allowed, through a special clause, to use for the duration of the contract some of the debtor's property – land, rooms of buildings – or even the personal service of the debtor himself or his legal dependents.[50] One common type of the antichretic contract was the *enoikêsis*. The contract allowed the creditor to dwell in, or even to rent to a third party,

[48] During the auction no one made a bid; literally: no higher bid and no *hyphesomenou*. Translating this word is very difficult. Suggestions are (see *ed. pr.* p. 30 on line 14) "even/still underbidding" (so Maehler), or "even/still reducing" (so Brashear), or "assuming the debt" (Wolff). This last variant is based on the idea that a third party at the auction would have assumed the debt along with the piece of real estate without paying the price. This is consistent with the idea of the mandatory pledge of forfeiture. Llewelyn (1994: 199 n. 7) proposed to translate: "there was no one at all to make a bid." This is attested in lexica and makes sense. Ptolemaios as the creditor in this state of affairs is awarded the object. The text does not mention whether he made a bid. This is not probable since after the distraint he had a lien on the property that then accrues to him on account of the forfeiture pledge.

[49] It happened as prescribed by the *diagramma*.

[50] In rare instances, in exchange for the rights of use granted to the creditor, the debtor was freed not only from paying interest but also from paying back the capital of the loan itself. Individual agreements grant the creditor's rights of use only in case of default by the debtor.

an apartment, room, or house belonging to the debtor. This type of contract was particularly favorable to the creditor, as it accorded him actual, tangible hold on the debtor's property. In some cases of *enoikêsis* (as in **5.5.1**), the creditor may have had a particular interest in the property concerned. This was, for example, the case, when the "loan" was given by a tenant to a lessor and the *antichrêsis* accorded him the right to possess the object of the lease.

The same holds for the second main type of *antichrêsis*, the *paramonê*. In this type of contract, in return for the loan, the debtor was obliged to perform some services for the creditor (**5.5.2–3**).[51] In these cases, the "loan" can be seen as a salary, paid in advance, and the contract as a contract of labor. The *paramonê* can thus be viewed as a work contract that consolidates the relationship between worker and employer through the act of loan (see discussion of **8.2.4** = **5.5.3**).

It is not always easy to determine in whose interest the *antichrêsis* came into being. We can conceive different scenarios: an impoverished debtor, eager to get a loan, places his dwellings or physical labor at the creditor's disposal, or a creditor, in need of real estate or personal service, grants the use of his capital to whoever could provide these. In only a few cases do we possess enough information about the contract's circumstances to contextualize them socially and economically.

A further example of a loan serving another purpose is the deposit: *parathêkê*. The *parathêkê* was used in Roman Egypt as a special type of open-ended loan that could be retrieved by the creditor at any time upon his sole discretion. The *parathêkê* has been considered a very harsh form of loan for the debtor: not only had he to return the loan promptly upon demand, he was also subject to a *duplum*, a fine of 100 percent, if he did not. Still, its open-ended nature rendered the *parathêkê* serviceable whenever long-term transfer was involved: this was the case particularly among business partners and family members. In addition, since the actual purpose of the loan was not named, a *parathêkê* could be used for documenting any type of loan if the parties preferred to leave the circumstances leading up to the debt unmentioned. It was thus an ideal means of carrying out prohibited transactions. Since, for example, soldiers on active service were not allowed to marry, and hence also could not receive dowries, they therefore used the *parathêkê* as a disguise for dowries that they received from their (illegitimate) wives (**5.5.4**).

The four documents discussed below illustrate how a document constructed as a loan contract could be used for a variety of agreements besides

[51] On *paramonê* contracts, see further Chapter 8 below.

that of the ordinary loan. Scholars who studied the *antichrêsis* and the *parathêkê* in the past focused on classifying the two institutions juridically. For generations, the *antichrêsis*, as attested in Roman jurisprudential sources, was considered a modified form of a pledge.[52] Yet the papyri show that the *antichrêsis* was in origin, and still in Roman times, a separate legal institution. Only in a few cases do we find an *antichrêsis* combined with a pledge. Generally the concession of rights of use does not create a pledge at all.[53]

Discussion concerning the *paramonê* formerly concentrated on how the agreement affected the personal status of the debtor, i.e., whether the debtor was reduced to a kind of servitude to the creditor. The clauses of the antichretic agreements (esp. **5.5.4**) can easily lead one to such a conclusion. Currently, however, this interpretation is rejected as excessively formal. Like any labor contract, the *paramonê* placed the debtor who worked for the creditor in a position of personal dependency, but the degree of this dependency could vary considerably.

Modern scholarship is more concerned with the social implications of antichretic contracts.[54] As discussed above, the *antichrêsis* could be adapted to many different purposes. It could secure a loan by binding the debtor personally to the creditor as in the *paramonê* contract. It could also serve as another kind of contract, for instance as a lease through inclusion of an *enoikêsis* clause. In light of the wide range of purposes for which antichretic agreements might be used, the circumstances of each contract must be evaluated individually on the basis of internal and other evidence.

5.5.1 Loan with antichretic lease

P.Mich. III 188 (Bacchias, 17 August AD 120). Image at Papyri.info.

The document is a loan with an antichretic lease agreement. Hermas receives from Tapekusis a loan of 300 drachmas. Instead of paying interest he grants her the right to occupy a building he owns in the village Bacchias. The Greek word *oikopedon*, in reference to the building-site, gives no clear idea of the nature of the property concerned. It could even mean a house that once existed or that is planned to be built.[55] Even so, the

52 See *Dig.* 13.7.33 (Marcian): "If the debtor pays back the money, he can use the action of pledge to recover the *antichrêsis*, for because this is a pledge he can use this word (i.e., the action of *pledge*)." Cf. *Dig.* 20.1.11.1 (Marcian).

53 See the still relevant work of Manigk (1910).

54 Cf. Jördens (1990: 272–95), Rupprecht (1992) and Tenger (1993: 61–95).

55 Cf. Daniel (2010: 158) and the extensive discussion of the meaning of *oikopedon* in this and other documents on 158–68.

building must have contained some habitable rooms, as is shown by the clause giving Tapekusis the right to live there herself or rent the property to others. The duration of the loan is not fixed in the contract. Apparently Hermas could return the money whenever he saw fit. This fact lends considerable support to the assumption that the real purpose of the contract was to accord Tapekusis the right to live in the house, and the "loan" was in fact the rent.

5.5.1 belongs to an archive of at least twenty-three texts that were collected by the creditor of this loan, Tapekusis, and her husband Horos.[56] Ten of these documents relate to the aforementioned property at Bacchias. As such, they allow us to reconstruct the history of the house and its owners over sixty years (AD 71 to 131).[57] During this time, the house was mostly held in Hermas' family in joint ownership, each share being inherited, divided, and sold repeatedly. Tapekusis had a special interest in the house: her family owned the neighboring estate to the west, and for a while also parts of the house itself. After Hermas' death, Tapekusis made another loan and *enoikêsis* contract with the new owner, Tauris.[58] Finally, sometime before AD 131, Tapekusis acquired the whole house through purchase.[59] Even more significant is that Tapekusis' archive contains five loans with *enoikêsis*, but not one rental agreement. It is conceivable that local practices or the use of model contract formulas influenced the choice of this form of contract rather than the parties' individual preferences.[60]

> In the fourth year of Emperor Caesar Traianus Hadrianus Augustus, in the month Kaisareios on the twenty-fourth, Mesore 24, in Bacchias of the Herakleides district of the Arsinoite nome. Hermas son of Ptolemaios, grandson of Ammonios, approximately eighty[-five?] years old, with a scar in the middle of his forehead, acknowledges to Tapekusis daughter of Horos, granddaughter of Katoites, approximately forty-five years old, with a scar on her upper lip toward the left, with her guardian, her

56 Cf. the description of the Horos and Tapekusis archive by R. Smolders at the Leuven Homepage of Papyrus Archives (www.trismegistos.org/arch.php).

57 *P.Mich.* XII 635 (AD 71), X 583 (AD 78), X 584 (AD 84), X 585 (AD 87), XI 605 (*c.* AD 117), III 188 (AD 120), XI 625 (AD 121), III 189 (AD 123), SB XXII 15850 (AD 126?) and *P.Mich.* III 180 (AD 131).

58 Cf. *P.Mich.* III 189 and the related payment of the property transfer tax in *SB* XXII 15850.

59 Since Tapekusis possessed all the documents related to the house, which were originally addressed to Hermas, there can be no doubt that she acquired the house at some point. In AD 131 she declared her ownership of an unspecified house acquired through purchase (*P.Mich.* III 180). Most likely the aforementioned house at Bacchias is meant in the declaration.

60 Closely related to our text is *P.Mich.* XI 625, dated 19 September AD 121, in which Tapekusis' payment of the property transfer tax for entering into the *enoikêsis* agreement with Hermas is recorded.

husband Horos son of Horos, approximately fifty years old, with a scar on his left eyebrow, that he, the declaring party, has received from her the sum of three hundred drachmas of the Emperor's minted silver coin, directly from her hand, out of her house; and in place of interest on this sum (*anti tôn toutôn tokôn*) he, the declaring party, has permitted that she and her relations and whosoever she should wish may dwell (*enoikein*), so long as he owes the aforementioned money, in the unit of the house-property (*oikopedon*) belonging to him in the aforementioned village, whose neighbors are, as they (*sc.* Hermas and Tapekusis) stated in agreement: to the south, the buildings of Katoites son of Menches and the joint owners including, along part of it, a common entrance and exit; to the north, the imperial road; to the west, buildings of the aforementioned Katoites and joint owners; to the east, the courtyard of Horos son of Katoites, grandson of Belles, and his brothers; and that he, the declaring party, and his relations guarantee to Tapekusis and her relations the terms of her dwelling with every guarantee (*bebaiôsis*), and he, the declaring party, will ensure that no one prevents either Tapekusis or her relations from dwelling there or renting it to others and collecting rents and using all its appurtenances without interference.

If it should appear that Tapekusis has paid the expense of maintenance or of reconstruction, and Hermas wishes to repay the aforementioned silver, he shall repay that (expense) along with the aforementioned silver, the responsibility resting on her, Tapekusis.

The subscriptions of the parties follow in second (Hermas') and third (Ammonios son of Dioskoros signing for the illiterate Tapekusis and Horos) hands.

(4th hand) Registered by the record office (*grapheion*) at Bacchias.

5.5.2 Loan with *paramonê*

P.Mich. x 587 (Tebtunis, AD 24/5). Image at Papyri.info.

The following document belongs to an archive of almost two hundred papyri that were collected by Kronion, head of the record office (*grapheion*) at Tebtunis, in the Arsinoite nome, where this agreement was written down.[61]

Pabelleous receives a loan of forty-eight silver drachmas from Harmiusis for the period of one year. Instead of interest, his daughter Kolleuthis will

[61] See the description of the archive of Kronon, son of Apion, by B. van Beek at the Leuven Homepage of Papyrus Archives (www.trismegistos.org/arch.php).

work for the creditor for the whole year. This is expressed through the statement, typical of *paramonê* clauses, that she will stay (*paramenein*) with him. Her work is not specified: she must fulfill all duties given to her by Harmiusis. The following security and penalty clauses, setting fines for theft, fraud, and damage, seem harsh: in addition to the repayment of the loan (with interest) Pabelleous must pay a penalty of fifty percent of the loan, reimburse the damage, and pay an additional fine of another hundred drachmas to Harmiusis as well as one hundred drachmas to the public treasury. Though these rigorous fines lay a heavy burden on Pabelleous and Kolleuthis, it must be remembered that similar clauses are also found in ordinary work contracts (see Chapter 8 below) and should therefore not be considered as peculiar to the *paramonê*.

Unlike routine labor contracts, and most *paramonê* agreements, in this contract Kolleuthis receives no payment for her work. Harmiusis pays for food and clothing, but Kolleuthis' salary is compensated only by the remission of interest on the loan. Calculating the interest shows how unfavorable the conditions of the agreement in fact were for the debtor. If we assume the standard interest rate of twelve percent, the yearly interest for the loan of forty-eight drachmas would be 5.76 drachmas, an absurdly small amount for a year's wage, even considering that the moneylender is supposed to pay for the necessities of his servant. Or, the other way around, if we assume a monthly wage of fifteen drachmas for Kolleuthis, the interest would reach the immense rate of 375 percent.[62]

We can conclude from this comparison that Pabelleous so desperately needed the forty-eight drachmas that he put his daughter's labor at the disposal of his creditor for practically nothing but the maintenance of the girl. Covering the living expenses of the girl for one year might, however, be an important motive for Pabelleous' agreement to the terms of this contract.

> [...] Pabelleous son of Onnophris, Persian of the *epigonê*, about forty years old, with a scar on the left side of his forehead, [acknowledges] to Harmiusis son of Onnophris, about twenty-six years old, with a scar on his left calf, that he has received from him directly from his hand, out of his house, forty-eight drachmas of minted silver, and that in place of interest on this sum and the cost of necessities and clothing, he, the

[62] The numbers used are highly hypothetical. Other wages for comparison can best be found in Drexhage (1991), who shows the great diversity of attested wages and illustrates the impossibility of calculating average wages.

declaring party, will present (to Harmiusis) his daughter Kolleuthis, who will reside with Harmiusis and his relations for one year from the above date, staying and doing all things asked of her, neither sleeping outside of Harmiusis' house nor leaving it during the day without his knowledge, but accompanying him everywhere throughout Egypt; nor may Pabelleous have the right to take his daughter away during that time, but if he should take her away, or she should willingly leave, or if they should otherwise violate any of the aforesaid terms, or if she should be caught stealing or damaging or embezzling anything belonging to Harmiusis or his relations, or fail to return intact anything she took to guard, unless it was taken (from her) by force, he, the declaring party, shall immediately pay to Harmiusis what he received from him as written above, the forty-eight drachmas of silver, with an additional fifty percent and with interest, as well as a fine of one hundred drachmas and (the same amount) for the treasury, and damages. And for each day she should neglect [. . .] (he shall pay) three bronze obols, and the principal, and fivefold the amount stolen, one and a half times the amount embezzled {one and a half times} and simple interest; but if she should not hand it over or not return it intact, (he shall pay) its value as assessed by Harmiusis. The right of execution against both the debtor and his property belongs to Harmiusis as if a judicial sentence had been delivered. At the end of this time (i.e., one year) the declaring party will return the aforementioned forty-eight silver drachmas; if he does not, he shall pay it with an additional fifty percent and the interest and a fine of an additional hundred silver drachmas and (the same amount) for the public treasury.

Signatory of the declaring party: Kollouthos son of Mieus, about 20 years old, with a scar on his right wrist.

I, Pabelleous son of Onnophris, Persian of the *epigonê*, acknowledge that I have received from Harmiusis forty-eight silver drachmas [. . .]

5.5.3 Loan with *paramonê*

P.Coll.Youtie II 92 (Antinoopolis [found at Aphrodito], 15 May AD 569). Editor's translation revised by J. G. Keenan. Image at Papyri.info.

The following text is another *paramonê* agreement, but from the Byzantine period. Martha, a seller of salted fish, received from Flavius Helladius, a member of the provincial elite, an open-ended loan of nine gold carats. As security for the debt she "mortgages" her fifteen-year-old sister Prokla, who must perform some lowly services for the creditor.

The document is of special interest because of its typically prolix Byzantine formulation. The first part of the contract is devoted to an extensive narration of the circumstances under which Martha's family sank into poverty, and to explaining why she was forced to take such drastic measures as handing over her sister. Her story, however, reveals a major paradox: Martha first describes the grueling work her sister had to endure for her former creditor; she praises her current contractual partner, Helladius, who delivered her from these hardships, but she then enumerates the humble and submissive circumstances under which her sister will work in his service.

From the legal viewpoint, two points are of particular interest. First, in contrast to earlier *paramonê* contracts, this antichretic agreement is formulated as a pledge, not as a contract of labor. This is remarkable because the *antichrêsis* was originally used to modify loan contracts. As such it did not imply a pledge of the given property. In addition, Prokla's future service is not regarded in the contract as antichretic, that is, as a return for the remission of interest. It would appear that, in this late document, either the terms have been confused or that *antichrêsis* has been tacitly assimilated to pledge. Second, Novel 134 §7 of Justinian (AD 556) prohibited creditors from receiving debtors' children as pledges or having them perform servile duties; the law inflicts on such creditors harsh monetary and corporal punishment.[63] This document, however, shows how ineffective imperial legislation was when confronted with the deeply rooted traditions in the provinces.

See also **8.2.4** below for further discussion of this document.

In the reign and consulship of our most divine lord Flavius Iustinus, the eternal Augustus (and) Emperor, the fourth year, Pachon the twentieth, at the beginning of the third indiction, at the most illustrious city of Antinous (i.e., Antinoopolis), to Flavius Helladius, the most illustrious secretary of the illustrious ducal staff in the area of the Thebaid, son of <BLANK SPACE> of excellent memory, originating from the fair city of the Panopolites, from me, here present, Martha daughter of Menas by my mother Thekla, salt-fish seller, herself also originating from the city of

[63] *Nov.* 134 §7: "Since we know that this kind of outrage is committed in different regions of our state, that creditors dare to accept children of debtors as pledge (*enechuron*) or for servile work (*doulikê hypêresia*) or to lease them out to others (*misthoun*), we prohibit this in every way and order that, if someone commits such an outrage, not only shall he be deprived of the debt, but he shall also be condemned to pay the same sum to the child whom he detained or to his parents, and he shall furthermore be subjected to corporal punishment (*sômatikê poinê*) by the local magistrates, since he dared to detain or lease out or receive in pledge a free person on account of a debt."

Antinous, acting without a male guardian but providing a signatory on her own behalf and witnesses, whose subscriptions immediately follow, to the present contract of pledge on the agreed upon conditions as set forth below, on all the terms contained in it, greetings. My father having fallen into the utmost poverty, and being well off(?) [. . .] long since, before having completing his life's service – Menas by name, nicknamed "the Bath-attendant" – and of necessity having then made a pledge of my orphan sister, more indigent (*sc.* of years, i.e., younger) than me, called Prokla, to the most illustrious lord Nonnos for one gold *solidus* pursuant to the deed of pledge made by him at that time to the most illustrious gentleman, and after his death, in these (circumstances) I spared no effort, until I repaid by my manual labor the half of the aforesaid one *solidus* to the said gentleman, in the desire to redeem my overworked sister, I, the above-written Martha, not having the means to repay it in full, but being blessed (to meet) Your Illustriousness moved by the love of God, have applied entreaties to It to lend the remaining amount for the redemption of this same orphan sister. Accordingly, I, the same Martha, acknowledge that I have received from your hand into my hands and have borrowed from you along with this deed of security the nine gold carats by the public standards of Antinoopolis, = 9 gold c. publ. std. Antin., and by the deposition of the guarantee and surety and full and unfailing repayment, I pledge to you now on the spot and have pledged as security and by right of pledge my said sister Prokla, being fifteen years old more or less, upon condition that she reside in your household, performing all servile offices and requirements of yours unremittingly, willingly and submissively and obediently, doing all things sincerely and without any attempt at flight or theft or any manner of recklessness whatsoever, at my own risk and my resources being at stake entirely to this end, until the settlement of the aforesaid debt of the nine gold carats; she, however, being fed and clothed (by you), is to reside with you respectfully until the repayment of these; and for your security I have drawn up this amicable deed based upon all the prescribed terms and issued it, and in answer to the formal question I gave my assent.

(*2nd hand*) † I, Aurelia Martha daughter of Menas the Bath-attendant, the aforesaid, have deposited this pledge of Prokla my sister instead of the nine gold carats, and I shall repay as aforesaid. I, Aurelius Victor son of Ioannes, of Antinoopolis, wrote on her behalf since she has little facility with letters.

(*3rd hand*) † I, Aurelius Kollouthos son of Kallinikos, by God's will notary, bear witness to the pledge, having heard it from its depositor.

5.5.4 Deposit concealing a dowry

BGU III 729 (= *M.Chr.* 167) (Alexandria, 3 [or 13] October AD 144)

The following document is a *synchôrêsis*, a contract drafted before a judicial authority, here the *archidikastês* of Alexandria. The agreement, between Petronia Sarapias and C. Julius Apolinarius, was formulated as a contract of deposit (*parathêkê*). Its format cannot be distinguished from that of a normal *parathêkê* contract, which is generally considered a type of loan. There can be no doubt, however, that the real purpose of the contract was to provide a dowry. Since soldiers were forbidden to marry, they could not acknowledge in writing the receipt of a dowry from their (illegitimate) wives. They therefore acknowledged the receipt of "deposits" instead.

The marital background can be traced in the identity of the parties: an unmarried woman appears as bailor and a soldier as bailee. The objects listed in the contract are typical dowry items: a woman's dress and gold jewelry.[64] Finally, and most decisively, in a receipt from 5 April AD 145 preserved in *P.Lond.* II 178 (= **4.2.1**), Petronia Sarapias confirms that she regained part of the dowry (*proix*) she had given C. Julius Apolinarius.

It is quite surprising that this *synchôrêsis* agreement, which so obviously served to circumvent the law, was drawn up before the *archidikastês* himself. We might have expected such an official to notice this legal sleight of hand. We know moreover from a record of proceedings, *P.Catt.* recto Col. 1, lines 5–13 (Alexandria, 5 January AD 117), that Roman judges were well aware of this practice. The prefect M. Rutilius Lupus there remarked (lines 9–10): "We know that the *parathêkai* are dowries." He accordingly rejected a soldier's widow's claim for the repayment of a "deposit." Apparently, the *archidikastês* was less strict in the case of Petronia and C. Julius Apolinarius. (See also **4.6.2a.**)

> To Dionysios son of Deios, former *stratêgos* of the city, *neôkoros* of the great Sarapis, one of the tax-exempt persons maintained in the Mouseion, priest, *archidikastês* and *curator* of the *chrêmatistai* and the other tribunals, from Petronia Sarapias, under the guardianship of her brother, Gaius Petronius Marcellus, and from Gaius Julius

[64] In the first century AD these types of items usually form part of the *parapherna*. Later on, gold jewelry is commonly given as *phernê* and the *parapherna* lost their financial importance; on this development see Yiftach-Firanko (2003: 129–82 and tables 7–10).

Apolinarius, soldier of the First Cohort of Armenians under the centurion Julianus.

Gaius Julius Apolinarius acknowledges that he has received from Petronia Sarapias as deposit, without any risk at all, women's garments valued at three hundred silver drachmas and gold jewelry, in kind, (weighing) a total of thirty-two *tetartai*, which he will keep safe by him and return to her immediately whenever she should request, or else pay according to the law of deposits, whereby Petronia Sarapias receives right of execution over the whole of the property of Gaius Julius Apolinarius as if from a legal judgment. We agree (?). In the eighth year of Emperor Caesar Titus Aelius Hadrianus Antoninus Augustus Pius, Phaophi 6 (or 16).

CHAPTER 6

Sale

Roger Bagnall, Mark Depauw, Éva Jakab, J. G. Manning, T. Sebastian Richter, and Uri Yiftach-Firanko

Introduction

In the Egyptian legal tradition the private conveyance by sale was conceived of as an oral agreement between two parties, or two groups of parties, in the presence of witnesses. Property rights were well developed in ancient Egypt before the Ptolemaic period. In order for a person to convey title to a piece of property, an equivalent value had to be exchanged. Thus the Demotic "sale contract" was termed a "document in exchange for silver" (above, **2.2**). This basic idea was valid for other types of conveyances, and was at times merely fictional, i.e., an actual exchange of property for an equivalent value did not always occur.

This basic principle of Egyptian law, "notwendige Entgeltlichkeit" ("necessary remuneration"), is paralleled in other ancient Near Eastern traditions.[1] If the surviving record is any guide, there was considerable evolution in the formalities of the written sale in ancient Egypt and, over time, an increase in the use of written instruments of sale.[2] Most conveyances were probably accomplished orally and therefore without need of a document. Before the first millennium BC, most sales recorded in writing simple memorialized oral agreements and were rudimentary.

By the time of the New Kingdom (1550–1069 BC) the variety of objects of sale increased. A major evolution in written contracts arose in the seventh century BC, at a time when the Demotic language and script began to be used. Legal phraseology became more complex and the conception more abstract. Formal written legal contracts probably replaced oral agreements, but nonetheless in their formulation still betrayed their oral roots. The evolution of Demotic contracts reached a peak by the late

[1] Seidl (1951: 47; 1968: 56).

[2] On the evolution of the Egyptian sale, see Menu (1988a, 1988b), on whom we rely here. See also Botta (2009) for a summary of Demotic sale and cession formulas.

fourth century BC, when well-developed clauses that protected the buyer became part of the standard instrument.

The main purpose of the real sale instrument was the preservation and guarantee of a title in property, with a chain of succession. The vendor in the sale was responsible for guaranteeing clear title, and the transaction was recorded in anticipation of future disputes. As we know from the Demotic legal manual *P.Mattha*, there was a formal procedure, known as a "public protest" (Muhs 2002), by which title could be cleared, a process that was undertaken before a formal trial could be held regarding the property. All documents that had previously been made with respect to the property in question were conveyed to the buyer at the time of the new sale. The oral nature of the transaction is stressed by the use of the verb "to say" that begins Demotic legal documents: "Party A has said to Party B: I have received a satisfactory price. . ." Recording sales, as in later Egyptian history (see **2.6**), may have been normative for unusual circumstances or for important property such as houses and land. In any case this is perhaps why sales of property and marriage contracts are preserved in family archives. Keeping such texts together protected the long-term property interests of the family. The degree to which the sale documents from Egypt reflect market transactions is the subject of ongoing discussion.

Objects of sale

The most common objects of sale were land, usually in small plots, and houses, or parts of houses, tombs, priestly stipends (shares of income derived from temple service), oxen, cows, and donkeys, and slaves (pre-Ptolemaic Demotic only). Sales of animals are exceedingly rare in both Greek and Demotic Ptolemaic texts although this is likely a function of the failure of this type of text to survive within family archives.[3] They are quite common in the Roman period (**6.4**). Animal sales were less formal instruments and generally of the narrow type, i.e., they were not large, broad texts consisting of a few very long lines. No doubt this was because such animal sales were ephemeral. Sales of important items such as land and houses were regularly drawn up as formal documents, such documents being important in proving long-term property rights interests and therefore more likely to be preserved in family "archives."[4]

[3] See Manning (2003a).

[4] On the distinction between archives and dossiers, see Vandorpe (2009a). It is a purely conventional modern distinction between texts that were gathered together for a particular purpose in antiquity

The text of a sale contract was written by a professional scribe and was written unilaterally from the point of view of the buyer. There was regional variation in the phrasing of the legal formula.[5] The contracts themselves were used as proof of clear title and all such records pertinent to the conveyance of a piece of property were handed over to the buyer at the time of the sale.

Greek law recognized one type of sale only: the sale for ready money, by which the delivery of the object and the payment of the consideration took place simultaneously. The written documentation of the act was meant to bear evidence of this act, and of the title of the purchase to the object, should it ever be challenged in court. The sale contract did not create new obligations whose future performance was to be enforced in a court of law (Pringsheim 1950). In any case, such obligations were rarely set out in writing.

The Greek sales on papyrus, like the Demotic, concern a wide variety of objects: agricultural land, vineyards, palm groves and even sacred land, houses, or their shares. In many cases the parties were family members: in *P.Mich.* v 272 Herakles sells a date-palm garden to Beris, his wife. In *P.Mich.* v 277 Kronion son of Labesis sells a house to his brother Labesis. In others the parties seem to be strangers, e.g., *P.Mich.* vi 428 by which Valeria Diodora conveys landed property to Gaius Julius Niger, a newly (?) discharged former cavalryman of the *ala veterana Gallica.*

Sale, even in the Roman period, presents a somewhat different aspect in the papyri from what we find in the Roman jurists. Except in the special case of the so-called sales on delivery, where we encounter a kind of mixed type of contract with many elements of loans, sales in the papyri are not undertakings to sell, with all of the complexities that can accompany such undertakings, but statements that a sale has taken place. They therefore reflect in large part the continuing domination of a Greek legal tradition, which Pringsheim characterized as follows (1950: 333):

> Greek legal imagination was not active enough to conceive a more progressive and abstract theory of sale. The conception of cash sale was never superseded by the idea of a binding contract of sale which created enforceable obligations on vendor and purchaser.[6]

and those texts that have been gathered together by scholars normally for the purposes of studying a particular family.

[5] On the clause variations, see Zauzich (1968).

[6] It should be noted that this remark is made at the beginning of a discussion of *arra* (or *arrabôn*), an agreement in which "the intending buyer gives to the intending vendor a part of the price and it is agreed that in case of non-performance the buyer shall lose his earnest, the vendor pay back the double amount" (Pringsheim 1950: 335). This type of transaction is not relevant for movables in the papyri.

Sales contracts were thus important to buyers mainly as proof that the rights to something had passed from one person to another (the distinction between ownership and possession hardly ever figuring explicitly). Many of the subjects we find in the *Digest* have for this reason no immediate relevance in the papyri. Even the later documents included here largely conform to long-established patterns.

Common sales in antiquity happened unrecorded as nowadays; the formal recording of a transfer of ownership was rather dependent on particular conditions. Many sales attested in the papyri are sales on delivery (cf. Ernst 1997 and below, **6.2.2**): the purchaser bought a quantity of crops of the coming harvest, of wine still being fermented, or of goods still to be produced, while the vendor received payment in advance (see the bilingual examples in **2.7.1**). This procedure implied indebtedness – in fact, sales on delivery are sometimes hardly distinguishable from loans in money to be paid off in kind (cf. section **5.4**) – and indebtedness required formal confirmation by the debtor. The motivation for recording sales could also be the high value of the purchase object or the long-lasting consequences of a sale, which might involve future generations, as was the case with sales of slaves and, above all, with sales of estates and buildings or parts of buildings. The prolixity of language is a notable feature of Byzantine contracts and is well illustrated below in **6.6**.

6.1 Demotic sales and cessions

Mark Depauw and J. G. Manning

We present here the two commonest types of sale, a sale of a house and a sale of land.[7] The first is well represented by *P.Fam.Theb.* 3 + 4, which belong to a group of thirty-two papyri found in a house during excavations in western Thebes (Dra-Abu-el-Naga) in 1922, the same year as the discovery of Tutankhamun's tomb. The texts have come to be known as the archive of Psenminis. The text is a typical "bipartite" contract consisting of a "sale" and a "cession" document. Both the sale and the cession are dated in the same year. Both texts also share the rather archaic feature of witness-copies, which means that in the sale six and in the cession four witnesses have copied out in full the entire text of the sale on the same papyrus sheet as the original text written by the professional scribe (Depauw 1999).

[7] Previous surveys in Seidl (1962: 116–21), Depauw (1997: 140–42), Manning (2003b).

6.1.1 Demotic sale and cession of a house

P.Fam.Theb. 3 + 4 (Thebes, March /April 307 BC). Image at *P.Fam.Theb.*, Plates 5–10.

Note that the correct witness list to this document is published by El-Amir (1959: 29) but labeled incorrectly.

Sale: Year 10, first month of *peret* of pharaoh Alexander son of Alexander. The smith of the temple of Amun, Pais son of Pamounis and Tarenetbastis, has said to the *kalisiris* (*an ancient military title*) of the estate of Amun Parates son of Panouphis and Taratis: "My heart is content with the price of my house, which is built and roofed, which is in the northern quarter of Thebes to the west of the enclosure wall of the temple of Montu lord of Waset. To its south: your house, which is built and roofed and your house (plot) that is vacant; its north: the house of Pateharpres son of Pachaas, which is built and roofed and which is in possession of his children, with the street of Pharaoh between them; its west:[8] your house, which is built and roofed and your courtyard which is at its entrance; its east: the rest of the above-mentioned house which measures two and a half ground cubits, that is 250 square cubits, that is two and a half ground cubits, which I have sold to the waxmaker Chesseus (Chonsuiou) son of Oteuris (Oudjahor). Those are the neighbors of this house. I have given it to you. It is yours. I do not have any claim at all against you concerning it. No man at all, myself included, will be able to exercise power over it except you from today onwards. The one who will come against you concerning it in my name or in the name of any man at all, I will cause that he is far from you, and I will cause it to be clear for you concerning every right, every title deed, any matter at all any day. Yours are their title deeds in any house in which they are. Every document that has been drawn up concerning it, and every document that has been drawn up for me concerning it, and every document by virtue of which I am entitled concerning it they belong to you and the rights conveyed by them. To you belongs that by virtue of which I am entitled concerning them. The oath (or) the proof that will be imposed on you in the courthouse with respect to the right conveyed by the foregoing document that I have drawn up

[8] The property boundaries here are out of the normal order: south–north–east–west.

for you to cause me to do it, I will do it without claiming any title or anything at all against you."

Scribal signature: Written by Psammetichus son of Iretouredj.

A list of sixteen witnesses is recorded on the verso. Beneath and to the left of the main text, six of the witnesses (a different list of names than in the cession – see below) write out the agreement in full as part of the act of witnessing. They are:

The god's father and *choachytês* Peteamun son of Harpaesis and Chensartais, while he is witness in year [. . .]
Pahen son of Petenefhotep and Mathot, while he is witness in year [. . .]
The singer of Amun Amunhotep son of Peteharpares and Taty, while he is witness in year [. . .]
Imhotep son of Montuemhat and Tahib, while he is witness in year [. . .]
Hor son of Esmin and Tykaptah, while he is witness in year [. . .]
Userwer son of Peteamunopet and Tykemeru

Cession: Year 10, first month of *peret* of pharaoh Alexander son of Alexander. The smith[9] of the temple of Amun, Pais son of Pamounis and Taremetbastis, has said to the *kalisiris* Parates son of Panouphis and Taratis: "I am far <from you> concerning your house, which is built and roofed, which is in the northern quarter of Thebes, to the west of the enclosure wall of the temple of Montu lord of Waset. To its south: your house, which is built and roofed, and your house, which is a building plot; to its north: the house of Peteharpres son of Pachaas, which is built and roofed and which is in the possession of his children, with the street of Pharaoh between them; to its east: the rest of the above-mentioned house, which measures two and a half ground cubits, which I have sold to the wax maker Chesseus (Chonsuiou) son of Oteuris (Oudjahor); to its west: your house, which is built and roofed, and your courtyard, which is at its entrance. Those are all the neighbors of this house, which is built and roofed, which you have bought from me, myself having made for you a document concerning money for it in year 10, first month of *peret* of Pharaoh, may he live forever. I do not have any claim at all on you concerning it. No man at all, myself included, will be able to exercise power over it except you from

[9] The Demotic here is ambiguous; the title refers to someone who works in metal.

today onwards. The one who will come against you concerning it in my name or in the name of any man <at all>, I will cause that he is far from you, you having a claim on me regarding the right of the document for money that I have made for you for the abovementioned house, which is built and roofed, in year 10, the first month of *peret* of Pharaoh, may he live forever and in eternity, to act for you according to its contents on every day, beside everything above, without any obstruction."

Scribal signature: Written by Psammetichus son of Iretouredj.

A list of sixteen witnesses is recorded on the verso, four of whom copy the entire text of the agreement on the recto, with the following introductions:

Imouthes son of Mentemes (Montemhates) and Thabis, while he is witness in year . . .
Amenothes son of Peteharpres and Tatia, while he is witness in year . . .
Paches son of Petenephotes and Maithotis, while he is witness in year . . .
Horos son of Sminis and Tayptahwer, while he is witness in year . . .

6.1.2 Demotic sale of land

P.Brit.Mus. Andrews 28 (Thebes, December 208 BC). Image: Figure 10.

Dating formula and a rather full description of the eponymous priests begin the text.

Year [15, third month] of the season *akhet*[10] (under) pharaoh Ptolemy, (son of) Ptolemy and Berenike, the Gods Euergetai, and his son Ptolemy; while Demosthenes son of Kratinos is priest of Alexander and of the gods who save and [the] Gods Adelphoi, the Gods Euergetai, the Gods Philopatores; while Diognis daughter of Philotas is *athlophoros* before Berenike Euergetis; while Glauke daughter of Zenodotos is *kanêphoros* before Arsinoe Philadelphos; while Heniokhos son of Lysanias is priest in the Theban nome of Ptolemy the god and of the

[10] There is no reason to assume with the editor that the first day of the month is implied by the fact that no specific day date is mentioned in the text.

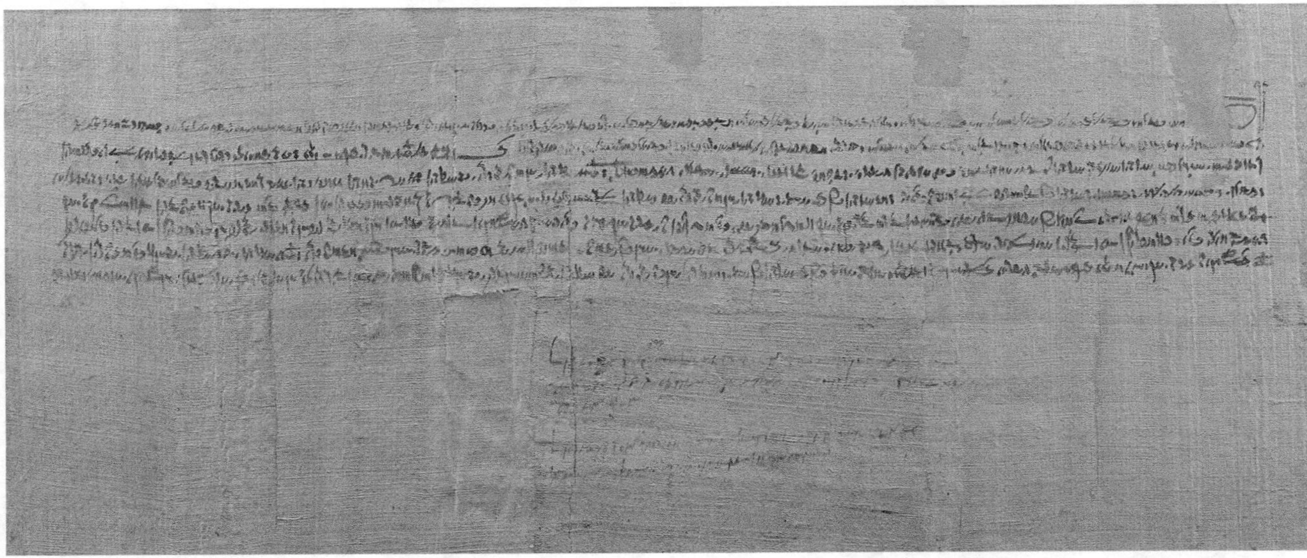

Fig. 10. Demotic land sale. *P.Brit.Mus. Andrews* 28 / *P.Brit.Mus. EA* 10392. Thebes, December 208 BC

Gods Philopatores. Has declared the Nubian Hellos son of Phennesis, his mother (being) Titos, to the woman Takhoumis daughter of Patous, her mother (being) Nekhthaus: "You have caused my heart to agree to the money for the value of one aroura of land (comprising) 31/32 arouras, (that is) one aroura of land again. I have given it to you; it belongs to you, (namely) this your one aroura of land aforementioned, besides the two arouras of land concerning which I drew up a document in your favor earlier, making three arouras of land (in all). I have received their value in money from your hand, it being complete and without any remainder; my heart agrees to it. I have no claim at all against you in respect of them. No person at all, not even me, will be able to exercise authority over them except you from this day onwards. As for anyone who shall proceed against you on account of them in my name or in the name of anyone at all, I shall cause him to be far from you. And I shall clear it for you from anything at all at any time. To you belong their documents, their titles in any place in which they are.[11] Every document that has been drawn up regarding them and every document that has been drawn up for me regarding them and (every) document by virtue of which I am entitled in respect of them, they belong to you and the rights conferred by them. To you belongs that by virtue of which I am entitled in respect of them. The oath (or) the proof that will be imposed upon you in the courthouse in respect of the rights conferred by the aforementioned document that I have drawn up for you, to cause me to swear it, I will swear it. You will be able to constrain me by virtue of the document for silver that I drew up earlier (regarding) the two other arouras of land, totaling three arouras of land, making two documents. And I shall act on your behalf (in) conformity with them at any time without alleging any title or anything at all against you." While the woman Titos daughter of Psenesis, his mother, has said: "Receive this document from the hand of Hellos son of Phennesis, my son aforementioned, regarding the one aroura of land aforementioned, besides the two arouras of land concerning which I drew up a document for you earlier, making three arouras of land (in all), while I have given approval to the document in question, making two documents. I am far from you regarding them without any force (being applied)." Petemenophis son of Petemestous, the scribe of the legal documents, has written this, in Pois in the northern section.

[11] On the conveyance of all prior deeds pertaining to the property, see Pestman (1983).

Greek subscription (fragmentary), registering the payment of the conveyance tax: [A] "Year 15 (month of) Hathor day 6 (or 3). There has been paid to the [. . .] in [. . .] by [. . .]"

[B] "Year 15 Hathor day 10 [. . .] by [. . .]"

A list of sixteen witnesses is recorded on the verso.

6.2 The different applications of the Demotic sale and cession contract

Mark Depauw and J. G. Manning

The basic form and content of a Demotic sale instrument were treated above (**2.2**). A distinctive feature of the sale instrument was that it typically consisted of two separate acts, one acknowledging receipt of a price, the other ceding all claims to the property being conveyed and promising the buyer to defend his rights to the conveyed property.[12] Thus the real sale transaction in Demotic law was conceived of consisting of two distinct transactions despite some of the overlap in phraseology.[13] In a real sale, these took place simultaneously on the same day and were often even recorded on the same sheet of papyrus. Nonetheless the two legal instruments remained quite distinct in legal conception and could be used separately for different types of transactions. This separation of legal acts reflects the history of the development of conveyance instruments during the first millennium BC, and the distinction between conveyance and real sale was maintained.

The term sale contract ("Kaufvertrag") to describe these instruments, while in standard use, is thus inaccurate, for historically they served to document many different types of transfers, from real sale to pledges (**5.1.1**) and divisions of family property.[14] "Conveyance" might be a more accurate term. It is generally believed that a real sale must have both a *sẖ (n) ḏbꜣ ḥḏ* and a *sẖ n wy* instrument. Some evidence from Ptolemaic family archives has suggested to some scholars that the *sẖ (n) ḏbꜣ ḥḏ* instrument alone may have been sufficient to convey real property rights since the conveyed property was subsequently resold.[15] At the same time, the existence of a

[12] For an analysis of this cession document, see Allam (1985).

[13] On the evolution of the concept of sale and the contractual forms in Demotic, see Menu (1988).

[14] For an example of this last type of transaction, see, e.g., *P.Moscow* 135 (Elephantine, 349 BC) discussed by Martin (1996: 356–59).

[15] So Depauw (2000: 4–6).

sale instrument alone may reflect other kinds of transactions, including pledges used in marriage agreements (**6.2.3**).

The sale text could be pledged in exchange for a loan, as in **6.2.1**. In these cases, an acknowledgement of the loan has with it an embedded sale instrument, which in some cases could be handed over to a third-party trustee or lender to ensure the enforcement of the agreement (cf. above, **5.1.1**). Like their Greek counterparts, the Demotic loan is secured by real property that substitutes for the value of the loan. Here in **6.2.1** no possession or use of the house appears to have been involved in exchange for interest payments, as was the case in what are termed antichretic loans (i.e., giving the use of pledged property instead of interest on the loan: **5.5** introduction with **5.5.1** as example). In the case of default upon an agreement, the mortgagee was obliged to write a "cession" in order to convey clear title to the pledged property. In other cases pledges of property or "mortgages" could be done by the use of the normal sale and cession instruments. We can infer that when we have a sale instrument and a quitclaim concerning the same property dated a year or two later, the use of these two instruments documents a loan and then a default with subsequent mandatory conveyance of the pledged property that was used to secure the loan (e.g., **5.1.1**). The transfer of property in advance of death could also be accomplished by the writing of a sale document (*sẖ [n] ḏbꜣ ḥḏ*). Such "sales" are referred to as "sales *propter mortem*."[16]

A unique group of three texts studied by Pierce (1972), one of which is presented below as **6.2.2**, shows that in the Ptolemaic period a sale, in this case involving grain, could be effected in advance of the commodity's delivery.[17] Unlike typical Ptolemaic-period Demotic sale contracts, which had long horizontal lines of writing, this document type had many shorter lines (the so-called "narrow format"). **6.2.2** forms part of a small archive of a merchant/creditor Harmakhis. These three documents studied by Pierce are unique among Demotic legal instruments, and the contract may have been influenced by Greek ideas, the result of the new realities of the Ptolemaic economy and its increase in market activity. In fact, there are many comparable contemporary Greek contracts that document cash payments against deferred delivery. Pierce's view (1972: 93) is that the Demotic texts are constructed as sales with deferred delivery conceived of as "'claims' within the framework of contemporary Egyptian law – a category which would roughly correspond to δάνειον in Greek texts and to the modern notion of credit." Thus these Demotic texts, with no close pre-Ptolemaic parallels, are probably conceptually modeled on Greek transactions.

[16] Pestman (1995b: 80–81), and **4.5.1** above. [17] See further Bagnall (1977).

6.2.2 records a transaction involving grain and money that looks like a market transaction, as opposed to many of the Demotic contracts that were non-market transactions within families or tight-knit social groups. The legal instrument is divided into two parts, conflating two well-known Demotic legal forms: first, an acknowledgement of debt, or a "claim" (Dem. *R*^{c}*-wḫ3*), and, second, an agreement in the form either of a letter (Dem. *š*^{c}*.t*) or a contract (Dem. *sẖ*) in which the debtor promises to pay off the debt with grain. According to the agreement, the grain is to be delivered during the harvest season.

Pierce suggested two alternative ways of understanding the contract. (1) It is a loan. The debtor, called a "farmer," was in need of cash. An instrument is drawn up midway through the agricultural cycle; money is lent (in the text the phrase is "you have given me the price (or 'value') of X amount of grain"); and repayment is deferred until the coming harvest, with the repayment accepted in kind. (2) The merchant here is a grain dealer. He initiated the transaction. The advance payment is speculation in the grain market. The payment here is midway through the agricultural cycle. Thus the producer of grain could insure himself against a glut in the grain market, and therewith lower prices, and the merchant could hope for a good return on his advance.

Pierce concluded that there was no easy way to decide between these alternative understandings. Either way, it is possible to understand the transaction as an attempt to lower transaction costs. In case (1), the farmer was able to repay his cash debt with his harvest, not having to sell something in order to raise cash. In case (2) the grain dealer anticipated the harvest, midway through the year he could see what the nature of the coming harvest was likely to be, and locked in a price in advance, thus avoiding a market transaction later on.[18]

6.2.1 Demotic mortgage in the form of a sale

P.Brit.Mus. Glanville 10525 (Thebes, 284 BC). Images at *P.Brit.Mus. Glanville*, Plates 3, 7, and 8.

The text is similar to **5.1.1** above. The document combines two different contract types, an acknowledgement of debt and an agreement to repay a cash loan within a specific time period. Upon failure to do so, the borrower agrees here in advance to sell his house. The house, then, served as

[18] Pierce (1972: 83–93), *P.Recueil* 4–6. Other loans of money repayable in kind may reflect similar kinds of transactions. See Devauchelle (1986).

collateral for the cash loan. At the end there is a contingent interest disclaimer by the borrower's wife stating that while she has a contingent claim to the property through her marriage, she is rescinding it for the purposes of the loan. Unusually, the contract has two witness lists with the same order of names. One is written on the same side of the papyrus as the contract; the other is written on the verso, in the normal place for witness lists. According to the editor, the witness list on the recto is written in the same scribal hand as that of the contract; on the verso are signatures of the witnesses themselves.

(1) Year 21, third month of *shemu* of pharaoh Ptolemy. Has said the lector-priest of the Ape[19] Palehu son of Djehuty-iir-dy-s, whose mother is Tsherenese, to the God's father Wesir-wer son of Nakht-hor-em-heb, whose mother is Tayenese: "You have a claim against me (in the amount of) 9 silver *kite*, making 4.5 *statêrs* you have given me, and I will repay you by the last day of year 22, third month of *shemu*. (2) If I do not pay you the silver *kite*, making 4.5 *statêrs*, mentioned above by the last day of the thrd month of *shemu*, you have caused my heart to agree to the price for (the sale of) my house that is built and roofed, which is in the northern district of Thebes in The-House-of-the-Cow. Its boundaries: south, the house of the *choachytês* Petenefhotep son of Aludj, which is built and roofed; north, the house of the woman Tayiw, (3) daughter of Petenefhotep, the royal road being between them; east, the house of the embalmer Harsiese son of Panas, which is built and roofed; west, the house of the woman Ta-hib daughter of Petenefhotep, which is built and roofed. These are the boundaries of the house. I have given it to you; it's yours, your house, which is built and roofed, as already specified above. I have no claim whatsoever (4) against you regarding it. No one at all including me will be able to exercise authority over it except you, from the first of the month of Mesore, year 22 on. Whoever will come against you on account of it, in my name or in anyone's name, I will cause him to be far from you. And I will clear it for you with respect to any deed or any matter at all at any time. Yours are all of the title deeds (of this house) in any house in which they are. Every document that has been made concerning it, and every document (5) that has been made for me concerning it, and every document to which I am entitled regarding it – they are yours, along

[19] A priest perhaps connected with the burial of the sacred animal associated with the god Thoth. See Glanville (1939: 13 n. c).

with the rights pertaining thereto. Yours is that which I am entitled to concerning them. The oath of proof that will be required of you in the court regarding the right of the aforementioned document, which I have executed for you so that I do it, I will do it." Additionally, the woman Tay-hor daughter of Horsiese, whose mother is Taubastet, says: "Accept (the document) from Pelehu (son of) Djehuty-iir-ty-s (6) my husband, mentioned above, for the house mentioned above to cause him to do according to everything above. My heart is satisfied with it, (even though) I have a claim on him, by the right of the documents that he executed for me to carry out its conditions at all times. I have renounced in your favor your house mentioned here, without citing any deed or any claim whatsoever against you." Written by Nesmin son of Pa-hib.

Witness list

6.2.2 Demotic sale with deferred delivery

P.Recueil 4 (= *P.Brookl. Dem.* 1; probably Memphis [Sakkara], 15 February 108 BC). Image at *P.Recueil*, Plate VII.

A rather full dating protocol, with a rather long list of eponymous priests/priestesses, begins the document. In contrast to **6.2.1**, which is almost one meter in length, **6.2.2** is a rather modest strip of papyrus of the so-called narrow format, with only twelve witnesses signing on the verso.

The translation closely follows Pierce's.

(1) [Year 9 month 1 of *peret*], last [day], of the kings Kleopatra and Ptolemy (2) [the Gods Philometores Soteres[20]] (and of) the priest of Alexander and the G[ods Soter]es and (3) [the Gods Philadelphoi and the] Gods Euergetai and the Gods Philopatores and the Gods Epiphanes and the God (4) [Eupator and the] [God] Philometor and the young God Philopator[21] [and the God Euergetes] and the (5) Goddess [Philo] metor and [the Gods Philometores Sot]eres, (who is) Ptolemy son of king Ptolemy (6) [and of the priestess of] the [Queen K]leopatra, the Goddess Euergetes Philometor [Soteira], Dikaiosune[22] (7) [Nike] phoros,[23] [and the sacred fo]al of Isis,[24] the great one, Nut, the god's

[20] The Demotic writes a variant of Greek *sotêr*: *nt lk hb*, lit. "who causes sorrow to cease." See Pierce (1972: 24).
[21] In Greek, *theos neos philopatôr*. See Pierce (1972: 30).
[22] "Lover of Justice." See Pierce (1972: 31).
[23] "Mistress of Victory."
[24] A title of the eponymous priest of Kleopatra III.

mother, and of the prieste[ss of Arsinoe], Philopator (8) and [the] [*stephanê*]*phoros*[25] [of the] queen, Kleopatra, the Goddess Euergetes Philometor Soteira, (9) Dikaiosune, Nikephoros, and the *phosphoros*, K[l]eopatra, the (10) Goddess Euergetês [Philometor Sôteira], Dikaiosunê, the mistress of victory, and the *kanêphoros* before (11) [Arsinoe, the brother-loving], and the *athlophoros* before Ber[enik]e, Euergetês, (12) [who] are in Ra[kote].[26] The farmer, resident of Pr-[. . .] in the district of Wen-[. . .], Teosphib, (13) the son of Harmais, whose mother is Tawe, has declared to the merchant, resident of the Anoubieion, which is in the dependencies[27] of Memphis, (14) Harmakhis son of Herienupis, whose mother is Tagombes: "You have given to me the value [. . .] (15) six and three-quarters [. . .] their half being three and three-eighths [. . .] making six and three-quarters [. . .] still, (16) on credit.[28] I have received them from you. My heart is satisfied [with them, there being no] remainder at all. I will (17) pay to you the seed grain that is specified above in full, all the seed grain being pure, unadulterated, (measured) by the *oipe*-measure (of) the dromos (of) Perhenanup (18) that is sound, together with its striker that is sound, measured, transported, and delivered to you, (or?) to your (19) house that is in Perhenanup, by year 9, first or second month of summer, making [two] months (delivery window) [(of) the year] (mentioned) above, without receiving (20) any credit (or) anything (else) further. (As for) the seed-grain thereof that I shall not [deliver] to you (by) the above-specified delivery (date) (mentioned) above, (21) I will deliver it to you increased by 50 percent in the following month, compulsorily (and) without delay, or on one day (22) within two days (of) any day that you discuss with me after its term of delivery (mentioned) above. (23) I will not be able to fix another date regarding them. I will not be able to say: 'I have given to you (24) seed grain concerning it,' without a receipt. All that is mine and all that I will acquire is the security (of) the right (25) (of) the instrument above. I will not be able to say: 'I have performed for you in accordance with everything above-mentioned,' while you have the instrument. Your agent (26) is the one who is to be believed regarding everything that he will say to me (in) the name of everything above-mentioned; and I will perform them (at) his request, compulsorily, (27) without delay." The servant of the falcon, resident of [. . .] the town

[25] A title of a priestess, lit. "Bearer of the Crown."

[26] The Egyptian name for Alexandria.

[27] See Martin (2009b: 163 n. xi) on the term.

[28] The phrase has been variously translated. See the discussion in *P.Recueil* II, p. 43); Pierce (1983: 198).

of the district above-mentioned, (28) Harm[akhis], the son of Onnophris, whose mother is Tsherenhap, has (also) said: "Do everything that is (written) above. My heart (29) is satisfied. You have a claim against me to perform for you according to everything that is (written) above (and) in accordance with what is written above, compulsorily, without delay." (30) They have said: "You have a claim against whichever of the two of us you want to perform the right (31) (of) the instrument [above. If you] want to make a claim against both of us, (then) you will." Written by Petosiris son of Necthous.

Greek registration docket: In Year 9, [on the 13th of] T[ybi, registered in the An(oubieion)] by [Hera]klei[des]

List of twelve witnesses on the verso

The various uses of the cession instrument

The following three examples of cessions not only demonstrate the polyvalent use of this type of document but also the diversity of their external appearance. **6.2.3** and **6.2.4** are impressive papyrus sheets with widths of 162 and 80 cm respectively, with witness-copies and a list of sixteen witnesses for the former and autograph subscriptions for the latter.

The examples furthermore illustrate the "rise and fall" of the cession. A cession clause is first found in documents in the course of the sixth century BC and later developed into a document of its own.[29] In the Ptolemaic period, cessions were common accompaniments to sales of houses and other real property (**6.1.1**), to such an extent that in notary contracts of the Roman period the cession was degraded to a formal, legally almost meaningless, element (**6.2.5**).

6.2.3 An early Demotic quitclaim

P.Tsenhor 15 (= Louvre AF 9761; Pestman 1994c: 85–87 no. 15) (Thebes, 494 BC). Image at *P.Tsenhor*, Plate XXX.

This document belongs to the archive of Tsenhor, a woman living in late sixth- to early fifth-century Thebes. In it she declares to a certain Tamenefonuchos that she distances herself from claims conveyed by a document made by him for her husband. It is one of the oldest examples of

[29] Vleeming (1991: 129–31 n. dd).

the clause "I am far from you," which is the crucial element in the type of documents studied in this section.

Year 28, the fourth month of the *akhet* season, of pharaoh Darius. The woman Tsenuris (Tsenhor), daughter of Sminis and Rourou, has said to Tamenefonuchos (Djedimenioufanch) son of Pefsachonsis (Payeftjaouaouychonsou): "You have caused my heart to agree with the rights conveyed by this document that you made for Psenesis son of Herirem, my husband, in year 19, the first month of *shemu*. I am far from you. The one who will come against you concerning it, in my name or in that of any man at all, I will cause that he is far from you. <If not,> I will give you 5 *kite* silver of the treasury of Ptah without any trial at all."[30]

Written by Haryothes son of Sarpokratis.

Witnesses: Amenothes son of Sminis
Nesherbes son of Haryothes

6.2.4 A Demotic quitclaim after judgment

P.Teos and Thabis 12 (Thebes, 30 July 306 BC). Image at *P.Teos and Thabis*, Plate 28.

This text also belongs to an archive, in this case that of the *choachytês* Teos and his wife Thabis. Its position in that collection of documents from the late fourth century BC is somewhat uncertain, since the woman Taous presenting this declaration to the owner of the archive is otherwise unknown. She states she no longer has any claims on certain objects for which she has taken Teos to court. The contents of this document are parallel to the preceding one, but it is no longer introduced by "you have caused my heart to agree . . .," the characteristic first clause of the type of document called "sale" in this period.

Taous daughter of Horos is the one who says to Teos son of Ioufaw: "I am far from you concerning the right to the things for which I have come against you, saying: 'You were for me representative of them in the house of [. . .].' You have done for me as agreed. The one who will come

[30] With this clause the declarant promises to fulfill the penalty clause without resorting to any kind of litigation at all.

against you concerning them in my name, I will cause that he is far from you."

Written by Inaros son of Amasis in year 11, the first month of *shemu*, day 25.

Four witnesses sign below.

6.2.5 An unregistered Demotic quitclaim

P.Brit.Mus. 262 (= Schentuleit 2001) (Soknopaiou Nesos [Fayyum], 21 November AD 11). Images at *Enchoria* 27 (2001), Plates 5–9.

P.Brit.Mus. 262 is now preserved in the British Library.[31] The papyrus, of which a Greek translation was made, which in turn was copied several times, is part of an archive compiled by Satabous for the lawsuit filed against him by a certain Nestnephis. The subject of the dispute was the house that was the subject of this cession, as well as some land in its immediate vicinity. The plaintiff claimed that the vendor Chairemon did not have any documents proving his own ownership and therefore had no right to sell the property. As a consequence Satabous' claims were non-existent, notwithstanding this cession and the related sale.

One of the problems Satabous faced was that apparently the notaries who had drafted the present agreement had neglected to send a copy to the central archives in Alexandria. This new rule introduced under the Romans thus technically rendered the contract invalid, despite the registration in the local notary's office. It is therefore not surprising that eventually Satabous was required to pay a fine of 500 drachmas.

Year 41 of the coming to power of Caesar the god, the son of the god, the third month of *akhet*, day 24. The servant of Neith, the hereditary prince and count, prophet son of a prophet, Chairemon son of Herodes and Tasis has said to the lord of purity, the supervisor of the lake "The Great Green one" of Nephersatis,[32] Satabous son of Herieus the younger and Satabous: "I am far from you concerning your house, which is built and roofed, which is equipped with beams and doors up to the top, and its bench, which is to the north, and its light-well and its

[31] For a study of the archive, see Hoogendijk (1994). For the first half of this text (the sale document) and the Greek subscriptions, see **3.2.1**.

[32] "The Great Green one of Nephersatis" is Lake Moeris in the Fayyum. See www.trismegistos.org/geo/detail.php?tm=1384.

> building plots, which are to the south, and everything that belongs to them, which is in the village of Sobek 'The Island of Soknopaios, the great god,' in the district of Herakleides in the nome of Arsinoe, and every measure that belongs to them. Their neighbors are: south, the enclosure wall of the village; north, the house of Horos son of Horos; west and east, the streets of Pharaoh. I do not have any claim at all on you concerning them from today onwards. The one who will come against you concerning them, I will cause that he is far from you, compulsorily and without delay, and I will cause that they are free for you from any document, any deed, or anything at all, from today onwards, you having a claim on me regarding the right of the document for money that I have made for you concerning them, to perform for you its right. And I will perform their right according to everything mentioned above," while the woman and priestess of Sobek Temsais daughter of Chairemon and Tamestasythmis, his wife, says: "Write and act according to everything that is written above. My heart is pleased with it."

Below the text are a Greek registration, an elaborate Greek autograph subscription of the vendor, and a shorter Demotic autograph subscription by the purchaser; no witnesses on recto or verso; there is no mention of any notary.

6.3 The Greek sale of real property

Éva Jakab

The six documents that follow illustrate the typical features of contracts recording sales of property. Nevertheless, the circumstances under which property was sold could vary greatly. In *P.Oxy* XIV 1634, for example, two Romans who had borrowed two talents and 3,600 drachmas from their wealthy neighbor were only able to defray their debt by selling their stone house and court, with a cellar underneath and appurtenances, probably under very unfavorable terms. This was obviously a sale forced upon the debtors by financial exigency. As seen below, however, other documents will suggest different circumstances in their backgrounds.

6.3.1 Sale of shares of a house

P.Oxy. I 99 (Oxyrhynchos, 4 September AD 55)

A sale document was usually issued in several copies. Each party received one, and a third copy was submitted for registration (*katagraphê*, below,

6.5). **6.3.1** is probably the copy kept by the purchaser. The contract opens with a detailed dating formula, set up by the *agoranomoi* (the public notaries), and an account of the place in which the document was composed. The clause also reports the names of the *agoranomoi.*

The document itself is a notarial deed drawn up by the *agoranomoi* and formulated in objective style: that is, the *agoranomoi* report in third person the already completed act of sale: "A has bought from B": "Tryphon has bought (*epriato*) from Pnepheros." Every document reports the parties to the transaction. Since the *agoranomoi* did not know the parties (although the parties to this sale, as relatives, must have been well known to each other), they identify them in close detail, reporting their ages, statures, complexions, face shapes, and scars. The document serves primarily the interests of the purchaser, as he needed it to establish his claim to ownership. Consequently, his name is given first. The object of the sale is recorded next. The document reports its location, including the boundaries and neighbors. In **6.3.1** it is the half share of a three-storied house close to the Serapeum (Temple of Serapis) in the city of Oxyrhynchos. The name of the street is given as well: "Temgenouthis." Since in antiquity doors or windows (and fixtures) could be owned separately, independently of the house, the document has to report the sale of the accessories and fittings as well.

The vendor is interested in stressing that he is the lawful owner of the object sold. Consequently, the contract reports how he acquired his title. Acquisition by inheritance may have been considered a stronger claim than acquisition by purchase. Inherited property has usually been in family possession for several years, maybe for generations; therefore it is not likely that an eviction would follow. In the present document the vendor inherited the property from his mother.

An agreement on the price is indispensable for the validity of the contract. Such a component is found, therefore, in virtually every document of sale. In **6.3.1** it is for thirty-two talents. We do not know if the consideration for the sale was paid through a bank or directly in cash between the parties. In the present case, a bank, that of Sarapion and associates, was in charge of collecting the conveyance tax (*enkyklion*). The receipt for this is copied immediately below the sale contract. It adds little to what is contained in the contract itself, most of it being verbatim repetition, and is not therefore included here. In the last sentence the vendor undertakes a guarantee for the sold half share of the house. This clause will be discussed below, **6.3.2**.

The translation follows that of the original edition.

Copy. The second year of Nero Claudius Caesar Germanicus Imperator, on the 6th of the month Sebastos, at Oxyrhynchos in the Thebaid, before the *agoranomoi* Andromachos and Diogenes. Tryphon son of Dionysios, about [. . .] years old, of middle height, fair, with a long face and a slight squint, and having a scar on his right wrist, has bought from his mother Thamounis' cousin, Pnepheros son of Papontos, also an inhabitant of Oxyrhynchos, about 65 years old, of middle height, fair, having a long face and a scar above his [. . .] eyebrow and another on his right knee – the document being drawn up in the street – one half of a three-storied house inherited from his mother, together with all its entrances and exits and appurtenances, situated by the Serapeum at Oxyrhynchos in the southern part of the street called Temgenouthis to the west of the lane leading to Shepherds' Street, its boundaries being on the south and east, public roads; on the north, the house of the aforesaid Thamounis, mother of Tryphon the buyer; on the west, the house of Tausiris, sister of Pnepheros the seller, separated by a blind alley, for the sum of 32 talents of bronze; and Pnepheros undertakes to guarantee the half share that is sold, perpetually, in every respect, with every guarantee.

6.3.2 Sale of a house

P.Oxy. IV 719, lines 13–29 (Oxyrhynchos, 14 June AD 193). Image at Papyri.info.

6.3.2 like **6.3.1** records a sale of house property. Papontos sells to Didymus half a share of two houses in the village of Ision Tryphonis in the Oxyrhynchite nome. The document is structured as a *cheirographon*, a legal document in the form of a letter, written by one of the parties in his own hand. As in many *cheirographa* (see Chapter 2 introduction and **2.1.4–8**), our document contains a "subjective" declaration by the vendor regarding the act of sale ("I acknowledge that I sold and ceded [the object of sale]"). If there was more than one vendor, the declaration was in the plural (e.g., *P.Oxy.* X 1276).

When put beside **6.3.1**, **6.3.2** shows some outstanding differences. In the former the *agoranomoi*, who most likely did not know the parties concerned, used a detailed formula for their physical identification (see **6.3.1** introduction). In the present deed the vendor wrote the document in his own hand; of course, he knew the buyers personally. Detailed description was therefore superfluous; brief description was enough. By contrast, the description of the object itself is as detailed in the *cheirographon* as it was in the *agoranomoi*'s document: a half share of two houses, one house with two stories and another one with a yard. There is also a detailed description of the location of the houses and of their boundaries and neighboring grounds. The price is two thousand silver drachmas. The vendor acknowledges that he has received it in full in cash, "from hand to hand" (*dia cheiros*), i.e., not through a bank.

Next comes the *bebaiôsis* or warranty clause – one of the important future obligations arising from the sale contract. The act of sale involves considerable risks for the purchaser. If the vendor is not the object of sale's owner, he cannot convey title to the purchaser. Consequently, if the lawful owner sues in court, the purchaser has no remedy. The *bebaiôsis* is meant to provide such a remedy; by it the vendor is required to defend the purchaser against claims by third parties.

Finally the vendor declares that the contract is valid on the condition that it be publicly registered. The text ends with a dating formula: in **6.3.1**, the *agoranomoi* document, the date was placed on the top, whereas in a *cheirographon* it is usually, as in **6.3.2**, placed at the end.

The translation follows that of the original edition.

Papontos son of Bithys and Tsenpachous, of Ision Tryphonis in the Oxyrhynchite nome, to Didymos son of Apollonios and Helene, a settler from Heliopolis, greeting. I acknowledge that I have sold and ceded to you from henceforth forever of my property in the said Ision Tryphonis in the southern part of the village a half share of two houses, one having two stories, the other a yard, owned jointly by me and my brother Paous, whose boundaries are: of the one with yard: on the south, an entrance and exit; on the north, the property of the heirs of Diogas; on the east, that of the heirs of Horos; on the west, a public road; and of the other: on the south, the property of Papontos son of Mouthis; on the north, that of Herakleides son of Horion; on the east, a public road; on the west, the property of Miusis son of Melas, at the price agreed upon between us for the cession, namely 2,000 drachmas of the imperial silver coinage, which sum I have received immediately from hand to hand [. . .]; and I guarantee the houses free from public and private debts and unaffected by persons' property-returns or any other claims, the right resting with you to cede to others and to manage and dispose of them as you choose. This contract, written by me, Papontos, in my own hand without erasure or insertion, is valid as though publicly registered. Year 1 of Gaius Pescennius Niger Justus Augustus, Payni 20 . . .

6.3.3 Sale of shares of a house

P.Mich. x 583 (Bacchias [Fayyum], 26 August AD 78). Image at Papyri.info.

6.3.3 was drawn up in a village *grapheion* (record office). (See, e.g., **2.1.3** with introduction.) The document opens with a clause reporting the date and place of its composition, then the formula "A sold to B." According to the usual style of "professional" documents the contracting parties are described in detail with all their distinguishing marks (see **6.3.1** introduction). The document records the sale by Maron to Hermas of a four-ninths share of a house with courtyard, which is reported to be *koinonikê* (condominium); i.e., it was owned in common and indivisible (*communio pro indiviso*, Taubenschlag 1955: 242). Maron inherited most of his share (one-third of the house) and purchased the rest.

The text describes the object of sale in more detail than the previous documents, including the measures of the house and its physical condition. An account of measures was required if the price was made per unit (e.g., per aroura), and the vendor declared the number of units that had been sold – a declaration that made him liable for this exact declaration of quantity. In **6.3.3**, the statement that "the measures of the entire area [are] whatever they may be" was meant to exclude the liability of the vendor for any subsequently measured increase in the size of the plot.

As for the account of the object's physical condition, the vendor reports that the house was badly preserved, partly in ruins. This declaration too may have been made to rule out any future suit by the purchaser on account of hidden defects of the house. Its insertion in this contract is surprising, since this kind of liability is known primarily in slave sales and mainly in Roman law. It is not credible that the edict of the *aediles curules* (curule aediles) for the slave market in Rome had influenced the present deed. The clause must have developed independently, as everyday scribal practice developed clauses that served the requirements of the individual parties.

An account of the boundaries and neighbors was followed by a confirmation that the vendor received the agreed price: 100 drachmas, in cash. The warranty (*bebaiôsis*) clause is very detailed. Finally, in the penalty clause, the vendor promises to pay all damages, double the price, and an additional 300 drachmas to the purchaser and to the treasury if he should breach the terms of the contract.

As in other notarial documents, the body of the document is followed by a *hypographê*, a handwritten confirmation by the parties of the terms of the contract. The present document contains the vendor's confirmation of the contract's terms; this is quite common. But the present document, in a section not included below, also contains a confirmation by the purchaser. "I, Hermas, have received the sale of the four-ninths of the sold house and courtyard which has partly fallen in ruin, as stated above." This was a receipt made by the purchaser confirming that a copy of the sale contract had been handed over to him.

The translation follows that at Papyri.info.

3rd interca(lary day).

The tenth year of the Emperor Caesar Vespasian Augustus, in the month Kaisareios, on the third intercalary day, at Bacchias in the division of Herakleides of the Arsinoite nome.

Maron, son of Hermas and grandson of Maron, about forty-seven years old, with a scar in the middle of his forehead, acknowledges to Hermas, son of Ptolemaios and grandson of Ammonios, about forty-four years old, with a scar in the middle of his forehead, that he [Maron] has sold to him in accordance with this agreement from the present day for all time the following property that belongs to him, Maron, the party of the first part, in the aforesaid village of Bacchias: a third share inherited from his mother and a purchased ninth share, making four-ninths of a commonly owned house and old courtyard that has partly fallen in ruins, the measurements of the entire area being whatever they may be, with their ancient foundations and their boundaries, and in such condition as they are; of all of which the neighbors are: on the south, lots belonging to Katoites, the son of Menches, and his associates, and for a certain distance a common entrance and exit, on which a door opens; on the north, a royal road; on the west, an old house belonging to the aforesaid Katoites, the son of Menches, and his associates; on the east, a courtyard of Horos, the son of Katoites and grandson of Belles, and his brothers, beyond which there is an old house. And he, the party of the first part, Maron, has received from Hermas the entire price agreed upon, in full, one hundred silver drachmas, forthwith from hand to hand out of the house; and both he, the party of the first part, Maron, and his representatives will guarantee to Hermas and his representatives the property sold in accordance with this sale with full guarantee for all time; and he will deliver the property unencumbered, unpledged, not offered as collateral, not alienated, and free from all debts, both public and private, and will see that it has been neither previously mortgaged nor previously sold to other persons, nor any part of it either, in any way whatsoever, and will see that no one hinders the purchaser, Hermas, or his heirs from exercising ownership and control over the purchases, as stated above, entering and departing, demolishing and constructing on the property however they choose, and furthermore, selling the property, mortgaging it to others, transferring it and using it in whatever way they choose, free from interference; and as regards the terms which have been set forth, let no one accuse or dispute with or proceed against the purchaser, Hermas, or his representatives in any way upon any pretext. And if the party of the first part, Maron, or his representatives violate any of the aforesaid terms or do not guarantee or deliver the property in accordance with the terms as they have been written, then, apart from the fact that any contrary action will be invalid and inadmissible in every way, let him further pay to Hermas forthwith the damages and double the price and a fine of an additional three hundred silver drachmas and the same amount to the treasury, and none the less the sale be valid. Both parties concerned ...

There follow Maron's acknowledgement (in a second hand), repeating the contract's terms verbatim; Hermas' acknowledgement (in a third hand; see introduction to **6.3.3**); and a restatement of the date, together with notation of registration in the record office of Bacchias and Hephaistias (again in the first hand).

6.3.4 Sale of a house at auction

SB v 7638 (= *P.Ryl.* IV 555) (Philadelphia [Fayyum], 6 or 9 February 257 BC)

Agricultural land and houses were the most expensive objects of sales. The vendor would aim at getting the best price for his land. If the property was to be sold outside the vendor's family, he would frequently prefer to seek a purchaser by auction. A public auction would serve to publicize the transaction and would also allow the vendor, in theory, to maximize the price. In Egypt, the sale by auction also involved the payment of earnest money, whether money itself or a valuable thing, an *arrabôn* (Pringsheim 1950), to signify the buyer's serious intentions to conclude the sale.[33] If unknown persons participated in bidding, a down payment was required

[33] The entire process of a public auction is detailed in *P.Eleph.* 14 (= *Sel.Pap.* II 233 = Bagnall and Derow 2004, no. 87, third century BC). On auctions in Demotic texts see Manning (1999).

as well: it created a liability on the part of the purchaser and supplied evidence of the parties' consent.

6.3.4, written in Greek, illustrates the importance of earnest money for the sale by auction. A house, probably in Canopus, is sold by auction. There are two bids, one by "the people of Antilochos" and another by Amyntas, the author of the letter. Amyntas claims that "we" have already paid earnest money, and (thus?) kept "the people of Antiochos" out of the way. Amyntas even claims that the house is already "ours," as they bought it for the enormous sum of two talents, 500 drachmas.

The entire amount was not paid at the time of sale, nor was its payment required. It was sufficient for the buyer to have conveyed earnest-money to the seller. Amyntas does not state the size of the *arrabôn*. Its size was apparently not relevant; its mere existence secured the future completion of the act. The phrase "the house is ours" does not mean that ownership passed to Amyntas with his payment of earnest-money, but that it is "as good as ours" (Pringsheim 1949): the house had been knocked down to Amyntas and he has given earnest money, an *arrabôn*, as evidence.

The *arrabôn* had an additional function. As stated in the introduction, the act of sale per se did not create future obligations. The parties used the *arrabôn* to create these obligations. A purchaser who paid an *arrabôn* assumed on that occasion some obligations. If he did not keep them, he was to lose the *arrabôn*. A vendor who received the *arrabôn* assumed some obligations as well. If he did not keep them he was obligated to return double the amount of the *arrabôn* received. The vendor's liability for the payment of the *duplum* seems to be a special feature of sales of immovables, derived from legal practice, in commonly used formulas (*lex contractus*). The vendor promises the repayment of the double *arrabôn* only in the case that he refuses to accept the full payment and to carry out the *katagraphê* (registration of transfer of ownership). See **6.5**.

The translation closely follows that of the Rylands editors; see also Papyri.info.

> [. . .] The gifts, which the letter carrier brought, consisting of [. . .] wheat and the new flax, we presented to the king. And you must know that the house of the gouty Nicanor at Canopus is ours for 2 talents, 500 drachmas. So if the people of Antiochos [. . .] importune you, take note that originally we came forward first and have paid earnest-money (*arrabôn*) and repulsed [. . .]; and of these same facts we notified him when he was here himself and his secretary Sosibios approached us on his behalf.
>
> Farewell. (Year) 27, Choiak 13.

6.3.5 Sale of agricultural land

P.Ryl. II 164, lines 1–15 (Hermopolis, 3 November AD 171)

Like **6.3.4**, **6.3.5** involves a down payment. The vendor, a woman whose name is lost, sells eleven arouras of katoikic land to Hermaios. We are not informed how the vendor got the land. In most cases landed property did not form part of a dowry (Rowlandson 1981): The regular dowry was administered in a wife's behalf. Therefore, to grant a wife the freedom to dispose of land, land was not included in her dowry, but given as a special gift if not acquired by her through inheritance. Acquisition by inheritance is likely in the present case. Yet even so the husband is not entirely excluded from his wife's affairs. Following a very common practice, he acts as his wife's guardian (Yiftach-Firanko 2003).

By the time the contract was drawn up the vendor had not received the entire price, only a first installment of 3,000 drachmas – itself a significant amount in terms of the second century AD. The partial payment of the price recalls, at first glance, the *arrabôn* of **6.3.4**. Yet a closer look reveals substantial differences: the 3,000 drachmas was not earnest money. Its existence is not meant to induce the parties to complete the act of sale at a later date as in **6.3.4**. The remaining sum (we do not know exactly how much) will be paid within a short period with the registration (*katagraphê*) of the act. Until the consideration is paid in full, the vendor remains the owner of the object, yet her consent to the sale, as well as her receipt of the first installment, obligates her to carry out the *katagraphê* once she receives the entire price (see below, **6.5**).

The deed reports that katoikic land for agricultural use, properly measured, was sold. The vendor reports the location of the land and its distinctive features: watering places, a quay of baked brick (building material), and a tenant currently occupying some of its parts. The land was subject to taxes and imposts and the contract sets out exactly when the buyer will become responsible for their payment. The body of the contract ends with the *bebaiôsis* clause: the vendor's obligation to warrant the purchaser against eviction.

> [. . .]arion daughter of Hexakon, granddaughter of Cornelius, Hermopolite woman, registered in the Western Fort district, with my husband Metokos son of Achilleus as guardian, to Hermaios son of Diogenes from the same city, greetings. I acknowledge that I have sold to you from the present day for ever the eleven arouras of katoikic

land not subject to encumbrance belonging to me in the [. . .] around Tertesmonis from the holding of Asklepiodoros, together with their yearly rentals, and will transfer these severally in good condition for sowing, in full, measured by the just measure used in the settlement, free from the cultivation of royal land and every impost whatever, contained in four and a half common and undivided plots in which are watering-places and a quay of baked brick, also common, at the price mutually agreed upon of [. . .] drachmas. From this sum I have here received from you from hand to hand three thousand drachmas, total 3,000 silver dr. The remaining [. . .] drachmas you will pay me by the 30th of the present month Hathyr of the current 12th year of Aurelius Antoninus the lord, and I will make the conveyance whensoever you please by an official deed through the record offices in Hermopolis, so that you may receive an assignment [of the properties] free from all (adverse?) possession, from the public dues on the holding and all additional levies from former times up to the past 11th year of [Marcus Aurelius Ant]oninus the lord for which I, the vendor, am responsible, while you are responsible for those from the present 12th year inclusive; and I will henceforth guarantee the said land with every guarantee . . .

6.3.6 Sale of a vineyard

P.Mich. v 274 (Tebtunis [originally Ibion Eikosipentarouron], AD 46–47)

6.3.6 is a Greek subscription to a contract recording the sale of a vineyard. There is just one purchaser, Horion son of Didymos, but at least two vendors, Heron son of Akousilaos and his sister Phariene. Horion's mother and wife appear among the declaring parties as well; they probably had to give their consent to the alienation of family property, as was commonly the case among native Egyptians. The editor remarks that the document is written by a "childish and ill-formed hand" and shows more errors in grammar and spelling than usual. It is likely that Heron wrote it himself.

The object of sale is a vineyard of one half an aroura with all its appurtenances. The vineyard's vines are said to be trained on trees, a common viticultural practice in antiquity. The vineyard is also reported to be equipped with farm buildings, with an irrigation canal, fishing and a dike, half of which devolves upon the purchaser with the act of sale. Most of the neighboring plots are vineyards as well. The vineyard was obviously located in a highly developed agricultural landscape.

The vendors acknowledge that they have received the consideration in full, paid at once, in cash. The price is not reported, probably because **6.3.6** is just a subscription to a more detailed sale contract that gave the exact sum. The vendors also pledge to warrant the purchaser against legal defects. Heron chose here a simple variation of the clause that points to public and private debts and claims. At the end of the contract Heron states that he wrote on behalf of his illiterate wife, a common clause. Such a clause was necessary, perhaps, because the wife also took on certain obligations in the contract and the statement was essential to make them enforceable.

> I, Heron son of Akousilaos, and my wife Thaesis daughter of Herakles, and my sister Phariene, and our mother Thermoutharion daughter of Pharos, with the guardians of each of the women, of Thaesis, me, her husband, and Phariene and Thermoutharion [. . .] acknowledge that we, Heron and my sister Phariene, have sold to Horion son of Didymos the vineyard that belongs to us, inherited from our father, in which the vines are trained on trees, consisting of one-half of an aroura in the class paying the tax of one-sixth, and all the appurtenances, among which there are a half share of the stone well and the windlass, and a share of the storeroom and of the irrigation canal and the fishing and the dike, and a half share of the supply of Greek reeds at the storehouse, all near Ibion Eikosipentarouron of the same division. The neighbors are: on the south and east, the holdings of the Maecenatian estate of Tiberius Claudius Caesar Augustus Germanicus Imperator; on the north, the vineyard of Didymion; and on the west, the vineyard of Kronion. And we have received from Horion the entire price agreed upon, in full, at once, from hand to hand out of the house, and we guarantee the sale on mutual security with every guarantee both from public debts of past time up to the seventh year and the seventh year also of Tiberius Claudius Caesar Augustus Germanicus Imperator and from private encumbrances and every claim forever as aforesaid. I, Heron, wrote also for my wife since she is illiterate.

6.4 Sales of movables

Roger Bagnall

The sales of movables presented here all come from the Roman period and are all composed according to the typical subjective homology formula (Chapter 2 introduction) of the period, with the exception of the terse **6.4.1**, which says: "I have sold" rather than "I acknowledge that I have sold." The length and complexity of the documents do not appear to be correlated to the date of composition, as early Roman animal sales like **6.4.4** and **6.4.5** are very fully developed. Rupprecht (1994: 115) has remarked that in general the care and detail shown in sale contracts are greater with objects of high value, but this is not always the case, as a comparison of the brief **6.4.1** (200 drachmas) and the much more extensive **6.4.4** (160 drachmas) indicates. It is striking that of the documents presented here, only **6.4.5**, the camel sale, gives any indication of the intervention of any institution in the composition and execution of the agreement. In that case, the third hand records payment of the purchase price through a bank deposit. For the rest, there is no indication of who composed the document. That is, they are *cheirographa* rather than deeds drawn up in the *agoranomeion* or any other official agency. This distinction is in general characteristic of sales of movables as compared to sales of land.

The bulk of these sales are of animals, principally donkeys, horses, and cows. Only a handful of sales of other movable objects survive, and there is no reason to believe that the surviving texts are not representative of the ancient situation in this respect. In all cases the price seems to have been paid in cash and the delivery of the object performed at the same time, and no sales effective on the realization of conditions are preserved. As Rupprecht has noted, the cash sales in the papyri create no obligations for either party except for the seller to defend the right to the object (with a partial exception of a warranty of slaves to be free from leprosy and epilepsy). None of the sales presented here creates any other obligation for the seller.

The reason for the existence of such documents in the case of animals is presumably much the same as in the case of slaves, although the public recording process of *katagraphê* (further below, **6.5**) known for slaves (as for land) is not attested for animals. The animals are identifiable individuals with distinguishing colors and marks rather than fungible quantities, and it is not difficult to imagine the case in which someone sold a donkey to which he had no right – although, considering that even children might be the object of disputes about identity, it might not be easy for a claimant to establish the identity of a particular gray donkey. But possessing the sale contract would have obvious value for the buyer if such a dispute did arise. Donkeys are in fact the animal most commonly sold.[34]

[34] See generally for these transactions Litinas (1999) with the earlier bibliography; an updated list can be found at www.philology.uoc.gr/ref/Sales_of_donkeys/2008-04-20_text.doc (accessed August 4, 2013).

With the last three of these sales, however, the question of the reason for the existence of the contracts is less easily disposed of. We may indeed wonder on the one hand how likely it was that a third party would lay claim to a loom, or on the other hand why such sales do not survive for other classes of capital equipment – granite millstones, for example, or olive presses. Such things could certainly be the object of contracts, for example in the division of estates, but we do not find sales concerning them. This is perhaps just an accident of preservation. The value of the loom sold in **6.4.6** is substantial, even if lack of prices from this period makes it hard to contextualize it exactly. It may have been worth something like sixty artabas of wheat. The triclinium sold in **6.4.7** is worth 500 drachmas, around twenty artabas at the time.

Most surprising of all is **6.4.8**, the sale of wood. The text is not fully preserved – the loss of any price originally given is particularly regrettable – but even as it stands it gives less information than we might imagine. The number of trunks or logs of each type of wood is not given except for willow and olive, and for none of them is the length or weight specified. Tree trunks were undoubtedly not quite a fungible good, but wood is so readily cut up that within a day or two after the sale it could become difficult to identify the item sold and thus ensure its conformity to the description in the document. It is possible that the lost second part of the document contained information that would allow us to divine the purpose of creating such a text. At all events, it is hard to avoid the conclusion that the creation of a sale contract of this sort, and perhaps for all movables, was legally optional, representing a form of protection for the buyer but not necessary for the actual transfer of possession and use.

The general problem of the reason for the existence of these sales can also be refocused by the virtual absence of such texts from the Ptolemaic period. Joseph Manning has called attention to the scarcity of donkey sales from the Hellenistic period (Manning 2002/03). He cites the Tebtunis papyrus published by Duttenhöfer (1996) as the sole Greek example currently known (a couple of other fragmentary animal sales are known; cf. Duttenhöfer 1996: 297 n. 2), and he publishes the first Demotic example. The Greek papyrus is a third-person (objective) homology in the form of a double document with six witnesses dated to 145 BC. The Demotic sale is probably from the Fayyum and is assigned by Manning to the late third century BC. It comes from a significantly different legal tradition than do the Greek sales, representing a bilateral agreement in which the price has not yet been paid. As Manning points out, animal sales are known from pre-Hellenistic times, and it is their scarcity in the

Ptolemaic period that is surprising. He cautions against too simplistic an explanation for the pattern of the documentation.

There is no indication that the Greek sales of movables served as transferable title deeds to the animals or other objects sold – that is, that they might have been passed with the object to a subsequent owner. In the case of animals this may be a moot point, but with a loom or similar object it might not be. It seems more likely, however, that a subsequent sale would have been the subject of its own sale document.

6.4.1 Sale of cows

P.Sarap. 10 (Hermopolis, 14 October AD 124). Image at Papyri.info.

This short document of sale contains only the barest essentials: the identities of the parties, the number and a very brief description of the animals, the price, an "as is" and irrevocability clause, without guarantee, and the date. The origins of the parties and place of the transaction are not stated, but the purchaser is from Hermopolis and the transaction probably took place there. The first cow is described as *thêlazousan*, which can refer either to the cow nursing or to the calf being nursed. The document lacks the recapitulation and signature (the *hypographê*, or subscription) at the end. That could in principle indicate that we have the seller's copy, where the need for the signature would be absent (the seller would not need to enforce the contract), but as it was part of the papers of the purchaser, this is unlikely to be the explanation in this case. Indeed, it also lacks the *kyria* clause indicating enforceability.

> Didymos son of Demetrios to Anoubion son of Sarapion, greetings.
> I have sold to you two cows, one colorless, a suckling female heifer, the other reddish-colored, and I have received from you the agreed-upon price from hand to hand, two hundred drachmas of money, total, 200 dr. of money, these cows being as is and unrejectable. Year nine of the Emperor Caesar Traianus Hadrianus Augustus, Phaophi 17.

6.4.2 Sale of a cow

P.Sarap. 11 (cf. *BL* XI 241) (Hermopolis, 1 March AD 128)

This short document of sale, from the same archive as **6.4.1**, gives the origins of the parties but is notably brief in describing the cow, of which only the gender and color are given. Unlike **6.4.1**, it does include a complete guarantee, expressed in the briefest of terms. Like it, however, it lacks an enforceability clause, a recapitulation, and a signature at the end.

> Harpaesis son of (*name lost*), from Hermopolis, registered in the district of West Fort, to Anoubion son of Sarapion, Hermopolite, greetings. I acknowledge that I have sold to you the one reddish cow belonging to me and I have received herewith from you the agreed-upon price of sixty-two drachmas of money, total, 62 dr. of money, and I shall guarantee (it) with every guarantee. Year 12 of the Emperor Caesar Traianus Hadrianus Augustus, Phamenoth 5.

6.4.3 Sale of a horse

P.Sakaon 62 (Theadelphia, 22 January AD 328). Image at Papyri.info.

The first party to this contract has a military title, the second is apparently a villager from Dionysias.[35] The contract contains a seller's guarantee but also an "as is" clause stating that the horse cannot be rejected by the buyer subsequently. Enforceability clauses and the stipulation are also present.

> Flavius Sabinus, soldier seconded in the camp of Narmouthis, belonging to the ex-*protectores* under the command of the *praepositus* Salvitius, acknowledges. I acknowledge that I have sold to Aurelius Capito son of NN, from the village of Dionysias, the russet mare belonging to me, who has shed her first teeth, for the price agreed-upon between us of one hundred thirty talents of money, in full, of the coinage of the Emperors, from hand to hand, and I guarantee with every guarantee. And the purchaser has received herewith this mare as is and not subject to rejection. The sale is enforceable, and having been asked the formal question, I agreed. After the consulate of Constantius and Maximus the most illustrious, Tybi 26.

[35] According to the edition he was *primipilarius* of Dionysias. This title, although to my knowledge never questioned, is implausible. *Primipilarius* was an official position in the imperial administration and not attached to a village. On the printed plate and the online image (http://ipap.csad.ox.ac.uk/Sakaon-bw/300dpi/P.Sakaon62.jpg; accessed August 4, 2013) the editor's reading seems to me inadequately supported by the traces. It seems more likely that instead of the title there was a patronymic, followed by *apo*, "from". I thank Rodney Ast for his discussion of this text.

(*2nd hand*) I, Flavius Sabinus, soldier, have sold my mare and I have received the price in full as aforesaid. I, Flavius Aunes, soldier of the same camp, wrote for him because he is illiterate.

6.4.4 Sale of a donkey

O.Ber. II 125 (Berenike, Red Sea, 26 July AD 61)

The papyrus records the sale of a male donkey by one Horos son of Komaros, to Nektharaus son of Haryothes, for 160 drachmas (i.e., 40 tetradrachms). The bulk of the contract is written in the practiced hand of a professional scribe; the seller, in a less developed hand, acknowledges receipt of the sum in cash. There is a final restatement of the date in a very fast hand.

The contract is a unique example of a donkey sale from the Eastern Desert. The majority of surviving donkey sales come from the Fayyum, where there existed several animal markets, such as those at Kerkesoucha and Alexandrou Nesos, dominated by local sellers and breeders. Smaller regional markets also existed, at which animals changed hands between private individuals, but they are the exception in the surviving evidence (Jördens 1995: 60–61). A large regional animal market in Berenike is unlikely, given the lack of agricultural activity in the area and the settlement's position as an endpoint, as opposed to a crossroads, for land travel. The animal was most likely used for local hauling and breeding; donkeys were not the principal means of transport over the long haul between Berenike and Koptos, where camels predominated (Bagnall 1985; Jördens 1995: 95; Oates 1988).

Animal sales typically do not include the so-called "non-aggression" clause (Litinas 1999: 198); but here the language is expansive and complex, more typical of a loan or lease than an animal sale, and includes this clause. The clause protects both the seller and his assigns and the buyer and his assigns. When such a clause is included it is often compressed, as in *P.Oxy.* XLIII 3143 (AD 305). By contrast, the normally present guarantee clause is absent, perhaps because it was seen as redundant.

The sale includes, unusually, the pack-saddle. The donkey's color is, as usual, given, but (more uncommonly) not an age. The animal is sold "as is."

[In Berenike] on the Red Sea, year 7, sacred, of Nero Claudius Caesar Augustus Germanicus Imperator, Mesore 2. Horos son of Komaros, grandson of Germullos, to Nektharaus son of Haryothes, greetings.

I acknowledge that I have sold to you a white male donkey belonging to me, with a pack-saddle, just as it is, not subject to rejection, and that I have herewith received from you from hand to hand out of your house the price of one hundred sixty drachmas in Ptolemaic and Imperial silver, total 160 dr.

If anyone should summon or proceed against you or your assigns on my behalf or against me or my assigns in any manner concerning the above-mentioned donkey or its price or any part thereof, I myself shall necessarily defeat the plaintiff at my own expense or I shall immediately and without delay pay in full the price that I have received from you and an equal sum to the Treasury, and whatever may have been exacted from you on this account or expenses you may incur.

This agreement shall be enforceable and legal concerning the sale wherever it is produced as if it were registered in the public record office.

(*2nd hand*) I, Horos son of Komaros, grandson of Germalos, have sold and have received the price of one hundred sixty drachmas, 160 dr., price of the male donkey belonging to me, as aforesaid.

Year 7 of Nero Claudius Caesar Augustus Germanicus [. . .]

(*3rd hand*) Year 7, sacred, of Nero Claudius Caesar Augustus Germanicus Imperator, Mesore 2.

6.4.5 Sale of a camel

P.Oxy. LVIII 3915 (Oxyrhynchos, 7–8 September AD 30). Image at Papyri.info.

The purchaser here is a freedman of an imperial freedman. The camel is almost fully described and comes with a saddle. The animal comes "as is" but the sale is guaranteed. A penalty to the Treasury as well as the buyer is provided in case of the failure of the seller to deliver on the guarantee.

[Anteis (?),] son of Titan, from Oxyrhynchos, to [Iulius] Florus Bola, freedman of Bola, freedman of the Deified Augustus, greetings. I acknowledge that I have sold to you the reddish camel belonging to me, which has shed its first teeth and has two brands, one on the right thigh and the other on the right side of the neck, along with its saddle, such as it is, and that I have received from you as a principal sum the four hundred forty drachmas of money in Imperial and Ptolemaic coinage agreed upon between us as its price, in full, through the bank of Sarapion son of Zoilos in the Serapeum in Oxyrhynchos, and I shall guarantee the sale for you with every guarantee or I shall repay the price that I received from you increased by a half and your damages and as penalty an additional [–] hundred drachmas, with an equal amount to the Treasury, with no prejudice at all to you, Florus, in collecting what I owe you in accordance with (other) deeds of security. The contract is enforceable. Year 17 of Tiberius Caesar Augustus, month of Sebastos, 10.

(*2nd hand*) I, Anteis son of Titan, have sold the camel and the saddle and I receive the price, the four hundred forty drachmas of money in full, and I shall guarantee with every guarantee, without prejudice to Florus in what I owe him according to securities, as aforesaid. I, Philonides son of Theon, wrote for him because he does not know letters. Year 17 of Tiberius Caesar Augustus, month of Sebastos, 10.

(*3rd hand*) Year 17 of Tiberius Caesar Augustus, month of Augustus, 11, the deposit took place through the (bank) of Sarapion son of Zoilos.

Back: Sale of a camel . . .

6.4.6 Sale of a loom

P.Oxy. XIV 1705 (Oxyrhynchos, 6 July AD 298). Image: Figure 11.

The high standing of the parties in this contract is remarkable: a soldier acting through a member of the local elite (a victor in the games) on the one hand, a woman of equestrian rank on the other. The loom, about 3 × 5 meters in size, had been acquired by the soldier earlier in the same regnal year and was in storage rather than in use.

Valerius Petermouthis, soldier, through me, Aurelius Sarapion son of Sarapion, from the brilliant and most brilliant city of the Oxyrhynchites, former ephebe and victor in sacred games, to Aurelia Eudaimonis alias Apollonia, *matrona stolata*, greetings. I acknowledge that I have sold to you herewith the loom for Tarsian cloth which I purchased from Aurelius Sarapammon son of Thonis, from Oxyrhynchos, in the present year in the month of Mecheir 8, with a length of ten cubits and width of six cubits, and all the equipment of whatever amount where it is stored, for the price agreed upon between us of two talents and one thousand drachmas of money in coinage of the Emperors, which I have herewith received from you in full from hand to hand, and on being asked the formal question by you concerning this payment I have assented; you will transport this loom and its equipment from here where it is stored and transport it wherever you wish without hindrance, and you are to possess and own, along with your descendants and successors,

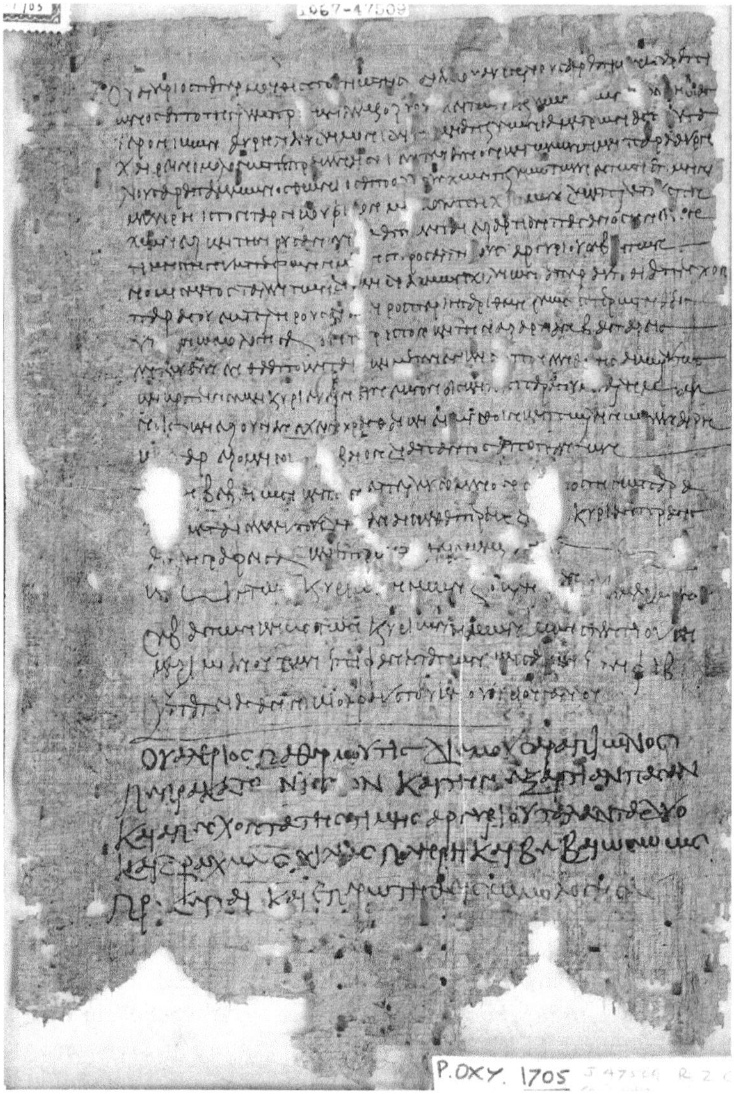

Fig. 11. Sale of a loom. *P.Oxy.* XIV 1705. Oxyrhynchos, July AD 298

and have the power to use and lease out and sell however you wish, and I shall provide it to you secure (*bebaion*) with every guarantee for all time from all risks, and I shall repel anyone who proceeds against you immediately at my own expense, as from a court proceeding. The sale is enforceable written in a single copy, and having been asked the formal question I assented. Year 14 and 13 of our lords Diocletian and Maximian Augusti and year 6 of our lords Constantius and Maximianus the most noble Caesars, Epeiph 12, in the consulate of Anicius Faustus and Virius Gallus.

(*2nd hand*) I, Valerius Pathermoutis,[36] through me, Sarapion, have sold the loom and all its equipment, and I have received the two talents and one thousand drachmas of money for its price in full, and I shall guarantee as aforesaid, and having been asked the formal question I assented.

6.4.7 Sale of a dining couch

P.Oxy. X 1277 (Oxyrhynchos, 9 August AD 255). Image at *Atti del XVII Congresso*, 3: 1127.

The seller in this unusual contract is a citizen of one of the Greek cities, a distinction that persisted even after all of the population was officially of Roman citizen status. The drafting is not impeccable: "as aforesaid" refers to nothing said earlier, and the clauses following the statement of the price appear in general rather hastily drafted.

Aurelia Sarapias daughter of Areios, citizen woman, acting without a guardian by right of children according to Roman custom, to Aurelius Theon son of Ammonios alias Aphynchis from Oxyrhynchos, greetings. I acknowledge that I have sold to you a dining couch with linen coverlets embroidered throughout and four pillows of [. . .] and linen of the same quality for a price of five hundred drachmas, total, 500 dr., which I have received herewith. The sale is enforceable, written in one clean copy, and I will guarantee, and I have had the question asked as aforesaid. Year 2 of the Emperors Caesars Publius Licinius Valerianus and Publius Licinius Valerianus Gallienus, Greatest Germanici, and Publius Licinius Cornelius Valerianus the most noble Caesar, Augusti, Mesore 16.

(*2nd hand*) I, Aurelia Sarapias, have sold the dining couch and its coverings and I have received the 500 dr. of the price and I shall guarantee and I have been asked the question as aforesaid. I, Aurelius Horigenes, wrote for my mother because she does not know letters.

[36] The scribe spells the seller's name Petermouthis, but the seller himself adopts a different spelling in the subscription.

6.4.8 Sale of wood

P.Stras. III 184 (Hermopolis, middle of the second century AD)

Unfortunately this unusual sale of wood is very fragmentary. The seller is from Oxyrhynchos. He has imported wood into the Hermopolite and sold it in Hermopolis to a local purchaser. Most of the clauses, regrettably, are lacking.

> Leonas son of Herakleides, from Oxyrhynchos, to Achilleus son of Sabourion, Hermopolite, greetings. I acknowledge that I have sold to you in Hermopolis the Great heath and olive and jujube and two willow beams of wood and seven trunks of olive wood, which I brought from the Oxyrhynchite nome in a boat and delivered to you in the harbor of [. . .] of Hermopolis . . .
>
> *Back:* Sale of wood of Leonas the Oxyrhynchite.

6.5 State registration of sales: the *katagraphê*

Uri Yiftach-Firanko

Land conveyances were subject in the Greek world to state supervision. In the course of the fourth century BC, and maybe even earlier, the supervision was made possible through the registration of the conveyances in a special archive. Such an archive is referred to by Theophrastos in his *nomoi* (128 Hense), and came down to us, in the most intact form, in the inscription *IG* xii.5 872 from late third-century BC Tenos (Faraguna 2000: 88–92). In the Hellenistic and Roman periods, *katagraphein* is a verb commonly used to denote the act of registration; the noun is *katagraphê*.

The *katagraphê* is also attested in Egypt. In third-century BC Alexandria it was prescribed by law as a precondition for a valid conveyance of title (see below, **6.5.3**). It is also attested outside Alexandria in a variety of sources from the Ptolemaic and the Roman periods. In this overview, I will present the workings and legal significance of the *katagraphê* in the Ptolemaic period and discuss some elements of its evolution after the Roman conquest.

The following five documents were chosen because of their concern with the *katagraphê*. The third-century BC sale contract **6.5.1** anticipates and prescribes the future act of registration; **6.5.2** records the act itself; and **6.5.3**, a law from the third century BC, is concerned with the *katagraphê* in the city of Alexandria. Each of these texts provides a glimpse of the workings and role of the *katagraphê* in the Ptolemaic period. Two further documents, **6.5.4** (payment of earnest money on the occasion of sale) and **6.5.5** (act of gift), shed light on its application in the early Roman period.

6.5.1 Sale of land

BGU XIV 2398 (= *BGU* X 1974) (Tholthis, Oxyrhynchite nome, 213/2 BC)

In the reign of Ptolemy son of Ptolemy and Berenike, the gods Euergetai, the tenth year, the priest of Alexander and the gods Soteres, and the gods Adelphoi, and the gods Philopatores being Pythangelos son of Philokleitos, and the *kanêphoros* of Arsinoë Philadelphos being Agathoklea daughter of Diognetos, in the month Gorpiaios at Tholthis in the Oxyrhynchite nome.

Aischylos son of Pytheas, Athenian of the *epigonê*, acknowledges that he has received from Pasis son of Petosiris, Oxyrhynchite, grandson of Thaues, two hundred drachmas in bronze money, produced to view in the presence of the reported witnesses, (which is) the value of a vacant lot that is adjacent to a building that belongs to him in the village Tholthis of the upper toparchy of the Oxyhrynchite nome, whose dimensions are from west to east, ten *pêcheis*, and on the north, from the building of Aischylos [to the south], eleven *pêcheis*, whose neighbors are: on the north, [. . .]; on the south, a canal; on the west, [. . .]; on the east, the two *pêcheis* and the property of Patsontis.

Let Aischylos give the sale document of the aforesaid place at the *agoranomeion* that is in the city of Oxyrhynchos within ten days of the day in which Pasis will give Aischylos notice, Pasis paying the incurred costs. If Aischylos does not give to the said Pasis the sale document according to these terms, let Aischylos pay Pasis as a penalty the three hundred drachmas, which are the value (of the asset) increased by half, and let Pasis have the execution right on Aischylos, acting according to the *diagramma*. Guarantor of the payment according to the above document is Eukleat[. . .] daughter of [. . .] with her husband, Aischylos son of Pytheas, acting as her guardian (*kyrios*). Let the document be valid wherever it is produced.

Witnesses.

The names of the witnesses are lost.

In the preceding text, Pasis gives Aischylos 200 bronze drachmas that are said to be the value of a vacant lot belonging to Aischylos in the village of

Tholthis. The payment is a first step in the acquisition of the land by Pasis, but in itself it does not accord him the title, or any other property right to the land. The scribe of **6.5.1** avoids designating Pasis "purchaser," Aischylos "vendor," and the act itself "sale." Pasis is also not accorded any of the elements that normally signify the conveyance of title in Greek sale contracts from Egypt, i.e., he is not entitled to dispose of the object, nor is Aischylos required to defend Pasis from future challenge to his possession (signaled in the so-called *bebaiôsis* clause).

The payment of the price accords Pasis merely the right to ask Aischylos to give him the *ônê* ("purchase") at the office of the *agoranomos* in Oxyrhynchos, the nome's *metropolis*. If Aischylos does not give Pasis the *ônê*, Pasis' remedy would be contractual only: the right to retrieve the consideration increased by a penalty of 50 percent. For now, Aischylos remains the owner of the land and can dispose of it in any manner he wishes: he can, for example, mortgage the land or sell it to a third party. Any act of alienation will be perfectly valid.

Things would only change after Aischylos and Pasis visit the *agoranomos* in the nome's capital, as anticipated in the earlier contract. The *agoranomos* will record the transaction in his files and issue for the parties a document that certifies the act of registration.

The contract is a double document (for which see **2.1.1** and **2.1.2** with **2.1** introduction). Here the translation is of the exterior text with one emendation from the interior.

6.5.2 Sale of land

P.Adl. 13 (Krokodilopolis, Pathyrite nome, 100 BC). Image at Papyri.info.

Column I: In the year 14, Payni 29, Panas sold to Pates his seventh proper share of 4 lots for 12 bronze talents.

Column II: In the reign of Ptolemy called Alexander and Berenike his sister, gods Philometores, in the 14th year under the priests and priestesses and the *kanêphoros* now in office, on the 29th of the month Payni, in Krokodilopolis, before Paniskos, the *agoranomos* of the upper toparchy of Pathyris.

Panas son of Pates, Persian of the *epigonê*, of those from Pathyris, about 45 (years) old, of middle size, honey-colored, with long straight hair, long-faced, straight-nosed, with a scar over his left eye, with a thin beard, sold his own seventh share, belonging to him and to the creditors, of 4 lots of undivided grain land above inundation level, in the northern plain of Pathyris, the first share of arouras, whatever (the size of the share) may be, the neighbors being: on the south, the land of Patephis son of Pemsais; on the north, the land of Pakoibis, in the possession of the sons of Phibis, the son of Panechates; on the east, the royal road; on the west, the land of Psemmonthes son of Panechates; besides another share, the neighbors being: on the south, the land of the before-written Pakoibis in the possession of the same people; on the north, the land of Tathotis daughter of Phibis; on the east, the royal road; on the west, the land of Nechoutes son of Pelaias, and the land of Poregebthis son of Eponychos; another share called of Phamounis, the neighbors being: on the south, the land of Pathotes son of Patous; on the north, the land of Patseous son of Phibis; on the east, the Nile; on the west, the land called of Haroeris; another share, whose neighbors are: on the south, the land of Onnophris son of Imouthes, which Petosiris, the priest, possesses; on the north, the land of Achonaibis son of Portis; on the east, a canal called "Telon's Canal"; on the west the desert, or whatsoever be the boundaries on all sides.

Pates son of Poëris, Persian of the *epigonê*, of those from the same village Pathyris, about 40 (years) old, of middling size, honey-colored, with long straight hair, long-faced, straight-nosed, with a scar on his forehead to the right, bought for 12 bronze talents. Buyer's agent and surety (*propôlêtês kai bebaiôtês*) of all things to do with this purchase is Panas, the vendor, whom Pates, the purchaser, accepted.

I, Paniskos, have transacted the business.

Column III: (*2nd hand*) Year 14, Payni 29. Paid into the bank at Krokodilopolis, of which (bank) Paniskos is head, for the 10 percent sales tax according to the <certificate> of Paniskos, who was present at the purchase, which (certificate) Apollonios the checking-clerk subscribes, by Pates son of Poëris, for the 4 shares of land above inundation level, whatever they may be, in the northern plain of Pathyris, whose neighbors are described in the preceding contract, which he bought of Panas son of Pates for 12 bronze (talents), tax 1 (talent), 1,200 (*sc.* drachmas).

Paniskos, banker, 1 (talent) 2,640 (*sc.* drachmas).

In contrast to **6.5.1**, **6.5.2** was issued on the occasion of the registration of a sale contract in the *agoranomos*' files. It consists of three main sections: Column 1 – a short account of the transaction, identical, in all probability, to its record in the files themselves; Column 2 – a detailed account of the act of sale, reporting the parties, the object, and the price (the act is said to take place before the *agoranomos*); and Column 3 – a confirmation of the payment of the conveyance tax (*amphiourion*).

The contents of this later document share some common features with **6.5.1**: it too gives a detailed account of the object of the transaction and of its value. Essentially, however, **6.5.2** is quite different from **6.5.1**. First, **6.5.1** was a private act taking place before witnesses but without the participation of a state institution; **6.5.2**, on the contrary, was recorded at the *agoranomeion*, which is usually (though not in this particular case) located in the *metropolis*. Second, the composition of the document coincides, follows, or is at least tightly connected with the payment of a conveyance tax, and it is assumed that the act was not complete without this payment (Pestman 1985d). Third, the act is actually termed "act of purchase" (*ônê*), and its terminology – "sold," "bought," "vendor," "purchaser" – is that routinely applied in regular contracts of sale (as, e.g., those issued outside Egypt, or in Egypt in the Roman period). The new document also reports the *propôlêtai* and *bebaiôtai* (translated in the Adler edition as "buyer's agents" and "sureties") – the persons, or in this case a person, who are to defend the purchaser against any future challenge to his title. When the *agoranomos* issues his certificate, then, the purchaser is designated *expressis verbis* as one and enjoys the benefits usually accorded a purchaser in a regular sale contract.

6.5.3 A law of the autonomous city of Alexandria

P.Hal. 1 Col. XI (Alexandria, third century BC). Image at Papyri.info.

The law as set forth in **6.5.3** describes for Alexandria procedures that are very close to those evident in the documentation from the *chôra* as exemplified in **6.5.2**. The law also relates the legal consequences of the act of registration.

> The purchase of land, a house, and building-sites. If someone buys from another person land, a house, or building-sites, or sells them to anyone, let him pay to the *tamiai* [– –] drachmas for each hundred, [but – – if the value of the asset is less than (?)] 50 let this payment be consecrated to Alexander. And let the *tamiai* record the acts of purchase by the demes and [the phratries in the (registers of) the] deme of the vendor, entering first the name [of the vendor], indicating his father and his deme, and then [the name of the purchaser] in the same

> manner, and the month and day [of the registration (?),] and what he purchased by name, [where it is located], and if the estate has some name, registering [also the guarantor (*propolêtês*)], and if they are many, all of them. And should they not do so, [let them carry liability]. And after the vendor gives the *amphourion* and [receives the act of purchase (?)], let him have against the purchaser no action not even [accusation regarding the] land, the house, or the building-sites. And to those who attempt to buy [in contravention of the law] let not the purchase, nor even the prescription have authority. [And if the vendor] did not receive some of the consideration, let him subscribe before [the act of sale] the amount owed him, or compose a new document before [the *thesmophylakes*]. Otherwise let him have no recovery.

The task of the *tamiai* is quite close to that of the *agoranomoi* in **6.5.2**. Once the conveyance tax is paid, they should register the sale, the identity of the parties, the date on which the registration took place, the details of the land, and the guarantors. They both refer to the vendor as *apodomenos* and to the purchaser as *priamenos*.[37]

6.5.3 reports the consequences of the act: in lines 252–55 (of *P.Hal.* 1 Col. XI) we read that after the *amphourion* is paid, and the details of the sale are reported, the vendor has no ground for legal action or suit against the purchaser regarding the piece of property. According to many scholars, the *amphourion* is the Alexandrian term for the conveyance tax – the very tax whose payment is prescribed at the beginning of the document (242–44). The "report" probably takes place on the same occasion: upon paying the tax the parties report to the *tamiai* the particulars of the sale – the same particulars that are later registered by the *tamiai* in their files. In other words, the report and the payment of the tax set the registration procedure in motion.

According to **6.5.3**, then, once the registration procedure was started, the vendor lost any claim towards the purchaser regarding the object of sale. The registration creates, therefore, in Alexandria a legal situation that is diametrically opposed to that manifested in **6.5.1**. In that contract the prospective buyer is accorded the right to initiate and enforce the registration, and to be compensated if it does not actually take place, but he does not acquire any right to the asset itself. In **6.5.3** the act of registration

[37] Note the aorist tenses. The only element that appears in **6.5.2** and is not counted among those recorded by the Alexandrian *tamiai* is the price.

deprives the vendor of all his claims on the object, meaning, in other words, that by now the purchaser has attained exclusive title.

6.5.3 is a part of the *politikoi nomoi*, the laws that were created for the city of Alexandria, and were, theoretically at least, applicable only in that city. Therefore, we cannot be certain that registration carried similar consequences for the real position of the object in the *chôra* as well. Such a supposition is supported, albeit indirectly, by the next section of the Alexandrian law of sale. Lines 255–56 (of *P.Hal.* 1 Col. XI) deny validity to any sale that does not conform to the law. The purchaser has no title to the object if the parties did not pay the conveyance tax and the *tamiai* did not register the act in their files. No sale, then, without a public act.

6.5.1 is not a public instrument. It is composed without the participation of a state official, and in the presence of private witnesses. The document also makes clear that the purchaser does not acquire any title. But what is perhaps more significant, it avoids any term that might identify it as an act of sale: no "vendor," "purchaser," "sale," or "purchase." Its authors acknowledge, in other words, that their private act cannot bring about a real sale and point this out through the cautious avoidance of any term or formulation that could give a different impression. This would be best explained if we assume that a sale without a public act was invalid in the *chôra* just as it was in the city of Alexandria.

This assumption is also supported by the overall Ptolemaic finding. All the Greek documents from that period that were titled in editions "land sale contracts" are either preliminary agreements on future registration typified by **6.5.1** (which are not really sale contracts, but just anticipate them), or, in the vast majority of cases, instruments issued by the *agoranomos* that follow the scheme of **6.5.2**. The absence of any other type of sale contract is best accounted for if we assume that in the course of the Ptolemaic period no sale instrument was accepted as valid except for those issued by the *agoranomos* on the occasion of the registration of sale.

The success of the Ptolemaic state in establishing the agoranomic act as the exclusive instrument for the documentation of land sales is one of its most impressive accomplishments in the area of private law. Since the registration was predicated on the payment of the conveyance tax, it forestalled tax evasion. The *agoranomos*' note of the sale was also kept in his files, accorded purchasers proof of the lawfulness of their acquisitions, and avoided, at least to some extent, the creation of future conflicting rights on the same object.

The Roman provincial government was also interested in monitoring real property rights. It accomplished this task, however, through a different, more complex mechanism: around AD 50 the provincial government created in each *metropolis* a new archive, the "acquisitions archive," or "property records office" (*bibliothêkê enktêseôn*), which was entrusted with keeping record of the legal position of landed properties within each nome (see **2.6**).

In the new system, instead of going all the way to the *agoranomos* in the *metropolis*, the parties turned to the *grapheion*, a local scribal office that was located in their village. The *grapheion* official informed the *bibliophylakes* – the officials in charge of the new archive – of the intended transaction and checked to be sure their files documented no conflicting rights. If there were no conflicting rights, the *grapheion* official issued the sale contract.

In the Roman period, then, the new *bibliothêkê enktêseôn* replaced the *agoranomeion* as the archive registering real property rights in the Egyptian *chôra*. The *katagraphê* lost the cause for which it was created three hundred years earlier. For this reason, according to the *communis opinio*, it soon declined and then disappeared as an independent institution (Wolff 1948).

This is not, in my view, entirely accurate. In his *Greek Law of Sale*, F. Pringsheim (1950) championed the view that in Greek law, the conveyance of title was brought about by the payment of the consideration. This may well have been the prevailing principle, but it could also be changed by law, as was the case in Ptolemaic Egypt: in Alexandria, and probably also in the *chôra*, not the payment of the consideration but the act of registration conveyed the title. This means that through registration the title could be conveyed when there was no consideration at all, or when it was paid by installments and it is not clear when exactly in the course of the transaction the purchaser was meant to become the owner of the asset.

Things changed to some extent in the Roman period. With the rise of the *grapheia* and the "acquisitions archive" the *katagraphê* indeed ceased to be a requirement in regular land sales; no sale contract issued in the *grapheia* ever anticipates the *katagraphê*. In its other uses – if the title was conveyed gratuitously, or the consideration was paid by installments – the *katagraphê* remains effective at least down to the end of the second century AD.

6.5.4 Sale of house and land

P.Vind.Sal. 4 recto (Soknopaiou Nesos, 15 November AD 11). Image at Papyri.info.

Chairemon son of Herodes, a priest, to Satabous son of Herieus the younger, greetings. I received from you as an earnest money (*arrabôn*) for my house and the adjacent vacant lot in Soknopaiou Nesos of the Great God three hundred drachmas of Ptolemaic silver currency out of a sum of seven hundred forty silver drachmas. And I will perform for you the *katagraphê* before the second day of Choiak of the present forty-first year of Caesar, upon receiving in addition the remaining four hundred forty silver drachmas. If you do not pay the money within the fixed period, you will lose the said *arrabôn*. But if I receive the money but do not perform the *katagraphê*, I will pay you twice the amount of the earnest money, and if I receive the money, I will perform the *katagraphê* and warrant the sale (*bebaiôsô*). Forty-first year of Caesar, Hathyr eighteenth.

(*One line in Demotic*)

The early Roman period yields seven documents recording the delivery of earnest money in connection with land sales.[38] Frequently the earnest money is termed *arrabôn* (*BGU* I 240, II 446, XI 2111; *P.Lond.* II 334, p. 211; *P.Mich.* II 121r, 2.9.1; *P.Vind.Sal.* 4r; *P.Wisc.* I 9). In contrast with regular contemporary sale contracts, among these documents the *katagraphê* was always anticipated: **6.5.4** is one of these cases. It forms part of a small family archive to which **3.2.1** and **6.2.5** also belong.

On the day the document was composed, Hathyr 18th, Chairemon son of Herodes received from Satabous son of Hiereus a sum of 300 drachmas out of a total of 740 drachmas, which is the value of a house and a vacant lot that he intended to sell her. Within two weeks, by Choiak 2, he would receive the rest. Then he would perform the *katagraphê*.

The arrangements made on the occasion of the payment of the first installment resemble those made in **6.5.1**. Both documents record the payment of the consideration: in **6.5.1** its entirety, in **6.5.4** roughly a half. Yet the authors of both documents avoid terminology that could imply that what they issue are actual sale contracts: they do not use the verbs "to buy," "to sell," or the nouns "sale" or "purchase." **6.5.4** records the obligation of the vendor to protect the title of the purchaser, but the obligation does not become effective immediately; it is only a consequence of the future *katagraphê*. Before the act of registration, the remedies of the prospective purchaser are in both cases contractual. If the vendor in **6.5.1** omitted the registration, the purchaser would receive the consideration plus fifty percent. In contrast, **6.5.4** provides for a payment of twice the amount of the earnest money.

[38] See **6.3.4** introduction for earnest money in auction sales.

Nevertheless, the incentives for the arrangement are quite different in the two cases. According to my earlier supposition, in **6.5.1** the *katagraphê* was indispensable for the conveyance of title upon the purchaser, for in the Ptolemaic period the conveyance could not be brought about by a private act. This was no longer the case in the Roman period; by the time **6.5.4** was composed the *katagraphê* was no longer required for the conveyance of title. But there were practical considerations for its use. According to Pringsheim (1950: 204–19), in Greek law the title was conveyed by the payment of the consideration. But what if, as in this case, there were several installments? What was the effect, for the property rights, of each installment? When did the purchaser finally get the full title?

In each case, the parties were at liberty to shape the transfer of title differently. In **6.5.4**, the vendor's obligation to guard the purchaser from challenge – a key element of the conveyance of title – should accrue at the final payment; this is also the case in *P.Mich.* II 121 2, IX 1 (Tebtunis, AD 42). In *BGU* II 446 (Herakleia, AD 169–177) it takes effect immediately after the first payment, while in *P.Wisc.* 9 (Oxyrhynchos, AD 183), the *bebaiôsis* will follow the final payment, but the surrender (*parachôrêsis*) of the asset is immediate. In this case too, then, the title may well have passed immediately. Yet regardless, or maybe because of the different individual strategies, an additional act was required that would indicate, once and for all, that the transaction was perfect, that the vendor forewent any right to the object, that the purchaser was the new absolute owner. This goal was reached through the act of registration; the *katagraphê* finalized the transaction.

Finally, gratuitous conveyance of title: the *katagraphê* was commonly used whenever there was no consideration whose payment could, according to Pringsheim, transfer the title. One main area of application was the procedure for foreclosure when a piece of land was given as security (*hypothêkê*) for a loan. If the debtor did not settle the debt, the land was to be possessed and appropriated by the creditor. The *katagraphê* was the act that conveyed upon the creditor the actual title.[39]

6.5.5 Gift of a vineyard

P.Mich. V 266 (Tebtunis [originally Ibion Eikosipentarouron(?)]), 31 January AD 38). Image at Papyri.info.

[39] See, e.g., *SB* IV 7379 (Ptolemais Euergetis, AD 177). See also the discussion at **5.4.6**.

Lysimachos son of Lysimachos, to Hero, my sister by the same father and mother, with Herodes son of Ptolemaios, her kinsman, as guardian (*kyrios*), greetings. I acknowledge that, as soon as you command me, I will register (*katagraphein*) for you through the *grapheion* at Tebtunis the vineyard of one and a half arouras with vines trained on trees that is in my possession near Ibion Eikosipentarouron, which vineyard I have purchased from Didymos, our common brother, who is also your husband. I am to receive nothing at all, and no guarantee (*bebaiôsis*) is forthcoming except for my descendants and those who shall bring suit in my name. Let the *cheirographon* be valid. The second year of Gaius Caesar Augustus Germanicus, Mecheir 5.

(*2nd hand*) I, Herakleides son of Maron, agree to render my daughter Arsinoë agreeable to the sale whenever it is completed as stated above without her receiving anything.

Year 2 of Gaius Caesar Augustus Germanicus, Mecheir 5.

The importance of the *katagraphê* in gifts can be illustrated by this text. Land gifts usually take place within the donor's family; frequently they are used for the redistribution of family assets, when, as a result of previous property arrangements, one family member received too much and others too little of the family assets.[40] This may well be the case in the present document. Lysimachos son of Lysimachos has bought from his brother Didymos a vineyard. Now, for some reason, he bestows the vineyard upon his sister Hero, who is also Didymos' wife. The present document records his intention to do so.

Still, **6.5.5**, much like **6.5.1** or **6.5.4**, does not record the conveyance of title itself: Hero is not accorded the right to dispose of the land or to the vendor's protection. The present document merely enables her to enforce the future registration of the asset recorded in this document. As in the two aforementioned cases, only the *katagraphê* will accord her the title.

Yet **6.5.5** also exhibits some peculiarities. Differently from **6.5.4**, in this case the performance of the *katagraphê* is not predicated on the payment of a consideration: Lysimachos expressly states that he will not ask for any money. Most remarkable, however, is a different feature: in the case of sale, the *katagraphê* created the vendor's obligation to defend the purchaser, unconditionally, against any challenge to his title. This obligation is reduced in the case of gift: Lysimachos vouches that he and his heir will not themselves sue Hero, but does not warrant her against a challenge by a

[40] Cf., e.g., *BGU* IV 1131 (Alexandria, 13 BC).

third person. Obviously, giving something for free also means a reduced accountability for the transferor.

Finally, the procedure itself: in the Ptolemaic period the *katagraphê* was performed in the *metropolis* at the office of an *agoranomos*, who registered the act in his files. This continued to be the case throughout the early Roman period; the *katagraphê* is still performed in the *metropolis*. It is never, however, attested in the villages. Still, a registration in the village is precisely what is anticipated in **6.5.5**: a *katagraphê* at the *grapheion* of Tebtunis. How can we explain this oddity? In the Ptolemaic period the *katagraphê* was the only lawful way to convey title on real estate. In the Roman period this could also be done at the local *grapheia*. Here it was not carried out through an act similar to the Ptolemaic *katagraphê* as reported in **6.5.2**, but through a regular sale contract (cf. above, **6.5.4**). These intricacies perhaps escaped the writer of **6.5.5**, who regarded any act of conveyance as *katagraphê*, even when technically speaking it was not.

The "improper" equation *katagraphê* = conveyance of title became entrenched in the legal language of the following century. In the third century, *homologô peprakenai kai katagegraphêkenai* ("I acknowledge that I have sold and transferred") becomes the routine formula in every land sale contract. Still, the real *katagraphê* – an act of registration by a state official that conveys title – continues to exist throughout the Roman period: cf., e.g., **6.3.1** (Oxyrhynchos, AD 55); **6.3.5** (Hermopolite nome, AD 171). The same procedure is also attested in this period, outside Egypt: cf. Gounaropoulou and Hatzopoulos (1998: 13) (third century AD?). With the legislation of Constantine it finally finds its way into Roman imperial law: according to *CTh* 8.12.3, probably from AD 323, a formal act of registration is required in the case of a gift, one of the areas where, according to my earlier supposition, the *katagraphê* was still vibrant in early Roman Egypt. The principle that was born in the Greek *poleis* of the fourth century BC was accepted into Roman law eight centuries later.

6.6 The Byzantine era: Greek, Coptic, and Arabic sales

T. Sebastian Richter

All six of the specimens selected here belong to the category of sale of real property. The earliest text of the selection, *P.Münch.* I 11 (**6.6.1**) from Syene, dated to AD 586, concerns a suite of rooms in a house located at that town. Although written by a trained lay scribe, not by a professional notary, it gives a nice example of the fully evolved technical skills of the

Greek Byzantine chancellery rhetoric, a prose meant to impress, but at the same time a functional style, exerted to make every relevant point of a legal event as certain as possible (cf. above, **2.7**). *P.KRU* 6 (**6.6.2**), forming part of the almost purely Coptic papyrological dossier of the Upper Egyptian town of Djême, is an eighth-century AD example of the same rhetorical style, now adapted to Coptic means of expression. Roughly contemporary to the latter, the Coptic document *P.Mon.Apollo* 24 (**6.6.3**) records a sale of pasture land, using a rather short and plain scheme. The document belongs to the large though badly dispersed archive of the monastery of Apollô south of Ashmunein, well known under the name of Bawît, one of the few sites providing papyrological as well as archaeological evidence. The following two items, *P.Lond.Copt.* I 673 (**6.6.4**) and *P.Teshlôt* 2 (**6.6.5**), belong to the rare specimens of late Coptic legal documents (cf. also the late Coptic lease *P.Lond.Copt.* I 487 = **7.4.7** below). The Hellenistic flavor of the earlier Coptic legal language has faded entirely; instead, single words and phrases of these latecomers mirror the scribes' acquaintance with Arabic legal terms and schemes, which may be exemplified by an Arabic deed of sale, *P.Cair.Arab.* I 57 (**6.6.6**).

6.6.1 Greek sale of parts of a house

P.Münch. I 11 (= Bavarian State Library, papyrus inv. 100, 2nd edn. D. Hagedorn) (Syene, 7 October AD 586). Images in *P.Münch.*, Plates XXII–XXV.

A complete papyrus scroll of 140 cm height and 32.5 cm width, consisting of eleven leaves pasted together; the text running in one column of eighty-one lines *transversa charta*, which means in vertical format, top down. The document is dated to the fifth regnal year of the Emperor Mauricius Tiberius, his third consulate, and a day date within the fifth year of indiction, corresponding to the 7 October AD 586, thus being in perfect accordance with Justinian's *Novella* 47 of 537, requiring a tripartite dating system for legal instruments, consisting of the regnal year (starting with the day of accession to the throne), the consulate (at that time mostly held by the emperors themselves), and the indiction year. This large document belongs to the private archive of a man called Aurelius Patermuthis who lived and worked at the late sixth- and early seventh-century town of Syene (modern Aswan), an important garrison near the southern border of the Byzantine empire. Aurelius Patermuthis was the son-in-law of Tapia, the daughter of Tsios and Mariam, who was the vendor in the present sale. A few years later (*P.Münch.* I 12), Aurelius Pathermouthis bought back Tapia's parts of the very house for the same price of five *solidi* from Flavius

Kyriakos, the addressee of the present sale, and on this occasion, **6.6.1** may have come into his archive. The elaborate, rhetorically stylized text (for this see above, **2.7**) is composed of a number of non-specific formulas at the beginning and end of the document, and a number of specific formulas in the deed corpus. The deed corpus starts with the vendor's declaration that he sells by free will, followed by a detailed description of the sale object and its location, a clause acknowledging the receipt of the sales price, a clause by which the vendor promises to indemnify the purchaser against any claim, and a penal clause against anybody who attempts to contest the present sale.

The translation by Porten and Farber (1996: 522–25) is followed.

Recto

Dating clause: † In the fifth regnal year of the reign of our most divine ruler Flavius Mauricius Tiberius, the eternal Augustus, the Imperator and greatest Benefactor, and the third year of the consulate of this very ruler of ours, in (the month) Phaophi the 10th, in the fifth year of indiction, at Syene.

Address: † Aurelia Tapia daughter of Tsios by my mother Mariam, acting without her husband as a guardian, originating from Syene, also bringing in a writing assistant, who thereafter signs on her behalf, and witnesses, who thereafter testify to this written, sure deed of sale upon her order †, to Flavius Kyriakos son of Menas, cavalryman of the *numerus* of Syene, greetings.

Deed corpus: I, the aforementioned Tapia, am declaring by this written sale document of mine, voluntarily and being convinced, without any fraud and fear and violence and deception and compulsion and robbery and flattery and contrivance, without any malice and malignity and knavery and any reduction, but with voluntary awareness and guileless decision and clear conscience and right-mindedness, in accordance with this unified/uniform/unilateral written record, that I have sold to you today and signed over to you, by the law of sale and in eternal possession and in every completest right to power, the half part belonging to me of an entire house, in the condition as it is, from the ground to the airspace, of which (house) the other half part belongs to Jacob, my departed husband; further, that I have simultaneously sold to you the half parts[41]

[41] Actually, the possession of these so-called "parts" is not real, but means the right to joint use.

belonging to me of all appurtenances, of the forecourt, of the portal and of the terrace and of the atria and of the oven – in short, entirely in accordance with the deed of sale formerly issued in my and my deceased husband's name; and this house is located at Syene at the southern side of the fort and at the lane of the public camel stable of the parcel-post of Philae and of the house of Abraamios son of Pachymios. The neighbors of the entire house of which I sold you the half part owned by me – from the chamber on the first floor northward to the public street, and from the dining room above it on the second floor westward to the plane of the terrace, and from the (chamber) beneath the terrace, or (so-called) *khrêre*,[42] on the first floor and from the southern dining room on the third floor northward to the common atrium, and from the airspace above it up to the airspace,[43] and from the eastern Great Hall up to the airspace and the half of all appurtenances from foundations to the airspace – are like this: on the south: the dark and narrow street and the house of Abraamios son of Pachymios; on the north: the public street; on the east: the house of Abraamios son of Pachymios; on the west: the house of Allamôn son of Patechnumios, and whosoever may be neighbor everywhere and from every side, as I also dictated by word of mouth. And I have nothing at all left unsold of this aforementioned half part of a house and all its appurtenances from the foundation up to the airspace, which came to me by lawful purchase from John, who is also called Paptsios, and to him by parental succession according to the validity of the earlier deed of sale, while the sales price which we agreed upon with each other and which pleased both of us comes to five *solidi* of minted, genuine gold according to the weight standard[44] of Syene, = 5 g(old) so(lidi) according to the weight standard of Syene, which complete and fair sales price I received from you, Kyriakos, the purchaser, from (your hand) to my hand out of your house, (here) at Syene, in full number and weight, on the present day. And I warrant you the sale by every warranty in every way against everybody who will proceed or make a claim against you. (As for) the one who will proceed or make a claim against you, I myself, the vendor, will reject him and clear up (the issue) for you at my own expense and expenditure according to the law of sale and warranty, so that you, Flavius Kyriakos, the purchaser,

[42] This word is a Greek transcription of the Egyptian designation of a certain part of houses somewhere under the staircases; cf. above, **3.4.2**.

[43] That means the space above it without limitation, e.g., in order to build up a further floor.

[44] Literally, "balance" or "scale."

henceforth shall be lord and proprietor and be governing and administering and constructing and selling and donating and reselling and exchanging and leaving to children and grandchildren and doing and acting with it in every way unhindered and unprevented, and (I declare) I will not take you to court or (even) try to take you to court, nor shall anybody else, acting on my behalf, be it from my heirs, children or grandchildren, or somebody of those being close to me by kinship on my father's side or on my mother's side, at this time or at any time in any way under any pretext, be able to take you to court or to sue or to bring about an arbitration against you for this issue. (As for) the one who shall dare to sue you or to make a claim against you or to infringe or to shake this deed of sale, this shall not be of advantage to him, but he shall pay twice the aforementioned sales price as a fine for violation, and nothing shall prevail against what is written in this deed of sale, but even reluctantly he shall abide by it as if it had been deposited in a public archive, because no compulsion nor any violence, deception or fraud is laid upon me, because it was rather agreeable to me like that, to have sold you the aforementioned half part of a house and the half part of all accompanying appurtenances, and to have received from you the complete sales price as inserted (in the text above), (namely) five *solidi* of gold according to the weight standard of Syene, and to have issued this deed of sale as a guarantee for you, being valid and sure and untearable and unshakeable and lawful wherever it will be produced and exhibited, bearing the signature of the one who signs for me on my request.

Stipulation: And in answer to the formal question face-to-face, I have personally given my consent, and I released (this deed).

(*2nd hand*) I, Aurelia Tapia daughter of Tsios by my mother Mariam, from Syene, the aforementioned, have sold the full half share of a house from foundation to airspace, with every right to it, and I have received from you the above-written price in full in five *solidi* of the weight standard of Syene, and I shall warrant this sale for you with every warranty, and all the things written herein are agreeable to me, as stated above. I, Flavius Theodoros son of Abraamios, soldier of the legion (*numerus*) of Syene, after she asked me, wrote on her behalf because she is not able to write +

There follow signatures of five witnesses, each signing in his own hand. Three are soldiers of the legion (*numerus*) of Syene, one an archdeacon of the church of St. Mary at Syene, one an *ekdikos* ("public defender") of the city (Latin *defensor civitatis*) of Apollonopolis, mentioning he has been present at Syene by pure chance.

Completion note by the scribe: (*8th hand*) † Written by me, Markos son of Apa Dios.

On verso, docket, mostly abbreviated: Sale of half part of a house from foundations up to airspace, sold by Tapia daughter of Tsios and her widowed mother Mariam, from Syene, at price of 5 gold *solidi* in the weight standard of Syene.

6.6.2 Coptic sale of a courtyard

P.KRU 6 (= London, British Library Or. 4872; Crum 1912: 22–23, no. 6; German translation by Till 1964: 96–98) (Djême, 14 August AD 758)

A papyrus scroll, 64 cm in height by 21.5 cm in width (3 *selides*, i.e., leaves pasted together); the text is written in thirty-eight lines *transversa charta*, i.e., in vertical format; on the back, a docket summarizing the record's content. After traces of a stamped protocol in Arabic indicating the fabrication year of the papyrus, as usual on the "end-paper" of papyrus scrolls, the written text starts with a dating formula that refers no longer to a Byzantine ruler (as still in **6.6.1**), but to a much more modest figure, a local dignitary of Djême. Its general structure, clauses, and single phrases strongly resemble those of the Greek **6.6.1** dated more than 150 years earlier (cf. above, **2.7**). The self-introduction of the issuer and addressee and the issuer's declaration of acting by free will are followed by a description of the sale object, a courtyard, whose location is specified by reference to its neighboring estates according to the four directions. The vendor acknowledges the receipt of the full sales price of two *trimesia* (= $^2/_3$ *solidus*), guarantees to forfend from the purchaser any claim against the sale, and imposes a penalty on anybody who should contest the sale.

Recto

Remains of the stamped protocol in Arabic: In the name of A[llah, the Merciful, the Compassionate . . .] in the year [. . .]

Invocation formula and issuing date: † (*Greek*) In the name of the holy and vivifying, consubstantial Trinity, of the Father and of the Son and of the Holy Spirit. Written in the month Mesore, 21st, 11th (year of) indiction.

† Under our master Flavius Komes son of the late Chaêl, the *dioikêtês* (administrator) of Kastron Memnonion.[45]

Introduction of the issuer and of the addressee, declaration of free will, and description of the sale object: † I, Senouthios son of the late Enoch, inhabitant of Kastron Djême in the district of the city of Ermont (i.e., Hermonthis), cause hereafter the signature of the one who will sign for me, and the honest and trustworthy witnesses to testify for me upon my own request and my order, I am writing without any fraud and fear and violence and deception and robbery and circumvention, no compulsion at all being laid upon me, but by my own, heartfelt desire and my decision. I sign over and sell to you, Aron son of the late Senouthios, my part of the courtyard (at the street) of the people of Pshoumare, which has come upon me from my late parents, the boundaries of which courtyard I will show you now according to its traditional position:

(in the) west: the house of Petros son of Zacharia,
(in the) east: the new street inwards to your house,
(in the) north: (the house of) David son of Kyriakos,
(in the) south: the public street and the main gate.

Receipt of the sales price and transfer of ownership: The sales price that we agreed upon with each other and that pleased both parties comes to two *trimesia* of gold – (*Greek*) total, *solidus* ⅔, two-thirds, (of) pure (gold), according to the weight standard of Kastron Memnonion. (*Coptic*) The complete sales price came to me, paid from hand to my hand, in good gold. As from now, it's up to you, Aron son of Senouthios, the purchaser and the one aforementioned above, that you shall come in and be lord and become proprietor of my part of this courtyard, being the fourth part (of it), from now until eternal times, yourself and everyone who will follow you.

Penalty clause: As to one who will dare to proceed against you, be it myself or a child of mine or a sibling of mine or (someone) on my father's side, or (someone) on my mother's side, firstly, that one shall not find any advantage, but he shall be alienated from the (oath by) the Father and the Son and the Holy Spirit; further, he shall be forced to agree (*lit.* "to come close") to this deed, apart from the fine and the penalty that will be fixed

[45] The Upper Egyptian town called Djême in Coptic, alternatively transliterated in English as Jême, bore the Greek name Kastron Memnonion after the two colossal statues of the pharaoh Amenophis III standing nearby, the so-called colossi of Memnon. The term Kastron, the Latin *castrum*, points to its earlier status as a Roman garrison; see Wilfong (2002).

upon him. For your surety now, I issued this deed of sale for you; it is sure, it is valid at every place where it will be produced. And in answer to the formal question I have personally given my consent (to this deed) as set forth.

Signatures of witnesses: (*2nd hand*) † I, Anastase son of Philôthis, I am witness; I, Leontios son of the late Aristophane, I wrote for him and I am witness. †

Completion note by the scribe: † (*Greek*) Written by me, Swai son of the late Philoth(eos) †.

Docket on verso: † Senouth(ios) son of Enoch, my part of the courtyard being at the street of the people of Pshoumare; its boundaries: (in the) west, the house of Petros (son of) Zach(aria); (in the) east, the street inwards; (in the) north, the house of David (son of) Phil.; (in the) south, the street inwards and the main gate. The sales price: *solidus* ⅔.

6.6.3 Coptic sale of an estate

P.Mon.Apollo 24 (= St. Petersburg, Papyrus Hermitage Museum inv. 13495, *P.HermitageCopt.* 7; ed. Jernstedt 1959: 35–42, no. 7; re-ed. Clackson 2000: 77–80, no. 24) (Bawît, eighth century AD)

A papyrus, 15 cm in height and 30 cm in width; text written in twelve lines plus two lines of the docket on the verso. Recorded is the transfer of ownership of an estate from the village/farmstead (*epoikion*) of Pôrahêw to the Hermopolite monastery of Apollô, illustrating the continuing existence of communal as well as monastic estates during the first century of Arabic rule of Egypt. In comparison to such elaborate texts as the Greek **6.6.1** and the Coptic **6.6.2**, the scheme of this document is conspicuously brief and plain. The estate to be sold is specified as to its quality and size. The receipt of the sales price of 1 and 5/6 *solidi* by the vendor and the transfer of the complete rights of ownership to the purchaser are stated. It is interesting to see that three of the four representatives of the village, among them two clerics, are unable to write and have to restrict themselves to signing with crosses.

Recto

Address: † We, the community of the farmstead of Pôrahêw, (represented) by me, Isitre, the *hiereus*,[46] the son of Viktor, together with the deacon

[46] The term *hiereus* designates an official with responsibility for policing and taxation; see Clackson (2000: 77) with reference to Gascou in *P.Sorb.* II 66–70.

Petre and the presbyter Anouph and Shenoute son of the late Phib and the remaining *epoikion* altogether, we are writing to master Athanase, the abbot (*proestôs*) of the monastery of Apa Apollô:

Deed corpus: After we have come to an agreement with you, and sold you three good fodder-arouras and twenty-five pasture-arouras in the field of our community, which we apportion to you by the *ba*-measuring line of the monastery – (*Greek, in figures*), that makes fodder-arouras 3 plus pasture-arourae 25 – (*Coptic*) we now acknowledge that we have received from you and have been paid out with our sales price according to what we have agreed with each other, namely 2 *solidi* less half a *trimêsion* – (*Greek, abbreviated, in figures*) total: go(ld) so(lidus) 1 (+) ½ (+) ⅓. Now then you are the master and you shall administer them in every way you want. As a surety now for your fatherhood, we issued this guarantee for you, we assent to it, swearing by God the Almighty and the salvation of those ruling over us that we shall watch for the validity of this guarantee in your favor.

Date, stipulation, and witness signs: † (*Greek, abbreviated*) Written in the month Tybi the 21st, 11th (year of) indiction.

(*2nd hand*) I, Isidre † *hiereus*, I assent †

+ + + I assent! (The crosses are) Petre the deacon's mark. †

+ + + I assent! (The crosses are) Anouph the presbyter's mark.

+ + + I assent! (The crosses are) Shenoute son of Phib's mark.

(*3rd hand*) I, Gennate son of Anop, inhabitant of Plêtem in the district of Kôs, I am witness (to) this document that I have heard by the issuer.

(*1st hand, Greek*) I, Mêna, the scribe, I am writing and testifying.

Docket on verso: † (*Greek*) Guarantee issued by Isitre and others of the *epoikion* Pouraêw; [. . .] as the purchase price (for) fodder (and) pasture (fields), 11th indiction(-year)

6.6.4 Late Coptic sale of two rooms

P.Lond.Copt. 1 673 (= London, British Library Or. 4927(15); ed. Crum 1905: 304–05, no. 673; re-ed. Richter 1999: 85–89) (Fayyum, AD 986/7)

A piece of parchment, 16 × 15 cm. Provenance from the Fayyum indicated by the Coptic dialect of the document. Dated to year 703 of the era of Diocletian, corresponding to AD 986/987. The laconic brevity of this document is a typical feature of late Coptic legal documents (cf. also **7.4.7** below), marking a clear break with the Byzantine chancellery tradition. The business events are no longer put as going to happen, but as having happened in the past, and the interlocutory style of the Greek *homologia* (cf. above, **2.7**) is replaced by the practice of speaking of the addressee in the third person. The document concerns the sale of two items of what is called *li* in Fayyumic Coptic, meaning a "room" or, in a technical sense, the "cell" of a monastery. As all participants in the present transaction bear ecclesiastical titles, the latter meaning may actually be the appropriate one. After a short description of the sale objects, the sales price of 2½ *solidi* is mentioned. The following witness list culminates in the appeal to the witness-ship of Jesus Christ, probably mirroring the contemporary standard phrase of Arabic legal documents *wakâfa billahi, Shîdâ* "and God suffices as witness" (Qur'an, Surah 48,28). The terse styling – note, e.g., that the location of the cells is not mentioned but simply taken for granted – points to a merely "internal" function and validity of the document.

> † (*Greek*) With God! (*Coptic*) In the name of God above all! It is I, the deacon Agau, who has given the two eastern dwelling cells to Apa Makoure, namely the cellar(?)[47]-cell and the dining room[48] being upon it, and the cell beside the road. The dwelling and the dining room and their storage rooms,[49] I sold them to him for 2 and a half *holokottinoi*; Apa Papnuti being witness; Apa Chaêl being witness, the archdeacon Sisini being witness, the deacon Houmisi being witness, the Lord Jesus Christ being witness upon all of us. According to the era (year) 703.[50]

6.6.5 Late Coptic sale of a house

P. Teshlôt 2 (= Leiden, Rijksmuseum van Oudheiden, F 1964/4.5; ed. Green 1985: 77–78, no. 5; re-ed. Richter 2000: 109–14, no. 2) (Dakhlût, AD 1023)

[47] The word *tarihy* used here is a loanword, perhaps borrowed from a Northwest Semitic language where a noun *darîh* with the meaning "vault, cellar, &c." exists. But the Greek word *tarikhion* "dried fish" would be a possible candidate too.

[48] The word *anteran* is borrowed from the Greek *andrôn*, meaning "men's apartment, banqueting-hall" (*LSJ* 129b); in older and middle Latin (*androna*) also the "passage between two courts of a house" (Du Cange 247a-b). Some rare Coptic instances (BL Or. 6203,53–54; BL Or. 6204,43) have *andrôn* in descriptions of a monastery's cell (*manshôpe*), consisting of "its cellars, its dining rooms (*andrôn*), its roofs."

[49] The Coptic word used here could also mean "threshing floor."

[50] "The era" (*pechronos*) means the "era of the martyrs" (*chronos martyrôn*), as the former era of Diocletian was called by Christians in later times. Starting with the first regnal year of Diocletian AD 284/5, its year 703 corresponds to AD 986/987.

An irregularly shaped piece of parchment, probably left over from the fabrication of a codex leaf; provenance according to internal evidence from Dakhlût, a village south of Hermopolis; dated to year 414 hijra, corresponding to AD 1023. The late Coptic sale document belongs to the private archive of a man called Raphael, son of the deacon Mêna, who spent his life in the south of Hermopolis, eventually living in the village of Dakhlût (called Teshlôt in Coptic); the extant parts of his archive bear evidence of his legal transactions, mainly the transfer of buildings over a forty-year period from AD 1022 to 1063. After the stereotyped invocation formula, the text starts with the introduction of the issuer and the affirmation of his soundness of mind. The purchaser is not directly addressed, but referred to in the third person. The sale object, a house, is specified as to its location. The vendor mentions its sales price of fourteen dinars from the emission of the present caliph Alî az-Zâhir, and acknowledges its receipt. The location of the house is described in the traditional way by indicating its neighbors in the four directions. The deed corpus is completed by a full date. The scribe and six witnesses have signed up with their own hands. The form of their statements is rendered from the witness formula of Arabic legal documents. Like many of the contemporary Arabic documents, **6.6.5** is written on parchment, the alternative writing support besides paper, after papyrus had gone out of use by the mid-tenth century.

In the name of God above all! I, Soutyrche,[51] son of Aplô,[52] inhabitant of Teshlôt, I am writing and assenting by my soul, while I am living, stable, and sound, while my mind is with me.

As for my house, (located) northwards from Apa Syrny[53] at Tylke:[54] I gave it to Raphael, son of the deacon Mina,[55] inhabitant of Paouêt,[56] for gold: 14 *holokottinoi*[57] of at-Tahir.[58] I received them from him,

[51] Late Coptic form of the Greek name Sôterichos.

[52] Late Coptic form of the Greek name Apollôs.

[53] Late Coptic form of the Greek name Serênos. It is quoted here as a place name, most likely the abridged name of a church or monastery of Apa Serênos.

[54] The modern village Dalga south of Hermopolis/Ashmunein.

[55] Raphael, son of the deacon Mina, is the holder of the Teshlôt archive.

[56] The site called Bawît.

[57] The term *holokottinos*, originally used in Coptic to name the *solidus*, the gold currency of the Byzantine emperors (in Greek called *nomisma*), was also the later Coptic designation of the Arabic gold currency, the *dînâr*.

[58] The Coptic word *attaheri* used here is a transcription of the Arabic adjective *at-tahiri*, "belonging to (the caliph) *at-Tahir*." In the Arabic terminology around coins and currency, names of caliphs served to

as the Lord is witness upon me. The southern boundary[59] is Apa Srny; the western boundary is the house of Thotôr[60] son of Makroben;[61] the eastern boundary is the garden of Sousinne; the northern boundary is the house of Myrkoure,[62] the inhabitant of Whitefield. Today, day 28 of (the month) Tôbe (of) this <year> 414.[63]

I, Hamôs, son of the deacon John, he (i.e., Soutyrche, the issuer) instructed me through his tongue. I wrote and witnessed for him.

(*2nd hand*) I, Petros (son of) Pigôsh, I am witness for (all) that is (written) in this document, (year) 414.

(*3rd hand*) I, Daniêl (son of) Aplô, I am witness for (all) that is (written) in this document in this year 414.

(*4th hand*) I, Chaêl (son of) Sousin, I am witness for (all) that is (written) in this document in this current year 414.

(*5th hand*) I, Apoulchair[64] (son of) Aplô, I am witness for (all) that is (written) in this document, this year 414.

(*6th hand*) I, Viktôr (son of) Sousinne, I am witness for (all) that is (written) in this document in (this year) 414.

(*7th hand*) I, Plothe[65] (son of) Thodôr, I am witness for (all) that is (written) in this document, this year 414.

6.6.6 Arabic sale of parts of a house

P.Cair.Arab. I 57 (= Cairo, Catalogue Général 38677, Ta'rîkh no. 1899; for the scheme and its terminology, cf. Frantz-Murphy 1981, 1985, 1988a, 1988b) (Tutun [Fayyum], June AD 952)

Paper, 26.5 × 15.1 cm. From the village Tutun in the southern Fayyum. Dated to the month Muharram of year 341 hijra = June AD 952. The document belongs to an assemblage of Arabic deeds of sale (*P.Cair.Arab.* I, 57, 58 and 59; *P.Mich.* inv. 5634 and 5635) related to each other by the same

specify different emissions of the *dînâr*, varying in weight and quality. The caliph Ali at-Tahir ruled AD 1021–36 – his *dînârs* were the most recent currency at the time when **6.6.5** was drawn up.

59 The Coptic text has *alhat*, a loanword borrowed from Arabic. The term *(al) hadd* meaning the "boundary (of an estate)" usually occurs in Arabic legal documents dealing with the location of estates or buildings; see below, **6.6.6**.

60 Late Coptic form of the Greek name Theodôros.

61 Late Coptic form of the Greek name Makrôbios.

62 Late Coptic form of the Greek name Merkourios.

63 The years in the Teshlôt archive are counted according to the era of the *hijra* of Muhammad. The *hijra* year 414 corresponds to AD 1023.

64 This man bears the Arabic name Abû-al-khair.

65 Late Coptic form of the Greek name Philotheos.

provenance from the Fayyum village Tutun and by certain persons occurring in all of them. The protagonists of the present document, as well as their parents, bear Arabized Coptic names, such as John, Shenoute, Petakos, Magdalena, Jôb, indicating that they were, or at least had been, Christians, using the Arabic language and Islamic law for doing business with each other, while the two witnesses, writing Arabic in their own hand, clearly were Muslims, as was required by the Islamic law of sale. The text is written in objective style, which means both the vendor who issued the document and the purchaser are referred to in the third person. The vendor is a woman, called Maqtalenâ daughter of Shenoude. The purchaser, Yohannes ibn Shenoude, is known also from two other Arabic deeds of sale, *P.Cair.Arab.* I 58 and 59, where he likewise buys parts of houses from fellow inhabitants of Tutun. After the introduction of the two parties, the sale object is described as to its constituents and its location. The sales price of one *dînâr* is mentioned, and its receipt by the vendor acknowledged. Then the transfer of the object and all appertaining rights of ownership is stated. In the following guarantee clause, Maqtalenâ, the vendor, takes responsibility for any claim against the sale, and finally she confirms her free will and soundness of mind.

The translation of A. Grohmann in *P.Cair.Arab.* I is followed.

Invocation and introduction of the parties: In the name of God, the Merciful, the Compassionate! This is what Yohannes ibn Shenoude ibn Batâqos bought from Maqtalenâ daughter of Shenoude ibn Ayyûb, who both are assigned to the inhabitants of Tutun in the district of the Fayyum:

Designation and description of the purchase object: (He has bought) her part of the residence divided between him and her, and this is the sixth (part) of it, four parts of four and twenty parts, with its boundary and its boundaries, and below it and above it, and inside and outside of it. Its southern boundary is the residence of Qufrâ, the man of Qambashâ; and its northern boundary is the highway and its eastern boundary is the residence of Hermina the daughter of Tamise, and its western boundary is the courtyard of the heirs of the sons of Bshai.

Acknowledgement of receipt of the sales price and transfer of the ownership from vendor to purchaser: He bought that from her for one *dînâr*, minted gold, of full new weight, of unadulterated minted gold. Maqtalenâ has taken this price without any remainder and in full, and she has removed herself from this part. And she delivered this to Yohannes ibn

Shenoude, and he took possession of it, and he took ownership of it, and that has become part of his property, possessed out of his right of possession. If he wishes he may sell, and if he wishes he may build, and if he wishes he may reside.

Exclusion of a claim by the vendor, and guarantee to indemnify the purchaser against any claim: Maqtalenâ daughter of Shenoude has no claim and no demand in this house after this recording, neither for any cause nor for any reason. She sold this according to the stipulation of the sale of Islam and its contract. And whatever there may be by way of a claim for an attachment to the property, or claims for a right in, or due from, the property, or (in case) someone shall come adventitiously because of a loan, or making a claim by inheritance, the execution of that and its clearance will be the obligation of Maqtalenâ daughter of Shenoude, for the worth to which it amounts, from her clear property.

Stipulation of the sale by the vendor in a state of free will and sound mind: Testimony was given to the affirmation of Maqtalenâ daughter of Shenoude, to all that is in this document, after it was read[66] to her, and she took note of it and confirmed that she understood it, being of sound mind and body and her actions legal, being willing, without being averse, not being compelled, (but being) the petitioner and the one desiring.

Issuing date: And that is in (the month) Muharram of the year one and forty and three hundred.

Witness list: And there have borne witness to this:

Abd al-Samad ibn Yusuf ibn Hârûn bore witness to the agreement of Maqtalenâ daughter of Shenoude, concerning all that is (written) in this document, and he wrote his testimony with his (own) hand, and this on its date.

Al-Yasa' ibn 'Omar ibn Mûsâ bore witness for the agreement of Maqtalenâ daughter of Shenoude, concerning the sale of her part of the residence described in this document, and he wrote with his (own) hand.

[66] In *P.Mich.* inv. 5634, ll. 14–15 and inv. 5635, ll. 13–14, the same paragraph is extended like this: "after it was read to him in Arabic and explained to him in foreign [i.e., Coptic] language."

CHAPTER 7

Leases

Cary J. Martin, T. Sebastian Richter, Jane Rowlandson, Ryosuke Takahashi, and Dorothy J. Thompson

Introduction

Leasing, in particular the leasing of land, is one of the best-attested private legal transactions in the papyrological evidence, abundantly attested across the boundaries of regions, periods, and languages of Egypt. While a large proportion of merely oral lease arrangements must always be taken into account (Mrsich 1994, Eyre 2004), there seems to have been a steady movement from oral to written agreements from the earliest attested lease-like documents of Egypt, cursive Hieratic and early Demotic texts of the seventh and sixth centuries BC, up to the Byzantine period, when the proportion of leases among the total of papyrus documents grew higher than ever before (Jördens 1999).

To date, about fifteen hundred Greek leases from the early third century BC to AD 708, the year of the latest datable Greek lease document, *P.Apoll.* 57, have been published. Among them are 450 documents from the Byzantine period. During the first century after the Arab conquest, the number of Greek lease documents dropped sharply; but in Coptic, which was gaining importance as a language of legal documents at that time, some sixty leases and about forty rent receipts are attested. These bear evidence of a certain continuity in agricultural work and its administration, at least on the local level. Land leases written in Arabic start with a document dated to AD 776. The sixty-two extant Arabic leases and 132 land-tax receipts from the later eighth to the mid-eleventh century, only recently studied in detail, differ greatly in form, content, and style from Byzantine leases. They bear witness to considerable alterations of crucial economic and legal concepts and to the transformation of a mainly private economy, an agricultural "capitalism" *avant la lettre*, to a rather state-dominated system of agricultural administration.[1]

[1] For the Ptolemaic period, thirty-one Demotic texts (twenty-three principal texts and eight fragments) are discussed in Felber (1997a) (plus P.Brit.Mus. EA 10595 from the Siut Archive, which he includes in his list but does not classify as an actual lease). His analysis does not include those documents that refer

The efforts of scholars in editing, analyzing, and interpreting, over many years, the large corpus of Greek leases has created one of the most important sources for the agricultural, social, and economic history of pre-modern Egypt. At the same time, this material is of great importance for the shaping of current ideas on the ancient economy as a whole. The range and complexity of issues intrinsically involved in this type of business – legal concepts of ownership and work, land tenure (or, more generally, access to natural resources), administration of agricultural work, access to agricultural profits, fiscal administration, development of rents and prices, irrigation strategies and technologies, the ecology of artificially shaped landscapes – make these leases an essential means for gaining insight into fundamental conditions of Egyptian life and society.

Unlike the Greek corpus with its wealth of documents from early Ptolemaic to Byzantine times, compiled and thoroughly studied over the last century, and the smaller Demotic corpus, which has had the attention of specialists for half a century, the Arabic corpus has only recently drawn attention, while the Coptic corpus has scarcely been analyzed until now.[2] With all this linguistically diverse but materially coherent evidence put together, the case of land-leasing would provide us with the rare opportunity for studying the social, legal, and economic development of an important sector of Egyptian society on a large scale and over the *longue durée*.

The vast majority of leases are leases of agricultural land, but a lease contract (*misthôsis*) could also be used for leasing other kinds of property, notably livestock (sheep and goats, geese, cattle), fishing rights, and buildings for habitation, agricultural, or industrial use, although leases of dwellings were not common until the Byzantine period. Hybrid forms are also found, like the *misthoprasia* (lease-sale) for ships (Rathbone 2007b), and the combined lease and receipt (*misthapochê*) that developed during

to leasing transactions, but are probably not actual documents of lease (e.g., *P.Ryl.* 34 and 41), or leases on ostraca, which are quite summarily written. To the material listed in Felber (1997a) can be added a further six Gebelen texts in the British Museum, which are in the process of publication, an unpublished fragment from the Fayyum, now in Michigan (*P.Mich.* 4244, 6, c; see Hughes 1952: 31), the partly translated *P.Moscow* 140 (Struve 1955: 52–54), and a group of texts from Tebtunis now in the Cairo Museum (*P.Cair.* 30613, 30615, 30626, 30631, and 31079) published by Spiegelberg (1906/8) (but see Hughes 1952: 31–33 for comments and interpretation). Of the texts discussed by Felber, eight are Theban, seventeen are from Gebelen (including seven of the fragmentary papyri), one is from Asyut (plus P.Brit.Mus. EA 10595), two are from Akoris, and two are from the Fayyum. There is one fragment for which no certain provenance can be established other than Upper Egypt. Chronologically, all the Ptolemaic Demotic papyri belong to the second and first centuries, but in the absence of firm evidence to the contrary it would be unwise to attempt to draw any conclusions, *ex silentio*, from the absence of third-century texts in the documentation (*contra* Mrsich 2003: 24–25 and 75).

2 An attempt to fill this gap will be made by Richter (forthcoming).

the Roman period (see **7.3.8**). In the later Roman period there began to appear, perhaps under the influence of the Roman *locatio-conductio operis*, leases of skilled work, particularly vineyard work and irrigation (**8.2.10–11**), characterized by the lessee's receipt of a wage rather than payment of rent. In practice this distinction between lease of an object subject to rent and that of work remunerated by a wage was commonly elided or confused; see the pottery lease below, **7.3.10**, and see **8.2.11**, a land lease in which the tenant received one-fifth of the crop and a cash wage; for sharecropping arrangements, see also **7.3.4** and **8.2.12**. A lease of work could also include a lease of arable land, **8.2.10**.

For the Ptolemaic period we possess a reasonable quantity of documentation written in Demotic, although this is not as plentiful as that for other categories of transaction.[3] The Ptolemaic land leases are principally written on papyrus but there are some on ostraca, small sherds of pottery or stone.[4] For Roman Egypt, on the contrary, we have only one Demotic papyrus and a few ostraca.[5] The four Demotic texts in **7.1** include Ptolemaic leases from the Fayyum (Philadelphia), Thebes, and Asyut, and the one Roman-period lease contract (from Tebtunis). They have been selected to illustrate the different structures and legal formulas found in the land leases and to highlight the regional differences that exist between texts from the Fayyum[6] and those from the Nile valley.[7] The relatively restricted number of texts available for study and the probably atypical circumstances that led, in any case, to the need for a written document mean that it is problematic to speak of a "typical" document of lease. The following introductory comments, however, will seek to give an overview of the Ptolemaic texts, with reference to the earlier leases and to the limited Roman material, and to describe the various clauses that are to be found in the documents.[8]

3 In his analysis of the documents of matrimonial property arrangements ("marriage documents") Lüddeckens (1960) had available to him seventy texts (more such documents have been published since). Zauzich (1968), in his analysis of documents of sale, included 159 texts (and again more texts have subsequently been published).

4 Two fragmentary Ptolemaic ostraca are published in Nur el-Din (1974: nos. 63–64). See also Kaplony-Heckel (1964: 30–31).

5 For Roman-period ostraca, see Mattha (1945, nos. 273–76), Nur-el-Din (1974, no. 65), and Wångstedt (1965, no. 44). The Late Demotic Gardening Agreement (Parker 1940) is not a legal document but either a very practiced scribal/school exercise or, perhaps more likely, a parody (or both); see Depauw (1997: 98) and Quack (2005: 169–70).

6 The leases from Akoris also show a number of points of agreement with Fayyumic practice; see Hughes (1952: 81 n. 19).

7 The Ptolemaic leases are typically quite detailed, while the information in the Roman-period Tebtunis lease (**7.1.4**) is comparatively slight, although it does include statements on the responsibility for taxes and the prepayment of the rent.

8 Hughes (1952) provides a very useful comparison of the Saite and Ptolemaic leases.

The Greek leases from the Ptolemaic period deal predominantly with kleruchic land, the important category of land allocated to Ptolemaic military settlers (see **7.2** and **7.3.2**).[9] Future work on kleruchic land, as indeed on other land categories in Hellenistic Egypt, is likely to concentrate on its changing legal and fiscal status over time and by area. Whereas earlier studies recognized the importance of change in tenure over time, the regional differences (see **7.2.5** introduction) were not given due recognition. The changes in charges made on this category of land are now becoming clearer, but there is more work to do on the taxes and dues charged at differential rates on kleruchic land (Préaux 1939: 400–03, for an introduction; more recent documentation continues simply to modify this picture). *Epigraphê* was the Greek term for the harvest tax. After the end of the revolt in the south in the second century BC, it was levied by royal officials on the produce of cultivated land in the Thebaid (Vandorpe 2000a) but not uniformly throughout the country.[10] The rate of the various artaba taxes levied on kleruchic land differed from time to time, according to nome, condition of the land, and kleruchic status.[11] The separate collection of dues paid by cavalry settlers was already known in the second half of the third century BC from *P.Petrie* III 108–112 but it now seems that, at least from the mid-second century BC, these were paid into a special account, the *hippikê prosodos* (*P.Lips.* II 124, line 1, with note), cf. the *hippikon logistêrion* involved in changes of registration in *BGU* VIII 1731, line 9; 1732, line 3; 1733, line 5 (first century BC, Herakleopolite nome). The publication of new texts like *P.Lips.* II 124, with the commentary of Duttenhöfer (2002), highlights the need for further study on the relationship between royal and military officials in the general administration and control of kleruchic land. Finally, and most important, it is clear that the integration of the Demotic with the Greek material will, as in the recognition of the Demotic term for land *en aphesei* (see **7.2.6** introduction), yield future results in this area.[12]

[9] They come predominantly from the Arsinoite and Oxyrhynchite nomes; see Herrmann (1958: 247–52) and Hennig (1967: 173–200). One notable exception is the Greek lease *PSI* IX 1021 that belongs to the predominantly Demotic Archive of Totoes in the Memnoneia; see Pestman in Boswinkel and Pestman (1978, no. 3). For some useful points of comparison between the Demotic and Greek leases, see Rowlandson (1996: 208–13).

[10] See *P.Lips.* II 124, line 36 (137 BC, or later), "in the nomes in which the harvest tax is paid."

[11] See *P.Tebt.* IV, pp. 11–12, for half-artaba and one-artaba taxes, *P.Lips.* II 124, line 87 with note for two-artaba taxes.

[12] Further on this subject see Crawford (1971: 53–85) (with the caution of **7.2.5** introduction); Verhoogt (1998: 107–48), both heavily Arsinoite in emphasis; Rupprecht (1984), on *parachôrêsis*.

By comparison with later periods, Ptolemaic leases in Greek were relatively homogeneous and standard in format, although we should not infer from this that they were rarely made; the series of at least eighteen lease abstracts from Tebtunis for 223/2 BC suggests otherwise (*P. Tebt.* III.1 815; cf. the eight leases in the register of contracts from Theogenis, *CPR* XVIII). But the number and certainly the complexity and variety of lease contracts do appear to increase in the Roman period in consequence of the expansion in the amount of private landed property, and the development of a moderately prosperous urban elite, whose landed properties were better suited to leasing out in parcels to local tenants than to the direct management employed by large estates.[13]

The implications of Roman rule for the development of lease contracts are much less straightforward to identify at a more detailed level. Apart from the replacement of witnesses by subscriptions as the means of authentication, it is hard to pinpoint Roman influence on the subsequent development of the various types of lease contracts. Leases exhibit few obviously "Roman" features even after the *Constitutio Antoniniana*, beyond the inclusion of the *stipulatio* clause that becomes a standard feature of leases (and other contracts) shortly afterwards.

There is still much scope for further research along the same lines as that already begun by Uri Yiftach-Firanko (forthcoming) to uncover the underlying reasons for the regional variations and changes in legal format and other characteristics. In particular, we need to look not only for general regional differences, and that between *metropolis* and village, but more closely at the specific local context to which the extant leases belong. Their survival (like that of all documentary papyri) is far from random, and is skewed by particular archives or other groups of texts, which can distort our perception of general regional trends. Close attention to the exact provenience of the documents, especially those that are part of private or official archives, is as important to furthering our understanding of legal history as it is in using the leases for economic and social analysis.

The above considerations aside, the standard content of all leases included identification of the lessor(s) and lessee(s), and the land or other object leased (often including the crops to be grown); the duration of the contract; details of the rent and how it was to be paid; and normally, clauses guaranteeing the rights and obligations of both parties. But both the diplomatic format of the documents and the conventions regarding the

[13] For an excellent treatment of the transition from Ptolemaic to Roman governance, see Monson (2012).

inclusion and order of particular clauses varied considerably with time and place. The double *syngraphê* with six witnesses, standard in the Ptolemaic period for both leases and other types of legal documents (**7.2.1**, **7.2.2**; cf. **5.2.2**), was replaced in the Roman period by a range of new formats, the parameters being whether they were notarial (**7.2.6**) or private documents, and objective or subjective in style.

The distinctive legal system of Alexandria apparently preferred the *synchôrêsis* format (**7.2.3**). In Oxyrhynchos, the so-called "private protocol" was typical ("x has leased to y": **7.3.8–9**). Elsewhere, the *homologia* was common ("x acknowledges that he has leased to y": **7.3.7**). The subjective style is exemplified particularly by the *cheirographon* (handwritten agreement), a private document in the form of a letter ("x to y, greetings. I have leased from you . . ."; cf. **7.3.6a**). A type of lease that from the start of the Roman period became gradually more common, until by the mid-third century it was predominant, was the *hypomnêma*, "offer of lease" ("I wish/undertake to lease from you . . .": **7.3.5**; **7.3.10–12**).[14]

The abandonment of the double document and change from authenticating contracts by witnesses to signed subscriptions resulted from administrative reforms in the late Ptolemaic and early Roman periods (Muhs 2005a: 97, Yiftach-Firanko 2008b and above, **2.1**). But the regional differences in the preferred diplomatic formats, and gradual nature of the spread of the *hypomnêma*, suggest that the detailed evolution of lease formats was prompted less by government action than by the particular socio-economic and scribal conditions in which the contracts were drawn up. Undoubtedly a major change was the move from types of documents drawn up in the *grapheion* or given some other form of public registration to private agreements, which at Oxyrhynchos had taken place at the very start of the Roman period with the use of the "private protocol." In the Arsinoite (and the Hermopolite) the progressive spread of the *hypomnêma* format (which originated in Ptolemaic bids for state land) had the same effect. Thus, while land leases composed almost one-quarter of all the contracts drawn up through the *grapheion* of Tebtunis in the year AD 45/6 (*P.Mich.* II 123; Rowlandson 1999: 141), second-century Arsinoite *grapheion* registers (much less complete) seem rarely to include leases (Yiftach-Firanko 2007: 1057 n. 26).

The simplified procedure involved in private agreements made good sense for what was essentially an ephemeral arrangement (in contrast to

[14] For further details on these formats, see Herrmann (1958: 20–39), Müller (1985: 18–82).

sales or other permanent dispositions of property), with one year the most common lease duration. Leases were rarely for more than four-year terms even at their peak average length in the Roman period, although renewals were not uncommon (see **7.3.6**). The private use of the lease *hypomnêma* seems to have originated with very short-term arrangements for harvesting tree crops, especially olives and dates, where speed was clearly more important than the security brought by public registration (Yiftach-Firanko 2007: 1055); but neither this nor the earlier view that the *hypomnêma* format reflects the increased social gap between landlord and tenant in the Roman period (cf. Yiftach-Firanko 2007: 1052) entirely explains the ever-increasing popularity of the *hypomnêma*, which by the end of the third century was the dominant format even in Oxyrhynchos.

The flexibility of the lease contract enabled it to accommodate considerable variation in the status of lessors and lessees. In the Roman period, typically the lessor was the wealthier and more literate party, but this situation could be reversed, particularly in the so-called "prodomatic" leases where rent was paid in advance and could thus function as loans. Similarly, while the balance of guarantee clauses normally provided greater legal protection to the lessor, most leases also provided some legal protection for the tenant (cf. Kehoe 1995).

7.1 Ptolemaic Demotic land leases

Cary J. Martin

The majority of Demotic instruments of lease were written in the period between the end of August and the beginning of November, i.e., just before work on the land was to begin.[15] There are some exceptions, which are probably to be explained as either due to individual requirements or as cases where the written documentation records an already existing state of affairs.[16] The leases normally run for one agricultural year, "from the water of regnal year X to (that of) regnal year Y," although in practice the work would only have commenced when the floodwaters receded.[17]

[15] This is also the case with the Greek documents; see the very useful table combining the Demotic and Greek material in Felber (1997b: 287–89).

[16] As, e.g., in *P.Tor.Botti* 43; see Pestman in Boswinkel and Pestman (1978: 10 n. j). *P.Reinach Dem.* 1 was probably written after the work had commenced and was to run for two harvests (following Felber 1997a: 127–28). See also the comments of Pestman (1961: 27 and 52) regarding the "marriage documents."

[17] See Felber (1997a: 126). In *P.Tor.Amen.* 17 the period of leasing is explicitly stated to be nine months. There are, however, exceptions, where the period of leasing was intended to run for longer; see, e.g., the texts mentioned in the preceding note, *P.Mil.Vogl.* III *Dem.* 1 (two years), *P. Reinach*

The documents are written as unilateral declarations, although there are two problematic cases that contain statements by both parties (**7.1.1** and *P.Reinach Dem.* 5).[18] In Upper Egypt the documents are drawn up with the lessee addressing the lessor: "you have leased to me."[19] In the Fayyum it is the lessor that speaks to the lessee: "I have leased to you." These texts also record the prepayment of rent, which is a feature of documents from the Fayyum, but rarely attested in Upper Egypt. The principle, established by Hughes,[20] that it was the party who was in the weaker economic position who had the document drawn up, still holds in the majority of cases.[21] When the texts mention prepayment of rent, this could refer either just to straightforward prepayment (called a "prodomatic" lease in Greek papyrology; see **7.3.7**) or to the use of the revenue of the land to repay a loan (an "antichretic" lease; see **5.5.1**).[22]

The act of leasing involves the transfer of usufruct for a limited period; it does not involve the transfer of ownership, which remains with the "landowner."[23] The lessors invariably belong to the priesthood.[24] The lessees sometimes carry priestly titles, but we also find here members of the military and people with Greek names, as well as individuals provided with so-called ethnic designations ("Greek born in Egypt," "man of Philae," etc., which probably had a military connection).[25] The introductory statement of leasing is followed by a description of the land concerned, typically accompanied by the mention of the neighboring plots to the south, north, east, and west (in order to clarify its location). The lessee is required to plough the land and the texts usually stipulate that he is responsible for providing all the seed, oxen, laborers, and farming implements.[26]

Dem. 5 (four years, originally three), and *P.Geb.Heidelberg* 14 (two years). The Cairo leases from Tebtunis published by Spiegelberg (1960/08) mentioned above (see n. 1) refer to periods of leasing of up to seven years.

18 On the concepts involved, see Herrmann (1975) and Mrsich (1994: 177–78), who summarizes the views of legal historians.

19 The word translated "lease" is the Demotic *sḥn*, which has a wide range of meanings, including "to hand over something to a person's care," "to commit," or "to entrust"; see Pestman *et al.* (1977, vol. 2: 102).

20 Hughes (1973: 152–53).

21 An exception is *P.Tor.Botti* 25C, which reads, line 15, "for whose taxes and rent I have already paid you in full," but which is nonetheless drawn up by the lessee in accordance with normal Upper Egyptian practice; see Hughes (1973: 159) and Felber (1997a: 118–19).

22 On the complicated question of prodomatic and antichretic leases, see Hughes (1973: 152–53), Felber (1997a: 209–10), Monson (2005: 82), Markiewicz (2005: 158–60), and Martin (2009b: 131 n. lvii). [See above, **5.5.1** (loan with antichretic lease), with **5.5** introduction, and **7.3.7** (prodomatic sublease) – eds.]

23 See the term *pꜣ nb n nꜣ ꜣḥw*, "the owner of the lands," in the Hermopolis Legal Code (Seidl 1973b: 14–16). Also relevant are the comments of Mrsich (2003: 86–87 and 108–10).

24 See the list in Felber (1997a: 99–106).

25 Felber (1997a: 106–14) and La'da (2007).

26 **7.1.1**, lines 11–12, and **7.1.3**, line 8; see Sethe and Partsch (1920: 170 § 41).

Different categories and sizes of land are the subject of the leases, but the land in question invariably belongs to the temple,[27] which is consistent with the lessors being members of the priesthood. It is, however, significant that, while the texts deal with the payment of rent to the lessor and taxes to the state, they rarely refer to any payment to the temple.[28] There are two possible explanations for this. The royal granaries were responsible for redistribution of part of the harvest to the temples (the *syntaxis*), so indirectly a proportion of the taxes going to the state was in effect going to the temple.[29] Alternatively, or in addition, we should consider the possibility that the rent to the lessor, who is a member of the priesthood, included part of the temple income. In this way, the priest's stipend is paid, either in whole or in part, not by the temple but by the farmer to whom he has leased the land on the temple's behalf.[30] In the pre-Ptolemaic period, however, the taxes on temple land were paid directly to the temples.[31] This may have also been the case in the early Ptolemaic period,[32] but certainly after the revolt of Hurgonaphor and Chaonnophris in 206/5–186 BC the state was directly controlling the collection. The limited data on the harvest tax that we possess for the third century would suggest that this was also the case in the period immediately leading up to the revolt.[33]

27 The land concerned often belongs to the "god's offering" of the relevant deity; see, e.g., **7.1.1**, line 4 ("of Amun"), and **7.1.3**, line 6 ("of Wepwawet").

28 Only two Ptolemaic texts explicitly mention temple taxes: *P.Ryl.* 34 and our **7.1.2** (our **7.1.4** dates to the Roman period); see Hughes (1952: 38–39 § aa). There are also certain texts that record land leased directly from the temple; see, e.g., Felber (1997a: 104–05). Also relevant is the "model" lease of garden land, P.Brit.Mus. EA 10648, which notes the payment by the lessee of the *apomoira* of one-sixth of the produce to the temple of Sobek; see Martin (2009a: 206 n. xx).

29 There are a number of Ptolemaic receipts that record the payment of the harvest tax for the temple *syntaxis*; see, e.g., Lichtheim (1957: 11–12) and Vandorpe (2000a: 182), who cites two Demotic receipts for the harvest tax in the Memnoneia that show that "part of the harvest tax of Pharaoh is handed over to the Egyptian priesthood." In the Roman period the situation is different. A series of receipts from Medinet Habu shows the rent (*ḥw ḥwv*) for temple lands (that were leased from the temple itself) being paid to the granary of the *stratêgos*; see Lichtheim (1957: 33–36).

30 Under this scenario the lessor is acting as an agent of the temple, not as the "real" owner of the land, although invariably he would de facto be this and over time the land would be viewed as his private property.

31 In the Saite leases the texts refer to the payment of taxes to the temple but never to the state; see Hughes (1952: 38 § aa).

32 The evidence for the third century BC is very limited; see Muhs (2005b: 61–62).

33 Vandorpe (2000a: 177). In an Elephantine text we see the *thebarch* instructing the *lesonis* of Chnum to proceed with the collection of the harvest of the god's offering on the basis of the previous year's survey and to have this delivered to the state granaries; see Martin (1996, no. C12). If the text were to date to 199 BC (216 BC is also possible), which is when Pharaoh regained possession of Thebes (Pestman 1995a: 105), the disruption caused by the troubles would explain why that year's survey had not taken place.

Ptolemaic texts from Upper Egypt typically state that it is the lessee who pays the taxes to the state,[34] while in the Fayyum and Akoris the lessor is responsible.[35] In Upper Egypt the tax is a harvest tax; in Middle Egypt and the Fayyum it is a land tax.[36] The Ptolemaic receipts-of-measuring from Upper Egypt, on the basis of which the harvest tax was calculated, are usually in the lessee's name (and typically only in the lessor's name when he cultivated the land himself).[37] This is, accordingly, consistent with the lessee's paying the taxes to the state granaries. It should be noted, however, that in a number of leases the lessee has to have the "receipt-of-payment" for the taxes from the royal granaries made out under the lessor's name.[38] So, although the tax-assessment on the leased land was made out in the lessee's name, the lessor in these cases knew that ultimately he would be held responsible for the taxes and therefore wanted the proof of payment in his name. The Ptolemaic leases do not provide any information on how much harvest tax was to be paid,[39] which in any case would not be known at the time the lease was written between the end of August and the beginning of November (see above) and could only be calculated later on, when the second survey of the crops grown on each field was taken (February/March).[40] The texts frequently contain a commitment by the lessee that he will farm the land, which is important because, if it were left uncultivated, not only would the lessor not receive his rent but also there would be no harvest to pay the taxes. In a number of texts there is an

[34] Exceptions include **7.1.2**, *P.Tor.Botti* 25C and *P.Bürg.* 9 (possibly, as the text was subsequently imperfectly corrected by the scribe; see Felber 1997a: 142 and 151–52). See also *P. Cairo* 30683+31012 (Felber 1997a: 72), where (line x+9) the lessees say that they are to pay the lessor the rent and "its harvest tax" (*ḥnʿ p3y=s šmw*), which means that here too it would appear (the text is fragmentary) that the lessor is responsible for paying the state. The lessor also pays the harvest tax in the Greek lease from the Archive of Totoes, but the situation here is atypical for a number of reasons; see Pestman in Boswinkel and Pestman (1978: 19 and 27 n. l).

[35] In one of the two Asyut papyri (**7.1.3**), the lessee pays, but in the summary *P.Brit.Mus. EA* 10595 the two parties pay together.

[36] For Ptolemaic land taxes and terminology, see Monson (2012: 172–84).

[37] In Demotic *iw-n-ḫy*. These have convincingly been identified with the *r.rḫ=w* documents by Vandorpe (2000a: 176 and 189; 2002a: 392). In **7.1.3**, lines 10–11, it would appear that the receipt-of-measuring is written for the lessor, as he has to show it to the lessee to determine the extent of cultivable land on which the rent of 3 artabas of wheat per aroura is to be calculated.

[38] E.g., *P.Berlin.Spieg.* 3102, line 16, and *P.Tor.Botti* 19, lines 6–7; see Sethe and Partsch (1920: 178–79 § 51–52). For examples of Ptolemaic harvest-tax receipts, see, e.g., n. 29 above; Wångstedt (1954: 40–41 and nos. 41–42; 1965, nos. 14–15); and Vleeming (1994, nos. 37–38).

[39] On the rates of harvest tax, see Vandorpe (2000a: 196) and the comments of Muhs (2005b: 61–62).

[40] The tax would be dependent on the location, the type and quality of the land, the crops grown on it, and the inundation; see Vandorpe (2000a: 175 and 185–87). The first survey was made to assess the size of the plot as soon as the land was sufficiently visible after the floodwaters had receded.

additional clause that gives the lessor protection against any loss caused by neglect on the part of the lessee.[41]

The rent is in nearly every case to be paid in produce rather than money.[42] In only a limited number of texts are both the size of the land and that of the rent given (or have survived), so calculating an average rent is problematic, particularly as the type of land would also affect the yield.[43] Although in most Ptolemaic leases the rent is given as a fixed amount, there are also a limited number of texts that are structured as sharecropping agreements, with a percentage of the product being delivered to the lessor.[44] Wheat is the usual crop that is cultivated,[45] but some texts stipulate specific products, including flax,[46] arakos,[47] spelt, barley, and the castor oil plant,[48] and in one text even onions and grass *inter alia*.[49] A time for delivery of the rent is stated in some papyri and this is usually in June or on occasion into July.[50] An allowance for a delay of one month is sometimes granted, but this incurs a penalty of an additional 50 percent.[51] It is often stated that the lessee cannot claim to have paid the rent unless he possesses a valid receipt.[52]

[41] Following Brinker *et al.* (2005: B, 834–35).

[42] The one exception is *P.Mil.Vogl.* III *Dem.* 1, where a cash payment is due (but for the year in question the land was not planted in grain). In *P.Reinach Dem.* 5, a lease of garden land, the lessee promises to pay in cash anything that he does not pay in produce from the harvest (with an increase of around one-and-a-quarter times the market value; see Boswinkel and Pestman 1982: 113 n. q). In the "model" lease P.Brit.Mus. EA 10648, front, line 11, which interestingly also concerns garden land, the rent is to be paid in either grain or money (although the reading is not entirely certain; Martin 2009a: 206 n. xix). It may simply be coincidence that both *P.Mil.Vogl.* III *Dem.* 1 and P.Brit. Mus. EA 10648 come from Tebtunis.

[43] Felber (1997a: 152–58) lists the evidence and makes some cautious observations. To his examples can be added that of *P.Brit.Mus. EA* 10648 (see preceding note), where the rent, if paid in cash, would be 2 *deben* on 10 arouras of garden land.

[44] See, e.g., **7.1.2**, where one-fifth of the produce is to be delivered to the lessor (but which includes the state taxes as well as the rent; in *P. Strassburg* 9 the rent is one-tenth, the lessee presumably being responsible for the taxes). In the Saite leases from Thebes the rent was calculated on a percentage basis, the normal division of the crop being one-third to the lessor and two-thirds to the lessee; see Vleeming (1991: 83 n. mm). In these texts the lessor was responsible for paying the taxes (to the temple, not the state; see n. 31). For a sharecropping lease of the Roman period, see **7.3.4**.

[45] See Felber (1997a: 152–54).

[46] **7.1.2** and *P.Tor.Botti* 30 (= Felber 1997a: 26–29).

[47] *P.Tor.Botti* 43 (see Pestman in Boswinkel and Pestman 1978: 11 n. l) and *P.Tor.Botti* 30.

[48] *P.Ryl.* 26.

[49] *P.Bürg.* 9.

[50] Felber (1997a: 157–58) provides an overview of the dates and notes some exceptions. The payment date of April/May in **7.1.2** is because the crop is flax and this would be harvested earlier.

[51] See, e.g., **7.1.1**, line 17.

[52] For examples of rental receipts, see Lichtheim (1957, no. 128), Nur el-Din (1974, nos. 66–72), and Devauchelle (1983: 135 (*ODL* 103), 139 (*ODL* 108), 139–40 (*ODL* 115), 140–1 (*ODL* 146), 142 (*ODL* 270), 143–4 (*ODL* 538+542), 146 (*ODL* 912), and 148–9 (*ODL* E 9075)).

Although the texts invariably state that the document is to run until the next inundation and dates are often specified for the delivery of the rent at the conclusion of the transaction,[53] an additional clause stipulates that the document remains in force until it has been returned: "I will not be able to say, 'I carried out for you the right (of) the lease which is above,' <while> the lease which is above is in your hand" (see **7.1.2**). In one document, the lessee explicitly says that he will leave the land and "give to you your lease."[54] Although it would appear that in most cases the document was kept by one of the two parties, when the text contains statements by both parties, it was presumably kept by a trustee.[55] The lessee often confirms that he will vacate the land at the end of the period of the transaction and the lessor will be able to lease it to whomever he wishes. The texts frequently state that the lessee cannot claim that the length of the lease has been extended.[56] His existing and future property is pledged as security of his commitments. Financial penalties ensue if the terms of the document are not adhered to or if the lessee is prevented from farming the land.[57]

It is improbable that every leasing transaction was recorded in writing,[58] so the obvious question is why in a certain number of instances the parties felt the need for a written document. In the case of the transactions that involve prepayment of rent, the text is also, in effect, a receipt, so the need for the transaction to be recorded in writing is here clear. For the other texts, we have to assume that there were particular circumstances that led one or both of the parties to require proof of the transaction.[59] In this respect, the evidence of the

53 Felber (1997a: 176–79). 54 P.Brit.Mus. EA 10496 (unpublished); see Martin (1986: 172).

55 See the introduction to **7.1.1** and Markiewicz (2005: 164–65).

56 E.g., **7.1.2**, lines 8–9; Felber (1997a: 180–84).

57 Felber (1997a: 185–95) for details; see **7.1.1**, lines 20–23, and **7.1.3**, lines 15–16. According to the Hermopolis Legal Code (Mattha and Hughes 1975, Donker van Heel 1990, and Stadler 2004), the lessor has to pay the lessee one-quarter of the harvest if he prevents him (i.e., the lessee) from cultivating the land. This is not a particularly severe penalty (see the evidence of the Saite leases, where the lessee typically kept two-thirds of the harvest [see n. 44], and Donker van Heel 1998: 96), which may be the reason why the documents mention a considerably larger penalty, i.e., the lessee required better protection than that provided by the law codes or case-law.

58 See Eyre (1999: 50–51). The state would not require any formal documentation between the two parties because the receipts-of-measuring were made out in the lessee's name (except when the lessor farmed the land himself) and the identity of the lessee would be known from the land survey; see Keenan and Shelton (1976: 7).

59 We can speculate on what these might have been, e.g., security, the need for clarity on the value of the rent, responsibility for paying the taxes, period of the leasing, dates for delivery of the rent, trustworthiness of the parties, and so forth. Written documentation, of course, would remove the case for any argument about who provided the seed or the oxen for ploughing.

Hermopolis Legal Code is worth highlighting[60] because here we find a series of cases of dispute and recommendations on how they should be resolved.[61] Also relevant are those temple-oaths that concern disputes concerning aspects of leasing transactions that had only been recorded orally.[62]

We also have to consider the reasons why, when the period of the transaction was over and the document accordingly returned to the relevant party, it was kept by the recipient. Perhaps the papyri were initially retained "just in case" some dispute subsequently arose and then remained in the archive because there was no requirement to sift through the old papyri (the same arguments would apply to the presence of loan documents many years after the repayment).[63] The documents would, however, also serve as proof of ownership of the land in question, i.e., the fact that he was able to lease the land would demonstrate that the lessor was the "owner" of it.[64] Usually the extant leases have been found in the archives of the lessor,[65] to whom they will have been returned at the end of the transaction, but one particular interesting anomaly is in the Archive of Amenothes, where the document was kept by the lessee, Amenothes, and not returned to the lessor. This has led to the conclusion that, in this instance at least, two copies of the document were probably drawn up. That this was the general practice in leasing transactions is a possibility, but certainly no more than that.[66] No record of a second document is found in any land lease, but in a lease of funerary properties and endowments there is mention of the existence of a reciprocal document.[67]

60 See n. 57.

61 Cols. I and II are concerned with the leasing of land. The examples in Col. II, lines 1–11, are listed under the heading of "seed-corn"; see Donker van Heel (1998: 95–96).

62 These are discussed in Mrsich (1994); see Grunert (1994: 394).

63 As Pestman remarked in the context of drafts of documents (1994a: 247), the Egyptians liked to possess a full documentation of their belongings and would have kept papyri "just in case."

64 Pestman (1981a: 146).

65 See, e.g., the leases in the Archive of Totoes from Deir el-Medineh; see Botti (1967) and Pestman (1981a). In many cases, of course, we have no details of provenance so there is no way of knowing where the document may have been kept.

66 So Pestman (1981a: 140–41).

67 P.Brit.Mus. EA 10384, line 23 (= *P. Malcolm*); see Martin (2009b: 120), "I am [behind you] through the lease which you made for me." On the other hand, the expression I am to "give to you your lease" (see n. 54) would argue in favor of one document being written and returned to the lessor at the end of the period of the transaction. The practice may have varied from place to place (and over time); see Pestman in Boswinkel and Pestman (1978: 20), who suggests that the *agoranomos* may have had two documents drawn up, one for each party.

7.1.1 Demotic lease of temple land

P.Brit.Mus. EA 10560 (Martin 1986) (Philadelphia, Fayyum, 5 September/4 October 190 BC). Image at *JEA* 72 (1986), Plates XIII–XIV.

Additional bibliography: Felber (1997: *passim* [see index, 232]), Mrsich (2003: 43–54).

This is the earliest example of a land lease from the Ptolemaic period and also the most unusual in that it contains declarations by both parties and then a joint statement. It comes from Philadelphia (Darb el-Gerza) in the Fayyum and concerns the leasing of three arouras of land belonging to the temple estate of Amun and located in the "Field of Tanis" (a village that lies roughly 10 km to the southwest of Philadelphia). In the first section of the text after the date (lines 6–26), the lessor is the addressor and the lease, following the custom in the Fayyum, is paid in advance. In lines 18–20 the prepayment of half the rent is acknowledged. So, in effect, the document also functions as a receipt for the lessee. The lease is to run for one year, and the lessee is to pay rent at the rate of 1⅓ artabas of wheat per aroura of land (in total four artabas). If this is not delivered by the last day of Payni (4 August), there will be a penalty charge of 50 percent. Responsibility for the state taxes lies with the lessor. If anyone tries to deprive the lessee of the land, the lessor is liable for a significant financial penalty. He pledges the security of his property if he does not act in accordance with the stipulations of the lease. A short line is then drawn and the text continues with a statement by the lessee (lines 26–29) in which he acknowledges that the land has been leased to him and that he will pay the rent, even if he leaves the land. The scribe then adds (lines 29–32) a joint declaration by the two parties in which they pledge their property as security, confirm that the lease will only be valid for the one year and that they will not be able to claim that they have fulfilled their obligations while the lease "stands" between them. On the back of the papyrus there are the names of twelve witnesses and also a one-line notation containing a short description of the contents.

As the document contains statements by both parties, as well as a joint declaration, it can hardly have been kept by either one of them. Although the text does not explicitly say, it seems most likely that the document was entrusted to a *ʿrbt* (= Greek *syngraphophylax*).[68] As it was tied and sealed, one can assume that it was only to be opened in the case of a dispute.

[68] A third-party keeper of the document.

In the following translations, a superscript "l.p.h." represents a Demotic abbreviation typically placed after the mention of Pharaoh, the living king, or the king's name, meaning "Life, Prosperity, Health."

Recto (1) Regnal year 15, fourth month of *shemu*, under Pharaoh$^{\text{l.p.h.}}$ P[to]lemy$^{\text{l.p.h.}}$, son of P[t]olemy [$^{\text{l.p.h.}}$,] and Ar<s>inoe, (2) the Gods Philopatores; the Priest (of) Alex[ander] and the Gods Adelphoi, the Gods Euergetai, the Gods (3) Philopatores, (and) the Gods Epiphaneis being Antipatros son of Dionysios; Batra (4) daughter of Hi[pp]alos being *athlophoros* before Berenice Euergetis; Athenodora (5) [being *kanê*]*phoros* before Arsinoe Philadelphos; (and) Eirene being the Prieste[ss of] Arsinoe Philopator.

(6) Said (the) guardian [of] the R[a]m [of] (the) Sobek-town of Philadelphia together with (the) Sobek-town of Perhat, (7) priest of Amenem[ope] of the te[mple] of Amenemope at Philadelphia that is above, Petesouchos son of Herieus, who is called (8) . . ., his mother [Cher]etanch, to (the) farmer Herakleides son of Kallistratos, his mother Kolluthes:

(9) "I have leased to you 3 (arouras of) land, [their half] 1½ (arouras of) land, making 3 (arouras of) land [again, of the] god's-[offering of] the Ram of the town that is above in the Field (10) of Tanis, whose neighbors are:

"[south], the Street of [Pharaoh$^{\text{l.p.h.}}$];

"[north], the god's-offering of Anubis;

"east, the canal;

"west, (11) the god's-offering of Harmotnis.

"Total of the neighbors of the lands that are above again.

"You are to fill them with cattle (and) equipment; you are to carry out all the agricultural (12) work with your equipment of free man . . . from year 15, fourth month of *shemu*, until year 16, third month of *shemu*, (13) makes one year of sowing.[69]

"You are to pay <to> me the rent of the lands that are above at the rate of 1⅓ artabas (of) wheat to 1 (aroura of) land, which amounts to 4 artabas (of) wheat, (14) their half 2, makes 4 (artabas of) wheat again.

"The rent (of) the 3 (arouras of) land that are above for the one year is to be all in seed-grain that is pure, unadulterated, (15) (and) measured

[69] If the period of leasing runs from 1 Mesore until 30 Epeiph that would be exactly one year; so Felber (1997a: 128).

by the receiving-measure of Pharaoh,[l.p.h.] and [its scraper],[70] which is sound, (and) transported (and) delivered to me (16) at my house that is (in) Philadelphia [in] year 16, first month of *shemu* (or) second month of *shemu*, compulsorily, without delay.

"As for the seed-grain thereof (17) that you[71] fail to deliver (in) its [time of] delivery that is above, you will deliver it with its additional one half[72] in the month after the said month, (18) compulsorily, without delay.

"You have given to me 2 artabas of wheat, their half 1, makes 2 artabas of wheat again, subject to claim. (19) I have received them from you, my heart being satisfied with them, they being complete without any remainder; I am to take them; I am (20) to credit them to your account within the days that are above of the one year that is above.

"If I hold back the lands that are above from you (21) (or) if any man on earth casts you out from them, I will cause that they are far from you. If I do not cause that they are far from you, (22) I will give to you money, 100 (*deben*), their half makes money, 50 (*deben*), makes money, [100 (*deben*)], again, in one day within five days of not causing that they are far from you, (23) which I will do, compulsorily, without delay. You are still behind me [to cause] that they are far from you in the one year that is above.

"Everything that is mine (24) together with that which I will acquire is the security of the right of the lease that is above.

"I will not be able to say: 'I have acted in accordance with every word above,' (25) while the lease stands between us. You are behind me to perform them in accordance with every word above, compulsorily, without delay; I am to cause to be far every (26) matter (of) Pharaoh[[l.p.h.]73] that will arise behind you concerning them (in the) name of the [lands] (in) the time which is above." – –

Herakleides who is above says (27) to Petesouchos son of Herieus who is above:

"You have leased to me the 3 (arouras of) land (of) the god's-offering of Amun that are above; I am to pay their rent in accordance with (28) that which is written that is above. If I abandon the lands that are above

[70] Greek *skutalê*; see Pestman *et al.* (1977, vol. 2: 47 n. p).

[71] The first and second person suffix pronouns have been confused here and the text has been emended accordingly. There is similar confusion in lines 19 (corrected from "you are to take them" to "I am to take them") and 25 (from "I am behind you" to "you are behind me"). The suggestions by Mrsich (2003: 48–51) to avoid these emendations are ingenious but not convincing; see Martin (2005: 490 n. 3).

[72] "Its one to one-and-a-half" = Greek *hêmiolia* (or *hêmiolion*); see Pierce (1972: 57 § 49). See also the introductions to **5.1.2** and **5.2** (in the framework of loans).

[73] "Every matter (of) Pharaoh," i.e., the land tax; see the introduction.

by [not work]ing them in the time that is above, I will pay to you their rent, (29) <in accordance with> that which is written that is above, compulsorily, without delay."

While they, the two people [who are above], say with one mouth:

"All and everything that is ours together with that which we will (30) acquire is the security of the right of the lease [that is above]. We will not be able to say, 'This is a lease that has changed (as to) year.' (31) We will not be able to say, 'We have acted in accordance with every word that is above,' while the lease that is above stands between us. One is behind his companion among us (32) to act in accordance with every word that is above, compulsorily, without delay."

(In the) writing of Petebastis son of Amenneus.

Verso: [A] lease that Petesouchos son of Herieus made for Herakleides for 3 (arouras of) land (of) the god's-offering (of) Amun (*seal*) for the crop (of) regnal year 16.

Twelve witness signatures

7.1.2 Demotic lease of temple land

P.Brit.Mus. EA 10230 (Reich 1914: 77–82; Felber 1997a: 7–15) (Thebes, 7 October 177 BC). Images at *P.Brit.Mus. Reich*, Plates XV–XVI and XVIII.

Additional bibliography: Pestman *et al.* (1977, vol. 2: 73–80), Brinker *et al.* (2005: A, 1–2).

This instrument of lease is drawn up by the lessee in accordance with standard Upper Egyptian practice. Both parties are members of the priesthood. The lessee is a *pastophoros* of Amun of Djême and the lessor the holder of a series of priestly offices attached to the burial-place of the Sacred Ibis and Falcon and the Sanctuary of the deified Amenothes son of Hapu. The object of the lease is high land that belongs to the temple estate of Amun and is located in an area on the west bank at Thebes. The land is to be cultivated with flax and the lease is to run for nine months (from 7 October to 2 July). The lessee is to pay one-fifth of the harvest to the lessor by 2 June at the latest.[74] This payment will include

[74] The period between sowing and harvesting for flax is about three months, depending on the purpose to which the fibers are to be put (the age of the plant at the time of harvest affects the use); see Vogelsang-Eastwood (2000: 270). The harvest time for flax at Thebes is considered to be around mid-March to mid-April; see Guglielmi (1977: 256) and Allen (2002: 134). Our text, however, suggests a slightly later two-month window for the harvest from the beginning of April to the end of May (line 6).

both rent and harvest tax.[75] Nothing can be taken from the land until this one-fifth is paid. The text states explicitly that the lessor is responsible for paying the taxes to the state and also to the temple.[76] The payment dates and the length of the period of the leasing are non-negotiable. The obligations to fulfil the terms of the leasing lie with the lessee and his children and remain in force as long as the document is in the lessor's possession. The existing and future property of the lessee is security for his commitments and the representative of the lessor has authorization over all matters.

Recto (1) Regnal year 5, first month of *akhet*, (day) 2, under Pharaoh$^{\text{l.p.h.}}$ Ptolemy$^{\text{l.p.h.}}$ son of Ptolemy$^{\text{l.p.h.}}$ and Kleopatra$^{\text{l.p.h}}$ the Gods Epiphaneis, and the Priest (of) Alexander$^{\text{l.p.h}}$ and the Gods Adelphoi, the Gods Euergetai, the Gods Philopatores, the Gods Epiphaneis and Pharaoh$^{\text{l.p.h.}}$ Ptole[my$^{\text{l.p.h.}}$] (2) Philometor, and the *athlophoros* (of) Berenice$^{\text{l.p.h.}}$ Euergetis, and the *kanêphoros* before Arsinoe$^{\text{l.p.h}}$ Philadelphos, and the Priestess (of) Arsinoe$^{\text{l.p.h}}$ Philopator, in accordance with those who are established in Alexandria; Hippalos son of Sosos being Priest (in) the Thebaid (of) Ptolemy$^{\text{l.p.h.}}$ Soter$^{\text{l.p.h.}}$ and (3) Ptolemy$^{\text{l.p.h.}}$ the God Epiphanes Eucharistos;[77] Kineas son of Dositheos being Priest (of) Pharaoh $^{\text{l.p.h.}}$ Ptolemy$^{\text{l.p.h.}}$ and Kleopatra$^{\text{l.p.h.}}$ his mother; and the *kanêphoros* before Arsinoe$^{\text{l.p.h.}}$ Philadelphos.[78]

Said (the) *pastophoros* (of) Amun (of) Djême Nesiahnefer,[79] son of Patymis, <his> mother Senminis, to (the) servant-of-the-god, priest (and) *pastophoros* (of) every office (and) every commission[80] (4) (of) the resting-place (of) the Ibis (and) the Falcon, which is in the necropolis (of) Djême, (and) the Sanctuary of (the) royal scribe Amenothes son of Hapu,[81] the great god, Amenothes son of Horos, his mother Senchonsis:[82]

75 This is unusual, as in Ptolemaic leases from Upper Egypt the lessee typically pays the harvest tax directly to the state; see the introduction.

76 Even though most of the Ptolemaic leases concern temple land, it is rare that mention is made of a payment to the temple; see the introduction.

77 For the translation of the epithet, see Depauw (2002: 115–16).

78 The final part of the protocol, "and the *kanêphoros* before Arsinoe$^{\text{l.p.h.}}$ Philadelphos," is omitted from Felber's translation.

79 The reading of the name is uncertain; see Thirion (1988: 131–32), on the name Iʿḥ-nfr, with reference to Ranke (1935: 13.6).

80 On this title, see Pestman *et al.* (1977, vol. 2: 84–85, n. h) and Muhs (2005b: 189 n. 43).

81 This sanctuary of Amenothes son of Hapu may be that installed on the upper (and later also the lower) terrace of the temple of Hatshepsut at Deir el-Bahari; see Łajtar (2006: 19–31).

82 On Amenothes, son of Horos, his titles and activities, see Łajtar (2006: 70–80).

"You have leased to me your share (of) high land in the 'Sand'[83] (in) the resting-place (of) the Ibis (of) the god's-offering (of) Amun (in) the places (in) the west (of) Thebes (in) Pestenemenophis,[84] which is assigned to[85] Djême, (in) the west (of) the Pathyrite nome,[86] on the southern side of the said 'Sand,' to which the share of Amenothes son of Thotsytmis (5) belongs.[87] Their neighbors:

"south, the land (that) is far before[88] (the) royal scribe Amenothes son of Hapu;

"north, the remainder (of) the said land (of the) 'Sand,' which is in the possession of Harsiesis son of Horos and you;

"east, the land (of) Psenchonsis son of Pabehet (and) Petechonsis, his children;

"west, the Street (of) Amun to Djême.

"Total (of) all the neighbors (of) the high land that is above, in which I made for you a lease for your high land (in the) 'Sand.'

"I am to harvest it[89] (6) as flax[90] land; I am to carry out all the work of flax farming in seed- (and) harvest-time;[91] you are to cite its accusation (of) any work of flax farming with me.

83 "The Sand" is a common name for a toponym and is found in a number of locations as well as at Thebes; see Pestman (1966: 316 n. 1), Cheshire (1987: 133), and Vleeming (1991: 57).

84 On Pestenemenophis, see Pestman in Boswinkel and Pestman (1978: 10 n. d and 199–200); to the examples cited can now be added *P.Louvre E* 9416, line 2 (Devauchelle 1987; "Amun" was overlooked in the transliteration) and *P.Brit.Mus. Andrews* 26, line 2 (Andrews 1990).

85 See Parker (1964: 98 n. d).

86 "The places in the West of Thebes" is probably the Perithebas (see Pestman 1993: 451–52). Initially the Perithebas and Pathyrite were both toparchies within one nome, but subsequently, during the first half of the second century BC, they became "true, independent nomes with their own toparchies"; so Vandorpe (1995a: 230). The evidence here would appear to suggest that, in 177 BC at least, the Perithebas was simply a toparchy within the Pathyrite nome; see Bataille (1952: 57 and 61).

87 This may be Tȝy, "to belong to" (Pestman 1993: 402), albeit in an Early rather than Middle Demotic form.

88 This presumably means that all the revenues belong to the god rather than the state; see Pestman *et al.* (1977, vol. 2: 78), Vandorpe (2000a: 190–91 n. 78), and Kaplony-Heckel (2001: 30–31).

89 While not attested to date in Demotic, the expression *ḥwy mḥ*, "to harvest flax" (see the next note), is known from hieroglyphic texts; see *Wb.* II: 121.6 and Hannig (2003: 551 and 781).

90 For the reading *mḥ*, "flax," see Quack (1999: 134).

91 The expression is conventionally rendered by "in winter (and) summer." Further on in this line, however, the text reads, "when harvest (*Šmw*) takes place in regnal year 5, the third month of the season of *pr.t* (or) fourth month of the season of *pr.t*," with the writing of *Šmw* identical to the earlier example in the line, but with *pr.t* written quite differently from the earlier example. As the second example of *Šmw* has to be a writing of the word for "harvest," this would suggest that the first example should also be so translated and *pr.t* in this clause taken as a reference to the act of sowing the crops rather than the winter season (so, originally, Thompson 1934: 75).

"When (the) harvest takes place in regnal year 5, third month of *peret* (or) fourth month of *peret*, I am to give to your representative [the one-fifth (in the) name] (of) the harvest tax (and) the rent of your flax-land that is above. Any flax (or) any plant that will grow in (7) your share (of) high land that is above, I am to give to you the one-fifth (of that) which will grow in it; you are to cause Pharaoh[l.p.h.], (and) the god to be far from me in your land that is above, while I will not be able to take any flax (or) plant out of your land that is above, without having [paid yo]ur one-fifth by regnal year 5, fourth month of *peret*, day 30, (and) I will not be able to give to you another time concerning it apart from the time that is above.

(8) "I will not be able to say, 'I gave you flax, money, (a) penalty, seed (or) anything on earth within the rent that is above,' without a valid receipt.

"I will not be able to say, 'I carried out for you the right (of) the lease that is above,' <while> the lease that is above is in your hand. It is on my head together with my children that the right (of) the lease that is above lies.

"When regnal year 5, first month of *shemu*, day 30, comes, I am to leave your share (of the) land that is above to you and you are to lease it (to) the person to whom you will wish to lease it. I will not be able to say, 'This is a lease which has changed (as to) year;' I am to act towards you in accordance with it at all times.

"All and everything that belongs to me together with that which I will acquire is security for every word that is above until I have acted for you in accordance with them. Your representative is the one who is to be believed concerning every word that he will speak with me (in the) name (of) every word which is above; and I am to do them at his request, without any blow."

(In the) writing (of) Amenothes son of Totoes, who writes (in the) name (of) the representatives of the prophetess of Djême.

Sixteen witness signatures on the verso

7.1.3 Demotic lease of temple land to a Greek cavalry officer

P.Brit.Mus. EA 10597 (Thompson 1934: 73–76; Felber 1997a: 61–64) (Asyut, 2 November 171 BC). Images at *P.Brit.Mus.Thompson*, Plates XXIX–XXX.

Additional bibliography: Brinker *et al.* (2005: A, 7–8).

This document belongs to the archive of the lector-priest Tefhapi that includes the proceedings of the famous lawsuit (Depauw 1997: 157). The lessor is Tefhapi himself and the lessee a Greek cavalryman, the owner of a *klêros* of eighty arouras. The lease is for Tefhapi's one-third part of two adjacent plots of land that in total amount to ten arouras that he owns with his brother Totoes[92] and that belong to the temple estate of Wepwawet. It is to run for one year. The lessee is responsible for paying the harvest tax to the royal granary. The rent is fixed at 3¾ artabas of wheat per aroura for one plot (= five artabas for Tefhapi's 1⅓ arouras) and at 3 artabas per aroura for the second plot, obviously reflecting the different quality of land.[93] The harvest is expected to be in May or June and the rent is to be delivered by the end of July. If it is late and only paid in August, a surcharge of 50 percent will be added. A receipt is required as proof of payment and also the return of the lease to the lessor. The lessee will incur a fine if he does not carry out the work, while the lessor will equally be fined if he prevents the lessee from farming the land.

Recto (1) Regnal year 11, first month of *akhet*, day 29, under Pharaoh$^{\text{l.p.h.}}$ Ptolemy$^{\text{l.p.h.}}$ son of Ptolemy and Kleopatra, the Gods Epiphaneis, (and) the Priest (of) Alexander and the Gods Adelphoi, the Gods Euergetai, the Gods Philopatores, (2) the Gods Epiphaneis and the Gods Philometores, (and) the *athlophoros* before Berenike Euergetis, the *kanêphoros* before Arsinoe Philadelphos, (and) the Priestess (of) Arsinoe Philopator, who are in Alexandria; (3) Hippalos son of Sosos being Priest (of) Ptolemy Soter in Ptolemais, which is in the Thebaid, and (of) Pharaoh Ptolemy, the God Epiphanes Eucharistos; Kineas son of Dositheos being Priest of Pharaoh (4) Ptolemy and Kleopatra, the Mother; (and) the *kanêphoros* before Arsinoe Philadelphos.

Said (the) Greek, cavalry-man (and) *ogdoekontarouros*[94] in the company of Nikandros, (5) Herakleides son of Ly[k]ophron, to (the) lector-priest in the necropolis of Taanch in Asyut, Tefhapi son of Petetumis, his mother Taoues:

"You have leased to me your one-third share of the grain-producing lands that are (shared) between you (6) and Totoes son of Petetumis, your brother, which are in the Field of the Southern High Land (of) Asyut,

[92] From P.Brit.Mus. EA 10595 we know that in the previous year the two brothers had leased their land together.

[93] In the preceding year the lessors were responsible for paying the harvest tax. The rent for this year, inclusive of the tax, was 5½ artabas per aroura for the six-aroura plot (= 33 artabas) and, probably (the reading is not entirely certain; Felber 1997a: 65 n. Z. 11), 12 artabas per aroura for the four-aroura plot (= 48 artabas).

[94] A cavalryman typically received a *klêros* of up to 100 arouras in the third century, but from the second century onwards these were often only nominal values, the actual size being much smaller; see Clarysse (1979: 731) and Van 't Dack (1988: 9–12).

which[95] belong to the god's-offering (of) Wepwawet, which makes two plots[96] of land. Their list:

"– one of them, on the south side, (7) which makes 4 arouras (of) land,

"– the other, on the north side, which makes 6 arouras (of) land,

"makes 10 arouras (of) land and their excess of measuring,[97] whose undivided one-third share belongs to you.

"I am to carry out the work on your one-third of the lands that are above from the water of year 10 to year 11, makes one year;

"I am to plough them; (8) I am to fill them with cattle, seed,[98] men, (and) all agricultural equipment for sowing (and) for harvest, as a free man.[99]

"When (the) harvest will come in regnal year 11, fourth month of *peret* (or) first month of *shemu*, I am to pay the harvest tax of the lands that are above to the granary (of) Pharaoh, (9) they being received by the grain-measures with which the grain (for) Pharaoh is received, and their installments, in accordance with that which the scribes (of) Pharaoh will calculate with me in respect of them;

"I am to give to you as the rent of the lands that are above, their list: the rent (10) for your one-third share of the lands that are on the south side 5 artabas (of) wheat, makes 2½ (artabas of) wheat, makes 5 artabas (of) wheat again; the plot that is on the north side, I am to give to you their rent at the rate of 3 (artabas of) wheat to 1 aroura (of) land, in accordance with the receipt-of-measuring that you will bring (11) to me in respect of them,[100] in wheat that [is pure], unadulterated, (and) without any chaff, and measured, carried, and delivered to your

95 Omitted in Felber (1997a: 61).

96 Note the use of the word *ḥt*, which appears to have the technical meaning of a "defined area" or a "plot of land measured and recorded in the land register"; see Meeks (1972: 61 n. 39).

97 This clause, "with their surplus/excess of measurement," is frequently added to the statement on the size of the land in many sales documents and some leases. There are two views on its meaning. Pestman (in Boswinkel and Pestman 1978: 17 n. f and 205) suggests that it refers to non-cultivable land that, although part of the plots in question, is of no importance to the parties involved in the transaction. Only the measurements of the land that could be cultivated are recorded in the document. An alternative, and the original, view is that the clause refers to the fact that the actual size of the plot could be affected by the annual Nile flood that would change the amount of cultivable land (hence the need for an annual inspection of the fields when the flood receded to measure the extent of the cultivation before the later measurement of the crops [see n. 40]); see Spiegelberg (1906: 203–04) and Grunert (1980: 56 n. c); see n. 100 below.

98 This strange group may be an idiosyncratic writing of *pr.t*.

99 Literally, "as my free man." The phrase usually reads "with my equipment of free man" (see **7.1.1**, line 12, and **7.1.4**, line 9). The scribe perhaps began to write "my equipment of free man" and then realized that he had already mentioned the equipment so he changed it to just "(a) free man," without deleting the "my."

100 Literally "with me in respect of them." It is interesting that the rent for the first plot of land is given as a specific number of artabas (as the number of arouras is fixed), while for the second plot the

storeroom in Pachyr, by the *oipe* of (the) capacity (of) 30 (*choinikes*), which is sound, without transportation costs.

"The wheat thereof that I will not give to you (12) by regnal year 11, second month of *shemu*, I will give it to you with its additional one half in third month of *shemu*, the month that[101] is after the said month, compulsorily, without delay; while I will not be able to give to you another time concerning them apart from the time that is above; and I am to give it to you accordingly, (13) while I will not be able to say, 'I gave to you wheat (or) anything on earth in respect of them,' without a valid receipt (and) while the lease that is above is in your hand; and while I will not be able to say, 'This is a lease that has changed (as to) year;' and I am to act towards you in accordance with it at all times.

"If I withdraw (14) by not carrying out the work on the lands that are above and I do not act for you in accordance with every word that is above, I will give to you money, 300 (*deben*), their half[102] money, 150 (*deben*), makes money, 300 (*deben*), again, in bronze, 24 (*kite*) makes 2 (obols), on one day within ten days of the said month, (15) and you are still behind me to act towards you in accordance with every word that is above, compulsorily, without delay.

"If you yourself hold back the lands that are above from me until regnal year 11, second month of *shemu*, day 30, you will give to me money, 300 (*deben*), makes money, 150 (*deben*), makes money, 300 (*deben*), again, in bronze, 24 (*kite*) to 2 (obols), (16) within ten days of the said month, and I am still behind you to leave them to me, compulsorily, without delay."

(In the) writing (of) Phatres son of Imouthes, who writes (at) Asyut and its places (in the) name (of) the priests (of) Wepwawet and the gods who dwell with him.

Sixteen witness signatures on the verso

7.1.4 Demotic lease of land from the Roman period

P.Tebt.Botti 1 (Botti 1957: 76–80) (Tebtunis, 8 July AD 4). Images at *Studi Calderini* II 76–77 pl. 1.

Additional bibliography: Hughes (1973: 157), Brinker *et al.* (2005: B, 771)

This is the only Demotic land lease written on papyrus from the Roman period published to date.[103] Although both lessor and lessee

amount is simply stated to be 3 artabas per aroura, the size clearly dependent on the assessment of the extent of cultivable land; see n. 97 above.

101 Omitted by Felber (1997a: 62).

102 Omitted by Felber (1997a: 62).

103 For Roman-period leases on ostraca, see n. 5.

are priests, the lease concerns 1½ arouras of land that belong to the state. The land is to be cultivated with wheat and covers the harvest of one year. The document is drawn up by the lessor in accordance with Fayyumic practice and acknowledges the prepayment of the rent. The lessor is responsible for paying the taxes to the state and to the temple.[104] The detail in the document is limited compared with what is found in the earlier Ptolemaic texts, but the structure of the text is consistent with earlier Ptolemaic practice.

Demotic: (1) Regnal year 33 (under) Caesar, the god, (2) the {the} son (of) the god, third month of *shemu*, day 14.

Said (3) (the) prince (and) *emneter*-priest[105] Marepsemis (4) (son of) Marresiou who is called Heron[106] (5) (to) (the) prince (and) *emneter*-priest Marsisouchos (son of) Marepsemis:

(6) "(I) have leased to you the 1½ (arouras of) land, (7) the (land) that is in the high land (of) "The Acacia," (8) land (of) Pharaoh,[l.p.h.107] you are to plough and you are to carry out all the (9) agricultural work with my equipment[108] (of) a free man; (10) you are to farm it (with) wheat (for) the crop (of) regnal year 34.

"Its (11) rent, you have paid (me). [You (12) have caused][109] that my heart is satisfied with it (as) money in advance, today.[110] (I) have received (it) from you. My heart is satisfied with it, it being (13) complete, without any remainder.

"(Concerning) any[111] thing on earth that [you will] (14) place (on) my head,[112] you will have authority [over it] (15) apart from me on account of it entirely. I am responsible vis-à-vis you to cause that they are clear for you (16) (from) any matter (of) Pharaoh, any matter (of the) temple (or) any matter on earth, (17) (in) accordance with the right (of)

[104] Taxes to the temple are rarely mentioned in the Ptolemaic leases; see n. 28.

[105] The reading and interpretation of this title are uncertain; see Schentuleit (2001: 135–36) and Quack (2013: 111–16).

[106] The reading is not certain.

[107] It is interesting to see that priests are leasing state land from each other and that they are required to pay taxes to both the state and the temple. On the question of the status of temple and private lands in Roman Egypt, see the discussion in Monson (2005) (his statement on our papyrus, p. 86, will have been written without the benefit of the reading of "Pharaoh" that was established by Pestman in Brinker *et al.* 2005: B, 771).

[108] Reading *grg*, "equipment" (as in **7.1.1**, line 12).

[109] The papyrus is damaged and the text not certain.

[110] For this expression to indicate prepayment of rent, see the references in n. 22.

[111] The *nb* is overlooked by Botti.

[112] The restoration is uncertain.

the lease (that) I made for you (for) the 1½ (arouras of) land (18) written above. My heart is satisfied with it."

(In the) writing (of) Harmiusis (son of) Harmiusis.[113]

Greek: Year 33 of Caesar, Ep[ei]ph, 14.

7.2 Kleruchic land in the Ptolemaic period

D. J. Thompson

Kleruchic land was land used by the Ptolemies, from early on, to settle their troops and tie them to their new home. The cultivation of the land together with the economic well-being of their soldiers and, in the case of the cavalry, the upkeep of their horses, were factors which may have influenced this policy. Like gift-estates (see **7.2.1**) or sacred land, kleruchic land was generally classified as land "in release" from the Crown, so subject to taxes but not to rents; see **7.2.5** and **7.2.6**, introductions.[114]

From the start royal initiative was prime; kleruchic land was granted by the king (see **7.2.1**). At first, kleruchic plots were held on a limited lifetime tenure. On death, a kleruch's land was reclaimed by the Crown, as in **7.2.2**. Other causes of reclamation are also known; for the non-payment of dues, see **7.2.4**, ruling 4. By the reign of Ptolemy IV, in a development as yet known only in outline, kleruchs acquired the right to leave their plots to their offspring. Grants were now made to the individual and his descendants, though on the holder's death were still temporarily resumed by the Crown until the registration of any sons took place (*W.Chr.* 336, lines 26–27 and 30–33 [218/217 BC]). By the late second century, the wording of **7.2.4**, rulings 2 and 3, is less equivocal: full possession is the rule, with the right to bequeath or alienate in other ways. Even sale of kleruchic land was possible in certain (unclear) circumstances: see **7.2.4**, introduction, with ruling 4. Normally, however, plots were exchanged through a process of cession (*parachôrêsis*); see **7.2.5** introduction. The final text, **7.2.6**, is a Demotic division of kleruchic property from 68 BC.

Holders of kleruchic land were in the third century known as kleruchs and distinguished by the number of arouras they held; see **7.2.3** for

[113] Harmiusis is probably the last member of a long line of document scribes attached to the temple of Tebtunis. Afterwards, the Demotic scribes appear to have been attached to the *grapheion*-offices; see Muhs (2005a: 94–95 and 100).

[114] Recent but still unpublished work by Andrew Monson on some Demotic texts from the third century BC (now in the Sorbonne papyrus collection) suggests that revision may be needed to the traditional picture of rent-free *klêroi*.

100-*aroura* cavalrymen. Later, from the reign of Ptolemy V, cavalry settlers were termed *katoikoi hippeis*. Their ranks might be replenished by transfer from other kleruchic classes, as for the *ephodos* of **7.2.3** (cf. Uebel 1968: 369). The extension of the kleruchy to members of the police, as later to Egyptian soldiers, is a feature of the second century BC. Increasingly grants were made from uncultivated land, with some exceptions.

If the tenure of kleruchic land depended on orders (*prostagmata*) of the king, in practice the *dioikêtês*, as the chief financial official of the administration, was regularly involved in changes of policy and overseeing new initiatives. Both the *dioikêtês* and the royal scribe could issue instructions (*chrêmatismoi*); see **7.2.5** and *P.Lips.* II 124, lines 79–80 (137 BC, or later). At times, especially in disputes over the quality of land or the levy of different dues, the conflict between differing sources of authority is documented; see *P.Meyer* 1.9–27 (144 BC) or *P.Lips.* II 124, lines 77–83, where the kleruchs claim that "the ordinance (*chrêmatismos*) of the *dioikêtês* is not stronger than (royal) commands and responses." For this category of land, as for others, the king's orders had superior legal force.

7.2.1 Extract from the "Revenue Laws" of Ptolemy Philadelphos

P.Rev. 36, lines 3–19 (= *W.Chr.* 249, *C.Ord.Ptol.* 17) (Fayyum, 259 BC). Image at Papyri.info.

The following extract in Greek is from the first of two papyrus rolls, originally from the Fayyum but now in the Bodleian Library, Oxford, which contain a compilation of Greek rulings known, since their first edition by Grenfell (1896), as the "Revenue Laws" of Ptolemy II. This section records a royal ruling of 14 June 263 BC on the levy of the one-sixth tax charged on the produce of vineyards and orchards and levied on certain categories of land to finance the cult of the deceased queen, sister of the king, Arsinoe Philadelphos.[115] Sacred land was not included in these provisions but kleruchic land, gift-estates (land termed *en dôreais*), and land of some others whose identity is unclear were to be charged the one-sixth tax. It should be noted that, although both categories might be termed "land in release" (*en aphesei*), in relation to this tax kleruchic land was treated differently from sacred land.

Kleruchic land is specified as "land from the king" and special arrangements for ascertaining the extent of this land are made for kleruchs (as for

[115] "Tax of one-sixth" is a direct translation of the Demotic *p3* $^1/_6$. Elsewhere this tax is known in Greek as *apomoira*.

those with land in related categories), who, as for the salt-tax levy, have the privilege of self-registration. Later, in 259 BC, the rate was lowered to one-tenth of the produce of vineyards for certain categories of kleruch, those on active service or who had their vineyards under cultivation.[116]

> The royal scribes in the [nomes throughout] the countryside shall, each for the nome for which he acts, register both the number of arouras consisting of vineyards and orchards and the produce from these, cultivator by cultivator, starting from year 22 (264/3 BC). They shall distinguish the sacred land and its produce so that the remainder of the land [may be known] from which the one-sixth tax is to be collected for (Arsinoe) [Philadelphos]. And they are to provide a report in writing on these for the agents working for [Satyros]. Similarly both the [kleruchs] holding vineyards or orchards on the plots (*klêroi*) that they have from the king and all others possessing vineyards or orchards, whether as part of gift-estates or cultivating them under some other regime, shall each for his part register his own land, both its size and its produce, and shall pay over the one-sixth of the produce to Arsinoe Philadelphos for the sacrifices [and] libations.

7.2.2 Extract from official correspondence on deceased cavalrymen

P.Hib. I 81, lines 12–18 (Hibeh, 7 February 238 BC). Image at Papyri.info.

This extract from a record of official correspondence under Ptolemy III derives from cartonnage from mummy 98 excavated at el-Hibeh in 1902 by Grenfell and Hunt, who in 1906 were the text's first editors. The text, written in Greek, lists deceased cavalrymen in the nearby Arsinoite nome whose *klêroi* should now return to the Crown, so illustrating the lifetime nature of the grant of a *klêros*, at least at this period. The military units to which these men belong were already known from elsewhere. The names Artemidoros and Asklepiades are both too common to allow identification with officials otherwise known, though Artemidoros may be the same as the representative of Stratios, recorded in *W.Chr.* 335, line 2 (243/2 BC), who writes on a similar subject earlier in the reign of Ptolemy III Euergetes I. Both military and civilian officials will have been involved in such

[116] *P.Rev.* 24, lines 5–7, 10, "(and the liability) for kleruchs who are on active service and who have planted their [own] plots (*klêroi*) . . . is one tenth (of the wine)." The workings of the different royal rulings to which this land category was subject are discussed by Koenen (1993: 66–69) and Clarysse and Vandorpe (1998).

changes of land-category. It is clear too that the organization of the return of *klêroi* to the Crown was on a nome-wide basis, with villages recorded here in two of the three divisions or *merides* (Herakleides, Themistos, and Polemon) that made up the Arsinoite nome.

Other examples of such orders make specific provision for the income from such plots, which on return to royal control had then to be paid to the Crown; see further *W.Chr.* 334 (244/3 BC) and 335 (243/2 BC).

Artemidoros to Asklepiades, greetings. The cavalrymen listed below have died. Therefore reclaim their holdings (*klêroi*) for the Crown.

At Herakleia in the Themistos *meris*:
In the troop of Damon, Leagros son of Dionysophanes, captain,
Philonides son of Artemidoros, decurion in the same troop.
At Hiera Nesos in the Polemon *meris*:
In the troop of Lichas, Ebryzelmis son of Zipyros, decurion.
Year 9, Hathyr 28 (17 January 238).

7.2.3 Official correspondence about a military reassignment

P.Tebt. I 32 (= *W.Chr.* 448) (Tebtunis [originally Kerkeosiris], 145 BC?). Image at Papyri.info.

This record of correspondence derives from the wrapping of a crocodile mummy excavated at Ûmm el-Baragât (ancient Tebtunis) in the south Fayyum by Grenfell and Hunt in the winter of 1899/1900. It was published by the same scholars with impressive speed and expertise in 1902. The text in Greek provides information on both the army and the role of kleruchic plots as a defining feature of the status both of cavalry settlers (*katoikoi hippeis*) and of other military or paramilitary offices, like the *ephodos* here. Asklepiades, an *ephodos* with a plot of twenty-four arouras which he acquired in year 34 of Philometor (148/7 BC, cf. *P.Tebt.* I 62, lines 91–99), was in year 36 (146/5 BC) transferred to the rank of *katoikos hippeus* in the *politeuma* (see **10.2** below) of the Cretans, forming part of the fifth hipparchy of cavalry settlers. Asklepiades' earlier appointment as *ephodos* was no longer relevant after his transfer, though his existing plot was apparently essential to his acceptance into his new position.

The order of events recorded here must be read in the reverse order. The first official involved was the secretary of the settler cavalry, Apollodoros, who was also *epistatês* with the honorific rank of "one of the first friends." He wrote to Sosos and Aigyptos, who then passed this on to Pankrates, in charge of the assignment (*syntaxis*) for the *katoikoi hippeis*. Pankrates forwarded a copy of this letter to the chief royal official in the nome, the royal scribe, and another copy to Aristippos, probably the *topogrammateus*, enclosing a copy of his letter to the royal scribe, with orders that the instructions be followed. Finally Aristippos sent a complete copy of the correspondence he had received to Eumelos, probably the village scribe of the village of Kerkeosiris, requesting the release of Asklepiades from his previous duties.

> Aristippos to Eumelos, greetings. Below is appended a copy for you of the letter addressed to me from Pankrates who is in charge of the assignment for the cavalry settlers (*katoikoi hippeis*).[117] You should aim, now, not to involve Asklepiades in the responsibilities of an *ephodos*.[118] Farewell. Year [3]6, Payni. (June/July 245 BC)
>
> Pankrates to Aristippos, greetings. I have appended for your information the copy of a letter we have written to [. . .], the royal scribe. Year 36, Phamenoth. (March/April 245 BC)
>
> To [. . .]. A copy is appended of the letter written to us by Sosos and Aigyptos, the [. . .] who are appointed by the *politeuma* of the Cretans,[119] relating to the affairs of Asklepiades, so that you are aware that he has changed [. . .], and to ensure that the instructions are carried out.[120]
>
> [Sosos] and Aigyptos to Pankrates, greetings. Since orders have been given through us that the settler cavalry [. . .] through us, Apollodoros, one of the "first friends,"*epistatês* and secretary of the settler cavalry,[121] has sent me from the 500 men who have been attached to the *politeuma* of the Cretans, Asklepiades son of Ptolemaios, a Macedonian of the regional *ephodoi*, on the grounds that he is in possession of a plot of 24 arouras in the neighborhood of Kerkeosiris in the Polemon *meris*. Please, therefore, enter him in the record, enlisting him into the fifth hipparchy[122] of the

[117] For the post, see *P.Lips.* II 124, line 43 with note (137 BC, or later). Pankrates is well known from other texts; see, for example, Criscuolo (2004).

[118] An *ephodos* was a policeman of superior rank to a *phylakitês* (with a *klêros* of twenty-four as opposed to ten arouras).

[119] A *politeuma* was an ethnic unit for army groups together with their families introduced under Ptolemy VI; in addition to their military function *politeumata* served as units of social organization and identity. As in army regiments in other societies and periods (see the Scots Guards in the UK), the particular ethnic identity could be acquired by incomers; Asklepiades was earlier a Macedonian. See further below, **10.2**.

[120] The word used here for "instructions," *prostetagmena*, may imply royal orders.

[121] On honorific ranks, such as "first friends" (*sc.* of the king), see Mooren (1977: 1–61).

[122] This hipparchy or divisional unit of cavalry was larger than the single *politeuma*; it included both Macedonians and Persians.

100-*aroura* men,[123] and report to Apollodoros. I have added below his physical description[124] and the name of his son.

He is about 22 years old, short, with honey-coloured skin and curly hair [. . .] His son is Ptolemaios aged five months [. . .]

On the other side: To Eumelos.

7.2.4 A series of royal rulings

P.Tebt. I 124, lines 23–45 (= *C.Ord.Ptol.* 54) (Tebtunis [originally Kerkeosiris] *c.*, 118 BC). Image at Papyri.info.

This listing of royal rulings was extracted from the wrappings of crocodile no. 20 from the crocodile cemetery at ancient Tebtunis in the south Fayyum. The Greek text translated here follows on from a very fragmentary petition made to Ptolemy VIII Euergetes II and his queens Kleopatra II and III by the settler cavalrymen in the Arsinoite nome, *P.Tebt.* I 124, lines 1–22. Those treated in these rulings are described as having entered the *katoikia*, i.e., the status of *katoikos hippeus*. Ruling 4 refers specifically to royal concessions, *philanthrôpa*, and ruling 5 to royal orders, *prostagmata*, which affect the status of kleruchs in relation to their land and the charges levied on it.

Ruling 1, with its protection of kleruchs from extra charges or legal prosecution, suggests a desire on the part of the Crown to retain the loyalty of the cavalry kleruchs who were militarily important. Rulings 2 and 3 illustrate how *klêroi* were now held in full possession. The Crown seems willing to ignore the way in which such plots may have been acquired. The background may have been a desire to pacify this group of settlers, to get the land cultivated and taxes paid at any cost, but these royal rulings are expressed in legal terms.

Ruling 4 specifies both outgoing and incoming *katoikoi*. Some ceded their land when they were unable to pay their dues; others lost their land in other ways, through confiscation, for instance, or, as recorded here, through cession to others in the forces. The new status as *katoikos* might be acquired by those who earlier held private land and who now joined the category, presumably by the purchase of *klêroi* (cf. *P.Lips.* I 124, line 78, for

[123] Despite an extensive run of later land surveys, there is no evidence that Asklepiades ever received any further land, as would be consonant with his new status as a holder of 100 arouras.

[124] An *eikôn*, a literate form of photo-ID, was regularly employed in legal transactions, see *C. Ptol. Sklav.* 8 lines 4–9 (176/5 BC), for slaves; *P.Petrie*[2] *Wills* pp. 49–55, in soldiers' wills.

"bought *klêroi*"), or by those who were transferred from police or other kleruchic categories, as in **7.2.3** above. The final provisions concern tax payments.

(1) That those who [. . .] should be freed from the payment of additional contributions, should receive pardon from accusations made against them, from any involuntary or unintentional offences committed, from any legal decisions they are subject to, and any prosecution made against them up to year 53 (118/7 BC).[125]

(2) That we and our descendants should remain in possession[126] of the plots (*klêroi*) that we occupy up to year 52 (119/8 BC) whatever they may be and in whatever way acquired without legal question or dispute for any reason whatsoever.

(3) And likewise those who for any reason whatsoever have been deprived of their plots, who have had them taken over, annulled or encroached upon, are equally to remain in full possession of them.

(4) And since some who have grown weak [. . .] or fallen into difficulties have ceded possession to [. . .], others have alienated their plots, yet others have divided their holdings with their comrades in arms,[127] given that the (new) holders may have transferred from private holdings and from other categories of possession into the rank of settlers in accordance with royal ordinance (*pr(ostetagmena)*), both these and their descendants are to remain in possession (of their *klêroi*) for all time; those who exploit these are not to be recorded in the category of kleruchs *kat' axiôma*[128] . . . and, in accordance with earlier (royal) concessions (*philanthrôpa*) they are not to be asked for the harvest taxes[129] and extraordinary levies that are raised as required.

(5) And likewise those too who up to the present time have been registered in the place of other kleruchs on the kleruchic registers by the intermediary of our *epistatai* and scribes according to our rulings (*prostetagmena*) and, entering the *katoikia* from being [private owners]

[125] For this combination of fiscal and penal aspects, see *UPZ* II 162.vii, lines 14–15, an amnesty decree of 118 BC.

[126] The Greek of line 7, *kyriôs echein*, denotes full possession.

[127] For cession of kleruchic land, *parachôrêsis*, see introduction to **7.2.5** below.

[128] The precise meaning of this is unknown; the term *kat' axiôma* clearly designates a fiscal category of kleruchs, see *P.Meyer* 1, line 25 (144 BC). The implication may be that they should not be treated as tenants paying rent but rather as kleruchs not liable to certain charges; see Préaux (1939: 477 n. 1).

[129] On the harvest tax (*shemu*), *epigraphê* in Greek, which was levied on kleruchic land at least in the Thebaid, see Vandorpe (2000a).

and members of other kleruchic categories, they are not to find themselves subjected to any charges other than those levied specifically on *katoikoi*.

7.2.5 Extract from a Greek land survey

P.Haun. inv. 407, lines 33–62 (Apollonopolite nome [Edfu], 119/8 BC)

This Greek survey of land in the Apollonopolite (Edfu) nome in Upper Egypt is preserved on a carbonized roll of papyrus probably coming from a central office in the nome capital. Now in Copenhagen, it is preserved under glass as a series of sheets, only legible through the use of infrared photography. The survey details kleruchic land immediately following land "in release" (*en aphesei*), which in this text includes dedicated and some other land (lines 1–32) but not kleruchic land; it is notable, however, that the two are later added together (line 249) suggesting a close link between these categories. This particular section is concerned with land assigned to kleruchs before the great revolt of the Thebaid which started in 207/6 BC. A large plot which once stood at well over 100 arouras was later transferred; the text records the re-registration (*metepigraphê*) of the land involved. This transfer took place between two cavalry settlers, described as *politikoi*, so perhaps living in the nome capital Apollonopolis or possibly the nearby city of Ptolemais, and was presumably made by the process of *parachôrêsis*, which is well documented in contemporary texts.[130] With the acquisition of such land came liability for taxes (cf. **7.2.4** above).

Crown officials involved in establishing land tenure are here detailed as the *oikonomos*, the royal scribe, and the local village scribe. The royal scribe is shown to have the power to issue instructions affecting kleruchic land (*chrêmatismos*, lines 45–7). The poor quality of much of the land granted to kleruchs is further illustrated by this text, which was first edited in his (as yet unpublished) dissertation by Christensen (2002).

Details of further kleruchic allotments follow this extract. Compared with elsewhere, kleruchic holdings in this nome were very few (only 3 percent of the land recorded in this text).

Kleruchic land (assigned) prior to year 16 (207/6 BC)[131] under the grandfather of the [king]

[130] See *P.Tebt.* I 30 (115 BC) and 31 (112 BC); *BGU* VIII 1731–1740 (first century BC); on *parachôrêsis*, see Rupprecht (1984).

[131] When the revolt in the south broke out.

Land of the settler cavalrymen (*katoikoi hippeis*) from the city (*politikoi*):
[The plot] of Sommounis son of T[– –] which is registered as having been transferred in [year . . .] to Ptolemaios son of Pasas, chief bodyguard[132] of the same settler cavalrymen of the city. A report (*paradeixis*) on this has been made by us, by Kastor who was *oiko[nomos]*, by Psempchoïs the representative of Hermias, who was then royal scribe, and by Piyris, who was village scribe, according to the instructions (*chrêmatismos*) of Hermias, who was then royal scribe, the copy of which was placed on record in year 29 (142/1 BC). The plot (*klêros*) belongs to an assignation prior to year 16. It is located in the area of Apollonopolis and consists of 140½ + ¼ (= ¾)[133] arouras from which have been deducted the land eaten away by the floodwater and the area found to be less on the occasion when the report was made as to the state of the land. We categorize 100 arouras of fertile land, of which 30 arouras have been sown.

7.2.6 Demotic division of family property (docket in Greek)

P.Moscow 123, lines 1–2 (= Malinine 1967: 73–79) (Akhmim [Panopolis], 17 April 68 BC). Image at Malinine (1967), Plate XX.

This division of family property is written in four long lines of Demotic followed by a brief record of registration in Greek, giving the date (year 13, Pharmouthi 11) and names of the contractors, on a papyrus roll which measures 267 × 22.5 cm. The roll forms part of the Golenischeff collection in Moscow and was edited by Malinine (1967). The text illustrates the degree to which kleruchic land had become the private property of its holder by the first century BC (cf. **7.2.4**). Here a cavalry settler, in Greek a *katoikos hippeus*, divides his land among five of his six sons. There is no indication in the text why the elder Pelilis should have received money instead of a share of the land of his father. The one daughter, named Siepmous like her grandmother, receives no part of the land but, as recorded later in the text, an allowance of wheat and a dowry. Elsewhere at this date, daughters are known to have inherited, perhaps in the absence of sons, cf. Ptolema in *BGU* VIII 1734 from the Herakleopolite nome. Like many kleruchic estates, this property near Akhmim (Panopolis) in Upper Egypt was divided among different locations. The kleruchic land

132 Chief bodyguard, *archisômatophylax* in Greek, is an honorific title: see Mooren (1977: 1–61). Ptolemaios, son of Pasas, whose title suggests he was a high-ranking officer or official in the area, had other land besides, amounting in all by the date of the survey to 218 arouras of kleruchic land.

133 With the exception of ⅔ fractions are always expressed in such units.

of this area, in contrast to that in the Edfu nome (see **7.2.5** [119/8 BC], introduction) but as in the Arsinoite (e.g., *P. Tebt.* I 63, lines 2–3 [115 BC]), is specified as "land in release" (*n w3y* in Demotic, *en aphesei* in Greek).

Year 13, fourth month of *peret*, day 11, of King Ptolemy (XII) the god who loves his father and who loves his sister (Theos Philopator Philadelphos), according to the (dynastic) priests, priestesses and the *kanêphoros* who are in post.[134]

Has declared Hatres son of Petephibis and of Siepmous, his mother, a cavalry settler who is numbered among the *katoikoi*, to the child of the cavalry settler numbered among the *katoikoi*, his eldest son Petephibis son of Hatres and of Thermouthis, his mother, my eldest son.

I have given to you, and to Hermon also called Totoes, son of Hatres, cavalry settler numbered among the *katoikoi*, and to Patoumis son of Hatres, to Pelilis the elder, son of Hatres, to Pelilis the younger, son of Hatres, and, finally, to Peteminpisais son of Hatres, that makes five persons whose mother is Thermouthis, my children, your younger brothers together with you, that makes (in total) 6 persons, my possessions as specified below, for each one of you.

Detailed list:

Petephibis son of Hatres, my eldest son, and Hermon also known as Totoes son of Hatres, two persons mentioned above (are to receive) my land in release providing income for a *katoikos* measuring 39 arouras, divided into three parcels as follows: two plots of these totaling 32 arouras lying in the Field of Tsmine; the other (third) plot measuring 7 arouras lying in the area of the Guard-Post to the north of Akhmim [. . . ; . . .] to be divided into halves – that is ¼ + ¼ – that is a half share again for each of the two after my death.

Patoumis son of Hatres, like Pelilis the younger, son of Hatres, and Peteminpisais son of Hatres, three persons mentioned above, (are to receive) my fields in release consisting of four plots, registered in the [. . .] of *Edfa* as follows: two plots of these lying in the field south of the Place of the Vineyard, the other two in the Field of *Pr-Gndb* – to make up the total, together with the extra which is registered there,[135] to be divided into thirds – that is $^{1}/_{6}$ + $^{1}/_{6}$ – or one-third again for each of the three, after my death.

[134] The dynastic priests and priestesses in Alexandria or Ptolemais used in official dating formulas are no longer specified by name at this date. I am grateful for the assistance of Mark Depauw.

[135] Additional land discovered after the survey of the field attracted a royal fine.

Pelilis the elder, the aforementioned son of Hatres, (is to receive) 100 talents – their half is 50 talents – that is 100 talents again payable (in bronze) at the rate of twenty-four bronze (obols) to two (silver) *kite* which he will raise from the debts owed me by others outside (the family), as an alternative to *his* share in my land after my death . . .

7.3 Greek leases in the Ptolemaic and Roman periods

Jane Rowlandson and Ryosuke Takahashi

The vast majority of surviving *misthôsis* contracts were made between private individuals; although farmers of public land freely used *misthôsis* contracts to sub-lease their parcels, the few surviving bids for the primary lease of public land suggest that these were exceptions, and that public land was normally held from the state without written contract (Rowlandson 2005; cf. **7.3.6**). Public officials also used written contracts to lease out confiscated or certain other types of property, such as that of orphans (**7.3.5**) or belonging to a city. Leasing generated other types of written document beyond the *misthôsis* contract itself, notably receipts for rent and applications to withdraw from a contract (**7.3.6a**, **b**; cf. **7.3.8**).

7.3.1 Lease of land of the Apollonios estate

P.Col. III 54 (= *SB* IV 7450, *Sel.Pap.* I 39; tr. *P.Col.* III 54, APIS (incl. Cols. 2 and 3), *Sel.Pap.* I 39, Austin 2006, no. 306; Orrieux, *Les papyrus de Zenon* (1983), 111–12) (Philadelphia [Fayyum], 31 August 256 BC). Images at *MAAR* 6 (1927), Plates 53 and 54; APIS (columbia.apis.p54); Papyri.info.

This text comes from the famous archive of Zenon, estate manager of Apollonios, the *dioikêtês* of Ptolemy II in the middle of the third century BC. The king had given Apollonios a gift-estate (*dôrea*) of 10,000 arouras situated near the newly founded town of Philadelphia in the Fayyum to develop for agriculture. The estate had already been divided by canals into rectangular irrigation basins, and here three Macedonian entrepreneurs lease 100 arouras from one of the basins for one year to sow wheat and barley for a fixed rent in wheat. Seed and expenses will be given in advance, to be repaid with the rent. Any default was subject to the 50 percent penalty commonly found in leases (Herrmann 1958: 147–48; cf. **7.3.3**). Like other Ptolemaic contracts, this contract bears the names of six witnesses, mostly fellow Greek immigrants settled in Philadelphia, one of whom became keeper of the contract (*syngraphophylax*).

Our text is not the original contract but a copy written on the first column of a papyrus some six years after the original lease, in preparation to sue the lessees, who had defaulted on most of the rent and other sums owed. The second column calculates the outstanding rent and expenses, which, with the additional 50 percent penalty for each of years 31 to 35, brought the total debt to over 2,500 artabas of wheat.[136] The third column (in a different hand, written in Xandikos of year 36 = June/July 250 BC) contains preparatory notes for proceeding with the claim against the lessee Theopompos, which it was anticipated would be held before the *stratêgos*, since there was currently no tribunal sitting in the Arsinoite nome. This example therefore demonstrates that the penalty clauses in leases were no empty threats, but could be enforced in the event of non-payment.

In the 30th year of the reign of Ptolemy son of Ptolemy Soter, when Alexander son of Leonidas is priest of Alexander and brother–sister gods, Prepousa daughter of Demetrios is *kanêphoros* of Arsinoe Philadelphos, in the month Panemos, or in Egyptian reckoning, Epeiph 10th. Hegesarchos son of Theopompos and Theopompos son of Hegesarchos and Nikodemos son of Hegesarchos, all three being Macedonians of the *epigonê*, have taken on contract from Zenon son of Agreophon, Caunian, in the entourage of Apollonios the *dioikêtês*, from the 10,000 arouras granted by the king to Apollonios the *dioikêtês* in the Arsinoite nome near Philadelphia, 100 arouras of arable land in the third basin reckoning from north to south, for one year, at $7^1/_8$ artabas in wheat per aroura, free of risk and not subject to deduction of any kind. There will be given as seed for the land bearing wheat one half an artaba per aroura,[137] and proportionately for the barley-bearing land, and for expenses one artaba of barley for each aroura, and for weeding half an artaba of barley, and for cutting brushwood, if the need arises, as much as is judged sufficient is to be given for each aroura. Hegesarchos and Theopompos and Nikodemos shall measure out the grain for the rent at the granary in Philadelphia in accordance with the (royal) ordinance on grain collection, in the month of Daisios of the 31st year, and likewise (they shall repay) whatever grain they receive for seed and weeding and expenses and whatever cash they borrow for cutting the brushwood or grain in place of cash, wheat at the rate of one artaba to one drachma two obols in bronze,

[136] I.e., *c.*70 artabas plus 5 × 347 artabas: the arithmetic is inaccurate.

[137] This contrasts with the usual provision of seed at one artaba per aroura throughout later leases.

and for the barley at a proportionate rate. Hegesarchos and Theopompos and Nikodemos shall sow two-thirds of land they have taken on in wheat and the remaining third in barley. If they do not do as they have agreed, Zenon shall be permitted to lease the land to others. For any damage that they may cause to the revenue of Apollonios or whatever they may owe in respect of rent and loans, they shall forfeit to Zenon immediately one and a half times the amount, and Zenon or another acting as his agent shall have right of execution upon them and their sureties and all their possessions, both individually and all together as in the case of debts to the Crown. Sureties set by the contract for payment are the contracting parties, each for one another, and Ammonios son of Theon, Cyrenaean, one of the *epergoi*.[138] The contract shall be valid wherever it is produced. Witnesses: Damis son of Kleon, Sostratos son of Kleon, both Heleneians; Theopompos son of Aristion, Thessalian physician; Diodoros son of Zopyros, Magnesian, in the entourage of Apollonios the *dioikêtês*; Agathinos son of Pyrrhos, Cyrenaean, one of the *epergoi*; Anosis son of Totorchois, Saite, village scribe of Philadelphia. Keeper of the contract, Damis.

7.3.2 Lease of half a *klêros*

P.Frankf. 2 (other copies of the same contract: *BGU* VI 1263, 1264, probably *BGU* XIV 2384) (Tholthis, 215/4 BC). Image at Papyri.info.

This lease belongs to a group of late third-century BC leases and loans found on mummy cartonnage, from the milieu of the military settlers in the villages of Tholthis and Takona in the north of the Oxyrhynchite nome. Here Eupolis, an Athenian private, leases half his military allotment (*klêros*) jointly to a Greek civilian (Alexander, Cyrenaean) and to Horos, a local Egyptian. Such a partnership is characteristic of this group of leases, and it has been suggested that the Greek civilian would supply the necessary capital for working the land while the Egyptian provided the labor (Bingen 1978 in 2006: esp. 210). The contract, a double document (see **2.1.1–2**) with witnesses typical of the Ptolemaic period, survives in at least three copies (four including the very fragmentary *BGU* XIV 2384). The translation here is of the interior text of *P.Frankf.* 2, but draws on the other versions to supplement the

[138] Meaning uncertain: perhaps an assistant worker (*Sel.Pap.* I 39) or a surety for subsidiary obligations (Orrieux, APIS).

readings. The most significant difference between the versions is that in *P.Frankf.* 2 the amount of rent is corrected from 146 to 126 artabas of wheat in total, whereas in *BGU* VI 1263 and 1264 it is simply stated to be 146 artabas. The contract does not specify what crop the lessees should sow, but the clause requiring the rent to be delivered in wheat grown in the land (i.e., not taken from storage) assumes that they would be cultivating wheat. The penalty on the lessees for non-delivery of rent (ten drachmas per aroura) is around twice the current market price for wheat (*BGU* XIV 2384 line 11n.), but the lessor is also liable to a large fine (1,000 drachmas of silver) if he fails to abide by the terms, as in other leases from this period (cf. Herrmann 1958: 154). None of the extant copies of this lease records the witnesses' names.

In the eighth year of the reign of Ptolemy son of Ptolemy and Berenike, Benefactor gods, when Ptolemaios son of Ptolemaios son of Stasikrates is priest of Alexander and the Saviour gods and brother–sister gods and Benefactor gods and Father-loving gods, and Arsinoe daughter of Sosibios is *kanêphoros* of Arsinoe Philadelphos, in the month of Peritios in Tholthis of the Oxyrhynchite nome. Eupolis, Athenian private of Philon's troop, has leased for one sowing and one harvest from the sowing in the ninth year, of which the crops will be in the tenth year, to Alexander son of Krates Cyrenaean of the *epigonê* and Horos son of P[. . .], Oxyrhynchite sacred slave[139] of Thoeris, the half of the fallow in his *klêros*, that is twenty-twoablouras, including seed free of risk at a rent of one hundred and twenty-six[140] artabas of wheat. Let Eupolis give them seed for each aroura one artaba of wheat according to their need. If Eupolis discovers that any of the land is larger than the twenty-two arouras by survey of the said share, let [them pay] to Eupolis rent including seed at eight artabas of wheat per aroura.[141] Let Alexander and Horos hand over the agreed rent to Eupolis in the month of Dystros of the tenth year, grain that is clean and without clods that was grown in the land, properly measured by the *chous* measure of Eupolis, and let them convey it to Eupolis' property at their own expense. If they do not pay over as agreed, let them pay a penalty to Eupolis of ten drachmas for each artaba of wheat. The stubble shall belong to Eupolis, and Eupolis shall have the chaff having threshed it himself,

[139] Greek *hierodoulos*, a status designation of someone bound to work on a temple estate.
[140] "Twenty-six" written above the line, corrected from "forty-six"; see *BGU* VI 1263, 1264.
[141] In *BGU* VI 1264, this clause precedes the previous one about seed provision, and omits "by survey."

and Eupolis shall have right of execution from Alexander and Horos acting in accordance with the (royal) ordinance. Eupolis shall own the crops until he has received what is his. Eupolis shall guarantee to Alexander and Horos the land and the crops sown in it according to the terms on which he has leased them. If Eupolis does not guarantee in accordance with what is written, let Eupolis pay a fine to Alexander and Horos of one thousand drachmas of silver, unless there is a royal hindrance.[142] Let this agreement be valid wherever it is brought.

Names of witnesses

7.3.3 Lease of a house in Alexandria

BGU IV 1116 (German translation [lines 1–32]: Metzger 1974: 29–30, no. 31; see also: Husson 1983, Müller 1985) (11 or 21 April 13 BC). Image at Papyri.info.

This text belongs to the only significant group of Alexandrian legal documents known, preserved on mummy cartonnage from Abusir el-Melek, and dating from the first few decades of Roman rule in Egypt.[143] Like many other documents in this group, it takes the form of a *synchôrêsis* (agreement) addressed to Protarchos, head of the Alexandrian tribunal to which contracting parties submitted their agreements for official registration. The contracts would then be filed by pasting the sheets together into a composite roll (*tomos synkollêsimos*).

The absence of close parallels, small handwriting, and numerous corrections make translation sometimes difficult, but the text is interesting not only for illustrating the format of Alexandrian legal contracts, but also for the active presence of Roman citizens and their protégés in the Alexandrian property market at this period (cf. Bowman 2001), and the light it throws on Alexandrian housing, to which archaeology has only recently begun to contribute significantly. Although the house itself may be primarily residential (the fittings mentioned could be domestic and sanitary in function), its street frontage consisted of shops or workshops that were also included in the terms of this lease. Alexandria possessed a sophisticated water supply from underground cisterns, which, as this text shows, was piped into even relatively modest private housing.

142 This clause (normal in Ptolemaic leases of *klêroi*) reflects the insecurity of tenure of kleruchic land at this period; if the kleruch went on active service or died, his *klêros* might revert to Crown land for later reassignment.

143 Mostly published in *BGU* IV (1050–60, 1098–1184), on which see Schubart (1913). Other leases from this group with English translation are Johnson (1936, nos. 213 [1117: bakery] and 72 [1120: cemetery garden]), and *Sel.Pap.* I 41 (1121: papyrus marsh). See also below, **8.2.6** (wet-nursing contract).

To be pasted (?)[144]

To Protarchos.

From Antonia Philemation, freedwoman of Antonius, with her guardian Gaius Julius Felix, and from Sarapion son of Aristeios, Persian of the *epigonê*. Concerning the matters under debate we agree on the following terms: Whereas Sarapion has leased from Antonia Philemation for a period of two years from Pharmouthi of the present 17th year of Caesar (= Augustus) the house belonging to her in the Delta (= 4th district of Alexandria) together with its associated shops facing the street, for a fixed rent per month of sixty drachmas of Ptolemaic silver, which he will pay to Antonia Philemation in full, each (installment) free of any deduction and expense [. . .] paying for the previous month on the 29th of each successive month. The maintenance and [? . . .] of the `public`[145] gaskets (?) and of watertight matting(?) and all the supply `and cutting off` and draining of the public water supply are the responsibility of Antonia Philemation; while the excrement in it is the responsibility of Sarapion, who has taken over the house complete with doors, windows and keys and free of excrement. He shall take on the lease for the agreed period, and take the profit as his own, having the right to introduce into or eject from it whomever he wishes, and to sub-lease to others the house with its associated shops facing the street, but he is not permitted to abandon the lease within the period, nor to fall behind with the monthly rent. And when the term is [completed], `he` will hand over the house with the [[and . . .]][146] doors and windows and keys contained in it, and additionally within the house, the mill and wooden pulley-system and wooden swing-beam in the wall and double night-stools[147] `in the swing-beam`, all as he received them apart from wear and tear. And if he infringes any of these terms, he will immediately be liable to arrest and imprisoned until he has paid whatever he owes for the rent increased by fifty percent, `and whatever he does not hand back he shall pay its value` plus the damages and expenses and a fine of 100 drachmas and the prescribed penalty, Antonia Philemation having the right of execution upon Sarapion and all his property as though by legal decision, all assurances produced by him and resort to protection being invalid and Antonia Philemation nonetheless having the right to remove Sarapion, if he breaks the contract, from the lease within the term and to lease out to

[144] See Pestman (1994b: 99).
[145] This word, and the others below enclosed in ` `, are added above the lines.
[146] Double brackets indicate a cancelation by the scribe.
[147] See Husson (1983: 42, 154–55).

others, and to exact the deficit as it stands at the date of reletting. But if he does everything in accordance with the terms, then Antonia Philemation shall give him secure possession of the lease for the term [[and pay in addition the remainder of the wages]],[148] or else she must forfeit the equivalent penalty. And Sarapion shall deduct for himself from the installments (?) of the rent of 60 dr., eight drachmas on account of [. . .]. And when Sarapion delivers the monthly rent to Antonia Philemation, he shall receive the [. . .] receipt from her slave Philargyros, and Antonia Philemation is to incur no risk with regard to the . . .

. . . 17th year of Caesar, Pharmouthi [.]6th.

7.3.4 Sharecropping lease of a vineyard

P.Soter 2 (*BL* VIII 412, X 250; German tr. *P.Soter.*, also reproduced in Drexhage *et al.* 2002: 236–37 [M 29]; see also Cadell 1994: esp. 115; *P.Louvre* I 36, pp. 173–74; Ruffing 1999) (Theadelphia, 18 August AD 71). Images at *P.Soter.* table II; Photographic Archive of Papyri in the Cairo Museum (http://ipap.csad.ox.ac.uk); Papyri.info.

This lease from the archive of the tenant farmer Soterichos employs the format of a public notarial contract (*syngraphê*): a notary wrote the body of the text, the parties appended their signatures, and then a copy was registered at the public office. The parties also kept their own copies; the surviving text is the one preserved by Soterichos in his family papers (see Smolders 2005).[149]

Unlike annual crops such as wheat or barley, grapevines are perennial and mismanagement in one year would ruin production in future. Therefore vineyard lease contracts tend to stipulate the obligations of the contracting parties in detail. Here the tasks of hoeing, pruning, fertilizing, repairing trellises to support the vines, and irrigation are carefully regulated.

Sharecropping arrangements are quite common in vineyard leases. Here the lessee's share of the produce is one-third and the cost of wine production is divided equally between the parties. The lessee can also profit from the surplus from the fruit trees, which were also used to train the vines, after he has paid the rent in kind to the lessor. Although the lessor is to

[148] This clause (like the other words marked in double square brackets) has been deleted on the papyrus, and clearly does not belong in this contract.

[149] We thank Dominic Rathbone for assistance with this text.

take two-thirds of the wine, she is liable for taxes and has to contribute to the costs of cultivation by providing donkeys and some necessary materials (reeds and ropes).

> Third year of the Emperor Caesar Vespasian Augustus, 25th of the month Kaisareios, in Theadelphia of the Themistos division of the Arsinoite nome. Thermoutharion daughter of [Sarapion], about twenty-five years old with a scar on the tip of her nose, with her husband Didymos son of Ptolemaios, about thirty-five years old with a scar on his left knee as her guardian, has leased to Soterichos son of Lykos, Persian of the *epigonê*, about twenty-five years old with a scar on the little finger of his left hand, the vineyard trained on trees belonging to her near the village, of half an aroura or whatever size it is. This lease is for three years from the coming fourth year, on terms that the lessee <shall have> one-third share of the annual fruits and produce yielded by the vines free from public taxes and every levy, all the cost of wine-making and of the wine to be drunk at the vat to be deducted jointly. It is not permitted to the lessee to vacate the lease within the term; and he must hoe the vineyard with two hoeings, one in winter in four spans in depth, clean, the other in summer with a single hoeing; and he must carry out a pruning of the vine that is moderate and sufficient, not cutting to excess. For the coming annual carting of earth and manure Thermoutharion shall provide donkeys, but the lessee will dig it in and distribute it; and each year he must construct anew from reeds eight five-pole trellises ("beds") and do maintenance on the rest, Thermoutharion providing the reeds and ties; and the lessee must each year carry out mechanical irrigation once every two days from the first of Pharmouthi until the coming of the inundation is apparent,[150] and he is to bear the expense of providing the dike-workman. All the fruit trees in the vineyard are for the lessee's use, from which he must give annually one thousand apples, and in the first year of the lease three-tenths <of an artaba> of thyme and in the remaining two years annually twice that amount of thyme, by the four-choinix dromos measure. And at the end of the term, the lessee must hand over the vineyard clear of rushes, scrub and every weed, and the walls standing. If the lessee infringes any of these conditions, let him pay twice the damage and expenses, plus a fine of five talents of bronze and no less; and on these terms Thermoutharion shall guarantee the lease, and free of taxes. Let this contract be binding.

[150] Literally "from foot": the exact meaning is uncertain; see Ruffing (1999: 139–40).

(*2nd hand*) I, Soterichos son of Lykos, Persian of the *epigonê*, have leased the vineyard on all the terms aforementioned. Nikandros son of Isidoros wrote on his behalf because he does not know letters.

(*3rd hand*) I, Thermoutharion daughter of Sarapion, with my guardian, my husband Didymos, have leased the vineyard to him on the [aforementioned] terms. I, [. . .] son of Phanias wrote on their behalf since they do not know letters.

(*4th hand*) A copy of the lease is registered. Year 3 of the Em[peror Vespasi]an Augustus, month of Kaisareios 25.

7.3.5 Application to lease the property of orphans

P.Amh. II 85 (= *M.Chr.* 274; tr. *P.Amh.* II; Johnson 1936, no. 73) (Hermopolis, 19 March AD 78). Image at Papyri.info.

The administration of the estates of orphaned children was supervised by public officials (here the *exêgêtês* of the Hermopolite nome), who leased them out to the highest bidder as illustrated by this text. The provision that the lease was conditional on no higher bid being offered within a statutory period is characteristic of land leased out under public administration (cf., e.g., *P.Oxy.* III 500), as, too, is the duration of five years, which reflects Roman practice. This contract (like its close parallel *P.Amh.* II 86) also differs from more typical agricultural leases in not following the pattern of the agricultural year for either its starting point or the date of rent payment. But, although it also does not mention the crops to be grown, the reference to the standard land taxes and the unusually full provisions in case of inundation failure make clear that the property is envisaged as primarily a landed estate.

To Hermaios son of Apollonios, of the Philoklaudian tribe and Althaian deme, *exêgêtês* of the Hermopolite nome, from Apollonios son of Ammonios and Horion son of Horion, Hermopolites. We voluntarily wish to lease for five years from the present tenth year of the Emperor Caesar Vespasian Augustus all the property of every kind left to his orphaned sons by Sarapion son of Kastor of Koussai, and whatever else I (*sic*) find to be owned by the orphaned sons of Sarapion, at a yearly rent, excluding the artaba-tax per aroura and the *naubion*, of six hundred drachmas of silver. If anything else is asked or exacted from us apart from the artaba-tax per aroura and the *naubion*, a deduction will be made to us from the aforesaid rent. We shall hand over the rent annually in the month of Phaophi to whomever you, the *exêgêtês*, appoint. If any of the land becomes uninundated, or washed away by the river, or sanded over, or eroded, from the coming eleventh year onwards, a proportionate deduction will be made to us from the aforesaid rent. If you agree to publish a copy of this for the customary ten days, as long as no one presents a higher bid, may the lease remain guaranteed to us for the period of five years without change. Tenth year of the Emperor Caesar Vespasian Augustus, Phamenoth 23. (*2nd hand*) I, Horion son of Horion, made this application. (*3rd hand*) I, Apollonios son of Ammonios, jointly made this application as stated.

Verso: Chou[. . .] lease of Apollonios son of Ammonios . . .

7.3.6 Prolonged leasehold of the Kronion family

The Kronion family from Tebtunis leased the same 25 (or 25.5) arouras of katoikic land near Kerkeesis from Eirene and her son Asklepiades, and later a certain Peteeus, for at least four decades (AD 109/10–150/1). Their archive contains seventeen documents concerning this long leasehold, including lease contracts, receipts for rent and tax, and notifications of cancellation of contracts.[151]

The two surviving lease contracts (*P.Kron.* 34 [AD 135] and 41 [AD 140]), with terms of six and seven years respectively, stipulate that the land was half arable and half pasture land (*ktamia*); the arable half was to grow wheat and fodder (as a fallow crop) in alternate years. In the years of wheat cultivation a rent in kind was to be paid. Although the surviving receipts (in *cheirographon* format: *P.Kron.* 27 [= **7.3.6a**], 28, and 33) date from outside the period of the surviving lease contracts, they seem to reflect similar conditions. Whether or not a contract specified who was responsible for paying the land taxes, in practice it was often the tenant who handed over the tax to the officials, as a phrase in the receipt translated below and several further receipts issued to the landowner but preserved in the Kronion archive suggest (*P.Kron.* 32, 37, 40, 43, 44, *SB* XIV 11864).

This leasehold was occasionally interrupted by cancellation requested by the tenant (*P.Kron.* 25, 29 [= **7.3.6b**], 42 [duplicate: *P.Mil.Vogl.* III 181], 45 [duplicate: *P.Mil.Vogl.* II 88]). The alleged grounds for cancellation were situations that made cultivation impossible in a given year, such as untimely breakout of water into the field. The cancellation seems to have been valid for

151 On the family and their archive, see also Rowlandson (1998: 125–33).

only the current year, the Kronion family resuming cultivation of the land from the next year. Lease cancellations show that, despite the gap of social and economic status between the landlord and tenant, tenants knew about and invoked a legal process when, for reasons beyond their control, they found difficulty in carrying out the terms of the lease (see further Kehoe 1995).

Eventually a certain Peteeus must have bought the land from Asklepiades or his mother, but the Kronion family continued to farm it (*P.Kron.* 45; AD 150/1).

7.3.6a Receipt for rent

P.Kron. 27 (= *P.Mil.Vogl.* III 168; *SB* VIII 9650; *Acme* 13 [1960]: 262; *BL* IX 116–17) (May/June AD 123, Tebtunis). Image at *P.Kron.*, Plate V.

Eirene daughter of Herakleides, with her son Asklepiades son of Asklepiades as her guardian, to Kronion, tenant farmer, greetings.
I have received from you the rent in kind for the present seventh year of the lord Hadrian Caesar, for the twelve and a half arouras of mine you farm near the village of Kerkeesis. You are liable for the artaba-tax and *naubion* of the arouras, for which you will give me receipt along with those for the other years that you have in hand.
I, Asklepiades, registered guardian of my mother Eirene.
Seventh year of the Emperor Caesar Trajan Hadrian Augustus, Payni [. . .]

7.3.6b Application to withdraw from lease

P.Kron. 29 (= *P.Mil.Vogl.* III 170; *SB* VI 9480 [2]; *Acme* 13 [1960]: 104ff.) (March–August AD 126, Tebtunis)

To Demetrios alias Menander, *basilikogrammateus* (royal scribe) of the Arsinoite (nome) Polemon division, also performing the duties of *stratêgos* of the said division, from Kronion son of Cheos from Tebtunis. I leased from Eirene daughter of Herakleides near the village of Kerkeesis twelve and a half arouras of *klêros* and twelve and a half arouras of pasture. But when I had carried out the agricultural work and sowing of all the arouras, it happened that the arouras were submerged by a breakout of water from the marshland in the past month of Phamenoth. I ask that a copy of this be handed over to [Eirene] through your assistant, so that she knows that I have no power to pay the rent for the present tenth year, it being sufficient for me to abide by this order.

7.3.7 Prodomatic sub-lease of public land

W.Chr. 359 (= *P. Flor.* I 20; cf. *BL* IV 29, VIII 124 – both concern the interpretation, not the reading; tr. Johnson 1936, no. 36) (Theadelphia, 9 August AD 127). Image at *P.Flor.* I, Plate V.

This contract (strictly an *epichôrêsis*, not a *misthôsis*) exemplifies a prodomatic lease, that is, one where the rent was paid in advance (*ek prodomatos*). Such contracts are not uncommon, particularly in leases of land involving fodder crops, and were made between farmers of public land in the Arsinoite nome. As here, they normally just record that the rent had been received, but not what it consisted of, giving rise to the suspicion that they are in fact concealed loans. Unquestionably in these cases, it was the lessor, not the lessee as usual in a lease contract, who was technically the indebted party (indicated here by Demas' status as Persian of the *epigonê*), and some such contracts seem to have the provision of credit as their main rationale (as is plausible in this case). But in other instances the same arrangement could be made for different reasons, such as the difficulty of predicting a fair price for fodder several months in advance.

This is one of the key texts once used to support the view that the state (in both the Ptolemaic and Roman periods) periodically revised all holdings of public land through a general *diamisthôsis* (leasing out); but it has now been shown that the redistribution of land envisaged here was a local, possibly one-off, event among the farmers themselves, not imposed by the state authorities (Hagedorn 1986; cf. Rowlandson 2005). In contrast, most sub-leases of public land show no indication that the lessor's tenure might be disrupted.

> Eleventh year of the Emperor Caesar Trajan Hadrian Augustus, sixteenth of the month Kaisareios, in Theadelphia of the Themistos division of the Arsinoite nome. Demas son of Horeion, Persian of the *epigonê*, about twenty-five years old, scar under his right shin, acknowledges to Horos son of Panesneus, about twenty-eight years old, scar to the right of his forehead, that he has conceded to him for the coming twelfth year of the lord Hadrian Caesar, in the public lands that he cultivates near Polydeukia in the so-called lands assigned,[152] one aroura by measurement from five arouras from whichever direction Horos chooses, to sow vetch-seed together with the mustard that will be planted,[153] Horos providing

[152] I.e., to Theadelphia; see later in the text, and Poethke (1969), Hagedorn (1986).

[153] As a second crop? Cf. Johnson (1936: 110).

seed and doing the sowing and weeding, but all the agricultural work and irrigation being the responsibility of the acknowledging party (= Demas); and the same acknowledging party has received from Horos the rent in advance and guarantees it with every guarantee. If it happens that the plain of the village is divided, Horos shall receive one aroura from whatever arouras Demas is allotted, whether this allocation is near Theadelphia or near Polydeukia . . . (*the papyrus breaks off*).

7.3.8 Lease of fishing rights with receipt

P.Turner 25 (*BL* VIII 498 [on interpretation of lines 26–28; see below]; tr. *P.Turner*; Italian: Migliardi Zingale 1992: 68–69, no. 33) (Oxyrhynchos, 28 December AD 161). Image at *P.Turner*, Plate XI.

This lease of fishing rights is also the earliest known *misthapochê*, a type of contract that combines in a single document both the lease and the receipt for rent paid in advance. Whereas some leases concern the right to fish in public canals or sluices (e.g., *P.Oxy.* XLVI 3268–70), here the fishing rights concern ponds located in private land, from a parcel formerly allotted to a Ptolemaic military settler ("the *klêros* of Krates").

Sarapion son of Hierax, mother Arsinoe, from Oxyrhynchos city, has leased to Philoxenos son of Apollonios from the same city, and Horos son of Ptollas from Seryphis, and Eutychos alias Vitlos son of Nophris from the (hamlet) of Episemou, the three of them, for the present year only, the catching of all fish that are in the ponds belonging to him near the said Seryphis in the *klêros* of Krates, at a rent of one hundred and seventy-two drachmas of silver, and eight drachmas for surcharge, which Sarapion acknowledges that he has received on the spot in full from the lessees, at the same time as the lease was written, the combined total of one hundred and eighty drachmas, the public dues of the land being Sarapion's responsibility. The lease having been confirmed,[154] this lease-receipt is binding. 2nd year of the lords Augusti Aurelii Antoninus and Verus, Tybi 2. (*2nd hand*) We, Philoxenos son of Apollonios and Horos son of Ptollas and Eutychos alias Vitlos, have leased the fishing and on the spot paid the

[154] See *BL* VIII 498: this clause, common in leases, normally refers to the future payment of rent being conditional on the confirmation of the lease (see **7.3.9**, **7.3.10**). It is therefore not appropriate in a *misthapochê*, where the rent has already been paid. It does not recur in later *misthapochai*, and here seems to reflect an early stage in the development of this new document type from a standard lease.

rent in full, that is, one hundred and eighty drachmas of silver as stated. I, Saras son of Philoxenos, wrote for them since they do not know letters.

Verso (downwards, along the fibres): (*3rd hand*) receipt [. . .] of fishing for the 2nd year, at a rent of 180 (drachmas).

7.3.9 Lease of land

P.Fouad 43 (= *BL* III 61, VIII 133; tr. *P.Fouad*) (Oxyrhynchos, AD 190/1). Image at *P. Fouad*, Plate IV.

This text is chosen because it includes clauses typical of Oxyrhynchite land leases from the Roman period, but also exhibits less usual features that merit comment (Rowlandson 1996: 202–79). Typical are the elaborate provisions for crop rotation between cereals and fodder, associated with a combination of rent in kind and money; the deduction from the rent in case of flood failure (only for the second year, since the current year's flood conditions must already have been known when the contract was drawn up); and the detailed prescription of how and where the rent in kind should be handed over. The two arable plots leased here are additional to a property (*ktêma*: probably a vineyard) that the lessees already lease from the same landlord. The seed loan (at 33 percent interest) to the tenants is unusual in Oxyrhynchite leases, although common in the Fayyum.

Serenus alias Dionysios son of Dionysios, ex-*exêgêtês* of the city of the Oxyrhynchites, has leased to Ptolemaios son of Papontos, mother Tayris, and to Antonius son of Thotsutmis, mother Kaipous, both residing in the village of Phoboou, for a period of two years from the present thirtieth year from what belongs to him near Phoboou on the south of the property <called> "Wheel," which the aforesaid hold on lease from the said Serenus, four and a quarter arouras on condition that `in the present year` they sow and plant them with wheat and barley at a total rent of twelve artabas of wheat and fourteen artabas of barley, and in the following year to plant with green fodder `for cutting and grazing` (*above the line*) at a rent of sixty drachmas per aroura. And in addition he has leased to the same men to the east of these eight arouras by survey on condition that in the present year they plant them with green fodder at a rent per aroura of twenty-four drachmas, and in the coming year to sow or plant with barley at a rent per aroura of eight artabas of barley. And the lessees acknowledge that they have received forthwith from the lessor for seed for the land four artabas of wheat at an interest rate of one third, all free of all risk, the public taxes on the land being the responsibility of the lessor, who will also own the crops until he receives what he is owed each year. If there is any flood failure in the coming year, an allowance will be made to the lessees. The lease having been confirmed, let the lessees hand over <what they owe> bringing the specified produce onto the threshing floor of Phoboou, the wheat new, clean, unadulterated, free of clods, free of barley, and sieved as if measured out to the public granary, and the barley complete, new, clean, free of clods, well threshed, without darnel and chaff, all by the landlord's *choinix*-receiving measure, including that for seed and interest, his agents doing the measuring for themselves, and he has the right of execution on both of them, being mutual sureties for payment, and from whichever one of them he chooses . . . (*papyrus breaks off*)

7.3.10 Lease of a pottery

P.Oxy. L 3597 (with trans.) (Oxyrhynchos, 22 September AD 260). Image at Papyri.info.

This is one of a small group of pottery leases that have aroused interest both for their legal aspects (Hengstl 1983) and for their detailed information on the practical and financial organization of pottery production (Cockle 1981, Mees 2002). Although explicitly described as a lease of the pottery (in the *epidochê* format), the arrangement here is in practice closer to a lease of work (cf. **8.2** below), in that, rather than paying a rent to the owner, the potter Claudianus is to receive a wage (in installments) in return for supplying the specified number of wine-jars. Although described as a "dependent," Claudianus is evidently able to enter into a legal contract with the owner of the estate for which he works, and it is envisaged that he will himself employ further labor to assist him. The note at the end of the signature shows that part of his previous year's obligations (and the corresponding raw materials provided to him) remain outstanding in the estate accounts.

To Septimius Eudaimon, gymnasiarch and councilor of Oxyrhynchos city, from Claudianus, dependent potter. I voluntarily undertake to lease for the present first year your third-share of a pottery for the production of wine jars that you possess in common with your brothers next to your estate near Sennis, and of the kilns in it and chambers and all appurtenances, on condition that I make for you from the winter manufacture so-called Oxyrhynchite four-*chous* jars to the number of eight thousand, one hundred double *keramia*, thirty two-*chous* jars, your men providing me in the pottery with black earth, sandy earth, friable earth and all the other necessities; I receiving as payment for the manufacture, firing and coating with pitch thirty-two drachmas per hundred jars, that is in total two thousand five hundred and sixty drachmas from which are deducted for the dues of myself, Claudianus, seven hundred drachmas. The remaining one thousand eight hundred and sixty drachmas I shall receive from you, from the present month Thoth up to and including Tybi, two hundred drachmas each month, (in) Mecheir three hundred drachmas, (and in) Epeiph and Mesore for the stoking, the remaining five hundred <and sixty?> drachmas. For the smoking of the jars and the stoking, you will provide for me in the pottery the necessary fuel, and the necessary pitch for coating them with pitch, you being present to supervise the pitching. And you will provide for me without interruption the necessary water for the cistern. [I shall make?] for you, in addition to the aforesaid, jars fired and coated with pitch to the number one hundred, and I shall receive as special payments two *keramia* of sour wine and one artaba of lentils. If my undertaking is confirmed, I shall carry out the manufacture of the jars and firing and pitching, providing myself with potters and all [assistance?]; and I shall hand over the pots in the month of Epeiph on the drying floors of the pottery, from the winter manufacture well-fired and pitched from rim to foot, satisfactory, not leaking, without repairs and blemishes; and at the end of the period I shall hand over the pottery as regards the part leased to me <free> from ash and potsherds, the right of execution belonging to you as appropriate. This undertaking is binding, and in answer to the formal question, I gave my assent. 1st year of the Emperors Caesars Titus Fulvius Iunius Macrianus and Titus Fulvius Iunius Quietus, Felices Augusti, Thoth 25.

(*2nd hand*) I, Septimius Eudaimon, have signed. There remain booked to him from the account of the 7th year: 150 jars, 21 double *keramia*, 3 two-*chous* jars; 1 talent of pitch.

7.3.11 Lease of "immortal" goats

P.Stras. I 30 (= Pestman 1994b, no. 67 [with trans.]; *P.Chept.* 12; *M.Chr.* 364; *Jur. Pap.* 40; *BL* VIII 413, XI 324) (Theadelphia, 7 September AD 276). Image at Pestman (1994b: 246).

This is one of twenty texts relating to a family based in the neighborhood of Theadelphia, who seem to have specialized in leasing sheep and goats, mostly from local large estates, although also from villagers, as here.[155] The lease does not explicitly mention that the lessee must have needed to supply a male goat to service the females, and to bear the cost of the goatherds' wages and the rent of pasture. In return, he would profit from the dairy produce, goat-hair, and any surplus kids. The adjective "immortal" (*athanatos*) in leases of sheep or goats means that the lessee had to return a herd of exactly the same number of beasts, replacing any lost during the term (Hengstl 1978b).

> To Aurelius Panneus son of Sepygos(?) from the village of Theoxenis, from Aurelius Pabous son of Kalamos from the village of Euhemeria. I wish to lease from you adult female goats, immortal, in number fifty-six, for two years from the present second year, at a rent in total each year of fourteen weaned kids, seven being male and the remaining female. I will make payment of the goats to you in the month of Payni each year.[156] And after the period, I will give you the goats, immortal, in the same condition as I have received them, if you decide to lease. In answer to the formal question, he gave his assent (*sic: for "I" and "my"*).
>
> Panneus about thirty-one years old, scar on the first finger of his right hand.
>
> (*2nd hand*) 2nd year of our lord Marcus Aurelius Probus Augustus, Thoth 10.

7.3.12 Lease of land

SB XII 10982 (= P.Mich. inv. 1352; see Shelton, *ZPE* 7 [1971]: 41–43, with English translation) (Tanis [Fayyum], 10 October AD 288). Image at Papyri.info.

Third-century land leases from the Fayyum are relatively few (compared to the third-century Oxrhynchite as well as to the Fayyum over the previous two centuries), and this example, with poor spelling and grammar, is typical in the low rent charged (cf. Drexhage 1991: 162–63). While containing all the clauses essential to the practical carrying out of the lease, it lacks the elaboration common in leases, such as specifying that the rent must be pure and unadulterated and the month in which it must be paid, and the guarantee clauses protecting the rights of both parties (contrast, e.g., *P.Tebt.* II 378).

[155] See Schwartz (1964) (= *P. Chept.*), Rathbone (1991: 202–11).

[156] "in the following year" is deleted here. Payni was the usual time for paying rent in kind on goats; they would just have been weaned: Rathbone (1991: 202).

To Aurelius Apollonios, honorably discharged veteran, from Aurelius Kornelios, from the village of Philadelphia. I wish to lease from you two and a half arable katoikic arouras near the village of Tanis in the Herakleides division, in a place called "Stone," for the present 5th and 4th year only, at the fixed rent for the two and a half arouras of five artabas of wheat, (total) 5 (artabas of wheat). And all the work and the construction of canals are the responsibility of me, the lessee, and all the public taxes and impositions are the responsibility of me,[157] the landowner. And after the time, I shall hand over the arouras to you in fallow.[158] And having been asked the formal question, I consented. And I shall give you the rent by the four-*choinix* measure on the threshing floors. (*2nd hand*) I, Aurelius Apollonios, have leased as stated.

(*1st hand*) 5th and 4th years of our lords Diocletian and Maximian Augusti, Phaophi 13th.

7.4 The Byzantine era: Greek, Coptic, and Arabic leases

T. Sebastian Richter

From a wealth of evidence, eight documents have been chosen for presentation below. The collection starts with two Coptic examples of leases of house property, *CPR* IV 114 (**7.4.1**) from Ashmunein and *O.Crum Ad.* 15 (**7.4.2**) from the Theban area. Like the Roman concept of *locatio-conductio*, the Greek notion of *misthôsis* included the leasing of objects both for simple use (*usus simplex*), as in the leasing of houses or apartments, and for yielding earnings (*usus fructus*), as in the leasing of land. While the designation of the documents themselves is always *misthôsis*, the designation of the rent varies in accordance with the different sorts of leasing (see Table 1). The rent to be paid for the leasing of house property was called *enoikion* in Greek and *shgor* in Coptic; in contrast, the rent to be paid for land-leasing was called *phoros* or *ekphorion* in Greek documents (see **7.4.3**), while its Coptic designation varied according to the document's provenance: In Coptic leases from the Fayyum (no example here), the old term *shom*, already attested in Demotic leases of this region (*šmw*), is preserved. Coptic leases from Ashmunein had borrowed the Greek term *phoros* (see **7.4.4**), and Theban documents used the Greek term *pakton* (**7.4.5**), which

157 If this reading is correct, it is a mistake for "you."

158 The lease does not specify the crop to be grown, but does this mean that the only crop of the year is to be a fallow crop (grass or legume), or that there is to be a second crop in the year, after wheat? The low rent perhaps suggests the former.

Table 1

MISTHÔSIS					
≈ *locatio conductio rei*				≈ *locatio conductio operis*	
usus simplex lease		*usus fructus* usufructuary lease		Contract for material and labor	
Term for "rent"		Term for "rent"		Term for "hire"	
Greek	Coptic	Greek	Coptic	Greek	Coptic
enoikion	*shgor*	*phoros*, *ekphorion*	Fayyum: *shom* Ashmunein: *phoros* Thebes: *pakton*	*misthos*	*beke*

was confined to a particular type of long-term agreement called *emphyteusis* (no example here) within the terminological system of Hermopolite documents.

One of the earliest datable Coptic lease documents, *BKU* I 48 (**7.4.6**) is a specimen of a particular Theban type of Coptic land lease, the so-called *epitropê* lease, which often contained a sharecropping arrangement instead of a fixed rent amount. By far the latest known Coptic lease, *P.Lond.Copt.* I 487 (**7.4.7**), issued in AD 900, is strongly influenced by Arabic documents, as can be seen by comparison with *Chrest.Khoury* II 29 (**7.4.8**, an Arabic lease of AD 938).[159]

7.4.1 Coptic *misthôsis*-lease of a part of a house

CPR IV 114 (= Vienna, papyrus collection of the National Library, inv. K 2569, Krall 1895, no. 125; re-ed. Till 1958: 108–09, no. 114 and Richter 2002c: 122–24, no. 3) (Ashmunein [Hermopolis], seventh century AD)

A papyrus 9 cm in height and 33 in width; text written in eight lines plus the docket on the verso. Both lessor and lessee are women. The Coptic clauses and phrases used to establish the agreement are renderings from the Greek *misthôsis*-scheme current in Hermopolis. The text starts with the introduction of the issuing party, the lessee, and the address to the lessor.

[159] In the translations below the spellings of the month names are given as they appear in Coptic; though different from, they will be easily identified with their Egyptian equivalents as transliterated through the Greek.

The entire body of the contract depends on the initial phrase, "I lease from you," recording the starting term of the lease (its duration was not fixed), the lease object, its appurtenances and location, the purpose of the leasing party, the amount of the rent (*shgor*), and the mode of its payment. The text closes with a stereotyped guarantee clause, the issuing date, and the lessee's stipulation.

Recto

Address form: † I, Kouper, the wife of the farmer John, I write to Lia, the daughter of [*blank*], the inhabitant of Shmoun:

Deed corpus: I lease from you as from today, the twentieth of the month Pakhons of this current eleventh year of indiction, your *exedra*-hall located on the first floor of the house, which opens westwards in the Street of Apa Gabriel, the street entrance opening westwards (too), and the joint use (*lit.*: share) of the cistern and of the stable and of the roof and of the remaining rights, and I will stay with you, and I will give you for the rent (*Coptic, amount in words:*) three *keratia* a year according to the exchange value, (*Greek, abbreviated, in figures:*) makes (in total) *k*(*eratia*) 3; and I give you that rent at the end of my year[160] as long as I will be staying with you.[161]

Closing form: As surety now, I have issued this *misthôsis*-deed. (*Greek, abbreviated:*) Wr(itten) (in the month) P(a)kh(ons), (day) 20, 11th ind(iction year) + + + (This is) Kouper's mark. † I, Kouper, I assent. I [. . .] son of [. . .], I have written for her, [. . .]

Docket on verso: The *misthô*(*sis*)-deed of K[ou]per; the rent is *k*(*eratia*) 3 †

7.4.2 Coptic lease of a house, written on an ostracon

O.Crum Ad. 15 (= Leipzig, Egyptian Museum of the University, inv. 504; Crum 1902, no. ad. 15, p. 23 (translation); re-ed. Richter 2002c: 136–37, no. 11, and Richter 2004) (probably Theban area, eighth century AD)

Written in ten lines on a reddish smooth potsherd of 9 cm in height and 12 cm in width. The lessee, being the issuing party, is a woman. She mentions an earlier conversation and gives an amazingly terse account of

160 "my year," i.e., a year counted from the starting term of the lease, the 20th of Pachon.

161 I.e., the duration of this lease was not specified, but left to the lessor's discretion. Other Byzantine leases had an explicit clause stating a term *eph' hoson chronon boulei* "as long as you like" (see Comfort 1934a).

the lease object, a house, which is referred to only by the expression "this house." Unlike the Greek and Coptic lease documents from Hermopolis, one of the larger towns of Byzantine and early Islamic Egypt, *O.Crum Ad.* 15 had a village background. Parts of the agreement could therefore have easily been settled in oral conversation and seemed unnecessary to put in writing. The details about the house as well as its location remain unstated. In the following clauses, likewise extremely short, the starting date and duration of the tenancy and the amount of rent (*shgor*) are fixed. The occurrence of the Arabic silver currency, the *dirham*, gives reason to date the piece to the eighth century, in conformity with the palaeography.

> *Invocation and address form:* In the name of God! It is I, Kyra,[162] (daughter of) Iethit,[163] who writes to Kometos:
>
> *Deed corpus:* Since I have spoken with you, you gave me this house, so that I dwell in it one year as from day twenty-four of (the month) Mechir up to day twenty-four of (the month) Mechir, and I give you its rent in the manner we have settled with each other, namely one *dirham* less two (corns of) barley.[164]
>
> *Closing form:* Kyra assents. (As for me,) Severos (son of) Mena, <she> asked me, I am writing for her.

7.4.3 Greek *misthôsis*-lease of arable land

P.Lond. III 1012 (cf. Herrmann 1958 and Hennig 1967) (Hermopolis, 7 September AD 633)

London, British Library, text written in forty-seven lines plus one line of the docket on the verso; from Hermopolis (Ashmunein); dated to the 23rd regnal year of the Emperor Herakleios, i.e., AD 633, which is a rather late date for a private legal document in Greek. The tenant, who is the issuer of the lease, and the lessor, its addressee, are identified as *geôrgoi* "farmers," and, in keeping with Byzantine custom, both bear the status designation Aurelius, pointing to Roman citizenship ultimately derived from the *Constitutio Antoniniana*, which is scarcely ever found in Coptic documents. In the deed corpus, introduced by

162 In Coptic contexts, the Greek word *kyra*, literally meaning "mistress," does often occur as a proper name.
163 A form of the Old Testament name Judith.
164 The mode of counting in "corns of barley" is inspired by the Arabic weight unit *hábba*.

and subordinated to the verb *homologô* "I declare" (cf. above, **2.7**), the starting day and duration of the lease, the sort, size, and location of the lease object – a plot of arable land – the agricultural work to be done by the lessee, and the amount as well as the quality of the rent (*phoros*) to be paid in kind in the month of Epeiph (June/July) are all recorded. The rights of use appertaining to the lease object include access to a cistern, a waterwheel, and an ox stable (no reference to whether with or without inhabitants), showing that this tenancy was not entirely dependent on the Nile flood but could be irrigated artificially by means of a waterwheel fed by a cistern driven by oxen (cf. also below, **7.4.4** and **7.4.5**).

Invocation: † In the name of the holy and vivifying and consubstantial Trinity, of the Father and of the Son and of the Holy Spirit!

Date: In the twenty-third year of the reign of our most divine, most gentle, god-crowned rulers Flavii Herakleios and Herakleios Neos Konstantinos, the eternal Augusti, the *imperatores* and greatest benefactors, in (the month) Thoth the 10th, in the seventh (year of) indiction †.

Address of the lessor and self-introduction of the tenant: † To Aurelius Daniel, the farmer, son of the late Christodoros, of Hermopolis †. From Aurelius Joseph son of Paul, of the mother Martha, farmer (as well), of the same city.

Deed corpus: I declare that I have willingly and voluntarily leased from you for one year, that means, (for) the crops of the – with God's will![165] – coming eighth (year of) ind(iction),[166] and only that![167] the three arouras of arable land belonging to you, corresponding to (*lit.* filling) 64 *hammata* according to the right measure(?) per each aroura, situated in the field called Tbôte in the landmark of the village Thynis under the protection of the Hermopolite nome, together with their right of use (*lit.* their share) of the cistern and of the waterwheel and the ox stable there, and of every right (of use), for sowing and planting of whatever produce I may choose,

165 A phrase due to the subsequent reference to future time, expressing a religious feeling of cautious reservation, just like the Latin *Dei voluntate*.

166 The expression "crops of an indiction" makes a statement as to the fiscal liability; see Comfort (1934b).

167 This expression stands in contrast to phrases like "and so forth" and "and from then forwards." It means the present tenancy cannot possibly be extended beyond the stipulated term of one season.

the rent being fifteen artabas of wheat, total, wheat art. 15; which rent I shall pay to you (in) new, clean, unadulterated, sifted (wheat), (measured) by your "Athenian" measure, and (which I) shall deliver for you to your house in Hermopolis by my own private beasts of burden and at my expense, in the month Epeiph of this same indiction year.

Kyria clause: The (present) lease is valid and guaranteed.

Stipulation clause: And in answer to the formal question I have given my consent. † (I,) Aur(elius) Joseph, so[n of Paul, have taken the lease as set forth.]

The expected witness signatures and the completion note of the notary are lost. On the verso are traces of the docket, mentioning the tenant's name.

7.4.4 Coptic *misthôsis*-lease of a "waterless aroura" of land

CPR IV 117 (Vienna, papyrus collection of the National Library, inv. K 3122; Till 1958: 112–13, no. 117) (Ashmunein [Hermopolis], seventh century AD)

Papyrus, 35.5 cm in height and 12 cm in width; text written in twenty-nine lines plus traces of the docket on the verso. The Coptic clauses and phrases are rendered from the Greek *misthôsis* scheme of Ashmunein. After the common opening formulas (a trinitarian invocation, the dating, and the introduction of the parties), the deed corpus, introduced by the Coptic equivalent of the Greek *homologô*-formula, gives the business details in the stereotyped order: first, the duration and starting date of the lease are fixed; thereafter the lease object is designated and specified as to its size, quality, and location, then the agricultural work to be done by the tenant is mentioned, and last, the amount of the rent (*phoros*) and the mode of payment are recorded. The plot of land is specified as a "waterless aroura," which means that it was located outside the inundated area. But as it was lying amidst an artificially irrigated field and surrounded by such fields, it may have been connected to water-lifting devices.

Opening form: Invocation, issuing date, self-introduction of the tenant and address of the lessor: [† In the name] of the Father a(nd) the Son [and the Holy Spi]rit! Written in the month [. . ., day *x* of the] current ninth year of indiction. [I,] the deacon [. . .,] son of the late Mêna who has been deacon too, the inhabitant of Schmûn, [I am writing to the] *dikaion* of my Lord, the Saint Theodore [of Pawôr]e,[168] (represented) by the most reverent deacon and estate manager Apa Viktor:

Deed corpus: I am glad and I agree, [being willing, without] regret, that I lease from you for three [consecutive] years, the space of time counted from the sowing [of this] current ninth [year] of indiction, the harvest however from – with God's will![169] – the tenth indiction, the belongings of the *dikaion* of this very monastery, (namely) one waterless aroura [. . .], located in Tsenoshîsh in the (artificially irrigated) field [which they call] "the field at the dike," according to its neighbors, [adjacent to its four sides] as follows: its southern side – the canal, its northern side – [the . . .] of the "field at the dike," its eastern side – the fields [. . .], its western side – the fields of the (artificially irrigated) field [. . .], and its neighboring etates are bordering on its four sides; [and that I shall] sow it with whatever produce I may choose, and shall harvest it, and that I shall [give you] for its cash-rent[170] five *keratia* a year; [(as to) this] cash-rent now, I am ready to give it [to you every] year in the month Hathor without any ambiguity.

Closing form and witness signatures: [For your surety now, I] issued this *misthôsis*-deed for you, honestly swearing [by God that I shall be watch]ful for you in accordance with its validity. (*2nd hand*) [I, . . .], this most humble deacon, son of the late Mena [who too has] been deacon, inhabitant of Shmoun, I assent † (*3rd hand*) [I, . . .]emon son of the late Kollouthe, inhabitant of Shmoun, [I am witness . . .] . . .

Traces of the docket on the verso

7.4.5 Coptic *misthôsis*-lease with waterless clause

O.CrumVC 33 (British Museum EA 44717, Crum 1939b, no. 33; tr. Crum 1939b: 17, Till 1964: 240–41; the *abrochos*-clause is dealt with by Richter 1998: 61) (Theban area [Taut], seventh/eighth century AD)

168 The landlord is a monastery, acting by its legal department, the so-called *dikaion*, which is represented by the person of an etate manager (*phrontistês*) in the rank of a deacon. Interestingly enough, the tenant, saying "the *dikaion* of my Lord the Saint Theodore," addresses not the monastery but its patron saint himself.

169 A phrase due to the reference to future time, expressing a religious feeling of reservation, just like the Latin *Dei voluntate*.

170 Literally, "rent in gold," as opposed to rent in kind. While the due date of the latter used to fall in a time shortly after the harvest, the payment of cash-rent was not terminated in such a manner. There are cases attested where the rent total was composed of an amount of money and an amount in kind, with two different due dates.

Text written in sixteen lines on a potsherd; from the *castrum* Taut in the area of Thebes. From the third century BC, the invention and improvement of water-lifting devices had made steady progress, but only in Byzantine times did the most effective watering machine, the waterwheel (called *mêchanê* or *kykleutêrion* in Greek, in Coptic *khoi*, nowadays in Arabic *sakîyah*) become increasingly widespread, lessening the risk of failure for the parties to agricultural leases. But in the present case, the tenancy is explicitly said to be lying "outside the artificially irrigated field," so that the success of agricultural work was entirely dependent on the height of the Nile flood. This might have caused the insertion of a so-called *abrochos*-[waterless, not inundated-]clause, setting a reduced rent amount to be paid in the case of a low flood (corresponding to the *remissio mercedis* "rent discount" of Roman law; cf. De Neeve 1983). When the agreement was issued at the first day of the month Thot, corresponding to 29 August, the irrigating and fertilizing waters of the Nile had just started to fill the artificial storage basins along the riverbanks. Despite an elaborate system of water-level measuring, there seem to have been residual doubts about whether or not the flood would reach certain areas in the region. For the first case, a sharecropping agreement was settled, otherwise, a low fixed rate of crops per aroura was to be paid by the tenant.

† We, Azarias son of Konon, in (the town of) Taut, and Iakob son of Isaak, inhabitant of the same *castrum*, are writing to the heirs of Tsia daughter of Tagia:

We have made a *misthôsis*-document for you concerning your fields which are located outside the artificially irrigated field of Mena, (son) of Kale, in the north of the ditch; and we sow them in the sowing of this eleventh indiction year at our expense and with our cattle and with our laborers; and we give you their rent (*pakton*), (being) one and a half artabas of [wheat] per aroura in the "small year," (or otherwise,) if they receive (inundation) water, the half (of the yield) [for you, the] (other) half for us. As a guarantee for you, we issued this *misthôsis*-document for you; it is secure. (*Greek*:) Written (in the month) Thoth the 1st, 11th (year of) indiction.

(*Coptic*:) [† We,] the afore[mentioned Az]arias and Iakob, [we] assent to this *misthôsis*-document as it stands.

7.4.6 Coptic *epitropê*-lease with sharecropping agreement

BKU I 48 (= Berlin, Papyrus Collection inv. P 865; Stern 1878: 19, no. 2; Revillout 1914: 23, no. 67; tr. Till 1964: 16; Hasitzka in *SBKopt.* II, no. 951) (Theban area, *c.* AD 600)

Text written in twenty-four lines on both sides of a slab of limestone; from the Theban area; around AD 600 (written in a third indiction year, such as 584, 599, or 614). The scheme is related to the Theban type of Coptic lease document called *epitropê* "commitment," but it differs from them by its particular societal attitude. Although the text starts with a common unilateral address formula and the usual promise by the tenant "that I sow your part of the fields," it continues, "and we work on it." Eventually the closing formulas are properly bilateral, saying: "we have drawn up this declaration together as an *epitropê*, we assent." Consequently, not only is a sharecropping agreement settled, as often in the Theban *epitropê* type of leases (and likewise in the Theban *misthôsis*-lease, e.g., **7.4.5** above), but any expenditure, from the seed to the land-tax, shall be paid for by both parties. The monk David who has written the ostracon is a well-known personality of early seventh-century Djême; he was one of the secretaries of Apa Abraham, the abbot of the local monastery of Phoibammon and at the same time the bishop of Hermonthis. For Abraham's dossier, see **3.4.3** (Ex. 2).

† It is I, Azarias son of Kyrikos, inhabitant of Ramow, who writes to Iakob son of Daniel, the monk.

After we agreed with each other that I shall sow your share of the fields (named:) "the clay[171] soil of the herdsmen," I am now ready to work on it without negligence; and we will work on it for half (of the yield) for each (of us); and the seed and the whole expenditure shall be paid in full from the common (i.e., the unshared crops), and (as for) the land-tax, we will pay it together, and (as for) the chaff, we will share it between us.

Together we issued this *epitropê*-declaration; we, Azarias and Iakob, we assent. I, David, this most humble monk, I have written this *epitropê* with my own hand on day five of (the month) Thot of the third year of indiction.

7.4.7 Late Coptic lease of a tenancy "without survey"

P.Lond.Copt. I 487 (= London, British Library, Or. 5287(1), Crum 1905; re-edited by Richter 2003) (probably Ashmunein, AD 900)

Written on a narrow, vertical piece of papyrus, 22.6 (H) × 6.5 (W) cm, which had been folded fourteen times in width and twice in length.

[171] "Clay soil" (in Coptic *ome*) as a sort of arable land is a peculiarity of Theban documents from the New Kingdom onwards.

Provenance presumably from Ashmunein. Dated 287 *hijra* = AD 900. This latest attested Coptic lease document is more than terse, it is almost telegraphic. Its scheme and its terminology are borrowed from contemporary Arabic leases. The text is issued by the lessor, as was usual in Arabic leases. It mentions nothing but the first names of the parties and of a third, unspecified person (perhaps a witness), the location of the tenancy (specified as one "without survey," cf. below, introduction to **7.4.8**), and the issuing date. Obviously, some important bits of information remain untold: we do not even learn anything about the term of this tenancy (which may have been one season) or the amount of rent to be paid. The use of Coptic as a language of legal documents was limited at that time to the narrow confines of Coptic village communities and their networks; the effectiveness of a document like the present one may have been small, not much above the oral agreements that seem to have been common in the case of the annual lease business (cf. Eyre 1997 and 2004).

//In the name of God! I, Anoup, I am writing to Phakeu:
After you asked me, I have given to you a tenancy without survey beneath the canal that carries water from the "dike of the Amîr" northwards. I, Anoup, I assent in this current year 287.
Papostolos (being witness), a tenancy.

7.4.8 Arabic lease of a tenancy "without survey"

Chrest.Khoury II 29 (= Vienna, papyrus collection of the National Library, Inv. Chart.Ar. 11314, *PERF* no. 955; descr. Karabacek, Krall, and Wessely 1894: 253, no. 955; ed. Grohmann 1950: 82–84, no. 1 + Plate II; re-ed. Grohmann and Khoury 1995: 101–03; for the scheme and its terminology cf. Frantz-Murphy 2001) (Ashmunein, AD 938)

Text written in nineteen lines on a leaf of paper, 21.3 cm in height and 10.5 cm in width. From Ashmunein. Dated 326 *hijra* = AD 938. Just like the late Coptic lease **7.4.7**, this Arabic document concerns a "tenancy without survey," an expression referring to certain irregularities in the official annual surveying of arable land on the banks of the Nile (cf. Frantz-Murphy 2001: 161). As under the conditions of flood-fed irrigation, both the location and size of fields varied considerably from year to year (cf. Eyre 2004). In the present case, the unspecified size of the leased-out fields must have been considerable; the extraordinarily high rent of 20 dinars would point to some 80,000 square meters. As usual in Arabic lease documents, which were always issued by fiscal agents formally acting as lessors, the state and its interest in land tax are much more visible than in the earlier Greek and Coptic land leases. While all issues of agricultural work are explicitly left to the tenant's discretion, his liability for correct and on-time tax payment is treated in great detail. The text starts and ends with an abstract, at least one of the two probably still visible after the paper was folded.

The translation of Grohmann and Khoury (1995) is followed.

Abstract: Tenancy that (previously) was in the hand of Rauh ibn Abd-al-Rahman, (including) everything within its boundaries in the last year, a tenancy without survey. Dinars: 20.

Invocation and address: In the name of god, the Merciful the Compassionate! Praise be to God, the Lord of the world! This is the record of Ali ibn Muhammad ibn Ahmad, the tenant in the island of Maqbala, for the year three hundred and twenty six. He wrote it for Muhammad ibn Ibrahim, the bean seller.

Deed corpus: Verily, you asked me and requested that I rent you the tenancy known as "Tenancy of Rauh ibn Abd-al-Rahman" from the soil of Maqbala, (that) you sow (on) it whatever you want, (as) a tenancy without survey, for twenty dinars' weight measure,[172] right, without discount,[173] according to the schedule[174] current in this area. You (may) sow (it) or you (may) leave (it) without work, its tax-in-money[175] is incumbent upon you, and on condition that you fulfill your tax-in-money together with the governor's (sultan's) – may God strengthen him! – installments and his expiry dates, so I grant you that. So sow with the blessing of God and his help, and you are responsible for that. And that (was written) in (the month) Dhu-l-Qa'da of the year three hundred and twenty-six, 326.

Summary: Tenancy of Rauh in the last year, a tenancy without survey. Dinars: 20.

[172] For the term *mithqâl* used here, see Frantz-Murphy (2001: 133–34).

[173] The term *sarf* "schedule, register" used here "should be understood as a discount given for paying in gold coins, dinars. Payment in crops, or even in coins other than gold dinars, would have involved an exchange rate. Payment made in dinars, the unit of account that did not have to be exchanged, would result in a discount, since there was no need to pay an exchange rate" – Frantz-Murphy (2001: 149).

[174] For the term *rasm* used here, see Frantz-Murphy (2001: 113–14).

[175] For the term *kharâjl* used here, see Frantz-Murphy (2001: 25–31).

CHAPTER 8

Labor

Brendan Haug, Andrea Jördens, and Sitta von Reden

Introduction

This chapter is concerned with the contractual relationship between laborers and employers. As it was elsewhere in the ancient world, the economic form that labor took ranged from fully free labor in the household, to paid wage labor, to slavery (Chapter 9).[1] As such, the texts that are presented here are generally concerned with free labor subject to certain contractual restrictions. Those restrictions, documented for example in the *paramonê* contracts (for which see also **5.5.2–3**), included the stipulation to remain in a particular place to work during the length of the contract.[2] The use of contracts to hire labor has an earlier history in the Ancient Near East. There was of course dependent labor particularly in agricultural work and domestic service (Chapter 9). In the periods covered by this volume, most labor arrangements were oral and therefore escape us entirely.

The preserved Ptolemaic contracts – only a few survive – are concerned generally with agriculture and related work, including the clearing of brushwood (**8.1.1**) and canal maintenance (**8.1.3**), or specifically with work in a so-called monopoly industry such as beer-making (not represented below). **8.1.2**, however, is a private agreement between two parties for the manufacture of a yoke and basket.

A much wider variety of labor agreements is represented in contracts of the Roman and Byzantine periods (**8.2**), while the more specific problem of the possibly dependent status of certain agricultural laborers (*enapographoi geôrgoi*) in the Byzantine-period papyri from Oxyrhynchos is illustrated and examined in **8.3**.

[1] On some of the interpretive problems involved, see Descat (2011).

[2] Demotic parallels for such texts from the Ptolemaic period, not treated here, are discussed by de Cenival (1973).

8.1 Ptolemaic (Greek) labor contracts

Sitta von Reden

In Ptolemaic Egypt, as in most other ancient societies, free contractual labor was common. Most agrarian labor was part of tenancy agreements (see Chapter 7) and sharecropping arrangements (**7.3.4**, **7.4.6**, **8.2.12**) that bear many similarities with labor contracts but are not treated in this section.[3] Some land was worked by farmers employed directly by the landowner, while special agrarian tasks, such as gardening, melioration work, and seasonal labor, were generally subject to work contracts. Outside the agrarian economy, temporary work contracts are attested for construction work, any type of manufacture, wet-nursing, and entertainment (music and dancing). For many other workers (scribes, managerial personnel, household staff, etc.) permanent employment was typical. Employees entered the household of the employer permanently and their employment is best approached in terms of a combination of patronage and contractual relationship.[4] There are some indications that the employer, apart from paying a salary in cash and in kind, was morally obliged to offer legal assistance, financial support, and monetary loans to his employee if needed.[5] Most types of free labor could be replaced by slave labor, and some slaves were hired out by their owners to work for others against a wage.[6] But slavery played a subordinate role in the economic life of Egypt and was largely confined to Greek households. (See Chapter 9 introduction.)

Certain labor contracts involved the forfeit of personal rights of the laborer or employee, most notably the right to leave the place of work or to seek asylum in a temple (i.e., the so-called *paramonê* contracts).[7] These contracts, of which only a few belong to the Ptolemaic period, have been much discussed by legal papyrologists. They usually contain the obligation to perform a specific task, or any work, in return for a loan, the interest of a loan, or an unrepaid debt. At the same time the person offering the work agrees not to leave the place of work for the period specified in the contract. It is questionable whether these contracts were a form of self-pledge,

[3] Both lease and labor contracts were regarded as forms of *misthôsis* (lease; letting for hire; see Aristotle, *Nicomachean Ethics* 1131a; Plato, *Laws* 759d; *Soph.* 219d). Both indeed share some contractual arrangements and legal consequences; Rupprecht (1995: 122–26), Wolff (1961: 149–54). See also Behrend (1970: 10–16).

[4] Pietowska (1975). [5] Von Reden (2007: 130–44).

[6] The practice is much better attested in Roman law: see Bürge (1999: 139–50). For Ptolemaic examples, see Scholl (1990).

[7] See **5.5.2** and **5.5.3** above. E.g., *CPR* XVIII 1, 1–13 (231/206 BC; Arsinoite nome); *CPR* XVIII 18 (231/206 BC, Arsinoite nome); *PSI* V 515 (251/0 BC, Arsinoite nome); see also Adams (1964).

an antichretic loan agreement (cf. **5.5.1**), or a labor contract.[8] Some texts suggest that a period of apprenticeship could be regulated in this way (*PSI* IV 424, third century BC, Arsinoite nome). Given that *paramonê* was stipulated in very different cases, it is likely that it was an agreement applied to a number of situations rather than one specific legal institution. Third-century BC Demotic papyri that detail third-party guarantees for specific work are clearly a related kind of contract. These papyri, known as "cautionnements," come from the Fayyum. The original editor (de Cenival 1973) categorized them into three basic types. The first, and most numerous, type was a third-party guarantee of a payment, probably a state tax. The second type involved third-party guarantees of appearance in a particular place and a promise not to seek asylum in a temple, while the third type was similar and involved a guarantee to work in a designated location for a specified period of time.

Labor in the Ptolemaic period was usually paid for in cash, or a combination of cash and kind, mostly bread (so-called *sitometria*, breads measured to a particular amount of grain used). Permanent employees could expect a clothing allowance that was paid annually in the form of a fixed sum of money. Oil could also be paid in kind, but it is not as frequently attested as *sitometria*. The commutation of parts of or the entire salary into kind or cash was frequently practiced.

There was no apparent distinction between public and private work contracts or forms of employment, or indeed between public and private *misthôsis* in Greek law.[9] Although the older literature tends to refer to public officials as civil servants, members of the administration did not enjoy particular rights of employment. On the contrary, we know that heavy financial burdens were imposed on even minor officials both at the moment of appointment and during their periods in office.[10] We also know that public officials were fully accountable and personally liable for the financial transactions they undertook (*SB* I 5680, Herakleopolite nome, 222/1 BC). Yet employment contracts within the administration are absent, and it is likely that royal or local instructions and a particular

[8] Wolff (1961: 150–52), Hengstl (1972: 12–14). A very interesting case is *CPR* XVIII 18 (231/206 BC), where the (relatively small) loan of 400 bronze drachmas (interest included) is said to be worked off by the debtor against ten years of work for payment in kind. The worker agrees to stay (*paramenein*) in the place of work and will receive a monthly grain and oil ration as well as an annual clothing allowance of 50 bronze drachmas (i.e., 500 drachmas in total). The editor *ad loc.* probably rightly concludes that this was de facto a labor contract styled as a loan agreement; see also *CPR* XVIII 1 (231/206 BC).

[9] Behrend (1970: 8–49).

[10] Verhoogt (1998: 54–67).

code of behavior acknowledged by the employee on oath or in writing provided the legal basis for the hierarchical labor relationships in the Ptolemaic administration.

Public and private work contracts were distributed by competitive bid. Larger projects, especially for irrigation and construction work, could be farmed out to a chief contractor who sub-employed the workforce (so-called *ergolabia* contracts; see **8.1.3**). Permanent employment in the private and public sectors seems to have required personal recommendation and general patronage. Moreover, the state and local administrations had the chance of recruiting labor on a compulsory basis (*leitourgiai*). In principle, every inhabitant of Egypt was liable for compulsory work, but in practice many were exempted, paying a small monetary tax in compensation. In the Ptolemaic period it was mostly strenuous labor, such as work on the irrigation system, in quarries, and construction work, for which *corvée* was used.

The provision of materials or work tools, or prepayment of parts or all of the salary could be agreed upon. Some documents in the Zenon archive suggest that such questions were negotiable (e.g., *P.Cair.Zen.* IV 59649; *PSI* IV 599, both third century BC, Arsinoite nome). But it is interesting to note that written labor contracts are attested only in those cases where capital was provided, salaries prepaid, or *paramonê* stipulated, and it is likely that labor contracts not including the transfer of capital or personal rights were concluded orally.[11]

Written labor contracts therefore represent exceptions rather than the norm in Ptolemaic labor relationships. In the first two contracts reprinted here it was the prepayment of money that justified a *syngraphê*; in the third it was the fact that public work was farmed out to a tenant-like *ergolabos*, which explains the written form of the initial contract. The employer appears in all cases as the contract's stronger party, while the employee had few enforceable rights against the employer. In the three cases cited this may have been justified by the prepayment of salary, but it is noteworthy that the employee was little secured against problems beyond his control occurring in the course of his work.[12] We also know that later installments for work in progress were sometimes delayed, causing damages to the contractual time schedule (e.g., *P.Petr.* II 13 (1), 256/5 BC,

[11] See *P.Mich.Zen.* 45 (252/1 BC, Arsinoite nome) where it is recommended that *bebaia* (guarantees, securities) should be requested from workers because money was to be prepaid for the completion of the work.

[12] According to Wolff (1961: 139–44), however, the laborer was secured against eviction from the land or work by third parties, as the contract of *misthôsis* included the temporary acquisition of rights over the object transferred.

Arsinoite nome; *P.Lond* VII 2038, mid-third century, Arsinoite nome). In such cases the employee had no contractual right to enforce payment in order to finish the work on time. Nevertheless, the weakness of the employee or contractor of work should not be overstated. *Paramonê* contracts, which used to be taken to illustrate the lack of freedom of Ptolemaic labor, were the exception, usually being the result of outstanding debts or loans. Permanent employees, moreover, had unwritten privileges such as access to legal and financial support. The right to seek asylum in a temple (*anachôrêsis*) was built into any labor relationship, unless it was explicitly forfeited.[13] And the employee had the chance to write letters of complaint or file a petition (*enteuxis*) with the king in cases where he had no enforceable rights against his employer.

Individual labor contracts must therefore be approached in a broader context of agrarian and social conditions, unwritten rules, customs, and the development of formal law under Ptolemaic rule. Moreover, a wide range of different labor and debt relationships was regulated by a very limited pool of contractual forms, which led to constructions in which rights and obligations swapped their functions. **8.1.2**, possibly a loan worked off in kind, or the much-discussed *paramonê* contracts offer the best illustration of the uncertainties that lie behind many Ptolemaic labor contracts.

8.1.1 Contract for land clearance

P.Cair.Zen. II 59182 (*BL* VI 27, X 37; Hengstl 1972: 53; Wolff 1961: 151–54; Rupprecht 1967: 73, 152) (Philadelphia [Fayyum], 4 October 255 BC). Image at Papyri.info.

This Greek text is a six-witness contract (cf. **5.2.2**) from the Zenon archive. This was the standard form in which full or temporary transfer of property was agreed between contractual parties using Greek law. As was usual in the third century BC, **8.1.1** appears in duplicate form, of which only the lower, unsealed version is reprinted here. For such "double documents," see also **2.1.1–2**.

Several Egyptian laborers, presented in groups, acknowledge the receipt of money at the rate of two drachmas per aroura for clearing of brushwood land that they have received (*eklambanein*). The receipt of the land included the right to occupy it and defend it against third parties.[14]

[13] Cadell (1983).

[14] For the rights of the lessee/laborer following from the terms *eklambanein/ekdidonai* (synonymous with *misthoun/misthousthai*), see Wolff (1961: 138).

They are required to return (*apodidonai*) the land in good condition and to Zenon's satisfaction within twenty-one days. The clause is constructed like a leasehold where, too, tenants are required to return the land or animals they have received (*eklambanein/paralambanein*) in good condition, e.g., *P.Mich.* I 66 (245 BC, Arsinoite nome); *P.Hamb.* IV 239 (third century BC, Oxyrhynchite nome), etc. The penalty of *hêmiolion* (50 percent more than received) in case of non-fulfillment of the contract was common both in loan and lease contracts.[15] The penalty clause, furthermore, contains the formula that execution should be as in cases of debts to the king (*hôs pros basilika*). This formula could be adopted both in public and private contracts and probably referred to a quicker way of enforcement.[16] The contract concludes with the list of six witnesses, all bearing Greek names apart from a village scribe. These were frequently Egyptians, or men who adopted Egyptian identities despite being Greek.

The papyrus belongs to the Zenon archive related to agricultural activities in the Fayyum between 260 and 240 BC. A number of much shorter Greek and bilingual receipts (*symbola*) in which individuals or groups acknowledge receipt of money for the same work are preserved from the year 257 BC (*P.Col.Zen.* I 22–28; *Pap.Lugd.Bat.* XX 3–10). They fall into two categories. Either a loan of four obols per aroura is acknowledged by tenants holding the land for a year or more, or temporary workers are paid (but not prepaid) directly by the estate at the rate of 2½ drachmas. It is likely that the more elaborate form of the present document was adopted because money was prepaid to temporary workers not bound to the estate by a tenancy contract.

> In the 31st year of the reign of Ptolemy son of Ptolemy the benefactor god, when Glaukon son of Eteokles was priest of Alexander and the brother–sister gods, and Berenike daughter of Nikanor *kanêphoros* of Arsinoe Philadelphos, on the 24th of the month Loios, which is the 14th of the Egyptian month Mesore, in Philadelphia in the Arsinoite nome.
>
> Etepheus, Nechtheneibis, Petenouris [*and two more*], five brothers living in the village of Sebennutes, have received from Zenon son of Agreophon, from Kaunos, in the service of Apollonios the *dioikêtês*

[15] Berger (1911: 102–03), Rupprecht (1967: 196–202).

[16] Rupprecht (1967: 105–06); Pringsheim (1950: 522); see *P.Col.Zen.* I 54, col. I (256 BC, Arsinoite nome), *P.Cair.Zen.* II 59173 (255/4 BC, Arsinoite nome); see *P.Hamb.* I 24 (222 BC, Arsinoite nome), where the formula appears in a public contract.

[*for a certain amount of* arouras *a certain amount of money*]; and Horos son of Haruotes [*and one more*], both living in Sebennutes for 10 arouras 20 drachmas; and Psenobastis son of Poklelios, and Petosiris son of [...] [*and one more*] for 5 arouras 10 drachmas; and Teoteles for 10 arouras 20 drachmas. This is for the cutting of the brushwood in the fields that they have taken up in the fourth basin. They will return the land clean and to Zenon's satisfaction by Gorpiaios, which is the first of the Egyptian month Thoth. If they do not return the land, they will pay to Zenon immediately the money received together with half more, and Zenon or his representative shall have the right of execution upon them and all their property as in cases of debts to the king

Witnesses of this contract are Sostratos son of Kleon, of Hellenion;[17] Diodoros son of Zopuros, Magnesian; Theopompos son of Aristion, the Thessalian; Harmodios son of Phokion, Kaunian; Styrax son of Apollonios, Argive; Anosis son of Totorchois, Saite, village scribe in Philadelphia.

8.1.2 Labor contract

P.Corn. 4 (Pathyris, 22 April 111 BC) (Seidl 1962: 146; Hengstl 1972: 54)

This fragmentary contract is comparable to the previous, but takes us to Pathyris in Upper Egypt, about thirty km to the south of Luxor. In Upper Egypt Greek *misthôseis* were drafted as single documents in the presence of an *agoranomos* in whose office the document was kept for the time of its duration. In the second century BC Pathyris accommodated a large Greek military settlement that entertained close connections with the Egyptian population of the town (see **3.1**). In this contract, the Egyptian carpenter Petes agrees with Horos, who claims immigrant descent but bears an Egyptian name, to make a yoke and a basket within nine months. In the lost section of the contract sanctions in the case of non-fulfillment were specified.

A striking aspect of this contract is the fact that the time provided for making rather unspecialized pieces of manufacture is exceedingly long. In connection with the previous, and because of the penalty clause, it is likely that some prepayment was agreed in the lost part of the contract. Possibly, it was a loan of money paid off in kind, rather than the work, that was the motivation behind this agreement.

17 A deme in Alexandria; *BL* VI 27.

Year 6, Pharmouthi 5, at Pathyris, in the presence of Ammonios the *agoranomos*. Petes son of Peatios, the carpenter, agrees with Horos son of Nechutes, Persian of the *epigonê*, that he will make a wagon yoke and a basket, both to satisfaction, by Tybi 3 of year 7. If he does not make them as written above, he will pay immediately . . . (*papyrus is damaged, then breaks off*)

8.1.3 Contract for maintenance of irrigation canals

P.Petrie III 43 (2) recto Cols. II–III, line 7 (*BL* III 146; Lewis 1986: 40–42; von Reden 2007: 205–26; Berger 1911: 166–79) (Krokodilopolis, 8 October 245 BC)

This text is part of a series of similar memoranda drawn up in Krokodilopolis under Theodoros, chief architect of the Arsinoite nome, during the 240s BC. They are all concerned with the public maintenance of the irrigation system in the Arsinoite nome. This one concerns the removal of silt that the Nile flood left behind when it receded in late September, causing obstruction in the water channels. It is not a work contract itself but an official note (with dating formula) referring to a public contract that had been given out by the administration. The contracting parties had been apparently the *oikonomos* of the Arsinoite nome and an *ergolabos* (contractor) who was in charge of a larger workforce. The administration in principle had the option of either requisitioning local *corvée* labor directly or farming out the work to a private contractor who sub-employed the laborers. Here the latter was adopted.

The arrangements are therefore close to those known from tax-farming contracts detailed in *P.Rev.*[18] Sureties had to be provided by the contractor; the contract was to be sealed in the presence of the sureties; working tools were provided by the administration; they had to be returned in full weight; payment was made in the bronze standard (i.e., 24 obols being reckoned to the *statêr* rather than 26 or more, as was the case when payment was made in the silver standard); and the usual penalty charge of *hêmiolion* plus any damages (*blabos*) resulting from the transfer of the work to a new contractor was stipulated. The *oikonomos*, in contrast, was advised to take the money from the oil monopoly (*elaïkê*) for whose collection he was responsible and personally liable. The payment in installments is explained mainly by the check it offered to the *oikonomos* on the

[18] Austin (2006, nos. 296 and 297).

contractor's work, but also by the fact that payments of the *elaïkê*, too, were paid into the treasury in installments.

Most interesting in this text is once again the prepayment of the salary to the contractor. Most contractual labor in the Ptolemaic period was paid after it was completed. Prepayment can be explained in this case by the fact that the *basilikon* was the financially stronger party, while the *ergolabos* could not be expected to advance the money he needed. The provision of capital (tools, seed, and money loans) to tenants was customary in Egypt, although it was generally a negotiable part of a contract.[19]

> In the second year of Ptolemy son of Ptolemy and Arsinoe, the brother–sister gods, when Tlepolemos son of Artapates was priest of Alexander and the brother–sister gods, and Ptolemais daughter of Thyion, *kanêphoros* of Arsinoe Philadelphos, on the 21st of the month Mesore at Krokodilopolis in the Arsinoite nome. A contract was farmed out from the royal treasury through Hermaphilos the *oikonomos* in the presence of Theodoros the architect and of Imouthes, the agent of the royal scribe Petosiris, to Ptolemaios [. . .] to clear out the sand from the irrigation channel at the canal near (the village of) Hephaistias alongside the boundary stone of the land of Timotheos, in order to secure the irrigation of the land of the kleruchic cavalrymen, for a distance of 50 *schoinia* [*c.* 7 lines missing]. They (the officials) shall pay half of the money assigned to the work in the third year out of the price of the produce of oil that they shall measure into the royal storehouses; but if they do not measure it in, they shall pay the money on demand together with half more. The contractors shall finish the work without interfering in any way with the irrigation of the land and providing themselves with all they need, within thirty days from which they receive the money. Thirteen spades shall be provided from the royal storehouses, whose price shall not be added to the account and which on completion of the work shall be returned at the same weight as when received. Half of the money shall be given to them as soon as they have sealed the contract in the presence of the sureties. The contract is to be given on the bronze standard at 24 obols to the *statêr*. When they have done the work for the money they have received [they shall receive the remainder . . .]; but if they do not perform the work or shall not act as is written, it shall be in the power of the person appointed for this purpose to put up the work for sale again and pay the workers daily. And the contractors mentioned above shall immediately pay any additional costs of the second sale, and all that may be expended on

[19] Hughes (1952: 2).

additional wages, and pay back the money which they have already received together with half more, and the loss incurred, and the king shall be notified. If not . . . (*the contract breaks off*)[20]

8.2 Roman and Byzantine labor contracts

Andrea Jördens

As in pre-modern societies generally, labor contracts in Roman and Byzantine Egypt would as a rule have been concluded orally. The conclusion of an agreement might have occasionally been strengthened by a specific gesture, such as a handshake, but this did not leave any trace in the tradition. The situation for written contracts, which survive in great numbers in the papyri, was different. Yet they should be viewed as exceptions, because they were concluded only when special circumstances rendered them necessary so that their content could be verified at any given time. This applied especially to long-term arrangements, as well as to contracts that depended on the fulfillment of a variety of conditions, not least when there was a clear status distinction between the parties and some otherwise existing requirements had to be secured through an obligation to work. Common to them all is that, at least from the perspective of one of the contracting parties, the oral agreement needed an appended written confirmation in order to enhance its reliability, whether for reasons specific to an individual, that is, to the economic or social status of the parties, or because of the complexity of the specific jobs contracted. Thus we find that extant labor contracts are primarily concerned, not with cases of ordinary work, but rather with exceptional circumstances. Accordingly, one frequently finds so-called mixed transactions, which chiefly combine loans and, in agriculture, leases, with work arrangements. In a broader sense, one might also include sales on delivery (*Lieferungskäufe*), especially when products, e.g., wine-jars, also had to be manufactured as part of the agreement (cf. **6.2.2**).[21] Because, however, compensation for this is regularly designated in the documents as the "price," such documents are treated in the present volume under contracts of sale, while an instance in which the use of a pottery workshop (**7.3.10**) is paid for expressly with manufactured wine-jars is treated as a contract of lease.

20 The last two sentences are reconstructed from another contract of this series, *P.Petr.* III 43 (2), recto Col. IV.

21 See further Kruit (1992b).

The labor contracts discussed in the following paragraphs have been chosen for their variety but also as a representative selection of this legal genre; references to any peculiarities will be made in the introductions to each text. The contracts, twelve in all, derive from both the Roman and Byzantine periods, since boundaries between the two epochs frequently imposed by political history remain inconsequential here. This is especially apparent in such contracts as the substitution in a liturgy (**8.2.7**) or the lease of labor (**8.2.10**) that seamlessly span the second to the fifth century AD. Substantive changes in other contracts are also difficult to observe. So at least in this area there can be no talk of the general Romanization of contract law that was earlier presumed. Correspondingly, the contracts below are arranged chiefly by theme, not chronologically. In the first four contracts various obligations to serve in an agricultural environment, in workshops, and in households are presented together. In all cases, payment is to be rendered in advance of the services, but there are some distinguishing characteristics. While the first example (**8.1.1**) involves an offset against later wages, the second (**8.2.2**) and third (**8.2.3**) concern loans that are to be repaid without interest upon termination of the work arrangement (so-called *Zinsantichrese*, "interest antichresis"). Nevertheless, the debtor/employee always receives an additional wage. In **8.2.4**, however, the loan as such is compensated for through labor. A term limit is as notably absent from this example as it is from **8.2.3**, in which the contractual relationship can be unilaterally terminated by the employee. In **8.2.2** the loan and period of service are limited to one year.

The next four contracts all concern working arrangements for which, in contrast to other sectors, contracts were probably drafted on a regular basis: apprenticeship contracts (**8.2.5**), wet-nurse contracts (**8.2.6**), contracts for substitutions in a liturgy (**8.2.7**), and contracts with entertainment artists, especially with musicians (**8.2.8**). Details specific to the contract type in all these cases led to the development of a set of juridical formulas. Thus, it is safe to assume that it was because of these details that the agreements were committed to writing: For apprenticeship contracts it was important to clarify in written form the relationship of the apprentice to the instructor and master, as well as specifics regarding room, board, etc. Detailed clauses about the expected conduct of the nurse are characteristic of wet-nurse contracts. In contracts for substitutions in a liturgy special value is placed upon the exemption of the liturgist from all subsequent burdens. The fewest specifics can be observed in contracts with artists, which are differentiated from all other contracts by their very brief time limits. With them, it can be assumed that the interest of both parties lay in reaching an agreement as early as possible, perhaps also in the coordination of target dates.

The last example (**8.2.8**) pertains to musical support offered during the harvest, which brings us to the remarkably wide complex of labor contracts in agricultural contexts. **8.2.9** concerns the transport of manure, without, however, specifying a time limit or volume, which is to be paid for according to transport units. **8.2.10** is a lease for labor in a vineyard, while **8.2.11** focuses on the land itself, whose irrigation the lessee promises to care for. In contrast to a normal lease of land, in both cases the lessee receives a wage. In addition to a cash wage, the lessee of **8.2.11** is promised a portion of the harvest, as is also the case in so-called sharecropping leases (*Teilpachten*), cf. **7.3.4**. In the sharing of the harvest between lessor and lessee, which is characteristic of this legal arrangement, the part belonging to the latter is construed as compensation for his work, as **8.2.12** also explicitly notes.

The translations of the texts presented here are based as far as possible upon the Greek originals; that they are often identical with previously published translations is only natural. The translations follow the Greek syntax, with one essential deviation: Independent of whether the contract is styled objectively (as in state and court notarial documents, see **8.2.1–2** and **8.2.6**, or in the private protocols, **8.2.5** and **8.2.7**) or subjectively (as in the *cheirographa* and the *tabellio*-documents that later replace them, see **8.2.3** and **8.2.4** and **8.2.8–12**), the body of the contract usually starts with the verb *homologein* "acknowledge"; this cannot be rendered in English syntax. To reflect the stressed initial position, the noun "acknowledgement" is used instead of the verb. Numbers, whether given in digits or written out in words, are rendered as they appear in the original document.[22]

8.2.1 Contract for labor in an olive mill

P.Fay. 91 (= *Sel.Pap.* I 17; tr. Johnson 1936: 456–57, no. 286; Campbell 1994: 224, no. 365, extract; Rowlandson 1998, no. 169; see Hengstl 1972: 35–44 §5; Jördens 1990: 130–84) (Euhemeria, 16 October AD 99). Image at Papyri.info.

This contract, concluded in the notary's office in Euhemeria, has been reproduced in numerous anthologies, since it is viewed as an example of a supposedly typical labor contract. In it Thenetkuis agrees with Epagathos,

[22] The author would like to thank Rodney Ast for his valuable assistance.

the steward of the properties of L. Bell(i)enus Gemellus, to work in his olive mill for the standard daily wage for such employment, with starting date still to be communicated to her. As an advance (*arrabôn*) she receives 16 drachmas, which will be reckoned up together with her later pay, but has to be paid back double if the contract is not fulfilled. That Epagathos has specially arranged for a state notarial document for such a routine transaction shows that contrary to first impressions we are in fact facing an extraordinary situation. Perhaps there was an acute shortage in the labor force at the time, so that Epagathos tried in this way to secure the services of Thenetkuis in advance. Nevertheless, she did not fulfill her obligation, as proven by the return of the *arrabôn* a good two years later, on 7 January AD 102. Apparently, her position was so strong that she could avoid repaying her 16 drachmas in double, as had been agreed upon in the contract. In the end, Epagathos must have been happy to get back at least this amount, even if after a two-year delay.

Phaophi the 18th, acknowledgement of Thenetkuis to Lucius.

The third year of the Emperor Caesar Nerva Traianus Augustus Germanicus, Phaophi the eighteenth, at Euhemeria in the division of Themistos of the Arsinoite nome. Acknowledgement of Thenetkuis daughter of Heron, laborer, a Persian woman, about twenty-six years old, with a scar on the right shin, with her guardian, her kinsman Leontas son of Hippalos, about fifty-four years old, with a scar on the forehead to the right, to Lucius Bellenus Gemellus, discharged from military service from the legions, about sixty-seven years old, with a scar on the left wrist, that she has received from him just now cash in hand, sixteen silver drachmas, as non-refundable *arrabôn*. Thus, Thenetkuis shall of necessity feed into the olive-press belonging to Lucius Bellenus Gemellus at Euhemeria from whatever day he will announce to her the olive fruits produced in this same third year, performing all that such a laborer should until the completion of the entire oil-making, receiving from Lucius Bellenus daily wages at the same rate as the other laborers in the village; and Lucius shall deduct the sixteen silver drachmas by installments from her future wages. If Thenetkuis does not act as aforesaid, she shall repay to Lucius the *arrabôn* two times, the right of execution being with Lucius Bellenus upon the acknowledging party and upon all that belongs to her as if in accordance with a legal decision. The signatory on behalf of Thenetkuis is Leontas, the aforesaid.

(*2nd hand*) I, Thenetkuis daughter of Heron, a Persian woman, with my guardian, my kinsman Leontas son of Hippalos, acknowledge that

I have received from Lucius the sixteen silver drachmas as *arrabôn*, and I shall feed olives into the olive-press from whatever day you shall announce to me, receiving from you, Lucius, wages at the same rate as the other laborers, and I shall perform everything as aforesaid. I, Leontas, wrote also on behalf of Thenetkuis, since she does not know letters.
(*1st hand*) Registered in the 3rd year, Phaophi the 18th, through Heron, in charge of the record office at Euhemeria.

(*3rd hand*) I, Lucius Bellenus Gemellus, through Epagathos, have got back the aforesaid, and I make no further claim.

(*in the left-hand margin, at right angles*) Sixteen silver drachmas. The fifth year of the Emperor Caesar Nerva Traianus Augustus Germanicus, Tybi the 12th.

8.2.2 Service contract for a swineherd

P.Oxf. 10 (*BL* IX 151; see Hengstl 1972: 9–34 § 4, esp. 15–16; Jördens 1990: 130–84) (Theadelphia, 30 December AD 98/117)

In this contract, which was signed in the notary's office in Theadelphia on 30 December in an unknown year of Trajan (in a leap year it would have been the 31st), Ares and his wife Thermuthas, both of whom come from the nome capital, declare that they have received twenty drachmas from the steward Epagathos, whom we know already from **8.2.1**. Since the contract on the *verso* is qualified as a *paramonê*, it is clear that we are dealing here with the so-called paramonial sum, which is the basis for an antichretic loan. The debtor thereby obligates himself, whether for the capital and interest or for the interest alone, to "remain/stay" (*paramenein*) with the creditor and to perform work for him. An additional wage can be granted, sometimes even board and clothing, especially if the capital must be paid back at the end of the agreed-upon term. In the present case, instead of paying interest Ares will tend the pigs of L. Bell(i)enus Gemellus for a period of one year beginning immediately, in return for a monthly wage of twenty drachmas. That this is explicitly designated as the "total amount" (*eis panta logon*) indicates that Ares was, in contrast to the frequent practice in this type of contract, obliged to provide for his own board and clothing, which is probably to be viewed in connection with his independent activity as a swineherd. Thus, the foundation of this contract upon a paramonial sum was of a purely formal character.

Remarkably, there are two penalty clauses which seem to contradict one another: If Ares should leave his duties beforehand, he must pay two drachmas for each outstanding day as well as one and a half times the paramonial sum. A second penalty clause, on the contrary, sets a doubling of the paramonial sum in case of a premature renunciation of the contract by Ares (a withdrawal by Bellienus Gemellus is apparently not considered). Since the general repayment clause stands between both these provisions at the end of the contract, it is possible that originally only the first variant had been agreed upon. Since a multiplication of the paramonial sum would thereby have occurred every ten days, which in actual fact could hardly have been realized, a decision was made to replace the first option with a second, simpler one. Whether in this process they merely forgot to delete the first penalty clause or both parties consciously decided to leave it in for the sake of deterrence cannot be decided with certainty.

The [. . .] year of the Emperor Caesar Nerva Traianus Augustus Germanicus, month of Dystros the 4th, Tybi the 4th, at Theadelphia in the division of Themistos in the Arsinoite nome. Acknowledgement of Ares son of Hermias, of the *metropolis*, registered, as he says, in the quarter "Bithynon and other places," a Persian of the *epigonê*, about thirty-two years old, with a scar on the right elbow, and his wife Thermuthas daughter of Leontas, a Persian woman, about thirty years old, with a scar on the left knee, with her guardian, her aforesaid husband, mutually guarantors for the payment, to Lucius Bellenus Gemellus, through Epagathos, about 35 years old, with a scar on the right shin, that they have received from him just now cash in hand, twenty silver drachmas, and instead of the interest Ares shall remain (*paramenein*) for one year from the aforesaid day herding the pigs, which Lucius has, bringing them to the proper roads and pastures and performing all that a herdsman should, he, Ares, receiving each month as total amount of wages twenty silver drachmas, there being no possibility for him to leave within the period. If he does leave, he has to pay for each day he abandons the pigs beforehand two drachmas and the silver one and a half times. And at the end of the period, he has to repay the aforesaid twenty silver drachmas. If he does leave before the (end of the) period, he shall repay the silver two times, the right of execution being with Lucius upon the acknowledging party and upon all that belongs to them as if in accordance with a legal decision. The signatory on behalf of the acknowledging parties is Heron son of Herakleides, about 53 years old, from Theadelphia.

(*2nd hand*) We, Ares son of Hermias, a Persian of the *epigonê*, and my wife Thermuthas daughter of Leontas, a Persian woman, with me as her guardian, mutually guarantors for the payment, acknowledge that we have received from Lucius Bellenus Gemellus, through Epagathos, twenty silver drachmas, upon condition of the *paramonê* of one of us, Ares, for one year herding the pigs, which Lucius has, receiving each month in total wages twenty silver drachmas, and at the end of the period we shall repay the silver. If I do leave before the (end of the) period, we shall repay the silver two times, as aforesaid. Heron son of Herakleides wrote on their behalf, since they do not know letters.

(*1st hand*) Registered through the record office at Theadelphia.

Verso: *Paramonê* of Ares . . . (and?) his wife for 20 drachmas.

8.2.3 Work in a tapestry-making workshop secured by an interest-free loan

P.Oxy. LXIII 4353 (see Jördens 1990: 271–95, 1997: 81; see also Fikhman 2000) (Oxyrhynchos, 14 April AD 304). Image at Papyri.info.

At first glance, this contract between a tapestry-weaver and the master of a tapestry-making workshop in no way exhibits any peculiarities: for a daily wage of 120 drachmas the weaver Heraklas agrees to join in working in Kephalon's workshop; for this he had already received an advance payment, *prochreia*, of two talents. Remarkably, however, a time limit on the contract has nowhere been set. Since Heraklas must pay back the *prochreia* the moment he leaves the workshop, it is therefore not an advance payment on his wages, but as with the paramonial sum discussed in **8.2.2**, an interest-free loan. The two talents, or 12,000 drachmas, here equal wages for 100 days, so that Heraklas, unlike Ares in **8.2.2**, cannot simply apply his last month's wages. It is also remarkable that Kephalon, for his part, is not bound by any comparable obligation: Kephalon not only does not promise not to dismiss Heraklas (in which event employees still retain a claim on the advance payments ceded to them), but not once does he even promise to employ him fully. Nevertheless, through the *prochreia* he apparently wanted to secure Heraklas' manpower for an extended period of time even if he could not provide work for him every day. Heraklas, on the contrary, probably no longer had the opportunity, or the necessity, to look elsewhere for employment opportunities, and he could, as long as he fulfilled his part of the contract, use the two talents according to his needs.

Under the consuls our lords the Emperors Diocletianus for the 9th time and Maximianus for the 8th time, Augusti. Aurelius Heraklas son of

Zoilas, mother Taaphynchis, of the illustrious and most illustrious city of the Oxyrhynchites, tapestry-weaver by trade, to Aurelius Kephalon son of Ammonios, mother [. . .]s, of the same city, master of a workshop of the same trade, greetings. Acknowledgement that I have received from (you) as *prochreia* two silver talents, total 2 talents, upon condition that I work with you in the tapestry-weaving workshop that you have in the same city, receiving from you daily as wages one hundred and twenty silver drachmas, and that I have no possibility to leave the workshop. If I do leave, I shall immediately pay to you the aforesaid two silver talents without interest and without any delay or excuse, the right of execution being with you upon me and upon all that belongs to me. The document of the *prochreia*, written in a single copy, is authoritative wherever it is produced and by whomsoever it is produced on your behalf, and in answer to the formal question I gave my assent. The 20th and the 12th year of our lords Diocletianus and Maximianus Augusti and Constantius and Maximianus the most noble Caesares, Pharmouthi the 19th.

(*2nd hand*) I, Aurelius Heraklas, have received the two talents as *prochreia* and shall repay as aforesaid, and in answer to the formal question I gave my assent.[23] I, Aurelius Agathos Daimon son of Dionysios, wrote on his behalf on request, since he said that he does not know letters.

8.2.4 Redemption of a sister bound by a service contract

P.Coll.Youtie II 92 (= *P.Cair.Masp.* I 67023; *Jur.Pap.* 12; *FIRA* III 12, upper part only; see Jördens 1990: 271–95) (Antinoopolis [found at Aphrodito], 15 May AD 569). Image at Papyri.info.

For a slightly different interpretation and the translation of the contract, see **5.5.3**.

This contract between the salt-fish seller Martha and Flavius Helladius, a secretary on the staff of the duke of the Thebaid,[24] falls outside the norm because of its detailed preamble. As described, Martha's now-deceased father was forced by poverty to take out a loan of one gold *solidus* from the rich man Nonnos, in return for which he gives over his still underage daughter Prokla into Nonnos' service. Because of the harsh labor conditions to which Prokla was subjected in Nonnos' household, Martha had tried to ransom her

[23] A remnant of the Roman verbal contract called *stipulatio* whereby the stipulating party asks a formal question and the other party responds in kind.

[24] The military and civil governor of this upper Egyptian province, especially used in the Byzantine period.

younger sister after their father's death. Nevertheless, the proceeds from Martha's own work were barely sufficient to cover even half the loan, and this is why Martha must now borrow the other half from Helladius. The nine gold carats she now borrows are the equivalent of one half *solidus*. For this loan Prokla again serves as security. From now on she will work for Helladius, from whom she will receive her board and clothing. A fixed date for repayment of the loan is not mentioned, but it is safe to assume that this once more depends on Martha's employment opportunities.

In principle, then, this is yet another contract of *paramonê* (cf. **5.5.3**) where performance of work serves as compensation for the interest on the loan. One difference, however, is that the person subject to *paramonê*, since she is taken into the employer's household, will also be fed and clothed. The loan aspects of the contract are also much more prominent here. This is mostly due to the legal terminology used in the contract, with repeated mention of "lending (out)," *(ek)danizesthai* and "pledging," *hypotithenai*. Correspondingly, both the old and the new contract are designated a "contract of pledge" (*hypothêkimaia syngraphê* or *hypothêkê*) or a "security document" (*asphaleia*); the borrowed sum is called a "loan" (*chreos*). Moreover, there is the dramatic description of the attendant circumstances that led to the change of employers.

All the same, the discrepancies in substance between **8.2.2**, **8.2.3**, and **8.2.4** are kept within bounds, even if the agreed-upon provision of work for the paramonial sum is not here to be rendered by the debtor himself, but by one of his dependents, since in earlier times family members or slaves were also occasionally used as workers subject to *paramonê*. Just as little weight is to be placed on the absence of any mention of a wage, because Prokla's maintenance as such may already be viewed as a form of compensation. A basic difference must above all be seen in the lack of reference to a specific date for repayment of the loan, for which **8.2.3** serves as the earliest example to date. The fact that these kinds of contracts with their ever tighter commitments to local magnates and the gradual loss of personal autonomy finally gained prominence in the Byzantine era sheds striking light on social changes at this time.

Formally this contract is a so-called *tabellio*-document, a type commonly found in the Byzantine period. Here the notarial signature is, surprisingly, lacking. Nevertheless, we can hardly conclude from this that the contractual agreement remained incomplete or was even rejected, because the notary at one and the same time assumed the function of a witness and might have deemed a second signature superfluous. But there were several other acts of negligence that, in view of the document's generally sophisticated presentation, are surprising: Thus, contrary to the announcement in the prescript, no witnesses besides the notary come into play, unless the writer of the actual contract (as opposed to the notary) should be regarded as such. Martha is designated as "also being a native of the city of Antinous," although Helladius originates from Panopolis lying about 150 km to the south (it may be that the previous mention of Antinoopolis as the place where the contract was drafted caused this confusion). Finally, Helladius' patronymic has not been entered in the space left blank for this purpose.

8.2.5 Weaver's apprenticeship contract

P.Oxy.Hels. 29 (see Hengstl 1972: 82–97 §10; Jördens 1990: 342–53; Bergamasco 1995) (Oxyrhynchos, 8 September AD 54). Image at *P.Oxy.Hels.*, Plate 19.

In this document, which is styled as a "private protocol" in technical terminology (Wolff 1978: 122–27), Apollonous gives her still underage grandson for two years to her son Heras for instruction in weaving. It seems that by the time the contract was drawn up (Sebastos 11 = 8 September) the grandson had already completed a probation period, since he had started his apprenticeship with Heras nearly one week earlier (Sebastos 5 = 2 September). In the meantime the parties seem to have agreed on the essential terms of the apprenticeship, which despite the interfamilial nature of the business arrangement were still formally recorded in the contract: During this time the youngster must obey Heras in every way. Food and clothing are to be provided by his grandmother, who is to receive from Heras a monthly allowance (in two annual payments for the clothing). Heras, for his part, undertakes the payment of all payable taxes. Should the grandson ever be absent – e.g., in case of sickness – he is required to make up for each day missed. Otherwise Apollonous must pay Heras one drachma per day, which in any case corresponds to a fifth of the monthly amount reserved to her for the maintenance of the youngster. In contrast to other contracts, this one does not explicitly establish that the youngster is not allowed to leave the workshop and residence of his master at any time during the apprenticeship period. This is probably because the grandson continued living with his grandmother, who both fed and clothed him. Perhaps everything (i.e., workshop and residence) was to be found in the same house, so that for this reason there was no potential for conflict between the parties. Any premature termination of the contract by either party is subject to a penalty.

Mutual acknowledgement of Apollonous daughter of Sarapion, with her guardian, her son Diogenes son of Didymos, and of her other son, the

brother of Diogenes, Heras son of the same Didymos, weaver, that Apollonous shall produce to Heras her daughter's son [. . .]onis alias Agelochos son of Harsiesis, who is still under age, for a period of two years, from the fifth of the present month Sebastos, to perform all that he is ordered by Heras in respect to the weaver's trade, which he himself shall teach him as he knows it, the boy being fed during the aforesaid period by Apollonous in return for the five silver drachmas which Heras shall deliver to her each month. The same Apollonous shall clothe the son (correctly: the grandson) during the two years in return for the twenty-four silver drachmas which Heras shall give to her, from which (amount) Apollonous on the spot acknowledges she has received from Heras twelve drachmas; the payment of the remaining twelve drachmas for the use of clothing shall be made by Heras to his mother in the month of Sebastos of the coming year. If the boy is required (to pay) poll tax or dike tax or pig tax or public dues on the trade, they shall be Heras' duty. If there are any days on which the boy is not at disposal, Apollonous shall produce him for an equal number (of days) after the period, or she shall pay one silver drachma for each day. The penalty for taking him away before the (end of the) period shall be one hundred silver drachmas and an equal sum to the Treasury. If Heras himself does not (?) teach the boy, he shall pay an equal sum as penalty, without prejudice to Heras and Diogenes in the rights (ensuing) from the acknowledgement which they made with each other, on all the terms contained in it.
This document is authoritative. The 15th year of Tiberius Claudius Caesar Augustus Germanicus the Emperor, month of Sebastos, the 11th.
(*2nd hand*) I, Apollonous daughter of Sarapion, shall produce my daughter's son for a period of two years and act as aforesaid. The 15th year of Tiberius Claudius Caesar Augustus Germanicus the Emperor, month of Sebastos, the 11th. I, Diogenes son of Didymos, have been registered as the guardian of my mother and wrote on her behalf since she does not know letters.

8.2.6 Wet-nursing contract

BGU IV 1106 (= *M.Chr.* 108, *CPJ* II 146, *CPGr.* I 5; tr. H. Metzger 1974: 32, no. 34, extract; Kraemer 2004: 125–26, no. 51; Jördens 2004; see Hengstl 1972: 61–69 §8; 1978a: 190–96, no. 77; Manca Masciadri and Montevecchi 1984) (Alexandria, 26 February 13 BC). Image at Papyri.info.

This wet-nursing contract was concluded in the form of the court notarial document used only in Alexandria, which, since it probably arose from a settlement of a dispute, was usually introduced by a common declaration of both parties to the *archidikastês*. In this agreement Theodote, who, to judge from her name, was probably of Jewish origin like her husband, agrees with the Roman Marcus Aemilius to nurse the slave baby named Tyche for a year and a half and to bring the child to Aemilius for periodic inspections. As is common, the child is described as "undying," i.e., in the event of the child's death, Theodote is obliged to nurse another child on the very same terms. She is to be paid eight drachmas per month and agrees she has received pay for the first nine months, that is, half the term of the contract, already upon conclusion of the contract's drafting.

A characteristic feature of the wet-nurse contracts lies in their detailed prescriptions regarding the moral conduct of the nurse, which deeply encroaches upon her privacy. This was probably based less on the unusual independence the nurse enjoyed during the fulfillment of her duties and more on the indirect or even direct effects of providing for the child, on which account sexual intercourse was especially forbidden her. All the more important therefore was it to bring her husband also into the agreement, be it only as guarantor, as in this example.

The chronological and geographical distribution of this type of contract is also noteworthy: while a higher-than-average number are encountered in the small group of contracts transmitted from Alexandria, there apparently are no wet-nurse contracts from the Byzantine period.

To Protarchos, in charge of the court, (*2nd hand*) from Marcus Aurelius son of Marcus, of the Claudian (?) tribe, and from Theodote daughter of Dositheos, a Persian woman, with her guardian and guarantor for the conditions set forth in the agreement, her husband Sophron son of [. . .-]arches, a Persian of the *epigonê*. With regard to the settled terms, Theodote agrees that she will for eighteen months from Phamenoth of the present 17th year of Caesar nurse and suckle in her own house in the city with her own milk pure and undamaged his foundling slave baby child Tyche which Marcus has entrusted to her, receiving from him each month as wages for the milk and the service as wet-nurse, besides the olive-oil, 8 silver dr.; and Theodote has received through her guarantor Sophron from Marcus cash in hand for the aforesaid eighteen months as wet-nurse's wages for nine months altogether seventy-two drachmas, and in case something should happen to the child within this (period), Theodote will take up another child and nurse it and suckle it and hold it at the disposal of Marcus for the same nine months, without receiving any wages at all, since she has undertaken to nurse it as "undying"; and being satisfied with the remaining wet-nurse's wages each month, she shall take the proper care of herself and of the child, not damaging her milk nor lying with a man nor conceiving nor suckling another child as well, and whatever she receives or is entrusted with, she will keep safe and repay when it is asked, or she shall pay the value of each thing, except in the case of a manifest loss, which will release her when it is proved. And she shall not leave the service as wet-nurse within the period. If she offends against something, she and Sophron may be seized and held until they pay the wet-nurse's wages they have received and whatever they received one and a half times and the damages and the costs and another 300 silver dr., the right of execution being upon both, being mutual guarantors for the payment, and upon one of them and upon whichever of them he may choose, and upon all that belongs to them as if in accordance with a legal decision, and all guarantees whatever they may produce and all (resort to) protection shall be invalid; but if she accomplishes everything, Marcus Aemilius shall provide her with the monthly wet-nurse's wages for the remaining nine months, and he shall not take the child away within the period, or he himself shall pay the same penalty.

Theodote shall bring the child before Marcus two (or three?) times per month that it may be inspected by him.

(*2d hand*) Theodote daughter of Dositheos and her husband Sophron for the slave child Tyche, for 18 months, from which (amount) she has received 8 dr. (each month) for 9 months, in the city.

8.2.7 Contract for substitution in a liturgy

P.Oxy. XXXVIII 2859 (see Hengstl 1972: 70–72 §9 11; Jördens 1990: 185–221) (Oxyrhynchos, 10 November AD 301). Image at Papyri.info.

A conspicuous feature of contracts for liturgy replacements is the emphasis on mutuality: references to social distinctions that customarily exist between employer and employee seem to have been consciously suppressed. Thus, in the present instance, the contracting parties make use of the *cheirographon*, which developed out of the private letter, but in what one might call a hybrid form, since both parties appear as both sender and recipient of the document. Consequently, the person being referred to at any given moment must be newly specified in the document's subjectively framed body.

8.2.7 concerns the task of driving a herd of donkeys and camels down the Nile at a still unspecified time. Because Sarapammon, who has been named *dekanos*, either cannot or will not fulfill this task, Paulos declares himself ready to take Sarapammon's place at a daily wage of 250 drachmas;

so far, he has already received 15,000 drachmas, the wage for two months' work. Should Paulos, contrary to expectation, return before the end of the two months, he must pay back the surplus sum; if he returns later, he is entitled to receive proportionate extra pay. It is not surprising that the term of the contract remains temporarily undetermined; this frequently can be observed elsewhere, depending on the type of liturgical task imposed. The extensive guarantee clauses are another characteristic feature of contracts concluded in this sphere. By these the substitute promises to free the liturgist from all burdens connected with the office or its administration – one of the liturgist's chief concerns. In contrast to liturgies involving taxation, **8.2.7** was not concerned with monetary claims. This is why "or penalty" was written but then deleted between "any trouble" and "or harm" in the latter half of the contract.

The Aurelii Sarapammon son of Heras, mother Isidora, chosen *dekanos*, and Paulos son of Horion, mother Helena, both from the illustrious and most illustrious city of the Oxyrhynchites, with his guarantor for his presence and appearance at the following service Aurelius Horion son of Horion, of the same city, to each other greetings. Acknowledgement that, on the one hand I, Paulos, instead of you, Sarapammon, shall go wherever I may be commanded, with the donkeys and camels and wand-bearers handed over to me, and shall undertake and fulfill the position of you the *dekanos* and I shall remain at the public orders until I am released fulfilling all that I may be ordered so that no blame or guilt result. I shall daily receive as wages from the following day, which is Hathyr the 15th, until I return two hundred and fifty silver drachmas, and I acknowledge on the spot that I have received for two months two talents three thousand silver drachmas. If I return within the two months' period, I shall return the silver that will become apparent in my possession. If being on the job the two months I should continue in the public service, you will provide me with the wages until I return, and (I have to act so) that you Sarapammon be corporeally free from any trouble (*cancelled*: or penalty) or harm in all matters in general pertaining to the service of *dekanos*; and that, on the other hand, I, Sarapammon, approve on these terms, and I shall pay the wages that will become apparent without any curtailment. If any inquiry in any way whatsoever arises about [. . .] (to) the *dekanoi*, I, Sarapammon, shall [. . .] in accordance with the share falling on me, and you, Paulos, be free from trouble in this matter. This document is authoritative, written in duplicate for each party to have a single copy, and in mutual answer to the formal question we gave our mutual assent. The 18th year and the 17th year of our lords Diocletianus and Maximianus

Augusti and the 10th year of our lords Constantius and Maximianus the most noble Caesars, Hathyr the 14th, in the consulship of Titianus and Nepotianus. (*2nd hand*) I, Aurelius Sarapammon, agree to all the aforesaid, and I shall pay the wages that will become apparent as aforesaid and in answer to the formal question I gave my assent.

8.2.8 Contract for services of a flutist at vintage time

CPR XVII A 19 (= *Stud.Pal.* XIII, pp. 6–7, *SB* I 5810, *Stud.Pal.* XX 78, *Sel.Pap.* I 22, Vandoni 1964: 39–40, no. 27; tr. Tedeschi 2002: 169–70; see Hengstl 1972: 45–51 §6, Heinen 1994) (Hermopolis, 20 December AD 321). Image at Papyri.info.

Contracts with performance artists constitute a special group of labor contracts. They are characteristically for short terms because the artists – musicians; dancers, too – were usually engaged for special events, as part of arrangements for festivals that lasted only a couple of days. Beyond wages and board, they often received payments for their travel expenses. In **8.2.8** a flutist agrees with a Hermopolitan landlord, Aurelius Adelphios, to accompany with his flute those involved in the gathering and pressing of grapes near the village Monyris. This may be why his wages are not more closely specified, but just said to be the "stated (wages)." The joyous association of music-playing and dancing with the vintage is an old one: cf. *Iliad* 18.561–572 (the shield of Achilles).

In the consulship of our lords Licinius Augustus for the 6th time and Licinius the most noble Caesar for the 2nd time. To Aurelius Adelphios, gymnasiarch and councilor of Hermopolis, (from) Aurelius Ps[. . .]is son of Kollouthos, mother Melitine, flutist, of Hermopolis, greetings. Acknowledgement that I have contracted and agreed with you the landlord to present myself at the village of Monyris and at the vintage of the vineyards located there, along with the appointed grape-treaders, and to minister without any blame to the grape-treaders and the others by my flute-playing and not leave the grape-treaders until the completion of the same vintage of the approaching auspicious tenth indiction; and for the flute-playing and the entertainment I shall receive the stated (wages) from those responsible. This agreement that I have issued in a single copy is authoritative, and in answer to the formal question I gave my assent. The aforesaid consulship, Choiak the 24th. (*2nd hand*)
I, Aurelius Ps[. . .]is, will fulfill the written (conditions) as aforesaid.
I, Aurelius Pinoution, assistant of Aniketos, wrote on his behalf since he does not know letters.

8.2.9 Contract for transportation of manure

P.Col. X 255 (= *SB* XVIII 13311) (Theadelphia, 10 May AD 131). Image at Papyri.info.

8.2.9 concerns the transportation of manure to a vineyard near Theadelphia, where the estates of L. Bellienus Gemellus, familiar from **8.2.1** and **8.2.2**, were also located. The wage promised to the animal-keeper Heron is calculated in cartloads, in which *sebakh*, if *ammos* can be interpreted this way, must have been lighter than dung, because for *sebakh* eight cartloads brought in eight obols, while with dung eight obols was the price of six cartloads. Even more striking than the missing time limit and form of remuneration is that both parties even decided to commit such a contract to writing in the first place. The explanation is probably best sought in the fact that, as in the case of Gemellus, a steward (who is here active on behalf of an Alexandrian landlord) was held accountable, whether he wanted to protect himself from eventual inquiries or saw profit in maintaining a working relationship with Heron for as long as possible.

To Claudius Apion, former *agoranomos* of Alexandria, through the manager (*phrontistês*) Philodespotes, (from) Heron son of Hermas, animal-keeper of the village of Theadelphia. Acknowledgement that I have undertaken the transport of dung and *sebakh* (?) to the vineyard belonging to your sons in the vicinity of the village called "of Spartianos" from the coming sixteenth year of Hadrianus Caesar the lord, upon condition that I receive from you as freight charges, on the one hand, for the transport of dung for each donkey eight obols per six freights, on the other hand, for the transport of *sebakh* (?) likewise for each donkey per eight freights eight obols. If I fall short as to transporting the dung, I shall repay to you the freight charges double; and if you fall short (in providing me with material?), I shall get the freight charges because we agreed upon [. . .]

Heron, about 50 years old, scar on the forehead. Year 15 of the Emperor Caesar Traianus Hadrianus Augustus, Pachon 15.

8.2.10 Lease of labor in a vineyard

P.Oxy. XLVII 3354 (*BL* X 153, Kloppenborg 2006: 528–34, no. 53; see Jördens 1990: 222–32; Jördens 1992) (Oxyrhynchos, 28 October AD 257). Image at Papyri.info.

In approximately one dozen leasing contracts, mainly from the Oxyrhynchite nome in middle Egypt but also from the neighboring Hermopolite nome, the object of the lease is not, as is typical, a piece of land, but the labor that is to be performed on a particular piece of land; correspondingly, the lessees receive a wage. Normally these contracts involve vineyards, which need especially intensive maintenance, as reflected in the contracts' extraordinarily rich details. Occasionally, only part of the work is assigned in this way, mainly in the area of irrigation. Since virtually no leasing contracts from Byzantine Oxyrhynchite survive, this type of contract may characterize the transition to self-administration of the great estate, which appears to have become virtually a hallmark of this nome (cf. **8.3**).

In **8.2.10** a father and son commit themselves for two years to perform all necessary labors for a female landowner in a vineyard consisting of six arouras near the village Senepta. The landowner is legally independent by virtue of the *ius liberorum* (see **4.3.3**). The wage due to workers, 360 drachmas per aroura, is to be paid monthly according to the progress of their work. On certain occasions additional payments in kind are to be added. Furthermore, the father and son agree to lease two arouras of grain land, for which they have to pay a fixed rent. The lessor is, as usual, responsible for all taxes. For a parallel, though not as detailed as **8.2.10**, see **8.3.1** below.

To Aurelia Sarapous daughter of Theon son of Theon, former *exêgêtês* of the city of the Oxyrhynchites, acting without a guardian in accordance with the *ius liberorum*, from the Aurelii [. . .] son of Sarapammon, mother Taaphynchis, and his son Hiereus, mother Taaphynchis, both of the hamlet of Nomou. We undertake by voluntary choice to lease from you for the period of two years, from the 1st of the present month Hathyr of the present 5th year, all the manual vine-growing operations and the watering of the vineyard belonging to you in the vicinity of Senepta, called Thaaut, of six arouras or however many it may be, and of the nearby reed-plantation, whatever its area in arouras may be. The operations for the vineyard are: the pulling up of reeds and their collection and transport; correct pruning; tying (the prunings) into bundles and binding and transport of the bundles; sweeping up of leaves and disposing of them outside the mud walls; (first) hoeing; trenching round; layering however many layers may be needed – and we shall stand in the reed-plantation in the front of the donkeys carrying earth so that the earth may be thrown where it should, as we might require these (donkeys) –; splitting of the reeds; reed work; (second) hoeing; thinning the shoots; the work of Pharmouthi (i.e., March/April); separating (the leaves); elevating (the shoots); thinning the foliage as necessary; watering and constant weeding, as well as all the other operations in the vineyard at their proper times; for the reed-plantation: watering; trenching round; spreading of dung. And we shall make the necessary matting for the treading-vat and the press, and the *kyltides* (?) for the (irrigation? pressing?) plant, and the testing of the jars which are to be used for the wine each year in the place from which they are transported; and when they have been filled with wine we shall place them in the drying-room, coat them (*sc.* with pitch), move them, and guard them as long as they stay there. And further, the one of us, Hiereus, will sleep in the farm-building without any interruption, and (we shall receive) as wages for all the operations in the vineyard three hundred and sixty silver drachmas per aroura, and we shall receive our wages each year altogether (as follows): in Hathyr (i.e., October/November) and Choiak (i.e., November/December), for pulling up reeds, two hundred drachmas; in Tybi (i.e., December/January), for pruning, four hundred drachmas; in Mecheir (i.e., January/February), for reed work, four hundred drachmas; in Phamenoth (i.e., February/March), one hundred and eighty drachmas; in Pharmouthi (i.e., March/April), two hundred and forty drachmas; in Pachon (i.e., April/May), one hundred drachmas; in Payni (i.e., May/June), for thinning the foliage, two hundred and forty drachmas; in Epeiph (i.e., June/July) and Mesore (i.e., July/August), (to be paid) annually in Thoth (i.e., August/September) and Phaophi (i.e., September/October) of the following year, the one hundred drachmas due each month. And we shall receive each year for the pruning one *keramion* of sour wine; and at harvest time, in consideration of our not leaving the watering and the thinning of the foliage, each year three artabas of wheat; and at the vintage each year, two *keramia* of new wine; and [. . .] we undertake to purchase half the fruits of the date-palms in the property for the stated rent (in money) and extra gifts each year; and further, to lease for the present year only from the (estate) belonging to you in the vicinity of the same Senepta, out of the plot of Dionysophantes, two arouras, one aroura to be sown in wheat, one aroura to be sown in barley, at a rent (in kind) of four artabas of wheat for the one in wheat and five artabas of barley for the one in barley, all being free of any risk. The public dues on the land shall be yours, the landlady's, duty, who shall also control the crops till you receive what is due to you each year. Our undertaking becoming valid, we shall of necessity perform all the operations in the vineyard and the reed-plantation at the proper times as set forth above, and the fertilization of the date-palms and trees, and (take) every care (of them), with your agents looking after all the operations so that the vineyard does not get damaged. And we shall pay the rent (in kind) for the land in the present year on the threshing floor of the place in new, clean, unadulterated produce free of clods and sieved, the wheat free of barley just as if it were being measured into the public granary, the barley well trodden and free of darnel and chaff, by your, the landlady's, receiving measure, with your agents measuring and adding two *choinikes* to each artaba, and for the date-palms the rent (in money) that will become apparent and the extra gifts each year in Thoth and Phaophi of the following year without any delay. And at the end of the period, we shall return the vineyard and the reed-plantation cared for with our operations, the vineyard free from rushes and weeds and all filth, the mud-walls [. . .], the trees living and flourishing, and we shall pay for whatever operation we should not accomplish or for any tree that withers through our carelessness double damages, the right of execution being with you upon us, being mutual guarantors for the payment, and upon whichever of us you may choose, and upon all that belongs to us. The undertaking is authoritative, and in answer to the formal question we gave our assent. The 5th year of the Emperors Caesars Publius Licinius Valerianus und Publius Licinius Valerianus Gallienus Germanici Maximi Pii Felices and Publius Licinius Cornelius Valerianus the most noble Caesar Augusti . . .

8.2.11 Contract for irrigation of a vineyard

P.Grenf. I 58 (= *BL* XI 86; see Jördens 1990: 260–70) (Hermopolis, *c.* AD 561)

Although **8.2.11** is styled as a lease, the parties agree (as in **8.2.9**) to perform certain agricultural tasks, here specifically the irrigation of the piece of land taken in lease. Since the date and the prescript are lost, we do not know precisely at what time of year the contract was concluded, but the sowing had, as it seems, already taken place. Presumably this was why no rent was required of the lessee – significantly, a baker – who instead received a wage in addition to part of the harvest. The lessor obviously wanted to secure for himself the lion's share of the harvest, but had to rely on help for the irrigation. Remarkably, the lessee's share, one-fifth, is also specified in a surface measure (arouras), suggesting perhaps that the work of the harvest fell upon him as well.

. . . of the city of the Hermopolites by Aurelius Banes son of Esaias, baker, of the village of Elias of the Hermopolite. Acknowledgement that by voluntary and free choice I have leased from you for one year only the field called "of Lechios" of however many arouras it may be. I am prepared to water this same field with my own animals that shall also be fed by me, without any ambiguity or negligence or disdain. It seemed (good) that I receive a fifth share of what is sown in the field, that is, three and a half and a quarter arouras, and one gold *solidus* less six carats. The lease is authoritative and valid, and in answer to the formal question I gave my assent. I, Aurelius Banes son of Esaias, the aforesaid, have leased as aforesaid. I, Aurelius Viktor son of Anastasios, wrote on request on his behalf since he does not know letters. † I, [. . .]las son of Iakubios, deacon, bear witness to the lease, having heard it from its depositors. † I, Aurelius Dioskoros son of Elias, bear witness to the lease, having heard it from its depositors. †

Through me, Viktor, by God's will notary.

Verso: Lease made by † Banes, baker, † regarding the field called "of Lechios."

8.2.12 Sharecropping lease

P.Lond. V 1694 (see Hengstl 1972: 73–77 §9 III; Jördens 1990: 233–59; Keenan 1985: 161–68) (Aphrodito, AD 516/7 or 531/2). Image at Papyri.info.

Sharecropping contracts (*Teilpachtverträge*), cf. **7.3.4**, **7.4.6**, are generally styled as leases in which lessor and lessee share the harvest according to a previously agreed-upon key; only by this feature are they distinguished from the lease contracts with fixed rents. Nevertheless, the lessor participates in this way in the lessee's labor, which is made explicit in contracts like this one from the village of Aphrodite (a.k.a. Aphrodito) in the Antaiopolite nome in Upper Egypt: in the sharing clause it is regularly stated that the farmer's share served as compensation for his labor (cf. below, "our labors").

Nearly all papyri from the Antaiopolite nome come from the village of Aphrodite, which is famous for the archive of the notary and poet Dioskoros. This is also true for **8.2.12**, in which Dioskoros' uncle, Besarion son of Dioskoros (the poet's homonymous grandfather), figures as sub-lessor of a piece of land owned by a local church ("the Holy New Church"). In contrast to the nomes lying farther north, the shares in the Antaiopolite tend to be of equal size, even in the so-called Byzantine period, which may point to a greater balance between the social groups here than in other parts of Egypt, most notably Oxyrhynchos.

. . . the Aurelii Mathias son of Ponnis and Ibeis son of Apollos, both of the village of Aphrodite of the Antaiopolite nome, to Aurelius Besarion son of Dioskoros, of the same village, greetings. Acknowledgement that we have leased from you on mutual guarantees for the present year only, the fruits (being) of the, by God's will, eleventh indiction, the field leased out by you to (*correctly*: to you by) the Holy New Church of however many arouras (it may be), located in the plain of the same village of Aphrodite in the plot of Hieras, with a pond and a cistern and trees and date-palms and all the rights according to its boundaries, upon condition that we farm it and perform all the manual operations with my (*correctly*: our) own expenses and animals without any disdain or negligence, and we shall cooperate in everything. The seed(-corn?) shall be supplied by you – and you receive it out of the common funds – whereas the seed of the green-crop is supplied by us, and we receive it out of the common funds. And when the proper (i.e., harvest) time has come, the yield of the different crops and the chaff shall be divided between us and you in half-shares, (one share) to us for our labors, (one share) to you for the rents. And you shall receive out of the common funds before the division of the green-crop at all the mowings (the yield) of half an aroura; and we shall supply to you fifty ripe good big cheeses suited for the landlord and six *koloba* of mustard; and we (shall) supply out of the common funds the price of the hurdles for the flocks without any ambiguity. The lease is authoritative and valid, and in answer to the formal question we gave our assent. The wages of the wooden (irrigation) plant and the expenses are supplied out of the common funds, and we shall perform the transport of your, the landlord's, share of the crops and the chaff to the village and the threshing-floor from your own threshing-floor. (*2nd hand*) † I, Aurelius Matheias son of Ponnis, the aforesaid, have leased as aforesaid. (*3rd hand*) † I, Aurelius [. . .]bais son of Apollos, the aforesaid, have leased as aforesaid. Aurelius Phoibammon . . .

8.3 Dependent labor: the case of the *enapographoi geôrgoi*

Brendan Haug

This section discusses the *enapographoi geôrgoi* (*coloni adscripticii*) in Egypt from the mid-fifth through the early seventh centuries AD. It is not intended as an introduction to wider debates on the nature and extent of the later Roman colonate, a task that lies outside the scope of this volume and requires substantial engagement with both the law codes and a massive bibliography. The discussion has been epitomized as the opposition between two schools: one positing the *coloni* as a middle stage in the development from Roman tenancy to medieval serfdom; the second perceiving in the *coloni* a post-classical decline and the inflexible, bureaucratic stratification of late Roman society.[25] More relevant for our purposes, a recent and essential contribution places the *coloni adscripticii / enapographoi geôrgoi* in the larger context of a supposed expansion of Byzantine agrarian capitalism and the attendant increase in direct exploitation and wage labor.[26] The modest aim of this chapter is to illustrate the general characteristics of Egyptian *enapographoi* through a selection of four documents representative of the corpus in which they appear.

It is crucial to note at the outset that *enapographoi* appear only in the papyri of the Oxyrhynchite nome.[27] Furthermore, the Oxyrhynchite documentation of our period is dominated by the papers of large landowners (*geouchoi*), especially the dossier of the Flavii Apiones (extensively documented from *c.* AD 540 on), a wealthy and powerful family whose history can be traced over six generations and which enjoyed close connections to the imperial house.[28] Indeed, the family produced one of the empire's final *consules ordinarii* in the person of Flavius Apion II (consul AD 539, died AD 579). It is from the documentation of the Apiones' extensive Oxyrhynchite holdings that we draw the majority of our attestations of *enapographoi geôrgoi*.[29] The smaller dossier of the contemporary local landowner Flavia Anastasia also preserves instances of *enapographoi* employed on her Oxyrhynchite holdings.[30] The history of the "Egyptian" colonate is thus a closely circumscribed, wholly local history heavily influenced by the practices of a powerful and perhaps atypical family estate. Consequently it is hazardous, despite the temptation, to generalize from the Oxyrhynchite data in an attempt to describe the whole of Egypt's agricultural labor regime.

25 Sirks (2008: 122). 26 Banaji (2007). On this controversial issue, see Hickey (2012: chapter 3).

27 One possible exception is *SB* XVIII 13949 (AD 541), a deed of surety in which a Herakleopolite *enapographos* acts as surety for his brother, also an *enapographos*. See Sijpesteijn (1985: 145–48) and Fikhman (1991: 10).

28 Gonis (2000: 95 and n. 8) on the corpus of Byzantine documents from Oxyrhynchos.

29 Estimates of the size of Apionic holdings in the Oxyrhynchite range from 25,000 arouras to at least 112,000 arouras or roughly 35 percent of arable land in the Oxyrhynchite. On the issue see briefly Hickey (2008: 96–98).

30 E.g., *P.Oxy.* LXIX 4757 (late sixth century AD). For Anastasia see van Haelst (1958, 1966). For recent additions to the dossier see *P.Oxy.* LXIX 4756–58. Other Oxyrhynchite landowners with *enapographoi* are Flavia Kyria (*P.Oxy.* XXXIV 2724 [AD 469] with Gonis 2002: 86–88), the Flavii Phoibammon and Samuel (*P.Oxy.* LXVIII 4697 [AD 489]), Flavius Ioannes *politeuomenos* (*P.Oxy.* XLIX 3512 [AD 492]), Flavius Dioskoros (*P.Oxy.* LXIII 4398 [AD 553]), Flavius Phoibammon a.k.a. Lamoson (*P.Wash.Univ.* I 25 [AD 530]), Flavii Philodemos and Ioannes (*SB* XVIII 13949 [AD 541]), Flavius Ioannes *vir clarissimus* (*P.Oxy.* LXIX 4755 [586]), Church of Saints [. . .] (*SB* XVIII 14006 [AD 635]).

The documents presented below sketch in outline the features and evolution of the singularly strict, tightly controlled labor regime obtaining in the Oxyrhynchite nome. In the Roman-period **8.3.1**, a lessee contracts to perform a precisely delineated schedule of tasks in a vineyard (cf. **8.2.10**). The following three texts represent document types common in the Byzantine Oxyrhynchite. In **8.3.2**, an *enapographos* acknowledges both the receipt of a waterwheel and his responsibilities on a piece of irrigated estate land. In **8.3.3**, the *enapographos* receives an advance on his wages in the guise of a loan, while **8.3.4** preserves a deed of surety in which a second party agrees to stand liable for an *enapographos* and make good any arrears in the former's dues.

8.3.1 Contract for vineyard labor

P.Oxy. XIV 1692 (tr. Kloppenborg 2006: 522) (Oxyrhynchos, 28 October AD 188)

Although *P.Oxy.* XIV 1692 predates the first appearance of *enapographoi* in the papyri by over two and a half centuries, it is useful in this context to observe a preexisting regime of close control over labor in the Oxyrhynchite. The text is a so-called lease of work (*misthôsis tôn ergôn*), a document type that originated in the Oxyrhynchite and seems to have spread to the nearby Hermopolite nome.[31] **8.3.1** is the earliest surviving example while the latest, *P.Oxy.* L 3582, dates to AD 442, two years after the appearance of the *enapographoi*. The bulk of the extant leases of work concern vineyard labor (*cheirika ampelourgika erga*), while a further two contract for work in irrigation (*hydroparochika erga*). In form *misthôseis tôn ergôn* closely resemble leases; in our example Apion "leases" (*emisthôsen*) vineyard labor on an unspecified number of arouras to one Amois for a single year. And yet these documents are more akin to labor contracts since the lessee does not pay rent (*phoros*) on the plot in question but rather agrees to perform a meticulously delineated set of manual tasks in return for compensation (*misthos*, a wage).

Although our text likely preserves the majority of Amois' responsibilities, the clauses detailing his *misthos* are entirely lost. A fuller example is the virtually complete *P.Oxy.* XLVII 3354, **8.2.10** in this volume, a two-year lease of vineyard labor and irrigation work on about six arouras. The lessees Aurelius NN and his son Aurelius Hiereus are to receive their total cash wages of 360 drachmas per aroura in installments plus additional wine and wheat for pruning, at harvest and during the vintage. It is worth noting

[31] On *misthôseis tôn ergôn* see Jördens (1990: ch. 4; 1992). See also Rowlandson (1996: 228–36), and Hickey (2012: 79–81).

that **8.3.1** expressly excludes pruning from the list of Amois' tasks. Insufficiently pruned vines will yield a large, poor-quality crop while leaving behind old unproductive wood, inhibiting future fruit production. It is likely that Apion left the responsibility to more experienced vinedressers.

> Apion son of Horion, ex-gymnasiarch of the city of Oxyrhynchos, has leased to Amois son of Amois, whose mother is Sambous, resident in Talao, for one year from the first of Hathyr of the present year 29, all the manual vineyard labor, apart from the pruning, from the vineyard and reed land belonging to him near Talao from the *klêros* of Ptolemaios son of Tryphon, however many arouras it is, both old and new. Tasks include the cutting of reeds and transporting them to the usual place; sweeping of leaves; the cutting and transporting of them outside the wall to the appropriate places; hoeing (around the vines); trenching; layering, in the places where it is required; cutting of new reeds for the reed-work; reed-work, with the landowner supplying reeds and sufficient bark; irrigation and continuous weeding; hoeing; thinning the shoots; separating of the leaves and raising the shoots, thinning the leaves. And (Amois) shall be present for the vintage and will mix the Pelousian (wine?), and will stand watch in the field, the accustomed [. . .] village [. . .] he will transfer(?) [. . .] the produce (?) as far as . . .

8.3.2 Receipt for a waterwheel

SB VI 9503 (= S. Daris, *Aegyptus* 37 [1951]: 92) (Oxyrhynchos, 6 December AD 440[32]). Image in Montevecchi (1988), Plate 95.

The following is a receipt (called a *cheirographia*, a deed or declaration) for a replacement wheel for an irrigator (Greek *mêchanê*; Arabic *sâqıya*) supplied to a *geôrgos* on an estate of the imperial house (*domus divina*).[33] Used in areas not reached by the Nile's annual inundation, *sawâqî* "were water-lifting devices . . . consisting of a pair of cog wheels at right angles, driven by one or two oxen."[34] Such *mêchanê* receipts are common in our period, the majority deriving from the dossier of the Apiones. Our text is, again, the earliest-known example of a type that is attested until AD 617

[32] Bagnall and Worp (1978: 226–27) date the text to AD 441. I accept the critique of N. Gonis at *P.Oxy.* LXVIII 4688, note to line 2.

[33] Tacoma (1998) provides a brief description of the document type and a table of the twenty-three examples then published. For the *domus divina* see now Azzarello (2012).

[34] Tacoma (1998: 123). For a more thorough discussion of the mechanics and technical vocabulary of waterwheels see Rathbone (2007a).

(*P. Oxy.* LXX 4801). Administrators on large estates, from whose context our receipts derive, provided replacement parts, e.g., wheels and axles, to peasants when irrigation machinery had broken down or had worn out. **8.3.2** adopts the form of a contract (*homologia*): the *geôrgos* acknowledges receipt of a wheel and agrees (*homologô*) to irrigate the plot under his charge, pay the rent due on it, and attend to all "appurtenant tasks (*panta ta anêkonta*)." Only single copies of *mêchanê* receipts were made. They were likely kept on record in the files of estate managers.[35]

8.3.2 is often considered the earliest attestation in the papyri of an *enapographos geôrgos* in the person of the recipient Aurelius Paulos. While *geôrgos* is preserved in line four, the original editor in a lacuna of line five restored *enapographos*. In view of the similarity of **8.3.2** to other *mêchanê* receipts the restoration is widely if not universally accepted. N. Gonis has recently raised several concerns (*P. Oxy.* LXVIII 4697, lines 6–7n.): It predates the earliest reference to an *enapographos* in the laws; the word order, with adjective following noun, is unusual;[36] and there are no additional attestations of *enapographoi* of the *domus divina*. Even if the restoration is incorrect, **8.3.2** is useful in charting the evolution of the *enapographoi* and their strong link to irrigation. In seventeen of the twenty-three *mêchanê* receipts listed in Tacoma (1998) the addressor is an *enapographos*. There are a further twelve *enapographoi* attested in the seventeen additional receipts published in *P. Oxy.* LXVII through LXX (in two additional texts the addressor is lost).[37] *Mêchanê* receipts without *enapographoi* are: *P. Oxy.* XVI 1987 (fully published in the appendix to *P. Oxy.* LXX), *P. Oxy.* LXX 4780, 4785, and 4789. There is no substantive difference between these receipts and those issued on behalf of *enapographoi*.

In the consulship of Flavius Anatolius *vir clarissimus*, Choiak 10.

To NN[38] the worshipful councilor of the splendid and most splendid city of the Oxyrhynchites, most esteemed administrator of the affairs for our most divine and most noble mistress Arcadia, from Aurelius Paulos son of Apphous from the hamlet of Kalpounios (*sic*) of the same nome of the same most divine house, *colonus* [*adscripticius*], greetings. Need having

[35] Ibid.

[36] But see, e.g., the petition *P. Oxy.* XXVII 2479, line 9, for the word order *geôrgos enapographos* – itself an unusual case.

[37] *P. Oxy.* XVI 1987; LXVIII 4696, 4697; LXIX 4755; LXX 4780, 4781–85, 4788, 4796–4801.

[38] Most likely Flavius Strategius, the earliest identified member of the Apion family and *curator* of imperial estates in Egypt.

now arisen for a large waterwheel for the irrigated estate plot under my charge,[39] which is called "New" and waters vineland and arable land, I departed for the city thinking that this would be provided to me and when Your Excellency provided the required new wheel of 36 cogs [. . .] and of the current month of Choiak of the present ninth indiction [. . .] as completion of the machine parts [. . .] I acknowledge upon receipt of this (waterwheel) that I will provide for the irrigation, pay the rent, attend to all appurtenant tasks, and as certification of the receipt of this large waterwheel I have made this declaration, which is valid, one copy having been made and having been asked I gave my consent.

(*2nd hand*) Aurelius Paulos son of Apphous, the aforementioned, made the deed for the large waterwheel and agrees. I, [. . .] Sarapion (son of) Horion,[40] having been asked, wrote on his behalf, since he is illiterate.

(*3rd hand*) Stephanos(?), accountant(?) of the city of the Oxyrhynchites [. . .] Flavius Phanias(?), steward . . .

8.3.3 Advance on wages

P.Oxy. I 194 (Oxyrhynchos, second half of sixth century AD). Image at Papyri.info.

P.Oxy. I 194 was originally published only as a description. The Greek text will be published by Todd M. Hickey elsewhere. For comparanda see the *descripta P.Oxy.* I 192 and 206, each fully published in Montserrat *et al.* (1994) (texts reprinted as *SB* XXII 15362 and 15367).

8.3.3 preserves a nearly complete *prochreia* agreement (see also **8.2.3**). The top of the papyrus is missing and the names of the addressor and addressee are lost, save for a patronymic and the name of the *epoikion* (estate residence) of Theagenes on the reverse. The *epoikion* is known from documents of the dossier of the Apiones, to which this text assuredly belongs. *Prochreia* agreements concern cash advances to agricultural laborers, often *enapographoi*,[41] and indicate with little specificity the labor to be performed in return. Such advances are couched in the terminology of a

[39] The wording – *tên hyp' eme despotikên mêchanên* – is vague. With reference to Apionic texts, Banaji (2007: 183–84) interprets the preposition *hypo* in similar contexts as "the assignment of individual (i.e., salaried) workers to specific plots" by the Apiones' central administration. In our text, however, Aurelius Paulos agrees to pay the rent (*phoros*, plausibly restored in line 12), which indicates a tenancy arrangement. See Hickey (2001: 111 with n. 144).

[40] Following in part the restoration of Youtie (1975b: 220).

[41] E.g., *P.Iand.* 48 (582), *P.Amh.* II 149 (sixth century AD).

loan and as such the advanced sum is not called a wage (*misthos*) but may be described as the principal (*kephalaion*), although this is not universal.[42] Unlike true loans, *prochreia* agreements neither specify interest on the "principal" nor offer precise schedules for repayment. **8.3.3** concerns the advance of one *solidus* on condition that it be returned whenever the lender should wish, a common formulation. In contrast, the near-contemporary *P.Oxy.* LXXI 4835 (21 March AD 574) preserves a loan of one *solidus* less five carats without interest. The contract, however, stipulates that the sum be repaid in Pachon (26 April/25 May), only a month or two after the initial loan. In the fifth-century *P.Oxy.* LXXI 4831 (AD 429) the debtor receives a single *solidus* to be repaid in about a month's time, but with the addition of half a *centenarium*[43] of "pure leafy woad" (*isatis*, indigo) as interest in kind.[44]

While the terms of *prochreia* agreements are relatively simple, their interpretation remains contested. They have been viewed as exploitative, in that the ill-defined repayment scheme placed recipients in a precarious position wherein the entire advance can be demanded back at will long after it had been spent on daily necessities. Additional advances would therefore increase ever further the dependency of heavily indebted laborers upon their employers.[45] Less malevolently, these documents have been interpreted as salary advances to hired laborers (as in **8.2.3** introduction), representative of an expansion of agricultural wage labor and its sophisticated deployment on Egyptian estates.[46] A further interpretation separates these documents from hired labor and connects them to lease contracts, as emerges particularly clearly in *P.Berl.Zill.* 7 (AD 574), in which one Aurelius Psaos leases an irrigated plot, its machinery, crops, and twelve dependent arouras while at the same time receiving an advance of one *solidus*. In the memorandum *P.Ant.* II 92 (fourth/fifth century AD) a landowner reminds himself to expel the lessee Papnouthios from a plot and demand back the items stipulated in the *misthôsis*, including reeds and a *prochreia* of unspecified substance and amount.[47]

42 Although not strictly a *prochreia* agreement, see *Stud.Pal.* III² 56 (sixth/seventh century) for an explicit advance of *misthos*.

43 *Centenarium* ("a hundredweight"): for references, see Daris (1991): 53.

44 For comparison's sake, see the true loans published in *P.Oxy.* LXXII.

45 So Jördens (1990: 281). See also Jördens (1985; 1997).

46 Banaji (2007: 183–88 and 198).

47 Mazza (2007; 2001: 125–28). Mazza cites in addition *P.Grenf.* I 59, *P.Amh.* II 149 (sixth century AD), *P.Oxy.* I 192 (= *SB* XXII 15362, AD 600/615), the latter two being advances to *enapographoi*. None of the three states explicitly that the recipients are lessees of the plots they farm and it can be argued that they are simply laborers.

If *prochreia* advances are to be linked with contracts for lease one wonders why there was need of additional documentation to solidify the terms of the relationship. In terms of hired labor, *prochreia* agreements do not clarify the laborer's expected duties in any real detail, in contrast with the precise delineation of tasks seen in a *misthôsis tôn ergôn* such as **8.3.1**. *Prochreiai* are thus critically deficient as actionable contracts since they lack the detail sufficient to lend them evidentiary force; this is clearly evident in the text presented here. It should be noted that our text references an earlier advance, perhaps recorded in a previous *prochreia* document. While cash advances could indeed be extended to lessees, it is less plausible that the *prochreia* agreement on its own had a concrete role in establishing the initial tenant–lessor or employer–employee legal relationship. In view of the nebulous terms of the agreements and the possibility of repeated advances, it is more likely that *prochreiai* were intended to provide the recipient with working capital to be spent in the completion of tasks more precisely enumerated in a separate agreement.

As with the similar *P. Oxy.* I 192 (= *SB* XXII 15362), our text mentions only an advance to an *enapographos* for an irrigated plot farmed by him (*eis tên hyp' eme geouchikên mêchanên*) either as a lessee or a wage laborer. No further elaboration is forthcoming and one cannot determine the recipient's position on the basis of the *prochreia* alone. Adscript status is not necessarily of help as it is now certain that the ostensibly poor and landless *enapographoi* could undertake leases.[48] Whatever the case, the close connection of *enapographoi* and water supply has been noted above and we see here in the deployment of *enapographoi* the continued desire on the part of landowners for ever-closer control over labor.

> [. . .] your *colonus adscripticius*, greetings. After the previous advance to me, yet again I acknowledge that I have received from Your Magnificence now immediately for the irrigated plot named Kariou farmed by me during the present first indiction on account of advances one *solidus* of gold at the private standard,[49] equals 1 *solidus* of gold at the private standard, and I acknowledge that I will return this to your magnificence whenever you wish without delay. The document is valid, one copy having been written, and having been formally asked I gave my consent.

[48] See *P. Oxy* LXVII 4615 (AD 505), the first published example of an *enapographos* as lessee.
[49] For the weight standards of *solidi* see *P. Oxy.* LXXII 4930, lines 13–16n.

(*2nd hand*) Aurelius Ptollion son of Souros(?): this contract of one *solidus* on account of advances as written above is satisfactory to me. Papnouthios wrote on his behalf as he is illiterate.

(*3rd hand*) Through me Papnouthios, notary.[50]

Verso: [. . .] son of Sourous from the *epoikion* Theagenis in the account of advance, one *solidus* of gold at the private standard.

8.3.4 Deed of surety

P.Oxy. XXVII 2478 (Oxyrhynchos, 25 November AD 595)

The deed of surety (*enguê eis parastasin*) is another well-attested type from our period.[51] The purpose of the *enguê* was to provide a landowner with the assurance that his laborers would remain on their plots and discharge their agricultural and financial responsibilities, neither fleeing their duties nor taking up positions under another employer. Since laborers paid their taxes through the intermediation of the landlord, the latter required a guarantee that he/she would not be left liable for the dues of absent individuals. In an *enguê* a guarantor or guarantors attest that the insured will perform his duties lest the guarantor(s) be obliged either to make up the ensured's unmet dues or pay a fine in *solidi*. As in the example below, the ensured party was often an *enapographos*. The guarantor might also be of adscript status, as in *P.Oxy.* LXX 4791 (AD 578), in which an *enapographos* provides surety for two brothers, both *enapographoi*.[52] While *enapographoi* are common in the sureties, neither party to the surety need be of adscript status, as demonstrated in a document from the dossier of Flavia Anastasia (*P.Oxy.* LXIX 4756 [AD 590]). Here Flavia Anastasia is acting in her capacity as pagarch while the parties to the surety are non-adscript villagers. It is thus clear that sureties are fiscal in nature; they exist to help protect the government's revenue, not simply to control a semi-servile labor force.

There is some confusion on the nature of the dues paid by the *enapographos* in our text, the *phoros*. Recently, Sirks (2008: 132), like the original editors, has understood *phoros* in our text to refer to tax payments, in this case reimbursement to the estate for capitation charges paid by it on behalf of the *enapographos*. More plausibly Banaji (2007: 97, cf. Hickey 2001:

[50] A Papnouthios writes on behalf of Oxyrhynchite illiterates from AD 570/1 (*P.Flor.* I 65) and AD 609 (*PSI* I 61). For the texts he subscribes see *P.Oxy.* LXVI 4635, line 39n. and LXX 4794, line 24n.

[51] For a list see Palme (2003: 531 n. 1); additional Oxyrhynchite examples in *P.Oxy.* LXVIII through LXX.

[52] In *P.Oxy.* LXX 4790 (AD 578) two guarantors, one an *enapographos*, give surety for a second *enapographos*.

87 n. 46) argues that since the orchard in question belongs to the estate (*geouchikon pômarion*) *phoros* must refer to a "rent" since it is unlikely that the *enapographos* would have been responsible for the taxes on a plot he did not own. This understanding of the *phoros* is reinforced by the use, later on in the text, of *ekphoria* ("produce").

Worth noting here is the private prison, the "jail of your honored house," mentioned in the text. Where such institutions were once regarded as attributes of mighty semi-feudal estates that were beyond the reach of an impotent government powerless to abolish them, they become less iniquitous if one views the estates as semi-public institutions. From this point of view, such prisons are an inevitable result of an estate empowered by the government to collect the taxes of those under its purview and possessed of the appropriate coercive apparatuses. For references see *P. Oxy.* LXIX 4756, note on line 20.

In the fourteenth year of the reign of our most divine and pious master, our greatest benefactor, Flavius Mauricius, the new Tiberius, perpetual Augustus and Emperor; in the thirteenth year of the consulship of the same, our most pious master; the thirtieth of Hathyr, fourteenth indiction.

To Flavius Apion the most renowned and most extraordinary consular, landowner here also in the illustrious city of the Oxyrhynchites, through Menas, slave, putting the formal question and supplying for his master, the same most renowned man, the conduct of and responsibility for (the transaction): I, Zacharias, steward of the Church of the Holy Resurrection, son of Anastasius of renowned memory, originating from this same city of the Oxyrhynchites, having signed below in his own hand, greetings.

I acknowledge with willing intent and from free choice, swearing the divine and august oath, that I give surety and pledge to Your Excellency through your representatives that Aurelius Pambrechios son of Paul and Thekla, your registered fruit-grower, originating from the hamlet Athlitou, the property of Your Excellency, on condition that he continually remain and abide on [. . .] estate-orchard and show all care and good cultivation to it without blame or hesitation or condemnation, and shall return the rent upon it every year and (perform) all the estate tasks usually presented by it; and if he is ever demanded from me by Your Excellency through your representatives on any day for any reason at all, I shall bring him forward and hand him over in a public place without recourse to any place of sanctuary or letter of safe conduct where I took charge of him, in the jail of your honored house; or if I do not do this, I acknowledge that I shall pay in full on his behalf from my own resources the rents of the same estate orchard at my own risk and that of all my property.

The surety, of which there is one copy, is valid and having been formally asked I gave my consent.

(*2nd hand*) Zacharias son of the blessed Anastasius, the above mentioned. The surety, as written above, is satisfactory to me.

While there is little work devoted solely to the *enapographoi* there has been much recent work on agriculture and aristocracy in Byzantine Egypt in which appear discussions of *coloni* in Egypt. Research on the colonate from the literary and legal sources also shows no signs of slacking.

The Egyptian adscript workforce was restricted to estate locales, the *epoikia* and *ktêmata*, with only four surviving texts referring to *enapographoi* in villages.[53] While there was no complete ownership of villages by Egyptian elites, the deficiencies of the estate-centered Oxyrhynchos papyri do not allow us to describe village life in a depth sufficient to provide counterbalance to the mass of central estate archives that provide us with the bulk of our evidence for the Byzantine Oxyrhynchite. Given these limitations we must attempt to gain a clearer sense of the numbers of the *enapographoi* and the extent and patterns of their deployment on large estates.

One minimalist reading sees the *enapographoi* as drawn from the same pool as the "tenants" of leases of work and most commonly used by *geouchoi* in specific agricultural tasks, including irrigation and vineyard labor, where a tighter degree of control than was available in a lease was desired. This particular argument sees the *enapographoi* as supplemental to widespread leasing on the estate of the Apiones.[54] If, however, the *enapographoi* are understood as "the mainstay of the Apion family's agricultural workforce,"[55] it follows that either the population of Byzantine Egypt was large enough to create a substantial pool of landless poor in search of work,[56] or that the growth of large estates had subsumed the land of smallholders, who were reduced to tied tenancy in order to survive. More work must be done on the demographic conditions in Egypt, especially in light of the Justinianic plague, before the first claim

[53] *P.Oxy.* XLIV 3204 (AD 588); *P.Oxy.* LXIX 4757 (late sixth century AD); *P.Oxy.* LXX 4787 (AD 564): all refer to *enapographoi* in villages under the pagarchic control of Anastasia (3204 and perhaps 4757) or the Apiones, presumably residents of estate holdings in the villages in question.

[54] Hickey (2012: 62–89). The author estimates that approximately 55 percent of the Apiones' vineyard land was let out on fixed-rent cash leases and that 90 percent of the estate's after-tax income (≈ 13,000 *solidi*) came from rents. See also Hickey (2007: 301–02).

[55] Sarris (2006: 62).

[56] Banaji (2007: 20) posits such a "demographic upswing" for the Byzantine East, although he ignores possible effects of the Justinianic plague.

can be substantiated.[57] The extent of Apionic and other aristocratic holdings in the Oxyrhynchite is also a matter of dispute (**8.3** introduction). This bears heavily upon the second issue, since the amount of land controlled by large estates directly correlates to the size of the adscript workforce.

Finally, in spite of the limited evidence for tenancy, the surviving lease contracts are sufficient to balance the claims by some for all-pervasive direct exploitation and wage labor.[58] Progress might be made on this front by attempting to locate *enapographoi* in the surviving annual accounts of the Apiones' estate.[59] Some fifteen entries survive for payment of a *synteleia* (*tês*) *kephalês* or capitation charge.[60] While it has been asserted that there is no evidence for a pre-Islamic Byzantine capitation charge,[61] the payment of taxes through a landlord as intermediary is a well-known attribute of the adscripticiate. If the *synteleia kephalês* is accepted as a pre-Islamic capitation charge, evidence for its payment is recorded from only seven of the forty-eight Apionic estate residences attested in the accounts, perhaps indicating a somewhat more restricted use of *enapographoi*.[62] And yet this must confront the fact that *enapographoi* are attested on some fifty Oxyrhynchite locales, admittedly not all of them pertaining to the Apiones.[63]

As mentioned earlier, the history of the *enapographoi* is the history of agricultural labor in one nome, largely restricted to the extensive holdings of one family. While it would be imprudent to impose conclusions drawn from the Oxyrhynchite data upon the rest of Egypt or the later Empire as a whole, the papyri at least preserve descriptive, first-hand evidence for the use of *coloni* in late Roman agriculture. A thorough investigation into the numbers, spread, and employment of the *enapographoi* on large estates will surely provide a different and welcome perspective on the debates surrounding the "colonate" as documented in the prescriptive legal sources.

[57] Rathbone (2001a) argues for a population no higher than 5 million in the Roman period, followed by a decline in the Byzantine period. For a recent assessment of urban population in Byzantine Egypt with consideration of the possible effects of the plague from comparative evidence see Alston (2001).

[58] Banaji (2007) and Sarris (2006). On tenancy and indirect exploitation see Mazza (2007) and Hickey (2012: 67–79).

[59] *P.Oxy.* XVI 2019 (AD 547/8 or AD 562/3); *P.Oxy.* XVI 1912 (AD 553/4–554/5?); *P.Oxy.* XVI 1913 (AD554/5?); *P.Oxy.* XVI 1914 (AD 556/7); *P.Oxy.* XVI 1911 (AD 556/7); *P.Oxy.* XVIII 2204 (AD 565/6); *P.Oxy.* LV 3804 (AD 565/6); *P.Oxy.* XVIII 2195 (AD 576/7); *P.Oxy.* XIX 2243 (a) (b) (AD 590/1); *PSI* VIII 954 (sixth century AD); *P.Oxy.* VI 999 (AD 616/7).

[60] Outside the accounts one receipt survives for payment of the *synteleia tês kephalês*, *P.Oxy.* X 1131 (fifth century AD). This still leaves us with the confusing situation of two recorded credits to an unspecified group for the *synteleia kephalês*: *P.Oxy.* XVI 1911, line 86 and *P.Oxy.* LV 3804, line 158. Both are credited to "those from [the *epoikion*] Trigêou."

[61] So Sijpesteijn (2007: 446). [62] Cf. Hickey (2012: 82–3).

[63] Survey of documents in the DDBDP and *P.Oxy.* LXIX–LXXII.

CHAPTER 9

Slavery in Greco-Roman Egypt

Y. Rotman, R. Scholl, and Jean A. Straus

Introduction

Anyone who has seen a spectacular movie set in Egypt, say, for example, *The Ten Commandments* starring Charlton Heston, will be forgiven for coming away with the impression that the land was full of slaves who spent all their time suffering while building pyramids and other massive structures. Herodotus (2.124), of course, reports a similar image of slave labor and pyramid building. So it is perhaps surprising to see in the preceding chapter (**8.1** introduction) that slavery in Ptolemaic Egypt was a negligible phenomenon and that such slaves as there were were mostly engaged in domestic service in Greek and hellenized Egyptian households. That would conform to what we know about pre-Ptolemaic practice, according to which slaves are found performing work in the non-agricultural sector, in households (see also of course Joseph's service to Potiphar in Genesis), in quarries, and in royal building projects. In agriculture, before the Ptolemies, many persons were bound to specific estates – to temple estates, or to the large estates of state officials – as "serfs" (Lloyd 1983: 315). Often the Egyptian terminology does not help us define exactly what the status of these workers was, but we may be safe in assuming that their status, like that of many workers in antiquity, was somewhere between fully free and fully enslaved. It was in the first millennium BC that the state began to recognize a particular institution that we may call slavery. It is documented in contracts of sale (Donker van Heel 1995: 177–82). The so-called self-sale to satisfy a debt (*P.Ryl.* 5 [569 BC]; see **5.1** above) and the seizure of debtors and/or their children continued to occur in the Ptolemaic period and beyond, not without attempts at regulation (e.g., **9.1.2**, **10.1.2**; cf. **5.5.3**, **9.3.1**).

But there was no need for large-scale agricultural slavery in a land full of laborers, some of whom brought their own specialized skills to bear on the agrarian economy (Chapter 8, *passim*).[1] Under such circumstances the scholarly interest in slavery as an object of historiographical investigation and as a social and legal phenomenon in Egypt is probably out of proportion to its importance as a demographic and economic phenomenon.

The introduction to **9.1** repeats the point about domestic slavery in hellenized households, but is rather more expansive on the imprint of slavery in Ptolemaic Egyptian society; for which **9.1.3**, which includes a rule on the registration of "houseborn" slaves, is an interesting bit of supporting evidence. The registration of slaves continues in the census returns of the Roman period (see **9.2.4**). As in the Ptolemaic period, slaves were mostly domestics, their numbers seem to have been relatively small, slave-owning families were a minority, and even among them the norm was to own one or two slaves; few owned more (Bagnall and Frier 1994: 48–49). If the Romans brought anything new, one thing was the increased opportunity for a slave's acquiring freedom through manumission (e.g., **9.2.5**; cf. **3.3** introduction, the testamentary manumissions in **3.3.1**). The impact of manumissions on the total numbers of slaves in Egypt is impossible to gauge, and the "numbers game" is in any case difficult to play. Some have argued for a drop in absolute numbers of slaves in the Byzantine period; others have said that the numbers held steady, it is only the nature of the evidence that changed (Bagnall 1993a; cf. **9.3** introduction).

For example, though not very numerous in the first place, the number of surviving sales of slaves drops off in the Byzantine period. Of these slave sales, most interesting are those sales and registrations of sales contracted outside Egypt for slaves who were to be imported. These begin with the sale from the Zenon archive of the seven-year-old Babylonian slave girl named Sphragis ("Seal," "Signet-Ring"), sold in Birta of the Ammanitis (modern Jordan) in 259 BC (*P.Cair.Zen.* I 59003, lines 11–22 = *Sel.Pap.* I 31). Sales and registrations of the Roman period include:

- the sale of a ten-year-old Galatian girl Abaskantis (the name begs avoidance of the Evil Eye) in the agora of Side in Pamplylia in AD 142 (*P.Turner* 22);
- the sale, also at the agora of Side in Pamphylia, of a twelve-year-old Phrygian girl Sambatis (now called Athenais) in AD 151 (*BGU* III 887 = *FIRA* III 133);

[1] On relative costs of slaves, see Scheidel (2005).

the sale of a seven-year-old boy named Abbas, also called "Lucky" (Eutyches; Felix in Latin), of Transeuphrates origin, possibly captured during the Emperor Verus' Parthian campaign, at Seleukia on the Syrian coast in AD 166 (*FIRA* III 132);

the request submitted in Oxyrhynchos in AD 237 for the registration of a nine-year-old Macedonian slave boy Zoilos, presumably purchased abroad (**9.2.2**);

the auction sale of a seven-year-old Moorish girl, *korasion*, on the island of Rhodes in the reign of Gordian III (AD 238–44) by sellers apparently from Caesarea in Mauretania (*P.Oxy.* L 3953, in Doric dialect; *ed. pr.* Oates 1969);

the registration of the sale of a seventeen-year-old female slave named Balsamea, by race Osrhoenian (by geography Mesopotamian), purchased in Phoenician Tripolis and registered in Oxyrhynchos in AD 252 (*P.Oxy.* XLII 3053);

the registration in Oxyrhynchos around AD 265 of a male slave named Prokopton, renamed Aptos, purchased in Bostra in Syria (*P.Oxy.* XLII 3054);

the sale of the fourteen-year-old Gallic slave boy Argoutis at Askalon on the Syrian coast in AD 359 (*BGU* I 316 = *FIRA* III 135).[2]

Finally, latest and longest by far, is the Greek notarial contract of sale (*SB* XVIII 13173 [AD 629?], *ed. pr.* Preisigke 1906) from Hermopolis for a twelve-year-old Nubian girl of the Alwan tribe. Named Atalous, she was to be renamed "Eutychia" ("Lucky," again; Fortunata in Latin; see also, in **8.2.6**, the female slave baby named Tyche). The current sellers had acquired their own right to Atalous "by right of sale" (*apo dikaiou ago* [*rasia*]*s*),[3] they having bought her from certain unnamed "slavedealers (*sômatemporoi*) of the Ethiopians" at an unspecified earlier date and unspecified place (presumably though not necessarily in Nubia).

The geographical spread of these scattered references is of obvious interest, as is the fact that the slaves whose ages have survived intact were "barbarian" children uprooted from their often very distant homes, owning nothing, not even, in some cases, their own names, a sure sign of their "social death" (Patterson 1982: 54–58). Of legal, or better, rhetorical, interest is the contrast between the simplicity of the Ptolemaic sale and the prolixity of the Byzantine (see Chapter 2). In the former

2 Also worth mention is *P.Oxy.* XXXVI 2771 (AD 323), a power of attorney (mandate) involving a female slave owned by a woman from Cos with obvious connections with Oxyrhynchos.

3 A new reading in line 24, verified against images kindly provided by Paul Heilporn.

(*P.Cair.Zen.* I 59003, 11–22 = *Sel.Pap.* I 31), between the date and the names of guarantor and witnesses, the transaction is simply put: "Nikanor son of Xenokles, a Knidian, one of those [[*canceled*: of Toubias' cavalrymen, kleruch]] in the service of Toubias, has sold (*apedoto*) to Zenon son of Agreophon, a Kaunian, one of those in the service of Apollonios the *dioikêtês*, a [Babylo]nian [slave girl (*paidiskê*)] whose name is Sphragis, about seven years old, for fifty drachmas." The Byzantine sale, even in its incomplete state (*SB* XVIII 13173), runs to over 160 lines (written *transversa charta*). One dozen-line stretch is worth particular note for its deployment of legal terminology. It sets forth the new owner's, Aurelia Isidora's, rights over Atalous/Eutychia as a complex series of articular infinitives (lines 54–65):

> ... perpetually, [for you] to have power over (*epikratein*) her and to control (*kurieuein*) and to own (*des[pozein]*) with every owner's right, to possess (*ktasthai*), to enjoy (*ne<me>sthai*), to have use of (*chrêsthai*) her and – God willing! – her children, to manage (*oikonomein*) and administer (*dioikein*) concerning her, to sell (*pôlein*), to mortgage (*hypothesthai*), to give as a gift (*charisasthai*), to exchange (*ant[ikatal]laxasthai*) for a dowry and in anticipation of marriage, to give as a gift (*dôrean didonai*) to one's children and grandchildren, to leave behind (*kataleipsai*) and pass on (*parapempein*) to your heirs, successors, and assigns, and to make (*poiein*) and do (*prattein*) absolutely everything regarding her that the laws (*nomoi*) order legally independent owners to accomplish (*diaprattesthai*) with respect to their own private property ...[4]

How far the above is a legitimate attempt by the notary to express rights of ownership as precisely and fully as possible (see Chapter 6); how much is for show or for justification of notarial fees; how much of the terminology is tautologous (e.g., *poiein* and *prattein*, cf. *diaprattesthai*); to what extent each infinitive is a distinct term referring to a distinct and identifiable legal institution; what one should make of the various rhetorical figures – assonance, alliteration, asyndeton, polysyndeton, word pairs (*oikonomein* + *dioikein*, *kataleipsai* + *parapempein*) and triplets; how many legal Latinisms lurk beneath the Greek – all this would require much more space to untangle than can be allotted here and belongs more appropriately in Chapter 2. It does seem, nevertheless, that the verbiage is a sign of the times, a sign, among other things, of the professionalization of the law in late antiquity.

[4] Translation uses Pierce (1995), reproduced by Burstein (1998: 118–20, no. 24), as its basis but both are based on Preisigke's *editio princeps* and both treat the sale as a sixth-century document.

9.1 Slaves and slavery in the Ptolemaic period

R. Scholl

Ptolemaic Egypt was part of the Hellenistic world, into which the Macedonian and Greek immigrants brought along with them their own culture. A part of that culture and way of life was slavery in Greek form. It belonged to the economy and society of their Greek homeland. We therefore find slavery in Egypt in all domains of human life, especially among Greeks and hellenized Egyptians. Although Ptolemaic Egypt is not normally viewed as a slave-owning society, slavery played an important role in the daily lives of Greeks in Egypt, particularly in trade, handicrafts, and household service. For certain jobs slaves were given over for training through apprenticeships. In these arrangements, slaves were to subsist upon food (*opsônion*) and clothing (*himatismos*) allowances, sometimes receiving sums of money for living expenses. In addition, the papyri give information about the purchase, manumission, and escape of slaves. We find slaves as property of the state, of the kings, and of private masters. Slaves can appear as components of inheritances and dowries.

The Ptolemaic state had to regulate the social relations of many different people and ethnic groups, free and servile, in Egypt as well as in outside possessions like Cyrenaica, Cyprus, Coele Syria, and Asia Minor, especially in the third century BC. The Ptolemaic kings did not change the law as they found it in Egypt and in the territories. Rather, they subordinated Greek law and Egyptian or "Demotic" law to their own law in the form of royal decrees and ordinances, *prostagmata* and *diagrammata* (*C.Ord.Ptol.*). But their legislation has not completely survived. We have only excerpts in texts like the famous Revenue Laws of Ptolemy Philadelphos. Such excerpts were made for specific legal cases; it is therefore difficult to use them as bases for generalizations. We must treat each case on its own terms.

The Ptolemaic state had an interest in all its subjects, including slaves. For this reason the Ptolemies, especially for purposes of taxation, included slaves when they registered the population of their domains. We have in **9.1.3** below just such a document. The Ptolemaic kings also intervened in the relationships between slave owners and slaves, notably within the sphere of criminal law through the different segments of the Ptolemaic legal system: royal law, Greek law (especially that of the Greek *poleis* Alexandria, Ptolemais, and Naucratis), and native law (see **9.1.1–2**). For works on Hellenistic and Ptolemaic slavery see, e.g., Pavlovskaja (1972) and Scholl (1995).

9.1.1 Rules on slaves in lawsuits

P.Lille I 29 (= *C.Ptol.Sklav.* 1) (Ghoran [Fayyum], third century BC). Image at *P.Lille* I, Plate VIII.

9.1.1 is one of the most important texts for the Ptolemaic law of slavery, especially for slaves involved in lawsuits. It is a compilation of paragraphs of different laws selected for a specific case.

The papyrus contains excerpts from the laws of a *polis*, which is unlikely to have been Alexandria because in Col. II, line 37 we find an order to bring the slave to Alexandria. That different terms for "slave" occur – *oiketês* in Col. I, lines 2 and 11; *sôma* in Col. I, line 13; *doulos* in Col. I, lines 19, 21, 27, 29, and in Col. II, line 6; *andrapodon* in Col. II, lines 30 and 34 – shows that the document is a compilation. In any case all these terms are commonly used to indicate a slave *stricto sensu*. Other pieces of evidence to indicate the text is a compilation are the *paragraphoi* and blank spaces between these digests, namely between lines 12 and 13, 26 and 27. Since proceedings of lawsuits followed the *nomoi*, we have to assume that the sections of this papyrus have mainly been excerpted from these *nomoi*. The royal law to which the *nomoi* were officially subordinated is in fact mentioned at Col. II, lines 11–12.

Section 1 (Col. I, lines 1–12) concerns a lawsuit against a slave as if he were a free person. If the slave is convicted, his master has the right to remonstrate. If the master does not win the appeal, he is to pay a penalty. The slave is to be punished according to the laws, except those slaves whom the *diagramma* excepts. The slave is also responsible for his own actions.

Section 2 (Col. I, lines 13–18) is not a general export ban for slaves, as it is often wrongly interpreted. All the paragraphs are in connection with a specific lawsuit. Therefore the interdiction of export, branding, etc., refers only to the slaves involved in this lawsuit. In some cases, however, the judge can make an exemption.

Section 3 (Col. I, lines 19–26) regulates the ability of slaves to bear witness. I assume that torture is to be applied only if the judge cannot decide from the presented proofs.

Section 4 (Col. I, line 27–Col. II, line 38) treats lawsuits against slaves and appropriate punishment. The law makes a distinction regarding the punishment, depending upon whether the slave is acting with or without his master's knowledge or incitement. If the master is not guilty, the slave is to be handed over to the plaintiff. He must punish him with flogging and brand him on the forehead and/or (there is a gap here in the papyrus) bring him to Alexandria and sell him into a foreign country. Perhaps the law gives a choice between existing punishments; or between the standard punishments and increased versions of them. This rule should prevent collusion between the plaintiff and the slave against the slave's former master.

(§1) If anyone on account of a wrong brought suit against the slave of another person as if he were a free person and has won the trial, the owner is to be allowed to file an appeal within 5 days, from the day on which the execution begins. And if the appeal is unsuccessful, the owner is to pay the tenth or the fifteenth part, and the execution is to be made according to the laws concerning the slaves, except those slaves whom the *diagramma* excludes.

(§2) Nobody is to be allowed either to sell slaves for export, or to brand, [or to flog] or [. . .] agree [. . .] judge. (*1 line lost*)

(§3) Slaves are allowed to bear witness. If the slaves have borne witness, the judges are to torture the slaves in the presence of the opponents, if they (*sc.* the judges) cannot decide from the evidence provided through documents.

(§4) Imputation(?) against slaves and punishment of the convicted. Whoever brings an accusation claiming to have been wronged by a slave or female slave is to inform the owner about the wrong face to face, in front of not less than two witnesses, and to bring suit in written form to the *nomophylakes*, and it is forbidden to [. . .] (*3–4 lines lost*) He (the plaintiff) is to bring suit against him according to the law. And if he agrees, the owner is to pay just the prescribed penalty. If he refuses, he is to defend himself on the grounds that neither on his order nor with his knowledge did the slave do wrong. If it is decided by the judge that the slave has acted legally [. . .] If it is decided by the judge that on the master's order or with the master's knowledge the slave has done wrong, (the master) is to act as a guarantor for the established penalty and the guilty is to pay also the fifth part of the established penalty to the opponent according to the law. If the master refuses to do this and it is decided by the judge that the master neither had knowledge nor ordered, the debtor is to be allowed to deliver the slave to the winner in the presence of the *nomophylakes* and he will be free of penalty. He is to take the slave and to flog him with not less than one hundred strokes and to brand him on the forehead as the *diagramma* orders (and/or) to carry him to Alexandria and to sell him for export.

9.1.2 More rules on slaves in a lawsuit

P.Hal. 1 Cols. VIII–IX (= *C.Ptol.Sklav.* 2) (Apollonopolite nome [originally Alexandria], 259–246 BC)

The famous Papyrus *P.Hal.* 1 (*Dikaiômata*) includes in 265 lines different laws collected for a specific lawsuit involving slaves. The text, containing the city law of Alexandria, dates to the later years of the reign of Ptolemy II. Excerpted below are the paragraphs that mention slaves.

The long first excerpt shows that there was a dual-penalty system whereby the punishment for slaves differed from that for free men. The free man was liable with his property: if he lost his case he paid money; the slave's punishment was corporeal: if convicted he was flogged. The master could change this punishment for his slave if he paid the slave's prescribed penalty. He himself could not buy off his own punishment. In this matter economic or social status was irrelevant: all that counted was the person's juridical status. The latter part of this excerpt lists various aggravations to battery based on time or place of assault and status dissonance between the parties concerned – similar to the Roman notion of *atrox iniuria* (Gaius, *Inst.* 3.225). The more severe punishment for slaves corresponds to common practice in Hellenistic law.

The short second excerpt bans slavery between Alexandrians. There is no explicit statement that an Alexandrian male cannot be a slave to a female Alexandrian, or that a male or female Alexandrian cannot be a slave to a foreigner or to a native Egyptian. Nevertheless we may assume that these forms of slavery were also (implicitly) forbidden by this rule. We also have to bear in mind that in the present lawsuit (for which these excerpts were made), one party is attempting to enslave his client's wife.

> *Col. VIII* (*Excerpt 1*) Threat with iron: If a free man has threatened a free man with iron or bronze or stone or [. . .] or wood, he is to pay 100 (drachmas) if he is defeated in a suit. But if a male slave or a female slave does such things against a free man or a free woman, he is to be flogged with not less than 100 strokes, or the master of the offender is to pay to the injured party double the penalty that is prescribed for a free man if he (*sc.* the master) is defeated in a lawsuit.
>
> *Col. IX* Injury in state of drunkenness: If anyone in a state of drunkenness injures somebody physically, or during the night, or in a temple, or in the market, he is to pay the double of the prescribed penalty.
>
> To the slave who has beaten a free man: If a male slave or a female slave has beaten a free man or a free woman, he is to be flogged with no fewer

than 100 strokes or the master is to pay for the slave double the penalty that is prescribed to be paid for a free man to pay, if he agrees. But if he refuses, the injured is to sue him for 100 drachmas for each stroke, but if he is cast in a suit, he is to pay the triple without estimation; in case of a higher number of strokes he is to make an estimation and sue. He is to pay triple what has been estimated by the court.

Col. X (*Excerpt 2*) Concerning (*sc.* Alexandrian) citizens, so that they not be slaves. The Alexandrian is not to be a slave to the Alexandrian, nor the female Alexandrian to the Alexandrian or the female Alexandrian.

9.1.3 Registration of households, including houseborn slaves

P.Harr. I 61, lines 1–15 (= *C.Ptol.Sklav.* 8) (Oxyrhynchos, May 176 BC/April 175 BC)

9.1.3 is a decree ordering the registration of slaves as part of the registration of the whole Egyptian population for tax purposes. All people are to register their children with the *agoranomoi*. The registration is free of charge at age 15. The mother's name is also to be declared; inclusion of the father's name must have been irrelevant and therefore left implicit. If the children are 15 years old, they have to be present in person to make a description of their own persons. Owners of houseborn slaves have to follow the same rules. If the deadline has not been respected, a penalty is to be paid to the city of Alexandria. Slaves by purchase are not mentioned, at least in the preserved text, but it cannot be excluded that they were mentioned in lines now lost. In any case they are registered in other ways (**9.1.4**).

This registration of the population follows the regulations of Ptolemy II Philadelphos in the third century BC. The single innovation is perhaps the fact that the penalty fee is here to be paid to the city instead of to the royal fiscus. We can assume that for this reason the city of Alexandria erected a golden image of the king, Ptolemy VI Philometor, to whom this favor was owed. The papyrus provides evidence for a form of *epikrisis* that is later known in Roman Egypt.

People who settle in Alexandria and in the country are to register [their children] to the *agoranomoi*, without payment, within the age of persons of 15 years, and are to add also the name of the children's mother on the register (*apographê*); if they reach the age of 15 years, they are to bring them to the *agoranomoi*, so that they may give the description of their own person. In the same way all [. . .] are to register their own houseborn slaves to the *agoranomoi* within 20 days, i.e., those until the age of 15, and to add in the same way the name of the mother; those over 15 years are to give the description of their own person. Those who are too late at the registration [as it is prescribed] are to make the registration and to pay to the city [a penalty to] the *agoranomoi* and to make the registration in accordance (with the laws). Because the king, Ptolemy, god Philometor, not only has greatly benefited our city Alexandria and all men, but [also because he . . .] wishing to do many useful things . . .

The text that follows is badly damaged and heavily restored, but does include reference to a decree for the making of a golden image of Ptolemy VI Philometor, as mentioned in the introduction to **9.1.3**, to sacrifices in his honor, and a golden crown.

9.1.4 Extract from a royal ordinance on taxes and fees on slave sales

P.Col. I 480, lines 1–22 (=Westermann 1929 with plate; *C.Ptol.Sklav.* 5) (Fayyum, *c.* 198/7 BC)

The approximate date is based upon reference to the gift estate (*dôrea*) of Dikaiarchos. The text consists of extracts from a royal ordinance about slaves (*ek tou diagrammatos tôn andrapodôn*). As in **9.1.1**, the word *andrapodon* signifies slave in general, without specifically connoting a slave captured in war. These extracts regulate the sale of slaves between private persons, and between the state and private persons, and the mortgage of slaves. The focuses are taxes and fees, which amount together on average to 20 percent of the sale price. The regulations for the purchase of slaves were only a part of this *diagramma*; the rest is lost. Included here are the first five of the seven regulations of Column 1. Only the upper left-hand corner of the second column survives.

The decree is divided into sections by means of *paragraphoi* (short horizontal strokes separating the various "paragraphs").

The first section establishes that the contractor of the sales tax on slaves and a supervisory official known as the *antigrapheus*, literally a "counter-signer," must collect from seller and buyer different taxes calculated upon the price of the slave. The seller offers an additional 1 percent fee, and to the city, a brokerage fee, *propôlêtikon* (called *propratikon* in §3), that is, a tax or fee to warrant that the sale is free of defect in title. If the state is the seller, this tax of course is not to be paid. The contracts of purchase are recorded with the *agoranomoi* (notaries). See Chapter 2 introduction.

The second section regulates the case of a single person paying all taxes.

The third section regulates sale at auction. The city receives fees for each bid and counterbid.

The fourth section regulates sale by the *praktôr xenikôn* ("collector of foreign debts"), i.e., by the state. This concerns slaves convicted of crimes, and persons enslaved as prisoners of war and now purchased by the state (cf. P.Mich. inv. 6947 = *C.Ptol.Sklav.* 9). In this case the state as owner and seller pays no tax or fee; the buyer must pay all.

The fifth section concerns slaves in the ownership of the state through debts of their masters to the fiscus, or slaves formerly free, but enslaved by the state as individual debtors to the state. In this case the seller must pay all taxes and fees.

[§1] From the *diagramma* upon slaves. The contractor for the tax upon slaves and the *antigrapheus* shall collect in respect to slaves whose sale contracts have been registered before the *agoranomoi*, upon the price at which they are registered, in silver, from the seller, including the one percent formerly reckoned for the gift estate of Dikaiarchos, per mina, 9 drachmas 2½ obols; and from the buyer, 8 drachmas 2[½] obols; total, per mina, 17 drachmas 5 obols; and for the city, a brokerage fee (*propôlêtikon*) from the seller, per slave, 4 drachmas 1 obol.

[§2] If anyone buys on the condition of paying all the taxes, they (the tax-contractor and the *antigrapheus*) shall collect, per mina, 20 drachmas 1 obol, and for the city per slave, 4 drachmas 1 obol.

[§3] If anyone possesses as a consequence of a bid or counterbid, he is to pay additionally to the city another brokerage fee (*propratikon*).

[§4] Upon (slaves) sold through the *praktôr xenikôn* the purchasers shall pay, per mina, 19 drachmas and 1 drachma as a crier's fee of one percent and 1 drachma per slave as a clerical fee for the gift-estate.

[§5] Upon (slaves) sold for the benefit of the royal treasury the purchasers shall pay, per mina, 16 drachmas 5 obols and 1 drachma as a crier's fee of one percent and 1 drachma per slave as a clerical fee for the gift estate of Dikaiarchos.

9.2 Slaves and slavery in the Roman period

Jean A. Straus

The conquest of Egypt by the Romans did nothing to change slaves' everyday lives. Technically, of course, there was a complete break in the domain of public law, where the Romans undertook full initiative, as well as in the legislative domain, where imperial constitutions (edicts, mandates, rescripts, decrees) and the prefect's edicts became sources of law. Nevertheless, in the present state of the documentation, there is no prefect's edict concerned with slavery in Roman-period Egypt (**10.4.6**, an edict of the *praeses* of the Thebaid, is dated to the fourth century), and only one imperial constitution is germane, namely, Augustus' constitution confirming the prefect's right to effect formal manumissions *vindicta* (*Dig.* 40.2.21, Modestinus; cf. Berger 1953: 577 s.v. Manumissio vindicta; *PSI* v 452.15, a rescript on fraudulent manumission, is dated to the fourth century). In judicial procedure, provincial *cognitio* was in use and ultimate justice belonged to the Roman authorities: the prefect of Egypt and delegated local officials. But slaves were not supposed to appeal to them since they could be neither plaintiffs nor defendants.

Measures taken by the conqueror did not directly affect peregrine private law. Indeed Romans accepted that Greek and Egyptian private laws in use under Ptolemaic rule should continue to be applied as local customs as long as they did not interfere with Roman public order. Pertinent are three documents, *PSI* vi 690, *SB* iii 6995 and 6996, where owners record their slaves as being in the category of "houseborn" (*oikogeneis*) slaves: all refer to Ptolemaic legislation and tax. If a local rule allowing settlement of differences by submitting one's case to the prefect was lacking, it was possible to appeal to Roman law. Such is the situation in *P.Oxy.* iv 706 = *M.Chr.* 81, concerned with relations between a patron and a freedman on which the *nomoi tôn Aigyptiôn* (Greek law applied in Egypt) remained silent. Roman citizens in Egypt were subject to Roman law, but did not always put into practice a pure Roman law. Moreover, after the *Constitutio Antoniniana*, peregrine local customs became Roman provincial customs or were accepted as official law of the empire. An example of the former is the (Greek) practice of manumission by notarial registration, unknown in Roman law (e.g., *P.Oslo* iii 129); of the latter, the efficacy of an emancipation performed by a joint owner (**9.2.5**).

The influence of the Roman conquest upon the law of slavery is above all noticeable in the realm of taxation. The creation of a class of fiscally privileged metropolitans gave birth to a process (called *epikrisis*) that served to identify persons of this status. As slaves followed their masters' fiscal status this process was applied to them too (**9.2.3**). Slaves were subject to poll-tax, tax on trades, tax upon Jews (if their masters were Jews, even if the slaves were not), and various other taxes. They were also subject to compulsory services such as repairing the dikes and cleaning out the canals.

As far as fiscal matters are concerned, slaves were thus regarded as human beings. Unions between free persons and slaves could suggest the same conception – but let us not be mistaken. It was never a question of legal marriage but rather of cohabitation (*contubernium*) or concubinage (*concubinatus*). Legal attitudes to the children born of such unions varied according to whether the servile spouse was a man or a woman. Indeed the Roman principle that "the child follows the womb" (*partus ventrem sequitur*) or takes its mother's "condition" (*condicio*: Gaius, *Inst.* 1.86) was applied: if the mother is free the child is free, if she is a slave he is a slave (**9.2.4**). But lots of children were undoubtedly the fruit of an ordinary "natural insemination" made by a slave (with the master's permission), or by the master himself, and wanted by the latter to replace or increase his slave livestock.

In this and in the rest of the papyrological documentation slaves are treated as things (*res*). They are sold, bequeathed, given in dowries or as gifts, left as security or divided up so that they come to be owned in fractions (**9.2.5**; also **9.2.4**). In all those deeds, the fisc puts slaves in the same category as goods and taxes them as such. So they are subject to the tax on property transfers (*enkyklion*). To insure that a thing and not a human being was put on sale the sold person underwent a special interrogation (*anakrisis*) (**9.2.2**). Ownership and transfer of slaves were subject to very strict controls on the Romans' part. Birth, death, transfer of ownership (by sale, gift, dowry, or legacy), and manumission of slaves were subject to all kinds of registrations. Slaves were listed in census returns too (**9.2.4**). Slaves' exit from Egypt was kept under close surveillance and export of slaves born in Egypt was perhaps prohibited (*BGU* V 1210, §§ 65–67, 69). When a slave had goods at his disposal (e.g., *P.Ryl.* II 144, *SB* XVI 12469), these were not under his ownership: either he was managing his master's goods or he had these goods in his possession as part of his *peculium*, which remained, strictly speaking, his master's property (e.g., *BGU* I 96, line 14; *PSI* IX 1040 = *FIRA* III 10, line 18). It is the same even when he seems to have some power (e.g., *BGU* IV 1116, *P.Oxy.* II 244): this power always derives from his master.

Finally, every slave, we assume, dreams of emancipation. Several modes of emancipation are found in Roman Egypt. The Greek type of manumission before a public notary has already been mentioned. To that we can add testamentary manumissions (e.g., *P.Tebt.* II 407; see also **3.3.1**), *manumissiones vindicta* (e.g., *P.Mich.* VII 462), and manumissions "among friends" (*inter amicos*) (*P.Oxy.* IX 1205 = *C.Pap.Jud.* III 473).

To sum up. As far as the law of slavery is concerned, the coming of Rome to Egypt is above all manifest in the Romans' strict control of slavery based upon fiscal interests. See further Pavlovskaja (1992), Straus (1988, 2004).

9.2.1 Investigation into the death of a slave

P.Oxy. III 475 (*BL* I 327, IX 180; Worp 2000: 190) (Oxyrhynchos, 3 November AD 182)

In Roman Egypt, as everywhere else, slaves were legally "things" (*res*) over which masters had absolute power, even the power of life and death. **9.2.1**, however, suggests that there were limits to the arbitrary treatment of slaves by masters. Here are the facts. During a feast in the Oxyrhynchite village of Senepta, the slave Epaphroditos died accidentally. His owner's father-in-law, Leonides alias Serenos, petitioned the *stratêgos* of the nome to send one of his assistants to conduct an investigation. The *stratêgos* appointed an assistant, enjoining him to go to Senepta, accompanied by a public physician, to examine the corpse, deliver a burial permit, and draw up a report (cf. **10.4.2–3**). Such a procedure could serve two different ends. First – although this is not evidenced in the papyri – the owner required authorization to bury his slave and to assure his own future freedom from taxation for that particular slave. The second was to establish the exact circumstances of death. If so, perhaps there is a link between this papyrus and a constitution of Antoninus Pius (AD 138–61) providing for penalties against a master who unjustifiably kills his slave: "For in accordance with a constitution of the Divine Antoninus Pius anyone who kills his slave without cause must not be punished less than one who kills another's slave" (Justinian, *Inst.* 1.8.2; also Gaius, *Inst.* 1.53). In this case the investigation would determine the circumstances of Epaphroditos' death to insure there was no willful homicide. Would a complaint have been lodged by Leonides alias Serenos because he suspected his son-in-law or anyone else had killed Epaphroditos? If so, this papyrus would illustrate some restriction on the master's power: he could be punished if the public physician concluded the slave had been murdered.

> Hierax, *stratêgos* of the Oxyrhynchite (nome), to Claudius Serenos, assistant. A copy of the request that has been presented to me by Leonides alias Serenos is sent to you so that, taking with you a public physician, you carefully examine the dead body in question and, having

delivered it over for burial, you come to a decision in writing. (*2nd hand*) I have signed. (*1st hand*) Year 23 of Marcus Aurelius Commodus Antoninus Caesar the lord, Hathyr 7.

(*3rd hand*) To Hierax, *stratêgos*, from Leonides alias Serenos who is styled as having Tauris for mother, of Senepta. At a late hour of yesterday the sixth while there was a festival in Senepta and cymbal-players were giving the performance as custom has it in front of the house of my son-in-law, Ploution the son of Aristodemos, his slave Epaphroditos aged about 8 years, wishing to lean over from the flat-roof of the said house to see the cymbal-players, fell and was killed. Presenting therefore this request I ask, if it please you, that you dispatch one of your assistants to Senepta so that the body of Epaphroditos may receive the suitable laying out and burial. Year 23 of the Emperor Caesar Marcus Aurelius Commodus Antoninus Augustus Armeniacus Medicus Parthicus Sarmaticus Germanicus maximus, Hathyr 7. I, Leonides alias Serenos, have presented (this request).[5]

9.2.2 Request for the interrogation of a slave (*anakrisis*)

PSI XII 1254 (*BL* IV 90) (Alexandria, 28 September–27 October AD 237)

In several documents concerning the slaves to be sold, it is said that these are subjected to *anakrisis*. This is a matter of procedure usually undertaken by the buyer of a slave in order to confirm that the latter really was a person of servile status and had not been illegally enslaved. This procedure is founded on legal measures and is required before a first sale of a slave in Egypt, regardless of his country of origin. It happens only once in the life of the slave and the certificate that attests it (also called *anakrisis*) is handed over from the seller to the buyer. The authorities concerned with *anakrisis* are numerous. *Anakrisis* is attested in Egypt from the end of the second century to the fourth century AD but the term is found as late as the sixth century in *Nov.* 142 of Justinian.

9.2.2 is a request for *anakrisis*. Aurelia Didymarion buys Zoïlos, a Macedonian slave aged about nine years who has arrived by sea in Alexandria. Since this slave is sold for the first time in Egypt he must be subjected to *anakrisis*. Therefore his buyer asks the Alexandrian authorities concerned with *anakrisis*, the *hypomnêmatographoi*, to make the required

[5] A different interpretation of this text is expressed in Heinen (2006).

interrogation in order to verify that Zoïlos is really a slave. (For the investigative procedure, see the report of *anakrisis* proceedings, *P.Herm.* 18, AD 323[?].) To prove the ownership rights of the seller, Marcus Aurelius Didymus, on the slave whom he sells to her, Aurelia Didymarion appends to her request a summary of the slave's sale contract. This sale took place one year previously (the slave was eight years old at the time) and outside Egypt (the payment is in *denarii*, Roman coins not in Egyptian circulation).

(*1st hand*) To the Aurelii Sarapion and Sarapion son of Ptolemaios, record-keepers (*hypomnêmatographoi*) in office, from Aurelia Didymarion and however she is styled. Upon buying from Marcus Aurelius Didymos and however he is styled a slave (named) Zoilos, Macedonian by race, imported by sea,[6] about nine years old, with a short scar under his chin, I request that he be subjected to *anakrisis* (*anakrithê[n]ai*) in accordance with the regulations. Farewell.

(*2nd hand*) Year 4 of the Emperor Caesar Gaius Julius Verus Maximinus, Pius, Felix, Augustus, Germanicus maximus, Dacicus maximus, Sarmaticus maximus, the holiest Caesar Augustus son of the Augustus, (month of) Phaophi.

(*1st hand*) I have attached below the copy of the sale to Marcus, the one who sold to me. It is:

Marcus Aurelius Didymos son of Apollonios and however he is styled has bought from Flavius Priscus, on faith and guarantee of Aemilius Eutyches, a slave boy, Zoilos by name, about eight years old, more or less, Macedonian by race for the price of three hundred silver *denarii*, and the other matters of the sale . . .

(*verso, 1st hand*) *Anakrisis* of the slave Zoilos for Aurelia Didymarion.

9.2.3 Selection of a slave boy (*epikrisis*)

P.Oxy. IV 714 (*BL* I 326, IV 59, V 76–77) (Oxyrhynchos, 14 February AD 122)

The Romans divided the population of Egypt into three legal classes: Roman citizens (*cives Romani*), peregrine citizens (*cives peregrini*) of the Greek cities (Alexandria, Naukratis, Ptolemais, later Antinoopolis), and non-citizen peregrines (*peregrini Aegyptii*, *Aigyptioi*). The first two classes

[6] *apo kataploou*: see *P.Turner* 40 (female Paphlagonian slave, age missing), *SB* VI 9145 (female Pontic slave, about 13); see *P.Turner* 40, line 9 note.

were exempt from the capitation tax (*capitatio, laographia*) to which all the male peregrines from 14 to 62 years old were subject. Within the last class some selected persons (*epikekrimmenoi*) paid a capitation tax at a reduced rate. They were the 6,475 *katoikoi* of the Arsinoite and selected metropolites of Arsinoë, Oxyrhynchos, Hermopolis, and Herakleopolis. These persons made up a Greek elite that descended from the Hellenes of the Ptolemaic period. For selected metropolites of Oxyrhynchos, the poll-tax was reduced still further from 16 to 12 drachmas, hence the name of *dôdekadrachmoi*, "twelve-drachma payers."

We do not know how membership in this privileged class of taxpayers was determined, but its origins probably go back to the reign of Augustus. We do know that the status of the selected metropolites was an inherited one. As such, the applicant had to prove that he descended both through his father and through his mother from the selected ones of his *metropolis* from the time of Augustus. To do this, his father or guardian had to initiate a procedure called *epikrisis* ("selection" or "examination") when the boy reached the tax-paying age of 14. A slave followed the fiscal status of his master. If this latter was subject to tax, the slave was subject too; if the owner was exempt from tax, his slave was also exempted; if the master paid tax at a reduced rate, his slave also paid at a reduced rate. In that case, the formal application had to be made by the slave's owner. In the following papyrus, Apollonios sends to the members of the Oxyrhynchite committee in charge of the *epikrisis* a request so that his slave, aged 13 years the previous year, may enjoy the reduced rate of the poll-tax that he himself enjoys in accordance with documents dated AD 117/8.

> To Philoneikos, *stratêgos*, Hermodoros, royal scribe, Dionysios, another Dionysios, keepers of the archives and officers in charge of the selection (*epikritai*), and to Apollonios ex-*exêgêtês*, scribe of the city, from Apollonios [. . .] of the city of the Oxyrhynchi, registered in the South Quay Quarter. I declare that [. . .], my houseborn slave born to the female slave [. . .], has reached the "thirteen years old" category in the past 5th year of Hadrianus Caesar the lord (AD 120/1). I therefore declare that I am a "twelve-drachma payer" by a poll-tax list of the 2nd year of Hadrianus Caesar the lord (AD 117/8) in the said quarter and I swear by the Emperor Caesar Traianus Hadrianus Augustus that I have made no false statement. Year 6 of the Emperor Caesar Traianus Hadrianus Augustus, Mecheir 20.
>
> (*2nd hand*) Registered by the officers in charge of the selection (*epikritai*), the same date.

9.2.4 House-to-house return with "married" free woman and slave man

P.Brux. I 19 (*BL* X 31; see also *BL* XI 51 but suggestions therein are not used here) (Arsinoite nome [Fayyum], AD 117/8)

With both taxation and control of the population registers in mind, the Roman government set up a fourteen-year cycle of census declarations, attested by the papyri from AD 61/2 to AD 257/8 (see Bagnall and Frier 1994: 2). Each inhabitant of Egypt had to be declared in a house-by-house return (*kat' oikian apographê*). The interval of fourteen years between censuses can be explained by the fact that boys were subjected to poll-tax and other capitation taxes from the age of fourteen. The registration was compulsory. Since the entire population of Egypt was registered, whatever their status, slaves also were recorded in the census declarations.

We can see this in **9.2.4**, which comes from Arsinoë, as proven by mention of the Hellenion quarter. The addressee is lost and we cannot guess his name and office because there are Arsinoite declarations addressed simultaneously to several officials: *stratêgos*, royal scribe, scribe of the village, etc. The information about the declarant and the first declared persons is also lost. Four slaves are registered: two males and two females. They are the equally shared property of two sisters: Laberia and Horaiane. The sisters probably inherited their parents' slaves. The joint ownership can be explained because it puts both joint owners on an absolutely equal footing. For example, the potential wages brought back by the slave weaver Dioskoros could be equally divided between both owners. By the same token, the costs brought about by the breeding of the little slave could be shared too. But the most interesting feature in this declaration is that the weaver Dioskoros, a slave, and Alexous daughter of Hermas have three children: Alexous, 8 years old, Taareotis, 6 years old, and Pasion, 1 year old. A male slave and a free woman accordingly have children and these are not declared as slaves. So they are freeborn (the same in *P.Ryl.* II 103). The Roman rule related to the children born of a union between a free person and a slave is applied: the child follows his mother's status. Nevertheless, although Dioskoros and Alexous belong to the same household, they cannot be legally married. They are only living together. But of course, this fact implies that the mistresses had given their consent, for whatever reasons.

[. . .] Dioskoros, slave of Laberia daughter of Pasion, as regards a half share, of the Hellenion quarter – the other half has been declared to belong to Horaiane her sister – at present weaver, considered here as if belonging to me, 29 years old, without distinguishing mark.

Another Dioskoros, slave of the aforesaid, likewise as regards a half share – the other half has been declared to belong to Horaiane her sister – unregistered but considered here among the newborn children of the year 1, 1 year old, without distinguishing mark.

Pasion son of Dioskoros, slave of Laberia whose mother is Alexous daughter of Hermas, unregistered among the newborn children of the year 1, 1 year old, without distinguishing mark.

And among others: Laberia daughter of Pasion son of Pasion whose mother is Alexandra daughter of Pasion . . . of the Hellenion quarter, wife of Theon, 32 years old.

Isidora, equally divided slave of Laberia and of her sister Horaiane, 49 years old.

Dioskorous called by surname Sarapous, slave of the said ones, 23 years old.

Alexous daughter of Hermas son of Hermas whose mother is Tasoucharion daughter of Syros, wife of the slave Dioskoros, 26 years old.

Alexous their daughter, 8 years old.

Taareotis, another daughter of the said ones, 6 years old [. . .].

9.2.5 One-third of a slave is manumitted, two-thirds are to be sold

P.Oxy. IV 716 (*BL* I 326, X 139) (Oxyrhynchos, 29 August–27 September AD 186)

Joint ownership of slaves is a common practice in Roman Egypt. **9.2.4** already attests the fact. **9.2.5** illustrates a very interesting case on legal practice related to slavery and manumission in Roman Egypt. Four children inherited a slave of their deceased father. Eudaimonis possesses one-sixth, Dionysios and Thaësis, one-half. They are minors. Their half-brother Diogenes had the remaining third share but he manumitted it. The minors' guardians request an auction sale of their wards' respective shares. So these shares come out of joint ownership. But the buyer will be the owner of only two-thirds of the slave, the remaining third share being free. Let us note that such a situation, attested in Greco-Roman law, would not be possible in Roman law. Indeed, if in Roman law one joint owner emancipated his share, the other joint owner would see his shares proportionately increased (see *Tituli ex corpore Ulpiani*, 1, 18: *communem servum unus ex dominis manumittendo partem suam amittit, eaque adcrescit socio*, "One owner, in manumitting a common slave, loses his share; this accrues to his partner"). It has been suggested that the aim of the sale was to reach a complete manumission: the slave himself, the *patronus* of the manumitted third share, or a benefactor would supply the requisite sum for a full manumission. A public auction, we presume, would safeguard the interests of the minors.

> To Asklepiades alias Sarapion, priest and *exêgêtês* in office, from Horion son of Panechotes son of Doras, his mother being Taous, from Apollonios son of Dorion son of Heras, his mother being Thaësis, and from Abaskantos freedman of Samos son of Herakleides, all three of the city of the Oxyrhynchi, guardians of minor children of Theon alias Dionysios, Eudaimonis her mother being Sintheus, and Dionysios and Thaësis their mother being Tauris, all three from the said city. There belong to the said minors: to Eudaimonis one-sixth, to Dionysios and Thaësis a half, in sum two-thirds of their father's slave Sarapion aged about 30 years, the remaining third of whom, belonging to their brother on their father's side, has been set free by him. We therefore present the request asking that, with regard to the aforesaid two-thirds belonging to the minors, a sale by herald should be held and that they be handed over to the highest bidder. Year 27 of the Emperor Caesar Marcus Aurelius Commodus Antoninus Pius Felix Augustus Armeniacus Medicus Parthicus Sarmaticus Germanicus maximus Britannicus, Thoth. (*2nd hand*) I, Horion son of Panechotes, have presented (this request). (*3rd hand*) I, Apollonios son of Dorion, have presented (this request). (*4th hand*) I, Abaskantos freedman of Samos son of Herakleides, have presented (this request). I, Diogenes son of Theon alias Dionysios, have written for him because he does not know letters.

9.3 Slaves and slavery in the Byzantine period

Y. Rotman

Modern research has traditionally considered that the political and social passage from the Roman empire to the Middle Ages brought with it a decline in the use of slaves. This is no longer a tenable position. The sources of the period show that slavery continued to hold an important position both in the Byzantine world and in the medieval Mediterranean civilizations that inherited the territories of the Roman empire. See recently Harper (2011). This was especially the case of Byzantium and the Arab world, both being what are termed today "slave-owning societies." Slaves were used in palaces, in the service of the rich, and in the service of people of moderate means. Slaves were present in both the city and the countryside. They performed rural tasks, took part in urban economic life, and were used in domestic services in their masters' households. Their socio-economic position depended as much on the position of their master as on the functions they themselves performed. Some slaves served as servants and housekeepers, while others worked their masters' fields. They shared these economic roles with laborers of free status, and hence had no economic position that could have defined them as a socio-economic stratum. They did, however, have in common a juridical status that set them apart from all other members of society. A person could be either a slave or a free person. A free person could be either a freeborn person or a manumitted slave (Gaius, *Inst.* 1.9–11). These Roman legal definitions continued to differentiate slaves from all other members of society all through late antiquity and the Middle Ages.

Izabela Bieżuńska-Małowist (1977: chapter 3) argues in her study on slavery in Greco-Roman Egypt that it did not hold an important place in Egyptian society in the Byzantine period. Slaves were used in all sorts of roles in both rural and urban milieus, but not to a great extent. This stands in contrast to other regions of the empire, namely Asia Minor, Syria, and Italy, where sources indicate a large use of slaves. As far as agriculture was concerned, Roger Bagnall (1993a) challenged this common view about the limited use of slaves in Egyptian rural society, showing that the ownership of a small number of slaves (one to four) was not uncommon on local family farms. His description of the Egyptian village, composed of relatively small parcels of land, explains why each family did not need more than a few slaves. As Jean Gascou showed (1985), in the Byzantine period the fiscal organization of the Egyptian countryside was controlled by powerful families and was based on the fiscal obligations of the Egyptian tenant farmers or of smallholders. In either case the farmers who owned slaves had no use for more than a few (Rotman 2000). The papyri from Byzantine Egypt that concern slavery are first and foremost documents that address the juridical status of slaves: sales, testaments with clauses on manumission, and other acts of manumission. Other documents may mention slaves, but with no reference to their status, thus making their identification impossible. We are left then with documents that directly concern the status of the persons in question.

A sale of two slaves, a mother and a daughter, is recorded in *P.Cair. Masp.* I 67120 of AD 567/8 (on this document see Urbanik 2010). Birth to a slave mother was, in fact, one of the major sources of slavery. Children born to slave mothers were deemed slaves of their mother's master. Such houseborn slaves were sold and bought within the empire, but slaves were also imported. This was a second chief source of slaves. A description of the sixth-century African trade in slaves from Ethiopia is given by Cosmas Indicopleustes in his *Christian Topography* (II, 64). This traffic is also seemingly attested in *SB* XVIII 13173 (*ed. pr.* Preisigke 1906), a Strasbourg papyrus dating to the seventh century, recording the sale of a twelve-year-old Nubian girl for four *solidi* (**9.1** introduction).

A testamentary emancipation (*manumissio per testamentum*) is to be found in *P.Cair.Masp.* III 67312, from AD 567, a will in which Flavius Theodoros manumits his slaves, male and female, leaving legacies of six *solidi* for each along with an annual stipend of twelve *solidi* (Keenan 2000: 617–25). Manumission is of course the act by which a slave loses his (or her) slave status, thus becoming a freedman – *apeleutheros* – and a free person – *eleutheros*.

The parallel act by which persons of free status were enslaved is also evidenced for Byzantine Egypt. Although the enslavement of freeborn persons was illegal under Roman and Byzantine laws, such acts were not rare. The following papyri from Byzantine Egypt address this phenomenon and manifest the problematic situation of the persons in question. Much more than acts of manumission these documents are illuminating for the definition of slavery, with two facets, one juridical, the other social. In other words, being a slave *de jure* and *de facto* did not always coincide, as will be shown below. This problem existed elsewhere in the empire. It is of major importance to the study of slavery and of the statuses of both slaves and free persons. Owing to the Gothic wars in Europe and the Vandal invasions in Africa many inhabitants of the empire found themselves captured and enslaved.

The subject of the status of the Roman war captive has been extensively examined by modern researchers (see Buckland 1970: 291–317; Kaser 1971: 290–91; Kaser 1975: 129–30; Kolendo 1987; Maffi 1992; Sanna 2001; Bradley 2004; Berrendonner 2006; Rotman 2009: chapter 2). The documents from Byzantine Egypt do not concern war captives, but rather persons whose free status was endangered without their leaving the empire. These documents attest to a real problem in Byzantine Egypt: people of free status who lost their freedom. Accordingly, presented below are three documents relevant to this problem: **9.3.1**, a letter dated to *c.* AD 330–340; **9.3.2**, a public declaration from the fourth–seventh centuries; and **9.3.3**, two copies of a juridical attestation from the sixth century.

All three documents concern, as one would expect at this time, a population that was thoroughly Christian. This is apparent in both their form and content. As these documents show, Christians, of whatever persuasion, brought new elements to the social definition of the individual by incorporating individuals into a religious community. This religious solidarity had a role to play in the definition of the individual as a free person. Nevertheless, Christianity did not change the institution of slavery. Indeed, slaves, whether Christian or not, continued to be bought and used by Christian masters, clergy and monks included (Garnsey 1996: 173ff.; Glancy 2002; Rotman 2009: chapter 4). See for example *P.Köln* III 157, from AD 589, by which a monk manumits his female slave.

9.3.1 Letter concerning the enslavement of a debtor's children

P.Lond. VI 1915 (= *Sel.Pap.* I 160) (Herakleopolite or Kynopolite nome, *c.* AD 330–340)

This is a letter written by a certain Herieous, a member of the Meletian community. He writes to the priest Paieous about the misfortunes of a fellow member of his community, a wineseller named Pamontheis. The latter did not have the money to pay his taxes, and hence borrowed the required sum. Since he used up the entire sum without being able to repay his debts, his creditors forced him to sell everything he owned, down to his clothes, and in addition enslaved his children. Herieous addresses this letter to the priest, asking him to help repay this man's debts so that he can buy back his children. This letter (together with its complementary *P.Lond.* VI 1916) attests to the fact that creditors could enslave the children of their debtors when the latter did not repay their debts. That Pamontheis' children were freeborn did not prevent their enslavement. Imperial legislation from the fourth century makes it clear that the parents had the right to sell their children into slavery. A *novella* of Valentinian (*Nov. Val.* 33) explains that this was mainly a desperate act of poor parents in hard times.

In a second letter (*P.Lond.* VI 1916) the same author applies to the generosity of the same priest and begs him to collect the necessary sum of money. The two letters make it clear that the enslavement of a debtor's children was a legal act of the creditors, since the author does not argue that the children can be redeemed through a juridical process. As their editor observed, this pair of letters attests to a new concept of community, a religious community. Its members, though they may live far from one another, as evidently in the present document, define themselves as brothers; they are expected to help redeem fellow members (in this case a fellow's children) who have lost their free status.

The creditor's right to enslave his debtor's children is also attested in hagiographic texts. This became a major problem in the Byzantine era. A *novella* of Justinian from AD 556 (*Nov.Just.* 134.7) attests to the fact that creditors used to enslave their debtors' children and profit from their work. The *novella* declares that such an act if carried on without the parents' consent is illegal, leaving to parents the right in practice to sell their children.

To brother Paieous, from Herieous, greetings in the Lord.

To those who fall upon misfortune the Word of God encourages us to render help, especially to our brothers. Therefore, since our brother Pamontheis has experienced extraordinary reversals and suffered extreme treatment at the hands of unmerciful and ungodly people so that he has, so to speak, been compelled to be deprived of our blessed hope: as a result of this it was necessary for us to submit to Your Brotherliness this very letter, clarifying his entire matter so that you, too, being informed of this, may help him, bearing in mind the saying of the blessed apostle: Do not ignore the weak, not only in the faith, but in worldly business.[7]

For this brother of ours happened to be a wineseller and was harassed by the magistrates (*archontes*) in his homeland (*patris*) to pay taxes beyond his means, and because of that he borrowed a lot of money, but when he had to pay it back he was unable to meet his debts. He was compelled by his creditors to sell everything he had, even the clothes that covered his shame. Even when these were sold, he was barely able to ante up half the money for his creditors, those merciless and godless men who seized his infant children, all of them together.

Accordingly, we extend this letter to you asking you to help him to the extent that you can so that he can recover them (*sc.* his children) from them (*sc.* his creditors).

From top to bottom on the left margin: [. . .] sons of our heavenly father [. . .]

Verso: [. . .] please help him urgently [. . .] because they have seized his children into slavery. Therefore do not neglect the [. . .] by all means.

Address, reverse side up: Deliver to Paieous priest from Herieous, brother.

[7] The apostle is presumably St. Paul, but the citation here does not match any known Pauline or other NT text. See, however, Rom. 14:1.

9.3.2 Husband's letter about his wife, a free person now enslaved

SB III 6097 (Alexandria?, fourth–seventh century AD)

In this fragmentary document the author states that he came to Alexandria on business whose nature is hard to determine due to gaps in the text. It is nevertheless clear that the reason for this journey is connected to the enslavement of his wife. That she was of free status is indicated by the fact that she is named his spouse (*gametês*). *Gamos* (marriage) in contrast to *contubernium* (concubinate) was only possible for men and women of free status. The author also states that he came to Alexandria to see a specific bishop, to whom he was referred by the bishop of his hometown. Three clergymen are mentioned: Abba Theodor[os] (of the author's home city), Apa Psoios (probably of Alexandria), and Apa Ioannes, possibly a priest (the reading is badly damaged). At least one of them could help in the matter of the enslavement of the author's wife. We may speculate that one of them (Psoios?) could provide testimony to her free status, having known her previously, or even having married the couple. Unlike **9.3.1** we have no indication as to the circumstances of this enslavement and the identity of the enslavers. Nevertheless, just as in **9.3.1**, the Christian community's organization is addressed when the problem is the enslavement of one of its members.

> I came downriver to the m[egalop]olis Alexandria to the [most] blessed bishop because of [my(?)] wife. Of that one who herself (itself?) had snatched her into [the status of?] slavery – for she was of free status. All the more[8] I came down because of Abba Theodor[os] of my city so that Aph[. . .] will inform him [. . .] me. Therefore when I came down to Alexandria, as [I] wrote, so that I might [find] an opportunity that the [same] bishop of my city [. . .] upriver(?) in the [. . .] of Apa Psoios and I have found there the [. . .] of my wife [. . .], for he is a priest [. . .] I therefore met him, [and] the same priest [. . .] the knowledge also of the [. . . from] the bishop in the name of the faithful martyrs of my city. For they made [. . .] saying that he said other things about [. . .] it is true that the same [. . .] I provide evidence [. . .] Apa Ioannes, pr[iest? . . .]

[8] Alternatively, by a different reconstruction of the text, "by boat."

9.3.3 Affidavit concerning a woman's free status

SB XVIII 13274 (= *P.Cair.Masp.* I 67089 + *P.Cair.Masp.* III 67204) (Aphrodito, sixth century AD?). Image at Papyri.info.

Two copies of the same text. The following translation was made from the unified text edited by Wenger (1922). An English translation is given in MacCoull (1992).

This is a fascinating text in that it portrays the social dynamics of a single household over three generations. The author, whose name we do not know, speaks of a family of servants of free status, all Christians, born to Jacob and Sophia. The couple came to work in the service of the author's father in his lifetime. The person principally in question in this document, Martha, the grandchild of Jacob and Sophia, was their only descendant; she was probably still living in the author's house when this document was written. The document is drawn up by the author to attest to the free status of Martha: "a freedom testimony" (*Freiheitszeugnis*), as Wenger called it. The author is, in fact, the only person who could still testify to it given the fact that he knows the life story of the entire family. Martha's other relatives had died, or had left for a monastery, or were enslaved illegally. Such was the case of her cousin Sophia and her children from a father of free status.

The author does not give any more information on the circumstances of their enslavement. He does, however, explain the situation of Martha that made him draw up the present statement: she was interrogated in the past and replied that she was a slave; there is a fear that this might happen again; she possesses a capital sum that might be the reason for the allegation of her being a slave. In other words, some third party considered she was not entitled, as a slave, to have such a sum. The author does not state who accused her, but his cautious formulation allows us to speculate that this was his son, Victor. This is why the author needs the latter's consent to the present statement. This is also why it is crucial that such a document be drawn up before the author's death. Such an act would prevent his son not only from harassing her, but also from enslaving her so as to take over her capital (a slave being incapable of ownership).

Exactly as in **9.3.2**, the present document concerns the illegal enslavement of free persons. In contrast to slaves and freedmen, freeborn persons had no documents to attest to their free status. According to the *Scriptores Historiae Augustae* (IV. Iul. Cap.: *M. Ant. Phil.* 9: 7–9) Marcus Aurelius ordered every father of free status in Rome as well as in the provinces to

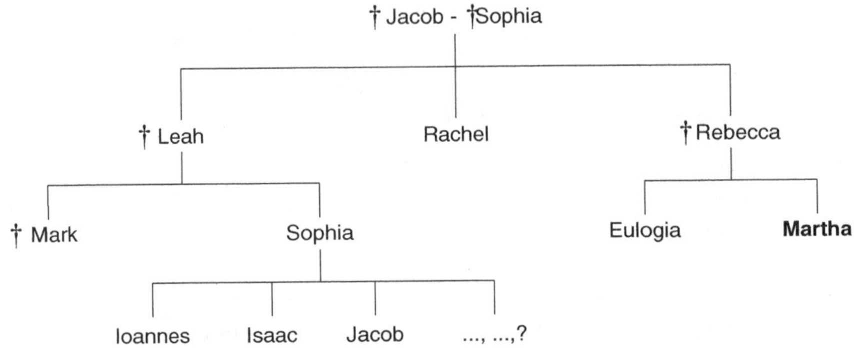

Fig. 12. Martha's family

register his children as freeborn. We have no indication that this imperial order, if it was not an invention of the *SHA*, was ever enforced. Such an act would have been extremely useful and would have corresponded to the modern use of identity cards.

As for slaves, a master had no proof of their servile status besides a contract of sale. The servile status of slaves born in their master's household was not recorded. But such a document was not in fact required to prove that a person was a slave. A person who was born in a household to free employers, as in the case of Martha's family (see Figure 12), could have easily been considered as a slave. Martha's grandparents, Jacob and Sophia, came to work in the employment of the author's father, probably under a *paramonê* contract, which settled their payment, but also attested to their free status (for the use of *paramonê* in the Byzantine period see *P.Strasb.* I 40 from AD 569 and *P.Ness.* 56 from AD 687; cf. e.g. **5.5.3**, **8.2.4**). Being born in the house, Martha had no such document and could not prove her free status, especially against a possible allegation of her future household's master (i.e., Victor). Against his word no witness could have proven the opposite, not even a local priest. This is exactly why Martha needs a written attestation to her free status from the present master of the household.

> It has been clearly established to everyone that neither time's passage nor attendant error will be able to diminish the freedom conferred upon men from above and by nature. For Jacob, originating from the city of Antaiopolites, and having lived no little time with my father, who is now with the saints, provided him with extraordinary care. There lived together with him also Sophia, his kindly wife, who stayed with her husband, the aforementioned Jacob, in the service (*paramenousa*) of my

master, who is among the saints, my father of blessed memory. And I never found any sign either from my father's side, or from another's side, nor any covenant, that they were slaves according to any title of law whatsoever. Afterwards, to the above-named Jacob and Sophia were born children, Leah and Rachel and Rebecca. To Leah were born Mark and Sophia. Leah reached the end of her life, as God willed, along with her son Mark. And Sophia, surviving daughter of the deceased Leah, gave birth to Ioannes and Isaac and Jacob and other children (born) of a free man. Those that drag her (*sc.* Sophia) together with her children into slavery shall see when they meet the terrifying tribunal of the Almighty. And this is enough about that matter.

Well then, to the above-mentioned Jacob and Sophia, as clearly stated above, were born Rachel and Rebecca and Leah. Rachel chose a monastic life, while Leah gave birth to Sophia who still lives, and Rebecca gave birth to Eulogia and Martha. But Eulogia chose a monastic life as well, while Martha, Eulogia's sister, the blessed Rebecca's daughter, is left behind living in my house. And lest at any given time by anyone of my likely successors, may the Divine protect my most eloquent son and heir, Victor, to a long life and enjoyment of his property. – well, then, lest anyone harass Martha as by chance being a slave, it is for this that I have come to this present agreement in writing, through which I understand and clearly acknowledge that she is in no way a slave, nor has she been born of a slave mother, in exactly the way I have previously related. But if, as is likely to happen, someone in the future should try to trouble her, in accordance with this written agreement, to which I took care that my most eloquent D.V., heir gave his assent – through it I insist that she now and henceforth assume for herself free persons' manners and to do what is fitting for free persons. For I heard her in the present time stating, when being asked concerning some capital belonging to her: "I am not of free status." And on account of this, fearing God's judgment and knowing the Savior's philanthropy, I expressed deepest regret and came to the present written agreement; by which written agreement I have insisted that she be known as free. But if someone, as is likely to happen, should try to say that she is a slave, through the present written agreement let her be free for the future, undisturbed by anyone, not even by my most eloquent and beloved heir, who has agreed by my request and decision to this written agreement. Therefore in the future, let no one cast suspicions and let no one consider that anyone is able to call her a slave, but let her be free as declared above, with no one able to damage the freedom given to her above.

CHAPTER 10

The judicial system in theory and practice

James G. Keenan, Chrysi Kotsifou, Joseph Mélèze Modrzejewski, Bernhard Palme, and Georg Schmelz

Introduction

This chapter presents an overview of the relationship between state institutions and the administration of justice. It is a complex topic that changed greatly over the period covered by this volume. There is, thus, considerable development both in terms of bureaucratic practice and also in terms of legal theory. In the case of legal procedure regarding trial proceedings, the Roman evidence is perhaps the fullest. For the Ptolemaic period the process is reasonably clear from the few court records we possess but we have to guess at some of the details.

In ancient Egypt the king was the center of all state institutions, and the guarantor of *Maat*, that crucial concept of the Egyptian state and of Egyptian law. The term has aptly been translated by Assmann (2002) as "connective justice." This sense of justice stressed balance or political order, and indeed the concept runs through both state institutions and private morality, binding the king to officials and to all people in Egypt. The concept of *Maat* and the king as the guarantor of justice prevailed, at least through the second century BC, when the ruling dynasty claimed legitimacy through Egyptian kingship and institutions such as the *laokritai*.

Throughout Egyptian history, including the periods covered by this volume, all persons had, in theory, the right to petition the king or, later, the prefect (a very busy person if *P. Yale* I 61 is a guide), or even the emperor (**10.3** introduction). Petitions or letters to various officials survive in great numbers from the later periods of Egyptian history. Some petitions led to trials; in most cases, however, petitions resulted in more informal resolution of disputes. In the Roman period, the emperor was the ultimate authority. But in normal circumstances in all periods justice was meted out at a more local level, in nome centers or in the village by various officials, village elders, even in some cases soldiers using their "police powers" (**10.3.4**), or by priests (**10.5.2**), a very ancient feature of Egyptian society.

The papyri offer excellent evidence for the continuity of local legal traditions and social practice, even after the promulgation of the *Constitutio Antoniniana* in AD 212. Certain communities retained specific legal institutions. These include the *politeumata* of the Ptolemaic period (**10.2**) and Roman soldiers, who were governed under a separate jurisdiction.

The subjects of the private wrongs investigated and/or adjudicated by some state officials documented in the papyri run the full range from murder investigations and baby-snatching (**10.3.1**) to less pressing, but perhaps no less dramatic, problems caused by arranged marriages (**10.5.4**).

We have included here texts that are at the beginning of the process of obtaining a trial before an official or group of officials, and the end results of such trials (**10.1.3**), including reports of court proceedings (**10.3.1–2** and **10.4.5**). But we have not included, for reasons of space, some of the best examples of court proceedings from the Ptolemaic period. Reports such as the Greek *UPZ* II 162, or the Demotic P.Brit.Mus. EA 10591 recto, differ in style from Roman reports (see **10.3**). They afford us a detailed window onto trial procedure and administration in civil proceedings, antecedent to the Roman period. For procedure in criminal law, the Roman period arrest warrants given below (**10.4.4**) provide evidence for local state institutions charged with the investigation of crimes.

The last two sections of the chapter take us into the Byzantine period and into the new world of Christian clerics and monks participating in arbitration and mediation processes. The status of the men documented in these dispute resolutions, tied as they were not to temples but to churches and monasteries, is new, but they preserve an ancient practice that goes back to the time of the pharaohs.

10.1 Ptolemaic justice

Joseph Mélèze Modrzejewski

Despite the contrary opinion formerly professed by some scholars, we are certain today that the Ptolemies did not strive to unify the legal rules throughout the kingdom. They preferred another solution to the problems created by the existence of legal rules of unequal weight and of various provenances. They did not work on the substance of the law itself but operated with an emphasis on the administration of justice. The originator of this judicial system was Ptolemy II Philadelphos, the second king of the dynasty (282–245 BC).

Thanks to research by Wolff (1960, 1970), the system is now well known. In the first instance, the king reserved the right of intervention in all litigations, either directly or indirectly, through the *chrêmatistai*, royal judges, itinerant at first, afterwards assigned to each nome as permanent judicial authorities. A double network of jurisdictions, each authorized to treat the cases falling within its specific nationally determined competence, blanketed the kingdom: for cases involving Greek-speaking immigrants, in the cities and in the *chôra*, the *dikastêria*, local law courts; for those involving the indigenous population, the courts of *laokritai* ("people's judges"), staffed by Egyptian priests.

In the application of the law, royal legislation had priority. However, the king was aware of the limits of his legislation, which was restricted to the administrative and fiscal field. He consequently decided in a decree (*diagramma*) that, in the absence of a rule of royal law, the judges ought to resort to the "civic laws," *politikoi nomoi*, the "national" laws of the litigants. If the latter did not give a solution that settled the litigation, they were to judge according to "the most equitable opinion," *gnomê dikaiotatê* – in modern parlance, "following their soul and conscience." In a similar fashion, the *laokritai* were to apply Egyptian law, the "law of the land," *nomoi tês chôras*.

Consequently, the Greek "common law" (legal *koinê*) followed by Greek-speaking immigrants became the official legal corpus for the local law courts, liable to judicial sanction. Egyptian law, for its part, the "law of the land," became the legal corpus for the courts of the *laokritai*. The two groups of *nomoi*, corresponding to the two groups of the population, had been raised to the status of "laws of the court," *leges fori*, for their respective tribunals. Greek versions facilitated the enforcement of legal prescriptions not originally formulated in Greek. As a further complication, the Torah of Moses in Greek translation (the Septuagint) became officially applicable to the Jews of Egypt as their "civic law." That Jewish Law, especially in family matters, was actually followed by the Jews in Ptolemaic Egypt and sanctioned by the authorities of Jewish autonomous communities is now confirmed by the material concerning the Jewish *politeuma* in Herakleopolis in the second century BC (*P.Polit.Jud.*; see **10.2.1**).

During the second century BC the original system progressively ceased to work. The local law courts disappeared. Egyptian *laokritai* had now to face the *chrêmatistai* who represented not a nationally determined jurisdiction but the royal government. Ptolemaic officials, who were entrusted with wide-reaching auxiliary competencies, tended to take the place of regular law courts. The judicial system of Ptolemy II, an original invention of the Hellenistic monarchy, did not survive the Roman conquest of Egypt in 30 BC.

10.1.1 A sentence of the *chrêmatistai*

P.Eleph.Wagner 1, Col. 1 (Elephantine, third century BC). Image at *P.Eleph.Wagner*, Plate 1.

A verdict of royal *chrêmatistai* in Elephantine – the first evidence of their judicial activity – sentencing two men, Mousaios, perhaps a Jew, and Nikias son of Nikanor, a Macedonian, to hard labor. Nikias' condemnation is related to an unlawfully accepted guardianship of a woman.[1]

Excerpt of the verdict given in the 7th year through the *chrêmatistai* (whose clerk is) Pasistrates son of Lophios.

"Because of all these (arguments) we decide to sentence Mousaios to hard labor. We likewise sentence to hard labor Nikias son of Nikanor, Macedonian, who is not presently here, because he has declared himself in writing to be the guardian of the lady Biote in her father's lifetime without being authorized by order (*prostagma*) of the King or of the *chrêmatistai*, but has allowed himself this status contrary to the laws (*nomoi*) which include a regulation (*programma*) on how to get married. Any willing party has permission to bring him before Ainesidemos."

10.1.2 Petition concerning usury and illegal detention

P.Col. IV 83 (Philadelphia [Fayyum], 245/4 BC). Image at Papyri.info.

This petition is part of a group of documents concerning the troubles of Antipatros, a resident of Philadelphia in the Fayyum, and his family. His wife, Simon, had borrowed seventy drachmas from a certain Nikon at the excessive interest rate of 6 percent per month (instead of 2 percent, the legal rate). For unexplained reasons Antipatros took his wife and their son and moved to Upper Hermopolis, where he opened a shop. Somewhat later, he returned to Philadelphia, attracted by the creditors' proposal to settle the case by interest-free repayment of the original principal. The creditor, however, appeared in Hermopolis; with threats of legal action, he induced the Lady Simon to follow him with her son and kept them in detention in some friend's house. Simon escaped to Philadelphia and joined her husband. They made depositions against Nikon, which are preserved in two other documents (*SB* III 6762 and 6763). Antipatros is now complaining against Nikon for two reasons: first, that the interest

[1] On this document, see Łukaszewicz (2003).

imposed was exorbitant; second, that the imprisonment of his son is illegal. He expects a sentence of the *chrêmatistai* ordering the restitution of the boy and the punishment of Nikon. Whether they obtained satisfaction is uncertain; their son may well have been pledged in the contract as a security for the loan, contrary to the royal legislation which forbade pledging free persons for private debts.

To King Ptolemy, greetings from Antipatros, one of the residents of Philadelphia. I am wronged by Nikon. For having lent seventy silver drachmas to my wife Simon at an interest rate of six drachmas per mina each month and having totaled (the interest) with the principal he drew up a contract of loan with her for 115 drachmas in which I myself was entered as security.

Afterwards, I left Philadelphia because I was falsely accused by Artemidoros, an agent of Apollonios the *dioikêtês*, and had opened a shop in Upper Hermopolis. Then, Nikon wrote a letter to Philadelphia to a certain Menestratos, our servant, in which he included the statement, made upon royal oath, that he will draw up an agreement with us for the principal by itself, namely, the seventy drachmas. When Menestratos wrote me at Hermopolis to come to Philadelphia and I sailed down there, Nikon sailed up to Hermopolis and said that he would hand my wife over to the *praktôr*[2] because of the loan unless she followed him of her own accord. Simon, prompted by fear, sailed down with Nikon together with her boy, and Nikon led them to Herakleopolis and shut them up with certain persons, apart from each other. Then Simon escaped by stealth; but the boy he holds in detention even now. And when we demand that he give him back, sometimes he acknowledges that he has seized him as pledge for the debt and is still holding him, sometimes he denies it. I beg you therefore, O King, to send my petition to the *chrêmatistai*, and if I prove that the allegations set forth in the petition are true, I beg that Nikon may meet with appropriate punishment both concerning the interest which he has set in the contract contrary to the regulation (*diagramma*) and because by his own authority he has confined and holds a free person; and I beg that the boy be restored to me in order that I, having fled to you for help, O King, may meet with justice.

Farewell.

[2] Here, this official is in charge of executing judgment for debts.

10.1.3 Trial in Krokodilopolis

P.Petrie III 21g (= *M.Chr.* 21) + *P.Gur.* 2 (= *Sel.Pap.* II 256; *C.P.Jud.* I 19) (Krokodilopolis [Fayyum], 9 August 226 BC). Image at *P.Petrie* III, Plate I.

On this trial, see Mélèze Modrzejewski (2003), briefly Gagarin (2008: 238–39).

Official report of a session of the local law court in Krokodilopolis. One Dositheos, a Jew born in Egypt, had sued Herakleia daughter of Diodotos, a Jewess, accompanied by her legal guardian, an Athenian born in Egypt. Dositheos accuses Herakleia of assaulting him in public and ripping his coat, causing him 200 drachmas' worth of damages. At the last minute, however, he lost his nerve and failed to appear before the court. Herakleia did not desist but, taking up her proper defense, produced, *inter alia*, an extract of a royal regulation, a *diagramma*, that served as a guide for the rendering of justice in the courts created by Ptolemy II Philadelphos for Greek-speaking immigrants.

In the reign of Ptolemy son of Ptolemy and Arsinoe, gods Adelphoi (siblings), in the 22nd[3] year (226/5 BC), the priest of Alexander and the gods Adelphoi and the gods Euergetai (benefactors) being the one officiating in Alexandria, the *kanêphoros* of Arsinoe Philadelphos being the one officiating in Alexandria, the 22nd of the month Dystros (8 March 225 BC), at Krokodilopolis in the Arsinoite nome, under the presidency of Zenothemis, the judges being Diomedes, Polykles, Andron, Theophanes, Maiandrios, Sonikos, Diotrephes. Polydeukes, the clerk of the court (*eisagôgeus*), having constituted us in accordance with the written order sent to him by Aristomachos, appointed to the office of *stratêgos* of the Arsinoite nome, of which the following is a copy:

"To Polydeukes, greetings. Herakleia has requested the king in her petition to form and swear in a court for her consisting of all the judges except such as either party may challenge in conformity with the *diagramma*. Year 21, Dystros 16 (which is) Pachon 19" (3 August 226 BC).

We have given verdict as below in the action brought by Dositheos against Herakleia according to the following indictment:

"Dositheus son of [. . .], Jew of the *epigonê* (born in Egypt), to Herakleia daughter of Diodotos, Jewess, as you in your [. . .] of yourself declared [. . .] on Peritios 22 of year 21, as I with other persons was entering the [. . .] of Apion [. . .] from the so-called house of Pasytis which is in Krokodilopolis in the Arsinoite nome opposite the so-called house of

[3] 22nd appears to be a scribal error for 21st.

Pasytis (*repeated by mistake*), you came to that place in the company of Kallipos the [. . .] and abused me saying that I had told certain persons that (you are a) [. . .] woman, and on my abusing you in return you not only spat on me but seizing the loop of my mantle [. . .] me and [. . .] until [. . .] the said Kallipos [. . .] you ceased your assaults [. . .] to which I have borne witness. Wherefore I bring an action of assault (*hubris*) against you for 200 drachmas, the assessment of damages being [. . .] drachmas. And as the injured party I by this indictment [. . .] The 21st year, the priest of Alexander and the gods Adelphoi and the gods Euergetai being Galestes son of Philistion, the *kanêphoros* of Arsinoe Philadelphos being Berenike daughter of Sosipolis, the 26th of the month Peritios. The suit will be placed against you on the agenda of the court sitting in the Arsinoite nome, of which Polydeukes is the clerk (*eisagôgeus*), on Peritios [. . .] of the 21st year. The indictment is in your hands as you have been personally summoned, the witnesses of the summons being [. . .] phanes son of Nikias, Thracian, official employee, Zopyros son of Symmachos, Persian of the *epigonê*."

Whereas this was the indictment and Dositheos neither appeared in person nor presented a written statement nor was willing to plead his case; and whereas Herakleia appeared with her guardian Aristides son of Proteas, Athenian of the *epigonê*, and put in both a written statement and justificatory documents (*dikaiômata*), and was willing to defend her case; and whereas the royal regulation (*diagramma*) which Herakleia handed in among the justificatory documents orders us to give judgment in a [. . .] manner on all points that any person knows or shows us to have been dealt with in the regulations of King Ptolemy (*diagrammata*), in accordance with the regulations; and on all points not dealt with in the regulations, but in the civic laws (*politikoi nomoi*), in accordance with these laws; and on all other points to follow the most equitable view (*gnomê dikaiotatê*); but when both parties have been summoned before the court and one of them is unwilling to put in a written statement or plead his case or acknowledge defeat (?) [. . .] he shall be judged guilty of injustice; [for these grounds] we have dismissed the case.

10.1.4 *Chrêmatistai* and *laokritai*

P.Tebt. I 5, lines 207–20 (Tebtunis, 118 BC). Image at Papyri.info.

This is one of a series of royal ordinances (*prostagmata*) promulgated in 118 BC to mark the end of a period of revolts and fighting in the royal family.

It deals with the sharing of jurisdiction between the *chrêmatistai* and the *laokritai.* In lawsuits between Greeks and Egyptians, the language of the written agreement is decisive for the choice of the court: the *chrêmatistai* are competent when the contract is written in Greek, but when the contract is written in Demotic, the case is to be decided by the *laokritai* in accordance with the Egyptian law.

> And they have decreed what follows about cases in which Egyptians and Greeks are opposed, namely cases of Greeks who bring actions against Egyptians, or of Egyptians who bring actions against Greek, with regard to all classes of litigants except the cultivators of Crown land and the tax-payers and all others involved in the revenues:
>
> Egyptians who make an agreement with Greeks by contracts written in Greek shall give and receive satisfaction before the *chrêmatistai*;
>
> However, all litigants who, being of Greek status, make agreements in contracts written in Egyptian shall give satisfaction before the *laokritai* in accordance with the local law.
>
> As to the suits of Egyptians against Egyptians, the *chrêmatistai* shall not drag them into their own courts, but they shall allow them to be decided before the *laokritai* in accordance with the local law.[4]

10.2 The *Politeuma*

Joseph Mélèze Modrzejewski

The *politeuma* (pl. *politeumata*) was a kind of military and religious organization, with some degree of internal self-regulation and judicial power, supposedly founded on an official authorization of the royal government. The papyrological and epigraphical sources known today document the *politeumata* of Greek-speaking immigrants from different regions of ancient Greece (the Boetians and the Cretans) and Asia Minor (the Phrygians, the Lycians, the Cilicians) as well as the hellenized Near East (the Jews and the Idumaeans). The most important single provenance is Herakleopolis, where a Jewish *politeuma* is attested in the second half of the second century BC (*P.Polit.Jud.*). The Herakleopolis file can be supplemented by two documents concerning *politeumata* other than Jewish ones. The first one (an inscription) is an honorific decree (**10.2.4**) issued by an assembly consisting of the *politeuma* of Memphite Idumaean

[4] The translation is based on my studies, Mélèze Modrzejewski (1975, 1979, reprinted in 2011a). For another interpretation, see Pestman (1985c).

mercenaries and of Idumaeans settled in Memphis who are "associated" with the *politeuma* (*hoi sumpoliteuomenoi*). The second one belongs to an official correspondence concerning a man who has been accepted as a member of the Cretan *politeuma* in the Fayyum (see **7.2.3** above). On this document, see Mandalake (2007).

The existence of a *politeuma* of Alexandrian Jews, a term mistakenly extended by modern scholars to the entire Jewish population of Alexandria, is uncertain. Only one literary source, the "Letter of Aristeas," employs this term (12.310) in connection with the Jews of Alexandria, opposing the "people of the *politeuma*" (*hoi apo tou politeumatos*) to the "leaders of the people" (*hêgoumenoi tou plêthous*). It clearly means that the *politeuma* is not synonymous with *plêthos*, i.e., the Jewish population of the city. According to the official terminology used in Herakleopolis, we would expect to hear about "the *politeuma* of the Jews of Alexandria" (*to en Alexandreiai politeuma tôn Ioudaiôn*). But such an expression does not appear in any known source. Nor do Alexandrian Jews describe themselves as members "of the *politeuma*" (*ek tou politeumatos*): they are *Alexandreis*, inhabitants of Alexandria in the broad sense of the term. Like the Idumaean *politeuma* in Memphis, a Jewish *politeuma* in Alexandria most likely represented only a small faction of the Jewish community, and probably was an ephemeral phenomenon in the second century BC, the presumed date of "Letter of Aristeas."[5]

10.2.1 "Citizens" and "strangers"

P.Polit.Jud. 1 (Herakleopolis, 7 October 135 BC). Image at Papyri.info.

A complaint by one member of the Jewish *politeuma* in Herakleopolis, who explicitly describes himself as such, against an individual described as "one of those from the harbor." The judicial powers of the leaders of the *politeuma* – the *politarchês* and the archons – applied also to people outside the group. The former are opposed as "citizens" (*politai*) to the "foreigners" (*allophyloi*).

> To Alexandros, the *politarchês*, and to the *politeuma* from Andronikos, a member of the *politeuma*. On the 12th of this month, Nikarchos, one of the inhabitants of the harbor, intentionally began a scuffle with me on the street: first, he violently and shamelessly injured and then

[5] See Lüderitz (1994), Cowey and Maresch (2001), Honigman (2003).

he leveled unjustified accusations against me in the presence of different persons, members of the *politeuma* (*politai*) as well as foreigners (*allophyloi*). That is why I request that you summon him and take the necessary measures towards him. [Farewell!]"

(*2nd hand*) Year 36 (of Ptolemy VIII Euergetes II), Thoth 12, in the [harbor].

Verso: Year 36, Thoth 12. From Andronikos vs. Nikarchos.

10.2.2 Juridical function of the oath

P.Polit.Jud. 3 (Herakleopolis, *c.* 140 BC). Image at Papyri.info.

A complaint by one Protomachos, who is not a member of the *politeuma*, against Euphranor, concerning a vineyard as part of a dowry (*phernê*) according to a marriage contract in the form of a "writ of cohabitation" (*synoikisiou syngraphê*). The petitioner refers to an "ancestral oath" (*horkos patrios*) in the form of a letter (*epistolê*) that complemented the original contract and made it valid according to Jewish law, the non-fulfillment of the contractual obligations protected by an oath being regarded as a contravention against the Third Commandment and thus a violation of ancestral law.

To the archons of the year [. . .] from Protomachos son of Demetrios.

In the month Pharmouthi, year 30 (of Ptolemy VIII Euergetes II), I presented a complaint to you against Euphranor concerning the oath he had sworn with respect to the dowry (*phernê*) promising to give me a part of the vineyard of a value of 3,000 silver drachmas[6] [immediately] after a writ of marriage (*synoikisiou syngraphê*) will be drawn up for this dowry, and to let me have it through the notary office (*archeion*). Whereas I honored [my commitment] and had [the writ of marriage] drawn up, Euphranor fails to honor his promise and does not let me have [part of the vineyard], but on the contrary [. . . That was why] you wrote a subscription (*hypographê*) to the [village elders] of T[. . .] in order that they take care [of my case] and bring the proceedings to completion. Those who were in charge of judging (*hoi krinantes*) have heard [the parties] and recorded their decision in a subscription, but as Euphranor did not comply with it, they handed him over to those

[6] The Greek text in the following short twelve lines is badly damaged. The translation attempts to reconstruct the sense of the passage.

who had to make him appear before you in accordance with the letter (*epistolê*), having attached to it the copy of the subscription (*hypographê*) as well as a copy of the oath he took for me in conformity with our ancestral tradition (*horkos patrios*).

Considering that Euphranor does not allow me to take possession of the aforesaid portion of the vineyard nor does he act correctly and treats me with contempt [as guilty of betrayal], I ask you, if it seems good to you, to have him led before you and to oblige him to do what is right in conformity with [the oath] and the subscription. If this is done, I will have received your help.

10.2.3 Unhappy bridal arrangement

P.Polit.Jud. 4 (Herakleopolis, 12 January 134 BC). Image at Papyri.info.

This is the most important document in the Herakleopolis file from a legal point of view. It is a complaint by one Philotas, a member of the *politeuma*, against Lysimachos, who had given his daughter Nikaia to him as a wife. After that Lysimachos changed his mind and gave his daughter to another man without receiving from Philotas the "customary bill of divorce" (*to eithismenon tou apostasiou bublion*). It contributes to the discussion on the attitude of Hillel the Elder (Tosefta Ketubbot 4:9, and parallels) and Philo of Alexandria (*De spec. leg.* 3.72) concerning the legal situation of the spouses during the period separating the two stages of Jewish marriage, *qiddushin* and *nissui'in*. In the time of Philo and Hillel, the pregnancy of Mary, the mother of Jesus, falls, from a judicial perspective, into the same category (Matt. 1:18–25). Thanks to the Herakleopolis papyrus, the texts of Philo, Hillel, and Matthew receive corroborating testimony from a document of unquestionable authority.[7]

Year 36 (of Ptolemy VIII Euergetes II), 19 Choiak. Concerning a marriage. We have given an order to issue a summons.

To the archons from Philotas son of Philotas, a member of the *politeuma*. In the current year, I betrothed Nikaia daughter of Lysimachos. The said father has promised by oath to give her to me (*sc.* as my wife) along with the dowry laid down for her, and with which I agreed. So after not only commitments (*horismoi*) were exchanged

[7] On this document, see Mélèze Modrzejewski (2005a), Kister (2002).

between us but also the ritual (*apoklusis*) according to the Law (*kata ton nomon*) [. . .], we parted on those terms. Not long afterwards, Lysimachos without good reason joined Nikaia to another man before receiving from me the customary bill of divorce (*biblion apostasiou*). Therefore, I request, if you consider it right, that you give the order to write to the Jews in the village to summon Lysimachos to appear before you, so that, if the matter is as I write, his case may be decided according to the Law, and at the same time he may be forced [. . .] to me . . .

Verso: Year 36, 19 Choiak. Philotas vs. Lysimachos.

10.2.4 A *politeuma* of the Idumaeans at Memphis

OGIS 737 (= *SB* v 8929) (Memphis, 112/1 BC)

A decree (*psephisma*) voted in the Upper Apollonieion at Memphis by a meeting (*synagogê*) of the *politeuma* of Idumaean soldiers and their civilian fellow compatriots from Memphis, in honor of Dorion son of Dorion, *stratêgos* and priest of saber-bearers (*machairophoroi*). As a token of gratitude for his action in favor of the Idumaeans and their shrine, his existing honors are confirmed for his life, and new honors are decreed: a palm-branch is to be presented to him at regular sacrifices, instructions are given to the priests and the psalmists to remember him in their chants, and at formal feasts of the *politeuma* he is to be crowned with a special crown. The *politeuma*, which is not to be confused with the Greeks in Memphis, together with its civilian associates, formed the Idumaean community in Memphis.[8] The Apollonieion is devoted to the cult of their national god Qos, identified with Apollo (see Thompson 1988: 100–02).

The sixth year (of Ptolemy IX Soter II), at the meeting of the *politeuma* and the Idumaeans of the city, which was held in the Upper Apollonieion:

"Whereas Dorion, *syngenês* (relative) of the King, *stratêgos*, and priest of the saber-bearers group, in numerous circumstances manifestly showed himself as their benefactor both publicly and privately to each one of them, and appearing devout towards the divinity he readily made generous and abundant expenses in plastering and whitewashing the above-mentioned temple, as it is obvious for everybody, it has been decreed that the honors he now enjoys will be his for life and, moreover,

[8] On Idumaeans in Egypt, see Rappaport (1969). On this inscription, Thompson Crawford (1984).

that at the regular sacrifices a palm-branch will be presented him, according to the ancestral custom, and that instructions will be given to the priests and the psalmists to remember him while executing their chants, and furthermore that at all regular feasts of the *politeuma* a choice crown will perpetually be awarded to him. This decree is to be engraved on a stone stele and placed in the most visible part of the temple; a copy of it is to be given to Dorion so that he may know the grateful response the city has given him."

10.3 Roman litigation: reports of court proceedings

Bernhard Palme

The emperor was the highest judicial authority in Egypt since its incorporation into the Roman empire. He could be approached through a rescript procedure. He could rule on legal issues brought to him by individual citizens, or delegate trials and rulings to local governors (Turpin 1991, Honoré 1994, Mourgues 1995). Appeal to the emperor was rare because of the exorbitant cost involved. Things were different if an emperor visited the province and could be approached by the local population. During the journey of Septimius Severus to Egypt in AD 200, for example, various disputes were pled before him and his decisions (*rescripta, apokrimata*) were subsequently published in Alexandria (*P.Col.* VI 123 = *SB* VI 9526). Normally, however, the prefect of Egypt is, as representative of the emperor, the responsible person for the centralized jurisdiction (Wolff 2002: 104–13). He officiates *in plano et pro tribunali*, that is, both on minor and major matters, both informally and formally, in Alexandria and at the annually held *conventus* (*dialogismos*, "assizes") in distinguished cities of the *chôra*, especially Pelusium and Memphis (Foti Talamanca 1979, Haensch 1997). Additionally, the *iuridicus Alexandreae* (*dikaiodotês*), the *archidikastês* and the *idios logos* all had, presumably, independent judicial authority.

The legal system of Roman Egypt was, of course, much more elaborate than that, and it developed over the centuries (Baade 1956, Seidl 1973a, Anagnostou-Cañas 1991). Court cases, conducted according to Roman law, had the *cognitio extra ordinem* form. The practice, which is evident from the papyri, exhibits a wide range in the structure of the proceedings, where the borders between legal procedure and administrative procedure become blurred. The actual spate of law cases to be contended with is shown in *P.Yale* I 61: during three days of a *conventus* in AD 210, the prefect had to conduct no fewer than 1,804 lawsuits. The legal cases, therefore, must have been prepared well in advance by the local authorities, usually the *stratêgoi* of the nomes (Witt 1977): an immediate ruling could only be made when the evidence was clear. The prefect referred all other cases back to the local authorities for the further gathering of evidence, in most cases to the *stratêgos*. Nevertheless, due to the large number of legal cases, the prefect delegated many suits, either at the very beginning or during the course of the proceedings, to *iudices pedanei*. These men were usually acting as *procuratores* (e.g., as *epistratêgoi* or *archidikastai*), military officers of equestrian status (**10.3.3**), or *stratêgoi* of the nomes (**10.3.1** and **10.3.2**), the latter primarily in cases involving *peregrini*. Except for criminal cases, only cases of high monetary stakes (as in *P.Oxy.* IV 706) or of great political significance (as in *FIRA* III 19a) were likely to reach a hearing before the prefect.

Local courts continued to exist into the second century alongside the courts of the governor (and *procuratores*) and heard minor cases. The courts of the *chrêmatistai* (Jörs 1915 and 1918) were active also after the Ptolemaic period until at least 6/5 BC (*SB* III 6663), and Demotic documents indicate trials, until late into the first century AD, in which the ruling was made dependent on a temple oath in the Ptolemaic manner (cf. the sworn declaration in **10.3.1**). In the second century, there still existed in Alexandria the court agency of the *chrêmatistai* and other *kritêria* (whose name indicates its Ptolemaic origin), which handled (at least) enforcement and certification issues. The so-called (Egyptian) *Law Code of Hermopolis* (*P.Mattha*), whose Demotic original was composed in the third century BC, was still copied in a Greek translation in the second half of the second century AD (*P.Oxy.* XLVI 3285). It wasn't until the *Constitutio Antoniniana* (AD 212) that all inhabitants of the empire became Roman citizens and thus were subject to Roman law – theoretically at any rate, for it is not clear how long Egyptian law(s), which appear in papyri as *hoi nomoi tês chôras* or *hoi tôn Aiguptiôn nomoi*, continued to be simultaneously in use (Wolff 2002: 113–49). Local legal traditions seem at least to have been integrated into "provincial law." "Provincial law," which is not identical with "imperial law," consists, on the one hand, of legislation enacted by the emperor or the prefect, and, on the other hand, of the legal practice of the prefect or designated procurators. Not least the Gnomon of the *Idios Logos* (*P.Oxy.* XLII 3014 [Oxyrhynchos, first century AD] and *BGU* V 1210 [Arsinoite, after AD 149]; extracts at **2.6.4** and **4.6.6**) shows that older, regional regulations were also considered by Roman officeholders. A methodic Romanization of private law in the courts did not take place. A separate jurisdiction existed solely for soldiers (Jung 1982; **10.3.3** and **10.3.5**). The people in the *chôra* willingly approached the officers stationed there with requests for legal aid or the hearing of evidence, although the soldiers possessed no legal competence (Peachin 2007: esp. 82–97; **10.3.4**).

The governor's dispensation of justice could not be opposed by either party in a dispute. The Roman officeholders presumably made judgments based essentially on Roman law, but they were free to take local practice and particularities into consideration (cf. the Gnomon). The proceedings began with the *editio actionis*, the disclosure of the matter of dispute with the defendant (Foti Talamanca 1979 and 1984). There was no strict regulation concerning the form of the *editio*, but as one had to prove that the *editio* had happened, one willingly undertook a "dispute announcement" (*litis denuntiatio*) through a court official. If proof of summons was presented and the defendant had failed to appear to the appointed court hearings, a ruling by default could be obtained. The oral hearing, where both parties presented their cases, was most important. In larger cases, lawyers (*synêgoroi*, *nomikoi*, *rhêtores*) almost always acted on behalf of clients and undertook the legal explanation of the circumstances. The parties had to cite the legal rules in their favor; relevant files or legal documents were read. Witnesses recorded their testimony in written form before the trial (e.g., *SB* V 7523 [Arsinoite nome, AD 153]). No documents indicating sworn statements from witnesses in oral form have come to light.

Trials were usually public: they were carefully recorded and the minutes were made accessible to the public before they were stored in archives (see **10.3.1**). It was first with the emergence of the "libellus" procedure in the fourth century (**10.3.6**) that lawsuits were possibly decided on the grounds of written documents (the complaint and evidence) only, without a hearing of the parties. The rulings of the judges are recorded most often in only a brief sentence in the transcripts. The judgments (*sententiae*) were presumably publicized by a notice from the governor (Haensch 1994). The enforcement of a ruling was left to the winner of the trial. That even an imperial judgment was hard to enforce when a weaker victorious plaintiff prevailed over a more powerful defendant is shown in *P.Cair.Masp.* I 67032 (= *Sel.Pap.* II 363 = *FIRA* III 179 [Constantinople, AD 551]), where two high-ranking *comites* engage to travel, for a fee, from Constantinople to the Thebaid in order to compel a judgment as *exsecutores*. Settlements out of court were regarded by the judges, especially in the Byzantine period, as a worthwhile goal (*P.Münch.* I 6; Syene, AD 583). The arbitration agreement (*compromissum*) and the settlement (*dialysis*) first appear in larger numbers in the fifth century (see below, **10.5–6**).

Most of the clues we have to case practice and hearing procedure in Roman Egypt come from court proceedings transcripts (Anagnostou-Cañas 2000).

Approximately 200 transcripts of this sort are known to date now from the Roman (Coles 1966: 55–63; Kelly 2011: 368–80) and approximately 60 from the Byzantine era (Thomas 1998: 132–34). Some of these are, however, very fragmentary.

The written accounts of the hearings before the courts of the prefect of Egypt, the procurators, or the delegated judges differ clearly from the forms of legal proceedings that were recorded during the time of the Ptolemies (Jörs 1915: 275–82). The narrative form dominated at that time, in which both the summations of the parties as well as the judgment were expressed in indirect address. The last examples of this style are: *P.Ryl.* II 65 (Oxyrhynchos, 67 BC?) and *BGU* VIII 1773 (Herakleopolis, 58 BC?). No documents exist from the final phase of the Ptolemaic reign and the first decades of Roman rule to illuminate when and how the conversion to the Roman type of protocol occurred. As noted above, the Ptolemaic courts of the *chrêmatistai* were still active in 6/5 BC; the Ptolemaic style of court transcripts survived into the early decades of Roman rule.

It is not until the middle of the first century AD that court proceedings transcripts again turn up in the papyrological evidence. They already display the characteristic Roman trait that speeches before the bench, in direct address, are recorded. This creates at least the impression that the entire case action was written down verbatim. It could be that this method was patterned on the practice used in Rome itself, where, since the middle of the first century AD at the latest, each communication in lawsuits was written down in shorthand (Seneca, *Apocoloc.* 9). Several very detailed transcripts from the second century AD (e.g., *P.Fam.Tebt.* 24 [Arsinoite nome, AD 124]; *P.Ryl.* II 77 = *Sel.Pap.* II 241 [Hermopolis, AD 192]), which contain lively and trenchant statements, speak in favor of the idea that legal proceedings were in fact transcribed verbatim. Most legal action transcripts, however, are kept short and confine themselves to the decisive remarks. The literal, stenographic notations were most likely transformed after the lawsuit into an abbreviated and selective clean copy in the relevant bureau.

Imperial-era case proceedings have the significant trait that they are not formally compiled as a single document, but are rather merely recorded as entries in the official minutes (*commentarii*, *hypomnêmatismoi*), which every officeholder in Roman Egypt kept. In these official journals, every official activity and even every official statement of the officeholder were documented – eventually also the cases negotiated before him. An original official journal with court transcripts is preserved in *W.Chr.* 41, Col. III 17–30 (= *Sel.Pap.* II 242 = *P.Par.* 69, Elephantine, AD 232). One could have an excerpt drawn up, for private or official purposes, concerning a single *causa* from the *commentarii* of the respective officeholder (*ex hypomnêmatismôn*, or *antigraphon hypomnêmatismou tou deinos*), which rendered the relevant passage in full wording. Practically all case transcripts from litigious proceedings before Diocletian's reign are such extracts from the official journals. Their composition and form follow defined patterns, which, despite the highly differing detail of the individual documents from the middle of the first until the end of the third century AD, remained standard (Coles 1966: esp. 29–54). A transcript is structured in four formal sections:

(1) Introductory formulas: Reference to the *commentarii*, from which the transcription is extracted; name and title of the officeholder and day date suffice to identify the exact section. The *causa* is stated by the names of the contending parties (A *pros* B, "Party A *vs.* Party B").
(2) Body of the proceedings, in which the actual trial, from the opening speech of the plaintiff (or his lawyer) through to the judgment, is rendered. The parties' pleas and objections as well as the remarks of the judge are recorded in *oratio recta*. When lawyers or witnesses are first mentioned, their roles are specified; after that they are just called by name. The presiding official, who was already mentioned in the introduction, is from then on only referred to with his title (e.g., *stratêgos*) or a simple name. It is not until the late Severan dynasty that it becomes customary to refer to the judge with a full form of address (*SB* I 5676 [Hermopolis, AD 232–33]). The direct addresses are commenced with *eipen*, though this introductory verb is often omitted by the end of the first century and from the middle of the third century nearly regularly abbreviated and expressed with: *ei(pen)*.
(3) The judgment (*krisis*) is the most important part of the transcript and is always begun on a new line. It is rendered in *oratio recta* which, especially at the beginning of the second century, accentuated the complete and literal rendition. The authority of the judge is emphasized by his full form of address.
(4) Concluding section: Following the verdict, further administrative measures can be referred to in a very succinct way. The official certification, from the beginning of the second century, by the *anegnôn* ("I have read / checked it") of a clerk follows frequently. The *subscriptio* (*hypographê*) of the scribe would have performed the same purpose.

Altogether transcripts dating from the imperial period are thus not a judicial record per se, but simply records of the activities and decisions of an officeholder. **10.3.1** and **10.3.2** may be considered typical examples from the early and middle Roman empire.

10.3.1 Court proceedings: trial before a *stratêgos* about baby-snatching

P.Oxy. I 37 (= *P.Lond.* III 746 descr., *M.Chr.* 79, *Sel.Pap.* II 257, *FIRA* III 170, *CPGr.* I 19 = *Jur.Pap.* 90) (Oxyrhynchos, 29 March AD 49). Image at *CPGr.* I 19, Plate XIX.

This extract from the official minutes of the Oxyrhynchite *stratêgos* Tiberius Claudius Pasion is the earliest extant example of court proceedings in the "Roman style." It has been reprinted in numerous papyrus anthologies because of the poignant legal dispute concerning the identity of a foundling. Pesouris, the plaintiff, picked up a male infant from a rubbish-heap in the seventh year of the reign of the Emperor Claudius (AD 46/7), and concluded a nursing contract with Saraeus, the defendant, to raise him as a slave child named Heraklas. Pesouris himself, however, did not act as signatory of the nursing contract, but had his son Theon sign. Subsequently Saraeus received the wages for a first and second year. The nurse also had her own infant son, who, at the time of the contract's conclusion, was already weaned. The legal dispute arose after one of the children died in AD 47/8. Pesouris took the surviving boy for himself and asserted that he was the foundling. Saraeus thereupon forced her way into Pesouris' home and retrieved the boy for herself. The judge in this lawsuit is the nome *stratêgos*, appointed by the prefect as in Roman times a *stratêgos* had no jurisdiction in his own right. After hearing the parties, the *stratêgos* announced his judgment: Because the boy resembled Saraeus, she should retain him as her own child, if she and her husband would declare in an affidavit that the foundling was dead. The earnings Saraeus received as a nurse had to be returned.

Because *P.Oxy.* I 37 belonged to the archive of the weaver Tryphon, one is in the exceptional position of being able to reconstruct the background and the continuation of the story from other records.[9] By AD 35 Saraeus had already been the nurse of Tryphon's daughter (*SB* XIV 11415); following Tryphon's separation from his wife Demetrous, Saraeus became his second wife. The anonymously addressed husband of Saraeus, in line 31 of the trial transcript, is therefore Tryphon. Saraeus' small son could be Apion, whose birthdate, known from his horoscope (*P.Oxy.* II 307), was 3 January AD 46. In the seventh year of Claudius (29 August AD 46 until 28 August AD 47), when the nurse contract for the foundling was concluded, Apion was between approximately 8 and 20 months old. Saraeus'

[9] Biscottini (1966), Piccolo (2003).

information is thus true; the *stratêgos*' decision to award her the child was correct. The return of the earnings was customary practice in nursing contracts: If the child died, the nurse lost the entitlement to compensation for work already performed. Even after the *stratêgos*' verdict Pesouris seems to have pestered Tryphon: In the petition *P.Oxy.* I 38 Tryphon even complains to the prefect about Pesouris' harassment.

P.Oxy. I 37 formally represents the type of imperial Roman court transcript described in the introduction to this section, which was integrated as a single entry in the minutes (*commentarii*) of the officeholder – here the *stratêgos* – and thereafter as an extract drawn up from the *commentarii* as an exact copy for Tryphon, which was found among his papers. The transcript follows the usual structure:

(1) Introductory formulas with the cross reference to the official minutes of the judge (*stratêgos*), date and place of the trial. The parties are introduced simply by name.
(2) Body of the trial: This begins with Pesouris' complaint, represented by the lawyer (*rhêtor*) Aristokles in direct speech. The plaintiff's *petitum* is not written but deducible from the contents. There follows, likewise in direct speech, the defendant's reply, which suppresses a counterclaim for acknowledgement of the child as their own. The suing party then presents the nurse contract (*trophitis*) and receipts for the paid nursing wage (*grammata*; *apochê*) as instruments of evidence.
(3) The judgment, spoken by the judging officeholder, who is only specified with his title (*stratêgos*). He renders a decision based on evidence, whereupon a written oath of assurance (*cheirographein*) as piece of evidence is required from the defendant. The verdict is also rendered in direct speech.

A fourth, concluding section, which would have contained the scribe's *subscriptio*, is not part of this copy.

> From the minutes of Tiberius Claudius Pasion, *stratêgos*. The ninth year of Tiberius Claudius Caesar Augustus Germanicus Imperator, Pharmouthi 3. At the court, Pesouris versus Saraeus.
>
> Aristokles, advocate for Pesouris, (said): "Pesouris, for whom I speak, in the 7th year of our lord Tiberius Claudius Caesar picked up from the garbage dump a male slave child named Heraklas. This he entrusted to the defendant. Thereupon a wet-nurse's contract was made as if for the son of Pesouris. She received her wages for the first year.

The payday for the second year came around and again she received them. (To show) that I speak the truth, there are her documents in which she acknowledges that she received payment. As the slave child was being starved, Pesouris took it away. Subsequently, finding an opportunity, she burst into my client's house and carried the slave child off, and she seeks to take for herself the slave child, pretending it is a freeborn person. I have here, firstly, the contract for nursing; I have, secondly, the receipt for the wages. I demand that these be recognized." Saraeus (said): "I weaned my own child, and the slave child of these people was entrusted to me. I received from them the whole eight *statêrs*. Subsequently the slave child died, [. . .] *statêrs* were left me being (still) unearned. Now they seek to take away my own child." Theon (said): "We have the documents relating to the slave child."

The *stratêgos* (said): "Since from its looks the child appears to be that of Saraeus, if she and her husband will make a sworn declaration in written form that the slave child entrusted to her by Pesouris has died, I give judgment in accordance with the decision of our lord the prefect that on paying back the money which she has received she shall have her own child."

10.3.2 Court proceedings: trial before a *stratêgos* about a loan and mortgage

P.Fam.Tebt. 19 (= *SB* VI 9252) (Arsinoite nome, 6 April AD 118). Image at Papyri.info.

This typical example of a second-century transcript records a court trial that took place before the *stratêgos* of the Polemon *meris*, a subdivision of the Arsinoite nome. The literal rendering of the events of the trial had (as in **10.3.1**) been originally recorded as a single entry in the official minutes (*commentarii*) and the copy of this entry lies before us. The text merits special attention because in the course of the trial the judge ordered a verdict, made eleven years previously in the same lawsuit, to be read from the *commentarii* of the judge from that time – the judge in charge of verdicts (*ho epi tôn kekrimenôn*), Cascelius Geminus. The relevant passage is then quoted by specific date (29 January AD 107) and read. It constituted the basis for the decision of the *stratêgos*. This detail sheds light both on the compilation and storage of records as well as on the recourse to previous judgments (and precedents).

The case concerns a trial based on a record of a loan (*daneion*) with corresponding clause of execution (on real security for loans see **5.4**).

Isidora received a small sum from Dieras as a loan (line 4) and in exchange provided land as security. Her son Kronion obviously functioned as surety. When repayment was not made, Dieras initiated all necessary legal steps (*enechyrasia*, *prosbolê*, and others), in order to bring the mortgaged land into his possession and ownership. Isidora and her son Kronion opposed these activities – they would have had to surrender their right of ownership to Dieras by way of a *synchôrêsis*-contract – so that he would have to conduct a trial before the judge Cascelius Geminus. Although the judge decided against the debtor and had Isidora as well as Kronion (temporarily) confined, they harvested the crops of the contested plots of land. Isidora and/or Kronion had obviously been released before Dieras had advanced to the seizure and acquisition of ownership of the mortgaged pieces of land. The sum owed had not been paid because the mortgage should have gone to Dieras.

After more than a decade the case was still not settled, which is the reason Dieras brought the matter to the *stratêgos* (whose transcript is presented here), to gain either the sum owed or the mortgage. Isidora, represented by her lawyer, accused Dieras in the trial of having seized two other arouras from her, which were mortgaged to another creditor, but signaled her willingness to repay the sum owed if the due date were extended. After the transcript of the proceedings before Cascelius Geminus was read, the *stratêgos* decided that Isidora should pay her debt on the next day (so without the requested extension); otherwise the mortgage is forfeited to Dieras. Afterward, Dieras again addressed the problem of the harvest, which at the time of the court proceeding, in Pharmouthi, was immediately impending. Kronion claimed this harvest with reference to the necessarily performed operations of farming (probably seed and cultivation). The *stratêgos* decided that Dieras should also receive the crops, but that the local *kômogrammateus* (village scribe) should arrange for compensation. With his verdict, the *stratêgos* did not allow Isidora a deadline extension for her debt, but he did afford her the possibility to reclaim her pieces of land if she repaid the sum she owed by the next day.

This transcript is also structured in four sections:

(1) Introductory formulas with reference to the *hypomnêmatismoi*, with date and trial location (*aula*, the place for public audiences).

(2) Body of the trial: begins without introduction of the parties directly with the description of the characteristics of the dispute by the plaintiff or, as the case may be, his lawyer. Isidora's rejoinder follows,

along with the judge's request for the reading of the earlier trial transcript before the assembly. Dieras' complaint is expressed in *oratio obliqua*; after that, the form of all statements – from the *stratêgos* as well as from both parties – changes remarkably to *oratio recta*. Neither of the speeches is introduced with *eipen*.

(3) The judgment: it is exceptional that following the *stratêgos*' judgment another objection from the plaintiff and reply from the defendant occurred, which the *stratêgos* accommodated with an additional judgment.

(4) The concluding section: the transcription closes with the usual notation of control, *anegnôn*.

Copy from the minutes of Apollonides, *stratêgos* of the Polemon *meris*, 2nd year of the Emperor Caesar Traianus Hadrianus Augustus, Pharmouthi 11, at the court.

Dieras son of Ischyrion, represented by Ammonios, his advocate, having said that he had lent to Isidora daughter of Lysimachus a small amount of money and not having recovered it he proceeded to distraint and execution and the consequent legal measures and brought everything to an end; that the matter was brought before chief judge Cascelius Geminus because she was recalcitrant and that he, deciding on the matter, also arrested her son Kronion, so that they would submit to the verdict; that they, (however), after the legal measures and the minutes which are against them, once more gathered the fruits of the estate, concerning which the legal measures have been fully taken. Isidora, represented by her advocate Soueros, having replied that she will pay to those who give up (their claim), if she meets with indulgence; but that he (Dieras) has snatched away two more arouras that were pledged to another creditor; that Dieras unduly asserts that he has taken the legal steps concerning these two arouras as well as concerning the others, and that now he claims that he has recovered the debt even without delay [. . .] make restitution of the arouras. And when Isidora asked for an extension (?), the *stratêgos* (said):

"Let the minutes of Cascelius Geminus be read." When these had been read, dated in the 10th year of the deified Traianus, Mecheir 4, (he said): "According to the minutes concerning this case and the fact that Kronion, the son of the debtor, was arrested with her, it seems reasonable to me that the whole debt will be paid back to Dieras tomorrow. If they do not pay back, I am of opinion that the legal decisions must be valid and unshaken, and the debtors shall have no claim on the land."

Dieras (said): "If only they will not collect the fruits once more, after your decision!" Kronion (said): "We made investments at our own cost." The *stratêgos* (said): "The village scribe shall ascertain how large the investments have been and he will take care that you get them back when he (Dieras) gathers the summer-harvest."

"I have read it."

10.3.3 A centurion as *iudex datus* in an intestate inheritance

P.Mich. III 159 (= *ChLA* V 280, *FIRA* III 64, *CPL* 212) (Arsinoite nome?, AD 37–43). Image at *TAPhA* 55 (1924), Plate IV; *ChLA* V p.11.

Papyri provide much evidence for the assignment of trials from the court of the prefect of Egypt to *procuratores*, *stratêgoi*, and other civilian officeholders. Occasionally also military officers are encountered as judges by special appointment, especially officers of equestrian rank. One such person, a commander of a cavalry unit, the *cohors I Flavia Cilicum equitata*, conducts an inheritance trial between Egyptians in the year AD 124, for example (*CPR* I 18 = *Stud.Pal.* XX 4 = *M.Chr.* 84 = *Jur.Pap.* 89). He deliberates with a legal expert (*nomikos*) and dictates the ruling (*apophasis*) thereafter, which is subsequently read. Presumably a comparable situation is recorded in the fragmentary minutes of proceedings *P.Tebt.* II 488 (Arsinoite nome, after AD 121/2), when a *tribunus* conducted a trial as an appointed judge. Another example of a military tribune as judge is presented in the extensive, but highly damaged, *M.Chr.* 90 (= *P.Oxy.* III 653b [Oxyrhynchos, AD 161]), which describes a suit for the confiscation of mortgaged land.

Besides military officers of equestrian rank centurions also were occasionally appointed as judges. An instructive example of a centurion acting as a *iudex datus* is found in **10.3.3**, describing an inheritance dispute among soldiers. A cavalryman named Dionysios, the son of Manlius, had died. His brother, a veteran also named Dionysios, now disputed with the sons of the sister of the deceased, his own nephews, the active cavalrymen Marcus Apronius and Marcus Manlius, over his brothers' inheritance. For the judge it was essential to ascertain the identity of the disputing parties, so the grade of relation to the deceased could be determined. Initially a *praefectus castrorum* was put in charge of the case, but he thereafter assigned (*dedisset*) the centurion P. Matius to act as judge with the explicit instruction to deliver a judgment (*iudicareque iussisset*). Matius, in turn, chose three decurions, lower-ranking soldiers, as assessors, conducted the case, and delivered the ruling. The selection of the consulted decurions is explained by the fact that the parties had come from, respectively, the *ala Apriana* and *ala Vocontiorum*, and two of the decurions were presumably officers of these units. P. Matius' decision conformed with Roman law: the brother is more closely related to the deceased than his nephews; the inheritance therefore goes to him. The legal dispute was carried out within the military sphere because all parties were soldiers.

Considerably later testimony to the appointment of a centurion as judge exists in *P.Oxy.* XIV 1637, from the years AD 256–61, which concerns the division of landholdings. The disputing parties in this and in the other texts cited above are civilians and the subject matter of the conflicts or legal actions is purely civil. The only lawsuit in a military setting is **10.3.3**. It seems, however, that at least in the case of some officers, the appointment as *iudex* occurred so frequently that they kept particular volumes of *commentarii* (*CPR* I 18 = *Stud.Pal.* XX 4 = *M.Chr.* 84 = *Jur.Pap.* 89: *ek tomou [hypo]mnêmatismôn [B]laisiou Ma[r]ianou*, commander of the *cohors I Flavia Cilicum equitata*).

> Whereas between Dionysius son of Manlius, a discharged cavalryman, whose cause in his absence was defended by Marcus Trebius Heraclides, a cavalryman in the *ala Apriana*, *turma* of Acamas, the son of the said Dionysius, and Marcus Apronius and Marcus Manlius, cavalrymen in the *ala Vocontiorum*, *turma* of Domesticus, there was a lawsuit concerning the nearness of relationship, as to which of them was the more nearly related so as to obtain possession of the property of Dionysius, the son of Manlius, a cavalryman in the *ala Apriana*, who was said to have died intestate; and whereas for that suit Lucius Silius Laetus, the prefect of the camp (*praefectus castrorum*), had appointed as judge Publius Matius, a centurion of the *legio III Cyrenaica*, and had ordered him to give judgment, the above-written Matius, a centurion of the *legio III Cyrenaica*, employed as his advisors Marcus Marcius Optatus of the Falerian tribe, the son of Publius, decurion of the *ala Xoitana*, and Lucius Herennius Valens, decurion in the *ala Apriana*, and Octavius Domesticus, decurion of the *ala Vocontiorum*, and, after the pleading had been completed on both sides and the surety bonds had been read through, rendered decision and in accordance with the decision announced that it seemed to him that Dionysius, the son of Manlius, was the brother of the Dionysius who is said to have died, but that Apronius and Manlius, who themselves have furnished bond of near relationship, were the sons of the sister of that Dionysius, and that the property of Dionysius, which is the subject in the suit,

seems to belong to Dionysius, the son of Manlius, a discharged cavalryman, and should be assigned to him [. . .]

10.3.4 Petition to a centurion

P.Mich. III 175 (tr. Bryen 2013: 243–44, no. 67) (Soknopaiou Nesos, 18 April AD 193). Image at Papyri.info.

As the directly manifest representatives of the government, the soldiers stationed in the *chôra* (mostly centurions, but also decurions or *beneficiarii*) became the point of contact for those seeking legal advice and who sought the immediate solution of a conflict by way of written petitions. More than fifty records of such petitions have emerged to date on papyrus, most of which come from the Arsinoite nome (Whitehorne 2004). Common to all petitions is that they were written by ordinary people and have daily problems as subject matter: theft, crop damage, property dispute, bodily harm, and the like. Complaints are occasionally levied on several offenses simultaneously, so that a differentiation between civil and criminal petitions is impossible. The appeals reflected the legal conceptions of the native population, which in no way allow for the categories of Roman law. Equally unspecified was the manner (if formulated at all) in which the addressed military were to intervene. In many cases they should find an immediate remedy for the problem and, for example, punish the wrongdoer or retrieve stolen property.

In contrast to previous research, which concentrated on the jurisdictional capacity of the military or surmised the usurpation of this, recent studies have shown that centurions performed no real judicial function in these matters, but that people approached them for either policing intervention or support preparatory to a trial. In a number of petitions the centurion was asked to initiate an inquiry and/or to produce a written report. This had the aim of recording evidence – for example, the consequences of bodily harm – with official attestation and putting it on the records for a lawsuit scheduled in the future. Sometimes the soldier should only relay the petition to the *praefectus Aegypti*, an *epistratêgos*, or another officeholder with judicial capacity. In these cases the petitioners obviously expected a carrying out of their appeal by obtaining the subscription of the prefect, the *epistratêgos*, etc. If in several cases a centurion was invoked as the judicial authority, and expected to find a ruling, it can hardly be considered proof of an informal adjudication performed by soldiers; it shows, rather, that in the population's conception there was no defined boundary between the conflict-solving, executive activity of the centurions and a legal adversarial proceeding before actual legal officials (Peachin 2007). Furthermore, it cannot be gathered from the petitions whether the soldiers granted these demands. One comes across petitions to centurions in Egypt very shortly after the integration of the country into the Roman empire (earliest evidence: *P.Oslo* II 30 [Arsinoite nome, 20 BC]). They apparently perpetuated the so-called Ptolemaic public official justice. Later on, soldiers (*beneficiarii*) in a similar role are known from other parts of the empire as well.

10.3.4, from the village Soknopaiou Nesos at the northwest edge of the Fayyum, may be considered a typical example of just such a petition to a centurion. A farmer, who at the same time is performing the duty of local priest, makes a complaint against his cousin, with whom he jointly uses an inherited piece of land for the storage of hay. The relative expelled the petitioner by use of force from the property. The petitioner now requests the centurion to restore justice by arresting the wrongdoer. The relevant formulation in line 22 (*tês apo [s]ou epi<ei>kias tuchein*) does not definitely say whether the petitioner expects a conviction or any other legal action from the centurion. The appeal is, as usual, structured as a letter: after the address of the receiver (the centurion) and naming of the sender (the petitioner) follows the description of the circumstances, the prehistory, and the offense, afterward the formulaic appeal to intervene and the greeting (*dieutuchei*). A second hand (a clerk from the centurion's office?) writes the date below.

To Ammonius Paternus, centurion, from Melas son of Horion, of the village of Soknopaiou Nesos, a priest of the god who is in the village. There belongs to me and to my cousins Phanesis and Harpagathes held in common and equally in the same village as an inheritance from our maternal grandfather a vacant plot surrounded with a wall where we stack our annual supply of hay. Now the one (cousin) Harpagathes died recently and although his share was inherited equally by both of us, yesterday, which was the 23rd, while I was stacking my hay in the place, Phanesis violently and shamelessly assaulted me and appropriated my hay, not allowing me to stack it in our share (but) attempting to exclude me therefrom and to claim for himself alone what belongs to me; not only this but he also offered me the most brutal treatment. Wherefore I beseech you to command him to be summoned so that I may be able to obtain the just judgment from you. Farewell.

(*2nd hand*) The first year of Publius Helvius Pertinax Augustus, Pharmouthi 23.

A result of the reforms of Diocletian and Constantine, with the separation of military and civil power, was the governor's more intense concentration on civil justice duties. In Byzantine literary sources, the governor (*praeses*) and *iudex* have become synonymous terms. From the time of Diocletian, Egypt had been partitioned into ever smaller administrative units. Under Justinian, as his 8th *Novella* (AD 535) and 13th *Edict* (AD 539) demonstrate, Egypt was ultimately subdivided into no fewer than seven provinces. There existed, therefore, in Byzantine Egypt, up to seven gubernatorial courts, which must have simplified court access as well as made the *conventus* unnecessary. The highest-ranking governor, the *praefectus Augustalis*, commanded, after all, fifty lawyers (*CJ* 2.7, 13 *pr.*). Moreover, in the old regional *metropoleis* (now *civitates*), a *defensor* (*ekdikos*) had, since the 330s, been appointed as judge for civil cases with low disputed values (*CTh* 1.29.5 [AD 373]).

Just as in the legal organization, a significant change is also evidenced toward the end of the third century – most probably before Diocletian's reign – in the recording of the trials. The written transcripts as excerpts from the *commentarii* disappear (latest example: *P.Mert.* I 26 [Oxyrhynchos, AD 274]), and in their place appears the individual transcript recording a specific *causa*. This development is located within a general reform, in which the official journals (and the *tomoi synkollêsimoi*) are discontinued and replaced by individual transcripts (*acta*, *hypomnêmata* and *gesta*, *ta pepragmena*). The trial itself is now the object of the record-taking of individual cases (Bickerman 1933). "Individual" transcripts usually begin directly (1) with the date and indication of place and courtroom (introduction). The body of the trial (2) then follows immediately with the plaintiff's plea, possibly the defendant's objection, and the speeches of the judge, all in direct speech. The terse judgment (3) concludes the document. Early examples for this new type of trial transcript are: *P.Sakaon* 31 (Arsinoite, AD 280/1, before the *epistratêgos*), *P.Oxy.* XII 1503 (Oxyrhynchos, AD 288/9, before the *praefectus*), *P.Oxy.* IX 1204, 11–28 (Oxyrhynchos after AD 299, before the *rationalis*), and *P.Oxy.* XVIII 2187, 14–32 (Oxyrhynchos, AD 304, before the *praefectus*). The variety of juridical officials concerned demonstrates that record-taking was standard practice after the reform.

The introduction of a Latin framework for the trial, which was still mainly conducted in Greek, is a second striking attribute of the new style for transcribing court cases. Here the introduction (1) of the record (date, place, etc.) is presented in the Latin language and script; likewise in Latin the mention of the judging official, whereby now, at each new address, his full name, rank, and official title are repeated. Especially in the fourth century, all of the judge's remarks, which are always introduced with an abbreviated *d(ixit)*, are in Latin, while lawyers and parties may have Latin names and be introduced with *d(ixit)*, but their speeches are recorded in Greek.

The earliest bilingual report of court proceedings from Egypt is *P.Ross.Georg.* V 18 (= *ChLA* XLVI 1395 [prov.?, AD 212/3]): Latin is herein only interlaced in the judge's speech and emphasized the distance between himself and the parties. Following this temporally isolated example (cf., however, from outside Egypt: *P.Dura* 128 = *ChLA* IX 383 [*c.* AD 245]; *SEG* XIII 625 [AD 200–37]; *SEG* XVII 759 [AD 216]; *SEG* XLIII 1028 [after AD 245]) the series of bilingual case transcripts begins with *P.Ryl.* IV 653 (= *P.Sakaon* 33 = *ChLA* IV 254 [Arsinoite nome, AD 318–20]) and *P.Sakaon* 34 (= *ChLA* XLI 1204 [Arsinoite nome, AD 321]): both before the *praeses Aegypti Herculiae*. In the latter, significantly, a Greek translation was written next to the Latin verdict of the *praeses*. The bilingual type of transcript – established in other Graecophone provinces already under the Severan emperors, as the examples outside Egypt show – seems to have been consistently implemented after its introduction. Several purely Greek transcripts from the fourth century (e.g., *P.Oxy.* LIV 3767 [Oxyrhynchos, AD 329?]; *P.Ross.Georg.* V 29 [provenance unknown, AD 360?]) come from subordinate courts (probably local courts in the *civitates*).

There are roughly sixty bilingual court proceedings from the later fourth and fifth centuries, including some very detailed exemplars (*SB* XVI 12692 [Arsinoite nome, AD 339]; **10.4.5** [Hermopolis, late 4th century]), though it is uncertain whether they recorded the trial verbatim or (more likely), as in the second- and third-century proceedings, they are abbreviated clean copies. An array of creative peculiarities are conspicuous in the bilingual transcripts, for instance, the preferred landscape format with extremely long lines (up to 50 cm). Further, the script sizes varied considerably, especially in the fifth century, according to the importance of the subject matter. The dating formula (often with the emperor's name) and the naming and the speeches of the judge (which are always found at the beginning of a line) are often double the size of the other (Greek) parts of the document. Only a few examples of Byzantine bilingual case transcripts are preserved completely (**10.3.6**).

To date there is no satisfying explanation for the mysterious disappearance of the bilingual transcripts around the middle of the sixth century (latest dated example: *P.Cair.Masp.* II 67131 = *ChLA* XLI 1197 [Antinoopolis?, AD 566/7]). A common interpretation was to see this as an indication of the termination of the gubernatorial courts in late Byzantine Egypt

(Schiller 1971: esp. 471), which had been displaced by private arbitral jurisdiction. But objections to this opinion have been raised (Simon 1971; Palme 2008).

10.3.5 Prefect's edict limiting access to military courts

P.Oxy. VIII 1101 (Oxyrhynchos, AD 367–70)

This papyrus conveys a copy of an edict, sent from Alexandria to Oxyrhynchos, from Tatianus, who later had a brilliant career at the imperial court in Constantinople (*PLRE* I, Tatianus 1 and 5). In the introductory sentences, the *praefectus* emphasizes the illegality of the practice, frequently undertaken by civilians in the *chôra*, of addressing petitions (*biblia*, line 10) to local garrison commanders (*praepositi*) and thus bypassing the regular, appropriate courts of the governor. This exactly addresses the very situation that is papyrologically attested in several dozen petitions to the centurions and *beneficiarii* (as in **10.3.4**) from the first century until the fifth century. Tatianus stresses the importance of the fact that the officer has authority only over his soldiers: he may neither judge civilians nor may he carry out executions against their property. Infringements against this were met with severe penalties: deportation for *humiliores*, loss of assets for *curiales*. He concedes, however, that a civilian is allowed to call a *praepositus* in case of conflict with a soldier, because otherwise he cannot take action against a military man. The papyrus text breaks off at the sanctions.

The edict is to be considered against the background of several constitutions in the *Codex Theodosianus* that regulated the privileged jurisdiction of the *militia* (cf. Palme 2006). Originally it had distinguished between civil and criminal trials, and furthermore, it had depended upon whether the soldier was the complaining or the defending party: *CTh* 2.1.2 (25 July AD 355) mandated that civil actions belonged, in any case, before the court of the civil governor, no matter which party the soldier was. The military court is only responsible if the soldier is the accused in a criminal case. *CTh* 9.2.2 (22 January AD 365) corroborates this basic principle and *CTh* 2.1.9 (27 November AD 397) – addressed to the *praefectus Augustalis* – inflicts severe punishment (as in the edict from Tatianus) upon the filing of a civil lawsuit with the military court first. *CJ* 3.13.6 (27 April AD 413) conveys the rule that civil suits against soldiers may also be brought before a military judge. As a plaintiff in civil matters, however, a soldier has to continue to turn to the civilian judge. This complies with the rule which **10.3.5**, approximately a half century earlier, had implemented. It therefore apparently anticipated the imperial legislation.

> Copy of an edict. Flavius Eutolmius Tatianus, *vir clarissimus*, prefect of Egypt proclaims: [My orders are not] based on information gained by [. . .] and from a few first-comers, but on reports about what happens in every city and their territory received in some way. I learn from petitions that some persons of civil status, without scruple, whether from malice or from the party's bad advice, in their desire thoroughly to worst their adversaries at law, have recourse to the local *praepositi*, presenting petitions to them and procuring exactions by their means from persons, as I said, of civil status. That this is forbidden by law is clear. For the *praepositus* has authority over soldiers, but not over civilians; it is enjoined on the governors of the province to [judge?] them and to receive their petitions. This, therefore, is for the future made clear by this announcement. Nevertheless, if any civilian has a difference with a soldier and relies on the vengeance of the *praepositus* and is confident of receiving assistance from him, let him petition; for he cannot obtain requisite assistance on the spot from anyone else. If, however, it is with a person of civil status, let him not attempt to do this. For should anyone ever be discovered leaving aside his proper court and having recourse to unauthorized persons, if he is a man of common rank, I order him to be deported, and if he is a *curialis*, I subject him to confiscation of property. Therefore I command the local *riparii* that, if they catch any civilian who has left his propert court and had recourse to *praepositi* [. . .]

10.3.6 Bilingual report of proceedings before the military court of a *dux*

P.Oxy. LXIII 4381 (= *ChLA* XLVII 1431) (Oxyrhynchos, 3 August AD 375). Image at Papyri.info.

This document is one of the few examples preserved intact of a bilingual court proceedings of the "individual" style. It features all formal distinguishing marks of this sort of record, as described above, **10.3.4** introduction (arrangement, size and styling of the script, etc.). The framing text and the judge's pronouncement are in Latin, the rest is in Greek. Though most of the bilingual proceedings come from civil courts of law, **10.3.6** is one of only three preserved trial transcripts conducted before the court of a military commander (the others: *P.Acad.* 56/1+2 + 57/1 [Antinoopolis, middle of fifth century AD?] and *ChLA* XLVII 1437 [Aphrodito, first half of sixth century AD]). The trial took place before Flavius Mauricius, a *comes primi ordinis* (Count of the First Rank), who held the office of *dux Aegypti* (military governor of Egypt).

The procedure of this trial *in secretario*, that is, not in public but in the official room of the *dux* in Alexandria, is depicted in the following way: The trial is opened with the request of the *officium* (the provincial office) to the *dux* to be allowed to read the statement of case (*libellus*). The *dux* tersely instructs it to be read and duly recorded in the files. Afterwards, an *officialis* (a member of the *officium*) reads the statement of case in Greek, which is recorded in its entirety. Another remark from the *dux* follows in Latin – probably the decision (*sententia*) through which he either dismisses the motion or issues the order for the summons of the opposing party (*conventio*) and ending the first negotiation.

Parallels to a similar trial introduction are found in the transcripts *P.Oxy.* XVI 1876–1879, *P.Thomas* 25, and *ChLA* XLIII 1247 (fifth century AD). These are early examples of a type of trial that is commonly denoted a "libellus" trial (Steinwenter 1925 and 1944, Wenger 1925), which becomes established in the sixth century as the customary type of trial record (Simon 1969). In this kind of trial the plaintiff submits a claim (*libellus conventionis*), which explains the matter in dispute and ends in the motion (*postulatio*) to summon the defendant. This simplified the preliminary proceedings considerably in contrast to the fourth and fifth centuries' routine act of summons of the *litis denuntiatio*, which entailed a series of steps and time limits (cf. *P.Oxy.* I 67 = *M.Chr.* 56 [Oxyrhynchos, AD 338]; *P.Lips.* I 33 = *M.Chr.* 55 [Hermopolis, AD 368]).

The following incidents led to the filing of a *libellus* claim by two non-commissioned officers of the cavalry unit of the *Mauri Scutarii*, the *ducenarius* Flavius Pelion and the *centenarius* or *circitor* Gounthos, who were stationed in Lykopolis. Both jointly own a camel stable in Oxyrhynchos, operated by people they trust. They bring action because, while they were away due to military service, the local tax collectors (two urban magistrates by the names of Crescentius and Theodoulos), wrongfully and with the use of pressure, collected the gold and silver trade levy (*collatio lustralis*, *chrysargyron*, lines 6 and 9) from their clients. The explanation of the case and the legal claims of the plaintiffs end with the request for the *dux* to prohibit the future infringement of their rights.

In light of the above-depicted rules regarding military courts (**10.3.5** introduction), the *causa* appears somewhat problematic. The soldiers are not the defendants, but rather the plaintiffs in a civil trial. The defendants are two public officials from Oxyrhynchos who are held responsible for the collection of taxes. The case is therefore exactly what the lawmakers from the fourth and fifth centuries strictly prohibited: soldiers suing civilians in a military court. According to the cited legal codes, both soldiers should have had to file their lawsuit, which had a financial background, unconditionally with the civil judge, therefore the governor. The case, nonetheless, was accepted by the *dux*; the *praescriptio fori*, the rule about court jurisdictions, was, according to this, not (always) adhered to by the public officials themselves.

After the consulship of our master Gratian, perpetual Augustus, for the 3rd time, and of Equitius, *vir clarissimus*, *comes*, on the 3rd day before the Nones of August, at Alexandria, in the *secretarium*.

Spoken from the *officium*: "Having in our hands a petition in the form which Pelion, *ducenarius*, submitted to Your Highness in public, we shall recite it, if you so command."

Flavius Mauricius, *vir clarissimus*, *comes primi ordinis* and *dux*, said: "Let it be read and entered in the records."

Recited from the *officium*: "From Flavius Pelion, *ducenarius*, and Flavius Gounthus, *centenarius* (*circitor*?) of the *numerus* of the *Mauri Scutarii* stationed in Lykopolis under Paulus, *praepositus*. It is Your Highness's custom to help all people, lord *dux*, but especially us soldiers, who are staying on even after our term of service. Our case, then, is of this kind. Certain persons, violent and audacious and disregarding the laws, while we were occupied with military service, have inflicted violence of no ordinary kind on our people in Oxyrhynchos. For although we possess no vineyards (?, *chôreia*) or (arable?) lands (*gêdia*) or indeed camels, they were powerful enough, while we were absent, as I (*sic*) said before, to practice extortion on the people belonging to us in respect of the *collatio lustralis*, which we have never had exacted from us on this pretext. We do possess, certainly, a property in the aforesaid city there in the shape of a camel stable that we hold for our own use. Since, therefore, we are taking care that those who belong to us may not suffer the same thing again from those to whom the exaction is entrusted, we flee for refuge to Your Highness, requesting and beseeching that you condescend to give orders to restrain for the future, through the attention of Crescentius, who has been put in charge of the peace, and of Theodoulos, *curialis* of the same city, those who conduct the administration of the same *collatio lustralis* from the unreasonable exaction that they are imposing on our people, in order that we may be able to carry out our military service faultlessly, so that, when we secure this, we may be able to acknowledge our very great thanks to Your Glorious Fortune, lord *dux*."

Flavius Mauricius, *vir clarissimus, comes primi ordinis* and *dux*, said: "If no [. . .] possessions [. . .] silver [. . .]."

Verso: Order of my lord *dux*.

10.4 Criminal procedure in the Roman period

James G. Keenan

The criminal law of the papyri has received comparatively little attention over the years.[10] The central and most frequently cited discussion therefore remains chapter 3 ("Penal Law") in Taubenschlag (1955). That chapter in turn makes liberal use of Taubenschlag's much earlier work (1916a). Taubenschlag, as one would expect from his career-long project, approached the abundant material in strictly juristic terms. He earnestly tried to impose order on the evidence by applying Romanist terminology. Methodical in his collecting of references on specific points, he presented them in extensive footnotes, but did not pause overmuch in analyzing single documents. Rather, he worked by means of definition, distinction, classification, and out-of-context illustration. Instead of speaking of crimes, he spoke of delicts, borrowed from Roman law as an umbrella term for all penal offenses. Strictly speaking, however, a delict was a misdeed prosecuted through a private lawsuit, which if successful was satisfied by the defendant's payment of a money penalty. As such, it is commonly taken as analogous to Common Law tort rather than to crime. More important at the moment than analogy, however, is that Taubenschlag applied the term delict to many papyrological examples that do not fit the legal definition (Bagnall 1991).

Today, reading Taubenschlag's densely packed chapter 3 drives one to conclude that the more he tried to impose terminological order on this material the more hopeless the endeavor became.[11] Meanwhile two historians (Baldwin 1963, Davies 1973: see Kelly 2002: 39–42) who used the papyrological evidence skipped juristically constructed niceties and simply made casual use of commonsense terms in reference to various crimes. In these anecdotal gatherings instances of murder are relatively infrequent (though see now the cases listed in *SB* XX 14085). In contrast, evidence for

[10] This contribution has benefited immensely from conversation and electronic correspondence with Ari Z. Bryen, especially from his valuable recommendations on documents for presentation and citation. I am likewise grateful to Bryen and to Benjamin Kelly for access to their Chicago and Oxford dissertations (Bryen 2008, Kelly 2002). See now Kelly (2011) and Bryen (2013).

[11] But see now *SB* XII 10929 with its Roman-law list of crimes and delicts under the jurisdiction of the prefect, including *atrox iniuria*.

thefts is abundant, covering so wide a variety of concrete circumstances with such an array of colorful terms that even for Taubenschlag (1955: 453, 456–57) it resisted juristic classification.

This is evidence that would repay investigation on a scale equal to that recently devoted to acts of violence (Kelly 2002, Bryen 2008). Accounts of violence, like those for theft – they often appear in combination (**10.4.5**, cf. **10.4.1** introduction; Kelly 2002: 57–58) – are abundant in the papyri. In the main they consist of petitions to assorted competent authorities.[12] In form, these include at least an address, a narrative of events, and a request for relief or satisfaction. Rarely does evidence survive for any kind of follow-up. We do not learn, that is, whether a given petition was successful (only – rarely – if it was ignored or failed); or whether a given criminal, as opposed to civil, case was settled by administrative intervention pursuant to a petition; or whether a complaint explicitly initiated by petition ever went to court.

This last eventuality, to calculate from the relevant documentary survivals (see **10.4.6** introduction), seems to have been exceptional. Evidence nevertheless does survive for the intermediate procedural steps (Kelly 2002: chapter 3). The aim here is to include these (**10.4.2–4**) as part of a "virtual" case beginning with a petition (**10.4.1**) initiating the process and ending with a trial (**10.4.5**) and a document pertinent to judicial procedure or sentencing (**10.4.6**). The reader should be cautioned that no such complete dossier illustrating these steps exists for any single attested case. What survive are almost always solitary documents, mostly copies of petitions, from what originally were small-sized personal dossiers or, less commonly, extensive official archives (cf. Haensch 1994, Anagnostou-Cañas 2000).

10.4.1 Petition about a violent attack

P.Oxy. LI 3620 (tr. Bryen 2013: 260–61, no. 101) (Oxyrhynchos, 2 February AD 326)

In this somewhat damaged petition Aurelius Thonius complains of an attack on his wife. He specifically requests the appointment of a midwife to examine and file a written report on his wife's condition. The report itself, technically a *prosphônêsis*, has not survived (**10.4.3** is an example). Thonius' concern to engage a midwife rather than a doctor may imply that his wife was pregnant. The presence of the word "gold" in a damaged context hints at a motive of robbery. The reference to torn clothing has been taken in

[12] There are 112 petitions on violence in Kelly's (2002) "Descriptive Catalogue"; over 150 Roman and Byzantine examples in Bryen (2008: Appendix 2).

other petitions, where the attackers were male, to imply sexual assault; but this, though imaginable, seems unlikely here. Of interest is the eventuality of a hearing in the court (*dikastêrion*) of the prefect of Egypt, normally resident in Alexandria when not on *conventus*. The vagueness of what the petitioner asks for in practical terms is typical.[13]

> In the consulship of our masters, Constantine Augustus for the 7th time and Constantius the most noble Caesar for the 1st time, Mecheir 8.
>
> To Aurelius Thonius and Aurelius Timotheos, both chiefs of the night watch (*nyktostratêgoi*) of the brilliant and most brilliant city of Oxyrhynchos, from Aurelius Thonius son of Onnophris from the same city. Yesterday, when my wife happened to be at home, a certain Tapesis together with her slave girl Victora, in the evening hours, though living in regions far distant from our house, made an attack and inflicted unspeakable acts of insult (*hybris*) on my wife, so that not only was her clothing torn, but her body [. . .] my wife [. . .] gold. Since, therefore, [. . .] I submit this petition (*biblidia*) requesting that [. . .] midwife be officially instructed by you to come and note her condition and report in writing; when the report has been made and the outrage (*atopêma*) investigated, they should provide guarantees (*enguai*) so that, if anything happens to my wife, the appropriate satisfaction (*ekdikia*) may be achieved at the immaculate court of my lord, the most renowned prefect of Egypt, Tiberius Flavius Laetus.

10.4.2 Application for an official medical examination

P.Oxy. LXI 4122 (Oxyrhynchos, 22 June AD 305)

Like **10.4.1**, this document, addressed to the chief executive officer (*logistês*) of Oxyrhynchos, requests a medical examination and written report, this time (as was more common) to be made by a public doctor (see also **10.4.3**). It refers to a narrative (*diêgêsis*) of the inciting incident as having already been made in a publicly displayed affidavit (*martyropoiêma*) – which any interested party could consult or copy.[14] This has not survived, but its existence apparently made a second full account of the attack unnecessary. Contrast **10.4.1** with its greater attention to narrative detail.

[13] In general, for the procedures involved in **10.4.1–3**, see Amundsen and Ferngren (1978), Torallas Tovar (2004a).

[14] See *BGU* III 970 (= *M.Chr.* 242), Anagnostou-Cañas (2000: 763–64, 771).

Under the consuls, our lords Constantius and Maximian, the most noble Caesars, for the 5th time.

To Aurelius Seuthes also called Horion, *logistês* (*curator civitatis*) of the Oxyrhynchite (nome), from Aurelius Hierax son of Asklepiades from the same city.

Of all the outrages committed illegally against my wife, Sarapias by name, by Pois and Tiron his brother-in-law and their wives and sons I have already made a full account (*diêgêsis*) through the affidavit (*martyropoiêma*) that I publicly posted. Therefore, since my herein mentioned wife was assaulted with blows and they struck [and wounded?] her arm, I necessarily present this petition (*biblia*), requesting that a public doctor be summoned through one of your assistants to examine together with the said assistant my wife's condition, and that they report to you in writing, and that this (*sc.* report) remain in your office for our evidence and security so that right of action (*ekdikia*) be preserved for me in the presence of the Greatness of the Gubernatorial Office.

Year 21 and 13 of our lords Diocletian and Maximian, Augusti, and Constantius and Maximian, the noblest Caesars, Payni 28.

(*2nd hand*) I, Aurelius Hierax son of Asklepiades, have submitted (*sc.* this document).

(*3rd hand*) I, Aurelius Horion, assistant of the *logistês*, have delivered (*sc.* it). Year 21 and 13, Payni 28.

10.4.3 Doctor's report

P.Oslo III 95 (Oxyrhynchos, 17 March AD 96). Image at *P.Oslo* III, Plate VII, c.

Some doctor's reports (*prosphônêseis*) amounted to death certificates (see **9.2.1**); others were based on examinations of living persons who had suffered injuries inflicted either by accident or by human intervention. They might subsequently figure as evidence in court (*P.Oxy.* XII 1502). The doctor here reports that a slave girl had had a middle finger injured; she showed signs of blood on one of her breasts; she was vomiting and feverish. Presumably she had gotten into a fight, or been attacked, but the doctor only reports on the physical results, not the circumstances or causes of her injuries. It does seem as if she got the worst of the encounter, especially if the damage to her finger was a defensive wound and not one resulting from, say, throwing an effective counterpunch to her opponent's chin.

To Peisis, *stratêgos*, from Theon son of Harpaesis, doctor, from Oxyrhynchos. On the twenty-first (Imperial) day of the month Pharmouthi of the fifteenth year of the Emperor Caesar Domitian Augustus Germanicus, orders were given to me by you through Loches the son of Onnophris, assistant, to examine Alexandra, slave of Claudia Dionysia. Therefore, having examined her, with the assistant in attendance, I found a wound on her middle finger, which I am tending to, and a clot of blood on her breast, and she was vomiting and running a fever. On this account I report. [Year 15 of the Emperor Caesar Domitian Augustus Germanicus, Pharmouthi x.]

10.4.4 Warrants

The following three documents, labeled **10.4.4a**, **10.4.4b**, and **10.4.4c**, of whose type nearly 140 have been published (a recent dozen: *P.Oxy.* LXXIV 5001–5012), are typically short. Texts of this type tend to be written on the scrap ends of papyrus rolls, rotated ninety degrees, with the resulting writing running against the fibers (Gagos and Sijpesteijn 1996; cf. *BGU* XVII 2701 introduction and Plate XXXIII). The results are papyri in the form of long rectangles, greater – sometimes significantly – in width than in height. They were necessarily folded: *P.Oxy.* XLII 3061 is a letter in which the writer, complaining of insult (*hybris*), asks to be assigned a desert guard (*erêmophylax*) "with a *diplôma*" (line 9), literally a doubled or folded document. The translation of **10.4.4a** attempts to reproduce the layout of the original as precisely as possible. All three chosen examples are typical in their urban provenance and in their being dispatched to police officials in regional villages. They must have been file copies or originals that were returned upon execution.

These orders almost never have dates. They are assigned by editors, relying on context, official titulature, and palaeography, to the second to fourth centuries. By formula, their texts will include references to the title of the sender of the order, indented or centered on the first line; the names and positions of the addressees, officials with local police power – titles will vary depending on time and place; instructions in the imperative mood: "Send," or, as in the following examples, "Hand over (*paradote*)" such-and-such a person; and the names of the persons on whose petitions or charges the orders have been authorized (U. Hagedorn 1979, Drexhage 1989). Thus, where this last detail is given, it is possible to view the orders as results of favorably received written petitions (e.g., *P.Mich.* V 228 = Rowlandson 1998, no. 229), or requests (again see *P.Oxy.* XLII 3061), or even (perhaps) oral complaints or demands. There were presumably charges for such services.

Traditionally called "orders for arrest" (e.g., Bülow-Jacobsen 1986), it has been objected that they do not employ Greek verbs that stand for our notion of "arrest" (see, however, **10.4.4b**, a more complicated than usual example in its reference to an earlier existing arrest). Thus it has been suggested (Gagos and Sijpesteijn 1996) that "summons" would be a better English term – but this too has its problems. A summons, though delivered by an agent, is normally issued directly to the person sent for and should include a statement of its purpose; but these orders, without stating particular purposes, were issued to local officials who were themselves made responsible for the appearance of the persons named. A label recently applied (Bagnall and Mitthof 2004: esp. 59), "order to send a person," while bland, is at least true to the full complement of these texts. Nevertheless, the texts chosen here all give signs that the persons "sent for" were after all subject to arrest – for theft in example **c** – so perhaps these at least should be called "warrants."[15] Once found, the persons in question were to be escorted (by a soldier in **10.4.4a**, an assistant in **10.4.4b**, a guard in **10.4.4c**) from the village to the city. Perhaps they were imprisoned on arriving in the city, but if so it should be noted that there was nothing in Egypt equivalent to modern penal systems and no custom of long-term incarceration. Rather, imprisonment was used for detention pending hearing or trial, or to compel a specific compliance (Taubenschlag 1959 vol. 2: 713–19; Torallas Tovar 2006), in effect, to use an American idiom, a form of "arm twisting."

10.4.4a Warrant

P.Oxy. I 64 (= *W.Chr.* 475) (Oxyrhynchos, third or early fourth century AD). Image: Figure 13

From the decurion
to the komarchs and the peace officer of the village of Teis.
Immediately hand over to the soldier sent by me:
Ammonis a.k.a. Alaker, on charges brought
by Ptollas, or come up yourselves (*sc.* to the city).

I have signed.

[15] *The Oxford Companion to Law* (Oxford 1980), p. 1290.

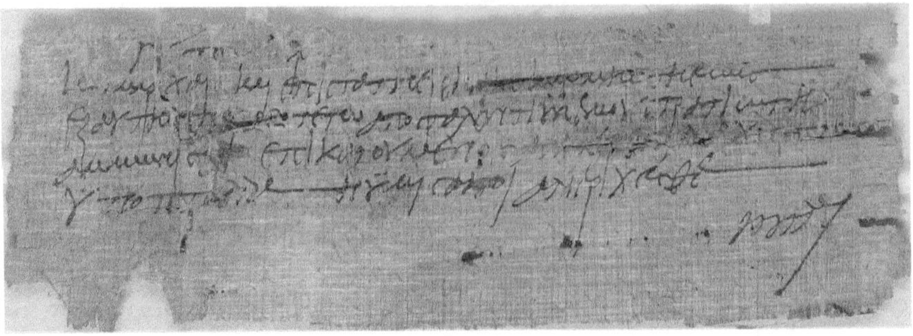

Fig. 13. Warrant for arrest. *P.Oxy.* I 64. Oxyrhynchos, third or early fourth century AD

10.4.4b Warrant

P.Oxy. I 65 (= *Sel.Pap.* II 232) (Oxyrhynchos, third or early fourth century). Image at Papyri.info.

From the *beneficiarius* on duty to the komarchs of the village of Terythis. Hand over to the assistant who has been sent (*sc.* by me): Pachoumis son of Pachoumis, whom you have arrested today and brought to your village, he being a resident of the city. If you have anything to say in his favor, come along with him and speak. But watch out that you do not detain the assistant.
I have signed.

10.4.4c Warrant

BGU XVII 2701 (Hermopolis, fourth century AD). Image at *BGU* XVII, Plate XXXIII.

From the peace officer (*eirenarchês*) to the komarchs and thief-catchers of the village of Senoabis. Immediately hand over to the guard sent (*sc.* by me): Panhelenes son of Silvanus, on charges brought by Telutis, mother of Sarapion, former *kosmêtês* of Alexandria, or come up yourselves (*sc.* to the city).

10.4.5 Bilingual report of judicial proceedings

P.Lips. I 40 (*ed. pr.* Mitteis and Wilcken 1906: 106–12, *ChLA* XII 518) (Hermopolis, late fourth century). Image at Papyri.info.

This report of judicial proceedings before the civil governor of the Thebaid is written in long lines in three columns on a papyrus roll, 31 cm high and 124 cm in breadth. Part of the first column and all of a second and third column survive. The columns are not numbered in the ancient text so it is impossible to say how many columns are lost from the beginning of the original record. The magistrate's decision (*krisis*) and much more are missing from the end.

The precise status of this report is a matter for conjecture. Most surviving reports were private copies made by interested parties from official copies, archived locally or in Alexandria (Coles 1966; Anagnostou-Cañas 2000: 764–67, 772; see **10.3.4** introduction). The present report has been corrected throughout by a second hand. Of special interest is the vividness of some of the dialogue, which gives it a sense of immediacy and authenticity.

10.4.5 is an extraordinarily well-preserved example of the fifty or so published "bilingual protocols" (cf. **10.3.6**).[16] In these the connecting frames assigned to the presiding magistrate are in heavily abbreviated Latin while the substance of what is reported as said in court is in Greek. Despite earlier instances, the bilingual protocol in its "fully developed form is an innovation of the reign of Diocletian," well known for his policy of fostering the use of Latin throughout the empire (*P. Oxy.* LI 3619 introduction). In the translation italic type is used to indicate the Latin passages in the original – except where italics are used for technical terms, Greek and Latin, within parentheses.

In an additional effort to reproduce its model, the lines of the translation are numbered continuously so as to represent the lengths of the original lines and the dispositions of words within them. Note, for example, how often lines begin with the Latin formula introducing questions and comments of the presiding magistrate. The line numbering will also facilitate use of the comments in the notes below.

Everything here relies heavily on the initial work of Mitteis and Wilcken (1906).

Dramatis personae (main characters only) and summary

Flavius Leontius Beronicianus, civil governor (*praeses*) of the Thebaid, presides over the hearing in an attempt to get at the facts of the case (Harries 1999: 122: "To get at the facts was the job of every *iudex* [judge]"; cf. 129). The focus of his interrogation, or *quaestio* (Harries 1999: 122–34), is **Acholius**, who is charged with having attacked and

[16] *P. Oxy.* LI 3619 introduction, published in 1984, lists thirty-nine instances.

robbed a city councilman named **Asyncritius**. As a slave, Acholius' testimony is extracted first under threat and later under application of torture. His master is **Sergius**, evidently the head of a military detachment (*contubernales*) headquartered in Hermopolis. Sergius is not present in court but is spoken for by his "partner," **Senecion**, apparently a high-ranking police officer, *supersta(tionarius)*. On the other side, **Philammon** (*Filammon* in Latin) primarily speaks for the victim, his son Asyncritius, who, apparently because he is still recuperating from his beating, is unable to be present. Philammon is assisted by an advocate named **Herminus**.

There seems no denying that a fierce struggle, or "battle," took place at night; Beronicianus is concerned to establish the number and identities of the alleged attackers. Acholius, though he claims Asyncritius was the instigator, at first admits to having been attended in the fracas by only one very small slave boy (whom he later, amusingly, rats out as having been the one who struck Asyncritius). He was joined by a third fellow slave, **Gorgonius**, so he says, only after the struggle was over. (He later concedes Gorgonius' presence and participation as the one who had restrained Asyncritius.) Philammon, on the other side, insists that "many" accomplices were involved throughout the attack, all apparently adults, including one who held Asyncritius' hands (Gorgonius), one who brained him with a rock (**Stercorius**), and another (unnamed) who kicked him – counting Acholius, "four" attackers in all. The attack was interrupted by the intervention of the "boys" (sons or slaves) of **Hermaion**, the *curator civitatis* (*logistês* in Greek), who is called as witness: his house was within earshot of the hubbub. He can attest only to two or three attackers – it was too dark to tell. After the attack Acholius and his sidekicks reportedly stole ten to twelve *solidi* of public moneys from Asyncritius. Acholius denies this too: rather, Asyncritius took off his cloak (with the money) and handed it over to a woman (perhaps his wife – the Greek word *gynê* is ambiguous); Acholius never saw it.

In the course of all this Senecion manages to bring before Beronicianus another, apparently unrelated case, claiming that thirty to forty rowdies had broken down the doors of his partner Sergius' house. (He perhaps suspects Acholius, as Sergius' slave, had some inside knowledge.) Whether theft followed the break-in is not made clear – but the possibility is implied since Sergius had custody of significant public moneys. This money could not, in any case, have been that which was violently lifted from the person of Asyncritius.

Column 1 is much damaged with only parts of lines and scattered words decipherable. Its connection to the other columns is nevertheless assured both by physical connection and by the identification of two of the speakers, Herminus the advocate and Acholius; also by references to testimony given by a slave, to a door, to a rock being snatched and thrown, and to an order for a witness to come forward. Problems throughout are occasioned by the various, sometimes ambiguous terms used for slaves.

Column II (1) "[. . .] Let him investigate whether he was alone, or a slave (*doulos*) was with him."

(2) *Fl(avius) Leontius Beronicianus, most brilliant man, civil governor of the Thebaid, said:* "Was the one who attacked alone, or were there others?"[17] *Filammon said:* "There were four, Stercorius and others. Let him tell who were with him; he knows

(3) his fellow slaves."

(4) *Fl(avius) Leontius Beronicianus, most brilliant man, civil governor of the Thebaid, said:* "Tell their names." *Filammon said:* "We do not know them. He himself knows them."

(5) *Fl(avius) Leontius Beronicianus, most brilliant man, civil governor of the Thebaid, said:* "How many household slaves (*oiketai*) joined with you in the attack?" *Acholius said:* "Alone with the boy (*paidion*) I was."

(6) *Fl(avius) Leontius Beronicianus, most brilliant man, civil governor of the Thebaid, said:* "Tell the truth." *Acholius said:* "Alone I was, with the boy (*paidion*)."

(7) *Fl(avius) Leontius Beronicianus, most brilliant man, civil governor of the Thebaid, said: Strip him; and after he had been stripped, he said:* "I was alone, plus that little boy who happens to be very young." *Filammon said:* "The *logistês* can say that there were many."

(8) *Fl(avius) Leontius Beronicianus, most brilliant man, civil governor of the Thebaid, said:* "Let the *logistês* whom they call as witness be brought in." *After Hermaion the* curator civitatis *of Hermopolis was brought in,*

(9) *Fl(avius) Leontius Beronicianus, most brilliant man, civil governor of the Thebaid, said:* "They have called you as witness to the events. And you as a free man shall tell the truth. What have you seen, or what has been dared?" *Hermaion the* curator *said*: "Very late,

(10) in the depth of the evening, I heard a noise (I happened to be at home) and I sent my boys (*paides*) to find out the cause. They went out and they found this Asyncritius being restrained(?) and beaten by thugs,

[17] Tenses of the verb "to be" in this line are present, but the sense calls for the imperfect. There are similar problems elsewhere in the text.

(11) and they made them put a stop to the ruckus (*ataxia*)."

(12)*Fl(avius) Leontius Beronicianus, most brilliant man, civil governor of the Thebaid, said:* "How many household slaves (*oiketai*) were there?" *Hermaion said*: "There were two there, or three; it was very late." *Senecion said:*[18] "Was the logistês summoned in order to say this? I request that the scribe come forward

(13) [and speak(?)]. There were many men who went up toward the house, there were thirty or forty." *Hermaion the* curator *said:* "If they had not been at my house, Asyncritius would have been long dead, by the Almighty."

(14) *Senecion said:* "You teach well! This house is near(?) the house of the *logistês*. The *logistês* is staying there."

(15) *Fl(avius) Leontius Beronicianus, most brilliant man, civil governor of the Thebaid, said:* "Who are those who dared this attack with you – name them." *Acholius said:* "There were two earlier, I and the little one; after that came my fellow slave (*syndoulos*) –

(16) after the fight – after the end of the fight." *Herminus the advocate said:* "A man worthy of credence has given testimony, a leading citizen (*prôteuôn*) of Hermopolis."[19]

(17) *Fl(avius) Leontius Beronicianus, most brilliant man, civil governor of the Thebaid, said:* "Tell the names of your fellow attackers." *Acholius said:* "The little boy (*paidion*) and Gorgonius, the one said to have held his (i.e., the victim's) hands."

(18) *Fl(avius) Leontius Beronicianus, most brilliant man, civil governor of the Thebaid, said:* "Are they free, or household slaves (*oiketai*)?" *Acholius said:* "They are slaves (*douloi*)."

(19) *Fl(avius) Leontius Beronicianus, most brilliant man, civil governor of the Thebaid, said:* "Whose slaves (*douloi*)?" *Acholius said:* "(They are slaves of) Sergius, my good master." *Senecion said:* "Their master is out of town. His house has suffered damage. I have testimony (*martyria*).

(20) Your Excellency sent the scribe and he saw that the doors had been hurled to the ground. I requested ten thousand times in memos (*hypomnêmata*) for the scribe to be brought in and to say who had done the damage.

18 Senecion's interruption and the following exchange with Hermaion, to the end of line 14, are puzzling. See also Senecion's other (even more intrusive) interruption to the proceedings at lines 39–44.

19 Who this anonymous "leading citizen" was remains a mystery; see also line 32. He had apparently given earlier oral testimony or been deposed in writing beforehand. Perhaps therefore the reference is to Hermaion, the *curator civitatis* (see lines 8–13).

(21) I certify that thirty or forty came up toward the house." *Filammon said:* "Not once, nor a second time, nor even a third time did he come to this city and rob us. Whom

(22) did they not attack?" *Senecion said:* "I am personally afraid since my partner (*hetairos*) is out of town. A public account (*dêmosios logos*) of the soldiers[20] is deposited there. The doors are on the ground. Let the scribe come,

(23) let him depose in the records (*hypomnêmata*) and identify those who came up[21] and who it is who came up (with them). For I did not find out who it is who came up (with them)." *Filammon said:* "The slave (*doulos*) admits that he restrained the hands

(24) of my son and beat him."

(25) *Fl(avius) Leontius Beronicianus, most brilliant man, civil governor of the Thebaid, said:* "Why did you attack the city councilman (*bouleutês*) in the evening and cause wounds to his brow?" *Acholius said:*

(26) "I beseech Your Excellency, I did not attack, but he himself attacked me! It was just my luck (*moira*) to meet up with him so late."

Column III (27) *Fl(avius) Leontius Beronicianus, most brilliant man, civil governor of the Thebaid, said:* "Who inflicted the wound?" *Acholius said:* "The little boy (*paidion*)."

(28) *Fl(avius) Leontius Beronicianus, most brilliant man, civil governor of the Thebaid, said:* "What says he who received the blow?" *Filammon said:* "One restrained his hands, another hurled him to the ground and wanted to 'separate'[22] him on account of the public

(29) money; the one restrained his hands, the other gave it to my son with a rock, another kicked him. His whole body was pummeled. By the Goddess (Pronoia)(!), he just about died."

(30) *Fl(avius) Leontius Beronicianus, most brilliant man, civil governor of the Thebaid, said:* "Say clearly, who was the one who struck him?" *Filammon said*: "This one's fellow slaves (*syndouloi*)."

(31) *Fl(avius) Leontius Beronicianus, most brilliant man, civil governor of the Thebaid, said:* "Did the one here present strike him, or another

[20] "soldiers": *Mannschaft* in Mitteis' translation, based on a Latin loanword in the Greek text, *contubernales*. "Logos" in this line, though literally referring to an "account," presumably refers to the actual money reckoned in the account.

[21] "came up" (three times in this line), apparently implying "to the house."

[22] "separate": the expression, which is peculiar, was taken by Mitteis to amount to an intent to commit murder.

one?" *Filammon said:*[23] "I don't know which of them. For they did not come against us by day, not to mention by night." *Herminus the advocate said:* "He himself confessed,

(32) namely the household slave (*oiketês*, i.e., Acholius), that one restrained his hands, others attacked and beat him. These matters have been deposed by a man worthy of credence, a leading citizen around Hermopolis, and it remains that punishment be carried out,

(33) punishment that is fitting, upon those who attacked the city councilman." *Senecion the police-chief said:* "Through rhetoric they are trying to get control of the plundered goods. The doors lie (*sc.* on the ground). There is testimony (*martyria*). For the ten thousandth time I have deposed that the doors lie (*sc.* on the ground)

(34) and I request that the scribe come in and say, 'The house is henceforth uninhabitable'."

(35) *Fl(avius) Leontius Beronicianus, most brilliant man, civil governor of the Thebaid, said:* "Well then the householder (*oiketês*) does not make these charges." *Senecion said*: "Your Excellency did not inquire. Your Excellency should investigate this."

(36) *Fl(avius) Leontius Beronicianus, most brilliant man, civil governor of the Thebaid, said* [here apparently turning from Senecion and looking at Acholius]*:* "Why did you attack Asyncritius?" *Acholius said:* "We did not attack, he's the one who attacked."

(37) *Fl(avius) Leontius Beronicianus, most brilliant man, civil governor of the Thebaid, said:* "In what places?" *Acholius said:* "In that street."

(38) *Fl(avius) Leontius Beronicianus, most brilliant man, civil governor of the Thebaid, said:* "Let Philammon say who are the ones who robbed the money from his son." *Filammon said:* "These slaves (*douloi*)."

(39) *Fl(avius) Leontius Beronicianus, most brilliant man, civil governor of the Thebaid, said:* "How much money?" *Filammon said:* "About ten gold pieces (i.e., *solidi*), or twelve." *Senecion the police chief said:* "The account (*logos*) of my partner Sergius is for one thousand four hundred in [sil]ver.[24]

(40) I request that Your Brilliancy order the scribe to be brought in and say, 'The doors lie on the ground and I have given my testimony'

[23] The syntax of Filammon's answer, at least as recorded, seems confused; he must have intended something like: "I don't know who did it. They didn't attack by day – it was night (and hard to see)."

[24] "Sergius" and "[sil]ver" are based on a very difficult editorial interpretation of what the scribe may have written.

(*written above the line:* I have received (the) scribe), and the scribe is ready to depose in the records (*hypomnêmata*) of what [. . .][25]

(41) who are the ones who attacked, let him name who it is. Thirty others, so he says, were with them. For I don't know because I was not with them. Let the scribe be examined."

(42) *Fl(avius) Leontius Beronicianus, most brilliant man, civil governor of the Thebaid, said:* "Let the scribe be brought in." *Gennadius the assistant record-keeper said:* "He was ordered to follow the chief of the night watch (*nyktostratêgos*) immediately according to the decree (*prostagma*) of Your Brilliancy on account of

(43) the presentation of those named by the city councilmen to the *kephalaiôtês.*"[26] *Senecion said:* "I have brought the scribe and I have handed him over to the *proximus.*"[27]

(44) *Fl(avius) Leontius Beronicianus, most brilliant man, civil governor of the Thebaid, said:* "What need do you have of the scribe?" *Senecion said:* "Your Excellency asked for witnesses that they attacked the house (*hospitium*) of my colleague (*kollêga*)."[28] *Filammon said:* "My son

(45) was in danger of dying from the blows."

(46) *Fl(avius) Leontius Beronicianus, most brilliant man, civil governor of the Thebaid, said* [apparently addressing Acholius]*:* "Why did you attack the city councilman?" *And he said to the* officium*:* "Let him be beaten." *And after he had been beaten with oxhide whips,*[29]

(47) *Fl(avius) Leontius Beronicianus, most brilliant man, civil governor of the Thebaid, said:* "Don't beat free men."[30] *And he said to the* officium*: "Spare him." And after he was spared,*

(48) *Fl(avius) Leontius Beronicianus, most brilliant man, civil governor of the Thebaid, said:* "Tell, where is the money that you snatched?"

[25] The whole line is puzzling. It is hard to determine exactly where in the translation to place the superlinear insertion.

[26] A tax-collector or the head of one of the city's craft guilds.

[27] An official on the governor's staff (*officium*).

[28] Note the shift to Latin loanwords for Greek terms used earlier (*hospitium* for *oikia* [house], *collega* for *hetairos* [partner]).

[29] *officium* in this line refers to anonymous, sub-clerical staff officers present in court; also in line 47. Note that the governor in this and the following lines gives instructions twice in Greek, once in Latin, a "code-switching" no doubt disconcerting to the witness (Adams 2003: 385–86). "Oxhide whips" is based on a transliterated Greek word (*buneuris*), "a local term, impossible to translate into Latin except by periphrasis" (Adams 2003: 445). For instructions to beat, see *P.Oxy.* IV 706 line 9 (*M.Chr.* 81), *P.Oxy.* LI 3619 line 24, **10.4.6** below, Bryen 2008: 125–26.

[30] A puzzling order, or counter-order, given the present context (a *slave* being interrogated or punished under torture) and the governor's just having himself given the order to beat. See above, line 7, where torture was prepared for but not inflicted.

Acholius said: "He (i.e., Asyncritius) stripped off his cloak (*himation*) and gave it to the woman (*or*: his wife) who was following him. I didn't see."

(49) *Fl(avius) Leontius Beronicianus, most brilliant man, civil governor of the Thebaid, said* [apparently to Filammon, if not to Herminus]*:* "Cross-examine him, because he stole your money." *Filammon said:* "After the fight he released my son's sleeve and snatched it; one restrained him and

(50) he confesses that Gorgonius bound his hands." *Herminus the advocate said:* "We ask that the household slaves (*oiketai*) who collaborated with him be made present." *Filammon said*: "Stercorius struck his head about the temples."[31]

(51) *Senecion said:* "Let him depose whether he was alone or others were with him, so that it may become clear to us, so that the scribe may come and speak."

10.4.6 Governor's edict on physical punishment

P.Oxy. IX 1186 (= Hengstl 1978a: 142–43, no. 54) (Oxyrhynchos, *c.* AD 385: *PLRE* I 426 s.v. Herodes 3). Image at Papyri.info.

Evidence for judicial sentencing in criminal cases is rare (Anagnostou-Cañas 1991: 123–40 and 2000: 772–77).[32] This is a likely result of a process, or "logic," of attrition (Kelly 2002: 89–93). In simplest terms, few cases initiated by petition ever made it to trial. Scholars relying on anthropological models (Bagnall 1989 = 2003: chapter v, Hobson 1993) have stressed a supposed preference for out-of-court settlements, with victims aiming to restore the social balance that had been upset by acts of violence. Others have recently argued for more concrete expectations – compensation *and* punishment, revenge, deterrence, or protection, depending on the case at hand (Kelly 2002: 69–81; Bryen 2008: 114–27). It is true nevertheless that victims used a fixed and generic vocabulary in reference to redress for themselves and punishment for the accused. The petitioner in **10.4.1**, for example, asks for appropriate "satisfaction" (*ekdikia*, perhaps suggestive of vengeance). In **10.4.5**, lines 32–33, Philammon, speaking in court for his badly beaten son, demands fitting "punishment" (*timôria*) without

[31] For Gorgonius, earlier named by Acholius as the one who had restrained Asyncritius, see line 17. For Stercorius, see line 2.

[32] Excepted from consideration here is the tantalizing but controversial codex, *BGU* 1024–27 (Keenan 1989). See the translation of *BGU* 1024, p. 6 in Rowlandson (1998, no. 208) – in high-flown rhetorical style, an Alexandrian senator, for murdering his girlfriend, is sentenced to execution by decapitation.

specifying what that might be. Reports of proceedings (Coles 1966; see **10.3.4** introduction, **10.4.5**) do sometimes preserve judgments (*kriseis*), but almost all of these concern cases of administrative and private law.[33]

The fragment presented here is not itself a judicial sentence, but an edict issued by the civil governor (*praeses*) of the Thebaid. It is possible to construe it as an edict on judicial torture during interrogation (*quaestio*) and as such relevant to **10.4.5** (line 46) and to the topic of "judicial savagery" in the Roman empire (MacMullen 1986, Harries 1999: 122–34). But the edict may also be viewed as an attempt to correct an abuse in "sentencing guidelines." In either case, the differential treatment of slaves and free men in in terms of corporal punishment is well known (Garnsey 1970: esp. 213–16). Relevant legal texts cited in the Oxyrhynchos editors' introduction are *Digest* 48.19.10.pr. ("In the matter of a slave the rule is that they are punished like men of the lower class (*humiliores*). For those reasons that a free man is beaten with rods (*fustes*), a slave is ordered to be beaten with whips (*flagella*) and returned to his master") and 48.19.28.2 ("Not all are customarily beaten with rods, but only those men who though free are of lower station (*tenuiores*); but men of higher standing (*honestiores*) are not subject to rods, and this is something that is specifically expressed in imperial rescripts"). Papyrus evidence includes *P.Wisc.* I 33 (AD 147), with its reference (line 20) to the corporal punishment of "the freeborn like slaves," and *SB* V 7523 (AD 153), the eyewitness testimony of Roman veterans to the beating and use of rods against a fellow veteran by order of the *stratêgos*.

> Aurelius Herodes, the most honorable governor of the Thebaid, states: Subjection to punishment through lashes, which is called *lêtar* [. . .] in the native language, is lamentable even for those of servile condition, even though not entirely prohibited; but for free men to endure such an outrage (*hybris*) is neither legal nor just . . .

10.5 Clerics as arbiters in Christian Egypt

Georg Schmelz

Arbitration in the Christian community is as old as Christianity itself, in spite of and because of its initial skepticism about human justice

[33] An exception is *P.Amh.* II 66 (AD 124): the *stratêgos* suspends a murder trial for want of cooperative witnesses.

and judgment.[34] Most New Testament passages about justice concern the day of the last judgment when the Lord will come again and sentence the world, including the Christians. For this reason the New Testament is against human judgment and against all attempts to settle disputes in everyday life. "Judge not that ye be not judged" (Matt. 7:1, Luke 6:37) is the main line in the New Testament.[35] But in practical community life rejecting any form of regulation was impossible: the early Christians faced conflicts and had to come to terms with them. Thus in Matt. 18:15–18 the following regulation is recommended: first, the two opponents should find a solution on their own. If this is not possible two or three brothers should help them solve their problem. If this attempt fails the dispute should be discussed in the church assembly, a process that might lead to excommunication (cf. 1 Tim. 5:19–20, Titus 3:10).

It is the Apostle Paul who combines in 1 Cor. 6 the principle of non-judgment and pragmatic solutions in community conflicts. Generally, Paul explains, it is preferable to suffer injustice than to have a conflict (1 Cor. 6:7). It is already a bad thing that there are any conflicts among the community members. It is even worse that Christians do not try to solve their problems within the community (1 Cor. 6:1, 6),[36] as Christians will at the end of all times – this is Paul's prediction – take part in the last judgment and judge even the angels (1 Cor. 6:2–3). Disputes should be settled by a wise man (1 Cor. 6:5), or a humble man (1 Cor. 6:4), who acts as an arbiter between the opponents.

Paul's recommendation to settle disputes not outside the community but in front of a brother was taken seriously,[37] as can be seen throughout the course of church history. To the extent that the bishop became the community leader, and later, during the Byzantine period, the city leader, he acquired jurisdiction over disputes. Bishops settling disputes are frequently mentioned in ancient Christian literature, with and without reference to 1 Cor. 6.

At the end of the first and beginning of the second century the episcopacy became the leading function in the parish. Regarding the bishop's juridical powers the First Letter of Clement (*c.* AD 96) takes an interim position in this development: the parish assembly has the last word but the bishop

[34] See Stein (1984: 479). [35] See also Rom. 2:1–3; James 4:12; see Käsemann (1964).

[36] Stein (1968) investigates whether these cases were brought in front of a Roman magistrate or a rabbi in the synagogue and finally decides for the rabbi.

[37] Dinkler (1967: 213–14) refers to similar regulations in Qumran and in Hellenistic mystery cults. These communities had rules to solve their conflicts without any external influence. For Jewish jurisdiction see Herrmann (1980: 79–82).

makes suggestions as to how the dispute can be settled.[38] For Ignatius of Antioch (died *c.* AD 110) the bishop is clearly the highest authority, whom all community members must obey. In his letters to the Christians in Tralles and Smyrna he reminds them of the bishop's position and refers to 1 Cor. 6:1–7. This implies that he does not want to have any litigation brought in front of a pagan judge.[39] Tertullian (died after AD 220) briefly mentions an ecclesiastical court in his *Apologeticum*.[40] Cyprian (died AD 258) reinforces the bishop's position as a *vicarius Christi*; referring to 1 Cor. 6 he sees it as strictly forbidden for any Christian to bring his problem to a pagan judge.[41] A bishop abusing his juridical authority is documented in the *Church History* of Eusebius: he mentions a letter from a synod accusing bishop Paul of Samosata of having accepted money for his sentences.[42]

It is commonly accepted among the Christian writers of the fourth and fifth centuries that the bishop should act as an arbiter. For Gregory of Nyssa (died AD 395) it is one of the bishop's duties to bring the adversaries together in peace so that they may live together again as friends.[43] Ambrose of Milan (died AD 397) recalls a situation in which he did not want to act as a judge in the first place. But because he wanted to obey the word of the Apostle in 1 Cor. 6 and since he was a friend to the opponents, he tried to settle their dispute.[44] Rufinus of Aquileia (died AD 410) reports from his time as a hermit on the Mount of Olives near Jerusalem that he attempted to bring to peace any conflict of which he became aware.[45] For St. Augustine (AD 334–430) settling disputes is, following 1 Cor. 6, one of the prime duties of the bishop,[46] but he understands it as a kind of paternal reconciliation.[47] John of Damascus (born *c.* AD 650, died before AD 754) also comments on 1 Cor. 6 as a reminder to reconcile adversaries within the community.[48]

38 See Gerke (1931: 61), Caspers (1954: 14).

39 Ignatius, *Ep. ad Tralles* 3.1 (*PG* 5.677); *Ep. ad Smyrn.* 8 (*PG* 5.713); see Mosiek (1965: 184).

40 Tertullian, *Apolog.* 39.4 (ed. Hoppe, *CSEL* 69); *adv. Marc.* 5.12 (*PL* 2.509); see Mosiek (1965: 184).

41 Cyprian, *Ep.* 66 *ad Florentinum* (ed. Hartel, *CSEL* 3/2); see Caspers 1954: 14; Cyprian, *Test. ad Iud.* (*PL* 4.788); see Vischer (1955: 22).

42 Eusebius, *HE* 7.30 (ed. Schwartz, GCS small edition, Leipzig 1955); see Mosiek (1965: 185).

43 Gregory of Nyssa, *De Vita S. Gregorii Thaumaturgi* (*PG* 46.926); see Caspers (1954: 9).

44 Ambrose, *Ep. Classis* 82 (*PL* 16.1332); see Caspers (1954: 10.46).

45 Rufinus, *Hist. Mon.* 16 (*PL* 21.437); see Caspers (1954: 10.46).

46 Augustine, *Enarr. in Ps.* 81 (*PL* 37.1045); see Caspers (1954: 47); Augustine, *Op. Mon.* 29 (*PL* 40.577); see Caspers (1954: 12).

47 Augustine, *Sermo* 355: *sed si pueri isti servi Dei sunt, litem hanc inter illos cito finimus. Audio illos ut pater . . .* (*PL* 39.1571); see Caspers (1954: 10).

48 John Damascenus, in *Ep. I ad Cor.* (*PG* 95.611–4); see Caspers (1954: 47); for the ancient Christian writers see also Herrmann (1980: 75–76) and Krause (1996: 48–50).

The synods of the first centuries found regulations for the legal status of clerics: the Third Synod of Carthage (AD 397) in canon 5 prohibited any cleric from going before a lay court.[49] This canon was reinforced in Chalcedon (AD 451): clerics should only apply to the bishop.[50] The most detailed source for the bishop's jurisdiction in early church history is the *didaskalia*, a mid-third-century church order probably written in Syria.[51] Questions of parish organization are dealt with in detail; how a bishop should settle disputes in the community is clearly regulated.[52] Monday is the day of jurisdiction. The bishop is assisted by priests and deacons who lead lives that could be examples for the others – but not by laymen. Both adversaries have to be present before the bishop, who together with his associates will carefully examine their motivations, their lifestyles, and their trustworthiness. When both sides are admitted to the episcopal court, the complainant can make his case first; then the accused has the right to defend himself. The burden of proof lies with the complainant; in case of doubt the innocence of the accused is presumed. To prove him guilty two or three witnesses are required (following the biblical account in Matt. 18:16, 2 Cor. 13:1 and Deut. 19:15). The judge is the bishop alone; he has to be correct, but merciful. Peaceful reconciliation is preferred to condemnation.

The *didaskalia* was read and followed in a vast area. It was translated into Syriac and Latin and forms, in a re-edited version, the first six books of the Apostolic Constitutions, the largest canonico-liturgical compilation of the early church, from which derived the Arabic and Ethiopic recensions of the *didaskalia*.[53]

It was under Constantine that Christianity became a legalized and privileged religion in the Roman empire and episcopal jurisdiction became part of the state law. Christians were no longer persecuted, the communities grew and prospered; the number of conflicts increased and the bishop had more disputes to settle. When Christianity became the prevailing religion in the Roman empire, episcopal jurisdiction was not just a minority affair any more, but took a place next to state law courts. The situation required clarifying the respective competences of the bishop and the state judge, and Constantine integrated the episcopal jurisdiction into Roman law as a form of arbitration.[54]

49 Mansi III 882; see Caspers (1954: 48).

50 Mansi VII 362; see Caspers (1954: 48).

51 Doepp (1998: 196), Achelis and Flemming (1904: 364–69).

52 Achelis and Flemming (1904: 269–71, 307–09), Plöchl (1953: 88–90), Caspers (1954: 9), Mosiek (1965: 185–94), Herrmann (1980: 81–86), Schöllgen (1998: 112–13, 130–34).

53 Doepp (1998: 196).

54 See Ziegler (1971: 167), Gaudemet (1989: 233–37), Kaser (1996: 528–29).

Arbitration had an important place in Roman law.[55] Even when a process was already in action before a judge, the two parties had the option to choose an impartial third person to act as an arbiter. They had to select this arbiter unanimously and agree beforehand to follow his decision. The arbiter was not bound to follow the law; he could not sentence only one side, but had to try to clear the case and give his opinion. If one side broke the declaration and failed to follow the arbiter's decision, the other side had no satisfaction unless the parties had previously agreed on a fine in their case. Because the opponents had unanimously chosen the arbiter, the arbiter's decision could not be taken to court.

The arbiter had to reconcile the two sides, which was just what the bishop had to do when settling disputes in the parish. He also had to bring the opponents to an agreement, not by his own opinion but by Christian love.[56] The main difference between the arbiter as Roman law sees him and the bishop is his position in the process: the bishop was not just any third party chosen by the opponents for their single case, but a community leader who was required regularly to settle disputes. And according to the *didaskalia* a regular agenda had developed for the process before the bishop.[57] Episcopal jurisdiction was a Christian institution similar to Jewish jurisdiction in the synagogue, where Jewish law was applied: Judaism was a *religio licita* with a privileged position in the Roman empire and Jewish jurisdiction had validity as an extraordinary form of litigation.[58]

Nevertheless, despite the differences between episcopal and secular practices, Constantine by *CTh* 1.27.1, a constitution of AD 333, defined episcopal jurisdiction as legal arbitration: the parties can apply to a bishop even if their case is already in front of a state judge: *etiamsi negotium apud iudicem sit inchoatum*. This quotation gives the main force of *CTh* 1.27.1: there was no need for regulations to enable the opponents to apply to a bishop, but it was necessary to prescribe that a process already in course before a state judge could be interrupted and be brought before a bishop, whose decision the state judge had to adopt.[59] *CTh* 1.27.1 is therefore no "introduction" or "approval" of episcopal jurisdiction in Roman law,[60] but rather an attempt to define the relation between religious and lay jurisdiction after Constantine's recognition of Christianity as a legal cult.

55 Caspers (1954: 18–21), Ziegler (1971: 109–42). 56 Caspers (1954: 21–22).

57 Herrmann (1980: 213). 58 Caspers (1954: 7–8), Ziegler (1971: 175–76), Herrmann (1980: 213).

59 Steinwenter (1950: 916), Caspers (1954: 18–21), Selb (1967: 171–85), Giradet (1975: 64–65), Herrmann (1980: 207–09).

60 See Lammeyer (1933: 194), Vismara (1937: 13–14), Klauser (1962: 173).

In AD 333, Constantine issued a further constitution on episcopal jurisdiction, the *constitutio ad Ablabium* (*Sirm.* 1). Since Gothofredus the genuineness of this constitution has been disputed.[61] Its main point, that a case can be brought before the bishop even over one side's objection (*etiamsi alia pars refragatur*), does not fit well into legal history. Later laws (*CJ* 4.7, 4.8) do not give the bishop this privileged position, so the regulation would have been revoked. It is in fact difficult to determine whether *Sirm.* 1 is genuine, however important the answer for the legal historical question of episcopal jurisdiction.[62] Gothofredus, Savigny, and de Francisci do not accept *Sirm.* 1 as genuine,[63] Haenel, Vismara, and Lammeyer do;[64] Caspers and Steinwenter think it contains interpolations.[65] Caspers sees especially the sentence *quicumque itaque litem habens ... etiamsi alia pars refragatur* as a later addition. It has – so Caspers – no logical connection to the preceding and following sentences. In his view grammatical features are also against this passage's being genuine.[66] If one leaves this passage of *Sirm.* 1 apart, this constitution just reconfirms *CTh* 1.27.1: the bishop is an arbiter who can be unanimously applied to by the opponents. The bishop should reconcile the adversaries, but he can also decide on a sentence that is to be prosecuted.[67]

Constantine's laws were confirmed by the emperors Arcadius and Honorius at the end of the fourth and the beginning of the fifth century, when Christianity became the state religion and the Roman empire was divided between East and West. *CJ* 4.7 (AD 398) allows the bishop to act as an arbiter when both sides apply to him unanimously (*si qui ex consensu apud sacrae legis antistitem litigare voluerint*).[68] *CJ* 4.8 (= *CTh* 1.27.2, AD 408) stipulates that, if both sides agree (*inter se consentientes*), they can come to the bishop, who will find a compromise between them.[69] This compromise has the value of a sentence from a state judge and is to be carried out by public authorities.[70]

In the Western Empire Valentinian in AD 455 again regulated the bishop's jurisdictional competency. He reconfirms in his *Novella* 35 a

[61] Denis Godefroy (Dionysius Gothofredus, 1549–1622) was the first editor of the *Corpus Iuris Civilis* (1583).

[62] See Selb (1967: 191–95), Herrmann (1980: 209), Kaser (1996: 528).

[63] De Francisci (1918: 51–53), Caspers (1954: 26).

[64] Haenel (1840, *non vidi*), Lammeyer (1933: 195), Vismara (1937: 23); for further literature see Selb (1967: 186–87).

[65] Steinwenter (1929/30: 660), Caspers (1954: 25–29).

[66] Caspers (1954: 28–29).

[67] Caspers (1954: 29), Ziegler (1971: 170), Herrmann (1980: 210), Gaudemet (1989: 231–32).

[68] Lammeyer (1933: 19), Steinwenter (1950: 916), Selb (1967: 197), Ziegler (1971: 170), Caspers (1954: 31).

[69] Caspers (1954: 32), Ziegler (1971: 172).

[70] Selb (1967: 205–06).

constitution from the emperors Arcadius and Honorius (*CTh* 16.11.1, AD 399) that restricted the bishop's legal competence to questions of religion.[71] All efforts undertaken by the church to insure that church officials should only be judged by a bishop were rejected. Like anybody else clerics could apply to the bishop, but only unanimously.

In the Eastern Empire Justinian put clerics and monks exclusively under the bishops' jurisdiction (*Nov.* 79.83).[72] *Nov.* 86.1.2 introduces a change in transferring proceedings from a state judge to a bishop: if somebody cannot accept the state judge's decision he can appeal to the bishop, and in an extreme case bishop and state judge can decide together.[73]

If we examine the emperors' constitutions attested in the papyri, we find a diverse picture that in many instances contradicts the law: not only bishops, but also priests and monks settle disputes, not only in their parishes but elsewhere as well. It is impossible to say with certainty whether they act officially or by their personal authority as spiritual fathers. It is also difficult to distinguish between cases of church discipline and those of worldly disputes.

The texts preserved on papyrus concern different types of cases: disputes about inheritance, landed property, and debts; disputes about marital problems as well. The documents come from different stages of the disputes in question: they give the sentence, they are the complaints from one side or they are writings by which the monk, priest, or bishop invites other people to take part in the process. Some documents show that not only the religious authority but also other clerics and laymen are in charge of settling the dispute. The documents never refer explicitly to the New Testament, the church fathers, or imperial constitutions, but the religious judges do have an elevated position and act as authorities superior to state judges. On the whole the cases documented in the papyri present a picture quite different from the theoretical regulations found in the constitutions of Roman law.

10.5.1 Bishop's decision about missing Christian books

P.Lips. I 43 (Lykopolis?, fourth century AD). Image at Papyri.info.

10.5.1 documents a case that may be seen as the classical form of episcopal jurisdiction: bishop Plousianos is the judge between Thaesis, a nun, and

[71] Caspers (1954: 34), Selb (1967: 204–05, 210–14), Ziegler (1971: 171).
[72] See Steinwenter (1950: 916).
[73] Steinwenter (1950: 916), Caspers (1954: 37), Hohlweg (1971: 55), Schweizer (1991: 163–64).

the heirs of Besarion. The papyrus is dated to the fourth century and comes possibly from Lykopolis, where a bishop Plousianos is attested from 325 until 347 (Worp 1994: 286–302).

Thaesis is accused of removing books, presumably from the inheritance of Besarion. She, like her opponents, was probably Besarion's heir, and their dispute concerned how to distribute what Besarion had left behind. Bishop Plousianos decides that the heirs of Besarion should present witnesses to testify to the theft, in which case Thaesis should return the books; or Thaesis should declare under oath that she did not steal the books. The question of theft being cleared, Besarion's property should be shared in equal parts between Thaesis and her opponents.

In this document, the bishop's decision is written down in short, precise form: date and place are given and so are the names of the persons involved (though the heirs of Besarion remain anonymous). The bishop sets out what has to be done and gives a deadline. What is attested in **10.5.1** is not the bishop's final decision, but just one step in the process: Besarion's heirs are to present witnesses to confirm the accusation. If the heirs are unable to find witnesses, Thaesis has the opportunity to confirm her position by oath.

The text shows the setting in which the process took place. Bishop Plousianos is sitting in the courtyard of his church. With him are not just Thaesis and Besarion's heirs. Also present are Dioskorides son of Hymnion, a city councilor; a second person, whose name is damaged; and a deacon (name lost). Probably the bishop was alone responsible for the decision. Dioskorides and the second (presumably) lay person were not present merely by coincidence, but had a certain (witnessing?) function. The deacon could have been the writer. The presence of one or more members of the city's ruling class suggests a public interest in the case. Lammeyer (1933: 200) and Dautzenberg (1971: 35) see all three as magistrates.

Pharmouthi 18 in the courtyard of the catholic church which is under Plousianos, most honorable bishop. In the process between the nun Thaesis and the heirs of Besarion the decision was pronounced by the said bishop Plousianos, serving as arbiter, in the presence of Dioskorides son of Hymnion, city councilor (*bouleutês*), and E[. . .] alias Herakleios son of Eith[. . . and NN], deacon, that either the heirs of Besarion should present witnesses charging Thaesis with having taken away Christian books, and that she should bring them back, or she should swear an oath that she never took any away, and thus all those things left behind in the house (should be divided) into two shares, Thaesis to have(?) one share and the heirs the other share; and this should happen before the thirtieth of the said (month) Pharmouthi.

10.5.2 Decision of the priest Sereu

P.Münch. I 14, lines 34–41 (Syene, 15 February AD 594). Image at *P.Münch.* I, Plates XXXI–XXXIV and XXXV (a).

In **10.5.2** the priest Sereu of Omboi settles a dispute between John son of James, and Patermouthis son of Menas, concerning James's estate. Patermouthis lived in Syene and first worked with his ship on the Nile; he was later a soldier. He owned several houses in Syene. John was also a soldier with some kind of family relation to Patermouthis. More documents are extant from Patermouthis and his family; most concern sales of property and inheritance disputes.[74] The texts of this archive are edited in *P.Münch.* I and *P.Lond.* V; for English translations see Porten (1996: 443–548); for the Coptic texts see Clackson (1995).

P.Münch. I 14 records in 111 lines John and Patermouthis' disagreement and Sereu's decision. The text was written by a notary and signed by witnesses; it presents the case and the process in great detail.

John and Patermouthis had been in dispute about the inheritance of James for a long time; they had earlier applied to different judges. After a first compromise in which he had declared himself fully satisfied, John applied to Kallinikos, *vicarius* of the city of Hermonthis,[75] accusing Patermouthis of having prevented his mother from giving him (John) four *solidi*. Patermouthis was fined seven *solidi*, but he sued John in turn. Finally they agreed to approach the priest Sereu as their arbiter. Upon careful consideration, Sereu decided that John had to pay five *solidi* to Patermouthis, but should receive four from his mother.

Lines 34–41 (**10.5.2**) show how the process before Sereu was conducted. According to these lines both parties were present before the priest Sereu. They explain the case's circumstances and put forward arguments in favor of their respective positions. Sereu listens to both parties, considers the circumstances and arguments that have been presented, and then renders his decision. In settling this dispute Sereu, unlike Plousianos in the preceding document, is functioning independently of any church organization.

[74] See Heisenberg, *P.Münch.*, Introduction, pp. 6–14, and Farber (1990).

[75] The *vicarius* was the second-in-command of the troops stationed in a town; see Gelzer (1913: 354–56), Rémondon (1961: 47).

He just happens to be in Syene when John and Patermouthis are arguing about James's estate. As the text puts it just before the excerpt given below, although he was a priest of the Holy Church of Omboi, he was "found by chance (*kata tuchên*) in this city of Syene." It appears there were no regulations about whether a cleric had the right to act as an arbiter in another diocese. For John and Patermouthis Sereu's decision is enough. His spiritual authority gives sufficient ground for his competence as an arbiter; an institutional authorization is unnecessary. It should be remarked that despite the informal character of this type of jurisdiction the case was not unimportant: Sereu here settles a long-lasting dispute that had previously been considered in other venues, one of them being that of the already-mentioned *vicarius* of Hermonthis.

> And then, when they came before his Godbelovedness, each side offered to him his own pleas of justification. He, after he had listened to what was in dispute between them, and after he had also gone through the settlements brought forward by Patermouthis, made for him and his wife Kako by the aforesaid John; and not only that, but after examining the arbitration-award given to John and his mother by the said most eloquent teacher (*grammaticus*) concerning the mortgage of the house, in which he awarded and decided that four *solidi* be given to John by his mother . . .[76]

10.5.3 Woman's letter to her spiritual father

O. Vind. Copt. 258 (Theban region, seventh–eighth century AD)

While John and Patermouthis applied to Sereu together, **10.5.3** documents a case in which one party comes to the arbiter first and later on the second party follows. The text, in Coptic, is preserved on an ostracon.

10.5.3 is a letter from a woman to a spiritual father: she reacts to an accusation put forward by her opponent, she explains her views of the case, and she promises her acceptance of the arbiter's decision. According to her description Anoup has planted a palm tree on her land. She complained to the priest and "the great men" of the village, and Anoup promised to take the palm tree away. But then he brought the case before the spiritual father, whom now the woman addresses. She writes the letter unprompted, probably after having heard that Anoup had accused her. She describes the

[76] Translation adapted from Porten (1996: 536–37).

case as she sees it and declares at the end of the letter that she will abide by the spiritual father's decision.

Like **10.5.2** above, the present case had a long history. The spiritual father addressed in **10.5.3** is the second arbiter; the priest and the great men of the village were the first. In **10.5.1** above, bishop Plousianos decided the case of Thaesis and the heirs of Besarion on his own; Dioskorides and the others were just attendants. In contrast, in the present matter of Anoup's palm tree, the village's "great men" and the priest were apparently on equal terms.

First I fall to your feet and kiss the footstool of the feet of your holy and in every way honored Fatherhood. Anoup came south and spoke some words to your Lordship about a little date palm that he had planted on my ground. Anyway, he spoke to you in truth or in lie. But there is no lie with the great men, the least with you, father of us all. And everybody in the whole village knows about this place that it is mine. So I brought together the priest and the great men of the village. And when I managed to make them speak against him, he said: "I will remove it." [. . .] then he went to court with me [. . .] as it comes [. . .] But whatever your Fatherhood will send us, I shall not disobey you. Farewell in the Lord, holy, honorable, Christ-loving father.
Your servant full of sins.

10.5.4 Conflict about a marriage

SB IV 7449 (= Bell 1924: esp. 140) (Oxyrhynchos, second half fifth century AD)

10.5.4 is another example of a one-sided process-opening before a spiritual father, documenting a conflict about a marriage.

With this letter Aurelia Nonna accuses Alypios, a monk, of having tried to give her daughter as a wife to one of his relatives. When the daughter resisted, the monk beat the mother. Aurelia Nonna complains to bishop Theodore, asks him to call Alypios to him and to judge between him and her. She promises she will accept the bishop's decision. Even if bishop Theodore was the ecclesiastical superior to the monk Alypios, this is not really a case of church discipline. The monk is active in a secular context in a matter that he certainly took as a family affair. Aurelia Nonna does not accept this and therefore addresses the bishop.

To the most holy and most pious Apa Theodore, bishop of the illustrious and most illustrious city of the Oxyrhynchites, from Aurelia Nonna of the village of Spania of the Oxyrhynchite nome. Alypios a monk, native of our village, who is our nephew, desired to give (in marriage) my little daughter to Apaion, also a relative of ours. And the administrators of our estate, who are unwilling to restore it to me, were eager to do this. Since therefore The[. . .], my daughter, (does not?) wish to marry him, and acting in defiance of his cloth, the monk beat me and tore my clothing and ruined it, therefore I beg your holiness to have compassion upon me and order him to be brought (before you), and for me to receive whatever decision you shall approve of, my lord, most holy bishop. I, Aurelia Nonna, have presented this petition.[77]

10.5.5 Arbitration by a bishop

BKU II 318 (Hermonthis, early seventh century AD)

Among the more than 2,400 papyri and ostraca in which bishops, priests, deacons, and monks are mentioned there are two groups of texts that document the office of the bishop in detailed context: the archive of bishop Pesynthios of Koptos and the archive of bishop Apa Abraham of Hermonthis. Both archives preserve interesting texts about settling disputes, but as there is no recent and reliable edition of the Pesynthios texts,[78] a case from the Apa Abraham archive will be presented here.

Apa Abraham (*floruit c.* AD 600) was the head of the Monastery of Phoibammon in Thebes and bishop of Hermonthis at the same time.[79] The monastery was built into the ruins of the ancient Egyptian temple of Queen Hatshepsut (Eighteenth Dynasty). When the Egyptologist Eduard Naville and his team excavated the temple in the nineteenth century,[80] many ostraca were found in the ground that was being cleared. Among these ostraca were the letters of bishop Apa Abraham.[81] They refer to the installation of clerics, to the celebration of the Eucharist, and to questions about baptism and marriage. The bishop finds regulations for church conflicts, excludes people from the Eucharist, expels clerics from the clergy and, in some cases, readmits them. The present selection, in Coptic, is unusual in that it documents a conflict that is not ecclesiastical but secular.

[77] Translation taken from Bell (1924: 142–43).

[78] The old edition is Revillout (1900, 1902, 1914); the texts from no. 61 (1902: 44) onwards do not belong to the Pesynthios archive; see Krause (1958: 10). A new edition is being prepared by J. van der Vliet – see van der Vliet (2002).

[79] Krause (1956: 21–29; 1969: 66).

[80] See Godlewski (1986: 13–20).

[81] Krause (1984: 750–51).

Bishop Apa Abraham acts as an arbiter between two parties, only one of whom is with him. The other is informed by this letter. A *lashane* (a village headman) has come to Apa Abraham together with the great men of his village, because he had a conflict with a certain Apa Victor and his great men. Apparently Apa Victor is a *lashane* himself and the letter documents a conflict between the two village heads or, more generally, between the two villages. Apa Abraham managed to persuade the *lashane* to make peace with Apa Victor. The *lashane* asked the bishop to inform Apa Victor that he was willing to make peace and that he (the *lashane*) would like to talk with Apa Victor. **10.5.5** is bishop Apa Abraham's letter to Apa Victor. This document of episcopal arbitration presents a bishop as peacemaker. As in the sense used by Christian writers of the fourth and fifth centuries Apa Abraham is not a judge in the strict sense of the word, but he tries, here successfully, to reconcile the two parties in the spirit of Christian love and peace.

As illustrated in this section, settlement of conflicts in the community is one of the continuities that pervade the history of Christianity. Biblical texts, early Christian writers, and church councils give normative and sometimes factual evidence for this praxis. When the Roman empire became Christian, settling disputes by clerics became a part of public life. The Roman emperors tried to define it juridically as arbitration by bishops. The papyri and ostraca show that there was a great variety of forms of dispute settlements. People addressed monks and priests as well as bishops, and they in turn decided on their own or in consultation with spiritual or secular authorities.

First I greet your sonship. The Lord bless you through God's mercy. God gave us the good *lashane* (i.e., village headman) and those who rule amidst the people. When therefore he came now to our humbleness with his brothers and the great men and all the people of the town, we asked their sonships for peace, that there would be peace amidst you together with them at once. For it is written: "Who destroys war, establishes peace." When we asked them for peace, they said, "Be so good as to write to them, 'We agree on peace.' Be so good as to send us the outcome of the matter as it is." May the Lord bless you and give you peace with those who are amidst you at once. Be so good to us and send me the outcome, how you want to talk to them by God. I pray for the well-being of all of you. Give it to my pious children, Apa Victor and all the great men together, from Abraham, the most humble.

10.6 Monks as mediators in Christian Egypt

Chrysi Kotsifou

In the *Historia Monachorum*, the following incident is recounted to Apa Paphnutius by a brigand:

> He [the brigand] found a beautiful woman wandering in the desert who was being pursued by agents of the governor and the city councilors because of her husband's arrears of taxes and was bitterly lamenting her vagabond life. He asked her why she was crying. She replied, "Do not ask me, master; do not question me in my misery but take me anywhere you wish as your handmaid. For my husband has often been flogged during the last two years because of arrears of taxes amounting to three hundred gold coins. He has been put in prison and my beloved three children have been sold as slaves. As for me, I have become a fugitive and move from place to place. I now wander in the desert but I am frequently found and flogged. I have been in the desert now for three days without eating anything." "I felt sorry for her," said the brigand, "and took her to my cave. I gave her the three hundred gold coins and brought her to the city, where I secured her release together with that of her husband and children." In the fashion of a true ascetic, Paphnutius replies, "I am not aware myself of having accomplished anything equal to this."[82]

Greek and Coptic letters from Byzantine Egypt offer a picture regarding monks as mediators that differs from Apa Paphnutius' modest self-assessment at the end of the foregoing report. Claudia Rapp notes that these letters reveal "the direct and largely unadulterated voice of the holy men and their correspondents," while at the same time, they provide a corrective to the literary creations of hagiographers.[83]

This section discusses the role of monks and holy fathers as mediators in Byzantine Egypt. Monks were actively involved in settling disputes, releasing prisoners, and intervening with the local magistrates for the benefit of people who felt they were wronged. The data are primarily derived from Greek and Coptic papyri and ostraca from the fourth to the early eighth century AD that contain letters and petitions to ascetics and heads of monastic communities. Besides the aforementioned issues, these papyri and ostraca also raise pertinent questions regarding prison conditions and the status of children in Byzantine Egypt. In searching for the reasons people resorted to monks to mediate their affairs, the ineffectuality of courts and judges is the first explanation to be offered. Contemporary opinion seems to have been that

[82] Festugière (1961: 102–04). Translation by Russel (1980: 95) (slightly modified in articulation).
[83] Rapp (1999: 67).

judges and wealthy landlords could not be trusted to be impartial or effective. Apa Shenoute, head of the White Monastery at the end of the fourth century and the beginning of the fifth, offers in his sermon *De Iudicio* a vivid picture of corrupt judges receptive to bribes, and of rich landlords careless about the residents of their lands and only concerned with giving their dogs expensive meat while poor people begged outside their doors.[84]

This phenomenon is also reflected in *CTh* 9.27.6 (AD 439), which states:

> The same Augusti (Gratian, Valentinian, and Theodosius) and Arcadius Augustus: An edict to the provincials.
>
> We order, we urge, that if any person honored by public office, any decurion, landholder, or finally even a tenant in bondage, or a person of any class whatever has suffered extortion in any manner at the hands of a judge, if anyone knows that a penalty has been remitted for a price or inflicted through depraved cupidity, finally, if anyone can prove that a judge has been unjust in any kind of case either during his administration or after his administration has been laid aside, the provincial shall come before the public officials, he shall report the crime, he shall prove his accusation, and when he proves his charge he shall obtain both victory and glory.[85]

Traianos Gagos and Peter van Minnen further elaborate on the settling of disputes outside courts, suggesting that the weaker parties in social terms stood a better chance in informal settings than in courts dominated by the peers of their socially stronger adversaries. They add that there is hardly any positive evidence for the use of the courts to settle disputes after about AD 500.[86] Two reasons seem probable. One is that going to court was procedurally complicated, costly, and time-consuming. Another is that Egyptians in the Byzantine period favored an approach based on personal relationships to solve problems between members of their communities, especially within their families.[87]

Arthur Schiller also proposed that the Council of Chalcedon (AD 451) and the subsequent schism of the Orthodox Church could be another reason for the Copts' preference for arbitration and mediation. He sums up his argument:

[84] Belhmer (1996: 11 and 39).

[85] On corrupt judges, see also Jones (1990: 517). He notes that there was one law for the poor and another for the rich, and that if the two parties were evenly matched in wealth and rank, justice might be impartially rendered. But if one of the parties was poor and the other rich and of rank, then courts favored the latter.

[86] Gagos and van Minnen (1994: 41); see Schiller (1971: 502).

[87] Gagos and van Minnen (1994: 42–43).

> The sole ray of hope for the lowly peasant or villager was the possibility of appeal to the emperor. Then, with almost one stroke, at the beginning of the sixth century, this prospect was removed. With the Emperors Justin and Justinian the orthodox tenets of the Council of Chalcedon gained full imperial support. Ever since the assemblage of the Council, followers of monophysitism had been in a position of peril. But now all chance of belief in their version of Christianity was denied the Copts. The deep religious feeling of these people at this period is well known. Is it not possible that the intensely fervid and religious Copts yielded to despair, and in their frustration thereafter shunned all unnecessary contact with government officials? . . . But the people would turn to the respected members of their own communities – and not in their capacity as minor local officials, but as trusted co-religionists – for aid as arbiters or as mediators in settling their little disputes, their family and inheritance troubles, the enforcement of their petty agreements, their rights in the little plots of land they claimed to own or lease and about which they were quarreling.[88]

This is a rather exaggerated view, however, because as Gagos and van Minnen note, "thoroughly 'orthodox' Christians elsewhere preferred private settlements too."[89] Nevertheless, we can assume that after the Council of Chalcedon, the followers of the Monophysite Church referred their cases to their Monophysite bishops and monks for settlement, while the Orthodox Egyptians went to their own bishops and monks.[90]

Besides monks, bishops were also approached to settle arguments outside court. In general, there were three ways to solve a dispute outside court in Byzantine and early Islamic Egypt, namely negotiation, arbitration, and mediation. When the disputants got together by themselves, solved their dispute without the intervention of a third party, and then put the terms of their own settlement in a deed, that was a negotiation. When the assistance of a third party for the settlement was asked for, then we have arbitration or mediation. The difference is that mediators had no power to compel compliance while the decision of an arbiter was supported by the authority vested in him by the parties who had chosen him as the final authority in their dispute.[91] In general monks served as mediators while bishops served as arbiters.

In **10.5**, Georg Schmelz analyzes state and Church law and their stipulations regarding the arbitral duties of bishops. In considering the papyrus evidence, he discusses the extent to which these laws were reflected in

[88] Schiller (1971: 501–02). [89] Gagos and van Minnen (1994: 43).

[90] For the role and activities of bishops after the Council of Chalcedon, see Wipszycka (2007).

[91] Allam (1992: 3) and Jones (1990: 517). See also Gagos and van Minnen (1994: 32).

everyday life. More specifically, he notes that during the reign of Justinian, if a party was not pleased with the decision of a state judge, then he (or she) could also apply to a bishop. Additionally, Schmelz concludes that the papyrological evidence shows that people applied to monks and priests as often as bishops; they decided alone or together with spiritual and secular authorities. But he points out that it is impossible to determine whether monks and priests acted officially or by their personal authority as spiritual fathers. My study of the letters addressed to monks requesting their mediation demonstrates that it was the latter case. Monks and ascetics acted as mediators based upon the spiritual authority that was vested in them by the Church, and most importantly by the lay community that surrounded them, and not because they were legally bound to do this. In addition there is no evidence, papyrological or hagiographical, to suggest that monks could legally force disputants to abide by their decisions.

The documents show that monastic fathers were repeatedly approached for mediation by a variety of people. The poor, widows, but also rich and powerful figures asked the monks' help in resolving hostile or potentially disruptive situations. This activity was one facet of monks' social interactions with lay people and of the charitable work they provided.[92]

Early on, the sources make it clear that the fathers who were approached were well established in their communities; often their fame had spread farther afield. Most, as the letters (in Greek and Coptic) to the ascetic Apa John suggest,[93] were also well educated and bilingual. The Apa John just mentioned was a famous monk whose status allowed him to engage with military and civil officials. Scholars have tried repeatedly to associate him with one or another of the holy fathers named John and known from hagiographical writings like Palladius' *Lausiac History*.[94] Constantin Zuckerman supports the theory that the Apa John in the papyri is the same as the John of Lykopolis that we know from the hagiographical writings of visitors to Egypt, such as Palladius and Cassian.[95] Claudia Rapp and Tim Vivian, on the contrary, would like him to be John

[92] The variety of social and economic interactions of monks and ascetics with their surrounding communities is too wide a topic to be discussed in this chapter. In the past decade, James E. Goehring (see Goehring 1999) has worked on all these aspects, and his treatment of both hagiographical and documentary sources has definitively proved that monastics did not spend their lives in complete isolation, away from everyday affairs and concerns.

[93] Zuckerman (1995: 189) explains that study of the letters to and from Apa John indicates that his native tongue was Coptic. For the most recent update on all the Greek and Coptic papyri that relate to the Apa John archive, see Choat and Gardiner (2006).

[94] Butler (1898–1904, vol. 2: 100–06).

[95] Zuckerman (1995: 190–91). Bagnall and Cribiore (2006: 204) seem also to share this belief.

of Hermopolis.[96] In either case, the fact remains that his archive offers valuable information about the number and variety of petitions for mediation that monks received.

This role of the holy men does not diminish in time: they were just as active in the eighth century AD as they were in the fourth. Petitioners had a firm belief in the monks' powers of intercession both with God and with the authorities in their area.[97] In a Coptic letter addressed to Apa John, *P.Ryl.Copt.* 311, the sender explains that he is asking for the father's help because "I know that which you shall say, God will grant it to you."[98] In addition, they expected monks to mediate on their behalf as part of the latter's charity work. In *P.NagHamm.* 68, this theme is stressed as the monk Harpokration asks father Sansnos to intervene and stop the harassment of another brother because of due rents; he specifies: "But be diligent, beloved, and come to the assistance of the brother; for thus it behooves your charity in Christ."

Despite all the social, political, and cultural circumstances that favored the intervention of monks, I believe that the most important factor was that monks from early on actually had the economic resources to bring to fruition these charity affairs. *P.Cair.Masp.* III 67312, the will of Flavius Theodore drafted on 31 March AD 567, is an excellent example of this situation. By his will Theodore bequeaths all his estates to the White Monastery; he further specifies that his houses in Antinoopolis are to be sold and the money used for the release of prisoners.[99]

96 Rapp (1999: 71–72) and Vivian (2005a: 347–49).

97 Brown (1982 [1971]) redefined the role of monks in their surrounding communities. He discussed for the first time the crucial role monks played as intercessors and mediators, and the great degree to which people around them, from all walks of life, depended on them. Although Brown studies primarily the case of Syria and the hagiographical writings that relate to that country, his results apply to Byzantine monasticism in the entire Mediterranean region. Also see Brown (1995: 55–78). Almost thirty years later, Rousseau (1999) reconsidered Brown's model; he tries in particular to put more emphasis on the function of the hagiographical literature in promoting the role of monks as mediators.

98 Claudia Rapp (1999: 72) explains that the men and women who approached these monks were emphatic and explicit in their belief that these men were holy and possessed the power of intercession. They were convinced that the exemplary ascetic lifestyle of these holy men assured their prayers of being heard by God. Further, Tim Vivian (2005a: 328) notes that the business requests in the papyri and ostraca "rather than detracting from the intercessory nature of faith – as if business somehow sullied prayer – make the letters doubly intercessory: many of the letters ask for intercessory prayer while many other letters ask the holy man to intercede in some business dealing – to supply some product, to intervene in a troubled business dealing, or to send some business to the writer – and other letters ask for both at the same time."

99 For monks and their help with prisoners, see below, **10.6.4**.

10.6.1 Letter for a prisoner's release

O.Crum Ad. 27 (Karnak, sixth–seventh century AD)

10.6.1 is a Coptic letter from Karnak, from the sixth or seventh century, written by Komes to Apa Jeremias asking him to intervene for the release of a prisoner. Komes concludes his letter by asking for the Apa's wishes for his own and his servant's health, a kind of blessing. The letter reads:

> Let your Fatherhood have pity on the prisoner. Truly, it is the time of work. I need him because I do not have anyone. Send me your (wishes for) the health by him, and send me the (wishes for) the health of the servant, so that he is healthy. But now more than all these things, I greet your Fatherhood. Give it to my beloved father, Apa Jeremias, from Komes.

10.6.2 Request from the villagers of Nesoi

P.Neph. 19 (Herakleopolite nome, Pathor, fourth century AD). Image at Papyri.info.

The mediation requests addressed to monks and ascetics cover a variety of situations. Fathers settled disputes between entire communities and between single individuals; they intervened for persons who were in trouble with the authorities. Some documents refer to tribulations faced by whole villages or communities for which the assistance of the holy father was essential for reestablishing peace. In *P.Mon.Epiph.* 216, the *lashane* (village headman) thanks a monk for an intervention that brought peace to the whole community, while in *P.Mon.Epiph.* 163, the *lashane*, with several other people from his village, entreats the father to mediate for the release of several of their brothers, who are imprisoned in a neighboring community.

In **10.6.2** the village of Nesoi asks father Paul to go to them and help them resolve a situation which apparently threatens to devastate their village. They conclude that they will not take any action until he goes to them. This insistence of the villagers that father Paul go in person to solve the crisis points up, first, that monks could mediate either in person, or through correspondence, or through another person; and, second, that the presence of the father was preferred and probably considered much more effective than just a word from him.

The editors of the archive to which **10.6.2** belongs reserve judgment as to what exactly is happening that is threatening these villagers, but it seems likely that the village of Nesoi was involved in a dispute over land.

The same kind of incident is recounted in the story of Apa Apollo in the *Historia Monachorum* when the ascetic had to restore peace between two villages that had come into armed conflict over the ownership of land.[100] Finally, a different possibility is illustrated in a letter of Besa, the successor of Apa Shenoute as head (*hêgoumenos*) of the White Monastery. In his letter "To the Dignitaries and People of the Villages," the abbot urges the presbyters, deacons, administrators, and headmen of various villages not to start a fight over a relic, "a piece of wood" as he calls it.[101]

> To my most honorable lord, Father Paul, from the community of the village of Nesoi. We entreat you, Lord Father, in the name of God and the whole village, not to consider (just) interceding,[102] but deem it worthy to come to us, so that they will not obliterate all of us, and if you wish something, order it and it will be done, and if you want them dead, we will carry it out ourselves. Because they are laying waste the whole village. But we, the whole village, entreat you not to set anything in motion. Come to us and what you want we will do. We pray for your health for many years.

10.6.3 Widow's petition to Apa John

P.Herm. 17 (tr. Bagnall and Cribiore 2006: 204) (Lykopolis [found in Hermopolis], *c.* AD 380). Image at Papyri.info.

Monks also concerned themselves with cases of a single person who had a dispute with another individual or was in trouble with the authorities. These people were from all walks of life. Noticeably, the *lashane* (village headman) of Djême often depended on Apa Epiphanius' intervention. Thus, in *P.Mon.Epiph.* 183, he writes to Epiphanius recounting losses and hardships endured, and begs for an investigation. In *P.Ryl.Copt.* 270, Porphyra asks the help of Apa John once again and mentions his interrogation at the *bêma* ("rostrum") of the prefect, while *P.Herm.* 10 is a letter written by John the anchorite and others to a man who may have been an ecclesiastic or an ascetic. They express their appreciation for his past help,

100 Festugière (1961: 58); Russel (1980: 74).

101 Kuhn (1956, vol. 1: 129–30 [text], vol. 2: 123–34 [translation]). For sixteen more letters from the Nepheros archive translated into English, see Vivian (2005b).

102 The verb is *entungkanô* whose meaning can be "converse with, talk to" but also "petition, appeal to." The latter is the way it is used at this point.

and ask him to intervene on their behalf with the judge in order to avoid a trial on a (purportedly) false charge.

The reasons monks were asked to mediate with local authorities on behalf of other people were varied and sometimes eccentric. To this group belongs **10.6.3**, the petition to Apa John, in Greek, from the widow named Leuchis.

The first editor of this letter took "them" to refer to prostitutes because its grammatical form is feminine. Bagnall and Cribiore (2006: 204) convincingly argue against this: despite the feminine form, "them" must refer to Gothic soldiers staying in Leuchis' house, no group of women having been mentioned before. It was an old custom to billet soldiers in the houses of ordinary people.

> To my lord the pious Apa John, Leuchis daughter of Malamos. Your goodness embraces all those without resources; and let your mercy extend to me too, lord. After God, I await your help, that you ask the tribune of the Goths to remove them from my house, since I am a widow woman. My lord, do it for God's sake.

10.6.4 Letter from an imprisoned recruit

P.Herm. 7 (tr. Vivian 2005a: 348) (Lykopolis [found in Hermopolis], fourth century AD). Image at Papyri.info.

Many petitions for intervention by monks refer to the release of prisoners. Four letters addressed to Apa John, the fourth-century ascetic from Lykopolis, concern prisoners. They are *P.Ryl.Copt.* 272, 310, 311, and *P.Herm.* 7 (**10.6.4**). Prisoners, or people writing in their behalf, write to monks begging them to pay the money required for their release. **10.6.4** is an exemplary petition. Once again, it is addressed in Greek to the famous Apa John (for whom, see above, **10.6** introduction). This time it is from a recruit called Psois.

In this case, Psois was a recruit who probably injured his finger on purpose to avoid being drafted.[103] This action did not work, and as a result he was imprisoned.[104] He then pledged his children in order to come up

[103] This action recalls the ruling in *CTh* 7.22.1: "If they should be judged useless for military service because their fingers have been cut off, We order them to be assigned, without any ambiguity, to the performance of the compulsory public services and duties of decurions."

[104] Zuckerman (1995: 186–87). He also explains that self-mutilation was against the law and various emperors had decreed against it. More specifically, Theodosius I (*CTh* 7.13.10) prescribed that fingerless candidates should be drafted nevertheless, at the rate of two for one valid recruit.

with the money to be released. Apa John was the one responsible for delivering the money and arranging this, but he had not succeeded. Therefore, Psois, in frustration, sent him this, begging for the monk's further action.

> To my master, beloved Apa John. I give thanks to God and to whoever will help me with you, through you and through God, for all souls live through you on account of your godliness [towards] the Almighty. So now help me: write a letter to Psois from Taetos, the tribune, to release me – if I have not already been released. I ask this because Psois' son has already demanded seven gold *solidi* from me and his assistant another gold *solidus*. You received money from me so I might be released, but they have not released me. I ask God that you either get me released or return to me the eight gold *solidi*. I am Psois son of Kyllos, from the village of Pochis in the Antaiopolite nome.
>
> Now, then, for God's sake do not neglect to do this, master, for you (*read* "I") have already put up my children as collateral to the moneylender for the gold and never serve in the army, being unfit for service. Because of my finger; I have a good reason for this; it has not festered, but it has not healed either. Deliver to my master, the anchorite John.

10.6.5 Letter concerning a prisoner's release

P.Mon.Epiph. 167 (Thebes, sixth–seventh century AD)

This is a Coptic counterpart to the preceding document, from the Monastery of Epiphanius at Thebes.

Most of the people mentioned in the text were imprisoned because they could not make the payments of their taxes or were otherwise in debt.[105] *P.Ryl.Copt.* 273 concerns a person imprisoned because his land was carried away by the river's water. Now he wants Apa John to intervene with the prefect so that he be given other fields so as to overcome his financial

[105] Torallas Tovar (2006: 105 n. 14). We have to assume that these prisoners were kept both in state and private prisons. Fikhman (1970: 129) explains that despite imperial law, large estates maintained their own armed troops and prisons. Van Minnen (2000) discusses the treatment of war prisoners in Graeco-Roman Egypt. He takes the noun *aixmalôtos* always to refer to war prisoners; thus his study also includes several documents that are in this section. See especially van Minnen (2000: 159 and 162). But *aixmalôtos* and *aixmalôsia* are very generic terms that just mean, respectively, "prisoner" and "captivity." There is nothing in my texts to limit these terms to indicating prisoners of war and imprisonment as a consequence of war.

burdens. Farmers were needed to work in the fields.[106] Long terms of incarceration would have been detrimental to the economy.[107] **10.6.1** made this explicit. Thus farmers' wives or children were often put in prison in their place.[108]

In order for the prisoners to convey the urgency of their situation and thus encourage the Apa to act as soon as possible, they describe sometimes how they were imprisoned for reasons unknown (*BKU* I 144); or they refer to themselves as "the poor who are imprisoned" (*O.CrumST* 374); or they claim they are dying from hunger while in custody (*O.Crum* 209, *P.Mon.Epiph.* 219).[109] In *P.Mon.Epiph.* 177, they also mention the tortures they endured, torments like hanging upside-down.

Monks and bishops through their acts of Christian charity were often the only hope for these prisoners. Canon law gave bishops the right to supervise prisons in an effort to provide for the protection of prisoners. The Canons of Pseudo-Athanasius consider visits to prison as a duty not only of the bishop but also of the presbyter (priest).[110] In *P.Oxy.* XIX 2238, we learn that the hospital of Oxyrhynchos, which belonged to the bishopric, possessed a prison, possibly for sick prisoners.

The references to children in these petitions to monks are meant to be poignant. One of the topics that prisoners regularly stress to their addressees is that their children had been used as security for their debts, and eventually were taken as slaves as a result of those debts. For example, *P.Lond.* VI 1916, from a Melitian archive,[111] dated *c.* AD 330–40, mentions among other things that "we desire to inform you concerning this beloved Pamonthius that he is in great straits and has suffered most shamefully at the hands of certain pitiless and godless men, that you too may help him [. . .] from your superfluity to dwell in the love which is in heaven. By all means then help him without hesitation, because creditors have carried off his children into slavery." In *P.Ryl.Copt.* 310, yet another letter addressed to Apa John, a widow laments: "And thereafter that merchant

[106] Torallas Tovar (2006: 105).

[107] Jones (1990: 521) notes that ordinary people could not count on immediate trial, and they could stay for months or years in prison.

[108] Torallas Tovar (2006: 105).

[109] Jones remarks that prisons were overcrowded and no food was provided. Prisoners had to depend on their friends and family for their sustenance (Jones 1990: 522; Torallas Tovar (2006: 108).

[110] Torallas Tovar (2006: 109–10) and van Minnen (2000: 158–59).

[111] The Melitian schism started when Melitius, bishop of Lykopolis in Upper Egypt, objected to the readmission of lapsed Christians as decreed by Peter I of Alexandria. Melitians were persecuted and Melitius himself was exiled. Papyrological evidence points to a thriving Melitian monastic community in the fourth century, and scattered evidence indicates that the sect survived until the eighth century (Timbie 1991).

too went north and constrained him and delivered him to the magistrate, a papa,[112] and he [. . .] him, saying, 'He is my debtor for 170,000 talents.' And he shut him up and maltreated him, till, against his will, he wrote, (making over) to him his children."

Jones remarks (1990: 853–54) that parents were forbidden to sell their children or pledge them for debt – although they frequently did so. The Emperor Constantine allowed food and clothing to the poor parents to prevent the selling of their children.[113] It is, however, only documents from the fourth and early fifth centuries AD, namely *P.Lond.* VI 1915 (**9.3.1**), 1916, *P.Herm.* 7 (**10.6.4**), and *P.Ryl.Copt.* 310, that mention children in this context. Can it be that this custom was subsequently abandoned?[114]

> This humble Isaac writes greeting his beloved brothers who are honored in all good ways, Abraham, and Peter, and their mother. Since afterwards you came into my humility (and) you said, "Release my brother so that he comes," now, be kind, do not throw the affair aside. According to what you said, "If my brother comes, God do His kindness." Now, do the charity and show your kindness to the poor prisoners, so that the beloved Lord Jesus Christ may bless you and all of your house. Truly, therefore, do not throw away our entreaty. Farewell in the Lord.

[112] The use of the term *papa*, father, in this document is ambiguous. In his edition Crum mentions that the term does not necessarily need to be an ecclesiastical title. Furthermore, the role of the prefix *rm* is unclear. Förster (2002: 608), however, claims that the term *papa* in Coptic documents was strictly an ecclesiastical title.

[113] See Richter (2005: 251–54).

[114] In the late Byzantine and early Islamic years in Egypt, children appear in another fascinating set of documents, namely the child donation documents, where male children were donated by their parents to monasteries. The latest treatment is Richter (2005).

Concordance

A. LIST OF TEXTS

2.1.1	*P.Cair.Zen.* I 59001
2.1.2	*P.Dion.* 14
2.1.3	*P.Tebt.* II 312
2.1.4	*P.Col.* IV 76
2.1.5	*P.Adl.* 4
2.1.6	*P.Oxy* XLIX 3487
2.1.7	*P.Sakaon* 64
2.1.8	*P.Ant.* I 42
2.1.9	*P.Oxy* II 277
2.1.10	*P.Ryl.* IV 600
2.1.11	*P.Corn.* 10
2.6.1	*P.Oxy* I 34 verso
2.6.2	*P.Oxy.* II 237 Col. VIII, lines 27–43
2.6.3	*BGU* III 959
2.6.4	*BGU* V 1210 §100
2.6.5	*P.Oxy.* XII 1475
2.6.6	*P.Fam.Tebt.* 15, lines 75–98
2.6.7	*P.Flor.* III 357
2.6.8a	*BGU* III 981 Col. I, lines 1–11
2.6.8b	*P.Lips.* I 123
2.7.1	*CPR* IV 34, lines 1–41
3.1.1	*P.Dryton* 19
3.1.2	*P.Dryton* 3
3.1.3	*P.Dryton* 34
3.1.4	*P.Dryton* 8
3.2.1	*P.Brit.Mus.* 262 + *M.Chr.* 181
3.2.2	*P.Ryl.* II 1617
3.2.3	*P.Mich.* V 301
3.3.1	*BGU* I 326
3.3.2	*CIL* XVI 122
3.3.3a	*M.Chr.* 309
3.3.3b	*P.Oxy.* LIV 3758, lines 134–55
3.3.3c	*P.Coll.Youtie* I 64, lines 18–20
3.3.3d	*P.Oxy.* XXII 2348, lines 50–56
3.3.4a	*FIRA* III 59

3.3.4b	*FIRA* III 60
3.3.5	*P.Oxy.* XII 1466
4.1.1	P.Louvre 2433
4.1.2	*BGU* IV 1052
4.1.3	*P.Cair.Masp.* III 67310 + *P.Lond.* V 1711
4.2.1	*P.Lond.* II 178
4.2.2	*P.Stras.* III 142
4.2.3	*P.Cair.Masp.* II 67153
4.2.4	*P.Cair.Preis.* 2–3
4.2.5	*P.Lond.* V 1651
4.2.6	*P.Lips.* I 41
4.3.1	*P.Vind.Bosw.* 6
4.3.2	*P.Oxy.* XXXIV 2710
4.3.3	*P.Oxy.* XII 1467
4.3.4	*CPR* VI 78
4.3.5	*P.Oxy.* IX 1208
4.4.1	*P.Diog.* 18
4.4.2	*BGU* I 90 *et al.*
4.4.3	*P.Petaus* 2
4.4.4	*P.Oxy.* XL 2913 Col. II
4.4.5	*P.Lond.* II 324
4.4.6	*SB* XXIV 15987
4.5.1	*P.Brit.Mus. Andrews* I
4.5.2	*P.Petrie* I^2 3, lines 9–38
4.5.3	*P.Dryton* 2
4.5.4	*P.Mil.Vogl.* II 84
4.5.5	*P.Oxy.* XXXVIII 2857
4.6.1a	*BGU* IV 1185
4.6.1b	*SB* VIII 9790
4.6.2a	*P.Catt.* recto Col. IV, lines 1–15
4.6.2b	*BGU* I 140
4.6.3	*BGU* I 19, lines 1–19
4.6.4	*CPR* I 18
4.6.5a	*SB* I 1010
4.6.5b	*SB* VI 9298a+b
4.6.6	*BGU* V 1210 §4
5.1.1	*P.Schreibertrad.* 14
5.1.2	*P.Dryton* 27
5.1.3	*P.Chic.Haw.* 10
5.1.4	*O.Tempeleide* 150
5.2.1	*P.Tebt.* III.1 817
5.2.2	*P.Dion.* 16
5.2.3	*P. Amh.* II 48
5.2.4	*P.Dryton* 21
5.3.1	*P.Kron.* 9
5.3.2	*SB* XII 10786
5.3.3	*P.Oxy.* XXVII 2471
5.3.4	*P.Oxy.* III 530, lines 1, 10–32
5.4.1	*Stud.Pal.* XX 2
5.4.2	*P.Tebt.* III.1 817

5.4.3	*P.Ryl.* II 177
5.4.4	*P.Oslo* II 40a
5.4.5a	*SB* XII 10804
5.4.5b	*DDD* III 23
5.4.6	*BGU* XIV 2376
5.5.1	*P.Mich.* III 188
5.5.2	*P.Mich.* X 587
5.5.3	*P.Coll.Youtie* II 92
5.5.4	*BGU* III 729
6.1.1	*P.Fam.Theb.* 3 +4
6.1.2	*P.Brit.Mus. Andrews* 28
6.2.1	*P.Brit.Mus. Glanville* 10525
6.2.2	*P.Recueil* 4
6.2.3	*P.Tsenhor* 15
6.2.4	*P.Teos and Thabis* 12
6.2.5	*P.Brit.Mus.* 262
6.3.1	*P.Oxy.* I 99
6.3.2	*P.Oxy.* IV 719, lines 13–29
6.3.3	*P.Mich.* X 583
6.3.4	*SB* V 7638
6.3.5	*P.Ryl.* II 164, lines 1–15
6.3.6	*P.Mich.* V 274
6.4.1	*P.Sarap.* 10
6.4.2	*P.Sarap.* 11
6.4.3	*P.Sakaon* 62
6.4.4	*O.Ber.* II 125
6.4.5	*P.Oxy.* LVIII 3915
6.4.6	*P.Oxy.* XIV 1705
6.4.7	*P.Oxy.* X 1277
6.4.8	*P.Stras.* III 184
6.5.1	*BGU* XIV 2398
6.5.2	*P.Adl.* 13
6.5.3	*P.Hal.* I Col. XI
6.5.4	*P.Vind.Sal.* 4 recto
6.5.5	*P.Mich.* V 266
6.6.1	*P.Münch.* I 11
6.6.2	*P.KRU* 6
6.6.3	*P.Mon.Apollo* 24
6.6.4	*P.Lond.Copt.* I 673
6.6.5	*P.Teshlôt* 2
6.6.6	*P.Cair.Arab.* I 57
7.1.1	P.Brit.Mus. EA 10560
7.1.2	P.Brit.Mus. EA 10230
7.1.3	P.Brit.Mus. EA 10597
7.1.4	*P.Tebt. Botti* 1
7.2.1	*P.Rev.* 36, lines 3–19
7.2.2	*P.Hib.* I 81, lines 12–18
7.2.3	*P.Tebt.* I 32
7.2.4	*P.Tebt.* I 124, lines 23–45
7.2.5	P.Haun. inv. 407, lines 33–62

7.2.6	*P.Moscow* 123, lines 1–2
7.3.1	*P.Col.* III 54
7.3.2	*P.Frankf.* 2
7.3.3	*BGU* IV 1116
7.3.4	*P.Soter* 2
7.3.5	*P.Amh.* II 85
7.3.6a	*P.Kron.* 27
7.3.6b	*P.Kron.* 29
7.3.7	*W.Chr.* 359
7.3.8	*P.Turner* 25
7.3.9	*P.Fouad* 43
7.3.10	*P.Oxy.* L 3597
7.3.11	*P.Stras.* I 30
7.3.12	*SB* XII 10982
7.4.1	*CPR* IV 114
7.4.2	*O.Crum Ad.* 15
7.4.3	*P.Lond.* III 1012
7.4.4	*CPR* IV 117
7.4.5	*O.CrumVC* 33
7.4.6	*BKU* I 48
7.4.7	*P.Lond.Copt.* I 487
7.4.8	*Chrest.Khoury* II 29
8.1.1	*P.Cair.Zen.* II 59182
8.1.2	*P.Corn.* 4
8.1.3	*P.Petr.* III 43 (2) recto Cols. II–III, line 7
8.2.1	*P.Fay.* 91
8.2.2	*P.Oxf.* 10
8.2.3	*P.Oxy.* LXIII 4353
8.2.4	*P.Coll.Youtie* II 92
8.2.5	*P.Oxy.Hels.* 29
8.2.6	*BGU* IV 1106
8.2.7	*P.Oxy.* XXXVIII 2859
8.2.8	*CPR* XVII A 19
8.2.9	*P.Col.* X 255
8.2.10	*P.Oxy.* XLVII 3354
8.2.11	*P.Grenf.* I 58
8.2.12	*P.Lond.* V 1694
8.3.1	*P.Oxy.* XIV 1692
8.3.2	*SB* VI 9503
8.3.3	*P.Oxy.* I 194
8.3.4	*P.Oxy.* XXVII 2478
9.1.1	*P.Lille* I 29
9.1.2	*P.Hal.* I Cols. VIII–IX
9.1.3	*P.Harr.* I 61, lines 1–15
9.1.4	*P.Col.* I 480, lines 1–22
9.2.1	*P.Oxy.* III 475
9.2.2	*PSI* XII 1254
9.2.3	*P.Oxy.* IV 714
9.2.4	*P.Brux.* I 19

9.2.5	*P.Oxy.* IV 716
9.3.1	*P.Lond.* VI 1915
9.3.2	*SB* III 6097
9.3.3	*SB* XVIII 13274
10.1.1	*P.Eleph.Wagner* 1, col. 1
10.1.2	*P.Col.* IV 83
10.1.3	*P.Petrie* III 21g + *P.Gur.* 2
10.1.4	*P.Tebt.* I 5, lines 207–20
10.2.1	*P.Polit.Jud.* 1
10.2.2	*P.Polit.Jud.* 3
10.2.3	*P.Polit.Jud.* 4
10.2.4	*OGIS* 737
10.3.1	*P.Oxy.* I 37
10.3.2	*P.Fam.Tebt.* 19
10.3.3	*P.Mich.* III 159
10.3.4	*P.Mich.* III 175
10.3.5	*P.Oxy.* VIII 1101
10.3.6	*P.Oxy.* LXIII 4381
10.4.1	*P.Oxy.* LI 3620
10.4.2	*P.Oxy.* LXI 4122
10.4.3	*P.Oslo* III 95
10.4.4a	*P.Oxy.* I 64
10.4.4b	*P.Oxy.* I 65
10.4.4c	*BGU* XVII 2701
10.4.5	*P.Lips.* I 40
10.4.6	*P.Oxy.* IX 1186
10.5.1	*P.Lips.* I 43
10.5.2	*P.Münch.* I 14, lines 34–41
10.5.3	*O.Vind.Copt.* 258
10.5.4	*SB* IV 7449
10.5.5	*BKU* II 318
10.6.1	*O.Crum Ad.* 27
10.6.2	*P.Neph.* 19
10.6.3	*P.Herm.* 17
10.6.4	*P.Herm.* 7
10.6.5	*P.Mon.Epiph.* 167

B. CONCORDANCE OF DOCUMENTS

The concordance provides references to the first publication named for each document. For other editions and for other available translations (e.g., in *Sel.Pap.*) the reader should consult the headings and introductions to the individual documents. Documents are classified below according to their principal language. Thus a Demotic document with a Greek docket will be listed as Demotic, but documents in which two languages are significantly present are classified as bilingual. Several of the documents listed as Greek are obviously translations from Latin. Consult the individual documents for details.

1. Greek

BGU I 19, lines 1–19	**4.6.3**
BGU I 90 *et al.*	**4.4.2**
BGU I 140	**4.6.2b**
BGU I 326	**3.3.1**
BGU III 729	**5.5.4**
BGU III 959	**2.6.3**
BGU III 981 Col. I, lines 1–11	**2.6.8a**
BGU IV 1052	**4.1.2**
BGU IV 1106	**8.2.6**
BGU IV 1116	**7.3.3**
BGU IV 1185	**4.6.1a**
BGU V 1210 §4	**4.6.6**
BGU V 1210 §100	**2.6.4**
BGU XIV 2376	**5.4.6**
BGU XIV 2398	**6.5.1**
BGU XVII 2701	**10.4.4c**
CPR I 18	**4.6.4**
CPR VI 78	**4.3.4**
CPR XVII A 19	**8.2.8**
M.Chr. 309	**3.3.3a**
O.Ber. II 125	**6.4.4**
OGIS 737	**10.2.4**
P.Adl. 4	**2.1.5**
P.Adl. 13	**6.5.2**
P.Amh. II 48	**5.2.3**
P.Amh. II 85	**7.3.5**
P.Ant. I 42	**2.1.8**
P.Brux. I 19	**9.2.4**
P.Cair.Masp. II 67153	**4.2.3**
P.Cair.Masp. III 67310 + *P.Lond.* V 1711	**4.1.3**
P.Cair.Preis. 2–3	**4.2.4**
P.Cair.Zen. I 59001	**2.1.1**
P.Cair.Zen. II 59182	**8.1.1**
P.Catt. recto Col. IV, lines 1–15	**4.6.2a**
P.Col. I 480, lines 1–22	**9.1.4**
P.Col. III 54	**7.3.1**
P.Col. IV 76	**2.1.4**
P.Col. IV 83	**10.1.2**
P.Col. X 255	**8.2.9**
P.Coll.Youtie I 64, lines 18–20	**3.3.3c**
P.Coll.Youtie II 92	**5.5.3**
P.Corn. 4	**8.1.2**

P.Corn. 10	**2.1.11**
P.Diog. 18	**4.4.1**
P.Dion. 14	**2.1.2**
P.Dion. 16	**5.2.2**
P.Dryton 2	**4.5.3**
P.Dryton 3	**3.1.2**
P.Dryton 8	**3.1.4**
P.Dryton 19	**3.1.1**
P.Dryton 21	**5.2.4**
P.Dryton 34	**3.1.3**
P.Eleph.Wagner 1, col. 1	**10.1.1**
P.Fam.Tebt. 15, lines 75–98	**2.6.6**
P.Fam.Tebt. 19	**10.3.2**
P.Fay. 91	**8.2.1**
P.Flor. III 357	**2.6.7**
P.Fouad 43	**7.3.9**
P.Frankf. 2	**7.3.2**
P.Grenf. I 58	**8.2.11**
P.Hal. 1 Cols. VIII–IX	**9.1.2**
P.Hal. 1 Col. XI	**6.5.3**
P.Harr. I 61, lines 1–15	**9.1.3**
P.Haun. inv. 407, lines 33–62	**7.2.5**
P.Herm. 7	**10.6.4**
P.Herm. 17	**10.6.3**
P.Hib. I 81, lines 12–18	**7.2.2**
P.Kron. 9	**5.3.1**
P.Kron. 27	**7.3.6a**
P.Kron. 29	**7.3.6b**
P.Lille I 29	**9.1.1**
P.Lips. I 41	**4.2.6**
P.Lips. I 43	**10.5.1**
P.Lips. I 123	**2.6.8b**
P.Lond. II 178	**4.2.1**
P.Lond. II 324	**4.4.5**
P.Lond. III 1012	**7.4.3**
P.Lond. V 1651	**4.2.5**
P.Lond. V 1694	**8.2.12**
P.Lond. VI 1915	**9.3.1**
P.Mich. III 175	**10.3.4**
P.Mich. III 188	**5.5.1**
P.Mich. V 266	**6.5.5**
P.Mich. V 274	**6.3.6**
P.Mich. V 301	**3.2.3**
P.Mich. X 583	**6.3.3**
P.Mich. X 587	**5.5.2**
P.Mil.Vogl. II 84	**4.5.4**
P.Münch. I 11	**6.6.1**
P.Münch. I 14, lines 34–41	**10.5.2**

P.Neph. 19	**10.6.2**
P.Oslo II 40a	**5.4.4**
P.Oslo III 95	**10.4.3**
P.Oxf. 10	**8.2.2**
P.Oxy. I 34 verso	**2.6.1**
P.Oxy. I 37	**10.3.1**
P.Oxy. I 64	**10.4.4a**
P.Oxy. I 65	**10.4.4b**
P.Oxy. I 99	**6.3.1**
P.Oxy. I 194	**8.3.3**
P.Oxy. II 237 Col. VIII, lines 27–43	**2.6.2**
P.Oxy. II 277	**2.1.9**
P.Oxy. III 475	**9.2.1**
P.Oxy. III 530, lines 1, 10–32	**5.3.4**
P.Oxy. IV 714	**9.2.3**
P.Oxy. IV 716	**9.2.5**
P.Oxy. IV 719, lines 13–29	**6.3.2**
P.Oxy. VIII 1101	**10.3.5**
P.Oxy. IX 1186	**10.4.6**
P.Oxy. IX 1208	**4.3.5**
P.Oxy. X 1277	**6.4.7**
P.Oxy. XII 1466	**3.3.5**
P.Oxy. XII 1467	**4.3.3**
P.Oxy. XII 1475	**2.6.5**
P.Oxy. XIV 1692	**8.3.1**
P.Oxy. XIV 1705	**6.4.6**
P.Oxy. XXII 2348, lines 50–56	**3.3.3d**
P.Oxy. XXVII 2471	**5.3.3**
P.Oxy. XXVII 2478	**8.3.4**
P.Oxy. XXXIV 2710	**4.3.2**
P.Oxy. XXXVIII 2857	**4.5.5**
P.Oxy. XXXVIII 2859	**8.2.7**
P.Oxy. XL 2913 Col. II	**4.4.4**
P.Oxy. XLVII 3354	**8.2.10**
P.Oxy. XLIX 3487	**2.1.6**
P.Oxy. L 3597	**7.3.10**
P.Oxy. LI 3620	**10.4.1**
P.Oxy. LIV 3758, lines 134–55	**3.3.3b**
P.Oxy. LVIII 3915	**6.4.5**
P.Oxy. LXI 4122	**10.4.2**
P.Oxy. LXIII 4353	**8.2.3**
P.Oxy.Hels. 29	**8.2.5**
P.Petaus 2	**4.4.3**
P.Petrie I^{2} 3, lines 9–38	**4.5.2**
P.Petrie III 21g + *P. Gur.* 2	**10.1.3**
P.Petrie III 43 (2) recto Cols. II–III, line 7	**8.1.3**
P.Polit.Jud. 1	**10.2.1**
P.Polit.Jud. 3	**10.2.2**

P.Polit.Jud. 4	**10.2.3**
P.Rev. 36, lines 3–19	**7.2.1**
P.Ryl. II 161	**3.2.2**
P.Ryl. II 164, lines 1–15	**6.3.5**
P.Ryl. II 177	**5.4.3**
P.Ryl. IV 600	**2.1.10**
P.Sakaon 62	**6.4.3**
P.Sakaon 64	**2.1.7**
P.Sarap. 10	**6.4.1**
P.Sarap. 11	**6.4.2**
PSI XII 1254	**9.2.2**
P.Soter 2	**7.3.4**
P.Stras. I 30	**7.3.11**
P.Stras. III 142	**4.2.2**
P.Stras. III 184	**6.4.8**
P.Tebt. I 5, lines 207–20	**10.1.4**
P.Tebt. I 32	**7.2.3**
P.Tebt. I 124, lines 23–45	**7.2.4**
P.Tebt. II 312	**2.1.3**
P.Tebt. III.1 817	**5.2.1**
P.Turner 25	**7.3.8**
P.Vind.Bosw. 6	**4.3.1**
P.Vind.Sal. 4 recto	**6.5.4**
SB I 1010	**4.6.5a**
SB III 6097	**9.3.2**
SB IV 7449	**10.5.4**
SB V 7638	**6.3.4**
SB VI 9298a+b	**4.6.5b**
SB VI 9503	**8.3.2**
SB VIII 9790	**4.6.1b**
SB XII 10786	**5.3.2**
SB XII 10804	**5.4.5a**
SB XII 10982	**7.3.12**
SB XVIII 13274	**9.3.3**
SB XXIV 15987	**4.4.6**
Stud.Pal. XX 2	**5.4.1**
W.Chr. 359	**7.3.7**

2. Latin

CIL XVI 122	**3.3.2**
P.Coll.Youtie I 64, lines 18–20	**3.3.3c**
P.Mich. III 159	**10.3.3**

3. Bilingual Greek and Latin

FIRA III 59	**3.3.4a**
FIRA III 60	**3.3.4b**
P.Lips. I 40	**10.4.5**
P.Oxy. XII 1466	**3.3.5**
P.Oxy. LXIII 4381	**10.3.6**

4. Demotic

DDD III 23	**5.4.5b**
O.Tempeleide 150	**5.1.4**
P.Brit.Mus. 262	**3.2.1**
P.Brit.Mus. 262 + *M. Chr.* 181	**6.2.5**
P.Brit.Mus. Andrews 1	**4.5.1**
P.Brit.Mus. Andrews 28	**6.1.2**
P.Brit.Mus. EA 10230	**7.1.2**
P.Brit.Mus. EA 10560	**7.1.1**
P.Brit.Mus. EA 10597	**7.1.3**
P.Brit.Mus. Glanville 10525	**6.2.1**
P.Chic.Haw. 10	**5.1.3**
P.Dryton 8	**3.1.4**
P.Dryton 27	**5.1.2**
P.Fam.Theb. 3 + 4	**6.1.1**
P.Louvre 2433	**4.1.1**
P.Moscow 123, lines 1–2	**7.2.6**
P.Recueil 4	**6.2.2**
P.Schreibertrad. 14	**5.1.1**
P.Tebt.Botti 1	**7.1.4**
P.Teos and Thabis 12	**6.2.4**
P.Tsenhor 15	**6.2.3**

5. Greek–Coptic (bilingual)

CPR IV 34, lines 1–41	**2.7.1**

6. Coptic

BKU I 48	**7.4.6**
BKU II 318	**10.5.5**
CPR IV 114	**7.4.1**
CPR IV 117	**7.4.4**
O.Crum Ad. 15	**7.4.2**
O.Crum Ad. 27	**10.6.1**
O.CrumVC 33	**7.4.5**

O.Vind.Copt. 258	**10.5.3**
P.KRU 6	**6.6.2**
P.Lond.Copt. I 487	**7.4.7**
P.Lond.Copt. I 673	**6.6.4**
P.Mon.Apollo 24	**6.6.3**
P.Mon.Epiph. 167	**10.6.5**
P.Teshlôt 2	**6.6.5**

7. Arabic

Chrest.Khoury II 29	**7.4.8**
P.Cair.Arab. I 57	**6.6.6**

Suggested reading for introductions to papyrology in English

Bagnall, R. S. (1993). *Egypt in Late Antiquity*. Princeton.
ed. (2009). *The Oxford Handbook of Papyrology*. Oxford.
Lewis, N. (1983). *Life in Egypt under Roman Rule*. Oxford.
(1986). *Greeks in Ptolemaic Egypt*. Oxford.
Pestman, P. W. (1994). *The New Papyrological Primer*. 2nd edn. rev. Leiden.
Turner, E. G. (1980). *Greek Papyri: An Introduction*. 2nd edn. Oxford.

Glossary of technical terms

In the glossary the linguistic origins of words and terms, or principal language of use, are noted in parentheses as: A = Arabic, E = Egyptian, G = Greek, L = Latin. Note that many technical Greek words are also found in Coptic (late Egyptian in a mostly Greek alphabet).

ab intestato (L)	Without valid last will and testament
actio furti (L)	The Roman-law action for theft
actio rerum amotarum (L)	The Roman-law "action for things removed," available to one spouse against another (the Romans were reluctant to call this theft)
aediles curules (L)	Anglicized as curule aediles; Roman magistrates created 367 BC. They were in charge of the marketplace, weights, measures, etc.; influential in the law of sale
agoranomos (G)	Plural, *agoranomoi*. Municipal official in Ptolemaic and early Roman Egypt; supervised the marketplace and served as notary in various transactions
agraphos gamos (G)	Literally, an "unwritten marriage," i.e., a valid marriage but one without written contract
akhet (E)	The first four months of the ancient Egyptian calendar, corresponding to the season of inundation/autumn
antichrêsis (G)	Loan whose creditor is granted use of pledged land or house property in lieu of interest
archeion (G)	Record office, archive

archidikastês (G)	Judicial official, chief judge based in Alexandria
aroura (G)	Standard unit of area for land in Egypt, *c.* ⅔ acre, 0.275 hectare
arrabôn (G)	Pledge, earnest-money in a contract of sale
artaba (E, G)	Persian loanword; Egyptian dry measure for wheat, barley, beans, etc.; capacity is variable
athlophoros (G)	Title of a priestess of Berenike II, literally "Bearer of the (Olympic) prize," common in Ptolemaic dating formulas
Aurelius (L, G)	Plural, Aurelii. Most individuals with this name are likely to have been recipients or descendants of recipients of Roman citizenship as a consequence of the *Constitutio Antoniniana*, AD 212 (q.v.)
basilikogrammateus (G)	"Royal scribe": second main official in the nome (q.v.) after the *stratêgos* (q.v.)
bebaiôsis (G)	Warranty, guarantee, assurance; in particular, promise of legal protection for the buyer provided by the seller in a contract of sale
beneficiarius (L)	Plural, *beneficiarii*. In the Byzantine period a staff officer of military status.
cheirographon (G)	A "handwritten," non-notarial contract; legal document in the form of a letter
choachytês (G)	Plural, *choachytai*. Egyptian priest, embalmer
choinix (G)	Plural, *choinikes*. $^1/_{40}$ or $^1/_{48}$ of an artaba (q.v.)
chôra (G)	Generally, the Egyptian "countryside" as distinct from Alexandria
chrêsis (G)	A type of loan
Constitutio Antoniniana (L)	Edict of Caracalla, AD 212, bestowing Roman citizenship on all free inhabitants of the empire
conventus (L)	In the Roman period, the prefect's judicial sessions at major cities outside Alexandria according to a fixed schedule
cretio (L)	Plural, *cretiones*. An heir's formal declaration of acceptance of an inheritance

curator civitatis (L)	Chief municipal official in fourth-century (AD) Egypt. The Greek equivalent is *logistês* (q.v.)
daneion (G)	A type of loan
deben (E)	Egyptian monetary unit found in Demotic documents, valued at 20 drachmas (q.v.)
dekanos (G)	An Egyptian police officer
diagramma (G)	Official decree
diagraphê (G)	Decree; also a receipt issued for payment of money
dînâr (A)	Gold coin of the Arab period, term borrowed from the Roman *denarius*
drachma (G)	Basic currency unit of Ptolemaic and Roman Egypt, specified as silver or bronze depending on circumstances
duplum (L)	As a penalty, double
eisagôgeus (G)	Officer ("introducer") in charge of bringing cases into court
embadeia G)	Procedure by which a creditor entered upon possession of pledged property
enoikêsis (G)	In lieu of interest, a creditor's right to occupy land or inhabit house property pledged as security for a loan (see *antichrêsis*)
ephebe (G)	A youth of the gymnasial class who had reached the age of puberty
epigonê (G)	"Descent," even if legally fictive, as in Persian of the *epigonê* (q.v.)
epikatabolê	Procedure by which a creditor entered upon possession of pledged property
epikrisis (G)	Procedure for certifying membership in the gymnasial class
epistratêgos (G)	Regional governor of the Thebaid (Upper Egypt) in the Ptolemaic period; in the Roman period, one of four territorial "sub-prefects" of equestrian rank
epitagma-unit (G)	Large cavalry detachment, several thousand strong, Ptolemaic period
epitropos (G)	Equivalent of the Latin *curator*, a legal guardian in private law

epoikion (G)	Rural settlement, smaller than and sometimes administratively attached to a village
ergolabos (G)	Contractor in an *ergolabia*-contract (work contract)
exêgêtês (G)	An official associated with the municipal gymnasium
gentilicium (L)	Originally, a Roman family, or "gentile," name; later a possible sign of Roman citizenship; see above s.v. Aurelius
Gnomon of the *Idios Logos*	A collection of rules or precedents assembled for the Roman fiscal official or procurator of equestrian rank in charge of the state account, or *Idios Logos*. The text, preserved primarily in *BGU* V 1210, dates to the second century AD, but some rules are much earlier (Ptolemaic, Augustan)
grapheion (G)	Plural, *grapheia*. Office where contracts were drawn up and registered
gymnasiarchos (G)	Chief official of a municipal gymnasium
hedna (G)	Bride-price, wedding-gift (*LSJ*)
hêmiolion (G)	50 percent penalty
hiereus (G)	Greek term for priest
hieros pôlos (G)	Greek term for a type of Egyptian priest
holokottinos	Coptic for *solidus* (q.v.)
homologia (G)	Generic term for agreement, contract, whether in subjective (1st person) or objective (3rd person) form
hypallagma (G)	A type of mortgage: debtor retains possession but creditor has special position against other claimants; see 5.4 introduction
hypêretês tagmatos (G)	Ptolemaic cavalry officer
hypomnêma (G)	Literally, "memorandum": a form of petition or, in other circumstances, a contractual offer
hypomnêmatographos (G)	Recorder of deeds, notary
hypothêkê (G)	A type of mortgage, officially certified in the creditor's favor; see 5.4 introduction
Idios Logos	See under Gnomon of the *Idios Logos*

indiction (L)	Term for the cycle of taxation, fixed at 15 years in AD 312; a standard component of dating formulas from then on into the Islamic period
iuridicus (L)	Judge
ius liberorum (L)	Augustan Roman-law right to legal independence for a free woman with three children, a freedwoman with four
kanêphoros (G)	Literally, "basket-bearer"; title of the priestess of Queen Arsinoe II, common in Ptolemaic dating formulas
katagraphê (G)	Property registration, effecting transfer of title
katalogeion (G)	Record-office in Alexandria
katoikic land (G)	Category of land assigned in the Ptolemaic period to cavalrymen of high rank; in the Roman period, a special category of private land
keramion (G)	Plural, *keramia*. Liquid measure for wine, olive oil, etc.; capacity unknown
keration (G)	Plural, *keratia*. Fraction (sometimes $^1/_{24}$) of a *solidus* (q.v.)
kite (E)	Egyptian monetary unit, equivalent to 2 drachmas (q.v.)
kleruch	Ptolemaic military settler to whom was allotted a "klêros," or parcel, of land
kolobon (G)	Plural, *koloba*. A measure, common in the Byzantine period, for wine, fodder, charlock, etc.
komogrammateus (G)	Village scribe
kosmêtês (G)	An official of the gymnasium
kratêsis (G)	The "conquest" of Egypt by Augustus in 31/30 BC; alternatively, possessory or ownership rights
kyrieia (G)	Proprietary rights
kyrios (G)	Male guardian, especially (as evidenced in the papyri) over women, in various legal settings
laographoi (G)	Roman period, collectors of poll-tax

Lex Julia (et) Titia (L)	Law of Augustus (date unknown) regarding the appointment of guardians for women by provincial governors (cf. *kyrios*)
Lex Laetoria (L)	Or *Plaetoria*. Roman law of 192/1 BC protecting legally independent minors (to age 25) from fraud
logistês (G)	Greek equivalent of *curator civitatis* (q.v.)
matrona stolata (L)	Roman wife of high status, entitled to wear a dress, *stola*, with purple hem
menein-contract (G)	A type of mortgage; see 5.4 introduction
meris/merides (G)	Subdivision(s) of a nome (q.v.), in particular the Arsinoite nome
metropolitan (G)	High-ranking citizen of a *metropolis*, or nome capital; in the Roman period entitled to pay poll-tax at a reduced rate
mina (G)	A Semitic loanword: unit of weight and currency worth 100 drachmas (q.v.)
naubion (G)	A cubic measure applied to earth, as a unit of labor (*LSJ*)
neôkoros (G)	Priestly title; temple warden
nome (G)	Regional administrative unit in Egypt; there were about forty of them, each with its own *metropolis* and chief executive officers, especially *stratêgos* (q.v.) and *basilikogrammateus* (q.v.)
nomisma, nomismation	Greek for solidus (q.v.)
nomophylax (G)	Plural, *nomophylakes*. In the Roman and Byzantine periods, a local police officer
numerus (L)	Military unit, Byzantine period, with a strength of about 500; the Greek equivalent is *arithmos*
oikonomos (G)	Plural, *oikonomoi*. A financial official in charge of a nome (q.v.), especially in the Ptolemaic period; in the Byzantine period, the economic overseer of a monastery
ônê en pistei (G)	A fiduciary sale: a form of security by which property is transferred to the creditor, but the debtor retains possession and right of redemption

paramonê (G)	A service or work contract, whereby one party becomes indentured to another
parathêkê (G)	Gratuitous contract for the safekeeping of cash and/or valuables; the Latin *depositum*, deposit
pastophoros (G)	A type of low-level Egyptian priest
patria potestas (L)	The theoretically absolute power of the Roman family-father (*paterfamilias*) over the members and property of his extended family or household (*familia*)
pêchus (G)	Plural, *pêcheis*. "Cubit": a measure for urban property lots; 100 × 100 *pêcheis* = 1 aroura (q.v.)
peculium (L)	The "nest egg" or assets set aside for slaves or sons in power (q.v. *patria potestas*) to operate with as if their own
peret (E)	The second third of the ancient Egyptian calendar, corresponding to the growing season of the agricultural year/winter
Persian of the *epigonê* (G)	A subordinate legal status assumed, e.g., by debtors in loans of the Ptolemaic and Roman periods
phosphoros (G)	A title of a priestess, lit. "Bearer of Fire"
phrontistês (G)	In private law, equivalent to the Latin *curator*, a guardian (cf. *epitropos*); alternatively, an estate steward (Roman period)
phylarch (G)	Chief officer of a *phylê*, one of the political divisions of the city of Oxyrhynchus
praeses (L)	A civil governor of an Egyptian province in the Byzantine period
praktôr xenikôn (G)	A type of tax-collector, also concerned with the execution of loans secured by mortgage and the auction sale of such property in cases of default
prasis epi lysei (G)	"Sale with right of redemption." A type of loan contract in which the lender is couched as the purchaser of the property that was pledged to secure the loan
praxis (G)	Right of action, execution, pursuant to a contract

prefect (L)	Roman governor of Egypt, an official of high equestrian rank, *Praefectus Aegypti*
prochreia (G)	Advance payment, advance loan
prytanis (G)	President, chief executive officer of a municipal council
pterophoros (G)	Plural, *pterophoroi*. Class of Egyptian priest, literally "wearing feathers" (on their heads)
riparius (L, G)	Plural, *riparii*. Village or metropolitan police officer, Byzantine period
Senatus consultum (L)	Plural, *Senatus consulta*. Decree of the Roman Senate (with the force of law)
sestertius (L)	Roman coin; 4 sestertii = 1 denarius
sextarius (L)	Plural, *sextarii*. A liquid measure, literally a "sixth" part, roughly a pint
shemu (E)	The last third of the ancient Egyptian calendar, corresponding to harvest season/summer
solidus (L)	Plural, *solidi*. Standard gold coin following Diocletian's currency reform at the end of the third century (AD), stabilized under constantine
statêr (G)	A measure of weight, but also a denomination of money, equivalent to 4 drachmas or the silver tetradrachm
stephanêphoros (G)	Literally, "crown-wearer." Priestess, common in Ptolemaic dating formulas
stolistês (G)	Plural, *stolistai*. Class of Egyptian priest, in charge of the sacred vestments
stratêgos (G)	Plural, *stratêgoi*. Chief administrator of a nome (q.v.) in the Ptolemaic and Roman periods
synchôrêsis (G)	Contract or agreement
syngraphê (G)	Contract or agreement
syngraphophylax (G)	Literally, "guardian of contracts," a notary
talent (G)	Unit of weight, but also a unit of (bronze) currency especially in the Byzantine period
tamias (G)	Plural, *tamiai*. Literally, a "treasurer," but also an official concerned with the registration of sales

testamenti factio (L)	Privilege of legally independent Roman citizens to make, take under, and witness a will
tetartai (G)	Taxes of 25 percent, Ptolemaic period; also, a unit of weight for gold
trimêsion (G)	Alternatively, *tremissis* (Latin loanword). One-third of a *solidus* (q.v.)

Works cited

Abbott, F. F. and A. C. Johnson (1926). *Municipal Administration in the Roman Empire*. Princeton.

Abbott, N. (1938). *The Kurrah Papyri from Aphrodito in the Oriental Institute*. Studies in Ancient Oriental Civilization 15. Chicago.

Achelis, H. and J. Flemming (1904). *Die ältesten Quellen des orientalischen Kirchenrechts II: Die syrische Didaskalia*. Texte und Untersuchungen zur Geschichte der altchristlichen Literatur. Neue Folge, x. Band, 2. Heft. Leipzig.

Adams, B. (1964). *Paramone und verwandte Texte: Studien zum Dienstvertrag im Rechte der Papyri*. Neue Kölner rechtswissenschaftliche Abhandlungen 35. Berlin.

Adams, J. N. (2003). *Bilingualism and the Latin Language*. Cambridge.

Allam, S. (1985). "Bemerkungen zur Abstandschrift," *Enchoria* 13: 1–5.

(1991). "Glossen zu einem schiedsrichterlichen Verfahren," *Mitteilungen des Deutschen Archäologischen Instituts, Abteilung Kairo* 47: 1–9.

(1992). "Observations on civil jurisdiction in late Byzantine and early Arabic Egypt," in *Life in a Multi-Cultural Society: Egypt from Cambyses to Constantine and Beyond*. Ed. J. H. Johnson. Studies in Ancient Oriental Civilization 51. Chicago. Pp. 1–8.

(1994a). "The agreement after judgement," in *Acta Demotica. Acts of Fifth International Conference for Demotists. Pisa, 4th–8th September 1993*. Egitto e Vicino Oriente 17. Pisa. Pp. 19–28.

ed. (1994b) *Grund und Boden in Altägypten (Rechtliche und sozio-ökonomische Verhältnisse). Akten des internationalen Symposions Tübingen 18.–20. Juni 1990*. Untersuchungen zum Rechtsleben im Alten Ägypten 2. Tübingen.

(2008). "Regarding the *EISAGOGEUS* (εἰσαγωγεύς) at Ptolemaic law courts," *JEgH* 1: 3–19.

Allen, J. P. (2002). *The Heqanakht Papyri*. Publications of the Metropolitan Museum of Art Egyptian Expedition 27. New York.

Alston, R. (1995). *Soldier and Society in Roman Egypt: A Social History*. New York.

(2001). "Urban population in late Roman Egypt and the end of the Ancient World," in *Debating Roman Demography*. Ed. W. Scheidel. Leiden. Pp. 161–204.

(2002). *The City in Roman and Byzantine Egypt*. London.

Amelotti, M. (1966). *Il testamento romano attraverso la prasi documentale*, vol. 1: *Le forme classiche di testamento*. Florence.
Amelotti, M. and G. I. Luzzatto (1972). *Le costituzioni giustinianee nei papiri e nelle epigrafi*. Milan.
Amelotti, M. and L. Migliardi Zingale (1985). *Le costituzioni giustinianee nei papiri e nelle epigrafi*. 2nd edn. Milan.
Amundsen, D. W. and G. B. Ferngren (1978). "The forensic role of physicians in Ptolemaic and Roman Egypt," *Bulletin of the History of Medicine* 52: 336–53.
Anagnostou-Cañas, B. (1991). *Juge et sentence dans l'Égypte romaine*. Paris.
(2000). "La documentation judiciaire pénale dans l'Égypte romaine," *Mélanges de l'École Française de Rome: Antiquité* 112: 753–77.
Andrews, C. A. R. (1990). *Ptolemaic Legal Texts from the Theban Area*. Catalogue of Demotic Papyri in the British Museum 4. London.
Arjava, A. (1996). *Women and Law in Late Antiquity*. Oxford.
(1997). "The guardianship of women in Roman Egypt," in *Akten des 21. internationalen Papyrologenkongresses, Berlin 13–19.8.1995*, vol. 1. Stuttgart. Pp. 25–30.
(1998). "Paternal power in late antiquity," *JRS* 88: 147–65.
(1999a). "Die römische Vormundschaft und das Volljährigkeitsalter in Ägypten," *ZPE* 126: 202–04.
(1999b). "Eine Freilassung aus der väterlichen Gewalt, CPR VI 78," *Tyche* 14: 15–22.
Assmann, J. (2002). *The Mind of Ancient Egypt: History and Meaning in the Time of the Pharaohs*. New York.
Austin, M. M. (2006). *The Hellenistic World from Alexander to the Roman Conquest: A Selection of Ancient Sources in Translation*. 2nd edn. Cambridge.
Azzarello, G. (2012). *Il dossier della "domus divina" in Egitto*. Archiv für Papyrisforschung Beiheft 32. Berlin.
Baade, E. C. (1956). *Jurisdiction in Roman Egypt*. Ph.D. dissertation, Yale University.
Bagnall, R. S. (1977). "Prices in 'sales on delivery'," *Greek, Roman and Byzantine Studies* 18: 85–96.
(1982). "Religious conversion and onomastic change in early Byzantine Egypt," *BASP* 19: 105–24. Reprinted as chapter 8 in Bagnall (2003).
(1985). "The camel, the wagon, and the donkey in Later Roman Egypt," *BASP* 22: 1–6. Reprinted as chapter 16 in Bagnall (2003).
(1987). "Conversion and onomastics: a reply," *ZPE* 69: 243–50. Reprinted as chapter 9 in Bagnall (2003).
(1989). "Official and private violence in Roman Egypt," *BASP* 26: 201–16. Reprinted as chapter 5 in Bagnall (2003).
(1991). "Response to Hans-Albert Rupprecht," in *Symposion 1990. Vorträge zur griechischen und hellenistischen Rechtsgeschichte = Papers on Greek and Hellenistic Legal History*. Ed. M. Gargarin. Cologne. Pp. 149–52.
(1993a). "Slavery and society in late Roman Egypt," in *Law, Politics and Society in the Ancient Mediterranean World*. Ed. B. Halperin and D. Hobson. Sheffield. Pp. 220–40. Reprinted as chapter 1 in Bagnall (2003).

(1993b). *Egypt in Late Antiquity*. Princeton.
(1995). *Reading Papyri, Writing Ancient History*. London.
(2003). *Later Roman Egypt: Society, Religion, Economy and Administration*. Aldershot, Hampshire, UK.
ed. (2007). *Egypt in the Byzantine World, 300–700*. Cambridge.
ed. (2009). *The Oxford Handbook of Papyrology*. Oxford.
(2011). *Everyday Writing in the Greco-Roman East*. Berkeley.
Bagnall, R. and R. Cribiore (2006). *Women's Letters from Ancient Egypt, 300 BC–AD 800*. Ann Arbor.
Bagnall, R. S. and P. Derow, eds. (2004). *The Hellenistic Period: Historical Sources in Translation*. New edn. New Malden, MA.
Bagnall, R. S. and B. Frier (1994). *The Demography of Roman Egypt*. Cambridge.
Bagnall, R. S. and F. Mitthof (2004). "Order to send a person," in *Gedenkschrift Ulrike Horak (P.Horak)*. Ed. R. Pintaudi. Papyrologica Florentina 34. Florence. Pp. 59–62.
Bagnall, R. S. and K. A. Worp (1978). "Ten consular dates," *ZPE* 28: 221–30.
Baldwin, B. (1963). "Crime and criminals in Graeco-Roman Egypt," *Aegyptus* 43: 256–63.
Banaji, J. (2007). *Agrarian Change in Late Antiquity: Gold, Labour, and Aristocratic Dominance*. 2nd rev. edn. Oxford.
Bataille, A. (1952). *Les Memnonia: Recherches de papyrologie et d'épigraphie grecques sur la nécropole de la Thèbes d'Égypte aux époques hellénistique et romaine*. Cairo.
Beaucamp, J. (1992). *Le statut de la femme à Byzance (4e–7e siècle)*, vol. 2: *Les pratiques sociales*. Travaux et mémoires du Centre de recherche d'histoire et civilisation de Byzance. Monographie 6. Paris.
(2007). "Byzantine Egypt and imperial law," in Bagnall (2007), pp. 271–87.
Behrend, D. (1970). *Attische Pachturkunden*. Vestigis 12. Munich.
Belhmer, H. ed. (1996). *Shenute von Atripe: De Iudicio* (Torino, Museo Egizio, Cat. 63000, Cot. iv). Turin.
Bell, H. I. (1924). "The *episcopalis audientia* in Byzantine Egypt," *Byzantion* 1: 139–44.
(1929). "The administration of Egypt under the 'Umayyad Khalifs," *Byzantinische Zeitschrift* 28: 278–86.
Bergamasco, M. (1995). "Le *didaskalikai* nella ricerca attuale," *Aegyptus* 75: 95–167.
Berger, A. (1911). *Die Strafklauseln in den Papyrusurkunden: ein Beitrag zum gräkoägyptischen Obligationenrecht*. Leipzig.
(1953). *Encyclopedic Dictionary of Roman Law*. Philadelphia.
Berrendonner, C. (2006). "Les prisonniers de guerre romains durant le conflit samnite," in *Guerre et diplomatie romaines*. Ed. E. Caire and S. Pittia. Aix-en-Provence. Pp. 157–73.
Bickerman, E. (1930). "Beiträge zur antiken Urkundengeschichte II," *Archiv* 9: 24–46.
(1933). "Testificatio Actorum. Eine Untersuchung über antike Niederschriften zu Protokoll," *Aegyptus* 13: 333–55.

Bieżuńska-Małowist, I. (1977). *L'esclavage dans l'Egypte gréco-romain. Seconde partie: période romaine*. Trans. J. Wolf. Warsaw.

Bingen, J. (1978). "The third-century B.C. land-leases from Tholthis," *ICS* 3: 74–80. Reprinted in Bingen (2006), pp. 206–12.

(2006). *Hellenistic Egypt: Monarchy, Society, Economy, Culture*. Edinburgh.

Biscottini, M. (1966). "L'archivio di Tryphon, tessitore di Oxyrhynchos," *Aegyptus* 46: 60–90; 186–92.

Bogaert, R. (1983). "Les *kollybistikai trapezai* dans l'Egypte gréco-romaine," *Anagennesis* 3: 21–64. Reprinted in Bogaert (1994), pp. 95–120.

(1984). "Les banques affermées ptolémaïques," *Historia* 33: 181–98. Reprinted in Bogaert (1994), pp. 59–75.

(1994). *Trapezitica Aegyptiaca: Recueil de recherches sur la banque en Égypte gréco-romaine*. Papyrologica Florentina 25. Florence.

Boswinkel, E. and P. W. Pestman (1978). *Textes grecs, démotiques et bilingues. Textes grecs et démotiques*. Pap.Lugd.Bat. XIX. Leiden.

(1982). *Les archives privées de Dionysios, fils de Kephalas*. Pap.Lugd.Bat. XXII. Leiden.

Botta, A. F. (2009). *The Aramaic and Egyptian Legal Traditions at Elephantine. An Egyptological Approach*. London.

Botti, G. (1957). "Papyri demotici dell'epoca imperiale da Tebtunis," in *Studi di onore de Aristide Calderini e Roberto Paribeni*. Vol. II. Milan. Pp. 75–86.

(1967). *L'archivio demotico da Deir el-Medineh*. Catalogo del Museo Egizio di Torino. Serie prima – monumenti e testi I. Florence.

Bowman, A. K. (2001). "Some Romans in Augustan Alexandria," in *Alexandrian Studies II in Honour of Mostafa el-Abbadi*. BSAA 46 [2000]. Cairo. Pp. 13–24.

Bowman, A. K. and D. W. Rathbone (1992). "Cities and administration in Roman Egypt." *JRS* 82: 107–27.

Bowman, A. K. and E. Rogan, eds. (1999). *Agriculture in Egypt from Pharaonic to Modern Times*. Proceedings of the British Academy 96. Oxford.

Bradley, K. (2004). "On captives under the Principate," *Phoenix* 58: 298–318.

Brashear, W. (1980). *Ptolemäische Urkunden aus Mumienkartonage*. BGU xiv. Berlin.

Bremen, R. van (1996). *The Limits of Participation: Women and Civic Life in the Greek East in the Hellenistic and Roman Periods*. Dutch Monographs on Ancient History and Archaeology 15. Amsterdam.

Brinker, A. A. den, B. P. Muhs and S. P. Vleeming (2005). *A Berichtigungsliste of Demotic Documents*. Studia Demotica VII a–b. Leuven.

Brown, P. (1982). "The rise and function of the Holy Man in Late Antiquity," in *Society and the Holy in Late Antiquity*. Berkeley. Pp. 103–52.

(1995). *Authority and the Sacred: Aspects of the Christianization of the Roman World*. Cambridge.

Bryen, A. Z. (2008). *Violence, Law, and Society in Roman and Late Antique Egypt*. Ph.D. dissertation, University of Chicago.

(2013). *Violence in Roman Egypt: A Study in Legal Interpretation*. Philadelphia.

Buckland, W. W. (1970). *The Roman Law of Slavery: The Condition of the Slave in Private Law from Augustus to Justinian*. Cambridge, MA. Reprint of 1908 Cambridge University Press edition.

Bülow-Jacobsen, A. (1986). "Orders for arrest," *ZPE* 66: 93–98.

Bülow-Jacobsen, A. and S. Ebbesen (1971). "Five Copenhagen papyri," *Cahiers de l'Institut du Moyen-Âge Grec et Latin* 6: 1–41.

Bürge, A. (1999). *Römisches Privatrecht: Rechtsdenken und gesellschaftliche Verankerung: eine Einführung*. Darmstadt.

Burkhalter, F. (1990). "Archives locales et archives centrales en Égypte romaine," *Chiron* 20: 191–216.

Burns, K. (2010). *Into the Archive: Writing and Power in Colonial Peru*. Durham, NC.

Burstein, S. (1998). *Ancient African Civilizations: Kush and Axum*. Princeton.

Butler, C., ed. (1898–1904). *Palladius, Lausiac History*. Texts and Studies 6. 2 vols. Cambridge.

Cadell, H. (1967). "Nouveaux fragments de la correspondance de Kurrah ben Sharik," *Recherches des Papyrologie* 4: 107–60.

(1983). "Sur quelques cas de grève dans l'Égypte lagide," *JESHO* 26: 22–32.

(1994). "Vocabulaire de l'irrigation: la Septante et les papyrus," in *Les problèmes institutionnels de l'eau en Egypte ancienne et dans l'antiquité méditerranéenne: Colloque AIDEA Vogüé 1992*. Ed. B. Menu. Cairo. Pp. 103–17.

Calderini, A. (1922). "Sei esemplari di un' unica scheda di censimento romano," *Aegyptus* 3: 341–45.

(1953). "Apatores," *Aegyptus* 33: 358–69.

Campbell, B. (1994). *The Roman Army 31 BC – AD 337*. London.

Carrié, J.-M. (1998). "Archives municipales et distributions alimentaires dans l'Égypte romaine," in *La mémoire perdue: recherches sur l'administration romaine*. Ed. C. Moatti. Collections de l'École Française de Rome 243. Pp. 271–302.

Caspers, P. (1954). *Der Güte- und Schiedsgedanke im kirchlichen Zivilgerichtsverfahren: Eine kirchenrechtliche Untersuchung über das Wesen der episcopalis audientia*. Düsseldorf.

Cenival, F. de (1972). "Une vente d'esclaves de l'époque d'Artaxercès III (P.Inv. Sorbonne Nos 1276 et 1277)," *Rev. d'Ég.* 24: 31–39.

(1973). *Cautionnements démotiques du début de l'époque ptolémaïque (P. Dem. Lille 34 à 96)*. Paris.

(1987). "Répertoire journalier d'un bureau de notaire de l'époque ptolémäique en démotique (P. dem. Lille 120)," *Enchoria* 15: 1–9.

Champlin, E. (1991). *Final Judgments: Duty and Emotion in Roman Wills 200 B.C.–A.D. 250*. Berkeley.

Chankowski, V. (2008). "Banking in the city. Reflections on the Greek papers," in *Pistoi dia tèn technèn: Bankers, Loans and Archives in the Ancient World*. Ed. K. Verboven, K. Vandorpe, and V. Chankowski. Studia Hellenistica 44. Leuven. Pp. xxix–xxxiii.

Cheshire, W. (1987). "A dictionary of Demotic toponyms," in *Aspects of Demotic Lexicography: Acts of the Second International Conference for Demotic Studies, Leiden, 19–21 September 1984*. Ed. S. P. Vleeming. Studia Demotica I. Leiden. Pp. 131–34.

Choat, M. and I. Gardiner (2006). "*P.Lond.Copt.* I 123: another letter to Apa Johannes?" *ZPE* 156: 157–64.

Christensen, T. (1998). "SB XIV 11355 – a reedition: copy of a census-return," *Archiv* 44: 29–37.

(2002). *The Edfu Nome Surveyed: P.Haun. inv. 407 (119–118 BC)*. Ph.D. dissertation, University of Cambridge.

Clackson, S. (1995). "Four Coptic papyri from the Patermouthis archive in the British Library," *BASP* 32: 97–116.

(2000). *Coptic and Greek Texts Relating to the Hermopolite Monastery of Apa Apollo*. Oxford.

(2010). "Coptic or Greek? Bilingualism in the papyri," in Papaconstantinou (2010), pp. 73–104.

Clarysse, W. (1979). "Egyptian estate-holders in the Ptolemaic period," in *State and Temple Economy in the Ancient Near East: Proceedings of the International Conference Organized by the Katholieke Universiteit Leuven from the 10th to the 14th of April 1978*. Ed. E. Lipinski. Vol. 2. OLA 6. Leuven. Pp. 731–43.

(1993). "Egyptian scribes writing Greek," *Cd'É* 68: 186–201.

(2003). "Tomoi Synkollēsimoi," in *Ancient Archives and Archival Traditions: Concepts of Record-keeping in the Ancient World*. Ed. M. Brosius. Oxford. Pp. 344–59.

(2010). "Bilingual papyrological archives," in Papaconstantinou (2010), pp. 47–72.

Clarysse, W. and K. Vandorpe (1998). "The Ptolemaic apomoira," in *Le culte du souverain dans l'Égypte ptolémaïque au IIIe siècle avant notre ère. Actes du colloque international, Bruxelles, 10 mai 1995*. Ed. H. Melaerts. Studia Hellenistica 34. Leuven. Pp. 5–42.

Cockle, H. M. (1981). "Pottery manufacture in Roman Egypt: a new papyrus," *JRS* 71: 87–97.

Cockle, W. E. H. (1984). "State archives in Graeco-Roman Egypt from 30 BC to the reign of Septimius Severus," *JEA* 70: 106–22.

Cohen, N. (1996). "A notice of birth of a girl," in *Classical Studies in Honor of David Sohlberg*. Ed. R. Katzoff *et al.* Ramat Gan. Pp. 385–98.

Coles, R. A. (1966). *Reports of Proceedings in Papyri*. Papyrologica Bruxellensia 4. Brussels.

Comfort, H. (1934a). "Late Byzantine land-leases *ἐφ' ὅσον χρόνον βούλει*," *Aegyptus* 14: 80–88.

(1934b). "The crops of an indiction in late Byzantine land-leases," *Aegyptus* 14: 429–46.

Cowey, J. M. S. and K. Maresch (2001). *Urkunden des Politeuma der Juden von Herakleopolis (144/3–133/2 v. Chr.) (P.Polit.Iud.). Papyri aus den Sammlungen von Heidelberg, Köln, München und Wien*. Sonderreihe Papyrologica Coloniensia 29. Wiesbaden.

Crawford, D. J. (1971). *Kerkeosiris: An Egyptian Village in the Ptolemaic Period*. Cambridge.

Criscuolo, L. (2004). "Papiri tolemaici dell'Università Cattolica di Milano," *Simblos: scritti di storia antica* 4: 7–23.

Crum, W. E. (1902). *Coptic Ostraca from the Collections of the Egypt Exploration Fund, the Cairo Museum and Others*. London.

(1905). *Catalogue of the Coptic Manuscripts in the British Museum*. London.

(1912). *Koptische Rechtsurkunden des achten Jahrhunderts aus Djême (Theben)*. Leipzig.

(1939a). *A Coptic Dictionary*. Oxford.

(1939b). *Varia Coptica*. Aberdeen.

Daniel, R. W. (2010). *Architectural Orientation in the Papyri*. Papyrologica Coloniensia 34. Paderborn.

Daris, S. (1991). *Il lessico latino nel greco d'Egitto*. 2nd edn. Barcelona.

Dautzenberg, V. (1971). *Die Gesetze des Codex Theodosianus und des Codex Justinianus für Ägypten im Spiegel der Papyri*. Diss. jur. Cologne.

Davies, R. W. (1973). "The investigation of some crimes in Roman Egypt," *Ancient Society* 4: 199–212.

De Neeve, P. W. (1983). "Remissio mercedis," *ZSS* 100: 296–339.

Depauw, M. (1997). *A Companion to Demotic Studies*. Papyrologica Bruxellensia 28. Brussels.

(1999). "Demotic witness-copy-contracts," *Rev.d'Ég.* 50: 67–105.

(2000). *The Archive of Teos and Thabis from Early Ptolemaic Thebes (P. Brux. dem. inv. E. 8252–8256)*. Monographies Reine Élisabeth, vol. 8. Turnhout.

(2002). "Two notes on the Demotic participle or how *i.ir* became theologically relevant," *Lingua Aegyptia* 10: 101–21.

(2003). "Autograph confirmation in Demotic private contracts," *Cd'É* 78: 66–111.

Descat, R. (2011). "Labour in the Hellenistic economy: slavery as a text case," in *The Economies of Hellenistic Societies, Third to First Centuries BC*. Ed. Z. H. Archibald, J. K. Davies, and V. Gabrielsen. Oxford. Pp. 207–15.

Devauchelle, D. (1983). *Ostraca démotiques du Musée du Louvre I: Reçus*. Bibliothèque d'Étude 92. Cairo.

(1986). "Pap. dém. Amiens 1 et 2," *Enchoria* 14: 57–65.

(1987). "Le papyrus démotique Louvre E 9416: une vente de terrain," *BIFAO* 87: 161–65.

Diethart, J. M. and K. A. Worp (1986). *Notarsunterschriften im byzantinischen Ägypten*. Mitteilungen aus der Papyrussammlung der Österreichischen Nationalbibliothek 16. Vienna.

Dijkstra, J. H. F. (2008). *Philae and the End of Ancient Egyptian Religion: A Study of Religious Transformation (298–642 CE)*. Leuven.

Dinkler, E. (1967). "Zum Problem der Ethik bei Paulus – Rechtsnahme und Rechtsverzicht," in Dinkler, *Signum Crucis: Aufsätze zum Neuen Testament und zur christlichen Archäologie*. Tübingen. Pp. 204–40.

Doepp, S. (1998). *Lexikon der antiken christlichen Literatur*. Freiburg.

Donahue, C. (2006). "Comparative law before the Code Napoléon," in *The Oxford Handbook of Comparative Law*. Ed. M. Reimann and R. Zimmermann. Oxford. Pp. 3–32.

Donker van Heel, K. (1990). *The Legal Manual of Hermopolis [P. Mattha]: Text and Translation*. Uitgaven vanwege de stichtung "Het Leids Papyrologisch Instituut" 11. Leiden.

(1994). "The lost battle of Peteamonip son of Petehorresne," in *Acta Demotica. Acts of Fifth International Conference for Demotists. Pisa, 4th–8th September 1993. EVO* 17. Pp. 115–24.

(1995). *Abnormal Hieratic and Early Demotic Texts Collected by the Theban Choachytes in the Reign of Amasis: Papyri from the Louvre Eisenlohr Lot*. Leiden.

(1998). "Use of land in the Kushite and Saite Periods (Egypt, 747–656 and 664–525 BC)," in *Landless and Hungry? Access to Land in Early and Traditional Societies. Proceedings of a Seminar Held in Leiden, 20 and 21 June, 1996*. Ed. B. Haring and R. de Maaijer. CNWS Publications 67. Leiden. Pp. 90–102.

Drexhage, H.-J. (1989). "Zu den Überstellungsbefehlen aus dem römischen Ägypten (1–3 Jh. n. Chr.)," in *Migratio et Commutatio: Studien zur Alten Geschichte und deren Nachleben. Festschrift Th. Pekary*. St. Katharinen. Pp. 102–18.

(1991). *Preise, Mieten / Pachten, Kosten und Löhne im römischen Ägypten bis zum Regierungsantritt Diokletians*. St Katharinen.

(2004). "Zu den Berufsbezeichnungen mit den Suffix -ής in der litterarischen, papyrologischen und epigraphischen Überlieferung," *Münstersche Beiträge zur Antiken Handelsgeschichte* 23.1: 18–40.

Drexhage, H.-J., H. Konen, and K. Ruffing (2002). *Die Wirtschaft des römischen Reiches (1.–3. Jahrhundert): eine Einführung*. Berlin.

Duttenhöfer, R. (1996). "Ein ptolemäischer Eselkauf mit neuer eponymer Priestertitulatur," *Cd'É* 71: 297–309.

ed. (2002). *Griechische Urkunden der Papyrussammlung zu Leipzig (P. Lips. II)*. Munich.

El-Amir, M. (1959). *A Family Archive from Thebes: Demotic Papyri in the Philadelphia and Cairo Museums from the Ptolemaic Period*. Cairo.

Erdmann, W. (1941). "Ehescheidung in Rechte der gräko-ägyptischen Papyri," *ZSS* 61: 44–57.

Ernst, W. (1997). "Gattungskauf und Lieferungskauf im römischen Recht," *ZSS* 114: 272–344.

Evans Grubbs, J. (2002). *Women and the Law in the Roman Empire: A Sourcebook on Marriage, Divorce and Widowhood*. London.

Eyre, C. (1997). "Peasants and 'modern' leasing strategies in ancient Egypt," *JESHO* 40: 367–90.

(1999). "The village economy in pharaonic Egypt," in Bowman and Rogan (1999), pp. 33–60.

(2004). "How relevant was personal status to the functioning of the rural economy in pharaonic Egypt?" in *La dépendance rurale dans l'antiquité égyptienne et proche-orientale*. Ed. B. Menu. Cairo. Pp. 157–86.

Faraguna, M. (2000). "A proposito degli archivi nel mondo greco: terra e registrazioni fondiarie," *Chiron* 30: 65–115.

Farber, J. (1990). "Family financial disputes in the Patermouthis archive," *BASP* 27: 111–22.

Feissel, D. and J. Gascou (2000). "Documents d'archives romains inédits du moyen Euphrate (IIIe s. après J.-C.): III. Actes divers et lettres (P. Euphr. 11 à 17)," *Journal des Savants*: 157–208.

Felber, H. (1997a). *Demotische Ackerpachtverträge der Ptolemäerzeit. Untersuchungen zu Aufbau, Entwicklung und inhaltlichen Aspekten einer Gruppe von demotischen Urkunden*. Ägyptologische Abhandlungen 58. Wiesbaden.

(1997b). "Die Daten in den demotischen Ackerpachtverträgen der Ptolemäerzeit und das landwirtschaftliche Jahr," in *Akten des 21. Internationalen Papyrologenkongresses, Berlin, 13.–19. 8. 1995*. Ed. B. Kramer *et al.* Archiv Beiheft 3. Vol. 1. Stuttgart. Pp. 281–89.

Festugière, A. D., ed. (1961). *Historia Monachorum in Aegypto*. Brussels.

Fikhman, I. F. (1970). "On the structure of the Egyptian large estate in the sixth century," in *Proceedings of the Twelfth International Congress of Papyrology*. Ed. D. H. Samuel. American Studies in Papyrology 12. Toronto. Pp. 127–32.

(1991). "Esclaves et colons en Égypte Byzantine," *Analecta Papyrologica* 3: 7–17. Reprinted in Fikhman (2006), pp. 281–91.

(2000). "Quelques rémarques sur P. Oxy. LXIII 4353," in *Timai Ioannou Triantaphyllopoulou*. Ed. J. Velissaropoulou-Karakosta, S. N. Troianos, K. A. Bourdara, M. P. Stathopoulos, and N. Klamaris. Athens. Pp. 381–88.

(2006). *Wirtschaft und Gesellschaft im spätantiken Ägypten: Kleine Schriften Itzhak F. Fikhman*. Ed. A. Jördens with W. Sperling. Historia Einzelschriften 192. Stuttgart.

Fischer-Bovet, C. (2011). "Counting the Greeks in Egypt. Immigration in the first century of Ptolemaic rule," in *Demography and the Graeco-Roman World: New Insights and Approaches*. Ed. C. Holleran and A. Pudsey. Cambridge. Pp. 135–54.

Förster, H. (2002). *Wörterbuch der griechischen Wörter in den Koptischen Dokumentarischen Texten*. Berlin.

Foti Talamanca, G. (1979). *Ricerche sul processo nell'Egitto greco-romano*, vol. 2.1: *L'introduzione del giudizio 1*. Milan.

(1984). *Ricerche sul processo nell'Egitto greco-romano*, vol. 2.2: *L'introduzione del giudizio 2*. Naples.

Fournet, J.-L. (1989). "Les emprunts du grec à l'égyptien," *Bulletin de la Société de Linguistique de Paris* 84: 55–80.

(2009). "The multilingual environment of Late Antique Egypt: Greek, Latin, Coptic, and Persian documentation," in Bagnall (2009), pp. 418–51.

Fournet, J.-L. and J. Gascou (2004). "Liste des pétitions sur papyrus des Ve –VIIe siècles," in *La pétition à Byzance*. Ed. D. Feissel and J. Gascou. Paris. Pp. 141–96.

Francisci, P. de (1915–1918). "Per la storia dell'episcopalis audientia fino alla Nov. XXX di Valentiniano," *Annali della Facoltà die Giurisprudenza della Università Perugia* 30: 45–90.

Frantz-Murphy, G. (1981). "A comparison of the Arabic and earlier Egyptian contract formularies, part I: The Arabic contracts from Egypt (3rd/9th–5th/11th centuries," *JNES* 40: 203–25, 355–56.

(1985). "A comparison of the Arabic and earlier Egyptian contract formularies, part II: Terminology in the Arabic warranty and the idiom of clearing/cleaning," *JNES* 44: 99–114.

(1988a). "A comparison of Arabic and earlier Egyptian contract formularies, part III: The idiom of satisfaction," *JNES* 47: 105–12.

(1988b). "A comparison of Arabic and earlier Egyptian contract formularies, part IV: Quittance formulas," *JNES* 47: 269–80.

(2001). *Arabic Agricultural Leases and Tax Receipts from Egypt, 148–427 A.H./765–1035 A.D. Corpus Papyrorum Raineri XXI*. Vienna.

Fraser, P. M. (1972). *Ptolemaic Alexandria*. 3 vols. Oxford.

Gagarin, M. (2008). *Writing Greek Law*. Cambridge.

Gagos, T. (2008). "*Compromissum*," *BASP* 45: 59–67.

Gagos, T. and P. J. Sijpesteijn (1996). "Towards an explanation of the typology of the so-called 'orders to arrest'," *BASP* 33: 77–97.

Gagos, T. and P. van Minnen (1994). *Settling a Dispute: Towards a Legal Anthropology of Late Antique Egypt*. Ann Arbor.

Garnsey, P. (1970). *Social Status and Legal Privilege in the Roman Empire*. Oxford.

(1996). *Ideas of Slavery from Aristotle to Augustine*. Cambridge.

Gascou, J. (1985). "Les grands domaines, la cité et l'état en Égypte byzantine," *Travaux et Mémoires* 9: 1–96. Reprinted in Gascou (2008), pp. 125–213.

(1989). "Les codices documentaires égyptiens," in *Les débuts du codex*. Ed. A. Blanchard. *Bibliologia* 9. Pp. 71–101. Reprinted in Gascou (2008), pp. 351–76.

(2008). *Fiscalité et société en Égypte byzantine*. Paris.

(2009). "Procès-verbal d'audience du juge Ammonios," *ZPE* 170: 149–55.

Gaudemet, J. (1989). *L'église dans l'empire romain (IVe–Ve siècles)*. 2nd edn. Paris.

Geens, K. (2008). "Financial archives of Graeco-Roman Egypt," in *Pistoi dia tèn technèn: Bankers, Loans and Archives in the Ancient World*. Ed. K. Verboven, K. Vandorpe and V. Chankowski. Studia Hellenistica 44. Leuven. Pp. 133–51.

Gelzer, M. (1913). "Altes und neues aus der byzantinisch-ägyptischen Verwaltungsmisere, vernehmlich im Zeitalter Justinians," *Archiv* 5: 346–77.

George, M., ed. (2005). *The Roman Family in the Empire: Rome, Italy and Beyond*. Oxford.

Gerke, F. (1931). *Die Stellung des ersten Clemensbriefes innerhalb der Entwicklung der altchristlichen Gemeindeverfassung und des Kirchenrechts*. Texte und

Untersuchungen zur Geschichte der altchristlichen Literatur IV. Reihe II, 47. Leipzig.
Giradet, K. (1975). *Kaisergericht und Bischofsgericht: Studien zu den Anfängen des Donatistenstreites (313–315) und zum Prozeß des Athanasius von Alexandrien (328–346)*. Bonn.
Glancy, J. A. (2002). *Slavery in Early Christianity*. Oxford.
Glanville, S. R. K. (1939). *Catalogue of Demotic Papyri in the British Museum*, vol. I: *A Theban Archive of the Reign of Ptolemy I, Soter*. London.
Godlewski, W. (1986). *Le monastère de St Phoibammon*. Warsaw.
Goehring, J. E. (1999). *Ascetics, Society, and the Desert: Studies in Early Egyptian Monasticism*. Harrisburg, PA.
Gonis, N. (2000). "A late Byzantine land lease from Oxyrhynchus: P.Oxy XVI 1968 revised," *Tyche* 15: 93–102.
(2002). "Studies on the aristocracy of Late Antique Oxyrhynchus," *Tyche* 17: 85–97.
(2005). "Some curious prescripts (native languages in Greek dress?)," *BASP* 42: 41–44.
Goody, J. (1990). *The Oriental, the Ancient, and the Primitive: Systems of Marriage and the Family in the Pre-Industrial Societies of Eurasia*. Cambridge.
Gounaropoulou, L. and M. B. Hatzopoulos, eds. (1998). *Epigraphes katô Makedonias (metaxu tou Vermiou orous kai tou Axiou potamou)*, vol. I: *Epigraphes Beroias*. Athens.
Green, M. (1985). "A private archive of Coptic letters and documents from Teshlot," *Oudheidkundige Mededelingen uit het Rijksmuseum van Oudheden te Leiden* 64: 61–122.
Grenfell, B. P. (1896). *Revenue Laws of Ptolemy Philadelphus, Edited from a Greek Papyrus in the Bodleian Library, with a Translation, Commentary, and Appendices*. With an introduction by the Rev. J. P. Mahaffy. Oxford.
Grenfell, B. P. and A. S. Hunt (1906). *The Hibeh Papyri Part I*. London.
Grohmann, A. (1934). *Arabic Papyri in the Egyptian Library*, vol. I: *Protocols and Legal Texts*. Cairo.
(1950). "Einige bemerkenswerte Urkunden aus der Sammlung der Papyrus Erzherzog Rainer an der Nationalbibliothek zu Wien," *Archiv Orientální* 18: 80–119.
Grohmann, A. (†) and R. G. Khoury (1995). *Chrestomathie de la papyrologie arabe: documents relatifs à la vie privée, sociale et administrative dans les premiers siècles islamiques*. Handbuch der Orientalistik, Abtg. I, vol. 2/2. Leiden.
Grunert, S. (1980). "Ägyptische Erscheinungsformen des Privateigentums zur Zeit der Ptolemäer: Grundeigentum," *Altorientalische Forschungen* 7: 51–76.
(1994). "Zur Definition 'Eigentum'," in *Grund und Boden in Altägypten (Rechtliche und sozio-ökonomische Verhältnisse). Akten des internationalen Symposions Tübingen 18.–20. Juni 1990*. Ed. S. Allam. Tübingen. Pp. 389–95.
Guglielmi, W. (1977). "Flachs," in *LexÄg* II. Pp. 256–57.
Haenel, G. (1840). *De constitutionibus quas Iacobus Sirmondus Parisiis A. MDCXXXI. edidit*. Leipzig.

Haensch, R. (1994). "Die Bearbeitungsweisen von Petitionen in der Provinz Aegyptus," *ZPE* 100: 487–546.

(1997). "Zur Konventsordnung in der Provinz Aegyptus und den übrigen Provinzen des römischen Reiches," in *Akten des 21. Internationalen Papyrologenkongresses, Berlin, 13.–19. 8. 1995*. Ed. B. Kramer, W. Luppe, H. Maehler, and G. Poethke. Vol. 1. Archiv Beiheft 3. Stuttgart. Pp. 320–91.

Hagedorn, D. (1979). "Marci Aurelii in Ägypten nach der Constitutio Antoniniana," *BASP* 16: 47–59.

(1986). "Flurbereinigung in Theadelphia?," *ZPE* 65: 93–100.

Hagedorn, U. (1979). "Das Formular der Überstellungsbefehle im römischen Ägypten," *BASP* 16: 61–74.

Hannig, R. (2003). *Ägyptisches Wörterbuch I: Altes Reich und Erste Zwischenzeit*. Hannig-Lexica 4. Kulturgeschichte der antiken Welt 98. Mainz am Rhein.

Hansen, V. (1995). *Negotiating Daily Life in Traditional China: How Ordinary People Used Contracts 600–1400*. New Haven.

Haran, M. (1996). "Codex, pinax and writing slat," *Scripta Classica Israelica* 15: 212–22.

Harper, K. (2011). *Slavery in the Late Roman World, AD 275–425*. Cambridge.

Harries, J. (1999). *Law and Empire in Late Antiquity*. Cambridge.

Harrison, A. R. W. (1968). *The Law of Athens I: The Family and Property*. Oxford.

Heinen, H. (1994). "Papyri und Archäologie," in *Proceedings of the 20th International Congress of Papyrologists 23–29 August 1992*. Ed. A. Bülow-Jacobsen. Copenhagen. Pp. 156–59.

(2006). "Amtsärztliche Untersuchung eines toten Sklaven. Überlegungen zu P. Oxy. III 475," in *Medicina e società nel mondo antico. Atti del convegno di Udine (4–5 ottobre 2005)*. Ed. A. Marcone. Florence. Pp. 194–202.

Hengstl, J. (1972). *Private Arbeitsverhältnisse freier Personen in den hellenistischen Papyri bis Diokletian*. Bonn.

(1978a). *Griechische Papyri aus Ägypten als Zeugnisse des öffentlichen und privaten Lebens*. Zurich.

(1978b). "Die athanatos-Klausel," in *Actes du XVe Congrès International de Papyrologie, Brussels, 29 August–3 September 1977*. Part 4. Pap. Brux. 19. Brussels. Pp. 231–39.

(1983). "Einige juristische Bemerkungen zu drei 'Töpferei-Mieturkunden'," in *Studi in onore di Arnaldo Biscardi*, vol. 4. Milan. Pp. 663–73.

Hennig, D. (1967). *Untersuchungen zur Bodenpacht im ptolemäisch-römischen Ägypten*. Munich.

Herrmann, E. (1980). *Ecclesia in Re Publica: Die Entwicklung der Kirche von pseudostaatlicher zu staatlich inkorporierter Existenz*. Frankfurt.

Herrmann, J. (1958). *Studien zur Bodenpacht im Recht der graeco-aegyptischen Papyri*. Münchener Beiträge zur Papyrusforschung und Antiken Rechtsgeschichte 41. Munich.

(1975). "Verfügungsermächtigungen als Gestaltungselemente verschiedener griechischer Geschäftstypen," in *Symposion 1971: Vorträge zur griechischen und hellenistischen Rechtsgeschichte*. Ed. H. J. Wolff. Akten der Gesellschaft für griechische und hellenistische Rechtsgeschichte 1. Cologne. Pp. 321–32.

Hickey, T. M. (2001). *A Public "House" but Closed: "Fiscal Participation" and Economic Decision Making on the Oxyrhynchite Estate of the Flavii Apiones*. Ph.D. dissertation, University of Chicago.

(2007). "Aristocratic landholding and the economy of Byzantine Egypt," in Bagnall (2007), pp. 288–308.

(2008). "An inconvenient truth? *P.Oxy*. 18.2196, the Apion estate, and *fiscalité* in the Late Antique Oxyrhynchite," *BASP* 45: 87–100.

(2012). *Wine, Wealth, and the State in Late Antique Egypt: The House of Apion at Oxyrhynchus*. Ann Arbor.

Hobson, D. W. (1993). "The impact of law on village life in Roman Egypt," in *Law, Politics and Society in the Ancient Mediterranean World*. Ed. B. Halpern and D. W. Hobson. Sheffield. Pp. 193–219.

Hohlweg, A. (1971). "Bischof und Stadtherr im frühen Byzanz," *Jahrbuch der österreichischen Byzantinistik* 20: 51–62.

Hölbl, G. (2001). *A History of the Ptolemaic Empire*. London.

Honigman, S. (2003). "Politeumata and ethnicity in Ptolemaic and Roman Egypt," *Ancient Society* 33: 61–102.

Honoré, T. (1994). *Emperors and Lawyers, with a Palingenesia of Third-Century Imperial Rescripts 193–305 A.D.* London.

Hoogendijk, F. A. J. (1994). "Het 'Nestnêphis-proces'. Een strijd tussen Egyptische priesters in de 1e eeuw n. Chr." *Hermeneus* 66: 255–62.

Hopkins, K. (1980). "Brother-sister marriages in Roman Egypt," *Comparative Studies in Society and History* 22: 303–54.

Huebner, S. (2007). "Brother-sister marriage in Roman Egypt: A curiosity of humankind or a widespread family strategy?," *JRS* 97: 21–49.

Hughes, G. R. (1952). *Saïte Demotic Land Leases*. Studies in Ancient Oriental Civilization 28. Chicago.

(1973). "Notes on Demotic leases of property," *JNES* 32: 152–60.

Hughes, G. R. and R. Jasnow (1997). *Oriental Institute Hawara Papyri: Demotic and Greek Texts from an Egyptian Family Archive in the Fayum (Fourth to Third Centuries B.C.)*. Oriental Institute Publications 113. Chicago.

Husson, G. (1983). *Oikia: le vocabulaire de la maison privée en Égypte d'après les papyrus grecs*. Paris.

Jasnow, R. (2003a). "Egypt: New Kingdom," in *A History of Ancient Near Eastern Law*. Ed. R. Westbrook, vol. 1. Leiden. Pp. 289–359.

(2003b). "Third Intermediate Period," in *A History of Ancient Near Eastern Law*. Ed. R. Westbrook, vol. 2. Leiden. Pp. 777–818.

Jernstedt, P. V. (1959). *Koptskije Teksty Gosudarstwenogo Ermitasha*. Moscow.

Johnson, A. C. (1936). *Roman Egypt to the Reign of Diocletian: An Economic Survey of Rome*, vol. 2. Ed. T. Frank. Baltimore.

Jones, A. H. M. (1951). "Review of Johnson and West, *Byzantine Egypt: Economic Studies*," *JHS* 71: 271–72.

(1964). *The Later Roman Empire 284–602: A Social, Economic and Administrative Survey*. Oxford.
(1990). *The Later Roman Empire 284–602*. 4th edn. Oxford.
Jördens, A. (1985). "P. Prag. I 34: Ein Arbeitsvertrag," *ZPE* 75: 164–66.
(1990). *Vertragliche Regelungen von Arbeiten im späten griechischsprachigen Ägypten, mit Editionen von Texten der Heidelberger Papyrus-Sammlung, des Istituto Papirologico "G. Vitelli," des Ägyptischen Museums zu Kairo und des British Museum, London (P. Heid. v)*. Heidelberg.
(1992). "Μίσθωσις τῶν ἔργων: ein neuer Vertragstyp," in *Proceedings of the xix International Congress of Papyrology, Cairo 2–9 September 1989*. Ed. A. H. S. El-Mosallamy, vol. 2. Cairo. Pp. 259–70.
(1995). "Sozialstrukturen im Arbeitstierhandel des kaiserzeitlichen Ägypten," *Tyche* 10: 37–100.
(1997). "P. Bodl. I 82: Ein προχρεία-Vertrag," *ZPE* 116: 81–84.
(1999). "Die Agrarverhältnisse im spätantiken Ägypten," *Laverna* 10: 114–52.
(2000). "Registrierungsgesuch aus Oxyrhynchos (sog. Geburtsanzeige)," in *Papyri in honorem Johannis Bingen octogenarii*. Ed. H. Melaerts. Studia Varia Bruxellensia ad Orbem Graeco-Latinum Pertinentia 5. Leuven. Pp. 389–400.
(2004). "Griechische Texte aus Ägypten," in *Texte aus der Umwelt des Alten Testaments*. Neue Folge, vol. 1. Gütersloh. Pp. 338–40.
Jörs, P. (1915). "Erzrichter und Chrematisten," *ZSS* 36: 230–339.
(1918). "Erzrichter und Chrematisten," *ZSS* 39: 52–118.
Jung, J. H. (1982). "Die Rechtsstellung der römischen Soldaten. Ihre Entwicklung von den Anfängen Roms bis auf Diokletian," in *Aufstieg und Niedergang der römischen Welt* II.14. Pp. 882–1013.
Kaimio, J. (1979). *The Romans and the Greek Language*. Societas Scientiarum Fennica, Commentationes Humanarum Litterarum 64. Helsinki.
Kaplony-Heckel, U. (1963). *Die demotischen Tempeleide*. 2 vols. Ägyptologische Abhandlungen 6. Wiesbaden.
(1964). *Die demotischen Gebelên-Urkunden der Heidelberger Papyrus-Sammlung*. Veröffentlichungen aus der Heidelberger Papyrus-Sammlung, neue Folge 4. Heidelberg.
(2001). "Theben-Ost III. Die r-rḫ=w-Tempel-Quittungen und ähnliche Texte. Erster Teil: Allgemeiner Teil und Texte Nr. 18–25," *ZÄS* 128: 24–40.
Karabacek, J., J. Krall, and C. Wessely (1894). *Führer durch die Ausstellung Papyrus Erzherzog Rainer*. Vienna.
Käsemann, E. (1964). "Sätze heiligen Rechts im Neuen Testament," in Käsemann, *Exegetische Versuche und Besinnungen*, vol. 2. Göttingen. Pp. 69–82.
Kaser, M. (1971). *Das römische Privatrecht*, vol. 1. Munich.
(1975). *Das römische Privatrecht*, vol. 2. Munich.
(1996). *Das römische Zivilprozessrecht*. Handbuch der Altertumswissenschaft, Abt. 10, Teil 3, Bd. 4, 2. Revised and enlarged edn. by K. Hackl. Munich.

Katzoff, R. (1970). "BGU 19 and the law of representation in succession," in *Proceedings of the Twelfth International Congress of Papyrology, Ann Arbor, 13–17 August 1968*. American Studies in Papyrology 7. Toronto. Pp. 239–42.
Katzoff, R. and D. Schaps, eds. (2005). *Law in the Documents of the Judaean Desert*. Leiden.
Keenan, J. G. (1970). "Two loans from Tebtunis," *BASP* 7: 77–86.
(1975). "On law and society in Late Roman Egypt," *ZPE* 17: 237–50.
(1978). "The Case of Flavia Christodote: Observations on PSI I 76," *ZPE* 29: 191–209.
(1981). "On village and polis in Byzantine Egypt," in *Proceedings of the XVI International Congress of Papyrology, New York, 24–31 July 1980*. American Studies in Papyrology 23. Chico, CA. Pp. 479–85.
(1985). "Notes on absentee landlordism at Aphrodito," *BASP* 22: 137–69.
(1989). "Roman criminal law in a Berlin papyrus codex (BGU IV 1024–1027)," *Archiv* 35: 15–23.
(1994). "The will of Gaius Longinus Castor," *BASP* 31: 101–07.
(1995). "The Aphrodito murder mystery: a return to the scene of the crimes," *BASP* 32: 57–63.
(2000). "Egypt," in *Cambridge Ancient History*, vol 14. Cambridge. Pp. 612–37.
(2001). "'Die Binnenwanderung' in Byzantine Egypt," *Greek, Roman & Byzantine Studies* 42: 57–82.
(2003). "Deserted villages: from the ancient to the medieval Fayyum," *BASP* 40: 119–39.
(2008). "'Tormented voices': *P.Cair.Masp.* I 67002," in *Les Archives de Dioscore d'Aphrodité cent ans après leur découverte. Histoire et culture dans l'Égypte byzantine*. Ed. J.-L. Fournet. Paris. Pp. 171–80.
(2009a). "History of the discipline," in Bagnall (2009), pp. 59–78.
(2009b). "Egypt's 'special place'," in *Jesuit Education and the Classics*. Ed. F. Benda, S. Byrne, and E. Cueva. Newcastle upon Tyne. Pp. 157–72.
Keenan, J. G. and J. C. Shelton (1976). *The Tebtunis Papyri IV*. London.
Kehoe, D. P. (1995). "Legal institutions and the bargaining power of the tenant in Roman Egypt," *Archiv* 41: 232–62.
Kelly, B. (2002). "*The Repression of Violence in the Roman Principate.*" D.Phil thesis, Oxford University.
(2011). *Petitions, Litigation, and Social Control in Roman Egypt*. New York.
Kister, M. (2002). "From Philotas to Hillel: 'betrothal' contracts and their violation," *Scripta Classica Israelica* 21: 57–60.
Klauser, T. (1962). "Bischöfe auf dem Richterstuhl," *Jahrbuch für Antike und Christentum* 5: 172–74.
Kloppenborg, J. S. (2006). *The Tenants in the Vineyard: Ideology, Economics, and Agrarian Conflict in Jewish Palestine*. Tübingen.
Koenen, L. (1993). "The Ptolemaic king as a religious figure," in *Images and Ideologies: Self-definition in the Hellenistic World*. Ed. A. Bulloch, E. S. Gruen, A. A. Long, and A. Stewart. Berkeley. Pp. 25–115.

Kolendo, J. (1987). "Les romains prisonniers de guerre des barbares au i[er] et au iie siècles," *Index. Quaderni camerti di studi romanistici. International Survey of Roman Law* 15: 227–34.
Kraemer, R. S. (2004). *Women's Religion in the Graeco-Roman World*. Oxford.
Krall, J. (1895). *Koptische Texte*, vol. 1: *Rechtsurkunden, Corpus Papyrorum Raineri Archiducis Austriæ ii*. Vienna.
Krause, J.-U. (1995). *Witwen und Waisen im römischen Reich*, vol. 3: *Rechtliche und soziale Stellung von Weisen*. Stuttgart.
(1996). *Gefängnisse im römischen Reich*. Stuttgart.
Krause, M. (1956). *Apa Abraham von Hermonthis. Ein oberägyptischer Bischof um 600*. 2 vols. Ph.D. dissertation, Berlin, Humboldt Universität.
(1958). "Zum Recht der koptischen Urkunden," *Orientalistische Literaturzeitung* 53: 5–12.
(1969). "Die Testamente der Äbte des Phoibammon-Klosters in Theben," *Mitteilungen des Deutschen Archäologischen Instituts Abteilung Kairo* 25: 57–67.
(1984). "Koptologie und Papyrologie," in *Atti del XVII Congresso Internazionale di Papirologia (Napoli, 19–26 maggio 1983)*, vol. 2. Naples. Pp. 735–53.
Kreller, H. (1919). *Erbrechtliche Untersuchungen auf Grund der gräko-ägyptischen Papyrusurkunden*. Leipzig. Reprinted Darmstadt 1970.
Kreuzsaler, C. and J. Urbanik (2008). "Humanity and inhumanity of law: the case of Dionysia," *JJurPap* 38: 119–55.
Kruit, N. (1992a). 'The meaning of various words related to wine: some new interpretations," *ZPE* 90: 265–76.
(1992b). "Local customs in the formulas of sales of wine for future delivery (a supplement to *P.Heid.* v)," *ZPE* 94: 167–84.
Kruse, T. (2002). *Der königliche Schreiber und die Gauverwaltung. Untersuchungen zur Verwaltungsgeschichte Ägyptens in der Zeit von Augustus bis Philippus Arabs (30 v. Chr.–245 n. Chr.)*. Archiv für Papyrusforschung und verwandte Gebiete. Beihefte 11. Munich.
Kuhn, K. H., ed. (1956). *Letters and Sermons of Besa, in Corpus Scriptorum Christianorum Orientalium 157–58*. 2 vols. Scriptores Coptici 21–2. Leuven.
Kupiszewski, H. (1953–54). "The *iuridicus Alexandreae*," *JJurPap* 7/8: 187–204.
La'da, C.A. (2007). "The Meaning of the Demotic Designations rmt Pr-iy-lq, rmt Yb and rmt Swn," in *Akten des 23. Internationalen Papyrologen-Kongresses, Wien, 22.–28. Juli 2001*. Ed. B. Palme. Pap. Vind. I. Vienna. Pp. 369–80.
Łajtar, A. (2006). *Deir el-Bahari in the Hellenistic and Roman Periods: A Study of an Egyptian Temple Based on Greek Sources. J Jur Pap*. Supplements 4. Warsaw.
Lammeyer, J. (1933). "Die 'audientia episcopalis' in Zivilsachen der Laien im römischen Kaiserrecht und in den Papyri," *Aegyptus* 13: 193–202.
Lefort, L.-T. (1950). *Concordance du Nouveau Testament sahidique*, vol. 1: *Les mots d'origine grecque*. Corpus Scriptorum Christianorum Orientalium 124, Subsidia 1. Louvain.
Lenger, M.-T., ed. (1964). *Corpus des Ordonnances des Ptolémées (C.Ord. Ptol.)*. Mémoires, Académie royale de Belgique 2nd series, vol. 57/5. Reissued with corrections in 1980. Brussels.

Lerouxel, F. (2006). "Les femmes sur le marché du crédit en Égypte romaine (30 avant J.–C.–284 après J.-C.): une approche néo-institutionnaliste," *Cahiers du Centre de Recherches Historiques* 37: 121–36.

(2008). "La banque privée romaine et le marché du crédit dans les tablettes de Murecine et les papyrus d'Égypte romaine," in *Pistoi dia tèn technèn: Bankers, Loans and Archives in the Ancient World. Studies in Honour of Raymond Bogaert*. Ed. K. Verboven, K. Vandorpe, and V. Chankowski. Studia Hellenistica 44. Leuven. Pp. 169–98.

(forthcoming). "Le rôle de la bibliothèque des acquêts (*bibliothêkê enktêseôn*) dans la diminution des coûts de transaction sur le marché du crédit en Égypte romaine," in *Legal Documents in Ancient Societies 2: Transaction Costs in the Ancient World*. Ed. D. Ratzan, D. Kehoe, and U. Yiftach-Firanko. Colloquium Held at the Center for Hellenic Studies, Washington DC, 27–28.9.2009.

Levy, E. (1925). *Der Hergang der römischen Ehescheidung*. Weimar.

Lewis, N. (1945). "The meaning of σὺν ἡμιολίᾳ and kindred expressions in loan contracts," *TAPA* 76: 126–39. Reprinted in Lewis (1995), pp. 17–30.

(1983). *Life in Egypt under Roman Rule*. Oxford.

(1986). *Greeks in Ptolemaic Egypt*. Oxford.

(1993). "The demise of the Demotic document: when and why," *JEA* 79: 276–81. Reprinted in Lewis (1995), pp. 351–56.

(1995). *On Government and Law in Roman Egypt: Collected Papers of Naphtali Lewis*. American Studies in Papyrology 33. Atlanta, GA.

Lichtheim, M. (1957). *Demotic Ostraca from Medinet Habu*. Oriental Institute Publications 80. Chicago.

Lippert, S. (2004). *Ein demotisches juristisches Lehrbuch: Untersuchungen zu Papyrus Berlin P 23575 rto*. Ägyptologische Abhandlungen 66. Wiesbaden.

(2008). *Einführung in die altägyptische Rechtsgeschichte*. Berlin.

Lippert, S. and M. Schentuleit (2006a). *Demotische Dokumente aus Dime*, vol. 1: *Ostraka*. Wiesbaden.

(2006b). *Demotische Dokumente aus Dime*, vol. 2: *Quittungen*. Wiesbaden.

(2010). *Demotische Dokumente aus Dime*, vol. 3: *Urkunden*. Wiesbaden.

Litinas, N. (1999). "*P.Lond.* III 1128: sale of a donkey," *ZPE* 124: 195–204.

Llewelyn, S. R. (1994). "The procedure of execution and the *prosbolê*," *New Documents Illustrating Early Christianity* 7: 197–232.

Lloyd, A. B. (1983). "The Late Period, 664–323 BC," in *Ancient Egypt: A Social History*. Ed. B. G. Trigger, B. J. Kemp, D. O'Connor, and A. B. Lloyd. Cambridge. Pp. 279–348.

Lüddeckens, E. (1960). *Ägyptische Eheverträge*. Ägyptologische Abhandlungen 1. Wiesbaden.

Lüderitz, G. (1994). "What is politeuma?" in *Studies in Early Jewish Epigraphy*. Ed. J. W. van Henten and P. W. van der Horst. Leiden. Pp. 183–225.

Łukaszewicz, A. (2003). "Quelques observations sur les chrématistes de Syène (P.Eleph. DAIK 1)," in *Symposion 1999: Akten der Gesellschaft für Griechische und Hellenistische Rechtsgeschichte* 14. Cologne. Pp. 433–42.

MacCoull, L.S.B. (1991). "Law, Coptic," in *The Coptic Encyclopedia*, vol. 5. Ed. A. A. Atiya. New York. Pp. 1428–31.
(1992). "A Cinderella Story from Byzantine Egypt: *P.Cair. Masp.* I 67089 and III 67294," *Byzantion* 62: 380–88.
(2009). *Coptic Legal Documents: Law as Vernacular Text and Experience in Late Antique Egypt.* Tempe, AZ.
MacMullen, R. (1986). "Judicial savagery in the Roman Empire," *Chiron* 16: 147–66. Reprinted as chapter 20 in MacMullen (1990).
(1990). *Changes in the Roman Empire: Essays in the Ordinary.* Princeton.
Maehler, H. (2005). "Greek, Egyptian and Roman law," *JJurPap* 35: 121–40.
Maffi, A. (1992). *Ricerche sul postliminium.* Milan.
Mairs, R. and C. J. Martin (2008–09). "A bilingual 'sale' of liturgies from the archive of the Theban choachytes: P. Berlin 5507, P. Berlin 3098 and P. Leiden 413," *Enchoria* 31: 22–67.
Malinine, M. (1967). "Partage testamentaire d'une propriété familiale (Pap. Moscou No. 123)," *Rev.d'Ég.* 19: 67–85.
Malouta, M. (2007). "The terminology of fatherlessness in Roman Egypt: ἀπάτωρ and χρηματίζων μητρός," in *Proceedings of the 24th International Congress of Papyrology, Helsinki, 1–7 August, 2004.* Ed. J. Frösén, T. Purola, and E. Salmenkivi. Vol. 2. Societas Scientiarum Fennica, Commentationes Humanarum Litterarum 122. Helsinki. Pp. 615–24.
(2009). "Fatherlessness and formal identification in Roman Egypt," in *Growing up Fatherless in Antiquity.* Ed. S. Hübner and D. Ratzan. Cambridge. Pp. 120–38.
Manca Masciadri, M. and O. Montevecchi (1984). *I contratti di baliatico.* Milan.
Mandalake, A. (2007). "The Cretan *politeuma* in Hellenistic Egypt," (in Greek) in *Yearbook of the Research Center for the History of Greek Law* 40. Athens. Pp. 56–83.
Manigk, A. (1910). *Gläubigerbefriedigung durch Nutzung: Ein Institut der antiken Rechte.* Berlin.
Manning, J. G. (1999). "The auction of Pharaoh," in *Gold of Praise: Studies in Honor of Edward F. Wente.* Ed. J. Larsen and E. Teeter. Studies in Ancient Oriental Civilization 58. Chicago. Pp. 277–84.
(2002/03). "A Ptolemaic agreement concerning a donkey with an unusual warranty clause. The strange case of P. Dem. Princ. 1 (inv. 7524)," *Enchoria* 28: 46–61.
(2003a). *Land and Power in Ptolemaic Egypt: The Structure of Land Tenure.* Cambridge.
(2003b). "Demotic law," in *A History of Ancient Near Eastern Law*, vol. 2. Ed. R. Westbrook. Leiden. Pp. 819–62.
(2010). *The Last Pharaohs: Egypt under the Ptolemies, 305–30 BC.* Princeton.
Marek, C. (2006). *Die Inschriften von Kaunos.* Vestigia 55. Munich.
Markiewicz, T. (2005). "Security for debt in the Demotic papyri," *JJurPap* 35: 141–67.
(2006). "Heqanakhte and the origins of hemiolion," *JJurPap* 36: 125–36.

(2008). "Bocchoris the lawgiver – or was he really?" *JEgH* 1: 309–30.
Martin, C. J. (1986). "A Demotic land lease from Philadelphia: P.BM 10560," *JEA* 72: 159–73.
(1996). "The Demotic texts," in B. Porten *et al.*, *The Elephantine Papyri in English: Three Millennia of Cross-Cultural Continuity and Change*. Leiden. Pp. 277–385.
(2005). "Review of T. Q. Mrsich, *Rechtsgeschichtliches zur Ackerverpachtung auf Tempelland nach demotischem Formular*," *Bibliotheca Orientalis* 62: 489–95.
(2009a). "How to write a Demotic legal document," in *Actes du IXe Congrès International des Études Démotiques*. Ed. G. Widmer and D. Devauchelle. Bibliothèque d'étude 147. Cairo. Pp. 195–222.
(2009b). *Demotic Papyri from the Memphite Necropolis in the Collections of the National Museum of Antiquities in Leiden, the British Museum and the Hermitage Museum*. Turnhout.
Mattha, G. (1945). *Demotic Ostraca from the Collections at Oxford, Paris, Berlin, Vienna and Cairo*. Cairo.
Mattha, G. and G. R. Hughes (1975). *The Demotic Legal Code of Hermopolis West*. Bibliothèque d'étude 45. Cairo.
Mazza, R. (2001). *L'archivo degli Apioni: terra, lavaro e proprietà senatoria nell'Egitto tardoantico*. Bari.
(2007). "Gli affitti fondiari dell'Ossirinchite nell'età tardoantica," in *Akten des XXIII. Internationalen Papyrologenkongresses, Wien, 22.–28. Juli 2001*. Ed. B. Palme. Vienna. Pp. 439–46.
Meeks, D. (1972). *Le grande texte des donations au temple d'Edfou*. Bibliothèque d'ètude 59. Cairo.
Mees, A. W. (2002). *Organisationsformen römischer Töpfer-Manufakturen*. Mainz.
Mélèze Modrzejewski, J. (1974). "A propos de la tutelle dative des femmes dans l'Égypte romaine," in *Akten des XIII internationalen Papyrologenkongresses, Marburg/Lahn, 2–6 August 1971*. Munich. Pp. 263–92.
(1975). "Chrématistes et laocrites," in *Le monde grec: pensée, littérature, histoire, documents. Hommages à Claire Préaux*. Ed. J. Bingen, G. Cambier, and G. Nachtergael. Brussels. Pp. 699–708.
(1979). "Chrématistes et laocrites," in *Symposion 1974. Vorträge zur griechischen und hellenistischen Rechtsgeschichte*. Gargnano am Gardasee, 5.–8. Juni 1974. Cologne. Pp. 375–91. Reprinted in Mélèze Modrzejewski (2011a), pp. 79–192.
(1981). "La structure juridique du marriage grec," *in Scritti in onore di Orsolina Montevecchi*. Ed. E. Bresciani. Bologna. Pp. 231–68.
(1988). "'La loi des Égyptiens': le droit grec dans l'Égypte romaine," in *Proceedings of the XVIII. International Congress of Papyrology, Athens 25–31 May 1986*. Ed. B. Mandilaras, vol. 2. Athens. Pp. 383–99.
(1989). "Entre la cité et le fisc: le statut grec dans l'Égypte romaine," *Symposion 1982: Vorträge zur griechischen und hellenistischen Rechtsgeschichte (Santander, 1.–4. September 1982)*. Cologne. Pp. 241–80.

(1995). "Law and justice in Ptolemaic Egypt," in *Legal Documents of the Hellenistic World: Papers from a Seminar*. Ed. M. J. Geller and H. Maehler. London. Pp. 1–19.

(2001). "The Septuagint as nomos: how the Torah became a 'civic law' for the Jews of Egypt," in *Critical Studies in Ancient Law, Comparative Law, and Legal History: Essays in Honour of Alan Watson*. Ed. J. W. Cairns and O. F. Robinson. Oxford. Pp. 183–99.

(2003). "Droit et justice dans l'Égypte des premiers Lagides," in *L'Orient méditerranéen, de la mort d'Alexandre au Ier siècle avant notre ère*. Ed. M.-T. Le Dinahet. Nantes. Pp. 281–302. Reprinted in Mélèze Modrzejewski (2011a), pp. 111–39.

(2005a). "La fiancée adultère. A propos de la pratique matrimoniale du judaïsme hellénisé à la lumière du dossier du politeuma juif d'Hérakléopolis (144/3–133/2 av. n.è.)," in *Marriage: Ideal – Law – Practice. Proceedings of a Conference Held in Memory of Henryk Kupiszewski*. Ed. Z. Służewska and J. Urbanik. *JJurPap* Supplement 5. Warsaw. Pp. 141–60. Reprinted in Mélèze Modrzejewski (2011b), pp. 231–49.

(2005b). "What is Hellenistic law? The documents of the Judaean desert in the light of the papyri from Egypt," in Katzoff and Schaps (2005), pp. 7–21.

(2011a). *Droit et justice dans le monde grec et hellénistique*. *JJurPap* supplement 10. Warsaw.

(2011b). *Un peuple de philosophes: Aux origines de la condition juive*. Paris.

Menu, B. (1988a). "Les actes de vente en Égypte ancienne, particulièrement sous les rois kouchites et saïtes," *JEA* 74: 165–81. Reprinted in Menu, *Recherches sur l'histoire juridique, économique et sociale de l'ancienne Égypte*, vol. 2. Cairo, 1998. Pp. 305–32.

(1988b). "L'Évolution du droit contractual en Égypte ancienne et la notion de vente à la fin du Moyen Empire," reprinted in *Recherches sur l'histoire juridique, économique et sociale de l'ancienne Égypte*, vol. 2. Cairo, 1998. Pp. 289–304.

Merklein, A. (1967). *Das Ehescheidungsrecht nach den Papyri der byzantinischen Zeit*. PhD dissertation, Friedrich-Alexander Universität, Erlangen. Nuremberg.

Mertens, P. (1958). *Les services de l'état civil et le contrôle de la population à Oxyrhynchos*. Brussels.

Metzger, H. (1974). *Nachrichten aus dem Wüstensand: Eine Sammlung von Papyruszeugnissen*. Zurich.

Meyer, E. A. (2004). *Legitimacy and Law in the Roman World: Tabulae in Roman Belief and Practice*. Cambridge.

Migliardi Zingale, L. (1992). *Vita privata e pubblica nei papiri d'Egitto: Silloge di documenti greci e latini dal I al IV secolo d.C.* Turin.

(1997). *I testamenti romani nei papiri e nelle tavolette d'Egitto: Silloge di documenti dal I al IV secolo d.C.* 3rd edn. Turin.

Miller, G. P., ed. (2010). *Economics of Ancient Law*. Cheltenham.

Mitteis, L. (1891). *Reichsrecht und Volksrecht in den östlichen Provinzen des römischen Kaiserreichs. Mit Beiträgen zur Kenntnis des griechischen Rechts und der spätrömischen Rechtsentwicklung*. Leipzig. Reprinted Hildesheim 1963.

Mitteis, L. and U. Wilcken (1906). "P. Lips. 13," *Archiv für Papyrusforschung* 3: 106–12.

Möller, G. (1921). "Ein ägyptischer Schuldschein der zweiundzwanigsten Dynastie," *Sitzungsberichte der Preussischen Akademie der Wissenschaften, phil-hist. Klasse*: 298–304.

Monson, A. (2005). "Sacred land in Ptolemaic and Roman Tebtunis," in *Tebtunis und Soknopaiu Nesos: Leben im römerzeitlichen Fajum. Akten des Internationalen Symposions vom 11. bis 13. Dezember 2003 in Sommerhausen bei Würzburg*. Ed. S. L. Lippert and M. Schentuleit. Wiesbaden. Pp. 79–91.

(2012). *From the Ptolemies to the Romans: Political and Economic Change in Egypt*. Cambridge.

Montevecchi, O. (1947). "Ricerche di sociologia nei documenti dell'Egitto greco-romano, VI. Denunce di nascita di greco-egizi," *Aegyptus* 27: 3–24.

(1975). "L'epikrisis dei greco-egizi," in *Proceedings of the XIV International Congress of Papyrologists, Oxford, 24–31 July 1974*. London. Pp. 227–32.

(1988). *La papirologia*. Reprinted with corrections with an appendix. Milan.

Montserrat, D. (1996). *Sex and Society in Graeco-Roman Egypt*, London.

Montserrat, D., G. Fantoni, and P. Robinson (1994). "Varia descripta Oxyrhynchita," *BASP* 31: 11–80.

Mooren, L. (1977). *La hiérarchie de cour ptolémaïque: Contribution à l'étude des institutions et des classes dirigeantes à l'époque hellénistique*. Leuven.

Mosiek, U. (1965). "Das altkirchliche Prozeßrecht im Spiegel der Didaskalie," *Österreichisches Archiv für Kirchenrecht* 16: 183–209.

Mourgues, J.-L. (1995). "Les formules 'rescripsi,' 'recognovi' et les étapes de la rédaction des souscriptions impériales sous le Haut-Empire romain," *Mélanges de l'École Française de Rome. Italie et Méditerranée* 107: 255–300.

Mrsich, T. Q. (1994). "Zum unbeurkundeten ägyptischen Verpachts-Geschäft griechisch-römischer Zeit," in *Grund und Boden in Altägypten (rechtliche und sozio-ökonomische Verhältnisse): Akten des internationalen Symposions Tübingen 18.–20. Juni 1990*. Ed. S. Allam. Tübingen. Pp. 177–87.

(2003). *Rechtsgeschichtliches zur Ackerverpachtung auf Tempelland nach demotischem Formular*. Vienna.

Muhs, B. (2002). "Clear title, public protests and P.Brux.Dem. 4," in *Acts of the Seventh International Conference of Demotic Studies, Copenhagen, 23–27 August 1999*. Ed. K. Ryholt. Copenhagen. Pp. 259–72.

(2005a). "The grapheion and the disappearance of Demotic contracts in early Roman Tebtunis and Soknopaiou Nesos," in *Tebtunis und Soknopaiu Nesos: Leben im römerzeitlichen Fajum, Akten des internationalen Symposions von 11. bis 13. Dezember 2003 in Sommerhausen bei Würzburg*. Ed. S. Lippert and M. Schentuleit. Wiesbaden. Pp. 93–104.

(2005b). *Tax Receipts, Taxpayers, and Taxes in Early Ptolemaic Thebes*. Oriental Institute Publications 126. Chicago.

Müller, B. J. (1968). *Ptolemaeus II. Philadelphus als Gesetzgeber*. Ph.D. dissertation, University of Cologne.

Müller, H. G. (1985). *Untersuchungen zur Misthôsis von Gebäuden im Recht der graeco-aegyptischen Papyri*. Nuremberg.

Nims, C. F. (1958). "A Demotic 'document of endowment' from the time of Nectanebo I," *Mitteilungen des Deutschen Archäologischen Instituts Kairo* 16: 237–46.

Nur el-Din, M. A. A. (1974). *The Demotic Ostraca in the National Museum of Antiquities at Leiden*. Leiden.

Oates, J. F. (1963). "The status designation *Persês tês epigonês*," *Yale Classical Studies* 18: 1–129.

(1969). "A Rhodian auction sale of a slave girl," *JEA* 55: 191–210.

(1972). "A sailor's discharge and the consuls of A.D. 209," *Phoenix* 30: 282–87.

(1988). "Sale of a donkey," *BASP* 25: 129–35.

Oréal, E. (1999). "Contact linguistique. Le cas du rapport entre le grec at le copte," *Lalies: actes des sessions de linguistique et de littérature* 19: 289–306.

Palme, B. (2003). "Pflichten und Risiken des Bürgen in byzantinischen Gestellungsbürgschaften," in *Symposion 1999: Akten der Gesellschaft für Griechische und Hellenistische Rechtsgeschichte 14*. Ed. G. Thür and F. J. Fernández Nieto. Pp. 531–55.

(2006). "Römische Militärgerichtsbarkeit in den Papyri," in *Symposion 2003: Vorträge zur griechischen und hellenistischen Rechtsgeschichte*. Ed. H.-A. Rupprecht. Vienna. Pp. 375–408.

(2008). "Law and courts in Late Antique Egypt," in *Aspects of Law in Late Antiquity Dedicated to A. M. Honoré*. Ed. B. Sirks. Oxford. Pp. 55–76.

(2009). "The range of documentary texts: types and categories," in Bagnall (2009), pp. 358–94.

Papaconstantinou, A. (2002a). "*Theia oikonomia*. Les actes thébains de donation d'enfants ou la gestion monastiques de la pénurie," in *Mélanges Gilbert Dagron*. Travaux et Mémoires 14. Paris. Pp. 511–26.

(2002b). "Notes sur les actes de donation d'enfant au monastère thébain de Saint-Phoibammon," *JJurPap* 32: 83–105.

ed. (2010). *The Multilingual Experience in Egypt from the Ptolemies to the 'Abbasids*. Farnham, Surrey.

Parker, R. A. (1940). "A late Demotic gardening agreement: Medinet Habu ostracon 4038," *JEA* 26: 84–113.

(1964). "A Demotic property settlement from Deir el Ballas," *JARCE* 3: 89–103.

Patterson, O. (1982). *Slavery and Social Death: A Comparative Study*. Cambridge, MA.

Pavlovskaja, A. I. (1972). "Die Sklaverei im hellenistischen Ägypten," in *Die Sklaverei in hellenistischen Staaten im 3.-1.Jh. v. Chr.* Übersetzung von M. Bräuer-Pospelova, I. Neander und R. Pollach. Ed. H. Bräuer and J. Vogt. Wiesbaden. Pp. 171–275.

(1992). *Die Sklaverei im römischen Ägypten*, in L. P. Marinovic, E. S. Golubcova, I. S. Sifman and A. I. Pavlovskaja, *Die Sklaverei in den östlichen Provinzen des römischen Reiches im 1.–3. Jahrhundert*. Stuttgart. Pp. 165–270.

Peachin, M. (2007). "Petition to a centurion from the NYU Papyrus Collection," in *Papyri in Memory of P. J. Sijpesteijn (P. Sijp.)*. Ed. A. J. B. Sirks and K. A. Worp with the assistance of R. S. Bagnall and R. P. Salomons. American Studies in Papyrology 40. Oakville, CT. Pp. 79–97.

Pearce, S. (2007). "Translating for Ptolemy: patriotism and politics in the Greek Pentateuch?," in *Jewish Perspectives on Hellenistic Rulers*. Ed. T. Rajak, S. Pearce, J. Aitken, and J. Dines. Berkeley. Pp. 165–89.

Pestman, P. W. (1961). *Marriage and Matrimonial Property in Ancient Egypt: A Contribution to Establishing the Legal Position of the Woman*. Pap.Lugd.Bat. IX. Leiden.

(1965). "Les archives privées de Pathyris à l'époque ptolémaïque. La famille de Pétéharsemtheus, fils de Panebkhounis," in Pap.Lugd.Bat. XIV. Leiden. Pp. 47–105.

(1966). "Review of U. Kaplony-Heckel, *Die demotischen Gebelên-Urkunden der Heidelberger Papyrus-Sammlung*," *Cd'É* 41: 313–20.

(1969). "The law of succession in ancient Egypt," in *Essays on Oriental Laws of Succession in Ancient Egypt*. Leiden. Pp. 58–77.

(1971). "Loans bearing no interest?" *JJurPap* 16–17: 7–29.

(1981a). *L'archivio di Amenothes figlio di Horos (P. Tor. Amenothes). Testi demotici e greci relativi ad una famiglia di imbalsamatori del secondo sec. a. C.* Catalogo del Museo egizio di Torino. Serie prima – monumenti e testi 5. Milan.

(1981b). "Nahomsesis, una donna d'affari di Pathyris. L'archivio bilingue di Pelaias, figlio di Eunus," in *Scritti in onore di O. Montevecchi*. Ed. E. Bresciani *et al.* Bologna. Pp. 295–315.

(1983). "Some aspects of Egyptian law in Graeco-Roman Egypt: title-deeds and ὑπάλλαγμα," in *Egypt and the Hellenistic World*. Ed. E. Van 't Dack, P. Van Dessel, and W. van Gucht. Studia Hellenistica 27. Leuven. Pp. 281–302.

(1985a). "Ventes provisoires de biens pour sûreté de dettes: 'onai en pistei' à Pathyris et à Krokodilopolis," in *Textes et études de papyrologie grecque, démotique et copte*. Ed. P. W. Pestman. Pap.Lugd.Bat. XXIII. Leiden. Pp. 45–59.

(1985b). "Le démotique comme langue juridique," in *Textes et études de papyrologie grecque, démotique et copte*. Ed. P. W. Pestmen. Pap.Lugd.Bat. XXIII. Leiden. Pp. 198–203.

(1985c). "The competence of Greek and Egyptian tribunals according to the decree of 118 B.C," *BASP* 22: 265–69.

(1985d). "Registration of Demotic contracts in Egypt. P. Par. 65; 2nd cent. B.C.," in *Satura Roberto Feenstra sexagesimum quintum annum aetatis complenti ab alumnis collegis amicis oblata*. Ed. J. Ankum, J. E. Spruit, and F. B. J. Wubbe. Fribourg. Pp. 17–25.

(1987). "'Public protests' in the Demotic family archive of Pchorchonsis," in *Miscel·lània Papirologica Ramon Roca-Puig*. Ed. S. Janeras. Barcelona. Pp. 271–81.

(1990). *The New Papyrological Primer*. Leiden.

(1992). *Il processo di Hermias e altri documenti dell'archivio dei choachiti (P. Tor. Choachiti)*. Catalogo del Museo Egizio di Torino, Serie Prima-Monumenti e Testi, vol. 6. Turin.

(1993). *The Archive of the Theban Choachytes (Second Century B.C.): A Survey of the Demotic and Greek Papyri Contained in the Archive*. Studia Demotica 2. Leuven.

(1994a). "Drafts of Demotic notarial documents," in *The Unbroken Reed: Studies in the Culture and Heritage of Ancient Egypt in Honour of A. F. Shore*. Ed. C. Eyre, A. Leahy, and L. Montagno Leahy. London. Pp. 243–67.

(1994b). *The New Papyrological Primer*. 2nd edn. rev. Leiden.

(1994c). *Les papyrus démotiques de Tsenhor (P. Tsenhor). Les archives privées d'une femme égyptienne du temps de Darius Ier*. Studia Demotica 4. Leuven.

(1995a). "Haronnophris and Chaonnophris: two indigenous pharaohs in Ptolemaic Egypt (205–186 B.C.)," in *Hundred-Gated Thebes: Acts of a Colloquium on Thebes and the Theban Area in the Graeco-Roman Period*. Ed. S. P. Vleeming. Pap.Lugd.Bat. XXVII. Leiden. Pp. 101–37.

(1995b). "Appearance and reality in written contracts: evidence from bilingual family archives," in *Legal Documents of the Hellenistic World: Papers from a Seminar*. Ed. M. Geller and H. Maehler. London. Pp. 79–87.

Pestman, P. W., J. Quaegebeur, and R. L. Vos (1977). *Recueil de textes démotiques et bilingues*. 3 vols. Leiden.

Petsas, P., M. L. Gounaropoulou, M. B. Hatzopoulos, and P. Paschidis, eds. (2000). *Inscriptions du sanctuaire de la Mère des Dieux Autochtone de Leukopétra (Macédoine)*. Meletemata 28. Athens.

Phang, S. E. (2001). *The Marriage of Roman Soldiers (13 BC–AD 235): Law and Family in the Imperial Army*. Leiden.

Piccolo, M. (2003). "Osservazione ad alcuni papiri dell'archivio di Tryphon," *Aegyptus* 83: 197–213.

Pierce, R. H. (1972). *Three Demotic Papyri in the Brooklyn Museum: A Contribution to the Study of Contracts and Their Instruments in Ptolemaic Egypt*. Oslo.

(1983). "Review of P. W. Pestman, *Recueil de Textes démotiques*," *Journal of Egyptian Archaeology* 69: 197–99.

(1995). "A sale of an Alodian slave girl," *Symbolae Osloenses* 70: 148–66.

Pietowska, M. (1975). *La skêpê dans l'Égypte ptolemaïque*. Warsaw.

Plöchl, W. M. (1953). *Geschichte des Kirchenrechts*, vol. 1. Vienna.

Poethke, G. (1969). *Epimerismos: Betrachtungen zur Zwangspacht in Ägypten während der Prinzipatzeit*. Brussels.

Porten, B. (1996). *The Elephantine Papyri in English: Three Millennia of Cross-Cultural Continuity and Change*. Leiden.

Porten, B. and J. Farber (1996). "The Greek texts," in Porten (1996), pp. 386–568.

Préaux, C. (1939). *L'économie royale des Lagides*. Brussels.

(1962). "Acte de divorce du Brooklyn Museum (P.Brooklyn gr. 4)," *Cd'É* 37: 323–33.

(1978). *Le monde hellénistique: La Grèce et l'Orient de la mort d'Alexandre à la conquête romaine de la Grèce (323–146 av. J.-C.)*. 2 vols. Paris.

Preisigke, F. (1906). "Ein Sklavenkauf des 6. Jahrhunderts (P. Gr. Str. Inv. Nr. 1404)," *Archiv* 3: 415–24.

Pringsheim, F. (1949). "The Greek sale by auction," in *Scritti in onore di Contardo Ferrini pubblicati in occasione della sua Beatifcazione*, vol. 4. Milan. Pp. 284–343.

(1950). *The Greek Law of Sale*. Weimar.

Quack, J. (1999). "Review of H. Felber, *Demotische Ackerpachtverträge der Ptolemäerzeit*," *Archiv* 45: 134–37.

(2005). *Einführung in die altägyptische Literaturgeschichte III: Die demotische und gräko-ägyptische Literatur*. Einführungen und Quellentexte zur Ägyptologie 3. Munster.

Quack, J. F. (2013). "Zu einigen demotischen Gruppen umstrittener Lesung order problematischer Ableitung," in *Aspects of Demotic Orthography: Acts of an International Colloquium held in Trier, 8 November 2010*. Ed. S. P. Vleeming. Studia Demotica XI. Leuven. Pp. 99–116.

Ranke, H. (1935). *Die ägyptischen Personennamen I: Verzeichnis der Namen*. Glückstadt.

Rapp, C. (1999). "For next to God you are my salvation: reflections on the rise of the holy man in late antiquity," in *The Cult of Saints in Late Antiquity and the Middle Ages: Essays on the Contribution of Peter Brown*. Ed J. Howard-Johnston and P. A. Hayward. Oxford. Pp. 63–81.

Rappaport, U. (1969). "Les Iduméens en Égypte," *Revue Philologique* 43: 73–82.

Rathbone, D. W. (1991). *Economic Rationalism and Rural Society in Third-century A.D. Egypt: The Heroninos Archive and the Appianus Estate*. Cambridge.

(1993). "Egypt, Augustus and Roman taxation," *Cahiers du Centre Glotz* 4: 99–112.

(2001a). "Poverty and population in Roman Egypt," in *Poverty in the Roman World*. Ed. M. Atkins and R. Osborne. Cambridge. Pp. 100–14.

(2001b). "The 'Muziris' Papyrus (SB XVIII 13167): financing Roman trade with India," in *Alexandrian Studies II in Honor of Mostafa el-Abbadi*. Alexandria. Pp. 39–50.

(2007a). "*Mêchanai* (waterwheels) in the Roman Fayyum," in *New Archaeological and Papyrological Researches on the Fayyum*. Ed. M. Capasso and P. Davoli. Lecce. Pp. 251–62.

(2007b). "Misthoprasia: the lease-sale of ships," in *Akten des 23. Internationalen Papyrologen-Kongresses. Wien, 22.–28. Juli 2001*. Ed. B. Palme. Vienna. Pp. 587–93.

Ray, J. D. (1994). "Literacy and language in Egypt in the Late and Persian periods," in *Literacy and Power in the Ancient World*. Ed. A. K. Bowman and G. Woolf. Cambridge. Pp. 51–66.

Rea, J. R. (1972). *The Oxyrhynchus Papyri*, vol. 40. London.

Reich, N. J. (1914). *Papyri juristischen Inhalts in hieratischer und demotischer Schrift aus dem British Museum*. Vienna.

Reinach, T. (1920). "Un code fiscal de l'Égypte romaine: le Gnomon de Idiologue (suite)," *Nouvelle Revue Historique du Droit Français et Étranger* 44: 5–134.

Remijsen, S. and W. Clarysse (2008). "Incest or adoption? Brother–sister marriage in Roman Egypt revisited," *JRS* 98: 53–61.

Rémondon, R. (1961). "Soldats de Byzance d'après un papyrus trouvé à Edfou," *RechPap* 1: 41–93.

Revillout, E. (1900). "Textes coptes. Extraits de la correspondance de St. Pésunthius évêque de Coptos et de plusieurs documents analogues (juridiques ou économiques)," *Révue égyptologique* 9: 133–77.

(1902). "Textes coptes. Extraits de la correspondance de St. Pésunthius évêque de Coptos et de plusieurs documents analogues (juridiques ou économiques)," *Révue égyptologique* 10: 34–47.

(1914). "Textes coptes. Extraits de la correspondance de St. Pésunthius évêque de Coptos et de plusieurs documents analogues (juridiques ou économiques)," *Révue égyptologique* 14: 22–32.

Richter, T. S. (1998). "*rmpou* und *rmpshire*. Zwei Komposita jüngerer Bildungsweise im koptischen Ostrakonbrief Ägyptisches Museum der Universität Leipzig Inv.-Nr. 1611," *ZÄS* 125: 56–62.

(1999). "Spätkoptische Rechtsurkunden neu bearbeitet: BM Or. 4917(15) und P.Med.Copto inv. 69.69," *JJurPap* 29: 85–92.

(2000). "Spätkoptische Rechtsurkunden neu bearbeitet (II): Die Rechtsurkunden des Teschlot-Archivs," *JJurPap* 30: 95–148.

(2002a). "Alte Isoglossen im Rechtswortschatz koptischer Urkunden," *Lingua Ægyptia* 10: 389–99.

(2002b). *Rechtssemantik und forensische Rhetorik: Untersuchungen zu Wortschatz, Stil und Grammatik der Sprache koptischer Rechtsurkunden*. Kanobos 3. Leipzig.

(2002c). "Koptische Mietverträge über Gebäude und Teile von Gebäuden," *JJurPap* 32: 113–68.

(2003). "Spätkoptische Rechtsurkunden neu bearbeitet (III): P.Lond.Copt. I 487, Arabische Pacht in koptischem Gewand," *JJurPap* 33: 213–30.

(2004). "O.Crum Ad. 15 and the emergence of Arabic words in Coptic legal documents," in Sijpesteijn and Sundelin (2004), pp. 97–114.

(2005). "What's in a story? Cultural narratology and Coptic child donation documents," *JJurPap* 35: 237–64.

(forthcoming). *Pacht nach koptischen Quellen: Beiträge zur Rechts-, Wirtschafts- und Sozialgeschichte Ägyptens in byzantinischer und früharabischer Zeit*. Warsaw.

Riedel, W. (1900). *Die Kirchenrechtsquellen des Patriarchats Alexandrien*. Leipzig.

Riedel, W. and W. E. Crum (1904). *The Canons of Athanasius of Alexandria – the Arabic and Coptic Versions*. Oxford.

Rochette, B. (1994). "Traducteurs et traductions dans l'Égypte gréco-romaine," *Cd'É* 69: 313–22.

(1996). "Sur le bilinguisme dans l'Égypte gréco-romaine," *Cd'É* 71: 153–68.

Rotman, Y. (2000). "Formes de la non-liberté dans la campagne byzantine aux VIIe–XIe siècles," *Mélanges de l'École Française de Rome* 112: 499–510.

(2009). *Byzantine Slavery and the Mediterranean World.* Trans. J. M. Todd. Cambridge, MA.

Rouillard, G. (1928). *L'administration civile de l'Égypte byzantine.* Paris.

Rousseau, P. (1999). "Ascetics as mediators and as teachers," in *The Cult of Saints in Late Antiquity and the Middle Ages: Essays on the Contribution of Peter Brown.* Ed. J. Howard-Johnston and P. A. Hayward. Oxford. Pp. 45–59.

Rowlandson, J. (1981). "Sales of land in their social context," in *Proceedings of the XVI International Congress of Papyrology, New York, 24–31 July 1980.* American Studies in Papyrology 23. Chico. Pp. 371–78.

(1996). *Landowners and Tenants in Roman Egypt: The Social Relations of Agriculture in the Oxyrhynchite Nome.* Oxford.

ed. (1998). *Women and Society in Greek and Roman Egypt: A Sourcebook.* Cambridge.

(1999). "Agricultural tenancy and village society in Roman Egypt," in Bowman and Rogan (1999), pp. 139–58.

(2005). "The organisation of public land in Roman Egypt," in *L'agriculture institutionnelle en Égypte ancienne: état de la question et perspectives interdisciplinaires.* Ed. J. C. Moreno García. Lille. Pp. 173–96.

Rowlandson, J. and R. Takahashi (2009). "Brother–sister marriage and inheritance strategies in Greco-Roman Egypt," *JRS* 99: 104–39.

Ruffing, K. (1999). *Weinbau im Römischen Ägypten.* St. Katharinen.

Ruffini, G. (2008). *Social Networks in Byzantine Egypt.* Cambridge.

Rupprecht, H.-A. (1967). *Untersuchungen zum Darlehen im Recht der graeco-aegyptischen Papyri der Ptolemäerzeit.* Münchener Beiträge zur Papyrusforschung und Antiken Rechtsgeschichte 51. Munich.

(1971). *Studien zur Quittung im Recht der graeco-ägyptischen Papyri.* Münchener Beiträge zur Papyrusforschung und Antiken Rechtsgeschichte 57. Munich.

(1984). "Rechtsübertragung in den Papyri. Zur Entwicklung von Parachoresis und Ekchoresis," in *Gedächtnisschrift für Wolfgang Kunkel.* Frankfurt am Main. Pp. 365–90.

(1985). "Zum Ehegattenerbrecht nach den Papyri," *BASP* 21: 291–95.

(1986). "Zur Frage der Frauentutel im römischen Ägypten," in *Festschrift für Arnold Kränzlein.* Ed. G. Wesener. Graz. Pp. 95–102.

(1989). "Erwin Seidl als Papyrologe," in *Akademische Gedachnisfeier für Professor Dr. Erwin Seidl 1905–1987 am 9. Dezember 1988.* Cologne. Pp. 8–15.

(1992). "Zur Antichrese in den griechischen Papyri bis Diokletian," in *Proceedings of the XIX International Congress of Papyrology, Cairo 2–9 September 1989*, vol. 2. Ed. A. H. S. El-Mosallamy. Cairo. Pp. 271–89.

(1994). *Kleine Einführung in die Papyruskunde.* Darmstadt.

(1995). "Die dinglichen Sicherungsrechte nach der Praxis der Papyri – Eine Übersicht über den urkundlichen Befund," in *Collatio Iuris Romani. Études dédiées à Hans Ankum*, vol. 2. Amsterdam. Pp. 425–36.
(1997). "Zwangsvollstreckung und dingliche Sicherheiten in den Papyri der ptolemäischen und römischen Zeit," in *Symposion 1995: Vorträge zur griechischen und hellenistischen Rechtsgeschichte (Korfu 1.–5. September 1995)*. Ed. G. Thür and J. Vélissaropoulos-Karakostas. Cologne. Pp. 291–302.
(2007a). "Urkundsformular und Wirklichkeit – Bemerkungen zur praktischen Bedeutung einer Urkundsklausel," in *Worte des Rechts – Wörter zu Rechtsgeschichte: Festschrift für D. Werkmüller zum 70. Geburtstag*. Ed. S. Buchholz and H. Lück. Berlin. Pp. 283–96.
(2007b). "Ludwig Mitteis (1859–1920)," in *Hermae: Scholars and Scholarship in Papyrology*. Ed. M. Capasso. Pisa. Pp. 67–70.
Russel, N., trans. (1980). *The Lives of the Desert Fathers*. Kalamazoo.
Sachers, E. (1932). "Tabellio," in *Real-Encyclopädie der classischen Altertumswissenschaft*. Zweite Reihe, Bd 4. Pp. 1847–63.
Salomons, R. P. (2006). "Testamentaria," *ZPE* 156: 217–41.
Sanna, M. V. (2001). *Nuove ricerche in tema di postliminium e redemptio ab hostibus*. Cagliari.
Sarris, P. (2006). *Economy and Society in the Age of Justinian*. Cambridge.
Scheidel, W. (1995). "Incest revisited: three notes on the demography of sibling marriage in Roman Egypt," *BASP* 32: 143–55.
(1996). *Measuring Sex, Age and Death in the Roman Empire: Studies in Ancient Demography. JRA* Suppl. 21. Ann Arbor.
(2005). "Real slave prices and the relative cost of slave labor in the Greco-Roman world," *Ancient Society* 35: 1–17.
Schentuleit, M. (2001). "Die spätdemotische Hausverkaufsurkunde P. BM 262. Ein bilingues Dokument aus Soknopaiu Nesos mit griechischen Übersetzungen," *Enchoria* 27: 127–54.
Schiller, A. A. (1931). "Coptic Law," *The Juridical Review* 43: 211–40.
(1932). "Koptisches Recht. Eine Studie auf Grund der Quellen und Abhandlungen," *Kritische Vierteljahresschrift für Gesetzgebung und Rechtswissenschaft* 25: 250–96.
(1938). "Prolegomena to the study of Coptic law," *Archives d'histoire du droit oriental* 2: 340–64.
(1964). "The interrelation of Coptic and Greek papyri: P.Bu. and P.BM inv. nos. 2017 and 2018," in *Studien zur Papyrologie und antiken Wirtschaftsgeschichte. Festschrift Friedrich Oertel*. Bonn. Pp. 107–19.
(1968). "The Budge Papyrus of Columbia University," *JARCE* 7: 79–118.
(1970). "The fate of imperial legislation in late Byzantine Egypt," in *Legal Thought in the United States of America under Contemporary Pressures*. Ed. J. N. Hazard and W. J. Wagner. Brussels. Pp. 41–60.
(1971). "The courts are no more," in *Studi in onore di Edoardo Volterra*, vol. 1. Milan. Pp. 469–502.
(1975). Review of Amelotti and Luzzatto 1972, in *Gnomon* 47: 582–87.

Scholl, R. (1990). *Corpus der ptolemäischen Sklaventexte.* 3 vols. Stuttgart.
(1995). "Zum ptolemäischen Sklavenrecht," in *Legal Documents of the Hellenistic World.* Ed. M. J. Gellner and H. Maehler in collaboration with A. D. E. Lewis. London. Pp. 149–72.
(2001). "'Freilassung unter Freunden' in römischen Ägypten," in *Fünfzig Jahre Forschungen zur antiken Sklaverei an der Mainzer Akademie 1950–2000.* Stuttgart. Pp. 159–69.
Schöllgen, G. (1998). *Die Anfänge der professionalisierung des Klerus und das kirchliche Amt in der Syrischen Didaskalie.* Münster.
Schubart, W. (1913). "Alexandrinische Urkunden aus der Zeit des Augustus," *Archiv* 5: 35–131.
Schubert, P. (1990). *Les archives de Marcus Lucretius Diogenes et textes apparentés.* Papyrologische Texte und Abhandlungen 39. Bonn.
Schwartz, J. (1964). "Une famille de chepteliers au IIIe s. p.C.," *Rech.Pap.* 3: 49–96.
Schweizer, C. (1991). *Hierarchie und Organisation der römischen Reichskirche in der Kaisergesetzgebung vom vierten bis zum sechsten Jahrhundert.* Frankfurt.
Seidl, E. (1951). *Einführung in die ägyptische Rechtsgeschichte bis zum Ende des Neuen Reiches.* Glückstadt.
(1962). *Ptolemäische Rechtsgeschichte.* 2nd edn. Glückstadt.
(1968). *Ägyptische Rechtsgeschichte der Saiten- und Perserzeit.* 2nd edn. Glückstadt.
(1973a). *Rechtsgeschichte Ägyptens als römischer Provinz.* St. Augustin.
(1973b). *Bodennutzung und Bodenpacht nach den demotischen Texten der Ptolemäerzeit.* Österreichische Akademie der Wissenschaften Philosophisch-Historische Klasse Sitzungsberichte 291: 2. Vienna.
Selb, W. (1967). "Episcopalis audientia von der Zeit Konstantins bis zur Nov. xxxv Valentians III," *ZSS* 84: 162–217.
Sethe, K. and Partsch, J. (1920). *Demotische Urkunden zum ägyptischen Bürgschaftsrechte vorzüglich der Ptolemäerzeit.* Leipzig.
Sheridan, J. A. (1996). "Women without guardians: an updated list," *BASP* 33: 117–31.
(1998). "Not at a loss for words: the economic power of literate women in late antique Egypt," *TAPA* 128: 189–203.
Sijpesteijn, P. J. (1965). "Die χωρὶς κυρίου χρηματίζουσαι δικαίῳ τέκνων in den Papyri," *Aegyptus* 45: 171–89.
(1985). "Five Byzantine papyri from the Michigan collection," *ZPE* 62: 133–49.
(2007). "The Arab conquest of Egypt and the beginning of Muslim rule," in Bagnall (2007), pp. 437–59.
Sijpesteijn, P. M. and S. Clackson (2009). "A mid-eighth-century trilingual tax demand-note related to the monastery of Apa Apollo at Bawit," in *Monastic Estates in Late Antique and Early Islamic Egypt: Ostraca, Papyri, and Essays in Memory of Sarah Clackson (P. Clackson).* Ed. A. Boud'hors, J. Clackson, C. Louis, and P. M. Sijpesteijn. Cincinnati. Pp. 102–19.
Sijpesteijn, P. M. and L. Sundelin, eds. (2004). *Papyrology and the History of Early Islamic Egypt.* Leiden.

Simon, D. (1969). *Untersuchungen zum justinianischen Zivilprozeß*. Münchener Beiträge zur Papyrusforschung und antiken Rechtsgeschichte 54. Munich.

(1971). "Zur Zivilgerichtsbarkeit im spätbyzantinischen Ägypten," *Revue internationale des droits de L'Antiquité* 18: 623–57.

(1987). "Hans Julius Wolff†," *Gnomon* 59: 83–84.

Sirks, A. J. B. (2008). "The colonate in Justinian's reign," *JRS* 98: 120–43.

(2011). "In memoriam Pieter Willem Pestman, 1933–2010," *Tijdschrift voor Rechtsgeschiedenis* 79: 189–97.

Smith, H. S. (1995). "Marriage and the family in ancient Egypt. I. Marriage and family law," in *Legal Documents of the Hellenistic World: Papers from a Seminar*. Ed. M. J. Geller and H. Maehler. London.

Smolders, R. (2005). "Soterichos and Didymos," www.trismegistos.org/archive/226.

Sosin, J. (2004). "Half again more," *Archiv* 50: 42–44.

Spiegelberg, W. (1906). "Demotische Miszellen," *Recueil de travaux relatifs à la philologie et à l'archéologie égyptiennes et assyriennes* 28: 187–204.

(1906/8). *Die demotischen Denkmäler 30601–31270, 50001–50022 II: Die demotischen Papyrus*. Catalogue général des antiquités égyptiennes du Musée du Caire. Strassburg.

Stadler, M. (2004). "Rechtskodex von Hermupolis (P. Kairo JE 89.127–30+89.137–43)," in *Texte zum Rechts- und Wirtschaftsleben*. Ed. B. Janowski and G. Wilhelm. Gütersloh. Pp. 185–207.

Stein, A. (1968). "Wo trugen die korinthischen Christen ihre Rechtshändel aus?" *Zeitschrift für die Neutestamentliche Wissenschaft* 59: 86–89.

(1984). "Gerichtsbarkeit, kirchliche, 1.1," *Theologische Realenzyklopädie* 12: 479–506.

Stein, P. (1986). "Obituary (Arthur Schiller)," *in Studies in Roman Law in Memory of A. Arthur Schiller*. Ed. R. S. Bagnall and W. V. Harris. Leiden. Pp. xv–xviii.

Steinacker, H. (1927/1975). *Die antiken Grundlagen der frühmittelalterlichen Privaturkunde*. Grundriss der Geschichtswissenschaft, Ergänzungsband 1. Leipzig.

Steinwenter, A. (1925). "Neue Urkunden zum byzantinischen Libellprozesse," in *Abhandlungen zur antiken Rechtsgeschichte: Festschrift für Gustav F. Hanausek*. Graz. Pp. 36–51.

(1929/30). "Zur Lehre von der episcopalis audientia," *Byzantinische Zeitschrift* 39: 660–68.

(1944). "Zur Frage der Gliederung des Libellprozesses," in *Festschrift für L. Wenger zu seinem 70. Geburtstag dargebracht von Freunden, Fachgenossen und Schulern*, vol. 1. Munich. Pp. 180–203.

(1950). "Audientia episcopalis," *Reallexikon für Antike und Christentum* 1: 915–17.

(1952). "Was beweisen die Papyri für die praktische Geltung des justinianischen Gesetzgebungswerkes?," *Aegyptus* 32: 131–37.

Steinwenter, A. (1955). *Das Recht der koptischen Urkunden.* Handbuch der Altertumswissenschaft 10.4.2. Munich.

Stern, L. (1878). "Sahidische Inschriften," *Zeitschrift für ägyptische Sprache und Altertumskunde* 16: 9–28.

Straus, J. A. (1988). "L'esclavage dans l'Égypte romaine," in *Aufstieg und Niedergang der römischen Welt* II.10.1. Pp. 841–911.

(2004). *L'achat et la vente des esclaves dans l'Égypte romaine: Contribution papyrologique à l'étude de l'esclavage dans une province orientale de l'Empire romain.* Munich.

Struve, V. (1955). "The significance of certain Demotic papyri of the State Museum of Fine Arts named after Pushkin for the history and culture of Ptolemaic Egypt," in *Reports of the Soviet Delegations at the X International Congress of Historical Science in Rome.* Moscow. Pp. 32–57.

Swarney, P. R. (1970). *The Ptolemaic and Roman Idios Logos.* American Studies in Papyrology 8. Toronto.

Tacoma, L. (1998). "Replacement parts for an irrigation machine of the Divine House at Oxyrhynchos," *ZPE* 120: 123–30.

Talbot, A.-M., ed. (1996). *Holy Women of Byzantium: Ten Saints' Lives in English Translation.* Washington, DC. www.doaks.org/resources/publications/doaks-online-publications/byzantine-studies/holywomen/talbch9.pdf

Taubenschlag, R. (1916a). *Das Strafrecht im Rechte der Papyri.* Leipzig.

(1916b). "Die Patria potestas im Recht der Papyri," *ZSS* 37: 177–230. Reprinted in Taubenschlag (1959), vol. 2, pp. 261–321.

(1929). "*Materna potestas* im gräko-ägyptischen Recht," *ZSS* 49: 115–28. Reprinted in Taubenschlag (1959), vol. 2, pp. 323–37.

(1930). "Geschichte der Rezeption des römischen Privatrechts in Ägypten," in *Studi in onore di P. Bonfante.* Pp. 367–440. Reprinted in Taubenschlag (1959), vol. 1, pp. 181–289.

(1937). "Prozesse aus Pacht-, Miet-, Dienst- und Werkverträgen in den griechischen Papyri," *Archiv* 12: 187–93. Reprinted in Taubenschlag (1959), vol. 2, pp. 461–69.

(1940/41). "The legislation of Justinian in the light of the papyri," *Byzantion* 15: 280–95. Reprinted in Taubenschlag (1959), vol. 2, pp. 69–89.

(1955). *The Law of Greco-Roman Egypt in the Light of the Papyri 332 B.C.–640 A.D.* 2nd edn. Warsaw.

(1959). *Opera minora*, vol. 1: *Allgemeiner Teil*, vol. 2: *Spezieller Teil.* Warsaw.

Tedeschi, G. (2002). "Lo spettacolo in età ellenistica e tardo antica nella documentazione epigrafica e papiracea," in *Dal restauro dei materiali allo studio dei testi: Aspetti della ricerca papirologica.* Ed. M. Capasso. Lecce. Pp. 87–187.

Tenger, B. (1993). *Die Verschuldung im römischen Ägypten (1.–2. Jh. n. Chr.).* St. Katharinen.

Thirion, M. (1988). "Notes d'onomastique: contribution à une révision du Ranke *PN* (sixième série)," *Rev.d'Ég.* 39: 131–46.

Thissen, H.-J. (1986). "Koptische Kinderschenkungsurkunden. Zur Hierodulie im christlichen Ägypten," *Enchoria* 14: 117–28.

Thomas, J. D. (1998). "P.Ryl. IV 654: the Latin heading," *Cd'É* 73: 125–34.
Thompson, D. J. (1988). *Memphis under the Ptolemies*. Princeton. (2nd rev. edn. 2012.)
(1994). "Literacy and power in Ptolemaic Egypt," in *Literacy and Power in the Ancient World*. Ed. A. K. Bowman and G. Woolf. Cambridge. Pp. 67–83.
(2009). "The multilingual environment of Persian and Ptolemaic Egypt: Egyptian, Aramaic, and Greek documentation," in Bagnall (2009), pp. 395–417.
Thompson, H. (1934). *A Family Archive from Siut from Papyri in the British Museum*. Oxford.
Thompson Crawford, D. J. (1984). "The Idumaeans of Memphis and the Ptolemaic Politeumata," in *Atti del XVII Congresso Internazionale di Papirologia (Napoli, 19–26 maggio 1983)*, vol. 3. Naples. Pp. 1069–75. (*See also* Thompson, D. J.)
Tiersma, P. M. (1999). *Legal Language*. Chicago.
Till, W. C. (1953). "Der griechisch-koptische Wiener Papyrus K 4912," *Aegyptus* 33: 193–208.
(1958). *Die koptischen Rechtsurkunden der Papyrussammlung der österreichischen Nationalbibliothek*. Vienna.
(1964). *Die koptischen Rechtsurkunden aus Theben*. Vienna.
Timbie, J. (1991). "Melitian schism," in *The Coptic Encyclopedia*. Ed. A. S. Atiya. Vol. 5. Pp. 1584–85.
Torallas Tovar, S. (2004a). "La practica forense en el Egipto romano," in *Homenaje a Pedro Laín Entralgo*. Ed. L. Gil. Madrid. Pp. 183–200.
(2004b). "Egyptian lexical interference in the Greek of Byzantine and Early Islamic Egypt," in Sijpesteijn and Sundelin (2004), pp. 63–98.
(2006). "Violence in the process of arrest and imprisonment in Late Antique Egypt," in *Violence in Late Antiquity: Perceptions and Practices*. Ed. H. A. Drake. Aldershot, UK. Pp. 103–12.
Treggiari, S. (1991a). *Roman Marriage: Iusti Coniuges from the Time of Cicero to the Time of Ulpian*. Oxford.
(1991b). "Divorce Roman style: how easy and how frequent was it?" in *Marriage, Divorce, and Children in Ancient Rome*. Ed. B. Rawson. Pp. 31–46.
Turpin, W. (1991). "Imperial subscriptions and the administration of justice," *JRS* 81: 101–18.
Uebel, F. (1968). *Die Kleruchen Ägyptens unter den ersten sechs Ptolemäern*. Abhandlungen der Deutschen Akademie der Wissenschaften zu Berlin. Klasse für Sprachen, Literatur und Kunst 3. Berlin.
Urbanik, J. (2002). "D. 24.2.4: … Pater tamen eius nuntium mittere posse: l'influsso della volontà del padre sul divorzio dei sottoposti," in *Euergesias Charin: Studies Presented to Benedetto Bravo and Ewa Wipszycka by Their Disciples*. Ed. T. Derda, J. Urbanik, and M. Węcowski. Warsaw.
(2005). "A priestly divorce in the seventh century Palestine: various legal orders at work (the case of P. Nessana III 57, a. 689)," in *Marriage: Ideal – Law –*

Practice: Proceedings of a Conference Held in Memory of Henryk Kupiszewski. Ed. Z. Służewska and J. Urbanik. Warsaw. Pp. 199–218.

(2007). "Compromesso o processo? Alternativa risoluzione dei conflitti e tutela dei diritti nella prassi della tarda antichità," in *Symposion 2005: Vorträge zur griechischen und hellenistischen Rechtsgeschichte*. Ed. G. Thür and E. Cantarella. Vienna. Pp. 377–97.

(2010). "P.Cairo Masp. I 67120 *recto* and the liability for latent defects in the late antique slave sales: or back to *epaphe*," *JJurPap* 40: 219–47.

Uxkull-Gyllenband, W. (1934). *Der Gnomon des Idios Logos. Zweiter Teil: Der Kommentar (BGU V)*. Berlin.

van den Boorn, G. P. F. (1988). *The Duties of the Vizier: Civil Administration in the Early New Kingdom*. London.

van der Kooij, A. (2007). "The Septuagint of the Pentateuch and Ptolemaic rule," in *The Pentateuch as Torah: New Models for Understanding Its Promulgation and Acceptance*. Ed. G. N. Knoppers and B. M. Levinson. Winona Lake, IN. Pp. 289–300.

van der Vliet, J. (2002). "Pisenthios de Coptos (569–632): moine, évêque et saint. Autour d'une novelle édition de ses archives," in *Autour de Coptos*. Ed. M.-F. Boussac. *Topoi. Orient Occident* Supplement 3: 61–72.

van Groningen, B. A. (1950). *A Family Archive from Tebtunis*. Pap.Lugd.Bat. VI. Leiden.

van Haelst, J. (1958). "De nouvelles archives: Anastasia, propriétaire à Oxyrhynchos," *Cd'É* 33: 237–42.

(1966). "De nouvelles archives: Anastasia, propriétaire à Oxyrhynchos," in *Atti del'XI Congresso Internazionale di Papirologia, Milano, 2–8 settembre 1965*. Milan. Pp. 586–90.

van Minnen, P. (2000). "Prisoners of war and hostages in Graeco-Roman Egypt," *JJurPap* 30: 155–63.

(2003). "Dioscorus and the law," in *Learned Antiquity: Scholarship and Society in the Near East, the Greco-Roman World, and the Early Medieval West*. Ed. A. A. Macdonald, M. W. Twomey, and G. J. Reinik. Leuven. Pp. 115–33.

(2007). "The millennium of Papyrology (2001–)?," in *Akten des 23. Internationalen Papyrologenkongresses, Wien, 22.–28. Juli 2001*. Ed. B. Palme. Vienna. Pp. 703–14.

van 't Dack, E. (1988). *Ptolemaica Selecta. Études sur l'armée et l'administration lagides*. Studia Hellenistica 29. Leuven.

Vandoni, M. (1964). *Feste pubbliche e private nei documenti greci*. Varese.

Vandorpe, K. (1995a). "City of many a gate, harbour for many a rebel: historical and topographical outline of Greco-Roman Thebes," in *Hundred-Gated Thebes: Acts of a Colloquium on Thebes and the Theban Area in the Graeco-Roman Period*. Ed. S. P. Vleeming. Pap.Lugd.Bat. XXVII. Leiden. Pp. 203–39.

(1995b). *Breaking the Seal: Sealing-Practices in Greco-Roman and Byzantine Egypt Based on Greek, Demotic and Latin Papyrological Evidence*. Leiden.

(1997). "Seals in and on the papyri of Greco-Roman and Byzantine Egypt," in *Archives et sceaux du monde hellénistique. Torino, Villa Gualino 13–16 Gennaio*

1993. Ed. M.-F. Boussac and A. Invernizzi. *Bulletin de Correspondance Hellénique*, Supplement 29. Pp. 231–91.

(1998). "Interest in Ptolemaic loans of seed-corn in the 'House of Hathor' (Pathyris)," in *Egyptian Religion: The Last Thousand Years. Studies Dedicated to the Memory of Jan Quaegebeur*. Ed. W. Clarysse, A. Schoors, and H. Willems. Part 2. OLA 85. Pp. 1459–68.

(2000a). "The Ptolemaic epigraphe or harvest tax (*shemu*)," *Archiv* 46: 169–232.

(2000b). "Two agoranomic loans with Demotic summary (Pathyris: P. Cairo 31023 and 31028; verso of P. Lond. III 1205)," in *Papyri in honorem Johannis Bingen octogenarii*. Ed. H. Melaerts. Leuven. Pp. 195–204.

(2002a). *The Bilingual Family Archive of Dryton, His Wife Apollonia and Their Daughter Senmouthis (P. Dryton)*. Collectanea Hellenistica 4. Brussels.

(2002b). "Apollonia, a businesswoman in a multicultural society (Pathyris, 2nd–1st centuries B.C.)," in *Le rôle et le statut de la femme en Égypte hellénistique, romaine et byzantine*. Ed. H. Melaerts and L. Mooren. Studia Hellenistica 37. Leuven. Pp. 325–36.

(2004). "A Greek register from Pathyris' notarial office: loans and sales from the Pathyrite and Latopolite nomes," *ZPE* 150: 161–86.

(2008). "Persian soldiers and Persians of the *epigone*: social mobility of soldiers-herdsmen in Upper Egypt," *Archiv* 54: 87–108.

(2009a). "Archives and dossiers," in Bagnall (2009), pp. 216–55.

(2009b). "The Ptolemaic period," in *A Companion to Ancient Egypt*. Ed. A. B. Lloyd. Chichester. Pp. 159–79.

Vandorpe, K. and W. Clarysse (1998). "A Greek winery for sale in a Fayyum Demotic Papyrus," in *The Two Faces of Graeco-Roman Egypt: Greek and Demotic and Greek-Demotic Texts and Studies Presented to P. W. Pestman*. Ed. A. M. F. W. Verhoogt and S. P. Vleeming. Pap.Lugd.Bat. XXX. Leiden. Pp. 127–39.

Vandorpe, K. and S. Waebens (2010). *Reconstructing Pathyris' Archives: A Multicultural Community in Hellenistic Egypt*. Collectanea Hellenistica 3. Brussels.

Veïsse, A.-E. (2004). *Les "revoltes égyptiennes." Recherches sur les troubles intérieurs en Égypte du regne de Ptolémée III Éuergete à la conquête romaine*. Studia Hellenistica 41. Leuven.

Verhoogt, A. M. F. W. (1998). *Menches, Komogrammateus of Kerkeosiris: The Doings and Dealings of a Village Scribe in the Late Ptolemaic Period (120–110 B.C.)*. Pap.Lud.Bat. 29. Leiden.

(2004). Review of Wolff (2002) in *Classical Review* 54/1: 224–26.

Vischer, L. (1955). *Die Auslegungsgeschichte von 1.Kor. 6.1–11*. Tübingen.

Vismara, G. (1937). *Episcopalis audientia: L'attività giurisdizionale del vescovo per la risoluzione delle controversie private tra laici nel diritto romano e nella storia del diritto italiano fino al secolo nono*. Milan.

Vivian, T. (2005a). "Holy men and businessmen: monks as intercessors in fourth-century Egypt," in T. Vivian, *Words to Live By: Journeys in Ancient and Modern Egyptian Monasticism*. Kalamazoo. Pp. 323–49.

(2005b). "Sixteen letters to Nepheros and his community," in T. Vivian, *Words to Live By: Journeys in Ancient and Modern Egyptian Monasticism*. Kalamazoo. Pp. 351–75.

Vleeming, S. P. (1981). "La phase initiale du démotique ancien," *Cd'É* 56: 31–48.

(1991). *The Gooseherds of Hou (Pap. Hou): A Dossier Relating to Various Agricultural Affairs from Provincial Egypt of the Early Fifth Century B.C.* Studia Demotica 3. Leuven.

(1994). *Ostraka Varia: Tax Receipts and Legal Documents on Demotic, Greek and Greek-Demotic Ostraka Chiefly of the Early Ptolemaic Period from Various Collections*. Pap.Lugd.Bat. 26. Leiden.

(1998). "A demotic Doppelurkunde," in *The Two Faces of Graeco-Roman Egypt: Greek and Demotic and Greek-Demotic Texts and Studies Presented to P. W. Pestman*. Ed. A. M. F. W. Verhoogt, P. W. Pestman, and S. P. Vleeming. Pap.Lugd.Bat. xxx. Leiden. Pp. 155–70.

Vogelsang-Eastwood, G. (2000). "Textiles," in *Ancient Egyptian Materials and Technology*. Ed. P. T. Nicholson and I. Shaw. Cambridge. Pp. 269–76.

Volterra, E. (1940). *La conception du mariage d'après les juristes romains*. Padua. Reprinted in Volterra (1991), pp. 3–68.

(1948). "Quelques observations sur le mariage des *filiifamilias*," *Revue internationale des droits de l'Antiquité* 1: 213–42. Reprinted in Volterra (1991). Pp. 97–126.

(1966). "Il senatoconsulto orfiziano e la sua applicazione in documenti egiziani del III secolo d. C.," in *Atti dell' xi Congresso Internazionale di Papirologia, Milano 2–8 settembre 1965*. Milan. Pp. 551–85.

(1975). "Precisazioni in tema di matrimonio classico," *Bulletino dell'Istituto di Diritto Romano «Vittorio Scialoja»* 78: 245–70. Reprinted in Volterra (1991), pp. 355–80.

(1980). "Ancora sulla struttura del matrimonio classic," in *De iustitia et iure: Festgabe Urlich von Lübtow*. Berlin. Pp. 147–53. Reprinted in Volterra, *Scritti giuridici*, vol. 5: *Le Fonti*. Naples (1993). Pp. 599–605.

(1991). *Scritti giuridici*, vol. 3: *Famiglia e successioni*. Naples.

von Druffel, E. (1915/1970). *Papyrologische Studien zum byzantinischen Urkundenwesen im Anschluß an P.Heidelberg 311*. Munich.

von Reden, S. (2007). *Money in Ptolemaic Egypt from the Macedonian Conquest to the End of the Third Century BC*. Cambridge.

Wallace, S. L. (1938). *Taxation in Egypt from Augustus to Diocletian*. Princeton.

Wångstedt, S. V. (1954). *Ausgewählte demotische Ostraka aus der Sammlung des Victoria-Museums zu Uppsala und der Staatlichen Papyrussammlung zu Berlin*. Uppsala.

(1965). *Die demotischen Ostraka der Universität zu Zürich*. Bibliotheca Ekmaniana 62. Uppsala.

Waszynski, S. (1905). *Die Bodenpacht. Agrargeschichtliche Papyrusstudien*, vol. 1: *Die Privatpacht*. Leipzig.

Watson, A. (1966). "The identity of Sarapio, Socrates, Longus, and Nilus in the will of C. Longinus Castor," *The Irish Jurist* 1: 313–15.

(1971). *The Law of Succession in the Later Roman Republic*. Oxford.
Wenger, L. (1922). "Ein christliches Freiheitszeugnis in den ägyptischen Papyri," in *Festgabe Albert Ehrhard*. Ed. A. M. Koeniger. Bonn. Pp. 451–78.
(1925). "Neue Libellpapyri," in *Raccolta Giacomo Lumbroso*. *Aegyptus* Suppl. B III. Milan. Pp. 325–34.
(1939). Review of Schiller (1938). *Archiv* 13: 281–82.
Westermann, W. L. (1929). *Upon Slavery in Ptolemaic Egypt*. New York.
Whitehorne, J. (2004). "Petitions to the centurion: a question of locality?" *BASP* 41: 155–69.
Wilcken, U. (1908). "Zu den Florentiner und Leipziger Papyri," *Archiv* 4: 423–86.
(1913). "Zu den Brautgeschenken in P. Lips. 41," *Archiv* 9: 186–88.
(1920). "Papyrus-Ukunden," *Archiv* 6: 403–06.
Wilfong, T. G. (2002). *Women of Jeme: Lives in a Coptic Town in Late Antique Egypt*. Ann Arbor.
Williams, M. (2005). "The Jewish family in Judaea from Pompey to Hadrian: the limits of Romanization," in George (2005), pp. 159–82.
Winlock, H. E. and W. E. Crum (1926). *The Monastery of Epiphanius at Thebes*. Part 1. New York.
Wipszycka, E. (2007). "The institutional church," in Bagnall (2007), pp. 331–49.
Witt, P. D. (1977). *The Judicial Function of the Strategos in the Roman Period*. Ph.D. dissertation, Duke University.
Wolff, H. J. (1948). "Registration of conveyances in Ptolemaic Egypt," *Aegyptus* 28: 17–96.
(1956). "Zur Romanisierung des Vertragsrechts der Papyri," *ZSS* 63: 1–28.
(1957). "Die Grundlagen des griechischen Vertragsrechts," *ZSav* 74: 26–72.
(1960). "Plurality of laws in Ptolemaic Egypt," *Revue internationale des droits de l'Antiquité* 7: 191–223.
(1961). "Zur Rechtsnatur der *misthosis*," in *Beiträge zur Rechtsgeschichte Altgriechenlands und des hellenistisch-römischen Ägypten*. Freiburg. Pp. 129–54.
(1962). *Das Justizwesen der Ptolemäer*. Munich.
(1970). *Das Justizwesen der Ptolemäer*. 2nd edn. Munich.
(1978). *Das Recht der griechischen Papyri Ägyptens in der Zeit der Ptolemäer und des Prinzipats*, vol. 2: *Organisation und Kontrolle des privaten Rechtsverkehrs*. Munich.
(1983). "Neue Juristische Urkunden VII – Neues Material zum Zwangsvollstreckungsrecht der Papyri," *ZSS* 100: 444–53.
(1998). *Vorlesungen über juristische Papyruskunde*. Berlin.
(2002). *Das Recht der griechischen Papyri Ägyptens in der Zeit der Ptolemaeer und des Prinzipats*, vol. 1: *Bedingungen und Triebkräfte der Rechtsentwicklung*. Ed. H.-A. Rupprecht. Munich.
Worp, K. (1994). "A checklist of bishops in Byzantine Egypt," *ZPE* 100: 283–318.
(2000). "A Note on P. Oxy. III 475.20," *ZPE* 133: 190.
Yiftach-Firanko, U. (2002). "Deeds of last will in Graeco-Roman Egypt," *BASP* 39: 149–64.

Yiftach-Firanko, U. (2003). *Marriage and Marital Arrangements: A History of the Greek Marriage Document in Egypt, 4th century BCE – 4th century CE.* Münchener Beiträge zur Papyrusforschung und antiken Rechtsgeschichte 93. Munich.

(2005). "Judaean desert marriage documents and ekdosis in the Greek law of the Roman period," in Katzoff and Schaps (2005), pp. 67–84.

(2007). "The rise of the hypomnema as a lease contract," in *Proceedings of the 24th International Congress of Papyrology, Helsinki, 1–7 August 2004*. Ed. J. Frösen *et al.* Vol. 2. Helsinki. Pp. 1051–61.

(2008a). "The *cheirographon* and the privatization of scribal activity in early Roman Oxyrhynchos," in *Symposion 2007: Vorträge zur griechischen und hellenistischen Rechtsgeschichte*. Ed. E. Harris and G. Thür. Vienna. Pp. 325–40.

(2008b). "Who killed the double document in Ptolemaic Egypt?" *Archiv* 54: 203–18.

(2009). "Law in Graeco-Roman Egypt: Hellenization, fusion, Romanization," in Bagnall (2009), pp. 541–60.

(forthcoming). "The *grammatikon*: transaction-costs in first-century CE Tebtynis," in *Legal Documents in Ancient Societies, Seminar II: Transaction Costs in the Ancient World: July 27–28, 2009*. Washington, DC.

Youtie, H. C. (1975a). "APATORES: law vs. custom in Roman Egypt," in *Le monde grec: Hommages à Claire Préaux*. Ed. J. Bingen *et al.*, Brussels. Pp. 723–40. Reprinted in Youtie, *Scriptiunculae Posteriores* (1981), vol. 1. Bonn.

(1975b). "Notes on subscriptions," *ZPE* 18: 213–23.

Zahrnt, M. (1988). "Antinoopolis in Ägypten. Die hadrianische Gründung und ihre Privilegien in der neueren Forschung," *Aufstieg und Niedergang der römischen Welt* 11.10.1. Pp. 669–706.

Zauzich, K.-T. (1968). *Die ägyptische Schreibertradition in Aufbau, Sprache und Schrift der demotischen Kaufverträge aus ptolemäischer Zeit.* 2 vols. Ägyptologische Abhandlungen 19. Wiesbaden.

(1983). "Demotische Texts römischer Zeit," in *Das Römisch-Byzantinische Ägypten: Akten des internationalen Symposions 26.–30. September 1978 in Trier*. Ed. G. Grimm, H. Heinen, and E. Winter. Aegyptiaca Treverensia 2. Mainz. Pp. 77–80.

Zilliacus, H. (1956). "Zu Stil und Wortschatz der byzantinischen Urkunden und Briefe," *Mitteilungen aus der Papyrussammlung der Österreichischen Nationalbibliothek* 5: 157–65.

(1967). *Zur Abundanz der spätgriechischen Gebrauchssprache*. Helsinki.

Zuckerman, C. (1995). "The hapless recruit Psois and the mighty anchorite, Apa John," *BASP* 32: 183–94.